THE
ENDURING DEBATE

CLASSIC AND CONTEMPORARY READINGS
IN AMERICAN POLITICS

Seventh Edition

THE
ENDURING DEBATE

CLASSIC AND CONTEMPORARY READINGS
IN AMERICAN POLITICS

Seventh Edition

Edited by
David T. Canon
John J. Coleman
Kenneth R. Mayer

W. W. NORTON & COMPANY
NEW YORK   LONDON

W. W. Norton & Company has been independent since its founding in 1923, when William Warder Norton and Mary D. Herter Norton first published lectures delivered at the People's Institute, the adult education division of New York City's Cooper Union. The Nortons soon expanded their program beyond the Institute, publishing books by celebrated academics from America and abroad. By mid-century, the two major pillars of Norton's publishing program—trade books and college texts—were firmly established. In the 1950s, the Norton family transferred control of the company to its employees, and today—with a staff of 400 and a comparable number of trade, college, and professional titles published each year—W. W. Norton & Company stands as the largest and oldest publishing house owned wholly by its employees.

Composition: Westchester Book Composition
Production manager: Ashley Horna
Manufacturing by Courier-Westford

Library of Congress Cataloging-in-Publication Data
The enduring debate : classic and contemporary readings in American politics /
edited by David T. Canon, John J. Coleman, Kenneth R. Mayer. — Seventh edition.
pages cm
Includes bibliographical references.
ISBN 978-0-393-92158-8 (pbk.)
1. United States—Politics and government.   I. Mayer, Kenneth R., 1960–
II. Canon, David T.
JK21.E53   2014
320.473—dc23   2013018540

W. W. Norton & Company Inc., 500 Fifth Avenue, New York, N.Y. 10110
www.wwnorton.com
W. W. Norton & Company Ltd., Castle House, 75/76 Wells Street, London W1T 3QT
1 2 3 4 5 6 7 8 9 0

Contents

Preface   xiii

PART I   The Constitutional System

CHAPTER 1   Political Culture   3

1 FROM *The Liberal Tradition in America: An Interpretation of American Political Thought Since the Revolution*—LOUIS HARTZ   3

2 FROM *The Creation of the American Republic 1776–1787*—GORDON S. WOOD   9

3 "Beyond Tocqueville, Myrdal, and Hartz: The Multiple Traditions in America"—ROGERS M. SMITH   17

DEBATING THE ISSUES: WHAT DOES IT MEAN TO BE AN AMERICAN?   27

4 "Sworn-Again Americans"—ERIC LIU   28

5 "What Does It Mean to Be an American?"—STEVEN M. WARSHAWSKY   37

6 "The Three Political Cultures"—DANIEL J. ELAZAR   41

CHAPTER 2   The Founding and the Constitution   53

7 "The Nature of American Constitutionalism," FROM *The Origins of the American Constitution*—MICHAEL KAMMEN   53

8 *The Federalist*, No. 15—ALEXANDER HAMILTON   62

9 FROM *An Economic Interpretation of the Constitution of the United States*—CHARLES A. BEARD   67

DEBATING THE ISSUES: HOW DEMOCRATIC IS THE CONSTITUTION?   73

10 "The Ratification Referendum: Sending the Constitution to a New Convention for Repair"—SANFORD LEVINSON   75

11 "We"—ERIC LANE AND MICHAEL ORESKES   84

CHAPTER 3   Federalism   98

12 The Federalist, No. 46—JAMES MADISON   98

13 FROM *The Price of Federalism*—PAUL PETERSON   103

14 "Jumping Frogs, Endangered Toads, and California's
Medical-Marijuana Law"—GEORGE J. ANNAS   112

DEBATING THE ISSUES: IMMIGRATION REFORM AND
STATE POWER   122

15 "State Sovereignty Is the Issue"—JAY SEKULOW   123

16 "Dismantling Federalism Is a Shortcut With a
Very Steep Price"—RICHARD PELTZ-STEELE   127

17 "The Debate Over Immigration Reform Is Not
Over Until It's Over"—KEVIN JOHNSON   129

CHAPTER 4   The Constitutional Framework and
              the Individual: Civil Liberties and
              Civil Rights   134

18 "The Perpetuation of Our Political Institutions"
—ABRAHAM LINCOLN   135

19 "Letter from Birmingham Jail"—MARTIN LUTHER
KING, JR.   141

20 "In Defense of Prejudice"—JONATHAN RAUCH   149

DEBATING THE ISSUES: SAME-SEX MARRIAGE   157

21 "The Marriage Ideal"—ROSS DOUTHAT   159

22 "The Libertarian Case Against Gay Marriage"
—JUSTIN RAIMONDO   161

23 "Objections to These Unions"—JONATHAN RAUCH   164

PART II   Institutions

CHAPTER 5   Congress: The First Branch   175

24 FROM *Congress: The Electoral Connection*
—DAVID R. MAYHEW   175

25 "U.S. House Members in Their Constituencies:
An Exploration"—RICHARD F. FENNO, Jr.   179

26 "Too Much of a Good Thing: More Representative Is Not
Necessarily Better"—JOHN R. HIBBING AND ELIZABETH
THEISS-MORSE   192

| DEBATING THE ISSUES: PORK-BARREL POLITICS   199

27 "Corporate Welfare and Earmarks"—CATO HANDBOOK
FOR POLICYMAKERS   200

28 "Inhofe: Earmarks Are Good for Us"—BRIAN FRIEL   204

29 "Earmarks Are a Model, Not a Menace"—JONATHAN
RAUCH   208

CHAPTER 6   The Presidency   212

30 "The Power to Persuade," FROM *Presidential Power*
—RICHARD NEUSTADT   212

31 "Perspectives on the Presidency," FROM *The Presidency in a
Separated System*—CHARLES O. JONES   222

| DEBATING THE ISSUES: PROSPECTS, POSSIBILITIES, AND PERILS
| IN OBAMA'S SECOND TERM   229

32 "Triumphant Obama Faces New Foe in 'Second-Term
Curse' "—ADAM CLYMER   230

33 "Beware Obama's Big Ideas"—TIM CAVANAUGH   233

34 "Second Chances"—AKHIL REED AMAR   235

CHAPTER 7   Bureaucracy   239

35 "The Study of Administration"—WOODROW WILSON   239

36 FROM *Bureaucracy: What Government Agencies Do and Why
They Do It*—JAMES Q. WILSON   248

DEBATING THE ISSUES: PRIVATIZATION OF GOVERNMENT
ACTIVITY   257

37 *"Federalist* No. 70: Where Does the Public Service Begin and
End?"—JANINE R. WEDEL   258

38 "Privatization"—CATO HANDBOOK FOR POLICYMAKERS   268

CHAPTER 8   The Judiciary   273

39 *The Federalist*, No. 78—ALEXANDER HAMILTON   273

40 "The Court and American Life," FROM *Storm Center: The Supreme
Court in American Politics*—DAVID O'BRIEN   280

41 *The Hollow Hope: Can Courts Bring About Social Change?*—GERALD N.
ROSENBERG   287

DEBATING THE ISSUES: INTERPRETING THE CONSTITUTION
—ORIGINALISM OR A LIVING CONSTITUTION?   293

42 "Constitutional Interpretation the Old-Fashioned Way"
—ANTONIN SCALIA   294

43 "Our Democratic Constitution"—STEPHEN BREYER   302

PART III   Political Behavior: Participation

CHAPTER 9   Public Opinion and the Media   317

44 "Polling the Public," FROM *Public Opinion in a Democracy*—GEORGE
GALLUP   317

45 "Choice Words: If You Can't Understand Our Poll Questions,
Then How Can We Understand Your Answers?"
—RICHARD MORIN   325

46 "News vs. Entertainment: How Increasing Media Choice
Widens Gaps in Political Knowledge and Turnout"
—MARKUS PRIOR   330

DEBATING THE ISSUES: THE FUTURE OF POLITICAL
JOURNALISM   337

47 "Goodbye to the Age of Newspapers (Hello to a New Era
of Corruption)"—PAUL STARR   338

48 "How to Save the News"—JAMES FALLOWS   346

CHAPTER 10   Elections and Voting   358

49 "The Voice of the People: An Echo," FROM *The Responsible Electorate*—V. O. KEY, JR.   358

50 "The Unpolitical Animal: How Political Science Understands Voters"—LOUIS MENAND   364

51 "Telling Americans to Vote, or Else"—WILLIAM GALSTON   373

| DEBATING THE ISSUES: VOTER IDENTIFICATION   377

52 "The Historical Context of Voter Photo-ID Laws" —CHANDLER DAVIDSON   378

53 "Requiring Identification by Voters"—HANS VON SPAKOVSKY   384

54 "Is There a Middle Ground in the Voter ID Debate?" —EDWARD B. FOLEY   389

CHAPTER 11   Political Parties   393

55 "The Decline of Collective Responsibility in American Politics" —MORRIS P. FIORINA   393

56 "Be Careful What You Wish For: The Rise of Responsible Parties in American National Politics"—NICOL RAE   404

DEBATING THE ISSUES: RED AMERICA VERSUS BLUE AMERICA —ARE WE POLARIZED?   415

57 "*What* Culture Wars? Debunking the Myth of a Polarized America"—MORRIS P. FIORINA   416

58 "How Divided Are We?"—JAMES Q. WILSON and MORRIS P. FIORINA's Letter in Response to Wilson   419

59 "Tea Minus Zero"—JOHN B. JUDIS   432

CHAPTER 12   Groups and Interests   440

60 "Political Association in the United States," FROM *Democracy in America*—ALEXIS DE TOCQUEVILLE   440

61 "The Alleged Mischiefs of Faction," from *The Governmental Process*—DAVID B. TRUMAN   444

62 "The Logic of Collective Action," FROM *Rise and Decline of Nations* —MANCUR OLSON   452

| Debating the Issues: Corporate and Labor Spending in Campaigns | 462 |

63 "The Decision That Threatens Democracy"—Ronald Dworkin   464

64 "*Citizens United* We Stand"—Bradley A. Smith   471

65 "How Much Has *Citizens United* Changed the Political Game?"—Matt Bai   476

PART IV   Public Policy

CHAPTER 13   Government and the Economy   485

66 "Call for Federal Responsibility"—Franklin Roosevelt   485

67 "Against the Proposed New Deal"—Herbert Hoover   490

68 "The Rise and Fall of the GDP"—Jon Gertner   495

| Debating the Issues: Is Income Inequality a Problem?   505

69 "Why We Can't Ignore Growing Income Inequality" —Timothy Noah   506

70 "Three Cheers for Income Inequality"—Richard A. Epstein   513

CHAPTER 14   Government and Society   519

71 "Providing Social Security Benefits in the Future: A Review of the Social Security System and Plans to Reform It"—David C. John   519

72 "American Business, Public Policy, Case Studies, and Political Theory"—Theodore J. Lowi   533

| Debating the Issues: Health Care Reform   540

73 "Grading Health Reform: Experts Assess Whether the Bill Delivers on Its Promises"—Marilyn Werber Serafini   541

74 "Repeal: Why and How Obamacare Must Be Undone" —Yuval Levin   547

75 "Even After Big Victory, Health Care Future Uncertain" —George E. Condon, Jr.   555

CHAPTER 15   Foreign Policy and World Politics   559

76 "The Age of Open Society"—GEORGE SOROS   559

77 "Reality Check"—PETER D. SUTHERLAND   562

DEBATING THE ISSUES: IS THE WORLD STILL A DANGEROUS
PLACE?   570

78 "Clear and Present Safety: The United States is More
Secure Than Washington Thinks"—MICAH ZENKO and
MICHAEL A. COHEN   571

79 "National Insecurity: Just How Safe Is the United States?"
—PAUL D. MILLER   582

APPENDIX

Marbury v. Madison (1803)   589

McCulloch v. Maryland (1819)   594

Barron v. Baltimore (1833)   599

Roe v. Wade (1973)   601

Brown v. Board of Education of Topeka, Kansas (1954)   605

United States v. Nixon (1974)   608

United States v. Lopez (1995)   612

The Declaration of Independence   619

The Federalist, No. 10—JAMES MADISON   623

The Constitution of the United States of America   629

Amendments to the Constitution   643

Acknowledgments   657

Preface

We compiled this reader with two goals in mind. The first was to introduce students to some of the classic works in political science, so that they could see how these historic arguments connected to the broad themes generally covered in college-level introductory courses in American government. We also introduce students to classic primary-source documents. We think there is great value in reading Woodrow Wilson, David Truman, and V.O. Key, along with primary documents such as the *Federalist Papers*, the writings of Dr. Martin Luther King, Jr., and a major speech by Franklin Roosevelt, among others in this book. We also include more recent classics by political scientists such as Richard Fenno, David Mayhew, Gerald Rosenberg, and Richard Neustadt. Combining these classic readings with more modern selections is a good way to show how the main themes in American politics endure. As the title suggests, many contemporary issues are similar to what earlier generations of Americans—and the Framers themselves—had to work out through existing political institutions and processes, or by changing those processes when they proved inadequate.

Our second goal was to expose students to debates on important contemporary political controversies. These debates give students examples of high-level political argumentation, showing how scholars and other expert commentators probe, analyze, attempt to persuade, and confront competing arguments. In some of the debates, authors directly challenge each other in a point/counterpoint format. In most of the debates the authors do not directly engage each other, but rather present a range of arguments on opposing sides of issues. For example, in this edition we have added new debates on immigration reform and state power, same-sex marriage, and income inequality. Our hope is that students will see the value of real argument and become discerning consumers of political information.

Finally, in addition to editing down selections to a manageable length while preserving the authors' central arguments, the book includes two pedagogical devices: the introduction to each article and debate, and discussion questions at the conclusion to each piece. The introductions provide students with the context of a given article or debate while briefly summarizing the arguments. The questions provide the basis for students to engage some of the main ideas of an article.

THE
ENDURING DEBATE

CLASSIC AND CONTEMPORARY READINGS
IN AMERICAN POLITICS

Seventh Edition

PART I

The Constitutional System

CHAPTER 1

Political Culture

1

From *The Liberal Tradition in America: An Interpretation of American Political Thought Since the Revolution*

Louis Hartz

Political culture refers to the orientation of citizens toward the political system and toward themselves as actors in it. This includes the basic values, beliefs, attitudes, predispositions, and expectations that citizens bring to political life. Given the great diversity of the American population, one might expect a similarly diverse array of thought within political culture, with rival sets of political values challenging each other. In his classic and influential work, Louis Hartz argues that in fact there is broad agreement in the United States around a set of political beliefs. Hartz refers to this as the "liberal tradition"; the terms "liberal consensus" and "American creed" have been used by other authors. "Liberal" here refers to its original meaning from eighteenth-century political and economic theory—a focus on the individual and minimizing government intervention in daily life. Within the liberal tradition, the beliefs in equality, private property, liberty, individualism, protection of religious freedom, and democracy are especially powerful. There is certainly debate over what these terms mean or how heavily to weigh one belief versus another when they are in conflict, and these clashes drive a wedge between the two major political parties. But social and political movements in the United States, such as the movements for black civil rights and women's rights, have generally not directly challenged these beliefs. On the contrary, most movements seek to show how their beliefs and principles are highly consistent with these basic American beliefs. Hartz argues that it is the nature of American history that has led to this unusual uniformity. Not having had a feudal stage, Americans also did not witness the revolutionary stages and ideologies that challenged feudalism in Europe. As Hartz puts it, "no feudalism, no socialism." This historical path does present some problems, in Hartz's view. Americans view liberalism as natural, as obvious. Americans are hardly aware of it as an ideology because it has been unchallenged. To Hartz, writing in the 1950s, this lack of awareness sometimes blinds Americans to policy alternatives, heightens their fears of social disharmony and "foreign" ideas, and makes it hard for Americans to understand other societies where a liberal tradition is not so dominant.

1. America and Europe

The analysis which this book contains is based on what might be called the storybook truth about American history: that America was settled by men who fled from the feudal and clerical oppressions of the Old World. If there is anything in this view, as old as the national folklore itself, then the outstanding thing about the American community in Western history ought to be the non-existence of those oppressions, or since the reaction against them was in the broadest sense liberal, that the American community is a liberal community. We are confronted * * * with * * * America skipping the feudal stage of history * * *. "Feudalism" refers technically to the institutions of the medieval era, and it is well known that aspects of the decadent feudalism of the later period, such as primogeniture, entail, and quitrents, were present in America even in the eighteenth century. "Liberalism" is an even vaguer term, clouded as it is by all sorts of modern social reform connotations, and even when one insists on using it in the classic Lockian sense, as I shall insist here, there are aspects of our original life in the Puritan colonies and the South which hardly fit its meaning. But these are the liabilities of any large generalization, danger points but not insuperable barriers. What in the end is more interesting is the curious failure of American historians, after repeating endlessly that America was grounded in escape from the European past, to interpret our history in the light of that fact. * * *

* * *

2. "Natural Liberalism": The Frame of Mind

One of the central characteristics of a nonfeudal society is that it lacks a genuine revolutionary tradition, the tradition which in Europe has been linked with the Puritan and French revolutions: that it is "born free," as Tocqueville said. And this being the case, it lacks also a tradition of reaction * * *. Its liberalism is * * * a "natural" phenomenon. But the matter is curiously broader than this, for a society which begins with Locke, and thus transforms him, stays with Locke, by virtue of an absolute and irrational attachment it develops for him, and becomes as indifferent to the challenge of socialism in the later era as it was unfamiliar with the heritage of feudalism in the earlier one. It has within it, as it were, a kind of self-completing mechanism, which insures the universality of the liberal idea. * * * It is not accidental that America, which has uniquely lacked a feudal tradition, has uniquely lacked also a socialist tradition. The hidden origin of socialist thought everywhere in the West is to be found in the feudal ethos. * * *

America has presented the world with the peculiar phenomenon, not of a frustrated middle class, but of a *"frustrated aristocracy"*—of men, Aristotelian-like, trying to break out of the egalitarian confines of middle-class life but suffering guilt and failure in the process. The South before the Civil War is the case par excellence of this, though New England of course exemplifies it also. * * * The Southerners were thrown into fantastic contradictions by their iconoclastic conservatism, by what I have called the "Reactionary Enlightenment," and after the Civil War for good historical reasons they fell quickly into oblivion. The South, as John Crowe Ransom has said, has been the part of America closest to Old World Europe, but it has never really been Europe. It has been an alien child in a liberal family, tortured and confused, driven to a fantasy life which, instead of disproving the power of Locke in America, portrays more poignantly than anything else the tyranny he has had.

* * * Here we have one of the great and neglected relationships in American history: the common fecklessness of the Southern "feudalists" and the modern socialists. It is not accidental, but something rooted in the logic of all of Western history, that they should fail alike to leave a dent in the American liberal intelligence. * * * Socialism arises not only to fight capitalism but remnants of feudalism itself, so that the failure of the Southern [feudalists], in addition to setting the pattern for the failure of the later Marxists, robbed them in the process of a normal ground for growth. * * *

Surely, then, it is a remarkable force: this fixed, dogmatic liberalism of a liberal way of life. It is the secret root from which have sprung many of the most puzzling of American cultural phenomena. Take the unusual power of the Supreme Court and the cult of constitution worship on which it rests. Federal factors apart, judicial review as it has worked in America would be inconceivable without the national acceptance of the Lockian creed, ultimately enshrined in the Constitution, since the removal of high policy to the realm of adjudication implies a prior recognition of the principles to be legally interpreted. * * * If in England a marvelous organic cohesion has held together the feudal, liberal, and socialist ideas, it would still be unthinkable there that the largest issues of public policy should be put before nine Talmudic judges examining a single text. But this is merely another way of saying that law has flourished on the corpse of philosophy in America, for the settlement of the ultimate moral question is the end of speculation upon it. Pragmatism, interestingly enough America's great contribution to the philosophic tradition, does not alter this, since it feeds itself on the Lockian settlement. It is only when you take your ethics for granted that all problems emerge as problems of technique. Not that this is a bar in America to institutional innovations of highly non-Lockian kind. Indeed, as the New Deal shows, when you simply "solve problems" on the basis of a submerged and absolute liberal faith, you can depart from Locke with a kind of inventive freedom that European Liberal reformers and even European socialists, dominated by ideological systems, cannot duplicate. * * *

Here is a Lockian doctrine which in the West as a whole is the symbol of rationalism, yet in America the devotion to it has been so irrational that it has not even been recognized for what it is: liberalism. There has never been a "liberal movement" or a real "liberal party" in America: we have only had the American Way of Life, a nationalist articulation of Locke which usually does not know that Locke himself is involved; and we did not even get that until after the Civil War when the Whigs of the nation, deserting the Hamiltonian tradition, saw the capital that could be made out of it. This is why even critics who have noticed America's moral unity have usually missed its substance. Ironically, "liberalism" is a stranger in the land of its greatest realization and fulfillment. But this is not all. Here is a doctrine which everywhere in the West has been a glorious symbol of individual liberty, yet in America its compulsive power has been so great that it has posed a threat to liberty itself. * * *

I believe that this is the basic ethical problem of a liberal society: not the danger of the majority which has been its conscious fear, but the danger of unanimity, which has slumbered unconsciously behind it: the "tyranny of opinion" that Tocqueville saw unfolding as even the pathetic social distinctions of the Federalist era collapsed before his eyes. But in recent times this manifestation of irrational Lockianism, or of "Americanism," to use a favorite term of the American Legion, * * * has neither slumbered nor been unconscious. It has been very much awake in a red scare hysteria which no other nation in the West has really been able to understand. And this suggests a very significant principle: that when a liberal community faces military and ideological pressure from without it transforms eccentricity into sin, and the irritating figure of the bourgeois gossip flowers into the frightening figure of an A. Mitchell Palmer or a Senator McCarthy. * * *

The decisive domestic issue of our time may well lie in the counter resources a liberal society can muster against this deep and unwritten tyrannical compulsion it contains. They exist. Given the individualist nature of the Lockian doctrine, there is always a logical impulse within it to transcend the very conformitarian spirit it breeds in a Lockian society * * *.

But the most powerful force working to shatter the American absolutism is, paradoxically enough, the very international involvement which tensifies it. This involvement is complex in its implications. If in the context of the Russian Revolution it elicits a domestic red scare, in the context of diplomacy it elicits an impulse to impose Locke everywhere. * * * Thus to say that world politics shatters "Americanism" at the moment it intensifies it is to say a lot: it is to say that the basic horizons of the nation both at home and abroad are drastically widened by it. * * * [W]hen has the nation appreciated more keenly the limits of its own cultural pattern as applied to the rest of the world? * * * [W]hen has the meaning of civil liberties been more ardently understood than now? * * * The outcome of the battle between intensified "Americanism" and new enlightenment is still an open question.

* * *

3. The Dynamics of a Liberal Society

So far I have spoken of natural liberalism as a psychological whole, embracing the nation and inspiring unanimous decisions. We must not assume, however, that this is to obscure or to minimize the nature of the internal conflicts which have characterized American political life. * * * What we learn from the concept of a liberal society, lacking feudalism and therefore socialism and governed by an irrational Lockianism, is that the domestic struggles of such a society have all been projected with the setting of Western liberal alignments. * * *

* * *

That society has been a triumph for the liberal idea, but we must not assume that this ideological victory was not helped forward by the magnificent material setting it found in the New World. The agrarian and proletarian strands of the American democratic personality, which in some sense typify the whole of American uniqueness, reveal a remarkable collusion between Locke and the New World. Had it been merely the liberal spirit alone which inspired the American farmer to become capitalistically oriented, to repudiate save for a few early remnants the village organization of Europe, to produce for a market and even to enter capitalist occupations on the side such as logging and railroad building, then the difficulties he encountered would have been greater than they were. But where land was abundant and the voyage to the New World itself a claim to independence, the spirit which repudiated peasantry and tenantry flourished with remarkable ease. Similarly, had it merely been an aspect of irrational Lockianism which inspired the American worker to think in terms of the capitalist setup, the task would have been harder than it was.

But social fluidity was peculiarly fortified by the riches of a rich land, so that there was no small amount of meaning to Lincoln's claim in 1861 that the American laborer, instead of "being fixed to that condition for life," works for "a while," then "saves," then "hires another beginner" as he himself becomes an entrepreneur. And even when factory industrialism gained sway after the Civil War, and the old artisan and cottage-and-mill mentality was definitely gone, it was still a Lockian* idea fortified by

---

*"Lockian" refers to John Locke, a British political theorist. Locke's ideas of individualism, liberty, property rights, and limited government influenced political leaders at the time of the American Revolution [Editors].

material resources which inspired the triumph of the job mentality of Gompers rather than the class mentality of the European worker. The "petit-bourgeois" giant of America, though ultimately a triumph for the liberal idea, could hardly have chosen a better material setting in which to flourish.

* * *

One cannot say of the liberal society analysis that by concentrating on national unities it rules out the meaning of domestic conflict. Actually it discovers that meaning * * *. The argument over whether we should "stress" solidarity or conflict in American politics misleads us by advancing a false set of alternatives.

* * *

DISCUSSION QUESTIONS

1. Do you agree with Hartz that Americans have a hard time understanding other societies because of ideological uniformity in the United States?

2. Do you think Hartz is correct in saying that Americans are in agreement on the values of the liberal tradition? Are there parts of American history or of society today that make you doubt his thesis?

3. Without limiting yourself to Hartz's observations, what do you think might be some of the advantages and disadvantages of a high degree of agreement on basic values for American society and politics?

From *The Creation of the American Republic 1776–1787*

Gordon S. Wood

In the 1960s, a group of historians took issue with the depiction of American society as fundamentally and uniformly liberal. Perhaps American society in the twentieth century was dominated by the liberal tradition, historians such as Gordon Wood argued, but in the colonial and revolutionary period, it was classical republicanism that most shaped public thought about politics. The liberal tradition emphasizes the primacy of the individual in society; classical republicanism draws individuals' attention to society and the community. The classical republican approach does not disagree that individuals have personal responsibility and need to work hard and diligently. It would, however, suggest that the point of self-improvement is to better serve the community and society. Individual liberty and freedom, which are paramount in the liberal tradition, might be more subject to societal and community limits in the classical republican view. Wood notes that in this view, politics is not primarily about achieving one's personal interest. Rather, the focus is on civic duty. Participation was expected, for the social good. Individuals are to be motivated not by self-interest but by morality and virtue. Although Wood argues elsewhere that classical republicanism failed in the 1780s and made way for liberal politics to become dominant and embraced by the Constitution, other historians suggest that the classical republican ideals continued to influence American politics through various reform movements over the course of U.S. history.

* * *

The Public Good

The sacrifice of individual interests to the greater good of the whole formed the essence of republicanism and comprehended for Americans the idealistic goal of their Revolution. From this goal flowed all of the Americans' exhortatory literature and all that made their ideology truly revolutionary. This republican ideology both presumed and helped shape the Americans' conception of the way their society and politics should be structured and operated—a vision so divorced from the realities of American society, so contrary to the previous century of American experience, that it alone was enough to make the Revolution one of the great utopian movements of American history. By 1776 the Revolution came to represent a final attempt, perhaps—given the nature of American society—even a desperate attempt, by many Americans to realize the traditional Commonwealth ideal of a corporate society, in which the common good would be the only objective of government.

*   *   *

To make the people's welfare—the public good—the exclusive end of government became for the Americans, as one general put it, their "Polar Star," the central tenet of the Whig faith, shared not only by Hamilton and Paine at opposite ends of the Whig spectrum, but by any American bitterly opposed to a system which held "that a Part is greater than its Whole; or, in other Words, that some Individuals ought to be considered, even to the Destruction of the Community, which they compose." No phrase except "liberty" was invoked more often by the Revolutionaries than "the public good." It expressed the colonists' deepest hatreds of the old order and their most visionary hopes for the new. * * *

From the logic of belief that "all government . . . is or ought to be, calculated for the general good and safety of the community," for which end "the most effectual means that human wisdom hath ever been able to devise, is frequently appealing to the body of the people," followed the Americans' unhesitating adoption of republicanism in 1776. The peculiar excellence of republican government was that it was "wholly characteristical of the purport, matter, or object for which government ought to be instituted." By definition it had no other end than the welfare of the people: *res publica*, the public affairs, or the public good. "The word *republic*," said Thomas Paine, "means the *public good*, or the good of the whole, in contradistinction to the despotic-form, which makes the good of the sovereign, or of one man, the only object of the government." * * *

Since in a free government the public good was identical with the people's welfare, a "matter of COMMON FEELING" and founded on the "COMMON CONSENT" of the people, the best way of realizing it in the Whig mind was to allow the people a maximum voice in the government. "That the great body of the people," as even the Tory William Smith of Philadelphia admitted, "can have any interest separate from their country, or (when fairly understood) pursue any other, is not to be imagined," "unless," as John Sullivan said, "we suppose them idiots or self-murderers." Therefore any government which lacked "a proper representation of the people" or was in any way even "independent of the people" was liable to violate the common good and become tyrannical. Most Whigs had little doubt of the people's honesty or even of their ability to discern what was good for themselves. It was a maxim, declared a New York patriot, "that whatever may be the particular opinions of Individuals, the bulk of the people, both mean, and think right." Was there ever any fear, James Burgh had gone so far as to ask, that the people might be *"too free* to consult the general good?" Of course even the most radical English Whigs admitted that the people might sometimes mistake their own interest and might often be unable to affect it even when they did correctly perceive it. Most Americans therefore assumed that the people, in their representational expression of their collective liberty in the houses of representatives, could not run the whole government. "Liberty, though the most essential requisite in government," Richard Price had written, "is not the only one; wisdom, union, dispatch, secrecy, and vigour are likewise requisite"—qualities best supplied by a magistracy and a senate.

Yet such governors and upper houses, however necessary, must be electively dependent on the people. Republicanism with its elective magistracy would not eliminate the problems of politics and the threat of power, but it did promise a new era of stability and cooperation between rulers and ruled. * * * For decades, and especially in recent years, the Crown's presence in America had played havoc with the colonists' political life and was the real source of that factious behavior of which royal officials had so repeatedly and unjustly accused them. "Every man that has lived any time in America, under regal government, knows what frequent, and almost continual opposition there is between the country interest and those in power." "By keeping clear of British government," the Americans could at last be rid of those "jars and contentions between Governors and Assemblies." By allowing the people to elect their magistracy, republicanism would work to "blend the interests of the people and their rulers" and thus "put down every animosity among the people." In the kind of states where *"their governors shall proceed from the midst of them"* the people could be surer that their interests exclusively would be promoted, and therefore in turn would "pay obedience to officers properly appointed" and maintain "no discontents on account of their advancement."

What made the Whig conception of politics and the republican emphasis on the collective welfare of the people comprehensible was the assumption that the people, especially when set against their rulers, were a homogeneous body whose "interests when candidly considered are one." Since everyone in the community was linked organically to everyone else, what was good for the whole community was ultimately good for all the parts. The people were in fact a single organic piece (*"for God hath so tempered the body that there should be no Schism in the body, but that the Members should have the same care for one another"*) with a unitary concern that was the only legitimate objective of governmental policy. This common interest was not, as we might today think of it, simply the sum or consensus of the particular interests that made up the community. It was rather an entity in itself, prior to and distinct from the various private interests of groups and individuals. As Samuel Adams said in 1776, paraphrasing Vattel, the state was "a moral person, having an interest and will of its own." Because politics was conceived to be not the reconciling but the transcending of the different interests of the society in the search for the single common good, the republican state necessarily had to be small in territory and generally similar in interests. Despite sporadic suggestions in the press for "a simple government" of a strong continental congress chosen "by the people, (not by their representatives)," and uniting all the people "in one great republick," few Americans thought that such an extensive continental republic, as distinct from a league of states, was feasible in 1776—however much they may have differed over the desirable strength of the expected confederation.

No one, of course, denied that the community was filled with different, often clashing combinations of interests. But apart from the basic conflict between governors and people these were not to be dignified by their incorporation into formal political theory or into any serious discussion of what ought to be. In light of the assumption that the state was "to be considered as one moral whole" these interests and parties were regarded as aberrations or perversions, indeed signs of sickness in the body politic. Although some eighteenth-century thinkers were in fact beginning to perceive the inevitability, even the desirability, of faction in a free state, most continued to regard division among the people as "both dangerous and destructive," arising "from false ambition, avarice, or revenge." Men lost control of their basest passions and were unwilling to sacrifice their immediate desires for the corporate good. Hence, "party differences," however much they may infect the society, could never ideally be admitted into the institutions of government, but "would be dropped at the threshold of the state house." The representatives of the people would not act as spokesmen for private and partial interests, but all would be "disinterested men, who could have no interest of their own to seek," and "would employ their whole time for the public good; then there would be but one interest, the good of the people at large."

*   *   *

Yet ironically it was precisely internal discord and conflict for which republics were most widely known. Throughout history "free republican governments have been objected to, as if exposed to factions from an excess of liberty." But this was because liberty had been misunderstood and falsely equated with licentiousness or the liberty of man in a state of nature which was "a state of war, rapine and murder." True liberty was "natural liberty restrained in such manner, as to render society one great family; where everyone must consult his neighbour's happiness, as well as his own." In a republic "each individual gives up all private interest that is not consistent with the general good, the interest of the whole body." For the republican patriots of 1776 the commonweal was all-encompassing—a transcendent object with a unique moral worth that made partial considerations fade into insignificance. "Let regard be had only to the good of the whole" was the constant exhortation by publicists and clergy. Ideally, republicanism obliterated the individual. "A Citizen," said Samuel

Adams, "owes everything to the Commonwealth." "Every man in a republic," declared Benjamin Rush, "is public property. His time and talents—his youth—his manhood—his old age—nay more, life, all belong to his country." "No man is a true republican," wrote a Pennsylvanian in 1776, "that will not give up his single voice to that of the public."

Individual liberty and the public good were easily reconcilable because the important liberty in the Whig ideology was public or political liberty. In 1776 the solution to the problems of American politics seemed to rest not so much in emphasizing the private rights of individuals against the general will as it did in stressing the public rights of the collective people against the supposed privileged interests of their rulers. "Civil Liberty," as one colonist put it, was not primarily individual; it was "the freedom of bodies politic, or States." Because, as Josiah Quincy said, the people "as a body" were "never interested to injure themselves," and were "uniformly desirous of the general welfare," there could be no real sense of conflict between public and personal liberty. Indeed, the private liberties of individuals depended upon their collective public liberty. * * *

Thus in the minds of most Whigs in 1776 individual rights, even the basic civil liberties that we consider so crucial, possessed little of their modern theoretical relevance when set against the will of the people. This is why, for example, throughout the eighteenth century the Americans could contend for the broadest freedom of speech against the magistracy, while at the same time punishing with a severe strictness any seditious libels against the representatives of the people in the colonial assemblies. Anyone who tried to speak against the interests of the people "should be held in execration. . . . Every word, that tends to weaken the hands of the people is a crime of devilish dye"; indeed, "it is the *unpardonable Sin* in politics." Thus it was "no *Loss of Liberty*, that court-minions can complain of, when they are silenced. No man has right to say a word, which may lame the liberties of his country." * * *

* * *

Even at the beginning, however, there were some good Whigs who perceived the inherent conflict between individual liberty and traditional republican theory. Ancient Sparta, William Moore Smith told the members of the Continental Congress in the spring of 1775, had demonstrated the problem. Knowing that luxury was the great enemy of republicanism and liberty, Lycurgus had sought to avoid the evil by eliminating wealth itself. But in doing so he undermined the very basis of freedom. "He seems not to have reflected that there can be no true liberty without security of property; and where property is secure, industry begets wealth; and wealth is often productive of a train of evils naturally destructive to virtue and freedom!" "Here, then," said Smith, "is a sad dilemma in politics." If the people "exclude *wealth*, it must be by regulations intrenching too far upon civil *liberty*." But if wealth is allowed to flourish, "the siren *luxury*" soon follows at its heels and gradually contaminates the whole society. "What is to be done in this case?" Must the society, "to secure the first of blessings, *liberty*," strangle wealth, the first offspring of liberty, in its birth and thus in effect destroy liberty as well? "Or, is there no proper use of *wealth* and *civil happiness*, the genuine descendants of *civil liberty*, without abusing them to the nourishment of *luxury* and *corruption*?" Smith, like other Whigs in 1776, thought there was an answer to the dilemma in the more enlightened policy and "purer system of *religion*" of this modern age—"to regulate the use of wealth, but not to exclude it."

*   *   *

The Need for Virtue

Perhaps everyone in the eighteenth century could have agreed that in theory no state was more beautiful than a republic, whose whole object by definition was the good of the people. * * * The very greatness of republicanism, its utter dependence on the people, was at the same time its source of weakness. In a republic there was no place for fear; there could be no sustained coercion from above. The state, like no other, rested on the consent of the governed freely given and not compelled. In a free government the laws, as the American clergy never tired of repeating, had to be obeyed by the people for conscience's sake, not for wrath's.

*   *   *

In a monarchy each man's desire to do what was right in his own eyes could be restrained by fear or force. In a republic, however, each man must somehow be persuaded to submerge his personal wants into the greater good of the whole. This willingness of the individual to sacrifice his private interests for the good of the community—such patriotism or love of country—the eighteenth century termed "public virtue." A republic was such a delicate polity precisely because it demanded an extraordinary moral character in the people. Every state in which the people participated needed a degree of virtue; but a republic which rested solely on the people absolutely required it. * * * The eighteenth-century mind was thoroughly convinced that a popularly based government "cannot be supported without *Virtue*." Only with a public-spirited, self-sacrificing people could the authority of a popularly elected ruler be obeyed, but "more by the virtue of the people, than by the terror of his power." Because virtue was truly the lifeblood of the republic, the thoughts and hopes surrounding this concept of public spirit gave the Revolution its socially radical character—an expected alteration in the very behavior of the people, "laying the foundation in a constitution, not without or over, but within the subjects."

This public virtue, "this endearing and benevolent passion," was "the noblest which can be displayed" and represented all that men of the eighteenth century sought in social behavior. "Its grand source" lay in the attitudes and actions of the individuals who made up the society, "in that charity which forms every social connection." In other words, public virtue, the willingness of the people to surrender all, even their lives, for the good of the state, was primarily the consequence of men's individual private virtues. * * * For most Americans in 1776 vicious behavior by an individual could have only disastrous results for the community. A man racked by the selfish passions of greed, envy, and hate lost his conception of order; "his sense of a connection with the *general* system—his benevolence—his desire and freedom of *doing good*, ceased." It seemed obvious that a republican society could not "be maintained without justice, benevolence and the social virtues." * * * Somehow, as a Boston writer argued * * * the individual's widening and traditionally weakening circles of love—from himself to his family to the community—must be broken into; men must be convinced that their fullest satisfaction would come from the subordination of their individual loves to the greater good of the whole. It was man's duty and interest to be benevolent. "The happiness of every individual" depended "on the happiness of society." * * * Once men correctly perceived their relation to the commonwealth they would never injure what was really their personal interest to protect and sustain.

Equality

*   *   *

Even the most radical republicans in 1776 admitted the inevitability of all natural distinctions: weak and strong, wise and foolish—and even of incidental distinctions: rich and poor, learned and unlearned. Yet, of course, in a truly republican society the artificial subsidiary distinctions would never be extreme, not as long as they were based solely on natural distinctions. It was widely believed that equality of opportunity would necessarily result in a rough equality of station, that as long as the social channels of ascent and descent were kept open it would be impossible for any artificial aristocrats or overgrown rich men to maintain themselves for long. With social movement founded only on merit, no distinctions could have time to harden. * * * And projected public educational systems would open up the advantages of learning and advancement to all.

Great consequences were expected to flow from such an egalitarian society. If every man realized that his associations with other men and the state depended solely on his merit, then, as former Massachusetts Governor Thomas Pownall told the Americans, there would be an end to the jealousy and the contentions for "unequal Dominion" that had beset communities from time immemorial. Indeed, equality represented the social source from which the anticipated harmony and public virtue of the New World would flow. "It is this principle of equality . . . ," wrote one Virginian in 1776, "which alone can inspire and preserve the virtue of its members, by placing them in a relation to the publick and to their fellow-citizens, which has a tendency to engage the heart and affections to both."

It was a beautiful but ambiguous ideal. The Revolutionaries who hoped for so much from equality assumed that republican America would be a community where none would be too rich or too poor, and yet at the same time believed that men would readily accede to such distinctions as emerged as long as they were fairly earned. But ironically their ideal contained the sources of the very bitterness and envy it was designed to eliminate. For if the promised equality was the kind in which "one should consider himself as good a man as another, and not be brow beaten or intimidated by riches or supposed superiority," then their new republican society would be no different from that in which they had lived, and the Revolution would have failed to end precisely what it was supposed to end. Indeed, although few Americans could admit it in 1776, it was the very prevalence of this ambivalent attitude toward equality that had been at the root of much of their squabbling during the eighteenth century.

*   *   *

Discussion Questions

1. Do classical republican values sound impractical for contemporary American politics? Or do you think these values have more influence in politics than someone like Louis Hartz would acknowledge?

2. What are the key components of the classical republican outlook, as presented by Wood? How do they differ from the liberal tradition?

3. Wood notes at several points that some of the strengths of republican thought would also prove to make it difficult for republicanism to thrive. Identify and describe these strengths.

3

"Beyond Tocqueville, Myrdal, and Hartz: The Multiple Traditions in America"

Rogers M. Smith

Where liberalism points to notions of equality, Rogers Smith argues that there is another tradition in American political thought that has been influential. He does not deny the significance in American political history of liberalism as described by Louis Hartz, or of classical republicanism as described by Gordon Wood. Smith, however, contends that an equally significant strand of thought, "ascriptive Americanism," has been important across U.S. history. In this way of thinking, society is a hierarchy, where some groups are on top and others are below. Those on top are deserving of the rights and benefits the liberal tradition can offer; those below are not. The most glaring examples of this pattern throughout American history were the treatment of racial minorities, especially blacks, and the structure of laws that denied women the same opportunities as men. Smith notes that those holding these illiberal views were not on the fringes of society but, rather, were probably the majority view at many times. We cannot, Smith argues, marginalize the impact of ascriptive Americanism or those who held these views. American public policy at the highest levels was influenced by its premises. Researchers at universities and other institutions aimed to show through science the inferiority of some races and groups to others. Moreover, the same individuals often held these illiberal views in tandem with their liberal or republican views. They expended great intellectual energy to make these views seem acceptable and consistent with fundamental American beliefs. American political culture, in Smith's view, combines the traditions of liberalism, classical republicanism, and ascriptive Americanism.

Since the nation's inception, analysts have described American political culture as the preeminent example of modern liberal democracy, of government by popular consent with respect for the equal rights of all. They have portrayed American political development as the working out of liberal democratic or republican principles, via both "liberalizing" and "democratizing" socioeconomic changes and political efforts to cope with tensions inherent in these principles. Illiberal, undemocratic beliefs and practices have usually been seen only as expressions of ignorance and prejudice, destined to marginality by their lack of rational defenses. * * *

[Alexis de] Tocqueville's thesis—that America has been most shaped by the unusually free and egalitarian ideas and material conditions that prevailed at its founding—captures important truths. Nonetheless, the purpose of this essay is to challenge that thesis by showing that its adherents fail to give due weight to inegalitarian ideologies and conditions that have shaped the participants and the substance of American politics just as deeply. For over 80% of U.S. history, its laws declared most of the world's population to be ineligible for full American citizenship solely because of their race, original nationality, or gender. For at least two-thirds of American history, the majority of the domestic adult population was also ineligible for full citizenship for the same reasons. * * *

The Tocquevillian story is thus deceptive because it is too narrow. It is centered on relationships among a minority of Americans (white men, largely of northern European ancestry) analyzed via reference to categories derived from the hierarchy of political and economic statuses men have held in Europe: monarchs and aristocrats, commercial burghers, farmers, industrial and rural laborers, and indigents. Because most European observers and British American men have regarded these categories as politically fundamental, it is understandable that they have always found the most striking fact about the new nation to be its lack of one type of ascriptive hierarchy. There was no hereditary monarchy or nobility native to British America, and the revolutionaries rejected both the authority of the British king and aristocracy and the creation of any new American substitutes. Those features of American political life made the United States appear remarkably egalitarian by comparison with Europe.

But the comparative moral, material, and political egalitarianism that prevailed at the founding among moderately propertied white men was surrounded by an array of other fixed, ascriptive systems of unequal status, all largely unchallenged by the American revolutionaries. Men were thought naturally suited to rule over women, within both the family and the polity. White northern Europeans were thought superior culturally—and probably biologically—to black Africans, bronze Native Americans, and indeed all other races and civilizations. Many British Americans also treated religion as an inherited condition and regarded Protestants as created by God to be morally and politically, as well as theologically, superior to Catholics, Jews, Muslims, and others.

These beliefs were not merely emotional prejudices or "attitudes." Over time, American intellectual and political elites elaborated distinctive justifications for these ascriptive systems, including inegalitarian scriptural readings, the scientific racism of the "American school" of ethnology, racial and sexual Darwinism, and the romantic cult of Anglo-Saxonism in American historiography. All these discourses identified the true meaning of *Americanism* with particular forms of cultural, religious, ethnic, and especially racial and gender hierarchies. Many adherents of ascriptive Americanist outlooks insisted that the nation's political and economic structures should formally reflect natural and cultural inequalities, even at the cost of violating doctrines of universal rights. Although these views never entirely prevailed, their impact has been wide and deep.

Thus to approach a truer picture of America's political culture and its characteristic conflicts, we must consider more than the familiar categories of (absent) feudalism and socialism and (pervasive) bourgeois liberalism and republicanism. The nation has also been deeply constituted by the ideologies and practices that defined the relationships of the white male minority with subordinate groups, and the relationships of these groups with each other. When these elements are kept in view, the flat plain of American egalitarianism mapped by Tocqueville and others suddenly looks quite different. We instead perceive America's initial conditions as exhibiting only a rather small, recently leveled valley of relative equality nestled amid steep mountains of hierarchy. And though we can see forces working to erode those mountains over time, broadening the valley, many of the peaks also prove to be volcanic, frequently responding to seismic pressures with outbursts that harden into substantial peaks once again.

To be sure, America's ascriptive, unequal statuses, and the ideologies by which they have been defended have always been heavily conditioned and constrained by the presence of liberal democratic values and institutions. The reverse, however, is also true. Although liberal democratic ideas and practices have been more potent in America than elsewhere, American politics is best seen as expressing the interaction of multiple political traditions, including *liberalism, republicanism,* and *ascriptive forms of Americanism,* which have collectively comprised American political culture, without any constituting it as a whole. Though Americans have often struggled over contradictions among these traditions, almost all have tried to embrace what they saw as the best features of each.

Ascriptive outlooks have had such a hold in America because they have provided something that neither liberalism nor republicanism has done so well. They have offered creditable intellectual and psychological reasons for many Americans to believe that their social roles and personal characteristics express an identity that has inherent and transcendant worth, thanks to nature, history, and God. Those rationales have obviously aided those who sat atop the nation's political, economic, and social hierarchies. But many Americans besides elites have felt that they have gained meaning, as well as material and political benefits, from their nation's traditional structures of ascribed places and destinies.

Conventional narratives, preoccupied with the absence of aristocracy and socialism, usually stress the liberal and democratic elements in the rhetoric of even America's dissenters. These accounts fail to explain how and why liberalizing efforts have frequently lost to forces favoring new forms of racial and gender hierarchy. Those forces have sometimes negated major liberal victories, especially in the half-century following Reconstruction; and the fate of that era may be finding echoes today.

My chief aim here is to persuade readers that many leading accounts of American political culture are inadequate. * * * This argument is relevant to contemporary politics in two ways. First, it raises the possibility that novel intellectual, political, and legal systems reinforcing racial, ethnic, and gender inequalities might be rebuilt in America in the years ahead. That prospect does not seem plausible if the United States has always been essentially liberal democratic, with all exceptions marginal and steadily eliminated. It seems quite real, however, if liberal democratic traditions have been but contested parts of American culture, with in-egalitarian ideologies and practices often resurging even after major enhancements of liberal democracy. Second, the political implications of the view that America has never been completely liberal, and that changes have come only through difficult struggles and then have often not been sustained, are very different from the complacency—sometimes despair—engendered by beliefs that liberal democracy has always been hegemonic.

* * *

The Multiple-Traditions Thesis of American Civic Identity

It seems prudent to stress what is not proposed here. This is not a call for analysts to minimize the significance of white male political actors or their conflicts with each other. Neither is it a call for accounts that assail "Eurocentric" white male oppressors on behalf of diverse but always heroic subjugated groups. The multiple-traditions thesis holds that Americans share a *common* culture but one more complexly and multiply consti-tuted than is usually acknowledged. Most members of all groups have shared and often helped to shape all the ideologies and institutions that have structured American life, including ascriptive ones. A few have done so while resisting all subjugating practices. But members of every group have sometimes embraced "essentialist" ideologies valorizing their own ascriptive traits and denigrating those of others, to bleak effect. Cherokees enslaved blacks, champions of women's rights disparaged blacks and immigrants, and blacks have often been hostile toward Hispanics and other new immigrants. White men, in turn, have been prominent among those combating invidious exclusions, as well as those imposing them.

Above all, recognition of the strong attractions of restrictive American-ist ideas does not imply any denial that America's liberal and democratic traditions have had great normative and political potency, even if they have not been so hegemonic as some claim. Instead, it sheds a new—and, in some respects, more flattering—light on the constitutive role of liberal democratic values in American life. Although some Americans have been willing to repudiate notions of democracy and universal rights, most have not; and though many have tried to blend those commitments with exclusionary ascriptive views, the illogic of these mixes has repeatedly proven a major resource for successful reformers. But we obscure the difficulty of those reforms (and thereby diminish their significance) if we slight the ideological and political appeal of contrary ascriptive traditions by portraying them as merely the shadowy side of a hegemonic liberal republicanism.

At its heart, the multiple-traditions thesis holds that the definitive feature of American political culture has been not its liberal, republican, or "ascriptive Americanist" elements but, rather, this more complex pattern of apparently inconsistent combinations of the traditions, accompanied by recurring conflicts. Because standard accounts neglect this pattern, they do not explore how and why Americans have tried to uphold aspects of all three of these heterogeneous traditions in combinations that are longer on political and psychological appeal than on intellectual coherency.

A focus on these questions generates an understanding of American politics that differs from Tocquevillian ones in four major respects. First, on this view, purely liberal and republican conceptions of civic identity are seen as frequently unsatisfying to many Americans, because they contain elements that threaten, rather than affirm, sincere, reputable beliefs in the propriety of the privileged positions that whites, Christianity, Anglo-Saxon traditions, and patriarchy have had in the United States. At the same time, even Americans deeply attached to those inegalitarian arrangements have also had liberal democratic values. Second, it has therefore been typical, not aberrational, for Americans to embody strikingly opposed beliefs in their institutions, such as doctrines that blacks should and should not be full and equal citizens. But though American efforts to blend aspects of opposing views have often been remarkably stable, the resulting tensions have still been important sources of change. Third, when older types of ascriptive inequality, such as slavery, have been rejected as unduly illiberal, it has been normal, not anomalous, for many Americans to embrace new doctrines and institutions that reinvigorate the hierarchies they esteem in modified form. Changes toward greater inequality and exclusion, as well as toward greater equality and inclusiveness, thus can and do occur. Finally, the dynamics of American development cannot simply be seen as a rising tide of liberalizing forces progressively submerging contrary beliefs and practices. The national course has been more serpentine. The economic, political, and moral forces propelling the United States toward liberal democracy have often been heeded by American leaders, especially since World War II. But the currents pulling toward fuller expression of alleged natural and cultural inequalities have also always won victories. In some eras they have predominated, appearing to define not only the path of safety but that of progress. In all eras, including our own, many Americans have combined their allegiance to liberal democracy with beliefs that the presence of certain groups favored by history, nature, and God has made Americans an intrinsically "special" people. Their adherents have usually regarded such beliefs as benign and intellectually well founded; yet they also have always had more or less harsh discriminatory corollaries.

To test these multiple-traditions claims, consider the United States in 1870. By then the Civil War and Reconstruction had produced dramatic advances in the liberal and democratic character of America's laws. Slavery was abolished. All persons born in the United States and subject to its jurisdiction were deemed citizens of the United States and the states in which they resided, regardless of their race, creed or gender. None could be denied voting rights on racial grounds. The civil rights of all were newly protected through an array of national statutes. The 1790 ban on naturalizing Africans had been repealed, and expatriation declared a natural right. Over the past two decades women had become more politically engaged and had begun to gain respect as political actors.

*   *   *

[Neither liberal or republican analyses] would have had the intellectual resources to explain what in fact occurred. Over the next fifty years, Americans did not make blacks, women, and members of other races full and equal citizens, nor did racial and gender prejudices undergo major erosion. Neither, however, were minorities and women declared to be subhuman and outside the body politic. And although white Americans engaged in extensive violence against blacks and Native Americans, those groups grew in population, and no cataclysm loomed. Instead, intellectual and political elites worked out the most elaborate theories of racial and gender hierarchy in U.S. history and partially embodied them in a staggering array of new laws governing naturalization, immigration, deportation, voting rights, electoral institutions, judicial procedures, and economic rights—but only partially. The laws retained important liberal and democratic features, and some were strengthened. They had enough purchase on the moral and material interests of most Americans to compel advocates of inequality to adopt contrived, often clumsy means to achieve their ends.

The considerable success of the proponents of inegalitarian ideas reflects the power these traditions have long had in America. But after the Civil War, * * * evolutionary theories enormously strengthened the intellectual prestige of doctrines presenting the races and sexes as naturally arrayed into what historians have termed a "raciocultural hierarchy," as well as a "hierarchy of sex." Until the end of the nineteenth century, most evolutionists * * * thought acquired characteristics could be inherited. Thus beliefs in biological differences were easily merged with the * * * historians' views that peoples were the products of historical and cultural forces. Both outlooks usually presented the current traits of the races as fixed for the foreseeable future. Few intellectuals were shy about noting the implications of these views for public policy. Anthropologist Daniel G. Brinton made typical arguments in his 1895 presidential address to the

American Association for the Advancement of Science. He contended that the "black, brown and red races" each had "a peculiar mental temperament which has become hereditary," leaving them constitutionally "recreant to the codes of civilization." Brinton believed that this fact had not been adequately appreciated by American lawmakers. Henceforth, conceptions of "race, nations, tribes" had to "supply the only sure foundations for legislation; not *a priori* notions of the rights of man."

As Brinton knew, many politicians and judges had already begun to seize on such suggestions. In 1882, for example, California senator John Miller drew on the Darwinian "law of the 'survival of the fittest'" to explain that "forty centuries of Chinese life" had "ground into" the Chinese race characteristics that made them unbeatable competitors against the free white man. They were "automatic engines of flesh and blood," of "obtuse nerve," marked by degradation and demoralization, and thus far below the Anglo-Saxon, but were still a threat to the latter's livelihood in a market economy. Hence, Miller argued, the immigration of Chinese laborers must be banned. His bill prevailed, many expressing concern that these Chinese would otherwise become American citizens. The Chinese Exclusion Act was not a vestige of the past but something new, the first repudiation of America's long history of open immigration; and it was justified in terms of the postwar era's revivified racial theories.

Yet although men like Miller not only sustained but expanded Chinese exclusions until they were made virtually total in 1917 (and tight restrictions survived until 1965), they never managed to deny American citizenship to all of the "Chinese race." Until 1917 there were no restrictions on the immigration of upper-class Chinese, and in 1898 the Supreme Court declared that children born on U.S. soil to Chinese parents were American citizens (*United States* v. *Wong Kim Ark* 1898). Birthplace citizenship was a doctrine enshrined in common law, reinforced by the Fourteenth Amendment, and vital to citizenship for the children of *all* immigrant aliens. Hence it had enough legal and political support to override the Court's recognition of Congress's exclusionary desires. Even so, in other cases the Court sustained bans on Chinese immigration while admitting the racial animosities behind them, as in the "Chinese Exclusion Case" (*Chae Chan Ping* v. *United States* 1889); upheld requirements for Chinese-Americans to have certificates of citizenship not required of whites (*Fong Yue Ting* v. *United States* 1893); and permitted officials to deport even Chinese persons who had later been judged by courts to be native-born U.S. citizens (*United States* v. *Ju Toy* 1905).

The upshot, then, was the sort of none-too-coherent mix that the multiple-traditions thesis holds likely. Chinese were excluded on racial grounds, but race did not bar citizenship to those born in the United States; yet Chinese ancestry could subject some American citizens to burdens, including deportation, that others did not face. The mix was not perfect from any ideological viewpoint, but it was politically popular. It maintained a valued inclusive feature of American law (birthplace citizenship) while sharply reducing the resident Chinese population. And it most fully satisfied the increasingly powerful champions of Anglo-Saxon supremacy.

From 1887 on, academic reformers and politicians sought to restrict immigration more generally by a means that paid lip service to liberal norms even as it aimed at racist results—the literacy test. On its face, this measure expressed concern only for the intellectual merits of immigrants. But the test's true aims were spelled out in 1896 by its sponsor, Senator Henry Cabot Lodge, a Harvard Ph.D. in history and politics. Committee research, he reported, showed that the test would exclude "the Italians, Russians, Poles, Hungarians, Greeks, and Asiatics," thereby preserving "the quality of our race and citizenship." Citing "modern history" and "modern science," Thomas Carlyle and Gustave le Bon, Lodge contended that the need for racial exclusion arose from "something deeper and more fundamental than anything which concerns the intellect." Race was above all constituted by moral characteristics, the "stock of ideas, traditions, sentiments, modes of thought" that a people possessed as an "accumulation of centuries of toil and conflict." These mental and moral qualities constituted the "soul of a race," an inheritance in which its members "blindly believe," and upon which learning had no effect. But these qualities could be degraded if "a lower race mixes with a higher"; thus, exclusion by race, not reading ability, was the nation's proper goal.

When the literacy test finally passed in 1917 but proved ineffective in keeping out "lower races," Congress moved to versions of an explicitly racist national-origins quota system. It banned virtually all Asians and permitted European immigration only in ratios preserving the northern European cast of the American citizenry. Congressman Albert Johnson, chief author of the most important quota act in 1924, proclaimed that through it, "the day of indiscriminate acceptance of all races, has definitely ended." The quota system, repealed only in 1965, was a novel, elaborate monument to ideologies holding that access to American citizenship should be subject to racial and ethnic limits. It also served as the prime model for similar systems in Europe and Latin America.

* * *

But despite the new prevalence of such attitudes on the part of northern and western elites in the late nineteenth century, the Reconstruction amendments and statutes were still on the books, and surviving liberal sentiments made repealing them politically difficult. Believers in racial inequality were, moreover, undecided on just what to do about blacks. * * * "Radical" racists * * * argued that blacks, like other lower races, should be excluded from American society and looked hopefully for evidence that they were dying out. Their position was consistent with Hartz's claim that Americans could not tolerate permanent unequal statuses; persons must either be equal citizens or outsiders. But * * * "Conservatives" believed * * * that blacks and other people of color might instead have a permanent "place" in America, so long as "placeness included hierarchy." Some still thought that blacks, like the other "lower races," might one day be led by whites to fully civilized status, but no one expected progress in the near future. Thus blacks should instead be segregated, largely disfranchised, and confined to menial occupations via inferior education and discriminatory hiring practices—but not expelled, tortured, or killed. A few talented blacks might even be allowed somewhat higher stations.

* * * The result was a system closest to Conservative desires, one that kept blacks in their place, although that place was structured more repressively than most Conservatives favored. And unlike the ineffective literacy test, here racial inegalitarians achieved much of what they wanted without explicitly violating liberal legal requirements. Complex registration systems, poll taxes, and civics tests appeared race-neutral but were designed and administered to disfranchise blacks. This intent was little masked. * * * These efforts succeeded. Most dramatically, in Louisiana 95.6% of blacks were registered in 1896, and over half (130,000) voted. After disfranchising measures, black registration dropped by 90% and by 1904 totaled only 1,342. The Supreme Court found convoluted ways to close its eyes to these tactics.

By similar devices, blacks were virtually eliminated from juries in the south, where 90% of American blacks lived, sharply limiting their ability to have their personal and economic rights protected by the courts. "Separate but equal" educational and business laws and practices also stifled the capacities of blacks to participate in the nation's economy as equals, severely curtailed the occupations they could train for, and marked them— unofficially but clearly—as an inferior caste. Thus here, as elsewhere, it was evident that the nation's laws and institutions were not meant to confer the equal civic status they proclaimed for all Americans; but neither did they conform fully to doctrines favoring overt racial hierarchy. They represented another asymmetrical compromise among the multiple ideologies vying to define American political culture.

So, too, did the policies governing two groups whose civic status formally improved during these years: Native Americans and women. * * *

* * *

This period also highlights how the influence of inegalitarian doctrines has not been confined to white male intellectuals, legislators, and judges. The leading writer of the early twentieth-century women's movement, Charlotte Perkins Gilman, was a thoroughgoing Darwinian who accepted that evolution had made women inferior to men in certain respects, although she insisted that these differences were usually exaggerated and that altered social conditions could transform them. And even as he attacked Booker T. Washington for appearing to accept the "alleged inferiority of the Negro race," W. E. B. DuBois embraced the widespread Lamarckian view that racial characteristics were socially conditioned but then inherited as the "soul" of a race. He could thus accept that most blacks were "primitive folk" in need of tutelage. * * *

The acceptance of ascriptive inegalitarian beliefs by brilliant and politically dissident female and black male intellectuals strongly suggests that these ideas had broad appeal. Writers whose interests they did not easily serve still saw them as persuasive in light of contemporary scientific theories and empirical evidence of massive inequalities. It is likely, too, that for many the vision of a meaningful natural order that these doctrines provided had the psychological and philosophical appeal that such positions have always had for human beings, grounding their status and significance in something greater and more enduring than their own lives. * * *

In sum, if we accept that ideologies and institutions of ascriptive hierarchy have shaped America in interaction with its liberal and democratic features, we can make more sense of a wide range of inegalitarian policies newly contrived after 1870 and perpetuated through much of the twentieth century. Those policies were dismantled only through great struggles, aided by international pressures during World War II and the Cold War; and it is not clear that these struggles have ended. The novelties in the policies and scientific doctrines of the Gilded Age and Progressive Era should alert us to the possibility that new intellectual systems and political forces defending racial and gender inequalities may yet gain increased power in our own time.

*   *   *

The achievements of Americans in building a more inclusive democracy certainly provide reasons to believe that illiberal forces will not prevail. But just as we can better explain the nation's past by recognizing how and why liberal democratic principles have been contested with frequent success, we will better understand the present and future of American politics if we do not presume they are rooted in essentially liberal or democratic values and conditions. Instead, we must analyze America as the ongoing product of often conflicting multiple traditions.

DISCUSSION QUESTIONS

1. According to Smith, what are some examples of how Americans in the late nineteenth century simultaneously held liberal and ascriptive Americanist views?

2. How would you know if belief in ascriptive hierarchy was as widespread as Smith contends? What kind of evidence would you look for?

3. How might advocates of liberalism, republicanism, and ascriptive Americanism define "the public good"?

DEBATING THE ISSUES: WHAT DOES IT MEAN TO BE AN AMERICAN?

What does it mean to be an American? This deceptively simple question is challenging to answer. Because the United States encompasses a vast array of ethnicities, religions, and cultures, it can be difficult to define "American" by reference to those criteria. The country's geography differs dramatically from area to area, and the economic way of life accordingly differs greatly as well. In many ways, diverse groups of Americans have experienced American history differently, so a common historical identity is not obviously the answer either. One popular argument is that the United States is united by a set of political ideals. As far back as the early nineteenth century, scholars have tried to identify the nature of American political culture: Is it a commitment to individualism? A belief in equality? A shared set of values about the appropriate role of government? Openness?

Eric Liu wonders whether Americans have lost their way in having any shared identity. To Liu, "America is always in flux, but the flux today seems more disorienting than usual." He sees contemporary Americans as having a shared identity influenced heavily by the ideas and images presented by various media, oriented around commercial touchstones such as the Super Bowl, and ultimately not one of permanence. And although America has a strong story and history dating from the Declaration of Independence onward, Liu argues that its grip on the public is weak and that "these days, talk of citizenship is thin and tinny." Believing that a robust sense of nationhood and civic life is important for the future, Liu contends that a new Americanization campaign is necessary to breathe life back into the American creed. The effort must avoid the problems of past efforts at Americanization, particularly efforts to minimize differences and diversity in the quest for national unity. The modern effort to promote the American creed, character, and culture should, in Liu's view, be led by progressives, rather than being seen by progressives as a threat.

Steven Warshawsky argues that American identity centers around a commonly held set of ideas that can be considered the American way of life. This way of life includes beliefs in liberty, equality, property rights, religious freedom, limited government, and a common language for conducting political and economic affairs. Although America has always been a nation of immigrants, from the original European settlers to the mass immigration of the late nineteenth and early twentieth centuries, Warshawsky sees assimilation into American political culture as critical to American national identity. He also notes that America, including the scope and reach of government, has changed dramatically over time. Warshawsky asks whether these changes have also changed what it means to be an American. He argues this is a difficult question but concludes that straying too far from the principles of the Founders means "we will cease to be 'Americans' in any meaningful sense of the word."

Daniel Elazar provides a different way of approaching the question of what it means to be an American. He argues that political beliefs in the United States are distributed unevenly across the country. In large part, this has to do with migration patterns. Once certain ethnic groups and nationalities predominated in a particular area, the institutions they built and the practice of politics tended to become ingrained with their political and cultural beliefs. Elazar sees three types of value systems across the country: moralism, individualism, and traditionalism. Moralism is focused on the community and engaging in politics to do good. Individualism focuses on individual rights and tends to view governing as a set of transactions among various individuals and groups. Traditionalism attempts to use government to preserve existing social arrangements. These three approaches vary in their prevalence across the country, and even within states there may be variation as to which of the three predominates. Some areas have a mixture of two of these value systems, whereas other areas are more purely of one type.

4

"Sworn-Again Americans"

ERIC LIU

Last December I went to Taiwan to visit my grandmother. Like the Republic of China itself, she had turned 100 earlier in the year. During the trip I spent a day at the National Palace Museum in Taipei. Set among lush, green, mist-draped mountains, the museum holds the world's most spectacular collection of Chinese artifacts—spirited away in wartime by the Nationalists who fled to Taiwan when Mao's Communists took over the mainland.

On display that morning was a centennial exhibit of 100 masterpieces from the museum's holdings: famous calligraphic scrolls, priceless porcelain vases, finely carved jadeite cabbages. Each exquisite object was surrounded by a welter of tourists, many from the mainland. Even more stirring than the exhibit was its ambition, the belief that something as vast as Chinese culture and tradition could be captured in a selection of iconic things. The objects, from across dynasties and millennia, *were* Chinese-ness; the exhibit, an act of re-Sinicization. It was heritage reinforcement for an audience presumed Chinese.

I wondered, on the long flight home, whether Americanness could be so captured and so reinforced. I don't doubt that the Smithsonian could create a comparable show with 100 special objects. What I doubt is whether we have today a strong enough sense of shared identity, of common cultural and civic roots, for such an exhibit to capture the country's imagination.

America is always in flux, but the flux today seems more disorienting than usual. As China emerges rapidly and confidently, as Americans begin to wonder aloud about relative decline, as the center of gravity in our electorate shifts away from white men, as globalization enables immigrants to stay more wedded than ever to their homelands and not their new land, as political paralysis calls into question the durability of our constitutional design—as all these trends converge, a question arises: What is the content of American identity?

Without bonds of blood or tribe or sect to pull its people together, America has always tended toward the centrifugal. We are held together by Black Friday and "I'm lovin' it," by bowl games and March Madness, by reality television and virtual water coolers. America's story of self today is not so much a story as a Twitter feed. Heavily mediated, mainly commercial, and shockingly perishable is the sense of the republic that our public has today.

Of course, from the Revolution onward, America has had available a real story and a great unifying force: the self-evident ideals enshrined in the Declaration of Independence, encoded, even if imperfectly, in the Constitution, and embodied in amendments that made citizenship of the United States something transcendent and vital. Because our country began as an idea, the status of the citizen here has always been more than simply ministerial. It is, at least in theory, a trust; half a social contract. Citizens are promised liberty, and we, in turn, promise to earn it—by sustaining it.

These days, however, talk of citizenship is thin and tinny. The word has a faintly old-fashioned feel to it when used in everyday conversation. When evoked in national politics, it's often accompanied by the shrill whine of a descending culture-war mortar. Hence the debates in recent years about birthright citizenship and whether such status ought to be denied to so-called "anchor babies," mostly of Mexican descent. Or, less seriously but no less menacingly, the efforts to push the President of the United States out of the boundaries of American citizenship with a fervently wished-for foreign birth certificate.

When citizenship is drained of content by a commoditizing market and polarized politics, America suffers. Our ability as a people to maintain the democracy we've inherited diminishes, as does our ability to adapt to new challenges. We have to revive a spirit of citizenship if we want to remain a people.

That is why it is time now for a movement to re-Americanize Americans. This means reanimating our creed, cultivating the character needed for civic life, and fostering a culture of strong citizenship. Each of these imperatives is subject to abuse and co-optation by those who take a narrow view of what this country is. Which is why I argue that a twenty-first-century Americanization movement must be catalyzed by progressives.

Americanization, Last Time

A hundred years ago, as the great wave of European immigration to the United States peaked, there was a push for Americanization that crossed sector and institution. In public schools, the curriculum was changed to emphasize more American history and to teach patriotic anthems and parables. In urban slums, settlement houses like Jane Addams's Hull House and hundreds like it taught immigrant adults how to speak English and to assimilate into the "melting pot" of the city. Historic preservation took on greater prominence. From the pulpit came more lessons about American providence. Genealogy became a phenomenon and "heritage" a cultural obsession.

Today, at the end of another great migration to the United States, the will to Americanize is much weaker. That is in part proper. The nineteenth-century Americanizers, in their frantic eagerness, were stifling even when they meant well. As the First World War approached, much of the earnest patriotism of the movement curdled into jingoism and nativism. Excluded altogether from the Americanizing embrace were most people of color, who, whether deemed black, brown, yellow, or red, were the anvil against which various European ethnicities were forged into dominant whiteness.

In ensuing generations, with the emergence of the civil rights movement and multiculturalism, the descendants of those new-century immigrants came to reject the melting-pot ideal and its obliteration of differences. They instead learned to embrace a cosmopolitan pluralism—an identity libertarianism—in which to be American is to be what you want. Out went assimilation, in came authenticity.

Much has been gained in this revolution. Identity libertarians have freed us all to express and create our true selves and enabled the marketplaces of ideas, style, cuisine, and commerce to benefit from real diversity. But what's been lost is the core of American citizenship. It's no exaggeration to say that America has never been more confused about what its own citizenship entails—and never more timid about imparting the values, knowledge, and skills needed to be a citizen in the broadest sense.

Citizenship in this nation is many things. It is a legal status conferred by the accident of birth or by the process of naturalization. It is a set of privileges and immunities. But it is also a cultural inheritance, an ethical standard, an implied set of responsibilities, a collective story and memory.

At its core, citizenship in America is an act of claiming. *What* is being claimed is a creed that emanates from the declaration and finds restatement in the Gettysburg Address and yet again in "I Have a Dream." *How* it is claimed is by a combination of collective belief and deeds.

To pour content again into the vessel of citizenship, we need to Americanize anew. To do that, we must reinvent the very notion of Americanization. What I write of is not a deracinating assimilation to a white man's way. It is not enforcement of partisan orthodoxy. It is taking profoundly seriously how we make an *unum* from the *pluribus*. It is about having confidence in what is exceptional about our experiment.

Americanization, This Time

The word "Americanization," like the word "exceptionalism," pushes the buttons of many people, especially on the left. To them, it can sound like a cover for white privilege and warmongering. It suggests arrogance and groupthink. In short, Americanization conjures up for some folks the worst of America.

But these connotations are not fixed. It is in our power to reshape them by recalling the best of America, including our capacity to face our history in full. Americanization should mean, "to keep trying to live up to our promise." Redeeming the idea of Americanization is the very kind of redemptive act that America stands for. Not "my country right or wrong," but, as the German immigrant and U. S. senator Carl Schurz said a century ago, "our country—when right to be kept right; when wrong to be put right."

This is true patriotism. To Americanize means to ask people to commit to a set of values. Rights come with responsibilities and opportunities with obligations. You have the right to burn the flag in America—but you should honor the fact that the flag symbolizes that right. You have to be willing to work hard and be enterprising—but if you are, you should be promised a fair chance at success. You are free to sustain the traditions of your ancestral lands—but you should contribute to the development of *this* land and its rituals.

A new Americanization movement will reinforce these principles. It will instill in young people a sense of why being here is special, even in a networked and transnationalizing age, and what they owe this country. It will sharpen for Americans of all ages a sense of appreciation and responsibility for the institutions of our democracy—and thus our ability to participate in those institutions. It will enable us to face an era of demographic transition with more unity of purpose. And it will prove to us and to the world that for all its profound and tragic flaws, the United States still has a confounding ability to convert its shortcomings into strengths and to remix itself.

This new Americanization program, importantly, is not just for immigrants. It is for everyone. It is for the longstanding citizens who have forgotten or never appreciated the full measure of their inheritance. It is for the chieftains of global companies who think their fates are no longer tied to the fate of this nation. It is for romantics of the far left and far right who think nations and states are obsolete until they need one—this one—to provide for their needs.

A new Americanization program must also be created by everyone. Government can be involved, but so must community foundations, schools, business leaders, union organizers, film and TV producers, social-media mavens. There should be a spirit of wiki to it all, of popular movement, with ideas emerging from the bottom up and not only from experts. Throughout, it should focus on three core elements of a civic religion: creed, character, and culture.

Creed

To be Americanized is first to be immersed in the tenets of our democratic faith, expressed in seminal texts, speeches, and stories, from Jefferson's time to our own.

> As the patriots of seventy-six did to the support of the Declaration of Independence, so to the support of the Constitution and Laws, let every American pledge his life, his liberty, and his sacred honor. . . . Let reverence for the laws . . . be preached from the pulpit, proclaimed in legislative halls, and enforced in the courts of justice. And, in short, let it become the political religion of the nation; and let the old and the young, the rich and the poor, the grave and the gay, of all sexes and tongues, and colors and conditions, sacrifice unceasingly upon its altars.

When a young Abraham Lincoln spoke these words at the Young Men's Lyceum in Springfield, he meant by "reverence for the laws" not mere obedience to authority. He meant reverence for democracy itself—and for the obligations that democratic freedom entails.

To Americanize is to be comfortable telling everyone that what separates this nation from others is that it has a *moral* identity. Others have history and tradition. We do too, but more than anything, our nation is dedicated to a proposition. That distinction cannot be emphasized enough. When Jefferson proclaimed the truth of human equality "self-evident," he was not recording a timeless fact; he was asserting one into being. His saying so, as he declared America, helped make it so.

It falls on us to keep it so. Only continuous renewal of a commitment to the creed keeps the creed alive. Naming it matters: rediscovering the words, saying them again, assaying their meaning. In classrooms, boardrooms, kitchens, and churches, in corner stores and today's settlement houses, on TV and on Twitter, it's time to shake off the sleep of cynicism and to awaken in earnest as Americans. It is time to appreciate the content of our creed as if we were all newcomers: with wonder and awe at the world-changingness of it all.

To reanimate the creed we need to focus in part on revitalizing civic education in our schools. The Campaign for the Civic Mission of Schools is one advocacy group working to do this. Even though public education in America is a matter largely left to the states, there can and should be a federal requirement that the basic texts and ideas of our nation's civic creed be taught, in an upward spiral of sophistication, every year from kindergarten to twelfth grade. After all, as Justice Sandra Day O'Connor notes, this was the very point of creating free and compulsory public education: to make citizens.

The responsibility belongs not only to schoolteachers or education policymakers. Leaders in every community should take it upon themselves to start contests and public conversations about the American creed: what's in it, what challenges it, how we honor it, how we have fallen short. The answers will be staggeringly varied—as they are on the DefineAmerican.com website started by the Pulitzer Prize-winning journalist (and undocumented immigrant) Jose Antonio Vargas—but they will have a unifying thread of *reckoning*.

Character

Our standard of citizenship in America is centered, constitutionally and rhetorically, on rights. But with rights come duties and with liberty, responsibility; else freedom decays into mere free-for-all. So a second dimension of a new Americanization is the cultivation of citizenship as a matter of character. This is citizenship in the sense of good or great citizenship: living in a pro-social way; showing up for one another; making an adaptive asset of our diversity. Civic character is therefore more than industry, perseverance, and other personal virtues. It is character in the collective: team-spiritedness, mutuality, reciprocity, responsibility, empathy, service, cooperation. It is acting as if you believed that society becomes how *you* behave—because it does. Character is the thread that ties creed and deed together. What acts instantiate our stated values? With what understanding of our system of self-government? Making what kind of contribution?

The cultivation of strong citizens does not happen automatically, any more than the cultivation of healthy plants does. Democracy is a garden in which the organisms are interdependent. Developing civic character is the work of gardening—of tending the plot. In a multiethnic market democracy like ours, we cannot rely on a myth of rugged individualism to hold us together. We have to seed and feed trust. We reap what we sow.

Educators need to teach not just civic facts and history but also the elements of civic character: what it means to be in union with others. That requires doing real things together and reflecting on the shared experience. In schools, it means more service learning that's tied to an understanding of American institutions. Take students to serve in a church food bank, for instance, but also discuss the civic role of faith-based groups. What can citizens make happen with and without government, with and without each other?

In government policy, cultivating civic character means adding more resources for AmeriCorps and other national service programs—but also grounding them more explicitly in elements of American citizenship. In parenting and child rearing, it means teaching and rewarding even the smallest acts of courtesy and cooperation because they compound. In philanthropy and community life, it means creating more opportunities for *adults* to learn how to do democracy.

During the Great Depression, grassroots citizenship schools like the Highlander Folk School in Appalachia emerged for just this purpose. Highlander is where Rosa Parks was trained to organize. It was where she learned that civic character is expressed in the choices we make. She was prepared by her teachers to make the right choice as a citizen when the time came. What institutions prepare us now?

Culture

As it happens, the Highlander School is also where an old black spiritual was adapted and then popularized into a movement anthem called "We Shall Overcome." American democracy makes us a promise that only we can keep. This faith requires a rich, suffusing culture of unity: anthems, rituals, colors, civic scripture set and reset in new creative contexts.

The third aspect of Americanization, then, is introducing Americans to the patterns of our civic culture—how we have governed ourselves, by law or custom, and lived in community over 200 years. One such pattern is promise, failure, and redemption. This is the foundational story of slavery and civil rights. Another is the generation of hybrid innovations from our miscegenated gene and meme pool. This is the story of American music, of Silicon Valley's ingenuity.

I believe the new Americanization agenda must reveal and express both these story patterns: the profound ways, past and present, that we have fallen short of our stated ideal; and our resilient, adaptive ability to take our failures as the stuff of new invention. Slavery's legacy is evident in de facto segregation and in the severe inequality of our schools. It is found too in the voice of every American, in the warp and woof of the American vernacular. *We Shall Overcome.*

To teach Americanness is to celebrate the ideal and the real as one, without irony or ambivalence. It is to use a shared language in public life—American English, with a democratic accent—so that we may transcend unshared private histories. It is to invoke a civic religion that infuses our many narratives with common purpose. In 1982, the liberal producer Norman Lear created a pageant for ABC called "I Love Liberty" that grabbed hold of both the cultural patterns I described above. With the Muppets and multicultural celebrities, with earnestness and absurdity, it depicted the turmoil and contradiction of our founding—and the insistent promise of our future.

We need to have the self-assurance to create new pageants, to invoke and remix the rituals and symbols our own way: the flag, the hymns, the oaths. We can't fear causing offense. A people scared to say the Pledge of Allegiance is nearly as unhealthy as one scared not to. What we must remember is that we get to continually reinvent and rewrite that pledge, this *culture.*

That's why recently I helped launch a civic-artistic project called Sworn-Again American. It mashes up aspects of a naturalization ceremony, a multicultural festival, and a revival tent to make a playful public experience in which Americans recommit to the content of their citizenship. What we should celebrate more than diversity is what we *do* with it. How do we bring everyone in the tent and create something together? In a twenty-first century way that activates our true potential, we all need to become sworn-again.

The Role of Progressives

What I've called for here may cause many progressives heartburn. I admit that this new Americanization agenda sounds like—indeed, is—something conservatives promote. But I disagree that it should be something *only* conservatives promote. Progressives should be front and center.

Why? The promise of American life is a promise of justice, requiring action not passivity, challenge not complacency; and is therefore progressive. The effort to nudge the country toward alignment with its stated ideals is asymptotic: We can keep halving the distance to perfection, but it remains infinitely out of reach. With the goal never fully attainable, the pursuit becomes then an act of faith, and therefore *progressive.* Progressivism is nothing if not the belief that something "more perfect" is worth striving for.

Some progressives contest the very idea of citizenship and dispute the need even for nation-states. They are too Utopian. Other progressives hold the American nation-state in low regard because of a track record of racism and war and empire. They are too cynical. They do not see that inherent in the hypocrisy of so many American acts—in fact, what makes hypocrisy hypocrisy and not mere iniquity—is the existence of a higher professed standard.

We are called still, all of us, to live up to that standard. The best tradition of the American left is a tradition of love for America: insistent, impatient, often disappointed, but unrelenting. And the best hope for America tomorrow is that across lines of left and right we find ways to articulate common purpose—not by glossing over hypocrisies but by unpacking them; by treating them as the beginning of a chapter rather than the end of the story.

It's time for a civic synthesis that speaks to the tension between a Western WASP inheritance and a diverse multicultural present; between words in marble and a more sordid reality; between liberty and equality;

freedom from and freedom to—because that tension is what is American. In every setting we can, progressives and conservatives must teach to the tension *together*. And progressives should initiate the dialectic—because in America we always have.

There are some progressives who say that conservatives, consumed with culture war, are incapable of teaching to the tension. Maybe. But they should take a look at *What So Proudly We Hail*, a recent anthology of American stories and songs whose editors include Leon Kass, the conservative scholar and former adviser to President George W. Bush. Every prefatory note in that collection speaks to the tension and complexity of American identity. Not a note incites culture war.

There are some conservatives who would double over laughing at the notion of progressives leading the charge to reanimate a love of American citizenship. But I would refer them to *A Patriot's Handbook*, a similar and similarly powerful anthology of civic religious texts assembled by Caroline Kennedy.

Together, these collections remind us that the most useful way to be progressive is to conserve: to honor and maintain the deeply revolutionary, once-in-a-world tradition of our creed and culture. And the most useful way to be conservative is to progress: to enable the American idea to adapt to changing times so that the idea itself may endure forever and ever.

Lines of Descent and Ascent

At the National Palace Museum, beholding those objects made epochs ago—ten or 12 Americas ago—I marveled at the continuity of the line. But that line of Chineseness, a shared sensibility expressed in brushstrokes and carvings and in ratios of form to space, is in the end rooted in the soil and heart of China.

A European, an African, or a black or white American can appreciate those lines. They cannot claim them. When an American of Chinese descent like me can, it only sharpens the realization that of the two identities I might claim, only one is by design universal. Only one is an open operating system inviting people from anywhere to rewrite the code. Only one asks humans to be better.

American exceptionalism in this age of great tectonic shifts does not depend on our forever having the largest economy or the mightiest military. It does depend on our having the planet's most adaptive and resilient concept of citizenship, one that rises above land and blood, that commits us to a national lifetime of striving, failing, renewing, striving again to dedicate ourselves to our proposition.

We live in a great country. It's time again to get religion about it.

"What Does It Mean to Be an American?"

Steven M. Warshawsky

"Undocumented Americans." This is how Senate Majority Leader Harry Reid recently described the estimated 12–20 million illegal aliens living in America. What was once a Mark Steyn joke has now become the ideological orthodoxy of the Democratic Party.

Reid's comment triggered an avalanche of outrage among commentators, bloggers, and the general public. Why? Because it strikes at the heart of the American people's understanding of themselves as a nation and a civilization. Indeed, opposition to the ongoing push for "comprehensive immigration reform"—i.e., amnesty and a guest worker program—is being driven by a growing concern among millions of Americans that massive waves of legal and illegal immigration—mainly from Mexico, Latin America, and Asia—coupled with the unwillingness of our political and economic elites to mold these newcomers into red-white-and-blue Americans, is threatening to change the very character of our country. For the worse.

I share this concern. I agree with the political, economic, and cultural arguments in favor of sharply curtailing immigration into the United States, as well as refocusing our immigration efforts on admitting those foreigners who bring the greatest value to—and are most easily assimilated into—American society. * * * But this essay is not intended to rehash these arguments. Rather, I wish to explore the question that underlies this entire debate: What does it mean to be an American? This may seem like an easy question to answer, but it's not. The harder one thinks about this question, the more complex it becomes.

Clearly, Harry Reid has not given this question much thought. His implicit definition of "an American" is simply: Anyone living within the geopolitical boundaries of the United States. In other words, mere physical location on Earth determines whether or not someone is "an American." Presumably, Reid's definition is not intended to apply to tourists and other temporary visitors. Some degree of permanency—what the law in other contexts calls "residency," i.e., a subjective intention to establish one's home or domicile—is required. In Reid's view, therefore, a Mexican from Guadalajara, a Chinese from Shanghei [sic], an Indian from Delhi, or a [fill in the blank] become "Americans" as soon as they cross into U.S. territory and decide to live here permanently, legally or not. Nothing more is needed.

This is poppycock, of course. A Mexican or a Chinese or an Indian, for example, cannot transform themselves into Americans simply by moving to this country, any more than I can become a Mexican, a Chinese, or an Indian simply by moving to their countries. Yet contemporary liberals have a vested interest in believing that they can. This is not just a function of immigrant politics, which strongly favors the Democratic Party (hence the Democrats' growing support for voting rights for non-citizens). It also reflects the liberals' (and some libertarians') multicultural faith, which insists that it is morally wrong to make distinctions among different groups of people, let alone to impose a particular way of life—what heretofore has been known as the American way of life—on those who believe, speak, and act differently. Even in our own country.

In short, diversity, not Americanism, is the multicultural touchstone.

What's more, the principle of diversity, taken to its logical extreme, inevitably leads to a *rejection* of Americanism. Indeed, the ideology of multiculturalism has its roots in the radical—and anti-American—New Left and Black Power movements of the 1960s and 1970s. Thus the sorry state of U.S. history and civics education in today's schools and universities, which are dominated by adherents of this intellectual poison. Moreover, when it comes to immigration, multiculturalists actually *prefer* those immigrants who are as unlike ordinary Americans as possible. This stems from their deep-rooted opposition to traditional American society, which they hope to undermine through an influx of non-western peoples and cultures.

This, in fact, describes present U.S. immigration policy, which largely is a product of the 1965 Immigration Act (perhaps Ted Kennedy's most notorious legislative achievement). The 1965 Immigration Act eliminated the legal preferences traditionally given to European immigrants, and opened the floodgates to immigration from less-developed and non-western countries. For example, in 2006 more immigrants came to the United States from Columbia, Peru, Vietnam, and Haiti (not to mention Mexico, China, and India), than from the United Kingdom, Germany, Italy, and Greece. And once these immigrants arrive here, multiculturalists believe we should accommodate *our* society to the needs and desires of the newcomers, not the other way around. Thus, our government prints election ballots, school books, and welfare applications in foreign languages, while corporate America asks customers to "press one for English."

Patriotic Americans—those who love our country for its people, its history, its culture, and its ideals—reject the multiculturalists' denuded, and ultimately subversive, vision of what it means to be "an American." While the American identity is arguably the most "universal" of all major nationalities—as evidenced by the millions of immigrants the world over who have successfully assimilated into our country over the years—it is not an empty, meaningless concept. It has substance. Being "an American" is *not* the same thing as simply living in the United States. Nor, I would add, is it the same thing as holding U.S. citizenship. After all, a baby born on U.S. soil to an illegal alien is a citizen. This hardly guarantees that this baby will grow up to be *an American*.

So what, then, does it mean to be an American? I suspect that most of us believe, like Supreme Court Justice Potter Stewart in describing pornography, that we "know it when we see it." For example, John Wayne, Amelia Earhart, and Bill Cosby definitely are Americans. The day laborers standing on the street corner probably are not. But how do we put this inner understanding into words? It's not easy. Unlike most other nations on Earth, the American nation is not strictly defined in terms of race or ethnicity or ancestry or religion. George Washington may be the Father of Our Country (in my opinion, the greatest American who ever lived), but there have been in the past, and are today, many millions of patriotic, hardworking, upstanding Americans who are not Caucasian, or Christian, or of Western European ancestry. Yet they are undeniably as American as you or I (by the way, I am Jewish of predominantly Eastern European ancestry). Any definition of "American" that excludes such folks—let alone one that excludes me!—cannot be right.

Consequently, it is just not good enough to say, as some immigration restrictionists do, that this is a "white-majority, Western country." Yes, it is. But so are, for example, Ireland and Sweden and Portugal. Clearly, this level of abstraction does not take us very far towards understanding what it means to be "an American." Nor is it all that helpful to say that this is an English-speaking, predominately Christian country. While I think these features get us closer to the answer, there are millions of English-speaking (and non-English-speaking) Christians in the world who are not Americans, and millions of non-Christians who are. Certainly, these fundamental historical characteristics are important elements in determining who we are as a nation. Like other restrictionists, I am opposed to public policies that seek, by design or by default, to significantly alter the nation's "demographic profile." Still, it must be recognized that demography alone does not, and cannot, explain what it means to be an American.

So where does that leave us? I think the answer to our question, ultimately, must be found in the realms of ideology and culture. What distinguishes the United States from other nations, and what unites the disparate peoples who make up our country, are our unique political, economic, and social values, beliefs, and institutions. Not race, or religion, or ancestry.

Whether described as a "proposition nation" or a "creedal nation" or simply just "an idea," the United States of America is defined by *our way of life*. This way of life is rooted in the ideals proclaimed in the Declaration of Independence; in the system of personal liberty and limited government established by the Constitution; in our traditions of self-reliance, personal responsibility, and entrepreneurism; in our emphasis on private property, freedom of contract, and merit-based achievement; in our respect for the rule of law; and in our commitment to affording equal justice to all.

Perhaps above all, it is marked by our abiding belief that, as Americans, we have been called to a higher duty in human history. We are the "city upon a hill." We are "the last, best hope of earth."

Many immigration restrictionists and so-called traditionalists chafe at the notion that the American people are not defined by "blood and soil." Yet the truth of the matter is, we aren't. One of the greatest patriots who ever graced this nation's history, Teddy Roosevelt, said it best: "Americanism is a matter of the spirit and of the soul." Roosevelt deplored what he called "hyphenated Americanism," which refers to citizens whose primary loyalties lie with their particular ethnic groups or ancestral lands. Such a man, Roosevelt counseled, is to be "unsparingly condemn[ed]."

But Roosevelt also recognized that "if he is heartily and singly loyal to this Republic, then no matter where he was born, he is just as good an American as anyone else." Roosevelt's words are not offered here to suggest that all foreigners are equally capable of assimilating into our country. Clearly, they aren't. Nevertheless, the appellation "American" is open to anyone who adopts our way of life and loves this country above all others.

Which brings me to the final, and most difficult, aspect of this question: How do we define the "American way of life"? This is the issue over which our nation's "culture wars" are being fought. Today the country is divided between those who maintain their allegiance to certain historically American values, beliefs, and institutions (but not all—see racial segregation), and those who want to replace them with a very different set of ideas about the role of government, the nature of political and economic liberty, and the meaning of right and wrong. Are both sides in this struggle equally "American"?

Moreover, the "American way of life" has changed over time. We no longer have the Republic that existed in TR's days. The New Deal and Great Society revolutions—enthusiastically supported, I note, by millions of white, Christian, English-speaking citizens—significantly altered the political, economic, and social foundations of this country. Did they also change what it means to be "an American"? Is being an American equally compatible, for example, with support for big government versus small government? The welfare state versus rugged individualism? Socialism versus capitalism? And so on. Plainly, this is a much harder historical and intellectual problem than at first meets the eye.

Personally, I do not think the meaning of America is nearly so malleable as today's multiculturalists assume. But neither is it quite as narrow as many restrictionists contend. Nevertheless, I am convinced that being *an American* requires something more than merely living in this country, English, obeying the law, and holding a job (although this would art!). What this "something more" is, however, is not self-deed, is the subject of increasingly bitter debate in this

Yet one thing is certain: If we stray too far from the lines laid down by the Founding Fathers and the generations of great American men and women who built on their legacy, we will cease to be "Americans" in any meaningful sense of the word. As Abraham Lincoln warned during the secession era, "America will never be destroyed from the outside. If we falter and lose our freedoms, it will be because we destroyed ourselves." Today the danger is not armed rebellion, but the slow erasing of the American national character through a process of political and cultural redefinition. If this ever happens, it will be a terrible day for this country, and for the world.

6

"The Three Political Cultures"

Daniel J. Elazar

The United States is a single land of great diversity inhabited by what is now a single people of great diversity. The singleness of the country as a whole is expressed through political, cultural, and geographic unity. Conversely, the country's diversity is expressed through its states, subcultures, and sections. In this section, we will focus on the political dimensions of that diversity-in-unity—on the country's overall political culture and its subculture.

Political culture is the summation of persistent patterns of underlying political attitudes and characteristic responses to political concerns that is manifest in a particular political order. Its existence is generally unperceived by those who are part of that order, and its origins date back to the very beginnings of the particular people who share it. Political culture is an intrinsically political phenomenon. As such, it makes its own demands on the political system. For example, the definition of what is "fair" in the political arena—a direct manifestation of political culture—is likely to be different from the definition of what is fair in family or business relationships. Moreover, different political cultures will define fairness in politics differently. Political culture also affects all other questions confronting the political system. For example, many factors go into shaping public expectations regarding government services, and political culture will be significant among them. Political systems, in turn, are in some measure the products of the political cultures they serve and must remain in harmony with their political cultures if they are to maintain themselves.

* * *

Political-culture factors stand out as particularly influential in shaping the operations of the national, state, and local political systems in three ways: (1) by molding the perceptions of the political community (the citizens, the politicians, and the public officials) as to the nature and purposes of politics and its expectations of government and the political process; (2) by influencing the recruitment of specific kinds of people to become active in government and politics—as holders of elective offices, members of the bureaucracy, and active political workers; and (3) by subtly directing the actual way in which the art of government is practiced by citizens, politicians, and public officials in the light of their perceptions. In turn, the cultural components of individual and group behavior are manifested in civic behavior as dictated by conscience and internalized ethical standards, in the forms of law-abidingness (or laxity in such matters) adhered to by citizens and officials, and in the character of the positive actions of government.

* * *

The national political culture of the United States is itself a synthesis of three major political subcultures. These subcultures jointly inhabit the country, existing side by side or sometimes overlapping one another. All three are of nationwide proportions, having spread, in the course of time, from coast to coast. Yet each subculture is strongly tied to specific sections of the country, reflecting the streams and currents of migration that have carried people of different origins and backgrounds across the continent in more or less orderly patterns.

Given the central characteristics that define each of the subcultures and their centers of emphasis, the three political subcultures may be called individualistic, moralistic, and traditionalistic. Each reflects its own particular synthesis of the marketplace and the commonwealth.

It is important, however, not only to examine this description and the following ones very carefully but also to abandon the preconceptions associated with such idea-words as individualistic, moralistic, marketplace, and so on. Thus, for example, nineteenth-century individualistic conceptions of minimum intervention were oriented toward *laissez-faire*, with the role of government conceived to be that of a policeman with powers to act in certain limited fields. And in the twentieth century, the notion of what constitutes minimum intervention has been drastically expanded to include such things as government regulation of utilities, unemployment compensation, and massive subventions to maintain a stable and growing economy—all within the framework of the same political culture. The demands of manufacturers for high tariffs in 1865 and the demands of labor unions for worker's compensation in 1965 may well be based on the same theoretical justification that they are aids to the maintenance of a working marketplace. Culture is not static. It must be viewed dynamically and defined so as to include cultural change in its very nature.

The Individualistic Political Culture

The *individualistic political culture* emphasizes the conception of the democratic order as a marketplace. It is rooted in the view that government is instituted for strictly utilitarian reasons, to handle those functions demanded by the people it serves. According to this view, government need not have any direct concern with questions of the "good society" (except insofar as the government may be used to advance some common conception of the good society formulated outside the political arena, just as it serves other functions). Emphasizing the centrality of private concerns, the individualistic political culture places a premium on limiting community intervention—whether governmental or nongovernmental—into private activities, to the minimum degree necessary to keep the marketplace in proper working order. In general, government action is to be restricted to those areas, primarily in the economic realm, that encourage private initiative and widespread access to the marketplace.

The character of political participation in systems dominated by the individualistic political culture reflects the view that politics is just another means by which individuals may improve themselves socially and economically. In this sense politics is a "business," like any other that competes for talent and offers rewards to those who take it up as a career. Those individuals who choose political careers may rise by providing the governmental services demanded of them and, in return, may expect to be adequately compensated for their efforts.

Interpretation of officeholders' obligations under the individualistic political culture vary among political systems and even among individuals within a single political system. Where the standards are high, such people are expected to provide high-quality government services for the general public in the best possible manner in return for the status and economic rewards considered their due. Some who choose political careers clearly commit themselves to such norms; others believe that an office-holder's primary responsibility is to serve him- or herself and those who have supported him or her directly, favoring them at the expense of others. In some political systems, this view is accepted by the public as well as by politicians.

Political life within an individualistic political culture is based on a system of mutual obligations rooted in personal relationships. Whereas in a simple civil society those relationships can be direct ones, those with individualistic political cultures in the United States are usually too complex to maintain face-to-face ties. So the system of mutual obligation is harnessed through political parties, which serve as "business corporations" dedicated to providing the organization necessary to maintain that system. Party regularity is indispensable in the individualistic political culture because it is the means for coordinating individual enterprise in the political arena; it is also the one way of preventing individualism in politics from running wild.

In such a system, an individual can succeed politically, not by dealing with issues in some exceptional way or by accepting some concept of good government and then by striving to implement it, but by maintaining his or her place in the system of mutual obligations. A person can do this by operating according to the norms of his or her particular party, to the exclusion of other political considerations. Such a political culture encourages the maintenance of a party system that is competitive, but not overtly so, in the pursuit of office. Its politicians are interested in office as a means of controlling the distribution of the favors or rewards of government rather than as a means of exercising governmental power for programmatic ends; hence competition may prove less rewarding than accommodation in certain situations.

Since the individualistic political culture eschews ideological concerns in its "business-like" conception of politics, both politicians and citizens tend to look upon political activity as a specialized one—as essentially the province of professionals, of minimum and passing concern to laypersons, and with no place for amateurs to play an active role. Furthermore, there is a strong tendency among the public to believe that politics is a dirty—albeit necessary—business, better left to those who are willing to soil themselves by engaging in it. In practice, then, where the individualistic political culture is dominant, there is likely to be an easy attitude toward the limits of the professional's perquisites. Since a fair amount of corruption is expected in the normal course of things, there is relatively little popular excitement when any is found, unless it is of an extraordinary character. It is as if the public were willing to pay a surcharge for services rendered, rebelling only when the surcharge becomes too heavy. Of course, the judgments as to what is "normal" and what is "extraordinary" are themselves subjective and culturally conditioned.

Public officials, committed to "giving the public what it wants," are normally not willing to initiate new programs or open up new areas of government activity on their own initiative. They will do so when they perceive an overwhelming public demand for them to act, but only then. In a sense, their willingness to expand the functions of government is based on an extension of the *quid pro quo* "favors" system, which serves as the central core of their political relationships. New and better services are the reward they give the public for placing them in office. The value mix and legitimacy of change in the individualistic political culture are directly related to commercial concerns.

The individualistic political culture is ambivalent about the place of bureaucracy in the political order. In one sense, the bureaucratic method of operation flies in the face of the favor system that is central to the individualistic political process. At the same time, the virtues of organizational efficiency appear substantial to those seeking to master the market. In the end, bureaucratic organization is introduced within the framework of the favor system; large segments of the bureaucracy may be insulated from it through the merit system, but the entire organization is pulled into the political environment at crucial points through political appointment at the upper echelons and, very frequently, also through the bending of the merit system to meet political demands.

* * *

The Moralistic Political Culture

To the extent that American society is built on the principles of "commerce" (in the broadest sense) and that the marketplace provides the model for public relationships, all Americans share some of the attitudes that are of great importance in the individualistic political culture. At the same time, substantial segments of the American people operate politically within the framework of two political cultures—the moralistic and traditionalistic political cultures—whose theoretical structures and operational consequences depart significantly from the individualistic pattern at crucial points.

The *moralistic political culture* emphasizes the commonwealth conception as the basis for democratic government. Politics, to this political culture, is considered one of the great human activities: the search for the good society. True, it is a struggle for power, but it is also an effort to exercise power for the betterment of the commonwealth. Accordingly, in the moralistic political culture, both the general public and the politicians conceive of politics as a public activity centered on some notion of the public good and properly devoted to the advancement of the public interest. Good government, then, is measured by the degree to which it promotes the public good and in terms of the honesty, selflessness, and commitment to the public welfare of those who govern.

In the moralistic political culture, individualism is tempered by a general commitment to utilizing communal (preferably nongovernmental, but governmental if necessary) power to intervene in the sphere of "private" activities when it is considered necessary to do so for the public good or the well-being of the community. Accordingly, issues have an important place in the moralistic style of politics, functioning to set the tone for political concern. Government is considered a positive instrument with a responsibility to promote the general welfare, although definitions of what its positive role should be may vary considerably from era to era.

As in the case of the individualistic political culture, the change from nineteenth- to twentieth-century conceptions of what government's positive role should be has been great; for example, support for Prohibition has given way to support for wage and hour regulation. At the same time, care must be taken to distinguish between a predisposition toward communal activism and a desire for federal government activity. For example, many representatives of the moralistic political culture oppose federal aid for urban renewal without in any way opposing community responsibility for urban development. The distinction they make (implicitly, at least) is between what they consider legitimate community responsibility and what they believe to be central government encroachment; or between communitarianism, which they value, and "collectivism," which they abhor. Thus, on some public issues we find certain such representatives taking highly conservative positions despite their positive attitudes toward public activity generally. Such representatives may also prefer government intervention in the social realm—that is, censorship or screening of books and movies—over government intervention in the economy, holding that the former is necessary for the public good and the latter, harmful.

Since the moralistic political culture rests on the fundamental conception that politics exists primarily as a means for coming to grips with the issues and public concerns of civil society, it embraces the notion that politics is ideally a matter of concern for all citizens, not just those who are professionally committed to political careers. Indeed, this political culture considers it the duty of every citizen to participate in the political affairs of his or her commonwealth.

Accordingly, there is a general insistence within this political culture that government service is public service, which places moral obligations upon those who participate in government that are more demanding than the moral obligations of the marketplace. There is an equally general rejection of the notion that the field of politics is a legitimate realm for private economic enrichment. Of course, politicians may benefit economically because of their political careers, but they are not expected to *profit* from political activity; indeed, they are held suspect if they do.

Since the concept of serving the community is the core of the political relationship, politicians are expected to adhere to it even at the expense of individual loyalties and political friendships. Consequently, party regularity is not of prime importance. The political party is considered a useful political device, but it is not valued for its own sake. Regular party ties can be abandoned with relative impunity for third parties, special local parties, or nonpartisan systems if such changes are believed to be helpful in gaining larger political goals. People can even shift from party to party without sanctions if such change is justified by political belief.

In the moralistic political culture, rejection of firm party ties is not to be viewed as a rejection of politics as such. On the contrary, because politics is considered potentially good and healthy within the context of that culture, it is possible to have highly political nonpartisan systems. Certainly nonpartisanship is instituted not to eliminate politics but to improve it, by widening access to public office for those unwilling or unable to gain office through the regular party structure.

In practice, where the moralistic political culture is dominant today, there is considerably more amateur participation in politics. There is also much less of what Americans consider to be corruption in government and less tolerance of those actions considered to be corrupt. Hence politics does not have the taint it so often bears in the individualistic environment.

By virtue of its fundamental outlook, the moralistic political culture creates a greater commitment to active government intervention in the economic and social life of the community. At the same time, the strong commitment to *communitarianism* characteristic of that political culture tends to channel the interest in government intervention into highly local-istic paths, such that a willingness to encourage local government inter-vention to set public standards does not necessarily reflect a concomitant willingness to allow outside governments equal opportunity to intervene. Not infrequently, public officials themselves will seek to initiate new gov-ernment activities in an effort to come to grips with problems as yet unper-ceived by a majority of the citizenry. The moralistic political culture is not committed to either change or the status quo *per se* but, rather, will accept either depending upon the morally defined ends to be gained.

The major difficulty of this political culture in adjusting bureaucracy to the political order is tied to the potential conflict between communitarian principles and the necessity for large-scale organization to increase bureaucratic efficiency, a problem that could affect the attitudes of moral-istic culture states toward federal activity of certain kinds. Otherwise, the notion of a politically neutral administrative system creates no problem within the moralistic value system and even offers many advantages. Where merit systems are instituted, they are rigidly maintained.

* * *

The Traditionalistic Political Culture

The *traditionalistic political culture* is rooted in an ambivalent attitude toward the marketplace coupled with a paternalistic and elitist conception of the commonwealth. It reflects an older, precommercial attitude that accepts a substantially hierarchical society as part of the ordered nature of things, authorizing and expecting those at the top of the social structure to take a special and dominant role in government. Like its moralistic counterpart, the traditionalistic political culture accepts government as an actor with a positive role in the community, but in a very limited sphere—mainly that of securing the continued maintenance of the existing social order. To do so, it functions to confine real political power to a relatively small and self-perpetuating group drawn from an established elite who often inherit their "right" to govern through family ties or social position. Accordingly, social and family ties are paramount in a traditionalistic political culture;

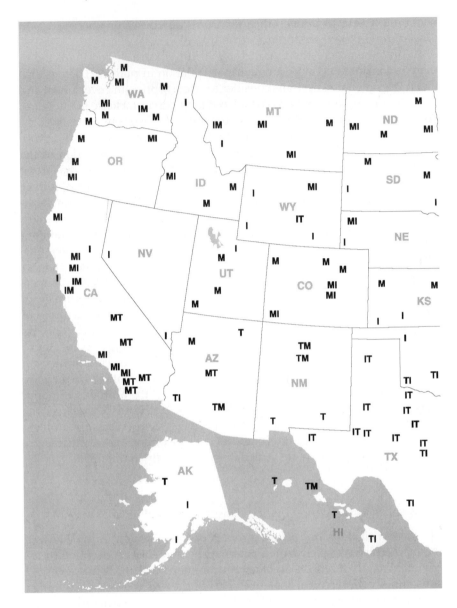

Map 1   The Regional Distribution of Political Cultures Within the States. *Source:* Daniel J. Elazar, *American Federalism: A View from the States*, 3d ed. (New York: Harper and Row Publishers, 1984), pp. 124–25. Reprinted by permission of HarperCollins Publishers.

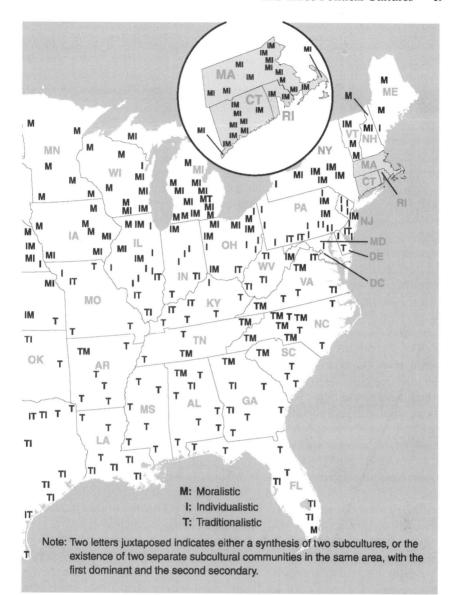

M: Moralistic
I: Individualistic
T: Traditionalistic

Note: Two letters juxtaposed indicates either a synthesis of two subcultures, or the existence of two separate subcultural communities in the same area, with the first dominant and the second secondary.

in fact, their importance is greater than that of personal ties in the individualistic political culture, where, after all is said and done, a person's first responsibility is to him- or herself. At the same time, those who do not have a definite role to play in politics are not expected to be even minimally active as citizens. In many cases, they are not even expected to vote. In return, they are guaranteed that, outside of the limited sphere of politics, family rights (usually labeled "individual rights") are paramount, not to be taken lightly or ignored. As in the individualistic political culture, those active in politics are expected to benefit personally from their activity, though not necessarily through direct pecuniary gain.

Political parties are of minimal importance in a traditionalistic political culture, inasmuch as they encourage a degree of openness and competition that goes against the fundamental grain of an elite-oriented political order. Their major utility is to recruit people to fill the formal offices of government not desired by the established power-holders. Political competition in a traditionalistic political culture is usually conducted through factional alignments, as an extension of the personalistic politics that is characteristic of the system; hence political systems within the culture tend to have a loose one-party orientation if they have political parties at all.

Practically speaking, a traditionalistic political culture is found only in a society that retains some of the organic characteristics of the pre-industrial social order. "Good government" in the political culture involves the maintenance and encouragement of traditional patterns and, if necessary, their adjustment to changing conditions with the least possible upset. Where the traditionalistic political culture is dominant in the United States today, political leaders play conservative and custodial rather than initiatory roles unless pressed strongly from the outside.

Whereas the individualistic and moralistic political cultures may encourage the development of bureaucratic systems of organization on the grounds of "rationality" and "efficiency" in government (depending on their particular situations), traditionalistic political cultures tend to be instinctively anti-bureaucratic. The reason is that bureaucracy by its very nature interferes with the fine web of informal interpersonal relationships that lie at the root of the political system and have been developed by following traditional patterns over the years. Where bureaucracy is introduced, it is generally confined to ministerial functions under the aegis of the established power-holders.

*   *   *

The Distribution and Impact of Political Subcultures

Map 1 on pages 48–49 shows how migrational patterns have led to the concentration of specific political subcultures in particular states and localities. The basic patterns of political culture were set during the period of the rural-land frontier by three great streams of American migration that began on the East Coast and moved westward after the colonial period. Each stream moved from east to west along more or less fixed paths, following lines of least resistance that generally led them due west from the immediately previous area of settlement.

* * *

Political Culture: Some Caveats

By now the reader has no doubt formed his or her own value judgments as to the relative worth of the three political subcultures. For this reason a particular warning against *hasty* judgments must be added here. Each of the three political subcultures contributes something important to the configuration of the American political system, and each possesses certain characteristics that are inherently dangerous to the survival of that system.

The moralistic political culture, for example, is the primary source of the continuing American quest for the good society, yet there is a noticeable tendency toward inflexibility and narrow-mindedness among some of its representatives. The individualistic political culture is the most tolerant of out-and-out political corruption, yet it has also provided the framework for the integration of diverse groups into the mainstream of American life. When representatives of the moralistic political culture, in their striving for a better social order, try to limit individual freedom, they usually come up against representatives of the individualistic political culture, to whom individual freedom is the cornerstone of their pluralistic order, though not for any noble reasons. Conversely, of course, the moralistic political culture acts as a restraint against the tendencies of the individualistic political culture to tolerate anything as long as it is in the marketplace.

The traditionalistic political culture contributes to the search for continuity in a society whose major characteristic is change; yet in the name of continuity, its representatives have denied African Americans (as well as Native Americans and Latinos) their civil rights. When it is in proper working order, the traditionalistic culture has produced a unique group of first-rate national leaders from among its elites; but without a first-rate elite to draw upon, traditionalistic political-culture systems degenerate into oligarchies of the lowest level. Comparisons like these should induce caution in any evaluation of a subject that, by its very nature, evokes value judgments.

It is equally important to use caution in identifying individuals and groups as belonging to one cultural type or another on the basis of their public political behavior at a given moment in time. Immediate political responses to the issues of the day may reveal the political culture of the respondents, but not necessarily. Often, in fact, people will make what appear to be the same choices for different reasons—especially in public affairs, where the choices available at any given time are usually quite limited. Deeper analysis of what is behind those responses is usually needed. In other words, the names of the political cultures are not substitutes for the terms *conservative* and *liberal*, and should not be taken as such.

* * *

DISCUSSION QUESTIONS

1. Should the United States, as Liu argues, engage in a new Americanization process? If so, how? What are the potential benefits and potential problems with such a process? Is it important for the country to have a sense of "shared values" or not?

2. Political scientists and historians often refer to "American exceptionalism," or the idea that the United States is unique. For example, compared to other democratic countries, Americans place more emphasis on individual rights, and the United States features much greater decentralization of political power across the branches and levels of government. Do these outcomes *require* the kind of shared beliefs discussed by Warshawsky?

3. Consider the definitions Elazar presents in his analysis. What would you say are the fundamental differences and similarities among the three approaches?

4. A visitor from another country asks you, "What does it mean to be an American?" What do you say?

CHAPTER 2

The Founding and the Constitution

7

"The Nature of American Constitutionalism," from *The Origins of the American Constitution*

MICHAEL KAMMEN

The Constitution is a remarkably simple document that has provided a framework of governance for the United States for more than 220 years. It establishes a shared sovereignty between the states and the federal government, a separation and checking of powers between three branches of government, qualifications for citizenship and holding office, and a delineation of the rights considered so fundamental their restriction by the government requires extensive due process and a compelling national or state concern. Yet the Constitution's simple text produces constant controversy over its interpretation and efforts to bend, twist, and nudge its application to changing economic markets, technology, social trends, and family structures. The document's durability and flexibility amidst conflict and social change is a tribute not only to the men who drafted the Constitution in 1787, but to the American people and their willingness to embrace the challenges of self-governance at the time of the Revolution and today.

In the following article Michael Kammen argues that in order to begin to understand the Constitution and the continuous debate surrounding its interpretation, we must look to the history of American constitutionalism. Informed by John Locke's Second Treatise of Government, *the British constitution, and a colonial experience deemed an affront to basic liberties and rights, Americans plunged into the writing of the Constitution as a means to delegate power from the sovereign people to their elected and appointed agents. It is, as Kammen notes, quite remarkable that the American states chose to draft state constitutions in the midst of a revolutionary battle for independence, rather than establish provisional governments. It is similarly remarkable that these state constitutions have grown significantly in length over the years and are so readily amended and even rewritten, in contrast to the relatively short and difficult-to-amend Constitution of the United States.*

Kammen suggests that the Constitution's simplicity and durability lies in both the historic need for compromise between conflicting interests, as well as the surprising common ground that nevertheless existed over basic principles: the need to protect personal liberty, the commitment to a republican form of government, and the importance of civic virtue for preserving citizen sovereignty. This embrace of basic governing principles could explain the deeper devotion to the U.S. Constitution, in contrast to the state documents, as well as the fear that an amended or completely altered Constitution might prove less malleable and accommodating for the governance of a diverse nation.

The Nature of American Constitutionalism

"Like the Bible, it ought to be read again and again." Franklin Delano Roosevelt made that remark about the U.S. Constitution in March 1937, during one of those cozy "fireside chats" that reached millions of Americans by radio. "It is an easy document to understand," he added. And six months later, speaking to his fellow citizens from the grounds of the Washington Monument on Constitution Day—a widely noted speech because 1937 marked the sesquicentennial of the Constitution, and because the President had provoked the nation with his controversial plan to add as many as six new justices to the Supreme Court—Roosevelt observed that the Constitution was "a layman's document, not a lawyer's contract," a theme that he reiterated several times in the course of this address.

It seems fair to say that Roosevelt's assertions were approximately half true. No one could disagree that the Constitution ought to be read and reread. Few would deny that it was meant to be comprehended by laymen, by ordinary American citizens and aspirants for citizenship. Nevertheless, we must ponder whether it is truly "an easy document to understand." Although the very language of the Constitution is neither technical nor difficult, and although it is notably succinct—one nineteenth-century expert called it "a great code in a small compass"—abundant evidence exists that vast numbers of Americans, ever since 1787, have not understood it as well as they might. Even the so-called experts (judges, lawyers, political leaders, and teachers of constitutional law) have been unable to agree in critical instances about the proper application of key provisions of the Constitution, or about the intentions of those who wrote and approved it. Moreover, we do acknowledge that the Constitution developed from a significant number of compromises, and that the document's ambiguities are, for the most part, not accidental.

Understanding the U.S. Constitution is essential for many reasons. One of the most urgent is that difficult issues are now being and will continue to be settled in accordance with past interpretations and with our jurists' sense of what the founders meant. In order to make such difficult determinations, we begin with the document itself. Quite often, however, we also seek guidance from closely related or contextual documents, such as the notes kept by participants in the Constitutional Convention held at Philadelphia in 1787, from the correspondence of delegates and other prominent leaders during the later 1780s, from *The Federalist* papers, and even from some of the Anti-Federalist tracts written in opposition to the Constitution. In doing so, we essentially scrutinize the origins of American constitutionalism.

If observers want to know what is meant by constitutionalism, they must uncover several layers of historical thought and experience in public affairs. Most obviously we look to the ideas that developed in the United States during the final quarter of the eighteenth century—unquestionably the most brilliant and creative era in the entire history of American political thought. We have in mind particularly, however, a new set of assumptions that developed after 1775 about the very nature of a constitution. Why, for example, when the colonists found themselves nearly in a political state of nature after 1775, did they promptly feel compelled to write state constitutions, many of which contained a bill of rights? The patriots were, after all, preoccupied with fighting a revolution. Why not simply set up provisional governments based upon those they already had and wait until Independence was achieved? If and when the revolution succeeded, there would be time enough to write permanent constitutions.

The revolutionaries did not regard the situation in such casual and pragmatic terms. They shared a strong interest in what they called the science of politics. They knew a reasonable amount about the history of political theory. They believed in the value of ideas applied to problematic developments, and they felt that their circumstances were possibly unique in all of human history. They knew with assurance that their circumstances were changing, and changing rapidly. They wanted self-government, obviously, but they also wanted legitimacy for their newborn governments. Hence a major reason for writing constitutions. They believed in the doctrine of the social contract (about which Jean-Jacques Rousseau had written in 1762) and they believed in government by the consent of the governed: two more reasons for devising written constitutions approved by the people or by their representatives.

The men responsible for composing and revising state constitutions in the decade following 1775 regarded constitutions as social compacts that delineated the fundamental principles upon which the newly formed polities were agreed and to which they pledged themselves. They frequently used the word "experiment" because they believed that they were making institutional innovations that were risky, for they seemed virtually unprecedented. They intended to create republican governments and assumed that to do so successfully required a fair amount of social homogeneity, a high degree of consensus regarding moral values, and a pervasive capacity for virtue, by which they meant unselfish, public-spirited behavior.

Even though they often spoke of liberty, they meant civil liberty rather than natural liberty. The latter implied unrestrained freedom—absolute liberty for the individual to do as he or she pleased. The former, by contrast, meant freedom of action so long as it was not detrimental to others and was beneficial to the common weal. When they spoke of *political* liberty they meant the freedom to be a participant, to vote and hold public office, responsible commitments that ought to be widely shared if republican institutions were to function successfully.

The colonists' experiences throughout the seventeenth and eighteenth centuries had helped to prepare them for this participatory and contractual view of the nature of government. Over and over again, as the circles of settlement expanded, colonists learned to improvise the rules by which they would be governed. They had received charters and had entered into covenants or compacts that may be described as protoconstitutional, i.e., cruder and less complete versions of the constitutional documents that would be formulated in 1776 and subsequently. These colonial charters not only described the structure of government, but frequently explained what officials (often called magistrates) could or could not do.

As a result, by the 1770s American attitudes toward constitutionalism were simultaneously derivative as well as original. On the one hand, they extravagantly admired the British constitution ("unwritten" in the sense that it was not contained in a single document) and declared it to be the ultimate achievement in the entire history of governmental development. On the other hand, as Oscar and Mary Handlin have explained, Americans no longer conceived of constitutions in general as the British had for centuries.

> In the New World the term, constitution, no longer referred to the actual organization of power developed through custom, prescription, and precedent. Instead it had come to mean a written frame of government setting fixed limits on the use of power. The American view was, of course, closely related to the rejection of the old conception that authority descended from the Crown to its officials. In the newer view—that authority was derived from the consent of the governed—the written constitution became the instrument by which the people entrusted power to their agents.

*   *   *

Issues, Aspirations, and Apprehensions in 1787–1788

The major problems that confronted the Constitution-makers, and the issues that separated them from their opponents, can be specified by the key words that recur so frequently in the documents that follow in this collection. The Federalists often refer to the need for much more energy, stability, and efficiency in the national government. They fear anarchy and seek a political system better suited to America's geographical expanse: "an extensive sphere" was Madison's phrase in a letter to Jefferson.

The Anti-Federalists were apprehensive about "unrestrained power" (George Mason's words), about the great risk of national "consolidation" rather than a true confederation, about the failure to include a bill of rights in the new Constitution, about the prospect of too much power in the federal judiciary, about the "tendency to aristocracy" (see the "Federal Farmer"*), about insufficient separation of powers, and a government unresponsive to the needs of diverse and widely scattered people.

Because the two sides disagreed so strongly about the nature of the proposed government—was it genuinely federal or really national?—it is all too easy to lose sight of the common ground that they shared, a common ground that made it possible for many Anti-Federalists to support the Constitution fully even before George Washington's first administration came to a close in 1793. Both sides felt an absolute commitment to republicanism and the protection of personal liberty, as we have already seen. Both sides acknowledged that a science of politics was possible and ought to be pursued, but that "our own experience" (Madison's view, though held by "Brutus"† also) ought to be heeded above all. A majority on both sides accepted the inevitable role that interests would play in public affairs and recognized that public opinion would be a powerful force. The phrase "public opinion" appears eleven times explicitly in *The Federalist* papers, and many other times implicitly or indirectly.

The desire for happiness was invoked constantly. Although admittedly a vague and elusive concept, it clearly meant much more than the safeguarding of property (though the protection of property belonged under the rubric of happiness in the minds of many). For some it simply meant personal contentment; but increasingly there were leaders, such as George Washington, who spoke of "social happiness," which referred to harmony among diverse groups. David Humphreys's "Poem on the Happiness of America" (1786) provides an indication that this notion had national as well as individual and societal connotations.

Although both sides believed that the preservation of liberty was one of the most essential ends of government, the continued existence of chattel slavery in a freedom-loving society created considerable awkwardness for the founders. In 1775–1776, when the revolutionaries had explained the reasons for their rebellion, they frequently referred to a British plot to "enslave" Americans. The constant invocation of that notion has puzzled many students because whatever the wisdom or unwisdom of imperial policy in general, there most certainly was no conspiracy in London to enslave America.

There really should be no mystery about the colonists' usage, however, because as good Lockeans they knew full well the argument in chapter four of John Locke's *Second Treatise of Government*, entitled "Of Slavery" (an argument reiterated in Rousseau's *Social Contract*). "The liberty of man in society," Locke wrote, "is to be under no other legislative power but that established by consent in the commonwealth, nor under the dominion of

*The pen name of Richard Henry Lee of Virginia, a noted Anti-Federalist [*Editors*].
†The pen name of Robert Yates, an Anti-Federalist [*Editors*].

any will or restraint of any law but what that legislative shall enact according to the trust put in it." The denial of *full* freedom quite simply meant "slavery."

Slavery and the international slave trade were discussed extensively in 1787 at the Constitutional Convention. By then, however, "slavery" was not often used as a theoretical and general synonym for unfreedom. It meant the permanent possession of one person (black) by another (white), usually for life, the slaveowner being entitled to own the children of his or her chattel as well. We must remember that the Convention met in secret session, and that the delegates agreed not to divulge information about their proceedings for fifty years. Consequently not very much was said publicly about slavery in 1787–1788 in connection with the Constitution. Not until 1840, when the U.S. government published James Madison's detailed notes on the Convention debates, did Americans learn just how much had been compromised at Philadelphia in order to placate South Carolina and Georgia. The Constitution essentially protected slavery where it existed, and remained mute about the legality of slavery in territories that might one day become additional states. Accommodation had prevailed in 1787, which meant, as it turned out, postponing for seventy-four years the moral and political crisis of the Union.

Legacies of American Constitutionalism

Although it is difficult for us fully to imagine the complexities of interest group politics, regional rivalries, and ideological differences in 1787, the instrumental achievement of that extraordinary Convention has generally been appreciated over the years. Even such a sardonic mind as H. L. Mencken's conceded as much. "The amazing thing about the Constitution," he wrote, "is that it is as good as it is—that so subtle and complete a document emerged from that long debate. Most of the Framers, obviously, were second-rate men; before and after their session they accomplished nothing in the world. Yet during that session they made an almost perfect job of the work in hand."

Their accomplishment was, indeed, remarkable. The distribution and separation of powers among three branches at the national level, and the development of federalism as a means of apportioning sovereignty between the nation and the states, have received broad recognition and the compliment of imitation by many other nations.

Equally appreciated is the fact that the U.S. Constitution is the oldest written national constitution in the world. (The Massachusetts Constitution of 1780, although amended and revised many times, is even older.) Its endurance is genuinely remarkable. We should therefore note that the framers deserve much of the credit for that endurance, not simply because they transcended their own limitations, * * * but because they contrived to restrict the ease with which the Constitution might be revised or reconsidered. There was considerable talk in 1787–1788 about holding a second convention in order to refine the product of the first. Anti-Federalists and many who were undecided wanted such a course of action. George Washington, however, regarded that idea as impractical. Hamilton, despite his dissatisfaction with many aspects of the Constitution, doubted whether a second convention could possibly be as successful as the first; and Madison feared a serious erosion of what had been accomplished in 1787.

It is easy to forget that the Philadelphia Convention vastly exceeded its authority, and that the men who met there undertook what amounted to a usurpation of legitimate authority. As [President] Franklin Delano Roosevelt pointed out on Constitution Day in 1937, contemporaries who opposed the newly drafted document "insisted that the Constitution itself was unconstitutional under the Articles of Confederation. But the ratifying conventions overruled them." The right of revolution had been explicitly invoked in 1776 and implicitly practiced in 1787. Having done their work, however, most of the delegates did not believe that it ought to be repealed or casually revised.

The complexity of changing or adding to the original document had profound implications for the subsequent history of American constitutionalism. First, it meant that in order to gain acceptance of their handiwork, the Federalists had to commit themselves, unofficially, to the formulation of a bill of rights when the first Congress met in 1789, even though many Federalists felt that such a list of protections was superfluous. They protested that a finite list of specified safeguards would imply that numerous other liberties might not be protected against encroachment by the government. The point, ultimately, is that promulgation of the U.S. Constitution required two sets of compromises rather than one: those that took place among the delegates to the Convention, and the subsequent sense that support for ratification would be rewarded by the explicit enumeration of broad civil liberties.

Next, the existence of various ambiguities in the Constitution meant that explication would subsequently be required by various authorities, such as the Supreme Court. The justices' interpretations would become part of the total "package" that we call American constitutionalism; but the justices did not always agree with one another, and the rest of the nation did not always agree with the justices. Those realities gave rise to an ongoing pattern that might be called conflict-within-consensus.

Some of those disputes and ambiguities involved very basic questions: What are the implications and limits of consent? Once we have participated in the creation of a polity and agreed to abide by its rules, then what? How are we to resolve the conflict that arises when the wishes or needs of a majority diminish the liberties or interests of a minority? This last question was the tough issue faced by the New England states in 1814, when they contemplated secession, and by South Carolina in 1828–1833 when a high tariff designed to protect northern manufacturing threatened economic distress to southern agricultural interests. And that, of course, was the thorny issue that precipitated southern secession and the greatest constitutional crisis of all in 1860–1861.

There is yet another ambiguity, or contradiction, in American constitutional thought—though it is less commonly noticed than the one described in the previous paragraph. As we have observed, the founders were not eager for a second convention, or for easy revisions or additions to their handiwork. They did provide for change; but they made the process complicated and slow. They did not believe that the fundamental law of a nation should be casually altered; and most Americans have accepted that constraint.

Nevertheless, on the *state* level Americans have amended, expanded, revised, and totally rewritten their constitutions with some frequency. A great deal of so-called positive law (i.e., legislative enactments) finds its way into state constitutions, with the result that many modern ones exceed one hundred pages in length. There is no clear explanation for this striking pattern of divergence between constitutionalism on the national and state levels. The curious pattern does suggest, however, that Americans have regarded the U.S. Constitution of 1787 as more nearly permanent than their state constitutions. Perhaps the pattern only tells us that achieving a national consensus for change in a large and diverse society is much more difficult than achieving a statewide consensus for change.

Whatever the explanation for this dualism in American constitutionalism, the paradox does not diminish the historical reality that writers of the federal as well as the first state constitutions all tried to establish charters clearly suited to the cultural assumptions and political realities of the American scene. Even though the founders explored the history of political thought in general and the history of republics in particular, they reached the commonsense conclusion that a constitution must be adapted to the character and customs of a people. Hence the debate in 1787–1788 over the relative merits of "consolidation" versus "confederation." Hence the concern about what sort of governmental system would work most effectively over a large geographical expanse. James Madison conveyed this sense of American exceptionalism several times in a letter to Thomas Jefferson (then U.S. minister to France) in 1788, when a bill of rights was under consideration.

On August 28, 1788, a month after New York became the eleventh state to ratify the Constitution, George Washington sent Alexander Hamilton a letter from his temporary retirement at Mount Vernon. The future president acknowledged that public affairs were proceeding more smoothly than he had expected. Consequently, he wrote, "I hope the political Machine may be put in motion, without much effort or hazard of miscarrying." As he soon discovered, to put the new constitutional machine in motion would require considerable effort. It did not miscarry because the "machine" had been so soundly designed. A concerted effort would be required, however, to keep the machine successfully in operation. That should not occasion surprise. The founders had assumed an involved citizenry; and the governmental system they created functions best when their assumption is validated. That is the very essence of democratic constitutionalism.

DISCUSSION QUESTIONS

1. In your view, what would Kammen think about recent efforts to amend the Constitution to ban abortion, ban gay marriage, mandate a balanced budget, protect the flag against desecration, and protect victims' rights?

2. Although the flexibility of the Constitution helps explain its longevity, that flexibility comes at a price: ambiguity and gaps in constitutional language. What are some examples of constitutional language that is ambiguous?

3. One reason that Kammen argues it is important to understand the origins of American constitutionalism is that many judges today use their understanding of the Founders' intentions to inform their decisions. To what extent should the Founders' intentions influence modern court decisions? What are the advantages and disadvantages of this "original intent" perspective on jurisprudence?

The Federalist, No. 15

ALEXANDER HAMILTON

Despite the deference given the Constitution today, it did not command instant respect in 1787. The fight for ratification was bitter between the Federalists (those who supported the Constitution) and the Anti-Federalists (who feared that the new national government would become too powerful).

The Federalist Papers, originally written as a series of newspaper editorials intended to persuade New York to ratify the Constitution, remains the most valuable exposition of the political theory underlying the Constitution. In The Federalist, *No. 15, reprinted below, Alexander Hamilton is at his best arguing for the necessity of a stronger central government than that established under the Articles of Confederation. He points out the practical impossibility of engaging in concerted action when each of the thirteen states retains virtual sovereignty, and the need for a strong central government to hold the new country together politically and economically.*

In the course of the preceding papers I have endeavored, my fellow-citizens, to place before you in a clear and convincing light the importance of Union to your political safety and happiness. * * * [T]he point next in order to be examined is the "insufficiency of the present Confederation to the preservation of the Union." * * * There are material imperfections in our national system and * * * something is necessary to be done to rescue us from impending anarchy. The facts that support this opinion are no longer objects of speculation. They have forced themselves upon the sensibility of the people at large, and have at length extorted . . . a reluctant confession of the reality of those defects in the scheme of our federal government which have been long pointed out and regretted by the intelligent friends of the Union.

We may indeed with propriety be said to have reached almost the last stage of national humiliation. There is scarcely anything that can wound the pride or degrade the character of an independent nation which we do not experience. Are there engagements to the performance of which we are held by every tie respectable among men? These are the subjects of constant and unblushing violation. Do we owe debts to foreigners and to our own citizens contracted in a time of imminent peril for the preservation of our political existence? These remain without any proper or satisfactory provision for their discharge. * * * Are we in a condition to resent or to repel the aggression? We have neither troops, nor treasury, nor government. * * * Is public credit an indispensable resource in time of public danger? We seem to have abandoned its cause as desperate and irretrievable. Is commerce of importance to national wealth? Ours is at the lowest point of declension. Is respectability in the eyes of foreign powers a safeguard against foreign encroachments? The imbecility of our government even forbids them to treat with us. . . . Is private credit the friend and patron of industry? That most useful kind which relates to borrowing and lending is reduced within the narrowest limits, and this still more from an opinion of insecurity than from a scarcity of money. * * *

This is the melancholy situation to which we have been brought by those very maxims and counsels which would now deter us from adopting the proposed Constitution; and which, not content with having conducted us to the brink of a precipice, seem resolved to plunge us into the abyss that awaits us below. Here, my countrymen, impelled by every motive that ought to influence an enlightened people, let us make a firm stand for our safety, our tranquility, our dignity, our reputation. Let us at last break the fatal charm which has too long seduced us from the paths of felicity and prosperity.

* * * While [opponents of the Constitution] admit that the government of the United States is destitute of energy, they contend against conferring upon it those powers which are requisite to supply that energy. * * * This renders a full display of the principal defects of the Confederation necessary in order to show that the evils we experience do not proceed from minute or partial imperfections, but from fundamental errors in the structure of the building, which cannot be amended otherwise than by an alteration in the first principles and main pillars of the fabric.

The great and radical vice in the construction of the existing Confederation is in the principle of LEGISLATION FOR STATES OR GOVERNMENTS, in their CORPORATE OR COLLECTIVE CAPACITIES, and as contradistinguished from the INDIVIDUALS of whom they consist. Though this principle does not run through all the powers delegated to the Union, yet it pervades and governs those on which the efficacy of the rest depends. Except as to the rule of apportionment, the United States have an indefinite discretion to make requisitions for men and money; but they have no authority to raise either by regulations extending to the individual citizens of America. The consequence of this is that though in theory their resolutions concerning those objects are laws constitutionally binding on the members of the Union, yet in practice they are mere recommendations which the States observe or disregard at their option. * * *

There is nothing absurd or impracticable in the idea of a league or alliance between independent nations for certain defined purposes precisely stated in a treaty regulating all the details of time, place, circumstance, and quantity, leaving nothing to future discretion, and depending for its execution on the good faith of the parties. * * *

If the particular States in this country are disposed to stand in a similar relation to each other, and to drop the project of a general DISCRETIONARY SUPERINTENDENCE, the scheme would indeed be pernicious and would entail upon us all the mischiefs which have been enumerated under the first head; but it would have the merit of being, at least, consistent and practicable. Abandoning all views towards a confederate government, this would bring us to a simple alliance offensive and defensive; and would place us in a situation to be alternate friends and enemies of each other, as our mutual jealousies and rivalships, nourished by the intrigues of foreign nations, should prescribe to us.

But if we are unwilling to be placed in this perilous situation; if we still will adhere to the design of a national government, or, which is the same thing, of a superintending power under the direction of a common council, we must resolve to incorporate into our plan those ingredients which may be considered as forming the characteristic difference between a league and a government; we must extend the authority of the Union to the persons of the citizens—the only proper objects of government.

Government implies the power of making laws. It is essential to the idea of a law that it be attended with a sanction; or, in other words, a penalty or punishment for disobedience. If there be no penalty annexed to disobedience, the resolutions or commands which pretend to be laws will, in fact, amount to nothing more than advice or recommendation. This penalty, whatever it may be, can only be inflicted in two ways: by the agency of the courts and ministers of justice, or by military force; by the COERCION of the magistracy, or by the COERCION of arms. The first kind can evidently apply only to men; the last kind must of necessity be employed against bodies politic, or communities, or States. * * * In an association where the general authority is confined to the collective bodies of the communities that compose it, every breach of the laws must involve a state of war; and military execution must become the only instrument of civil obedience. Such a state of things can certainly not deserve the name of government, nor would any prudent man choose to commit his happiness to it.

There was a time when we were told that breaches by the States of the regulations of the federal authority were not to be expected; that a sense of common interest would preside over the conduct of the respective members, and would beget a full compliance with all the constitutional requisitions of the Union. This language, at the present day, would appear as wild as a great part of what we now hear from the same quarter will be thought, when we shall have received further lessons from that best oracle of wisdom, experience. It at all times betrayed an ignorance of the true springs by which human conduct is actuated, and belied the original inducements to the establishment of civil power. Why has government been instituted at all? Because the passions of men will not conform to the dictates of reason and justice without constraint. * * *

In addition to all this * * * it happens that in every political association which is formed upon the principle of uniting in a common interest a number of lesser sovereignties, there will be found a kind of eccentric tendency in the subordinate or inferior orbs by the operation of which there will be a perpetual effort in each to fly off from the common center. This tendency is not difficult to be accounted for. It has its origin in the love of power. Power controlled or abridged is almost always the rival and enemy of that power by which it is controlled or abridged. This simple proposition will teach us how little reason there is to expect that the persons intrusted with the administration of the affairs of the particular members of a confederacy will at all times be ready with perfect good humor and an unbiased regard to the public weal to execute the resolutions or decrees of the general authority. * * *

If, therefore, the measures of the Confederacy cannot be executed without the intervention of the particular administrations, there will be little prospect of their being executed at all. * * * [Each state will evaluate every federal measure in light of its own interests] and in a spirit of interested and suspicious scrutiny, without that knowledge of national circumstances and reasons of state, which is essential to a right judgment, and with that strong predilection in favor of local objects, which can hardly fail to mislead the decision. The same process must be repeated in every member of which the body is constituted; and the execution of the plans, framed by the councils of the whole, will always fluctuate on the discretion of the ill-informed and prejudiced opinion of every part. * * *

In our case the concurrence of thirteen distinct sovereign wills is requisite under the Confederation to the complete execution of every important measure that proceeds from the Union. It has happened as was to have been foreseen. The measures of the Union have not been executed; and the delinquencies of the States have step by step matured themselves to an extreme, which has, at length, arrested all the wheels of the national government and brought them to an awful stand. Congress at this time scarcely possess the means of keeping up the forms of administration, till the States can have time to agree upon a more substantial substitute for the present shadow of a federal government. * * * Each State yielding to the persuasive voice of immediate interest or convenience has successively withdrawn its support, till the frail and tottering edifice seems ready to fall upon our heads and to crush us beneath its ruins.

PUBLIUS

DISCUSSION QUESTIONS

1. Do you think the national government is sufficiently held in check as Hamilton argues? Or is the exercise of its authority so vast as to give credence to the Anti-Federalist fears? To put it another way,

would the framers be surprised or pleased with the scope of government powers today?

2. According to Hamilton, what are the weaknesses of a "league" compared to a government?

3. What is the significance of Hamilton's statement that "we must extend the authority of the Union to the persons of the citizens?"

From *An Economic Interpretation of the Constitution of the United States*

Charles A. Beard

One of the longest running debates over the Constitution focuses upon the motivation of the Founders in drafting the document. Was the motivation ideological, based upon beliefs of self-governance, the nature of a social contract, and the role of representation? Or was the motivation primarily economic, based upon a need to preserve economic interests that were threatened under the system of governance of the Articles of Confederation? And if the motivation was economic, what economic interests divided the Anti-Federalists from the Federalists in their opposition to or support for the Constitution?

One of the earliest and most controversial efforts to answer the question was written by Charles Beard in 1913. Beard argued that those who favored the Constitution and played the primary role in its drafting were motivated by the need to better protect their substantial "personality" interests—money, public securities, manufactures, and trade and shipping (or commerce)–in contrast to their opponents, who were primarily debtors and small farmers (with small real estate holdings). Not only was its motivation less than democratic, Beard argued, but the Constitution was ratified by only one sixth of the male population because voting was limited to property owners.

Subsequent critiques of Beard have pointed out that there were far more economic interests than mercantilists and farmers; that having a certain set of economic interests did not dictate the political views of the framers; and that ideas such as republicanism and liberty were more important in shaping the Constitution than the founders' economic interests. Nonetheless, the idea that economic interests influence political outcomes resonates today.

The requirements for an economic interpretation of the formation and adoption of the Constitution may be stated in a hypothetical proposition which, although it cannot be verified absolutely from ascertainable data, will at once illustrate the problem and furnish a guide to research and generalization.

It will be admitted without controversy that the Constitution was the creation of a certain number of men, and it was opposed by a certain number of men. Now, if it were possible to have an economic biography of all those connected with its framing and adoption,—perhaps about 160,000 men altogether—the materials for scientific analysis and classification would be available. Such an economic biography would include a list of the real and personal property owned by all of these men and their families; lands and houses, with incumbrances, money at interest, slaves, capital invested in shipping and manufacturing, and in state and continental securities.

Suppose it could be shown from the classification of the men who supported and opposed the Constitution that there was no line of property division at all; that is, that men owning substantially the same amounts of the same kinds of property were equally divided on the matter of adoption or rejection—it would then become apparent that the Constitution had no ascertainable relation to economic groups or classes but was the product of some abstract causes remote from the chief business of life— gaining a livelihood.

Suppose, on the other hand, that substantially all of the merchants, money lenders, security holders, manufacturers, shippers, capitalists, and financiers and their professional associates are to be found on one side in support of the Constitution and that substantially all or the major portion of the opposition came from the non-slaveholding farmers and the debtors—would it not be pretty conclusively demonstrated that our fundamental law was not the product of an abstraction known as "the whole people," but of a group of economic interests which must have expected beneficial results from its adoption? Obviously all the facts here desired cannot be discovered, but the data presented in the following chapters bear out the latter hypothesis, and thus a reasonable presumption in favor of the theory is created.

* * *

The purpose of such an inquiry is not, of course, to show that the Constitution was made for the personal benefit of the members of the Convention. Far from it. Neither is it of any moment to discover how many hundred thousand dollars accrued to them as a result of the foundation of the new government. The only point here considered is: Did they represent distinct groups whose economic interests they understood and felt in concrete, definite form through their own personal experience with identical property rights, or were they working merely under the guidance of abstract principles of political science?

* * *

The Disfranchised

In an examination of the structure of American society in 1787, we first encounter four groups whose economic status had a definite legal expression: the slaves, the indentured servants, the mass of men who could not qualify for voting under the property tests imposed by the state constitutions and laws, and women, disfranchised and subjected to the discriminations of the common law. These groups were, therefore, not represented in the Convention which drafted the Constitution, except under the theory that representation has no relation to voting.

How extensive the disfranchisement really was cannot be determined. In some states, for instance, Pennsylvania and Georgia, propertyless mechanics in the towns could vote; but in other states the freehold qualifications certainly excluded a great number of the adult males.

In no state, apparently, had the working class developed a consciousness of a separate interest or an organization that commanded the attention of the politicians of the time. In turning over the hundreds of pages of writings left by eighteenth-century thinkers one cannot help being impressed with the fact that the existence and special problems of a working class, then already sufficiently numerous to form a considerable portion of society, were outside the realm of politics, except in so far as the future power of the proletariat was foreseen and feared.

When the question of the suffrage was before the Convention, Madison warned his colleagues against the coming industrial masses: "Viewing the subject in its merits alone, the freeholders of the Country would be the safest depositories of Republican liberty. In future times a great majority of the people will not only be without landed [property], but any other sort of property. These will either combine under the influence of their common situation; in which case, the rights of property and the public liberty will not be secure in their hands, or, which is more probable, they will become the tools of opulence and ambition; in which case there will be equal danger on another side."

* * *

It is apparent that a majority of the states placed direct property qualifications on the voters, and the other states eliminated practically all who were not taxpayers. Special safeguards for property were secured in the qualifications imposed on members of the legislatures in New Hampshire, Massachusetts, New York, New Jersey, Maryland, North Carolina, South Carolina, and Georgia. Further safeguards were added by the qualifications imposed in the case of senators in New Hampshire, Massachusetts, New Jersey, New York, Maryland, North Carolina, and South Carolina.

While these qualifications operated to exclude a large portion of the adult males from participating in elections, the wide distribution of real property, created an extensive electorate and in most rural regions gave the legislatures a broad popular basis. Far from rendering to personal property that defence which was necessary to the full realization of its rights, these qualifications for electors admitted to the suffrage its most dangerous antagonists: the small farmers and many of the debtors who were the most active in all attempts to depreciate personalty [private property] by legislation. Madison with his usual acumen saw the inadequacy of such defence and pointed out in the Convention that the really serious assaults on property (having in mind of course, personalty) had come from the "freeholders."

Nevertheless, in the election of delegates to the Convention, the representatives of personalty in the legislatures were able by the sheer weight of their combined intelligence and economic power to secure delegates from the urban centres or allied with their interests. Happily for them, all the legislatures which they had to convince had not been elected on the issue of choosing delegates to a national Convention, and did not come from a populace stirred up on that question. The call for the Convention went forth on February 21, 1787, from Congress, and within a few months all the legislatures, except that of Rhode Island, had responded. Thus the heated popular discussion usually incident to such a momentous political undertaking was largely avoided, and an orderly and temperate procedure in the selection of delegates was rendered possible.

* * *

A survey of the economic interests of the members of the Convention presents certain conclusions:

A majority of the members were lawyers by profession.

Most of the members came from towns, on or near the coast, that is, from the regions in which personalty was largely concentrated.

Not one member represented in his immediate personal economic interests the small farming or mechanic classes.

The overwhelming majority of members, at least five-sixths, were immediately, directly, and personally interested in the outcome of their labors at Philadelphia, and were to a greater or less extent economic beneficiaries from the adoption of the Constitution.

1. Public security interests were extensively represented in the Convention. Of the fifty-five members who attended no less than forty appear on the Records of the Treasury Department for sums varying from a few dollars up to more than one hundred thousand dollars. [A list of their names follows.]

It is interesting to note that, with the exception of New York, and possibly Delaware, each state had one or more prominent representatives in the Convention who held more than a negligible amount of securities, and who could therefore speak with feeling and authority on the question of providing in the new Constitution for the full discharge of the public debt: [list of names]

2. Personalty invested in lands for speculation was represented by at least fourteen members: [list of names]

3. Personalty in the form of money loaned at interest was represented by at least twenty-four members: [list of names]

4. Personalty in mercantile, manufacturing, and shipping lines was represented by at least eleven members: [list of names]

5. Personalty in slaves was represented by at least fifteen members: [list of names]

It cannot be said, therefore, that the members of the Convention were "disinterested." On the contrary, we are forced to accept the profoundly significant conclusion that they knew through their personal experiences in economic affairs the precise results which the new government that they were setting up was designed to attain. As a group of doctrinaires, like the Frankfurt assembly of 1848, they would have failed miserably; but as practical men they were able to build the new government upon the only foundations which could be stable: fundamental economic interests.

*　*　*

Conclusions

At the close of this long and arid survey—partaking of the nature of catalogue—it seems worthwhile to bring together the important conclusions for political science which the data presented appear to warrant.

[1.] The movement for the Constitution of the United States was originated and carried through principally by four groups of personalty interests which had been adversely affected under the Articles of Confederation: money, public securities, manufactures, and trade and shipping.

[2.] The first firm steps toward the formation of the Constitution were taken by a small and active group of men immediately interested through their personal possessions in the outcome of their labors.

[3.] No popular vote was taken directly or indirectly on the proposition to call the Convention which drafted the Constitution.

[4.] A large propertyless mass was, under the prevailing suffrage qualifications, excluded at the outset from participation (through representatives) in the work of framing the Constitution.

[5.] The members of the Philadelphia Convention which drafted the Constitution were, with a few exceptions, immediately, directly, and personally interested in, and derived economic advantages from, the establishment of the new system.

[6.] The Constitution was essentially an economic document based upon the concept that the fundamental private rights of property are anterior to government and morally beyond the reach of popular majorities.

[7.] The major portion of the members of the Convention are on record as recognizing the claim of property to a special and defensive position in the Constitution.

[8.] In the ratification of the Constitution, about three-fourths of the adult males failed to vote on the question, having abstained from the elections at which delegates to the state conventions were chosen, either on account of their indifference or their disfranchisement by property qualifications.

[9.] The Constitution was ratified by a vote of probably not more than one-sixth of the adult males.

[10.] It is questionable whether a majority of the voters participating in the elections for the state conventions in New York, Massachusetts, New Hampshire, Virginia, and South Carolina, actually approved the ratification of the Constitution.

[11.] The leaders who supported the Constitution in the ratifying conventions represented the same economic groups as the members of the Philadelphia Convention; and in a large number of instances they were also directly and personally interested in the outcome of their efforts.

[12.] In the ratification, it became manifest that the line of cleavage for and against the Constitution was between substantial personalty interests on the one hand and the small farming and debtor interests on the other.

[13.] The Constitution was not created by "the whole people" as the jurists have said; neither was it created by "the states" as Southern nullifiers long contended; but it was the work of a consolidated group whose interests knew no state boundaries and were truly national in their scope.

DISCUSSION QUESTIONS

1. Do you think the Framers were governed by self-interest or a commitment to principle, or some combination, when they drafted the Constitution? Explain your answer.

2. What does Beard's argument say about the use of historical evidence to support one's argument? How can historical evidence be misused and how can historians, or even readers of history, sort out what "really" happened in any specific context?

3. Think of current examples of wealthy people in politics. Do they tend to support positions that would enhance their own economic position? Can you think of examples of wealthy politicians who do not behave this way?

Debating the Issues: How Democratic Is the Constitution?

Veneration for the Constitution is a classic American value; indeed, it is often said that the essence of being an American is a set of shared values and commitments expressed within the four corners of that document, most notably equality and liberty. The Constitution is the embodiment of those values, celebrated as the first, and most enduring, written constitution in human history. We celebrate the first words of the preamble, "We the people," salute the framers as men of historic wisdom and judgment, and honor the structures and processes of government.

We also note the practical wisdom of the framers, in their ability to reconcile competing tensions in creating a government powerful enough to function, but not at the risk of giving majorities the right to trample minority rights. Political theory at the time held that efforts to create democracies inevitably devolved into one of two end results: either mob rule, as majorities took control and used their power to oppress political minorities; or autocracy, as elites assumed control and did not give it up. The many carefully considered elements of constitutional structure—bicameralism, the balance between federal and state power, the equilibrium of checks and balances—have lasted for more than two centuries. And apart from one exceptional period of civil war, the structures have channeled political conflict peacefully.

Is that veneration truly warranted? Sanford Levinson, a professor at the University of Texas Law School, thinks not. He considers the Constitution to be a seriously flawed document in need of fundamental change. As originally written, the Constitution came nowhere near the aspirations of the Preamble, explicitly allowing slavery, and even after amendments retains several antidemocratic elements, including the electoral college; the vastly unequal representation in the Senate, in which Wyoming (population 576,000) has the same voting power as California (population 38 million, over sixty-five times as large); and lifetime tenure for judges. These features fail to live up to the Preamble, which Levinson considers to be the foundation of the rest of the Constitution—the whole point of the constitutional enterprise. Levinson points out that several key figures of the American founding—Thomas Jefferson especially—believed that the Constitution would require frequent updating. This was the purpose of Article V, which sets out the process for amending the document. And, Levinson notes, many of the features of the Constitution that we venerate were not thought through but were instead the product of pure compromise, in which the framers took vastly inconsistent positions when necessary in order to secure sufficient support for ratification. So, far from being a philosophically perfect document or system, the Constitution created a cumbersome and inequitable system, one that no other democratic system has chosen to copy since.

The problem with amending the Constitution is that the features Levinson considers most offensive—especially the unequal representation in the Senate—are virtually impossible to change. Article V specifies that no state can be deprived of its equal representation in the Senate without its consent (something that no state could ever be expected to do). The only recourse is a constitutional convention, in which delegates would consider fundamental reform. Levinson regards this as essential in order to allow the national government to respond to the challenge of modern economic and political times.

Eric Lane and Michael Oreskes take the more traditional stance that the Constitution is fine as it is; they argue that it is the people who must change. The key problem is that people do not understand the purpose of checks and balances or other features of the Constitution that frustrate their policy demands. But the Constitution is not just a mechanism for giving each of us what we want: the Constitution, they argue, is a vehicle for protecting liberty and providing the opportunity for individuals to pursue what they want through political and economic freedom. Instead of evaluating our legislators by how well they fulfill their constitutional duties, we base our evaluation on how much pork they can deliver to the folks at home. We are looking for an institutional fix through constitutional change when the problem is that our own fidelity to constitutional principles is waning. Evidence that the Constitution got it right comes from the fact that it produced the richest, freest, and most powerful country that has ever existed.

If there is one area of agreement between Levinson and Lane and Oreskes, it is that democracy is fragile, though they arrive at that conclusion for different reasons: Levinson because government fails to give the public what it wants, Lane and Oreskes because we are using our power to demand the wrong things.

"The Ratification Referendum: Sending the Constitution to a New Convention for Repair"

Sanford Levinson

The U.S. Constitution is radically defective in a number of important ways. Unfortunately, changing the Constitution is extremely difficult, for both political and constitutional reasons. But the difficulty of the task does not make it any less important that we first become aware of the magnitude of the deficiencies in the current Constitution and then turn our minds, as a community of concerned citizens, to figuring out potential solutions. This [reading] is organized around the conceit that Americans [should] have the opportunity to vote on the following proposal: "Shall Congress call a constitutional convention empowered to consider the adequacy of the Constitution, and, if thought necessary, to draft a new constitution that, upon completion, will be submitted to the electorate for its approval or disapproval by majority vote? Unless and until a new constitution gains popular approval, the current Constitution will continue in place."

Although such a referendum would be unprecedented with regard to the U.S. Constitution, there is certainly nothing "un-American" about such a procedure. As Professor John J. Dinan has noted in his recent comprehensive study of what he terms "the American state constitutional tradition," fourteen American states in their own constitutions explicitly give the people an opportunity "to periodically vote on whether a convention should be called." Article XIX of the New York Constitution, for example, provides that the state electorate be given the opportunity every twenty years to vote on the following question: "Shall there be a convention to revise the constitution and amend the same?" Should the majority answer in the affirmative, then the voters in each senate district will elect three delegates "at the next ensuring general election," while the statewide electorate "shall elect fifteen delegates-at-large." It should occasion no surprise that one author has described such a "mandatory referendum" as a means of "enforcing the people's right to reform their government."

It is no small matter to give people a choice with regard to the mechanisms—as well as the abstract principles—by which they are to be governed. The imagined referendum would allow "We the People of the United States of America," in whose name the document is ostensibly "ordain[ed]," to examine the fit between our national aspirations, set out in the Preamble to the Constitution, and the particular means chosen to realize those goals.

I am assuming that those reading this * * * are fellow Americans united by a deep and common concern about the future of our country. * * * I hope to convince you that, as patriotic Americans truly committed to the deepest principles of the Constitution, we should vote yes and thus trigger a new convention. My task is to persuade you that the Constitution we currently live under is grievously flawed, even in some ways a "clear and present danger" to achieving the laudable and inspiring goals to which this country professes to be committed, including republican self-government.

I believe that the best way to grasp the goals of our common enterprise is to ponder the inspiring words of the Preamble to the Constitution:

> We the People of the United States, in Order to form a more perfect Union, establish Justice, insure domestic tranquility, provide for the common defence, promote the general Welfare, and secure the Blessings of Liberty to ourselves and our Posterity, do ordain and establish this Constitution for the United States of America.

It is regrettable that law professors rarely teach and that courts rarely cite the Preamble, for it is *the single most important part* of the Constitution. The reason is simple: It announces the *point* of the entire enterprise. The 4,500 or so words that followed the Preamble in the original, unamended Constitution were all in effect merely means that were thought to be useful to achieving the great aims set out above. It is indeed the ends articulated in the Preamble that justify the means of our political institutions. And to the extent that the means turn out to be counterproductive, then we should revise them.

It takes no great effort to find elements in the original Constitution that run counter to the Preamble. It is impossible for us today to imagine how its authors squared a commitment to the "Blessings of Liberty" with the toleration and support of chattel slavery that is present in various articles of the Constitution. The most obvious example is the bar placed on Congress's ability to forbid the participation by Americans in the international slave trade until 1808. The most charitable interpretation of the framers, articulated by Frederick Douglass, is that they viewed these compromises with the acknowledged evil of slavery as temporary; the future would see its eradication through peaceful constitutional processes.

One might believe that the Preamble is incomplete because, for example, it lacks a commitment to the notion of equality. Political scientist Mark Graber has suggested that the reference to *"our* Posterity" suggests a potentially unattractive limitation of our concerns *only* to members of the American political community, with no notice taken of the posterity of other societies, whatever their plight. Even if one would prefer a more explicitly cosmopolitan Preamble, I find it hard to imagine rejecting any of the overarching values enunciated there. In any event, I am happy to endorse the Preamble as the equivalent of our creedal summary of America's civil religion.

There are two basic responses to the discovery that ongoing institutional practices are counterproductive with regard to achieving one's announced goals. One is to adjust the practices in ways that would make achievement of the aims more likely. This is, often, when we mean by the very notion of rationality: One does not persist in behaviors that are acknowledged to make more difficult the realization of one's professed hopes. Still, a second response, which has its own rationality, is to adjust the goals to the practices. Sometimes, this makes very good sense if one comes to the justified conclusion that the goals may be utopian. In such cases, it is a sign of maturity to recognize that we will inevitably fall short in our aims and that "the best may be enemy of the good" if we are tempted to throw over quite adequate, albeit imperfect, institutions in an attempt to attain the ideal.

Perhaps one might even wish to defend the framers' compromises with slavery on the ground that they were absolutely necessary to the achievement of the political union of the thirteen states. One must believe that such a union, in turn, was preferable to the likely alternative, which would have been the creation of two or three separate countries along the Atlantic coast. Political scientist David Hendrickson has demonstrated that many of the framers—and many other theorists as well—viewed history as suggesting a high probability that such separate countries would have gone to war with one another and made impossible any significant measure of "domestic tranquility." Hendrickson well describes the Constitution as a "peace pact" designed to prevent the possibility of war. If there is one thing we know, it is that unhappy compromises must often be made when negotiating such pacts. Of course, American slaves—and their descendants—could scarcely be expected to be so complacently accepting of these compromises, nor, of course, should *any* American who takes seriously the proclamation of the Pledge of Allegiance that ours is a system that takes seriously the duty to provide "liberty and justice for all."

Not only must we restrain ourselves from expecting too much of any government; we must also recognize that the Preamble sets out potentially conflicting goals. It is impossible to maximize the achievement of all of the great ends of the Constitution. To take an obvious example, providing for the "common defence" may require on occasion certain incursions into the "Blessings of Liberty." One need only refer to the military draft, which was upheld in 1918 by the Supreme Court against an attack claiming that it constituted the "involuntary servitude"—that is, slavery—prohibited by the Thirteenth Amendment. We also properly accept certain limitations on the freedom of the press with regard, say, to publishing certain information—the standard example is troop movements within a battle zone—deemed to be vital to American defense interests. The year 2005 ended with the beginning of a great national debate about the propriety of warrantless interceptions of telephone calls and other incursions on traditional civil liberties in order, ostensibly, to protect ourselves against potential terrorists.

Even if one concedes the necessity of adjusting aims in light of practical realities, it should also be readily obvious that one can easily go overboard. At the very least, one should always be vigilant in assessing such adjustments lest one find, at the end of the day, that the aims have been reduced to hollow shells. It is also necessary to ask if a rationale supporting a given adjustment that might well have been convincing at time A necessarily continues to be present at time B. Practical exigencies that required certain political compromises in 1787 no longer obtain today. We have long since realized this about slavery. It is time that we apply the same critical eye to the compromise of 1787 that granted all states an equal vote in the Senate.

To criticize that particular compromise—or any of the other features of the Constitution that I shall examine below—is not necessarily to criticize the founders themselves. My project—and, therefore, your own vote for a new convention, should you be persuaded by what follows—requires no denigration of the founders. They were, with some inevitable exceptions, an extraordinary group of men who performed extraordinary deeds, including drafting a Constitution that started a brand-new governmental system. By and large, they deserve the monuments that have been erected in their honor. But they themselves emphasized the importance—indeed, necessity—of learning from experience.

They were, after all, a generation that charted new paths by overturning a centuries-long notion of the British constitutional order because it no longer conformed to their own sense of possibility (and fairness). They also, as it happened, proved ruthlessly willing to ignore the limitations of America's "first constitution," the Articles of Confederation. Although Article XIII of that founding document required unanimous approval by the thirteen state legislatures before any amendment could take effect, Article VII of the Constitution drafted in Philadelphia required the approval of only nine of the thirteen states, and the approval was to be given by state conventions rather than by the legislatures.

The most important legacies handed down by the founding generation were, first, a remarkable willingness to act in bold and daring ways when they believed that the situation demanded it, coupled with the noble visions first of the Declaration of Independence and then of the Preamble. Both are as inspiring—and potentially disruptive—today as when they were written more than two centuries ago. But we should also be inspired by the copious study that Madison and others made of every available history and analysis of political systems ranging from ancient Greece to the Dutch republic and the British constitutional order. We best honor the framers by taking the task of creating a republican political order as seriously as they did and being equally willing to learn from what the history of the past 225 years, both at home and abroad, can teach us about how best to achieve and maintain such an order. At the time of its creation, we could legitimately believe that we were the only country committed to democratic self-governance. That is surely no longer the case, and we might well have lessons to learn from our co-ventures in that enterprise. To the extent that experience teaches us that the Constitution in significant aspects demeans "the consent of the governed" and has become an impediment to achieving the goals of the Preamble, we honor rather than betray the founders by correcting their handiwork.

Overcoming Veneration

* * * I suspect * * * that at least some readers might find it difficult to accept even the possibility that our Constitution is seriously deficient because they venerate the Constitution and find the notion of seriously criticizing it almost sacrilegious.

In an earlier book, *Constitutional Faith*, I noted the tension between the desire of James Madison that Americans "venerate" their Constitution and the distinctly contrasting views of his good friend Thomas Jefferson that, instead, the citizenry regularly subject it to relentless examination. Thus, whatever may have been Jefferson's insistence on respecting what he called the "chains" of the Constitution, he also emphasized that the "Creator has made the earth for the living, not the dead." It should not be surprising, then, that he wrote to Madison in 1789, "No society can make a perpetual constitution, or even a perpetual law."

Jefferson and Madison might have been good friends and political associates, but they disagreed fundamentally with regard to the wisdom of subjecting the Constitution to critical analysis. Jefferson was fully capable of writing that "[w]e may consider each generation as a distinct nation, with a right, by the will of its majority, to bind themselves, but none to bind the succeeding generation, more than the inhabitants of another country." His ultimate optimism about the Constitution lay precisely in its potential for change: "Happily for us, that when we find our constitutions defective and insufficient to secure the happiness of our people, we can assemble with all the coolness of philosophers, and set it to rights, while every other nation on earth must have recourse to arms to amend or restore their constitutions." * * *

Madison, however, would have none of this. He treated 1787 almost as a miraculous and singular event. Had he been a devotee of astrology, he might have said that the stars were peculiarly and uniquely aligned to allow the drafting of the Constitution and then its ratification. Though Madison was surely too tactful to mention this, part of the alignment was the absence of the famously contentious Jefferson and John Adams. Both were 3,000 miles across the sea, where they were serving as the first ambassadors from the new United States to Paris and London, respectively. Moreover, it certainly did not hurt that Rhode Island had refused to send any delegates at all and therefore had no opportunity to make almost inevitable mischief, not to mention being unable to vote in an institutional structure where the vote of one state could make a big difference. And, if pressed, Madison would presumably have agreed that the Constitutional Convention—and the ratifying conventions thereafter—would never have succeeded had the delegates included American slaves, Native Americans, or women in the spirit of Abigail Adams. She had famously—and altogether unsuccessfully—told her husband that leaders of the new nation should "remember the ladies." One need not see the framers in Philadelphia as an entirely homogeneous group—they were not—in order to realize that the room was devoid of those groups in America that were viewed as merely the *objects*, and not the active *subjects*, of governance.

Madison sets out his views most clearly in the *Federalist*, No. 49, where he explicitly takes issue with Jefferson's proposal for rather frequent constitutional conventions that would consider whether "alter[ation]" of the constitution might be desirable. Madison acknowledges the apparent appeal, in a system where "the people are the only legitimate fountain of power," of "appeal[ing] to the people themselves." However, "there appear to be insuperable objections against the proposed recurrence to the people." Perhaps the key objection is that *"frequent appeal to the people would carry an implication of some defect in the government [and] deprive the government of that veneration which time bestows on every thing, and without which perhaps the wisest and freest governments would not possess the requisite stability."* Only "a nation of philosophers" can forgo this emotion of veneration—and, therefore, feel free of guilt-ridden anxiety about the idea of constitutional change. However, "a nation of philosophers is as little to be expected as the philosophical race of kings wished for by Plato."

Madison is thus fearful of "disturbing the public tranquillity by interesting too strongly the public passions." The success of Americans in replacing a defective Articles of Confederation with a better Constitution does not constitute a precedent for future action. We should "recollect," he says, "that all the existing constitutions were formed in the midst of a danger which repressed the passions most unfriendly to order and concord." Moreover, the people at large possessed "an enthusiastic confidence . . . in their patriotic leaders," which, he says, fortunately "stifled the ordinary diversity of opinions on great national questions." He is extremely skeptical that the "future situations in which we must expect to be usually placed" will "present any equivalent security against the danger" of an excess of public passion, disrespect for leaders, and the full play of diverse opinions. In case there is any doubt, he writes of his fear that the "*passions*, therefore, not the *reasons*, of the public would sit in judgment."

Madison's view of his fellow Americans was far closer to that of Alexander Hamilton, with whom he had coauthored the *Federalist*. One can doubt that Madison expressed any reservations when hearing Hamilton, addressing his fellow delegates to the Philadelphia convention on June 18, 1787, denounce the conceit that "the voice of the people" is "the voice of God." On the contrary, said Hamilton: "The people are turbulent and changing; they seldom judge or determine right." Although Madison was not opposed to constitutional amendment as such, he clearly saw almost no role for a public that would engage in probing questions suggesting that there might be serious "defects" in the Constitution. Only philosophers (like himself?) or, perhaps, "patriotic leaders" could be trusted to engage in dispassionate political dialogue and reasoning. In contrast, the general public should be educated to feel only "veneration" for their Constitution rather than be encouraged to use their critical faculties and actually assess the relationship between the great ends set out in the Preamble and the instruments devised for their realization.

* * *

This is a mistake. To the extent that we continue thoughtlessly to venerate, and therefore not subject to truly critical examination, our Constitution, we are in the position of the battered wife who continues to profess the "essential goodness" of her abusive husband. To stick with the analogy for a moment, it may well be the case that the husband, when sober or not gambling, is a decent, even loving, partner. The problem is that such moments are more than counterbalanced by abusive ones, even if they are relatively rare. And he becomes especially abusive when she suggests the possibility of marital counseling and attendant change. Similarly, that there are good features of our Constitution should not be denied. But there are also significantly abusive ones, and it is time for us to face them rather than remain in a state of denial.

Trapped Inside the Article V Cage

The framers of the Constitution were under no illusion that they had created a perfect document. The best possible proof for this proposition comes from George Washington himself. As he wrote to his nephew Bushrod two months after the conclusion of the Philadelphia convention over which he had presided, "*The warmest friends and the best supporters the Constitution has do not contend that it is free from imperfections*; but they found them unavoidable and are sensible if evil is likely to arise there from, the remedy must come hereafter." Sounding a remarkably Jeffersonian note, Washington noted that the "People (for it is with them to Judge) can, as they will have the advantage of experience on their Side, decide with as much propriety on the alteration[s] and amendment[s] which are necessary." Indeed, wrote the man described as the Father of Our Country, "I do not think we are more inspired, have more wisdom, or possess more virtue, than those who will come after us."

Article V itself is evidence of the recognition of the possibility—and inevitable reality—of imperfection, else they would have adopted John Locke's suggestion in a constitution that he drafted for the Carolina colonies that would have made the document unamendable. It is an unfortunate reality, though, that Article V, practically speaking, brings us all too close to the Lockean dream (or nightmare) of changeless stasis.

As University of Houston political scientist Donald Lutz has conclusively demonstrated, the U.S. Constitution is the most difficult to amend of any constitution currently existing in the world today. Formal amendment of the U.S. Constitution generally requires the approval of two-thirds of each of the two houses of our national Congress, followed by the approval of three-quarters of the states (which today means thirty-eight of the fifty states). Article V does allow the abstract possibility that amendments could be proposed through the aegis of a constitutional convention called by Congress upon the petition of two-thirds of the states; such proposals, though, would still presumably have to be ratified by the state legislatures or, in the alternative, as was done with regard to the Twenty-first Amendment repealing the prohibition of alcohol required by the Eighteenth Amendment, by conventions in each of the states. As a practical matter, though, Article V makes it next to impossible to amend the Constitution with regard to genuinely controversial issues, even if substantial— and intense—majorities advocate amendment.

As I have written elsewhere, some significant change functionally similar to "amendment" has occurred informally, outside of the procedures set out by Article V. One scholar has aptly described this as a process of "constitutional change off-the-books." Yale law professor Bruce Ackerman has written several brilliant books detailing the process of "non-Article V" amendment, and I warmly commend them to the reader. Yet it is difficult to argue that such informal amendment has occurred, or is likely to occur, with regard to the basic *structural* aspects of the American political system with which this book is primarily concerned.

It is one thing to argue, as Ackerman has done, that the New Deal worked as a functional amendment of the Constitution by giving Congress significant new powers to regulate the national economy. Similarly, one could easily argue that the president, for good or for ill, now possesses powers over the use of armed forces that would have been inconceivable to the generation of the framers. Whatever the text of the Constitution may say about the power of Congress to "declare war" or whatever the original understanding of this clause, it is hard to deny that many presidents throughout our history have successfully chosen to take the country to war without seeking a declaration of war (or, in some cases, even prior congressional approval of any kind). Ackerman and David Golove have also persuasively argued that the Treaty Clause, which requires that two-thirds of the Senate assent to any treaty, has been transformed through the use of "executive agreements." Although such agreements are unmentioned in the text of the Constitution, presidents have frequently avoided the strictures of the Treaty Clause by labeling an "agreement" what earlier would have been viewed as a "treaty." Thus, the North American Free Trade Agreement did not have to leap the hurdles erected by the Treaty Clause; instead, it was validated by majority votes of both the House of Representatives and the Senate.

These developments are undoubtedly important, and any complete analysis of our constitutional system should take account of such flexibility. But we should not overemphasize our system's capacity to change, and it is *constitutional stasis* rather than the potential for adaptation that is my focus.

*   *   *

* * * One cannot, as a practical matter, litigate the obvious inequality attached to Wyoming's having the same voting power in the Senate as California. Nor can we imagine even President George W. Bush, who has certainly not been a shrinking violet with regard to claims of presidential power, announcing that Justice John Paul Stevens—appointed in 1976 and embarking on this fourth decade of service on the Supreme Court at the age of eighty-six—is simply "too old" or has served "long enough," and that he is therefore nominating, and asking the Senate to confirm, a successor to Justice Stevens in spite of the awkward fact that the justice has not submitted his resignation.

In any event, * * * the Constitution makes it unacceptably difficult to achieve the inspiring goals of the Preamble and, therefore, warrants our disapproval. * * *

Although I am asking you to take part in a hypothetical referendum and to vote no with regard to the present Constitution, I am *not* asking you to imagine simply tearing it up and leaping into the unknown of a fanciful "state of nature." All you must commit yourself to is the proposition that the Constitution is sufficiently flawed to justify calling a new convention authorized to scrutinize all aspects of the Constitution and to suggest such changes as are felt to be desirable. The new convention would be no more able to bring its handiwork into being by fiat than were the framers in Philadelphia. All proposals would require popular approval in a further national referendum. This leaves open the possibility that, even after voting to trigger the convention, you could ultimately decide that the "devil you know" (the present Constitution) is preferable to the "devil you don't" (the proposed replacement). But the important thing, from my perspective, is to recognize that there are indeed "devilish" aspects of our present Constitution that should be confronted and, if at all possible, exorcised. To complete this metaphor, one might also remember that "the devil is in the details." * * *

11

"We"

Eric Lane and Michael Oreskes

We live in a remarkable political age. More people than ever before in history, possibly a majority of all the people on earth, live under governments that could reasonably be described as democracies. The enormity of this can only be grasped by going back * * * to that moment in the late 1700s when democracy as we now know it barely existed in the world. Indeed, the word *democracy* was essentially an insult, a synonym for *mob rule*. Yes, there were places where the king had ceded some measure of power to aristocracies or even to semirepresentative parliaments. There were also commercial cities in Europe that had allowed considerable popular participation in decision making.

But nowhere was there anything like what a group of men, desperately trying to save their fledgling country, invented in Philadelphia in the summer of 1787. They wrote "a Constitution which . . . has brought such a happy order out of so gloomy a chaos," James Madison said of his handiwork many years later. They wrote a Constitution that invented a new kind of representative government. It ushered in what we can now see as the Age of Democracy in which "representative government bottomed on the principle of popular sovereignty . . . has become the political norm." In a recent book on the rise of democracy, the British scholar John Dunn finds Madison's pride understandable given the far-reaching effects of his invention: "It secured the new Republic extremely effectively, and, as we now know, for a very long time. In doing so, it turned the United States into the most politically definite, the best consolidated and the most politically self-confident society on earth. It also, over time . . . opened the way for it to become overwhelmingly the most powerful state in human history."

Quite an impressive summer's work.

But where are we in the life span of this invention? The American experiment has now lasted longer than any democracy in history. (Athens, for example, lasted only around 170 years as a democracy.) It has also spawned and inspired many others to pursue democracy. After much spillage of words and blood across the twentieth century, there is no longer even a serious intellectual challenger to representative democracy as the best and most legitimate way to organize government. What a long way we have come from 1787! "The United States is now the oldest enduring republic in world history, with a set of political institutions and traditions that have stood the test of time," wrote the historian Joseph J. Ellis.

The framers would have been stunned by this success. They knew the lessons of history were against them. They had learned from experience that individuals set free pursued their own interests. Large numbers of individuals pursuing their own interests led to chaos. Chaos invited dictators, homegrown or external, to intervene to restore order, snuffing out the very liberty people had fought to establish. They understood this cycle from their reading and, more, from the first eleven years of their own nation, which by 1787 seemed to them to be descending into the gloomy chaos Madison wrote of later.

That is why they saw democracy as "fragile."

Fragile because the framers had come to understand that in pursuit of their self-interests, Americans, like everyone else, would be willing to trample the "democracy" of others thus endangering their own.

Fragile because it was dependent on the broad participation of Americans in the nation's political processes.

Fragile because it was dependent on the willingness of Americans to acquiesce to the results of such a process.

Fragile because of the Constitution's delicate arrangement of checks and balances.

Fragile because it was a system for institutionalizing compromise. There would always be citizens searching for a more perfect system, some system that promised more wealth, or more security, or more equality, or a more glorious future, or just more of whatever it is they particularly wanted.

That was the challenge the framers confronted in 1787. People wanted what they wanted for themselves. The framers' solution, wonderfully modern and, in 1787, totally original, was to adopt a more realistic view of people and adapt their design for government to that view. They enlisted vice "on the side of virtue." They set out to prove how a representative democracy could operate without special public virtue, how "an avaricious society can form a government able to defend itself against the avarice of its members." In other words, this was not a government as good as its people. It was a government designed to produce results better than the desires of each individual person! And that is how the people ensured their own liberty. Out of many one, *E Pluribus Unum.*

To accept democracy as it emerged from Philadelphia meant to accept, as Franklin said, that this was no perfect system, just the closest to perfection a human design could come.

The framers worried that their new democracy would last only a few years. But amazingly it succeeded. Two hundred and twenty years later, the many offshoots of modern representative democracy have triumphed around the world. How ironic, then, that its original American version, with its complicated checks and balances, faces meaningful challenge in the place where it was born.

This is not the first such challenge in American history, of course, and we hope not the last. It won't be if we face it, as previous generations faced their constitutional challenges. The challenge takes new forms each time. But at heart the issue is always the same: We want what we want, and we are convinced that the system that is stopping us is wrong, flawed, broken or outmoded.

This is the essence of our present challenge. The bond between government and governed has become strained. Americans are deeply frustrated with the workings of their government. They see it as unresponsive, unrepresentative, ineffective, crippling. Can you image even a handful of Americans acknowledging today that the purpose of their government is to produce results better than the desires of the people as individuals? Not likely.

We Americans love the framers. We consume books about them and revere their words. But we have lost our connection to what they actually invented and how that invention over time created in us what we have come to call a Constitutional Conscience. We have lost the narrative thread that connects us to the story of our constitutional democracy. That story tells us two things. First, how the framers learned a series of lessons between 1776 and 1787 and used these lessons to craft our government, the blueprint for which became the Constitution. And second, how we, the people, created a Constitutional Conscience from the essential meaning of that Constitution—its freedoms and its processes and tradeoffs—and guided by these principles were then able to adapt time and again through our history to an evolving America.

This narrative thread is vital to us. It is the story that makes us Americans, ties us to our government and ties our government to us. Without it we have begun, without being totally conscious of what we are doing, to drift away from our constitutional system. We are drifting away because our knowledge of our system has grown thin. From the 1960s onward, according to Derek Bok, civic education has been declining and by the 1980s had nearly vanished. "It is striking how little energy is devoted to trying to engage citizens more actively in the affairs of government. Civic education in the public schools has been almost totally eclipsed by a preoccupation with preparing the workforce of a global economy. Most universities no longer treat the preparation of citizens as an explicit goal of their curriculum."

Reports have documented this steady decline in civic understanding. In 1998, the Department of Education found that 75 percent of high school seniors were "not proficient in civics; one third lacked even a basic comprehension of how the government operates, while only 9 percent could give two reasons why citizens should participate in the democratic process." A report in 2002 concluded "that the nation's citizenry is woefully under-educated about the fundamentals of our American Democracy."

This lack of connection is producing a dangerous spiral of frustration and disenchantment. On the one hand, Americans take the existence of our democracy for granted, while, on the other hand, being frustrated with its workings. This produces a dangerous spiral of frustration and disenchantment. Observed Bok: "Americans have expectations for politics and the political process that are often unrealistic. Convinced that presidents can often accomplish more than is humanly possible, that legislators should be able to arrive at sensible decisions without prolonged disagreement or controversy, and that politicians should refrain from pandering to the voters yet still reflect the views of their constituents, the public seems fated to endure repeated disappointment over the government and those who run it."

Some Americans respond to this disappointment by demanding changes in the system, others by distancing themselves from the system, which leaves those who stay engaged more powerful to push for the agenda they want.

Those demands for change come in two basic forms, although proponents of each argue that their proposals would make the system more democratic by shifting power. There are the Lloyd Cutlers, Oliver Norths and Dick Cheneys who want to shift more power to the president so he can either force the rest of the government to respond or just act without being fettered by the process. And there are others who want to shift more power directly to citizens so they can force government to respond, or simply go around the process. That they want such changes is within their rights. But any meaningful argument for them must occur in the context of the lessons the framers learned long ago. Without this context, we risk making changes that dismantle what has been proven right about our system and even endanger the freedoms it was built to guarantee.

It might be helpful to restate those lessons, in a simple form that everyone can paste on their refrigerator.

The framers boiled their experience down to a Constitution. We have boiled their experience down to these five lessons.

1. Everyone is selfish. This is not to say that people cannot act well or perform acts of great nobility. But essentially people act to achieve their own self-interest, particularly at the level at which government operates: regulating conduct and redistributing wealth. People are, however, willing to trade one benefit for another and sometimes even sacrifice a narrow interest for a broader one that they feel will ultimately do them more good. The government's job is to find those areas of common ground. That is where we can build a common good.

2. Government is the steam valve of society. It funnels and relieves the pressures that build from competing interests.

3. Political process is more important than product. Consensus around a flawed plan can still produce great progress. (The Constitution itself is the best example.) But a "perfect plan" without consensus will only produce conflict and deadlock. (The Clinton health care debacle is one example.) Respect for the system is thus a vital prerequisite for progress. When respect is in such short supply, it is no surprise that progress is, as well.

4. The strength of consensus is directly related to the breadth of representation and the depth of deliberation. A sound-bite society where civic education has vanished has little basis for forging strong consensus.

5. Every interest is a special one. The founders would no doubt be amazed by the scale and power of modern corporations and trade unions. But they would have no difficulty at all with the idea that everyone has wants and desires and that these drive their views and their allegiances to groups and factions. To them, the only meaningful definition of the *common good* would be the agreement that emerged from an inclusive political and legislative process to resolve competing (special) interests.

Our world is very different from that of the framers. People have powers now they could not have dreamed of then. Information, the lifeblood of democracy, moved then at the speed of sail. It moves now at the speed of light.

But there is no evidence that people have changed. Therefore, we see no reason to abandon the lessons the framers formed about people or the system they built from those lessons. Indeed, some of the changes, most particularly the speed with which society can now move, only reinforce the need for care in our political deliberations and for the speed bumps in the process that prevent us from rushing to judgment. That is what the framers built for us.

Recent experience reminds us that we make mistakes as a country when we move away from how our system was built to work. When people say now they wish the Congress and the media had done more to question the march to war in Iraq, they are saying, too, that they wish the leaders of Congress and of the press had done more to assert their authority, and fulfill their responsibilities, under, respectively, Article I and the First Amendment to the Constitution. Even many proponents of the war concede now that the checks and balances did not work well. We believe this failure was due to the weakening of our sense of constitutional roles, of our Constitutional Conscience.

We as Americans need to continue to remind ourselves of the framers' concern that democracy was fragile.

So far, unlike in the past, no one is openly arguing for an abandonment of democracy. Indeed, what many Americans think we need is what they see as more democracy. Both the proponents of strengthened presidential power and the proponents of direct democracy argue that their proposals would make the system more representative of the general public: the president as the only nationally elected official, and direct democracy as the only means to involve Americans more directly in the decision-making processes. Either way, the argument is for a more direct engagement and less entanglement in Washington process. We understand those feelings. They rise historically from a treasured strain of American belief running back to, at least, Tom Paine, the Declaration of Independence and the Articles of Confederation.

But we must not forget the warning of the framers that the most likely undoing of democracy would be in the name of more democracy.

That thought is why we wrote this book. We wanted to pick up the dropped narrative thread of the American democratic story, to remind ourselves that the democratic thinking of 1776 is only the first half of our legacy. The second half was born of Madison and his colleagues in 1787. The framers in 1787 saw liberty and direct democracy is inadequate on their own to ensure the very democracy they purported to further. For in the real world in which government works, this directly democratic perspective translates into one group getting its way over the interest of other groups or one branch, whether a powerful legislature or monarchical president, getting too much power over everyone else.

The framers' ideas transformed the thirst for liberty into a real nation. Madison and his colleagues invented a form of government whose purpose, as the historian Gordon Wood summed it up, was not to transcend our differences but to reconcile them.

Americans' current frustration and anger with their government is sapping their commitment to the principles that have made the country work. Rather than drift away from the Constitution, we should renew our connection to it. We should remember that consultation and process and debate are good things, even when they slow and complicate decisions. Most of all, we should remind each other that compromise is a show of strength, not weakness. Reaffirming these constitutional principles will actually address our frustration better than inventing something different, or more accurately, returning to what did not work between 1776 and 1787.

People say that what they want is compromise and consensus. The framers believed in that. It is why the most important and radical word in the Constitution was the first word, *We*. The government was the people and is the people. The power of each branch of government is a grant from the people, and each branch to one degree or another is accountable to them. Nothing like this had ever been created before. One British political leader, comparing the evolution of Britain's unwritten constitution to the seemingly overnight drafting of the U.S. Constitution, called the latter "the most wonderful work ever struck off at a given time by the brain and purpose of man."

But Americans in practice, in the grind of life, are no longer seeing it this way. For one thing, they do not connect their desire for consensus with the Constitution's governmental design. For another, they routinely, and predictably, define the consensus they want as the achievement of their own goals, not something larger. Americans' demands on government are today broad and deeply diverse. And when they are in an uncompromising mood, when they are divided fifty-fifty, red from blue, their representative government reflects this division, and it stalls.

The problem is not that government is unrepresentative. The problem, if you want to call it that, is that the government is very representative. The message we are hearing is that our government does not work. The message we should be hearing is that our government is a reflection of our own divisions. What we need is not a new system of government. We need a renewed willingness to work out our differences and find compromises, consensus and that other now-popular phrase, common ground.

The purpose of American-style democracy is not to guarantee each of us what we want individually. It is to give each of us as large an opportunity as possible to pursue what we want within the limits the Constitution and our Constitutional Conscience impose on us. This tension between individual liberty and community restraint has over time produced a great deal of good for a great many people and worked better than any alternative yet tried. It is still the best system for our sprawling, complicated nation.

To say that ours is the best system is not to say that it is a perfect system. It is not and never will be perfect. It can't be. It is composed of we, the people, with all our flaws. That is the point. We make it work. Our drive. Our demands. Our participation! In 1888, the poet and editor James Russell Lowell remarked on the "splendid complacency" he found among his fellow Americans who were "neglectful" of their "political duties." He traced this neglect back to a widespread but mistaken belief that the framers of the Constitution had "invented a machine that would go of itself." Lowell said he admired the ability of Americans to let "confidence in our luck" and "absorption with material interests" subsume attention to the state of our democracy.

*   *   *

These problems have been building for years. By the end of the 1980s, politicians in Washington were in open despair that the political system was unable to deal with the problems facing the country.

The political deterioration has grown steadily worse. Not surprisingly, since it is our most representative branch of government, the dysfunction is most visible in the Congress. In a nation of citizens so lacking in an understanding of our system, it is hardly surprising that, increasingly, the men and women they send to Washington don't make an adherence to constitutional principles an important part of their daily work. "People revere the Constitution yet know so little about it—and that goes for some of my fellow senators," said the Senate's top institutionalist, Robert Byrd of West Virginia.

The framers counted on a balance of power between Congress and the president. They were, critically, intended to watch each other. But * * * Congress has wavered in the exercise of its constitutional duty.

The weakness of the legislature throws off the whole design of the system. The strong reassertions of presidential prerogatives would not have surprised the framers. They would have expected this, although some may have been surprised at the degree. "You must . . . oblige [the government] to control itself," Madison wrote. The American system counts on each branch asserting its authority, just as it counts on each individual to press his or her wishes. Balance is essential to the framers' design, but to find the right balance each participant has to push and pull. The danger comes when one branch pushes and the other folds.

*   *   *

The imbalance we refer to here is far more than the common instinct of members of Congress trying to protect a president of the same party. To some extent, this will always happen. But American history is marked with examples of members of Congress of each party asserting their institutional, constitutional role and challenging a president of their own party. Senator Harry S. Truman investigated President Roosevelt's administration, and Senator Lyndon B. Johnson investigated president Truman's administration. It was a Republican senator, Howard Baker, whose incessant questions crystallized the belief that a Republican president knew more about Watergate than he had told. And it was a Democratic senator, Daniel Patrick Moynihan, who blocked the Democratic president and his wife from their plan to overhaul American health care. Moynihan's critique was a classic defense of constitutional process. The Clintons drafted their plan, Moynihan complained, behind closed doors and failed to consult the Congress or build a consensus. And a few Republican legislators had begun challenging President George W. Bush's Iraq policy by the end of 2006.

But over the last few years on Capitol Hill, the Republican leadership seemed to disown the institutional role in the constitutional design. * * * Without amending the Constitution, both Senator Bill Frist and Speaker Dennis Hastert effectively gave President Bush the parliamentary type of system that Lloyd Cutler had so desperately wanted for President Carter. They operated as the president's floor leaders in the Congress, rather than as his separate and coequal partners in government.

Congress of course is not a piece of machinery. It is 535 individual members. They are the ones who decide how assertive to be. The single most important factor in that decision is the question of how assertive American voters expect them to be. Senator Frist and Speaker Hastert followed their path because it was easy, because they did not feel political pressure to assert their institutional roles under the Constitution. We can blame the voters for not pressuring the leaders. Or we can blame the leaders for not leading the citizens. Both are true. If two of the top elected figures in the country have such little regard for the institutional obligations handed down to them, how can we expect ordinary Americans to pay attention to the Constitution? Yet it is also hard to ask politicians to exercise institutional responsibilities that we give them no credit for exercising.

Both sides of the problem are an outgrowth of how far we have fallen away from an intimate knowledge of or connection to our Constitutional Conscience. We judge our politicians heavily by what we want and how well they deliver. We measure them in the present tense alone. We don't praise honest men and women for taking clear stands on constitutional principle or exercising those institutional responsibilities. We want to know what they have done for us lately; not what they have done to faithfully exercise the responsibilities given them by the Constitution. And how could it be otherwise, for we have little idea what those responsibilities are. * * *

The 2006 election sent a message to the incumbents in Congress. In very much the way the Federalists were tossed out in 1800, after President Adams failed to stop a Federalist Congress from plunging forward with the reviled Sedition Act, the Republicans were tossed out of Congress in 2006 for failing to check a Republican president's plunge into an unpopular war. Elections, as vital as they are, are in effect a last resort—the voters passing judgment after the fact. The system was designed to produce better results before the fact, when it is allowed to work. Whether you in the end supported or opposed American entry into Iraq, that decision, and more particularly the decision of the president and Congress, would have been stronger and more effective if it had been subject to more oversight in Congress and more debate in public. Perhaps you think the more effective policy would have been to stay out of war. Or perhaps you wish the war and its aftermath had been more effectively executed. As it turned out, Congress did not watch over the president, and the country got neither peace nor effective war. In both 1800 and 2006, the election produced dramatic shifts because classic checks and balances failed and thus produced policies that angered the voters. The election results were a punishment. But punishment by itself did not correct the more basic reasons the system of checks and balances failed.

The downward spiral will continue unless we get to the root of the problem. And what is the root of the problem? All of us, Americans, and each of us. A public opinion survey once asked Americans to "suppose the President and Congress have to violate a Constitutional principle to pass an important law the public wanted. Would you support them in this action?" Only 49 percent of the public said no. The other half were a mix of yes (22 percent) and undecided or neither (29 percent). Even on a simple statement of a bedrock principle of our system, we are divided. That is a shaky foundation on which to rest the most important government on earth.

Why does our constitutional commitment seem so thin? At one level, we have come to mistake longevity for permanence. We take for granted the existence of what not so long ago was remarkable and revolutionary. We assume that because we have been a free and successful democracy for our lifetimes and our parents' and grandparents' lifetimes that we will remain such for our children's and our children's children's lifetimes, too. That alone would be worrisome. When citizens take their democracy for granted, they undermine its most basic tenet. Democracy dissolves without the commitment to it of its citizens. That loss of commitment is what the framers most feared.

In our own time, the historian Sean Wilentz put it this way: "Democracy is never a gift bestowed by benevolent, far seeing rulers who seek to reinforce their own legitimacy. It must always be fought for, by political coalitions that cut across distinctions of wealth, power, and interest. It succeeds and survives only when it is rooted in the lives and expectations of its citizens and continually reinvigorated in each generation. Democratic successes are never irreversible."

But instead of reinvigorating our representative government, current generations are disparaging it. We are not fighting for it. Instead, we as a people are frustrated with the day-to-day workings of government and restlessly search for some "fix" for the system.

Perhaps our confidence in the permanence of our democracy has left us feeling free to attack its workings. To a point, that is healthy. The system was built for robust debate, and it has survived a great deal of it. But robust debate requires engagement and information. It requires the debaters to have some context, some sense of shared ground.

Where do we find that common ground? By looking behind the trouble signs. We said that taking our democracy for granted while also being frustrated with our government seems almost contradictory. We said "almost" because in fact we believe they rise from the same source.

Americans don't know their own government anymore. They don't know their own history. We take our democracy for granted because we don't understand how hard it was to build it, how much courage (not just on the battlefield) it took to preserve it, and how close it came to failure on several occasions from the Alien and Sedition Acts, through the Civil War to the Great Depression. And we are frustrated with how it works today because no one is explaining that how it works (most of time) is how the framers, benefiting from the real-life experience of the early nation, designed it to work. Defending the system is not a politically popular thing to do. And in our hurry-up society, no one wants to sit still long enough to hear explanations of the system, let alone defenses. This is frightening. The framers expected flaws to emerge in their design. They expected fixes to be needed.

What is dangerous now is that the debate over the system has lost the context of how the system got to be what it is. In an environment where citizens do not particularly understand the system's basic design, many of the fixes are actually challenges to the overall design. Madison and his colleagues envisioned the Senate, with its members chosen for longer terms from entire states, as a balance and a check to the House, with its larger membership with shorter terms from narrower constituencies. Together they would check the president, with a term halfway between that in the House and that in the Senate. Yet today former senator Gravel is running for president on the express platform of creating a national system of referendum to circumvent the Congress. His campaign is welcome to the extent that it encourages a debate that teaches Americans about the design of the Constitution. Americans are free to change that design. But they should understand what they are doing and what they are abandoning if they do.

We hope the result will be an embrace of improvements, rather than a dismantling of constitutional principles. But if only 49 percent of the country is willing to speak up for a fundamental constitutional principle, we are perilously close to undoing the system itself. The wrong crisis at the wrong moment could push us over the edge before we realize what we have done. Indeed, all that protects us in this situation is the framers' prescience in creating a system where a majority of one is not enough to make radical changes. But then of course we become frustrated that we can't get the change we want, and the spiral starts all over again.

Thomas Jefferson said that the tree of liberty needs to be refreshed from time to time with the blood of patriots and tyrants. What a wonderful bit of Jeffersonian poetry. But we think something less dramatic, but perhaps harder in its own way, is needed right now. We as Americans need to tend our own garden. We need to renew not just our faith in but our understanding of the system the framers gave us. That understanding requires more than some sound bites about liberty and freedom. We need to embrace that our liberty and freedom flow directly from less glamorous but still vital ideas, such as compromise, and checks and balances, and representation and process. A dash of humility would not hurt either.

Two of our most important modern presidents, Franklin Roosevelt and Ronald Reagan, each saw the importance of renewing our understanding of American constitutional government.

Roosevelt became president in the middle of the worst crisis of American democracy since the Civil War. The link between the American political system and its economic success had snapped. Around the world, dictatorships of the left and the right were on the rise. There were people who came to FDR—serious, important people—to advise him that he might have to take authoritarian powers himself. Looking back, we came much closer than many people realize to the loss of our democracy. But we did not lose it, thanks to the resolve of FDR and the strength in the American people of what we have come to describe as our Constitutional Conscience. Four years later, Roosevelt, in his first fireside chat of his second term as president, said he hoped the American people had reread their Constitution in the last few weeks. "Like the Bible," he said, "it ought to be read again and again." Ironically, Roosevelt made this remark in a speech in which he argued for a plan to weaken the Supreme Court and strengthen the power of the presidency and the Congress by putting more of his appointees on the Court. It is a testament to the strength of our Constitutional Conscience that Roosevelt's way of arguing for this plan was to present it as a defense of the Constitution, not an infringement of it. The system stopped him anyway, and even without those expanded powers he guided the country out of the Depression. The Court-packing plan he outlined in that fireside chat has vanished into history. It turns out that the more important notion of that speech was Roosevelt's insistence that we reconnect with the Constitution regularly.

Half a century later, Ronald Reagan was saying farewell after eight years as president. He had come to office in the midst of a crisis of confidence. Watergate, stagflation, the Iran hostage crisis, the residue of the 1960s had combined to shake Americans' faith in their country. Reagan had worked with considerable success to rebuild that faith. As he said farewell, he took pride in that accomplishment. But he recognized that the job was only partly done: "This national feeling is good, but it won't count for much and it won't last unless it is grounded in thoughtfulness and knowledge. An informed patriotism is what we want. And are we doing a good enough job teaching our children what America is and what she represents in the long history of the world? Those of us who are over thirty-five or so years of age grew up in a different America. We were taught, very directly, what it means to be an American. And we absorbed, almost in the air, a love of country and an appreciation of its institutions."

But as America prepared to enter the 1990s, Reagan warned, the fashion had changed. "Younger parents aren't sure that an unambivalent appreciation of America is the right thing to teach modern children. And as for those who create the popular culture, well-grounded patriotism is no longer the style. Our spirit is back, but we haven't reinstitutionalized it."

Roosevelt and Reagan are the touchstone presidents of the American Century. In some ways they could not represent more different political moments. The first brought a powerful centralized federal government into our domestic lives. The other drew the line to limit it. Yet across the half century that separated them, they each affirmed the centrality of connecting Americans to their democratic heritage.

"So we've got to teach history based not on what's in fashion but what's important," said Reagan. He concluded: "If we forget what we did, we won't know who we are. Let's start with some basics: more attention to American history and a greater emphasis on civic ritual."

We agree. Indeed, we think we owe it to the framers and all succeeding Americans who have struggled for the Constitution to renew our connection to our own history. But even more, we owe it to the future, which will be shaped by our actions.

There is a strong sense that we have become selfish and self-involved as a people. It is hard to say whether we are more self-interested than Americans at the time the Constitution was written. It was written because the framers thought we were very selfish, and they decided they could not fight human nature, only harness it. That was the genius of their system. It accepted us for who we are and yet still offered the optimistic vision that we could, as a nation, compromise our differences to agree to do great things.

We are all for ideas to make us less selfish or self-interested. But we are with the framers in doubting that human nature can be fundamentally changed.

They were right that our more selfish impulses can be channeled. Americans throughout their history have understood that it was in their own interest, ultimately, to preserve this system that balanced everyone's demands. That understanding is what we mean by our Constitutional Conscience. It is what Sean Wilentz is talking about when he describes coalitions that cut across lines of wealth, power and interest. It is noble to try to make people different. We admire those who try. But politics is the art of the possible. The framers made it possible for us to live together in liberty and community. The 220-year history of our Constitution is a history of Americans repeatedly rekindling their belief that their own interests are served by this system that grants extensive liberty in exchange for a willingness to compromise and tolerate differences. We Americans need to rekindle that belief once more.

If this [reading] has one message, it is that there is nothing about our past success that guarantees our future success. Each generation must do that for itself. Nevertheless, this is a hopeful message, because we are not alone in our struggle. We have been given a great gift and with it a great responsibility. We are the inheritors of the longest democratic tradition in the world. We still hold in great respect the men who began that tradition and the men and women who carried it forth and bequeathed it to us. That respect is a resource for us now. The struggles we are having, the frustrations we are feeling, are exactly the struggles and frustrations the framers anticipated when they designed our democracy. We can lean on them and their experience. By reaching backward to them and their ideas, we can move forward.

DISCUSSION QUESTIONS

1. Most of the time, people become critical of the Constitution when they don't get the policy results they want. When Congress fails to pass legislation because of the power of small-state senators, when the Supreme Court issues a ruling they oppose, when the president makes a decision regarding the use of force that they oppose, the immediate impulse is to blame the system and call for change that would make the preferred policies more likely. Is this a valid reason for wanting the system to change?

2. The Constitution was written over two hundred years ago by a group of white men who had very "unmodern" views about democracy and equality. On what basis should we be bound by the decisions that they made? What is the foundation of constitutional fidelity? What would be the result if each generation were permitted to remake the rules?

3. Often, opinions about the Constitution divide along philosophical lines. On one side are people who believe that the most important purpose of a constitution is to limit government size and power. On the other are people who believe that the Constitution must protect rights and promote equality (which almost always involves expanding the size and power of government). Who has the better case? Why?

CHAPTER 3

Federalism

12

The Federalist, No. 46

James Madison

Some of the most divisive and bitter political battles in our nation's history have occurred over interpretations of the constitutional principle of federalism—the division of powers and functions between the state governments and the national government. The struggle for desegregation and the civil rights of minorities, the legalization of abortion, the selective incorporation of the Bill of Rights into the Fourteenth Amendment, slavery and the Civil War all ultimately turned on the question, Who has the authority to govern: the states, or the national government? Our federal system is a delicate balance of power and shared responsibility between nation and states, each with constitutional authority to pass laws, levy taxes, and protect the interests and rights of citizens. It is a dynamic balance of power, easily destabilized by economic crises, political initiatives, and Supreme Court rulings, but often resolved in more recent years by the question, Who will pay the price for implementing and enforcing government policy?

The "double security" that James Madison discussed in The Federalist, *No. 51 did not satisfy those who feared that the national powers would encroach on state sovereignty. In* The Federalist, *No. 46, Madison went to great lengths to reassure the states that they would continue to wield a high degree of power, arguing that "the first and most natural attachment of the people will be to the governments of their respective states." While recognizing the potential for conflicts between state and federal governments, Madison concluded that the power retained by the states would be sufficient to resist arrogation by the newly established national government.*

I proceed to inquire whether the federal government or the State governments will have the advantage with regard to the predilection and support of the people. Notwithstanding the different modes in which they are appointed, we must consider both of them as substantially dependent on the great body of the citizens of the United States. * * * The federal and State governments are in fact but different agents and trustees of the people, constituted with different powers and designed for different purposes. The adversaries of the Constitution seem to have lost sight of the people altogether in their reasonings on this subject; and to have viewed these different establishments not only as mutual rivals and enemies, but as uncontrolled by any common superior in their efforts to usurp the authorities of each other. These gentlemen must here be reminded of their error. They must be told that the ultimate authority, wherever the derivative may be found, resides in the people alone, and that it will not depend merely on the comparative ambition or address of the different governments whether either, or which of them, will be able to enlarge its sphere of jurisdiction at the expense of the other. Truth, no less than decency, requires that the event in every case should be supposed to depend on the sentiments and sanction of their common constituents.

Many considerations * * * seem to place it beyond doubt that the first and most natural attachment of the people will be to the governments of their respective States. Into the administration of these a greater number of individuals will expect to rise. From the gift of these a greater number of offices and emoluments will flow. By the superintending care of these, all the more domestic and personal interests of the people will be regulated and provided for. With the affairs of these, the people will be more familiarly and minutely conversant. And with the members of these will a greater proportion of the people have the ties of personal acquaintance and friendship, and of family and party attachments; on the side of these, therefore, the popular bias may well be expected most strongly to incline.

The remaining points on which I propose to compare the federal and State governments are the disposition and the faculty they may respectively possess to resist and frustrate the measures of each other.

It has been already proved that the members of the federal will be more dependent on the members of the State governments than the latter will be on the former. It has appeared also that the prepossessions of the people, on whom both will depend, will be more on the side of the State governments than of the federal government. So far as the disposition of each towards the other may be influenced by these causes, the State governments must clearly have the advantage. But in a distinct and very important point of view, the advantage will lie on the same side. The prepossessions, which the members themselves will carry into the federal government, will generally be favorable to the States; whilst it will rarely happen that the members of the State governments will carry into the public councils a bias in favor of the general government. A local spirit will infallibly prevail much more in the members of Congress than a national spirit will prevail in the legislatures of the particular States.

* * * What is the spirit that has in general characterized the proceedings of Congress? A perusal of their journals, as well as the candid

acknowledgments of such as have had a seat in that assembly, will inform us that the members have but too frequently displayed the character rather of partisans of their respective States than of impartial guardians of a common interest; that where on one occasion improper sacrifices have been made of local considerations to the aggrandizement of the federal government, the great interests of the nation have suffered on a hundred from an undue attention to the local prejudices, interests, and views of the particular States. I mean not by these reflections to insinuate that the new federal government will not embrace a more enlarged plan of policy than the existing government may have pursued; much less that its views will be as confined as those of the State legislatures; but only that it will partake sufficiently of the spirit of both to be disinclined to invade the rights of the individual States, or the prerogatives of their governments.

Were it admitted, however, that the federal government may feel an equal disposition with the State governments to extend its power beyond the due limits, the latter would still have the advantage in the means of defeating such encroachments. If an act of a particular State, though unfriendly to the national government, be generally popular in that State, and should not too grossly violate the oaths of the State officers, it is executed immediately and, of course, by means on the spot and depending on the State alone. The opposition of the federal government, or the interposition of federal officers, would but inflame the zeal of all parties on the side of the State, and the evil could not be prevented or repaired, if at all, without the employment of means which must always be resorted to with reluctance and difficulty. On the other hand, should an unwarrantable measure of the federal government be unpopular in particular States, which would seldom fail to be the case, or even a warrantable measure be so, which may sometimes be the case, the means of opposition to it are powerful and at hand. The disquietude of the people; their repugnance and, perhaps, refusal to co-operate with the officers of the Union; the frowns of the executive magistracy of the State; the embarrassments created by legislative devices, which would often be added on such occasions, would oppose, in any State, difficulties not to be despised; would form, in a large State, very serious impediments; and where the sentiments of several adjoining States happened to be in unison, would present obstructions which the federal government would hardly be willing to encounter.

But ambitious encroachments of the federal government on the authority of the State governments would not excite the opposition of a single State, or of a few States only. They would be signals of general alarm. Every government would espouse the common cause. A correspondence would be opened. Plans of resistance would be concerted. One spirit would animate and conduct the whole. The same combinations, in short, would result from an apprehension of the federal, as was produced by the dread of a foreign yoke; and unless the projected innovations should be voluntarily renounced, the same appeal to a trial of force would be made in the one case as was made in the other.

The only refuge left for those who prophesy the downfall of the State governments is the visionary supposition that the federal government may previously accumulate a military force for the projects of ambition. The reasonings contained in these papers must have been employed to little purpose indeed, if it could be necessary now to disprove the reality of this danger. That the people and the States should, for a sufficient period of time, elect an uninterrupted succession of men ready to betray both; that the traitors should, throughout this period, uniformly and systematically pursue some fixed plan for the extension of the military establishment; that the governments and the people of the States should silently and patiently behold the gathering storm and continue to supply the materials until it should be prepared to burst on their own heads must appear to everyone more like the incoherent dreams of a delirious jealousy, or the misjudged exaggerations of a counterfeit zeal, than like the sober apprehensions of genuine patriotism. Extravagant as the supposition is, let it, however, be made. Let a regular army, fully equal to the resources of the country, be formed; and let it be entirely at the devotion of the federal government: still it would not be going too far to say that the State governments with the people on their side would be able to repel the danger.

Besides the advantage of being armed, which the Americans possess over the people of almost every other nation, the existence of subordinate governments, to which the people are attached and by which the militia officers are appointed, forms a barrier against the enterprises of ambition, more insurmountable than any which a simple government of any form can admit of.

Let us not insult the free and gallant citizens of America with the suspicion that they would be less able to defend the rights of which they would be in actual possession than the debased subjects of arbitrary power would be to rescue theirs from the hands of their oppressors. Let us rather no longer insult them with the supposition that they can ever reduce themselves to the necessity of making the experiment by a blind and tame submission to the long train of insidious measures which must precede and produce it.

The argument under the present head may be put into a very concise form, which appears altogether conclusive. Either the mode in which the federal government is to be constructed will render it sufficiently dependent on the people, or it will not. On the first supposition, it will be restrained by that dependence from forming schemes obnoxious to their constituents. On the other supposition, it will not possess the confidence of the people, and its schemes of usurpation will be easily defeated by the State governments, who will be supported by the people.

On summing up the considerations stated in this and the last paper, they seem to amount to the most convincing evidence that the powers proposed to be lodged in the federal government are as little formidable to those reserved to the individual States as they are indispensably necessary to accomplish the purposes of the Union; and that all those alarms which have been sounded of a meditated and consequential annihilation of the State governments must, on the most favorable interpretation, be ascribed to the chimerical fears of the authors of them.

Publius

Discussion Questions

1. Is Madison right when he states that people are more attached to their state governments than to the national government? Why or why not? If not, would it better facilitate the democratic process if they were more attached to state governments?

2. Would your answer change at all during different political times? For example, were people more attached to the national government in the wake of the terrorist attacks on our country than they were before September 11, 2001? Do people lose their faith in the national government during tough economic times?

From *The Price of Federalism*

Paul Peterson

In this concise overview of American federalism, Paul Peterson argues that both the early and more modern system of shared sovereignty between the national government and the states have had their disadvantages. From the early period of "dual federalism" to the more modern system of a dominant national government, the battle over national and state government jurisdiction and power has led to bloodshed and war; the denial of political, social, and economic rights; and regional inequalities among the states.

Nevertheless, Peterson argues, there are advantages to federalism. Federalism has also facilitated capital growth and development, the creation of infrastructures, and social programs that greatly improved the quality of life for millions of Americans. Once the national government took responsibility for guaranteeing civil rights and civil liberties, the states "became the engines of economic development." Not all states are equally wealthy, but the national government has gradually diminished some of these differences by financing many social and economic programs. One battle over the proper form of federal relations involved welfare policy in the 1990s. Republicans in Congress wanted to give back to states the power to devise their own programs, whereas most Democrats and President Clinton initially wanted to retain a larger degree of federal government control. However, President Clinton eventually agreed to end welfare as an entitlement and return substantial control over the program to the states. The long-term verdict on this landmark legislation is still an open question. There is considerable debate over the proper balance between federal and state funding for the state-level welfare programs.

These same debates have cropped up in more recent years in homeland security policy. Ideally, this policy would be run at the national level, and resources would be allocated to parts of the country that pose the greatest security risks. However, every state wants its share of the federal pie, so resources are not always allocated in the most efficient manner. Federalism also poses challenges for coordinating policy for "first responders" in a time of crisis: Who is responsible for coming to the aid of people in distress: local, state, or national agencies?

The Price of Early Federalism

As a principle of government, federalism has had a dubious history. It remains on the margins of political respectability even today. I was recently invited to give a presentation on metropolitan government before a United Nations conference. When I offered to discuss how the federal principle could be used to help metropolitan areas govern themselves more effectively, my sponsors politely advised me that this topic would be poorly received. The vast majority of UN members had a unified form of government, I was told, and they saw little of value in federalism. We reached a satisfactory compromise. I replaced "federal" with "two-tier form of government."

Thomas Hobbes, the founder of modern political thought, would have blessed the compromise, for he, too, had little room for federalism in his understanding of the best form of government. Hobbes said that people agreed to have a government over them only because they realized that in a state of nature, that is, when there is no government, life becomes a war of all against all. If no government exists to put malefactors in jail, everyone must become a criminal simply to avoid being a victim. Life becomes "nasty, brutish and short." To avoid the violent state of nature, people need and want rule by a single sovereign. Division of power among multiple sovereigns encourages bickering among them. Conflicts become inevitable, as each sovereign tries to expand its power (if for no other reason than to avoid becoming the prey of competing sovereigns). Government degenerates into anarchy and the world returns to the bitter state of nature from which government originally emerged.

The authors of *The Federalist* papers defended dual sovereignty by turning Hobbes's argument in favor of single sovereignty on its head. While Hobbes said that anything less than a single sovereign would lead to war of all against all, *The Federalist* argued that the best way of preserving liberty was to divide power. If power is concentrated in any one place, it can be used to crush individual liberty. Even in a democracy there can be the tyranny of the majority, the worst kind of tyranny because it is so stifling and complete. A division of power between the national and state governments reduces the possibility that any single majority will be able to control all centers of governmental power. The national government, by defending the country against foreign aggression, prevents external threats to liberty. The state governments, by denying power to any single dictator, reduce threats to liberty from within. As James Madison said in his defense of the Constitution, written on the eve of its ratification,

> The power surrendered by the people is first divided between two distinct governments, and then the portion allotted to each subdivided among distinct and separate departments. Hence a double security arises to the rights of the people. The different governments will control each other, at the same time that each will be controlled by itself. [*The Federalist*, No. 51]

Early federalism was built on the principle of dual sovereignty. The Constitution divided sovereignty between state and nation, each in control of its own sphere. Some even interpreted the Constitution to mean that state legislatures could nullify federal laws. Early federalism also gave both levels of government their own military capacity. Congress was given the power to raise an army and wage war, but states were allowed to maintain their own militia.

The major contribution of early federalism to American liberties took place within a dozen years after the signing of the Constitution. Liberty is never established in a new nation until those in authority have peacefully ceded power to a rival political faction. Those who wrote the Constitution and secured its ratification, known as the Federalists, initially captured control of the main institutions of the national government: Congress, the presidency, and the Supreme Court. Those opposed to the new constitutional order, the antifederalists, had to content themselves with an opposition role in Congress and control over a number of state governments, most notably Virginia's.

The political issues dividing the two parties were serious. The Federalist party favored a strong central government, a powerful central bank that could facilitate economic and industrial development, and a strong, independent executive branch. Federalists had also become increasingly disturbed by the direction the French Revolution had taken. They were alarmed by the execution of thousands, the confiscation of private property, and the movement of French troops across Europe. They called for the creation of a national army and reestablished close ties with Britain.

The antifederalists, who became known as Democratic-Republicans, favored keeping most governmental power in the hands of state governments. They were opposed to a national bank, a strong presidency, and industrial government. They thought the United States would remain a free country only if it remained a land of independent farmers. They bitterly opposed the creation of a national army for fear it would be used to repress political opposition. Impressed by the French Revolution's commitment to the rights of man, they excused its excesses. The greater danger, they thought, was the reassertion of British power, and they denounced the Federalists for seeming to acquiesce in the seizure of U.S. seamen by the British navy.

The conflict between the two sides intensified after George Washington retired to his home in Mount Vernon. In 1800 Thomas Jefferson, founder of the Democratic-Republican party, waged an all-out campaign to defeat Washington's Federalist successor, John Adams. In retrospect, the central issue of the election was democracy itself. Could an opposition party drive a government out of power? Would political leaders accept their defeat?

So bitter was the feud between the two parties that Representative Matthew Lyon, a Democratic-Republican, spit in the face of a Federalist on the floor of Congress. Outside the Congress, pro-French propagandists relentlessly criticized Adams. To silence the opposition, Congress, controlled by the Federalists, passed the Alien and Sedition Acts. One of the

Alien Acts gave President Adams the power to deport any foreigners "concerned in any treasonable or secret machinations against the government." The Sedition Act made it illegal to "write, print, utter, or publish . . . any false, scandalous and malicious writing . . . against . . . the Congress of the United States, or the President."

The targets of the Sedition Acts soon became clear. Newspaper editors supporting the Democratic-Republicans were quickly indicted, and ten were brought to trial and convicted by juries under the influence of Federalist judges. Matthew Lyon was sentenced to a four-month jail term for claiming, presumably falsely, that President Adams had an "unbounded thirst for ridiculous pomp, foolish adulation, and selfish avarice." Even George Washington lent his support to this political repression.

Federalism undoubtedly helped the fledgling American democracy survive this first constitutional test. When the Federalists passed the Alien and Sedition Acts, Democratic-Republicans in the Virginia and Kentucky state legislatures passed resolutions nullifying the laws. When it looked as if Jefferson's victory in the election of 1800 might be stripped away by a Federalist-controlled House of Representatives, both sides realized that the Virginia state militia was at least as strong as the remnants of the Continental Army. Lacking the national army they had tried to establish, the Federalists chose not to fight. They acquiesced in their political defeat in part because their opponents had military as well as political power, and because they themselves could retreat to their own regional base of power, the state and local governments of New England and the mid-Atlantic states.

Jefferson claimed his victory was a revolution every bit as comprehensive as the one fought in 1776. The Alien and Sedition Acts were discarded, nullified not by a state legislature but by the results of a national election. President Adams returned to private life without suffering imprisonment or exile. Many years later, he and Jefferson reconciled their differences and developed through correspondence a close friendship. They died on the same day, the fiftieth anniversary of the Declaration of Independence. To both, federalism and liberty seemed closely intertwined.

The price to be paid for early federalism became more evident with the passage of time. To achieve the blessings of liberty, early federalism divided sovereign power. When Virginia and Kentucky nullified the Alien and Sedition Acts, they preserved liberties only by threatening national unity. With the election of Jefferson, the issue was temporarily rendered moot, but the doctrine remained available for use when southerners once again felt threatened by encroaching national power.

The doctrine of nullification was revived in 1830 by John C. Calhoun, sometime senator from South Carolina, who objected to high tariffs that protected northern industry at the expense of southern cotton producers. When Congress raised the tariff, South Carolina's legislature threatened to declare the law null and void. Calhoun, then serving as Andrew Jackson's vice president, argued that liberties could be trampled by national majorities unless states could nullify tyrannical acts. Andrew Jackson, though elected on a state's rights ticket, remained committed to national supremacy. At the annual Democratic banquet honoring the memory of Thomas Jefferson, Calhoun supporters sought to trap Jackson into endorsing the doctrine. But Jackson, aware of the scheme, raised his glass in a dramatic toast to "Our federal union: it must be preserved!" Not to be outdone, Calhoun replied in kind: "The union, next to our liberty, most dear!"

A compromise was found to the overt issue, the tariff, but it was not so easy to resolve the underlying issue of slavery. In the infamous Dred Scott decision, the Supreme Court interpreted federalism to mean that boundaries could not be placed on the movements of masters and slaves. Northern territories could not free slaves that came within their boundaries; to do so deprived masters of their Fifth Amendment right not to be deprived of their property without due process of law. The decision spurred northern states to elect Abraham Lincoln president, which convinced southern whites that their liberties, most dear, were more important than federal union.

To Lincoln, as to Jackson, the union was to be preserved at all costs. Secession meant war. War meant the loss of 1 million lives, the destruction of the southern economy, the emancipation of African Americans from slavery, the demise of the doctrine of nullification, and the end to early federalism. Early federalism, with its doctrine of dual sovereignty, may have initially helped to preserve liberty, but it did so at a terrible price. As Hobbes feared, the price of dual sovereignty was war.

Since the termination of the Civil War, Americans have concluded that they can no longer trust their liberties to federalism. Sovereignty must be concentrated in the hands of the national government. Quite apart from the dangers of civil war, the powers of state and local governments have been used too often by a tyrannical majority to trample the rights of religious, racial, and political minorities. The courts now seem a more reliable institutional shelter for the nation's liberties.

But if federalism is no longer necessary or even conducive to the preservation of liberty, then what is its purpose? Is it merely a relic of an outdated past? Are the majority of the members of the United Nations correct in objecting to the very use of the word?

The Rise of Modern Federalism

The answers to these questions have been gradually articulated in the 130 years following the end of the Civil War. Although the states lost their sovereignty, they remained integral to the workings of American government. Modern federalism no longer meant dual sovereignty and shared military capacity. Modern federalism instead meant only that each level of government had its own independently elected political leaders and its own separate taxing and spending capacity. Equipped with these tools of quasi-sovereignty, each level of government could take all but the most violent of steps to defend its turf.

Although sovereignty and military capacity now rested firmly in the hands of the national government, modern federalism became more complex rather than less so. Power was no longer simply divided between the nation and its states. Cities, counties, towns, school districts, special districts, and a host of additional governmental entities, each with its own elected leaders and taxing authority, assumed new burdens and responsibilities.

Just as the blessings bestowed by early federalism were evident from its inception, so the advantages of modern federalism were clear from the onset. If states and localities were no longer the guarantors of liberty, they became the engines of economic development. By giving state and local governments the autonomy to act independently, the federal system facilitated the rapid growth of an industrial economy that eventually surpassed its European competitors. Canals and railroads were constructed, highways and sewage systems built, schools opened, parks designed, and public safety protected by cities and villages eager to make their locality a boomtown.

The price to be paid for modern federalism did not become evident until government attempted to grapple with the adverse side effects of a burgeoning capitalist economy. Out of a respect for federalism's constitutional status and political durability, social reformers first worked with and through existing components of the federal system, concentrating much of their reform effort on state and local governments. Only gradually did it become clear that state and local governments, for all their ability to work with business leaders to enhance community prosperity, had difficulty meeting the needs of the poor and the needy.

It was ultimately up to the courts to find ways of keeping the price of modern federalism within bounds. Although dual sovereignty no longer meant nullification and secession, much remained to be determined about the respective areas of responsibility of the national and state governments. At first the courts retained remnants of the doctrine of dual sovereignty in order to protect processes of industrialization from governmental intrusion. But with the advent of the New Deal, the constitutional power of the national government expanded so dramatically that the doctrine of dual sovereignty virtually lost all meaning. Court interpretations of the constitutional clauses on commerce and spending have proved to be the most significant.

According to dual sovereignty theory, article 1 of the Constitution gives Congress the power to regulate commerce "among the states," but the regulation of intrastate commerce was to be left to the states. So, for example, in 1895 the Supreme Court said that Congress could not break up a sugar monopoly that had a nationwide impact on the price of sugar, because the monopoly refined its sugar within the state of Pennsylvania. The mere fact that the sugar was to be sold nationwide was only "incidental" to its production. As late as 1935, the Supreme Court, in a 6-to-3 decision, said that Congress could not regulate the sale of poultry because the regulation took effect after the chickens arrived within the state of Illinois, not while they were in transit.

Known as the "sick chicken" case, this decision was one of a series in which the Supreme Court declared unconstitutional legislation passed in the early days of President Franklin Roosevelt's efforts to establish his New Deal programs. Seven of the "nine old men" on the Court had been appointed by Roosevelt's conservative Republican predecessors. By declaring many New Deal programs in violation of the commerce clause, the Supreme Court seemed to be substituting its political views for those of elected officials. In a case denying the federal government the right to protect workers trying to organize a union in the coal industry, the Republican views of the Court seemed to lie just barely below the surface of a technical discussion of the commerce clause. Justice George Sutherland declared, "The relation of employer and employee is a local relation . . . over which the federal government has no legislative control."

The Roosevelt Democrats were furious at decisions that seemed to deny the country's elected officials the right to govern. Not since Dred Scott* had judicial review been in such disrepute. Roosevelt decided to "pack the court" by adding six new judges over and above the nine already on the Court. Although Roosevelt's court-packing scheme did not survive the political uproar on Capitol Hill, its effect on the Supreme Court was noticeable. In the midst of the court-packing debate, Justices Charles Hughes and Owen Roberts, who had agreed with Sutherland's opinion in the coal case, changed their mind and voted to uphold the Wagner Act, a new law designed to facilitate the formation of unions. In his opinion, Hughes did not explicitly overturn the coal miner decision (for which he had voted), but he did say: "When industries organize themselves on a national scale, . . . how can it be maintained that their industrial labor relations constitute a forbidden field into which Congress may not enter?" Relations between employers and their workers, once said to be local, suddenly became part of interstate commerce.

The change of heart by Hughes and Roberts has been called "the switch in time that saved nine." The New Deal majority that emerged on the court was soon augmented by judges appointed by Roosevelt. Since the New Deal, the definition of interstate commerce has continued to expand. In 1942 a farmer raising twenty-three acres of wheat, all of which might

---

*In *Dred Scott v. Sanford* (1857), the Court declared the antislavery provision of the Missouri Compromise of 1820 to be unconstitutional [*Editors*].

be fed to his own livestock, was said to be in violation of the crop quotas imposed by the Agricultural Adjustment Act of 1938. Since he was feeding his cows himself, he was not buying grain on the open market, thereby depressing the worldwide price of grain. With such a definition of interstate commerce, nothing was local.

The expansion of the meaning of the commerce clause is a well-known part of American political history. The importance to federalism of court interpretations of the "spending clause" is less well known. The constitutional clause in question says that Congress has the power to collect taxes to "provide for the . . . general welfare." But how about Congress's power to collect taxes for the welfare of specific individuals or groups?

The question first arose in a 1923 case, when a childless woman said she could not be asked to pay taxes in order to finance federal grants to states for programs that helped pregnant women. Since she received no benefit from the program, she sued for return of the taxes she had paid to cover its costs. In a decision that has never been reversed, the Supreme Court said that she had suffered no measurable injury and therefore had no right to sue the government. Her taxes were being used for a wide variety of purposes. The amount being spent for this program was too small to be significant. The court's decision to leave spending issues to Congress was restated a decade later when the social security program was also challenged on the grounds that monies were being directed to the elderly, not for the general welfare. Said Justice Benjamin N. Cardozo for a court majority: "The conception of the spending power . . . [must find a point somewhere] between particular and general. . . . There is a middle ground . . . in which discretion is large. The discretion, however, is not confided to the Court. The discretion belongs to Congress, unless the choice is clearly wrong."

The courts have ever since refused to review Congress's power to spend money. They have also conceded to Congress the right to attach any regulations to any aid Congress provides. In 1987 Congress provided a grant to state governments for the maintenance of their highways, but conditioned 5 percent of the funds on state willingness to raise the drinking age from eighteen to twenty-one. The connection between the appropriation and the regulation was based on the assumption that youths under the age of twenty-one are more likely to drive after drinking than those over twenty-one. Presumably, building more roads would only encourage more inebriated young people to drive on them. Despite the fact that the connection between the appropriation and the regulation was problematic, the Supreme Court ruled that Congress could attach any reasonable conditions to its grants to the states. State sovereignty was not violated, because any state could choose not to accept the money.

In short, the courts have virtually given up the doctrine of judicial review when it comes to matters on which Congress can spend money. As a consequence, most national efforts to influence state governments come in the form of federal grants. Federal aid can also be used to influence local governments, such as counties, cities, towns, villages, and school districts. These local governments, from a constitutional point of view, are mere creatures of the state of which they are part. They have no independent sovereignty.

The Contemporary Price of Federalism

If constitutional doctrine has evolved to the point that dual sovereign theory has been put to rest, this does not mean that federalism has come to an end. Although ultimate sovereignty resides with the national government, state and local governments still have certain characteristics and capabilities that make them constituent components of a federal system. * * * Two characteristics of federalism are fundamental. First, citizens elect officials of their choice for each level of government. Unless the authority of each level of government rests in the people, it will become the agent of the other. Second, each level of government raises money through taxation from the citizens residing in the area for which it is responsible. It is hard to see how a system could be regarded as federal unless each level of government can levy taxes on its residents. Unless each level of government can raise its own fiscal resources, it cannot act independently.

Although the constitutional authority of the national government has steadily expanded, state and local governments remain of great practical significance. Almost half of all government spending for domestic (as distinct from foreign and military) purposes is paid for out of taxes raised by state and local governments.

The sharing of control over domestic policy among levels of government has many benefits, but federalism still exacts its price. It can lead to great regional inequalities. Also, the need for establishing cooperative relationships among governments can contribute to great inefficiency in the administration of government programs.

Discussion Questions

1. What is the constitutional basis for federalism?

2. How has the relationship between state governments and the national government changed since the early years of the Republic?

3. Does a federal system serve our needs today? Does the federal government have too much power relative to the states? What would be the advantages and disadvantages of a reduced federal presence in state matters?

14

"Jumping Frogs, Endangered Toads, and California's Medical-Marijuana Law"

George J. Annas

From welfare reform to health care, educational funding to inner-city development, state governments have sought more control over public policy within their borders. In the 1970s and 1980s, when this devolution of power to the states was called "New Federalism," the debate was pretty simple. Republicans favored devolution because state governments were "closer to the people" and could better determine their needs. Democrats resisted the transfer of power from Washington, fearing that many states would not adequately care for and protect minorities and poor people, or protect the environment without prodding from Washington. To the extent that the courts got involved in the debate, they tended to favor the transfer of power to the states.

The debate over developing power from the national government to the states has grown increasingly complicated in the past several years: the partisan nature of the debate shifted, the Courts have played a larger, but inconsistent role, and issues of "states' rights" increasingly tend to cut across normal ideological and partisan divisions. While Republicans continued to favor greater state control, a Democratic President, Bill Clinton, supported devolution to the states in several areas in the 1990s, especially welfare policy. Since the mid-1990s, the Supreme Court has played a central role in the shift of power to the states, but two recent cases involving medical marijuana (Gonzales v. Raich) and assisted suicide (Gonzales v. Oregon) show how the typical debate between national and state power can shift when a moral dimension is introduced.

In both cases, state voters supported liberal policies (approving medical marijuana in California and assisted suicide in Oregon). Therefore, the "states' rights" position on federalism in these cases represented the liberal perspective, which in partisan terms means mostly Democratic, rather than the conservative positions on race, labor, market regulation, and welfare that state-centered federalism is typically associated with. What's a good liberal or conservative to do? Social liberals supported the medical marijuana law (and thus the minority in Raich) and the assisted suicide law in Oregon (the majority in Gonzales). Moral conservatives were the opposite (pro-Raich, anti-Gonzales).

However, on the central question of federal versus state power, which has been a central ideological divide in this nation since the Federalists and Anti-Federalists battled it out at the Constitutional Convention, liberals and conservatives would have to flip their views. So a national-power liberal would have supported the Raich *decision and opposed the* Gonzales *decision (the opposite of the social liberal), whereas a state-power conservative would have opposed* Raich *and supported* Gonzales *(which is the reverse of a moral conservative's positions). That means that a national power liberal and the moral conservative would have the same views (national power would be used to regulate medical marijuana and assisted suicide), while states' rights advocates share the views of the social liberals (because voters in California approved medical marijuana and Oregon voters supported assisted suicide).*

Somewhat surprisingly, there was almost no consistency among the eight justices who voted on both cases (William Rehnquist was replaced by John Roberts between the two cases): only Justice O'Connor supported the states' rights position in both cases, and Scalia voted as a moral conservative (which runs strongly counter to his previously articulated views on national power and federalism). All of the other six justices mixed their views. The Court as a whole was inconsistent on the question of federalism as well: in the medical marijuana case, the Court upheld Congress's power to prohibit the medical use of marijuana under the Controlled Substances Act. But in the assisted suicide case, the Court said that Congress did not give the U.S. attorney general the power under that same law to limit the drugs that doctors in Oregon could prescribe for use in an assisted suicide.

George Annas looks at the medical marijuana case (and touches on the assisted suicide case) from the perspective of doctors. Writing in the New England Journal of Medicine, *one of the leading medical journals in the nation, Annas points out the "most interesting, and disturbing aspect of the case to physicians" is the Court's reference to "unscrupulous physicians who overprescribe when it is sufficiently profitable to do so." Annas says that such cases are rare and that the California law was narrowly written to make sure that such abuses would not occur. Eighteen states currently allow medical marijuana and in 2012 voters in Colorado and Washington legalized the use of marijuana, despite the fact that it is still illegal under federal law. President Obama initially said that he would not make it a priority to enforce federal law in states where marijuana was used for medical reasons. However, he later reversed course, cracking down on dispensaries that were taking advantage of state laws, indicating that the problem of unscrupulous physicians may be more widespread than Annas recognizes. This article is also very useful for its excellent overview of Congress's commerce clause powers and its importance in federalism cases.*

Mark Twain wasn't thinking about federalism or the structure of American government when he wrote "The Celebrated Jumping Frog of Calaveras County." Nonetheless, he would be amused to know that today, almost 150 years later, the Calaveras County Fair and Jumping Frog Jubilee not only has a jumping frog contest but also has its own Frog Welfare Policy. The policy includes a provision for the "Care of Sick or Injured Frogs" and a limitation entitled "Frogs Not Permitted to Participate," which stipulates that "under no circumstances will a frog listed on the endangered species list be permitted to participate in the Frog Jump." This fair, like medical practice, is subject to both state and federal laws. Care of the sick and injured (both frogs and people) is primarily viewed as a matter of state law, whereas protection of endangered species is primarily regulated by Congress under its authority to regulate interstate commerce.

Not to carry the analogy too far, but it is worth recalling that Twain's famous frog, Dan'l Webster, lost his one and only jumping contest because his stomach had been filled with quail shot by a competitor. The loaded-down frog just couldn't jump. Until the California medical-marijuana case, it seemed to many observers that the conservative Rehnquist Court had succeeded in filling the commerce clause with quail shot—and had effectively prevented the federal government from regulating state activities. In the medical-marijuana case, however, a new majority of justices took the lead out of the commerce clause so that the federal government could legitimately claim jurisdiction over just about any activity, including the practice of medicine. The role of the commerce clause in federalism and the implications of the Court's decision in the California medical-marijuana case for physicians are the subjects I explore in this article.

The Commerce Clause

The U.S. Constitution determines the areas over which the federal government has authority. All other areas remain, as they were before the adoption of the Constitution, under the authority of the individual states. Another way to say this is that the states retain all governmental authority they did not delegate to the federal government, including areas such as criminal law and family-law matters. These are part of the state's "police powers," usually defined as the state's sovereign authority to protect the health, safety, and welfare of its residents. Section 8 of Article I of the Constitution contains eighteen clauses specifying delegated areas (including the military, currency, postal service, and patenting) over which "Congress shall have power," and these include the commerce clause—"to regulate commerce with foreign nations, and among the several states, and with the Indian tribes."

Until the Great Depression (and the disillusionment with unregulated markets), the Supreme Court took a narrow view of federal authority that could be derived from the commerce clause by ruling consistently that it gave Congress the authority only to regulate activities that directly involved the movement of commercial products (such as pharmaceuticals) from one state to another. Since then, and at least until 1995, the Court's interpretation seemed to be going in the opposite direction: Congress was consistently held to have authority in areas that had almost any relationship at all to commerce.

Guns in Schools and Violence Against Women

Under modern commerce clause doctrine, Congress has authority to regulate in three broad categories of activities: the use of the channels of interstate commerce (e.g., roads, air corridors, and waterways); the instrumentalities of interstate commerce (e.g., trains, trucks, and planes) and persons and things in interstate commerce; and "activities having a substantial relation to interstate commerce." The first two categories are easy ones in that they involve activities that cross state lines. The third category, which does not involve crossing a state line, is the controversial one. The interpretation question involves the meaning and application of the concept of "substantially affecting" interstate commerce.

In a 1937 case that the Court characterized as a "watershed case" it concluded that the real question was one of the degree of effect. Intrastate activities that "have such a close and substantial relation to interstate commerce that their control is essential or appropriate to protect that commerce from burdens and obstructions" are within the power of Congress to regulate. Later, in what has become perhaps its best-known commerce-clause case, the Court held that Congress could enforce a statute that prohibited a farmer from growing wheat on his own farm even if the wheat was never sold but was used only for the farmer's personal consumption. The Court concluded that although one farmer's personal use of homegrown wheat may be trivial (and have no effect on commerce), "taken together with that of many others similarly situated," its effect on interstate commerce (and the market price of wheat) "is far from trivial."

The 1995 case that seemed to presage a states' rights revolution (often referred to as "devolution") involved the federal Gun-Free School Zones Act of 1990, which made it a federal crime "for any individual knowingly to possess a firearm at a place that the individual knows, or has reasonable cause to believe, is a school zone." In a 5-to-4 opinion, written by the late Chief Justice William Rehnquist, the Court held that the statute exceeded Congress's authority under the commerce clause and only the individual states had authority to criminalize the possession of guns in school.

The federal government had argued (and the four justices in the minority agreed) that the costs of violent crime are spread out over the entire population and that the presence of guns in schools threatens "national productivity" by undermining the learning environment, which in turn decreases learning and leads to a less productive citizenry and thus a less productive national economy. The majority of the Court rejected these arguments primarily because they thought that accepting this line of reasoning would make it impossible to define "any limitations on federal power, even in areas such as criminal law enforcement or education, where states historically have been sovereign."

In 2000, in another 5-to-4 opinion written by Rehnquist, using the same rationale, the Court struck down a federal statute, part of the Violence against Women Act of 1994, that provided a federal civil remedy for victims of "gender-motivated violence." In the Court's words:

> Gender-motivated crimes of violence are not, in any sense of the phrase, economic activity. . . . Indeed, if Congress may regulate gender-motivated violence, it would be able to regulate murder or any other type of violence since gender-motivated violence, as a subset of all violent crime, is certain to have lesser economic impacts than the larger class of which it is a part.

The Court, specifically addressing the question of federalism, concluded that "the Constitution requires a distinction between what is truly national and what is truly local. . . . Indeed, we can think of no better example of the police power, which the Founders denied to the National Government and reposed in the States, than the suppression of violent crime and vindication of its victims."

Medical Marijuana in California

The next commerce-clause case involved physicians, albeit indirectly, and the role assigned to them in California in relation to the protection of patients who used physician-recommended marijuana from criminal prosecution. The question before the Supreme Court in the recent medical-marijuana case (*Gonzales v. Raich*) was this: Does the commerce clause give Congress the authority to outlaw the local cultivation and use of marijuana for medicine if such cultivation and use complies with the provisions of California law?

The California law, which is similar to laws in at least nine other states, creates an exemption from criminal prosecution for physicians, patients, and primary caregivers who possess or cultivate marijuana for medicinal purposes on the recommendation of a physician. Two patients for whom marijuana had been recommended brought suit to challenge enforcement of the federal Controlled Substances Act after federal Drug Enforcement Administration agents seized and destroyed all six marijuana plants that one of them had been growing for her own medical use in compliance with the California law. The Ninth Circuit Court of Appeals ruled in the plaintiffs' favor, finding that the California law applied to a separate and distinct category of activity, "the intrastate, noncommercial cultivation and possession of *cannabis* for personal medical purposes as recommended by a patient's physician pursuant to valid California state law," as opposed to what it saw as the federal law's purpose, which was to prevent "drug trafficking." In a 6-to-3 opinion, written by Justice John Paul Stevens, with Justice Rehnquist dissenting, the Court reversed the appeals court's opinion and decided that Congress, under the commerce clause, did have authority to enforce its prohibition against marijuana—even state-approved, homegrown, noncommercial marijuana, used only for medicinal purposes on a physician's recommendation.

The majority of the Court decided that the commerce clause gave Congress the same power to regulate homegrown marijuana for personal use that it had to regulate homegrown wheat. The question was whether homegrown marijuana for personal medical consumption substantially affected interstate commerce (albeit illegal commerce) when all affected patients were taken together. The Court concluded that Congress "had a rational basis for concluding that leaving home-consumed marijuana outside federal control" would affect "price and market conditions." The Court also distinguished the guns-in-school and gender-violence cases on the basis that regulation of drugs is "quintessentially economic" when economics is defined as the "production, distribution, and consumption of commodities."

This left only one real question open: Is the fact that marijuana is to be used only for medicinal purposes on the advice of a physician, as the Ninth Circuit Court had decided, sufficient for an exception to be carved out of otherwise legitimate federal authority to control drugs? The Court decided it was not, for several reasons. The first was that Congress itself had determined that marijuana is a Schedule I drug, which it defined as having "no acceptable medical use." The Court acknowledged that Congress might be wrong in this determination, but the issue in this case was not whether marijuana had possible legitimate medical uses but whether Congress had the authority to make the judgment that it had none and to ban all uses of the drug. The dissenting justices argued that personal cultivation and use of marijuana should be beyond the authority of the commerce clause. The Court majority disagreed, stating that if it accepted the dissenting justices' argument, personal cultivation for recreational use would also be beyond congressional authority. This conclusion, the majority argued, could not be sustained:

> One need not have a degree in economics to understand why a nationwide exemption for the vast quantity of marijuana (or other drugs) locally cultivated for personal use (which presumably would include use by friends, neighbors, and family members) may have a substantial impact on the interstate market for this extraordinarily popular substance. The congressional judgment that an exemption for such a significant segment of the total market would undermine the orderly enforcement of the entire [drug] regulatory scheme is entitled to a strong presumption of validity.

The other primary limit to the effect of the California law on interstate commerce is the requirement of a physician's recommendation on the basis of a medical determination that a patient has an "illness for which marijuana provides relief." And the Court's discussion of this limit may be the most interesting, and disturbing, aspect of the case to physicians. Instead of concluding that physicians should be free to use their best medical judgment and that it was up to state medical boards to decide whether specific physicians were failing to live up to reasonable medical standards—as the Court did, for example, in its cases related to restrictive abortion laws—the Court took a totally different approach. In the Court's words, the broad language of the California medical-marijuana law allows "even the most scrupulous doctor to conclude that some recreational uses would be therapeutic. And our cases have taught us that there are some unscrupulous physicians who overprescribe when it is sufficiently profitable to do so."

The California law defines the category of patients who are exempt from criminal prosecution as those suffering from cancer, anorexia, AIDS, chronic pain, spasticity, glaucoma, arthritis, migraine, and "any other chronic or persistent medical symptom that substantially limits the ability of a person to conduct one or more major life activities . . . or if not alleviated may cause serious harm to the patient's safety or physical or mental health." These limits are hardly an invitation for recreational-use recommendations. Regarding "unscrupulous physicians," the Court cited two cases that involve criminal prosecutions of physicians for acting like drug dealers, one from 1919 and the other from 1975, implying that because a few physicians might have been criminally inclined in the past, it was reasonable for Congress (and the Court), on the basis of no actual evidence, to assume that many physicians may be so inclined today. It was not only physicians that the Court found untrustworthy but sick patients and their caregivers as well:

> The exemption for cultivation by patients and caregivers [patients can possess up to 8 oz. of dried marijuana and cultivate up to 6 mature or 12 immature plants] can only increase the supply of marijuana in the California market. The likelihood that all such production will promptly terminate when patients recover or will precisely match the patients' medical needs during their convalescence seems remote; whereas the danger that excesses will satisfy some of the admittedly enormous demand for recreational use seems obvious.

Justice Sandra Day O'Connor's dissent merits comment, because it is especially relevant to the practice of medicine. She argues that the Constitution requires the Court to protect "historic spheres of state sovereignty from excessive federal encroachment" and that one of the virtues of federalism is that it permits the individual states to serve as "laboratories," should they wish, to try "novel social and economic experiments without risk to the rest of the country." Specifically, she argues that the Court's new definition of economic activity is "breathtaking" in its scope, creating exactly what the gun case rejected—a federal police power. She also rejects reliance on the wheat case, noting that under the Agricultural Adjustment Act in question in that case, Congress had exempted the planting of less than 200 bushels (about six tons), and that when Roscoe Filburn, the farmer who challenged the federal statute, himself harvested his wheat, the statute exempted plantings of less than six acres.

In O'Connor's words, the wheat case "did not extend Commerce Clause authority to something as modest as the home cook's herb garden." O'Connor is not saying that Congress cannot regulate small quantities of a product produced for personal use, only that the wheat case "did not hold or imply that small-scale production of commodities is always economic, and automatically within Congress' reach." As to potential "exploitation [of the act] by unscrupulous physicians" and patients, O'Connor finds no factual support for this assertion and rejects the conclusion that simply by "piling assertion upon assertion" one can make a case for meeting the "substantiality test" of the guns-in-school and gender-violence cases.

It is important to note that the Court was not taking a position on whether Congress was correct to place marijuana in Schedule I or a position against California's law, any more than it was taking a position in favor of guns in schools or violence against women in the earlier cases. Instead, the Court was ruling only on the question of federal authority under the commerce clause. The Court noted, for example, that California and its supporters may one day prevail by pursuing the democratic process "in the halls of Congress." This seems extremely unlikely. More important is the question not addressed in this case—whether suffering patients have a substantive due-process claim to access to drugs needed to prevent suffering or a valid medical-necessity defense should they be prosecuted for using medical marijuana on a physician's recommendation. Also not addressed was the question that will be decided during the coming year: whether Congress has delegated to the U.S. attorney general its authority to decide what a "legitimate medical use" of an approved drug is in the context of Oregon's law governing physician-assisted suicide. What is obvious from this case, however, is that Congress has the authority, under the commerce clause, to regulate both legal and illegal drugs whether or not the drugs in question actually cross state lines. It would also seem reasonable to conclude that Congress has the authority to limit the uses of approved drugs.

Federalism and Endangered Species

Because *Gonzales v. Raich* is a drug case, and because it specifically involves marijuana, the Court's final word on federalism may not yet be in. Whether the "states' rights" movement has any life left after medical marijuana may be determined in the context of the Endangered Species Act. Two U.S. Circuit Courts of Appeals, for example, have recently upheld application of the federal law to protect endangered species that, unlike the descendants of Mark Twain's jumping frog, have no commercial value. Even though the Supreme Court refused to hear appeals from both of the lower courts, the cases help us understand the contemporary reach of congressional power under the commerce clause. One case involves the protection of six tiny creatures that live in caves (the "Cave Species")—three arthropods, a spider, and two beetles—from a commercial developer. The Fifth Circuit Court of Appeals noted that the Cave Species are not themselves an object of economics or commerce, saying: "There is no market for them; any future market is conjecture. If the speculative future medicinal benefits from the Cave Species makes their regulation commercial, then almost anything would be. . . . There is no historic trade in the Cave Species, nor do tourists come to Texas to view them." Nonetheless, the court concluded that Congress had the authority, under the commerce clause, to view life as an "interdependent web" of all species; that destruction of endangered species can be aggregated, like homegrown wheat; and that the destruction of multiple species has a substantial effect on interstate commerce.

The other case, from the District of Columbia Court of Appeals, involves the arroyo south-western toad, whose habitat was threatened by a real-estate developer. In upholding the application of the Endangered Species Act to the case, the appeals court held that the commercial activity being regulated was the housing development itself, as well as the "taking" of the road by the planned commercial development. The court noted that the "company would like us to consider its challenge to the ESA [Endangered Species Act] only as applied to the arroyo toad, which it says has no 'known commercial value'—unlike, for example, Mark Twain's celebrated jumping frogs [sic] of Calaveras County." Instead, the court concluded that application of the Endangered Species Act, far from eroding states' rights, is consistent with "the historic power of the federal government to preserve scarce resources in one locality for the future benefit of all Americans."

On a request for a hearing by the entire appeals court, which was rejected, recently named Chief Justice John Roberts—who at the time was a member of the appeals court—wrote a dissent that was not unlike Justice O'Connor's dissent in the marijuana case. In it he argued that the court's conclusion seemed inconsistent with the guns-in-school and gender-violence cases and that there were real problems with using an analysis of the commerce clause to regulate "the taking of a hapless toad that, for reasons of its own, lives its entire life in California." The case has since been settled. The development is going ahead in a way that protects the toad's habitat.

The Future of the Commerce Clause

Twain's short story has been termed "a living American fairy tale, acted out annually in Calaveras County." In what might be termed a living American government tale, nominees to the Supreme Court are routinely asked to explain their judicial philosophy of constitutional and statutory interpretation to the Senate Judiciary Committee. Asked about his "hapless toad" opinion during the Senate confirmation hearings on his nomination to replace Rehnquist as chief justice, Roberts said: "The whole point of my argument in the dissent was that there was another way to look at this [i.e., the approach taken by the Fifth Circuit Court in the Cave

Species case]. . . . I did not say that even in this case that the decision was wrong. . . . I simply said, let's look at those other grounds for decision because that doesn't present this problem." These hearings provide an opportunity for all Americans to review their understanding of our constitutional government and the manner in which it allocates power between the federal government and the fifty states. To the extent that this division of power is determined by the Court's view of the commerce clause, a return to an expansive reading of this clause seems both likely and, given the interdependence of the national and global economies, proper.

Of course, the fact that Congress has authority over a particular subject—such as whether to adopt a system of national licensure for physicians—does not mean that its authority is unlimited or even that Congress will use it. Rather, as Justice Stevens noted, cases such as the California medical-marijuana case lead to other central constitutional questions, as yet unresolved. These questions include whether patients, terminally ill or not, have a constitutional right not to suffer—at least, when their physicians know how to control their pain.

DISCUSSION QUESTIONS

1. *What would you do?* If you were a state legislator or a judge, how would you decide these issues? Specifically, as a matter of policy, do you think that doctors should be able to prescribe marijuana to alleviate pain? Should they be able to prescribe lethal drugs to be used by terminally ill patients? What about as a matter of law? Do you agree with the Supreme Court's decisions on these issues?

2. Do you support a state-centered or nation-centered perspective on federalism? Now go back and look at your answers to the last questions. Did you take positions that were consistent with your views on federalism or as a policy concern?

3. What does Mark Twain's jumping frog represent in Annas's article? Which Supreme Court case breathed life back into the frog? Why?

Debating the Issues: Immigration Reform and State Power

Immigration policy is one of the new areas of conflict in federalism. Who has the power to control the flow of illegal immigrants across borders: the national or state governments? It would seem to be a power of the national government, but what happens when states believe that the national government is not enforcing its own laws? Do states have the right to fill the breech? The recent *Arizona v. United States* case helped answer some of these questions, but left one other important question unanswered, at least for now.

The central constitutional question in this case concerns national supremacy—the pre-emption of state law by federal law when there is a conflict between the two. For example, the clause in the Arizona law that made it a criminal offense for employers to hire illegal immigrants is only a civil violation under national law; it was presumed, then, that the national law would hold, not the state law. Kevin Johnson explains that this well-established principle of federal pre-emption held in three of the four sections of the Arizona law. However, the controversial status check—or "show your papers"—provision of the state law was upheld by the Supreme Court because Arizona was simply enforcing the federal law. Johnson argues that this part of the case could have been decided as a civil rights claim rather than on the basis of federalism and pre-emption. However, he says that the Obama administration did not want to assert that Arizona residents and citizens were being denied equal protection of the laws under the Fourteenth Amendment because that argument would have been more difficult to prove than preemption. Johnson also speculates that President Obama may not have wanted to be seen as "playing the race card" during an election year.

The split verdict on different sections of the law meant that reactions to the decision were all over the map, ranging from those who saw it as a reaffirmation of Congress's role in immigration policy to those who thought it was more favorable to the states. Jay Sekulow is clearly in the latter camp, saying, "The Supreme Court's decision in *Arizona v. United States* represents an important victory for Arizona and proponents of the States' authority to protect their borders and citizens when the federal government fails to do so." Sekulow is pleased that the Court did not adopt a simple view of preemption, but rather made a distinction between active enforcement and non-enforcement of laws by the executive branch. States should be allowed to step in to enforce the intent of Congress when the executive branch is not enforcing the law.

On the other hand, Richard Peltz-Steele concludes that the Arizona decision (along with the Supreme Court's decision on the Affordable Care Act) reflect a "dismantling federalism [that] is a shortcut with a steep price." Peltz-Steele is sympathetic to Justice Scalia's dissenting opinion, which argued the majority opinion "deprives States of what most would consider the defining characteristic of sovereignty: the power to exclude from the sovereign's territory people who have no right to be there. Neither the Constitution itself nor even any law passed by Congress supports this result." Peltz-Steele is concerned that state governments are losing too much power to control their own policies.

While this was not a central point of debate between the various authors in this section, it is important to note that other constitutional scholars have reached a very different conclusion than Peltz-Steele concerning the implications of the Supreme Court's decision upholding most of "Obamacare." Rather than seeing this as another blow to federalism, this perspective points out that the Supreme Court may have limited future efforts by Congress to impose broad policy agendas on the states. In striking down the "coercive federalism" basis for the expansion of Medicaid (that is, states would have lost federal support if they did not expand health care for the poor) and in arguing that the commerce clause could not provide the constitutional basis for the individual mandate to buy health insurance, the Court strengthened the position of the states in their future battles with Congress over policy.

15

"State Sovereignty Is the Issue"

JAY SEKULOW

The Court's decision to uphold the immigration status check provision is a big win for state sovereignty. But in the end, does President Obama's selective enforcement of immigration law win the day? It was a little more than one week ago when President Obama actually changed immigration law by simply issuing a directive—an order to stop deporting many young illegal immigrants who were brought to the United States as children.

The Supreme Court's decision in *Arizona v. United States* represents an important victory for Arizona and proponents of the States' authority to protect their borders and citizens when the federal government fails to do so. Granted, the Court's holding that some of the Arizona law (SB 1070)'s provisions are preempted by federal immigration policy is disappointing (for the reasons Justice Scalia explained in his dissenting opinion). But, the Court's holding that the immigration status check provision (Section

2(B)) is not preempted by federal law represents an important rejection of the position that States are powerless to counteract the negative impact that illegal immigration has on their citizens when the President, Attorney General, or other federal Executive Branch actors choose not to enforce, or to otherwise disregard, duly enacted federal immigration laws.

Summary of Section 2(B) and the Court's Decision

Section 2(B) of SB 1070 states that, "[f]or any lawful stop, detention or arrest" made by Arizona law enforcement officers, "where reasonable suspicion exists that the person is an alien and is unlawfully present in the United States, a reasonable attempt shall be made, when practicable, to determine the immigration status of the person." Section 2(B) also states that "[t]he person's immigration status shall be verified with the federal government pursuant to 8 U.S.C. section 1373(c)," which requires the Immigration and Nationalization Service to verify the citizenship or immigration status of any individual when requested to do so by state or local law enforcement agencies.

In addition, if the lawful status of an arrested person cannot be presumed or determined, the status verification must occur "before the person is released." A person is presumed to be lawfully present if he presents a valid Arizona driver's license, tribal identification, or identification from any unit of government in the United States that requires proof of lawful presence. Section 2(B) expressly states that law enforcement officers "may not consider race, color, or national origin in implementing the requirements of this subsection except to the extent permitted by the United States or Arizona Constitution."

The Department of Justice (DOJ) argued that Section 2(B) conflicted with federal law enforcement objectives for two reasons: 1) The provision requires immigration status checks in some situations that the Attorney General would not likely have the individual removed; and 2) The provision could justify prolonged detentions while status checks are conducted. The Court rejected these arguments, noting that Arizona law enforcement officers generally contact Immigration and Customs Enforcement (ICE), which is required by federal law to respond to requests made by state officials to verify an individual's immigration or citizenship status and operates a support center for this purpose 24 hours a day, 7 days a week. * * * In addition, the Court concluded that hypothetical concerns that prolonged detentions may be authorized under Section 2(B) were premature, as Section 2(B) could be interpreted to avoid those concerns. The Court stated, "[h]owever the law is interpreted, if § 2(B) only requires state officers to conduct a status check during the course of an authorized, lawful detention or after a detainee has been released, the provision likely would survive preemption—at least absent some showing that it has other consequences that are adverse to federal law and its objectives." * * *

Justice Scalia concurred in the decision to uphold Section 2(B) but dissented from the Court's decision to invalidate other provisions of the law. He stated that the majority opinion "deprives States of what most would consider the defining characteristic of sovereignty: the power to exclude from the sovereign's territory people who have no right to be there. Neither the Constitution itself nor even any law passed by Congress supports this result." * * * (Scalia, J., dissenting in part). He said that accusing Arizona of contradicting federal law by enforcing provisions that the President declines to enforce "boggles the mind." * * * Justice Scalia also noted that the States would not have agreed to ratify the Constitution if it included a provision that prevented the States from taking action to defend their borders if the President declined to enforce immigration laws. * * *

Analysis

Scholars, pundits, and politicians from all corners are sure to spin the Court's decision in various ways, but the importance of the Court's holding concerning Section 2(B) cannot be denied. It not only affirms a level of State sovereignty to enact provisions like Section 2(B), but it also (at least indirectly) reestablishes that Congress, not the Executive Branch, is the ultimate source of federal immigration policy.

Opponents of SB 1070 essentially argued that *any* State provision (including the entirety of SB 1070) that seeks to enforce federal immigration law, or to otherwise protect States from the harmful effects of large-scale illegal immigration, is necessarily preempted by federal law. This is especially true if the Attorney General or the Department of Justice claims that the State provision undermines the Executive Branch's decision to under-enforce (or not enforce) federal statutes, even where the State provision is identical to, or otherwise mirrors, federal statutes. Under this view of preemption, the Executive Branch may effectively wrest *de facto* control of immigration law from Congress by both adopting a policy of under-enforcement or non-enforcement of federal statutes and actively fighting any State attempts to pursue Congress's stated goals.

If the Court had adopted this simplistic if–then approach to preemption (if the DOJ opposes a State law that touches upon some immigration matter, citing law enforcement concerns, then it must be preempted), State efforts to mitigate the deleterious effects of the federal government's failure to combat illegal immigration could be ground to a halt. Importantly, the Court's decision upholding Section 2(B) rejected DOJ's claim that a conflict between a State law and *the Attorney General's preferences* is necessarily a conflict *with federal law* for purposes of preemption. This may (and should) have major implications for the inevitable future battles over State provisions that mirror federal statutes that the Executive Branch objects to. As a basis for a preemption argument, the DOJ stated that, under Section 2(B) "the officers must make an inquiry even in cases where it seems unlikely that the Attorney General would have the alien removed. This might be the case, for example, when an alien is an elderly veteran with significant and longstanding ties to the community." The Court responded by stating, "Congress has done nothing to suggest it is inappropriate to communicate with ICE in these situations, however. Indeed, it has encouraged the sharing of information about possible immigration violations. . . . The federal scheme thus leaves room for a policy requiring state officials to contact ICE as a routine matter." In other words, an Executive Branch preference that ICE not be contacted for an immigration status check in certain situations *does not establish a conflict*, for purposes of preemption, between a state law requiring ICE to be contacted and federal statutes encouraging such contacts.

Conclusion

The Court's decision in *Arizona v. United States* is just one chapter (albeit an important one) in the ongoing story of how the federal, state, and local governments wrestle with the hot-button issue of illegal immigration. Importantly, the Court did not carve the States out of the story entirely by adopting a blanket rule that whatever the Executive Branch says in informal memos or court documents about a State provision represents federal "law" with preemptive power.

In light of the Court's decision, States will continue to enact provisions that are designed to remain consistent with federal statutes while mitigating the problems caused by the federal government's failure to adequately address illegal immigration. The Executive Branch will likely continue to attempt to elevate its (often unwritten) policy of under-enforcement or non-enforcement of federal immigration statutes to the level of federal "law" that would create a conflict between state statutes and identical, or nearly identical, federal statutes. The courts will continue to interpret the fine line between federal law that preempts state law and mere Executive Branch preferences that do not. That the States remain major players concerning this issue is a big defeat for the Executive Branch and its attempt to effectively rewrite immigration law through non-enforcement and litigation against the States.

16

"Dismantling Federalism Is a Shortcut With a Very Steep Price"

RICHARD PELTZ-STEELE

Recent decisions from the Supreme Court delivered a one-two punch to American federalism. While media focus on the political impact of the immigration and healthcare decisions on the elections, our constitutional system is reeling from a blow of greater proportion.

In the first high-profile decision, Arizona substantially lost its battle to maintain a state immigration enforcement system. The dispute arose from the gap between what the Feds say and what they do, specifically the failure to police immigration to the satisfaction of Arizona taxpayers.

The decision in *Arizona v. United States* was mostly about federal preemption of state law. And preemption law is notoriously fuzzy: "eye of the beholder" unfortunately characterizes the Court's approach. The majority saw the Arizona case as an instance of Congress so thoroughly "occupying the field" that no room remained for state law. Justice Thomas, in a concise dissent, reasoned that Congress had not precluded state law such as Arizona's, which merely echoes federal law.

Whatever one thinks of Justice Scalia's dissent, he got the facts right. The difference between majority and dissenter perceptions turns in part on whether the President's *inaction* in enforcing federal immigration law has preemptive significance. And certainly, as Scalia wrote, the framers would have abhorred this result; the states always have cherished their borders. One columnist wryly noted that the framers would not have signed a constitution abolishing slavery.

True, but that deficiency of our Constitution was addressed through amendment. No amendment yet has erased state borders.

Preemption always poses a fuzzy question, but the Court's ruling against Arizona takes a bite out of state power. Expansive federal *inaction* was read to displace a traditionally sound exercise of state police power that only sought to complement federal law—as written. The states now seem more than ever at the mercy of the federal government and its deep pockets to decide what is and is not the province of the state electorate.

So what local policy decisions will next take up residence between Capitol Hill and K Street? Healthcare, it seems. In *NFIB v. Sebelius*, the

Court substantially upheld the national healthcare initiative advanced by the President, including the controversial individual mandate.

The Court majority rejected the mandate as an exercise of Commerce Clause power. But leaving academic jaws agape, the majority capitalized on a marginal, throw-it-at-the-wall-and-see-if-it-sticks government argument that the penalty for failure to comply with the mandate was not a penalty at all—rather, a tax within the power of the Taxing Clause (as well as the Sixteenth Amendment, a further flimsy stretch).

The majority's use of the Taxing Clause dealt another blow to federalism. Again pundits derided the dissent, this time for getting hung up on the infamous hypothetical of government-compelled broccoli consumption and stubbornly failing to acknowledge that the individual decision *not* to buy health insurance (*inaction* again) is itself a regulable commercial act.

The problem of federalism can get lost in the shuffle. But in using the Taxing Clause, the Court offered precious little in the way of limiting principles. Indeed, the Taxing Clause now seems poised to become Congress's favorite new toy to run circles around the Commerce Clause and its carefully erected barriers to federal omnipotence. Whatever mandates formerly defied the reach of Congress may now be offered to individuals as a "choice," and persons lacking the wisdom to choose correctly may be "taxed" accordingly. Congress need not even use the word "tax"; the Justices will strain their eyes to find a tax wherever a penalty lies.

Citizens refusing to buy their shares of broccoli admittedly seems far-fetched. Imagine instead a domestic airline industry on the brink of collapse. A federal bailout compels all persons to buy airline tickets—or to invest in troubled banks, or to subscribe to failing newspapers—it's the patriotic choice, after all. Agoraphobic? Prefer to keep money under the mattress and get your news from TV? No problem; the "tax" on noncompliance comes due April 15.

Federalism is not an anachronism. The "United States" has—have—survived because of a well-drawn balance between sovereign states and the federal government. This system of "vertical separation of powers" is one of our essential checks and balances, right along with the three branches of government ("horizontal separation of powers") that kids learn about in grade school. Imbalance in this formula can spell catastrophe; think Civil War or European financial collapse.

Immigration and healthcare are critical public policy problems, but they are not intractable. Congress and the President have ample constitutional power at their disposal to achieve meaningful reforms without running roughshod over the States. Dismantling federalism is a shortcut with a steep price.

17

"The Debate Over Immigration Reform Is Not Over Until It's Over"

Kevin Johnson

On one of the last days of the 2011 term, the Supreme Court decided *Arizona v. United States* and determined the constitutionality of four provisions of the controversial Arizona immigration enforcement law known as S.B. 1070. The case had received a great deal of attention from Court watchers—and not just those interested in immigration. Indeed, it had a little something for just about everybody, from federalism to civil rights to election-year politics . . .

The Decision: States Have Some Immigration Enforcement Power

In many respects, the Supreme Court's decision in *Arizona v. United States* will be far from satisfying to many. Unlike lawsuits brought by other plaintiffs challenging S.B. 1070, the U.S. government challenged the Arizona law solely on the ground that it violated the Supremacy Clause of the U.S. Constitution, which makes federal law the "supreme law of the land." The body of law at issue is known as federal preemption doctrine, which is far from scintillating to most law professors, much less the general public.

In addressing the U.S. government's preemption challenge, the U.S. Court of Appeals for the Ninth Circuit had agreed with the district court that four provisions of S.B. 1070 impermissibly intruded on the federal power to regulate immigration law. The four provisions struck down include:

(1) Section 2(B), which requires state and local police to check the immigration status of persons about whom they have a reasonable suspicion of being undocumented;

(2) Section 3, which would have made it a crime not to complete or carry an "alien registration document" (and is directly contrary to the Court's decision in *Hines v. Davidowitz*);

(3) Section 5(C), which *criminalizes* the conduct of undocumented *employees* and goes well beyond the *civil* sanctions that U.S. immigration law allows to be imposed on employers of undocumented workers; and

(4) Section 6, which allows for a warrantless arrest if the "officer has probable cause to believe [that a person] has committed any public

offense that makes the person removable from the United States" under federal immigration law.

The Supreme Court, in a majority opinion by Justice Kennedy that was joined by Chief Justice Roberts and Justices Ginsburg, Breyer, and Sotomayor, affirmed the Ninth Circuit's ruling with respect to three of the four provisions. Justice Kagan, the former Solicitor General, took no part in the consideration or decision in the case.

At the outset, the majority emphasized that "[t]he Government of the United States has broad, undoubted power over the subject of immigration and the regulation of aliens" and that "[t]he federal power to determine immigration policy is well settled." After reaffirming federal primacy over immigration, the Court applied conventional federal preemption precedent. It carefully parsed each of the four sections individually, struck down Sections 3, 5(C), and 6, and upheld Section 2(B). In upholding that lone section, the Court found that there were adequate safeguards in place, including the law's ban on racial profiling, which saved it from being invalidated on its face.

It is important to note that, in upholding Section 2(B), the Court emphatically left the door open to future claims challenging its application: "This opinion does not foreclose other preemption and constitutional challenges to the law as interpreted and applied after it goes into effect."

Not even able to agree among themselves, Justices Scalia, Thomas, and Alito all filed separate opinions concurring in part and dissenting in part. Most jarring was Justice Scalia's dissent, which would have upheld S.B. 1070 in its entirety. Besides expressing unhappiness with the Obama Administration's immigration enforcement policies, Justice Scalia contended that the framers of the Constitution understood that the states had sovereign power over immigration. He stated sarcastically that "[i]f securing its territory in this fashion is not within the power of Arizona, we should cease referring to it as a sovereign State."

Avoiding the Civil Rights Concerns

Since the passage of S.B. 1070, Section 2(B) alone generated a firestorm of controversy. It, like many of the other new immigration enforcement laws passed by the States, requires state and local police to verify the immigration status of anyone whom they have a "reasonable suspicion" is undocumented. Critics claimed that S.B. 1070 would increase racial profiling of Latinos in law enforcement, a serious civil rights concern.

The majority's federal preemption analysis in *Arizona* allowed the Court to conveniently side-step this most frequently voiced public concern with the Arizona law. In so doing, the Court was aided by the parties.

Unlike the challenges to the Arizona law brought by civil rights groups, the U.S. government—the only plaintiff whose claims were before the

Supreme Court—did not include a claim that S.B. 1070 violated the Equal Protection Clause of the Fourteenth Amendment. The administration consciously wanted to avoid any claim of racial profiling. Indeed, during oral argument, Solicitor General Donald Verrilli unequivocally admitted in response to questioning from the Justices that racial profiling was not at issue in the case. Arizona, of course, would have no reason to disagree. The Justices eagerly seized on the admission that racial profiling was not at issue in the case to duck the race issue and write a treatise-like opinion on federal preemption.

There are at least two possible explanations for the U.S. government's strategy to avoid making the case a racial profiling case:

First, a claim of racial profiling presumably would be based on the Equal Protection Clause of the Fourteenth Amendment. To prevail on an equal protection claim, the U.S. government would have to prove that the state of Arizona acted with a "discriminatory intent" in enacting S.B. 1070. . . . This is a heavy burden, especially in a challenge to the constitutionality of a law on its face as opposed to as it has been applied.

Second, the Obama Administration may have wanted to avoid appearing to play the proverbial "race card" in challenging S.B. 1070 as a form of racial discrimination. Such reluctance would seemingly grow as the 2012 presidential election nears. It was relatively easy to avoid race and civil rights concerns when the parties were willing and when a readily available, and far less contentious, legal argument (federal preemption) was at hand.

In the end, the decision in *Arizona v. United States* centered on the power of the federal vis-à-vis state government over immigration. However, many critics of the state immigration enforcement laws like those in Arizona, Georgia, and South Carolina are less worried about state intrusion on federal power and much more concerned that the laws would encourage discrimination against Latinos, including lawful immigrants and U.S. citizens. Ultimately, a gaping disconnect exists between the Court's resolution of the case on legal technicalities and the civil rights concerns of certain segments of the public.

The Impact of Arizona v. United States

Only time will tell on what the real impact will be of the Supreme Court's decision in *Arizona v. United States* on the enforcement of the U.S. immigration laws. Several possibilities come to mind.

The Court's decision would appear to be far from the end of the matter with respect to the lawfulness of Section 2(B) of Arizona's S.B. 1070. We can expect challenges to that section as it is applied by the police, including claims by U.S. citizens of Mexican ancestry who are stopped and questioned about their immigration status by state and local law enforcement authorities. Racial discrimination in the criminal justice system has long been a problem in Arizona. In May, the U.S. Department of Justice brought a civil rights action against the Maricopa County Sheriff's Office, and celebrity Sheriff Joe Arpaio, for allegedly engaging in a "pattern of unlawful discrimination" against Latinos and immigrants.

It does seem clear after *Arizona v. United States* that there is a narrow space for the states to enforce the U.S. immigration laws. The decision may encourage more states to pass laws copycatting Section 2(B) and other lawful provisions of S.B. 1070 and perhaps even attempt to more aggressively "assist" the U.S. government in enforcing the immigration laws.

The Court's decision to uphold Section 2(B) will allow state and local governments on a daily basis to be involved in immigration enforcement as officers enforce the ordinary criminal laws. This will ensure that the decision has a significant impact in Arizona, but also in other states with laws similar in important respects, such as Alabama, Georgia, and South Carolina.

At the same time, the Court's careful review of the specific provisions of S.B. 1070 makes it clear that states do not have a blank check in terms of immigration enforcement. State leaders thinking about their own S.B. 1070 would need to think about the benefits of a largely symbolic—and possibly politically popular—law compared to the costs of enforcement (as well as litigating challenges to the law).

Importantly, nothing in the Court's decision suggests any change in the Court's approach to the run-of-the-mill immigration case, in which it looks to the text of the statute and the reasonableness of the agency's interpretation of the statute. Immigrants in recent years have prevailed in a *majority* of the Court's immigration decisions in the last few years.

Although immigrant rights advocates may be disappointed and restrictionists may be jubilant, it would be hazardous to read too much into *Arizona v. United States*. The newest Justice, Elena Kagan, did not participate in the decision, and future cases will push beyond the boundaries of the decision. For example, Alabama's H.B. 56, which goes further than S.B. 1070 by barring undocumented students from public colleges and universities and requiring school districts to collect immigration status information of K–12 students and parents, touches on education and raises many different legal and civil rights issues. . . .

In conclusion, the Supreme Court has cracked open the door to new state legislation, new claims of racial discrimination, and new lawsuits. States are likely to test the boundaries of *Arizona v. United States* with new, if not improved, immigration enforcement legislation. Litigation over the constitutionality of the laws is likely to continue. The lasting solution to the proliferation of state immigration enforcement laws, which is beyond the power of the Supreme Court, is for Congress to enact comprehensive immigration reform that has the support of the public. Perhaps the publicity over *Arizona v. United States* will prod Congress to act. Until it does, we can expect the status quo to continue.

DISCUSSION QUESTIONS

1. Who do you think should control immigration policy, the national government or the states? What if the executive branch is under-enforcing the law? Should states be able to step in and enforce congressional law?

2. Do you see the Arizona decision as a blow to states' rights, or a reaffirmation of their role in the formation of immigration policy?

3. The Arizona case is known as a "facial test" of the policy rather than an "as applied" test. That is, the law had not been applied yet, so the constitutionality of the law had to be determined "on its face." Once the law is applied, do you think that the "show your papers" part of the law will be upheld?

CHAPTER 4

The Constitutional Framework and the Individual: Civil Liberties and Civil Rights

In the next two selections, Abraham Lincoln and Martin Luther King, Jr., take opposing points of view about how to achieve peaceful change in a civil society. What happens when the fight for justice and equality comes into conflict with the rule of law? Are people ever justified in breaking laws for what they perceive to be the greater good? Is civil disobedience justified in some contexts?

In a speech that he delivered twenty-three years before becoming president, Lincoln argues that the laws must be followed, as without adherence to laws we have no civil society. Change, Lincoln stresses, must come from working within the system. King disagrees, arguing that while people have a moral obligation to follow just laws, they have an equally compelling duty to break unjust laws through nonviolent means. In his "Letter from Birmingham Jail," which he addressed to more conservative religious leaders in the civil rights movement who were concerned about his tactics, King outlined procedures for distinguishing between just and unjust laws, and for resisting those laws that are unjust. It is ironic that despite Lincoln's admonitions about working within the system, it was under his leadership that the nation fought its bloodiest war precisely because the central issues of states' rights and slavery could not be solved within the system. King, on the other hand, who argued in favor of breaking unjust laws, was actually instrumental in putting pressure on Congress (the "system") to change those laws that he and others in the civil rights movement considered unjust.

Current battles over abortion and the environment show the debate between Lincoln and King to be timeless. Activists in both policy areas have been decried as "radical" or "extremist" because of occasional civil disobedience against legal activities. Some environmentalists have prevented lumber harvesting by putting spikes in trees; some pro-life activists have blocked women's access to abortion clinics. And in the abortion case, as in the Lincoln-King debate, issues of civil rights and civil liberties intersect.

18

"The Perpetuation of Our Political Institutions"

Abraham Lincoln

In the great journal of things happening under the sun, we, the American People, find our account running, under date of the nineteenth century of the Christian era. We find ourselves in the peaceful possession, of the fairest portion of the earth, as regards extent of territory, fertility of soil, and salubrity of climate. We find ourselves under the government of a system of political institutions, conducing more essentially to the ends of civil and religious liberty, than any of which the history of former times tells us. We, when mounting the stage of existence, found ourselves the legal inheritors of these fundamental blessings. We toiled not in the acquirement or establishment of them—they are a legacy bequeathed us, by a *once* hardy, brave, and patriotic, but *now* lamented and departed race of ancestors. Theirs was the task (and nobly they performed it) to possess themselves, and through themselves, us, of this goodly land; and to uprear upon its hills and its valleys, a political edifice of liberty and equal rights; 'tis ours only, to transmit these, the former, unprofaned by the foot of an invader; the latter, undecayed by the lapse of time and untorn by usurpation, to the latest generation that fate shall permit the world to know. This task of gratitude to our fathers, justice to ourselves, duty to posterity, and love for our species in general, all imperatively required us faithfully to perform.

How then shall we perform it? At what point shall we expect the approach of danger? By what means shall we fortify against it? Shall we expect some transatlantic military giant, to step the ocean, and crush us at a blow? Never! All the armies of Europe, Asia and Africa combined, with all the treasure of the earth (our own excepted) in their military chest; with a Buonaparte for a commander, could not by force take a drink from the Ohio, or make a track on the Blue Ridge, in a trial of a thousand years.

At what point then is the approach of danger to be expected? I answer, if it ever reach us, it must spring up amongst us. It cannot come from abroad. If destruction be our lot, we must ourselves be its author and finisher. As a nation of freemen, we must live through all time, or die by suicide.

I hope I am over wary; but if I am not, there is, even now, something of ill-omen amongst us. I mean the increasing disregard for law which pervades the country; the growing disposition to substitute the wild and furious passions, in lieu of the sober judgment of Courts; and the worse than savage mobs, for the executive ministers of justice. This disposition is awfully fearful in any community; and that it now exists in ours, though grating to our feelings to admit, it would be a violation of truth, and an insult to our intelligence, to deny. Accounts of outrages committed by mobs, form the everyday news of the times. They have pervaded the country, from New England to Louisiana; they are neither peculiar to the eternal snows of the former, nor the burning suns of the latter; they are not the creature of climate—neither are they confined to the slaveholding, or the non-slaveholding States. Alike, they spring up among the pleasure hunting masters of Southern slaves, and the order loving citizens of the land of steady habits. Whatever, then, their cause may be, it is common to the whole country.

It would be tedious, as well as useless, to recount the horrors of all of them. Those happening in the State of Mississippi, and at St. Louis, are, perhaps, the most dangerous in example and revolting to humanity. In the Mississippi case, they first commenced by hanging the regular gamblers; a set of men, certainly not following for a livelihood, a very useful, or very honest occupation; but one which, so far from being forbidden by the laws, was actually licensed by an act of the Legislature, passed but a single year before. Next, negroes, suspected of conspiring to raise an insurrection, were caught up and hanged in all parts of the State: then, white men, supposed to be leagued with the negroes; and finally, strangers, from neighboring States, going thither on business, were, in many instances, subjected to the same fate. Thus went on this process of hanging, from gamblers to negroes, from negroes to white citizens, and from these to strangers; till, dead men were seen literally dangling from the boughs of trees upon every road side; and in numbers almost sufficient, to rival the native Spanish moss of the country, as a drapery of the forest.

Turn, then, to that horror-striking scene at St. Louis. A single victim was only sacrificed there. His story is very short; and is, perhaps, the most highly tragic, of anything of its length, that has ever been witnessed in real life. A mulatto man, by the name of McIntosh, was seized in the street, dragged to the suburbs of the city, chained to a tree, and actually burned to death; and all within a single hour from the time he had been a freeman, attending to his own business, and at peace with the world.

Such are the effects of mob law; and such are the scenes, becoming more and more frequent in this land so lately famed for love of law and order; and the stories of which have even now grown too familiar, to attract any thing more than an idle remark.

But you are, perhaps, ready to ask, "What has this to do with the perpetuation of our political institutions?" I answer, it has much to do with it. Its direct consequences are, comparatively speaking, but a small evil; and much of its danger consists, in the proneness of our minds, to regard its direct as its only consequences. Abstractly considered, the hanging of the gamblers at Vicksburg was of but little consequence. They constitute a portion of population that is worse than useless in any community; and their death, if no pernicious example be set by it, is never matter of reasonable regret with anyone. If they were annually swept from the stage of existence by the plague or small pox, honest men would, perhaps, be much profited by the operation. Similar too, is the correct reasoning, in regard to the burning of the negro at St. Louis. He had forfeited his life, by the perpetration of an outrageous murder, upon one of the most worthy and respectable citizens of the city; and had he not died as he did, he must have died by the sentence of the law, in a very short time afterwards. As to him alone, it was as well the way it was, as it could otherwise have been. But the example in either case was fearful. When men take it in their heads today, to hang gamblers, or burn murderers, they should recollect, that, in the confusion usually attending such transactions, they will be as likely to hang or burn someone who is neither a gambler nor a murderer as one who is; and that, acting upon the example they set, the mob of tomorrow, may, and probably will, hang or burn some of them by the very same mistake. And not only so; the innocent, those who have ever set their faces against violations of law in every shape, alike with the guilty, fall victims to the ravages of mob law; and thus it goes on, step by step, till all the walls erected for the defence of the persons and property of individuals, are trodden down, and disregarded. But all this even, is not the full extent of the evil. By such examples, by instances of the perpetrators of such acts going unpunished, the lawless in spirit are encouraged to become lawless in practice; and having been used to no restraint, but dread of punishment, they thus become absolutely unrestrained. Having ever regarded Government as their deadliest bane, they make a jubilee of the suspension of its operations; and pray for nothing so much as its total annihilation. While, on the other hand, good men, men who love tranquility, who desire to abide by the laws, and enjoy their benefits, who would gladly spill their blood in the defence of their country; seeing their property destroyed; their families insulted, and their lives endangered; their persons injured; and seeing nothing in prospect that forebodes a change for the better; become tired of, and disgusted with, a Government that offers them no protection; and are not much averse to a change in which they imagine they have nothing to lose. Thus, then, by the operation of this mobocratic spirit, which all must admit is now abroad in the land, the strongest bulwark of any Government, and particularly of those constituted like ours, may effectually be broken down and destroyed—I mean the *attachment* of the People. Whenever this effect shall be produced among us, whenever the vicious portion of population shall be permitted to gather in bands of hundreds and thousands, and burn churches, ravage and rob provision-stores, throw printing presses into rivers, shoot editors, and hang and burn obnoxious persons at pleasure, and with impunity, depend on it, this Government cannot last. By such things, the feelings of the best citizens will become more or less alienated from it; and thus it will be left without friends, or with too few, and those few too weak, to make their friendship effectual. At such a time and under such circumstances, men of sufficient talent and ambition will not be wanting to seize the opportunity, strike the blow, and overturn that fair fabric which for the last half century has been the fondest hope of the lovers of freedom, throughout the world.

I know the American People are *much* attached to their Government; I know they would suffer *much* for its sake; I know they would endure evils long and patiently, before they would ever think of exchanging it for another. Yet, notwithstanding all this, if the laws be continually despised and disregarded, if their rights to be secure in their persons and property are held by no better tenure than the caprice of a mob, the alienation of their affections from the Government is the natural consequence; and to that, sooner or later, it must come.

Here then, is one point at which danger may be expected.

The question recurs, "how shall we fortify against it?" The answer is simple. Let every American, every lover of liberty, every well-wisher to his posterity, swear by the blood of the Revolution never to violate in the least particular the laws of the country; and never to tolerate their violation by others. As the patriots of seventy-six did to the support of the Declaration of Independence, so to the support of the Constitution and Laws, let every American pledge his life, his property, and his sacred honor; let every man remember that to violate the law is to trample on the blood of his father, and to tear the character of his own, and his children's liberty. Let reverence for the laws be breathed by every American mother to the lisping babe that prattles on her lap—let it be taught in schools, in seminaries, and in colleges; let it be written in Primers, spelling books, and in Almanacs; let it be preached from the pulpit, proclaimed in legislative halls, and enforced in courts of justice. And, in short, let it become the *political religion* of the nation; and let the old and the young, the rich and the poor, the grave and the gay, of all sexes and tongues, and colors and conditions, sacrifice unceasingly upon its altars.

While ever a state of feeling, such as this, shall universally, or even, very generally prevail throughout the nation, vain will be every effort, and fruitless every attempt, to subvert our national freedom.

When I so pressingly urge a strict observance of all the laws, let me not be understood as saying there are no bad laws, nor that grievances may not arise, for the redress of which, no legal provisions have been made. I mean to say no such thing. But I do mean to say that, although bad laws, if they exist, should be repealed as soon as possible, still while they continue in force, for the sake of example they should be religiously observed. So also in unprovided cases. If such arise, let proper legal provisions be made for them with the least possible delay; but, till then, let them, if not too intolerable, be borne with.

There is no grievance that is a fit object of redress by mob law. In any case that arises, as for instance, the promulgation of abolitionism, one of two positions is necessarily true; that is, the thing is right within itself, and therefore deserves the protection of all law and all good citizens; or, it is wrong, and therefore proper to be prohibited by legal enactments; and in neither case, is the interposition of mob law, either necessary, justifiable, or excusable.

* * *

But this state of feeling *must fade, is fading, has faded,* with the circumstances that produced it.

I do not mean to say, that the scenes of the revolution *are now* or *ever will* be entirely forgotten; but that like everything else, they must fade upon the memory of the world, and grow more and more dim by the lapse of time. In history, we hope, they will be read of, and recounted, so long as the bible shall be read; but even granting that they will, their influence *cannot be* what it heretofore has been. Even then, they *cannot be* so universally known, nor so vividly felt, as they were by the generation just gone to rest. At the close of that struggle, nearly every adult male had been a participator in some of its scenes. The consequence was, that of those scenes, in the form of a husband, a father, a son or a brother, *a living history* was to be found in every family—a history bearing the indubitable testimonies of its own authenticity, in the limbs mangled, in the scars of wounds received, in the midst of the very scenes related—a history, too, that could be read and understood alike by all, the wise and the ignorant, the learned and the unlearned. But *those* histories are gone. They *can* be read no more forever. They *were* a fortress of strength; but, what invading foeman could *never do*, the silent artillery of time *has done*; the leveling of its walls. They are gone. They *were* a forest of giant oaks; but the all-resistless hurricane has swept over them, and left only, here and there, a lonely trunk, despoiled of its verdure, shorn of its foliage; unshading and unshaded, to murmur in a few more gentle breezes, and to combat with its mutilated limbs, a few more ruder storms, then to sink, and be no more.

They *were* the pillars of the temple of liberty; and now that they have crumbled away, that temple must fall, unless we, their descendants, supply their places with other pillars, hewn from the solid quarry of sober reason. Passion has helped us; but can do so no more. It will in future be our enemy. Reason, cold, calculating, unimpassioned reason, must furnish all the materials for our future support and defence. Let those materials be molded into *general intelligence, sound morality,* and, in particular, *a reverence for the constitution and laws:* and, that we improved to the last; that we remained free to the last; that we revered his name to the last; that, during his long sleep, we permitted no hostile foot to pass over or dese-crate his resting place; shall be that which to learn the last trump shall awaken our WASHINGTON.

Upon these let the proud fabric of freedom rest, as the rock of its basis; and as truly as has been said of the only greater institution, *"the gates of hell shall not prevail against it."*

19

"Letter from Birmingham Jail"

Martin Luther King, Jr.

My Dear Fellow Clergymen:
  While confined here in the Birmingham City Jail, I came across your recent statement calling my present activities "unwise and untimely." Seldom do I pause to answer criticism of my work and ideas. If I sought to answer all the criticism that cross my desk, my secretaries would have little time for anything other than such correspondence in the course of the day, and I would have no time for constructive work. But since I feel that you are men of genuine goodwill and that your criticisms are sincerely set forth, I want to try to answer your statement in what I hope will be patient and reasonable terms.

I think I should indicate why I am here in Birmingham, since you have been influenced by the view which argues against "outsiders coming in." I have the honor of serving as president of the Southern Christian Leadership Conference, an organization operating in every Southern state, with headquarters in Atlanta, Georgia. We have some eighty-five affiliate organizations across the South, and one of them is the Alabama Christian Movement for Human Rights. Frequently, we share staff, educational, and financial resources with our affiliates. Several months ago the affiliate here in Birmingham asked us to be on call to engage in a nonviolent direct-action program if such were deemed necessary. We readily consented, and when the hour came we lived up to our promise. So I, along with several members of my staff, am here because I was invited here. I am here because I have organizational ties here.

But more basically, I am in Birmingham because injustice exists here. Just as the prophets of the 8th century B.C. left their villages and carried their "thus saith the Lord" far afield, and just as the apostle Paul left his village of Tarsus and carried the gospel of Jesus Christ to the far corners of the Greco-Roman world, so am I compelled to carry the gospel of freedom beyond my own hometown. Like Paul, I must constantly respond to the Macedonian call for aid.*

Moreover, I am cognizant of the interrelatedness of all communities and states. I cannot sit idly by in Atlanta and not be concerned about what happens in Birmingham. Injustice anywhere is a threat to justice

---

*See Acts 16:9 [*Editors*].

everywhere. We are caught in an inescapable network of mutuality, tied in a single garment of destiny. Whatever affects one directly affects all indirectly. Never again can we afford to live with the narrow, provincial "outside agitator" idea. Anyone who lives inside the United States can never be considered an outsider anywhere within its bounds.

You deplore the demonstrations taking place in Birmingham. But your statement, I am sorry to say, fails to express a similar concern for the conditions that brought about the demonstrations. I am sure that none of you would want to rest content with the superficial kind of social analysis that deals merely with effects and does not grapple with underlying causes. It is unfortunate that demonstrations are taking place in Birmingham, but it is even more unfortunate that the city's white power structure left the Negro community with no alternative.

* * *

You may well ask, "Why direct action? Why sit-ins, marches, etc.? Isn't negotiation a better path?" You are quite right in calling for negotiation. Indeed, this is the very purpose of direct action. Nonviolent direct action seeks to foster such a tension that a community which has constantly refused to negotiate is forced to confront the issue. It seeks so to dramatize the issue that it can no longer be ignored. My citing the creation of tension as part of the work of the nonviolent resister may sound rather shocking. But I readily acknowledge that I am not afraid of the word "tension." I have earnestly opposed violent tension, but there is a type of constructive, nonviolent tension which is necessary for growth. Just as Socrates felt that it was necessary to create a tension in the mind so that individuals could shake off the bondage of myths and half-truths and rise to the realm of creative analysis and objective appraisal, so must we see the need for nonviolent gadflies to create the kind of tension in society that will help men rise from the dark depths of prejudice and racism to the majestic heights of understanding and brotherhood.

The purpose of our direct-action program is to create a situation so crisis-packed that it will inevitably open the door to negotiation. I therefore concur with you in your call for negotiation. Too long has our beloved Southland been bogged down in a tragic effort to live in monologue rather than dialogue.

* * *

We have waited for more than 340 years for our constitutional and God-given rights. The nations of Asia and Africa are moving with jet-like speed toward gaining political independence, but we still creep at horse-and-buggy pace toward gaining a cup of coffee at a lunch counter. Perhaps it is easy for those who have never felt the stinging darts of segregation to say "Wait." But when you have seen vicious mobs lynch your mothers and fathers at will and drown your sisters and brothers at whim;

when you have seen hate-filled policemen curse, kick, and even kill your black brothers and sisters with impunity; when you see the vast majority of your 20 million Negro brothers smothering in an air-tight cage of poverty in the midst of an affluent society; when you suddenly find your tongue twisted as you seek to explain to your six-year-old daughter why she can't go to the public amusement park that has just been advertised on television, and see tears welling up when she is told that Funtown is closed to colored children, and see ominous clouds of inferiority beginning to form in her little mental sky, and see her beginning to distort her personality by unconsciously developing a bitterness toward white people; when you have to concoct an answer for a five-year-old son asking, "Daddy, why do white people treat colored people so mean?"; when you take a cross-country drive and find it necessary to sleep night after night in the uncomfortable corners of your automobile because no motel will accept you; when you are humiliated day in and day out by nagging signs reading "white" and "colored"; when your first name becomes "nigger," your middle name becomes "boy" (however old you are), and your last name becomes "John," and your wife and mother are never given the respected title "Mrs."; when you are harried by day and haunted by night by the fact that you are a Negro, never quite knowing what to expect next, and are plagued with inner fears and outer resentments; when you are forever fighting a degenerating sense of "nobodiness"—then you will understand why we find it difficult to wait. There comes a time when the cup of endurance runs over, and men are no longer willing to be plunged into an abyss of injustice where they experience the bleakness of corroding despair. I hope, sirs, you can understand our legitimate and unavoidable impatience.

You express a great deal of anxiety over our willingness to break laws. This is certainly a legitimate concern. Since we so diligently urge people to obey the Supreme Court's decision of 1954 outlawing segregation in the public schools, at first glance it may seem rather paradoxical for us consciously to break laws. One may well ask, "How can you advocate breaking some laws and obeying others?" The answer lies in the fact that there are two types of laws: just and unjust. I agree with St. Augustine that "an unjust law is no law at all."

* * *

Let us consider some of the ways in which a law can be unjust. A law is unjust, for example, if the majority group compels a minority group to obey the statute but does not make it binding on itself. By the same token, a law in all probability is just if the majority is itself willing to obey it. Also, a law is unjust if it is inflicted on a minority that, as a result of being denied the right to vote, had no part in enacting or devising the law. Who can say that the legislature of Alabama which set up that state's segregation laws was democratically elected? Throughout Alabama all sorts of devious methods are used to prevent Negroes from becoming registered voters, and there are some counties in which, even though Negroes constitute a majority of the population, not a single Negro is registered. Can any law enacted under such circumstances be considered democratically structured?

Sometimes a law is just on its face and unjust in its application. For instance, I have been arrested on a charge of parading without a permit. Now there is nothing wrong in having an ordinance which requires a permit for a parade. But such an ordinance becomes unjust when it is used to maintain segregation and to deny citizens the First Amendment privilege of peaceful assembly and protest.

I hope you are able to see the distinction I am trying to point out. In no sense do I advocate evading the law, as would the rabid segregationist. That would lead to anarchy. One who breaks an unjust law must do so *openly, lovingly,* and with a willingness to accept the penalty. I submit that an individual who breaks a law that conscience tells him is unjust and who willingly accepts the penalty of imprisonment in order to arouse the conscience of the community over its injustice is in reality expressing the highest respect for law.

*　*　*

I must make two honest confessions to you, my Christian and Jewish brothers. First, I must confess that over the past few years I have been gravely disappointed with the white moderate. I have almost reached the regrettable conclusion that the Negro's great stumbling block in his stride toward freedom is not the White Citizen's Counciler or the Ku Klux Klanner but the white moderate who is more devoted to "order" than to justice; who prefers a negative peace which is the absence of tension to a positive peace which is the presence of justice; who constantly says "I agree with you in the goal you seek, but I cannot agree with your methods"; who paternalistically believes he can set the timetable for another man's freedom; who lives by a mythical concept of time and who constantly advises the Negro to wait for a "more convenient season." Shallow understanding from people of goodwill is more frustrating than absolute misunderstanding from people of ill will. Lukewarm acceptance is much more bewildering than outright rejection.

I had hoped that the white moderate would understand that law and order exist for the purpose of establishing justice and that when they fail in this purpose they block social progress. I had hoped that the white moderate would understand that the present tension in the South is a necessary phase of the transition from an obnoxious negative peace, in which the Negro passively accepted his unjust plight, to a substantive and positive peace, in which all men will respect the dignity and worth of human personality. Actually, we who engage in nonviolent direct action are not the creators of tension. We merely bring to the surface the hidden tension that is already alive. We bring it out in the open where it can be seen and dealt with. Like a boil that can never be cured so long as it is covered up but must be opened with all its pus-flowing ugliness to the natural medicines of air and light, injustice must be exposed, with all the tension its exposure creates, to the light of human conscience and the air of national opinion before it can be cured.

*   *   *

You speak of our activity in Birmingham as extreme. At first I was rather disappointed that fellow clergymen would see my nonviolent efforts as those of an extremist. I began thinking about the fact that I stand in the middle of two opposing forces in the Negro community. One is a force of complacency made up of Negroes who, as a result of long years of oppression, are so completely drained of self-respect and a sense of "somebodiness" that they have adjusted to segregation, and of a few middle-class Negroes who, because of a degree of academic and economic security and because in some ways they profit by segregation, have unconsciously become insensitive to the problems of the masses. The other force is one of bitterness and hatred, and it comes perilously close to advocating violence. It is expressed in the various black nationalist groups that are springing up across the nation, the largest and best-known being Elijah Muhammad's Muslim movement. Nourished by the Negro's frustration over the continued existence of racial discrimination, this movement is made up of people who have lost faith in America, who have absolutely repudiated Christianity, and who have concluded that the white man is an incorrigible "devil."

I have tried to stand between these two forces, saying that we need emulate neither the "do-nothingism" of the complacent nor the hatred of the black nationalist. For there is the more excellent way of love and nonviolent protest. I am grateful to God that, through the influence of the Negro church, the way of nonviolence became an integral part of our struggle.

If this philosophy had not emerged, by now many streets of the South would, I am convinced, be flowing with blood. And I am further convinced that if our white brothers dismiss as "rabble-rousers" and "outside agitators" those of us who employ nonviolent direct action and if they refuse to support our nonviolent efforts, millions of Negroes will, out of frustration and despair, seek solace and security in black nationalist ideologies—a development that would inevitably lead to a frightening racial nightmare.

*   *   *

Let me take note of my other major disappointment. Though there are some notable exceptions, I have also been disappointed with the white church and its leadership. I do not say this as one of those negative critics who can always find something wrong with the church. I say this as a minister of the gospel, who loves the church; who was nurtured in its bosom; who has been sustained by its spiritual blessings and who will remain true to it as long as the cord of life shall lengthen.

When I was suddenly catapulted into the leadership of the bus protest in Montgomery, Alabama, a few years ago, I felt we would be supported by the white church. I felt that the white ministers, priests, and rabbis of the South would be among our strongest allies. Instead, some have been outright opponents, refusing to understand the freedom movement and misrepresenting its leaders; all too many others have been more cautious than courageous and have remained silent and secure behind stained-glass windows.

In spite of my shattered dreams I came to Birmingham with the hope that the white religious leadership of this community would see the justice of our cause and with deep moral concern would serve as the channel through which our just grievances could reach the power structure. But again I have been disappointed.

I have heard numerous Southern religious leaders admonish their worshipers to comply with a desegregation decision because it is the *law*, but I have longed to hear white ministers declare, "Follow this decree because integration is morally *right* and because the Negro is your brother." In the midst of blatant injustices inflicted upon the Negro I have watched white churchmen stand on the sideline and mouth pious irrelevancies and sanctimonious trivialities. In the midst of a mighty struggle to rid our nation of racial and economic injustice I have heard many ministers say, "Those are social issues with which the gospel has no real concern," and I have watched many churches commit themselves to a completely otherworldly religion which makes a strange, unbiblical distinction between body and soul, between the sacred and the secular.

We are moving toward the close of the twentieth century with a religious community largely adjusted to the status quo—a taillight behind other community agencies rather than a headlight leading men to higher levels of justice.

*   *   *

But the judgment of God is upon the church as never before. If today's church does not recapture the sacrificial spirit of the early church, it will lose its authenticity, forfeit the loyalty of millions, and be dismissed as an irrelevant social club with no meaning for the twentieth century. Every day I meet young people whose disappointment with the church has turned into outright disgust.

Perhaps I have once again been too optimistic. Is organized religion too inextricably bound to the status quo to save our nation and the world? Perhaps I must turn my faith to the inner spiritual church, the church within the church, as the true *ecclesia* and the hope of the world. But again

I am thankful to God that some noble souls from the ranks of organized religion have broken loose from the paralyzing chains of conformity and joined us as active partners in the struggle for freedom. They have left their secure congregations and walked the streets of Albany, Georgia, with us. They have gone down the highways of the South on torturous rides for freedom. Yes, they have gone to jail with us. Some have been kicked out of their churches, have lost the support of their bishops and fellow ministers. But they have acted in the faith that right defeated is stronger than evil triumphant. Their witness has been the spiritual salt that has preserved the true meaning of the gospel in these troubled times. They have carved a tunnel of hope through the dark mountain of disappointment.

I hope the church as a whole will meet the challenge of this decisive hour. But even if the church does not come to the aid of justice, I have no despair about the future. I have no fear about the outcome of our struggle in Birmingham, even if our motives are at present misunderstood. We will reach the goal of freedom in Birmingham and all over the nation, because the goal of America is freedom.

*   *   *

Before closing I feel impelled to mention one other point in your statement that has troubled me profoundly. You warmly commended the Birmingham police force for keeping "order" and "preventing violence." I doubt that you would have so warmly commended the police force if you had seen its angry dogs sinking their teeth into six unarmed, nonviolent Negroes. I doubt that you would so quickly commend the policemen if you were to observe their ugly and inhuman treatment of Negroes here in the City Jail; if you were to watch them push and curse old Negro women and young Negro girls; if you were to see them slap and kick old Negro men and young boys; if you were to observe them, as they did on two occasions, refuse to give us food because we wanted to sing our grace together. I cannot join you in your praise of the Birmingham Police Department.

It is true that the police have exercised discipline in handling the demonstrators. In this sense they have conducted themselves rather "nonviolently" in public. But for what purpose? To preserve the evil system of segregation. Over the past few years I have consistently preached that nonviolence demands that the means we use must be as pure as the ends we seek. I have tried to make clear that it is wrong to use immoral means to attain moral ends. But now I must affirm that it is just as wrong, or perhaps even more so, to use moral means to preserve immoral ends. Perhaps Mr. Connor and his policemen have been rather nonviolent in public, as was Chief Pritchett in Albany, Georgia, but they have used the moral means of nonviolence to maintain the immoral end of racial injustice. As T. S. Eliot has said, there is no greater treason than to do the right deed for the wrong reason.

I wish you had commended the Negro sit-inners and demonstrators of Birmingham for their sublime courage, their willingness to suffer and their amazing discipline in the midst of great provocation. One day the South will recognize its real heroes. . . . One day the South will know that when these disinherited children of God sat down at lunch counters they were in reality standing up for what is best in the American dream and for the most sacred values in our Judeo-Christian heritage, thereby bringing our nation back to those great wells of democracy which were dug deep by the founding fathers in their formulation of the Constitution and the Declaration of Independence.

DISCUSSION QUESTIONS

1. What are the main points of disagreement between the King and Lincoln views?

2. Many of those involved in social protest movements (from anti-abortion protestors to environmental activists) draw parallels between their efforts and King's legacy of civil disobedience, in an effort to establish their right to disobey laws they find unjust. Are such applications of King's argument legitimate? Why or why not?

20

"In Defense of Prejudice"

Jonathan Rauch

Some political theorists argue that democracies must not only prevent the intrusion of government on basic liberties, but also must play a positive role in bolstering and protecting the rights of all their citizens. The challenge is admirable but difficult, as governments in practice are often faced with trade-offs between the two values. Consider free speech, a right enshrined in the First Amendment. The right to speak freely is fundamental to democratic governance. Yet it is not absolute. Is there a line where my right to speak freely impinges upon your wish not to hear what I have to say, particularly when my words are perceived as offensive, harmful, and prejudicial? What role should the government play in drawing the line, if any? Should it limit speech in order to protect others from the insult words can bring? If there is such a line, who decides where it is drawn?

In the following article Jonathan Rauch stands "in defense of prejudice" and in opposition to those who call for government regulation of speech that is insulting to or stigmatizes individuals based on their sex, race, color, handicap, religion, sexual orientation; or national and ethnic origin. In the workplace, universities, public school curricula, the media, and criminal law, speech is increasingly regulated by codes aimed at eradicating prejudice. Rauch argues that regulating speech this way is foolish. In his view, the only way to challenge and correct prejudice is through the free flow of speech, some of which we might not want to hear. Government best protects liberty when it works to preserve rather than prevent the free flow of speech, no matter how distasteful or hurtful that speech may be.

The war on prejudice is now, in all likelihood, the most uncontroversial social movement in America. Opposition to "hate speech," formerly identified with the liberal left, has become a bipartisan piety. In the past year, groups and factions that agree on nothing else have agreed that the public expression of any and all prejudices must be forbidden. On the left, protesters and editorialists have insisted that Francis L. Lawrence resign as president of Rutgers University for describing blacks as "a disadvantaged population that doesn't have that genetic, hereditary background to have a higher average." On the other side of the ideological divide, Ralph Reed, the executive director of the Christian Coalition, responded to criticism of the religious right by calling a press conference to denounce a supposed outbreak of "name-calling, scapegoating, and religious bigotry." Craig Rogers, an evangelical Christian student at California State

University, recently filed a $2.5 million sexual-harassment suit against a lesbian professor of psychology, claiming that anti-male bias in one of her lectures violated campus rules and left him feeling "raped and trapped."

In universities and on Capitol Hill, in workplaces and newsrooms, authorities are declaring that there is no place for racism, sexism, homophobia, Christian-bashing, and other forms of prejudice in public debate or even in private thought. "Only when racism and other forms of prejudice are expunged," say the crusaders for sweetness and light, "can minorities be safe and society be fair." So sweet, this dream of a world without prejudice. But the very last thing society should do is seek to utterly eradicate racism and other forms of prejudice.

I suppose I should say, in the customary I-hope-I-don't-sound-too-defensive tone, that I am not a racist and that this is not an article favoring racism or any other particular prejudice. It is an article favoring intellectual pluralism, which permits the expression of various forms of bigotry and always will. Although we like to hope that a time will come when no one will believe that people come in types and that each type belongs with its own kind, I doubt such a day will ever arrive. By all indications, *Homo sapiens* is a tribal species for whom "us versus them" comes naturally and must be continually pushed back. Where there is genuine freedom of expression, there will be racist expression. There will also be people who believe that homosexuals are sick or threaten children or—especially among teenagers—are rightful targets of manly savagery. Homosexuality will always be incomprehensible to most people, and what is incomprehensible is feared. As for anti-Semitism, it appears to be a hardier virus than influenza. If you want pluralism, then you get racism and sexism and homophobia, and communism and fascism and xenophobia and tribalism, and that is just for a start. If you want to believe in intellectual freedom and the progress of knowledge and the advancement of science and all those other good things, then you must swallow hard and accept this: for as thickheaded and wayward an animal as us, the realistic question is how to make the best of prejudice, not how to eradicate it.

Indeed, "eradicating prejudice" is so vague a proposition as to be meaningless. Distinguishing prejudice reliably and nonpolitically from non-prejudice, or even defining it crisply, is quite hopeless. We all feel we know prejudice when we see it. But do we? At the University of Michigan, a student said in a classroom discussion that he considered homosexuality a disease treatable with therapy. He was summoned to a formal disciplinary hearing for violating the school's policy against speech that "victimizes" people based on "sexual orientation." Now, the evidence is abundant that this particular hypothesis is wrong, and any American homosexual can attest to the harm that the student's hypothesis has inflicted on many real people. But was it a statement of prejudice or of misguided belief? Hate speech or hypothesis? Many Americans who do not regard themselves as bigots or haters believe that homosexuality is a treatable disease.

They may be wrong, but are they all bigots? I am unwilling to say so, and if you are willing, beware. The line between a prejudiced belief and a merely controversial one is elusive, and the harder you look the more elusive it becomes. "God hates homosexuals" is a statement of fact, not of bias, to those who believe it; "American criminals are disproportionately black" is a statement of bias, not of fact, to those who disbelieve it.

Who is right? You may decide, and so may others, and there is no need to agree. That is the great innovation of intellectual pluralism . . . We cannot know in advance or for sure which belief is prejudice and which is truth, but to advance knowledge we don't need to know. The genius of intellectual pluralism lies not in doing away with prejudices and dogmas but in channeling them—making them socially productive by pitting prejudice against prejudice and dogma against dogma, exposing all to withering public criticism. What survives at the end of the day is our base of knowledge.

*   *   *

Pluralism is the principle that protects and makes a place in human company for that loneliest and most vulnerable of all minorities, the minority who is hounded and despised among blacks and whites, gays and straights, who is suspect or criminal among every tribe and in every nation of the world, and yet on whom progress depends: the dissident. I am not saying that dissent is always or even usually enlightened. Most of the time it is foolish and self-serving. No dissident has the right to be taken seriously, and the fact that Aryan Nation racists or Nation of Islam anti-Semites are unorthodox does not entitle them to respect. But what goes around comes around. As a supporter of gay marriage, for example, I reject the majority's view of family, and as a Jew I reject its view of God. I try to be civil, but the fact is that most Americans regard my views on marriage as a reckless assault on the most fundamental of all institutions, and many people are more than a little discomfited by the statement "Jesus Christ was no more divine than anybody else" (which is why so few people ever say it). Trap the racists and anti-Semites, and you lay a trap for me too. Hunt for them with eradication in your mind, and you have brought dissent itself within your sights.

The new crusade against prejudice waves aside such warnings. Like earlier crusades against antisocial ideas, the mission is fueled by good (if cocksure) intentions and a genuine sense of urgency. Some kinds of error are held to be intolerable, like pollutants that even in small traces poison the water for a whole town. Some errors are so pernicious as to damage real people's lives, so wrongheaded that no person of right mind or goodwill could support them. Like their forebears of other stripe—the Church in its campaigns against heretics, the McCarthyites in their campaigns against Communists—the modern anti-racist and anti-sexist and anti-homophobic campaigners are totalists, demanding not that misguided ideas and ugly expressions be corrected or criticized but that they be eradicated. They make war not on errors but on error, and like other totalists they act in the name of public safety—the safety, especially, of minorities.

The sweeping implications of this challenge to pluralism are not, I think, well enough understood by the public at large. Indeed, the new brand of totalism has yet even to be properly named. "Multiculturalism," for instance, is much too broad. "Political correctness" comes closer but is too trendy and snide. For lack of anything else, I will call the new anti-pluralism "purism," since its major tenet is that society cannot be just until the last traces of invidious prejudice have been scrubbed away. Whatever you call it, the purists' way of seeing things has spread through American intellectual life with remarkable speed, so much so that many people will blink at you uncomprehendingly or even call you a racist (or sexist or homophobe, etc.) if you suggest that expressions of racism should be tolerated or that prejudice has its part to play.

The new purism sets out, to begin with, on a campaign against words, for words are the currency of prejudice, and if prejudice is hurtful then so must be prejudiced words. "We are not safe when these violent words are among us," wrote Mari Matsuda, then a UCLA law professor. Here one imagines gangs of racist words swinging chains and smashing heads in back alleys. To suppress bigoted language seems, at first blush, reasonable, but it quickly leads to a curious result. A peculiar kind of verbal shamanism takes root, as though certain expressions, like curses or magical incantations, carry in themselves the power to hurt or heal—as though words were bigoted rather than people. "Context is everything," people have always said. The use of the word "nigger" in *Huckleberry Finn* does not make the book an "act" of hate speech—or does it? In the new view, this is no longer so clear. The very utterance of the word "nigger" (at least by a non-black) is a racist act. When a *Sacramento Bee* cartoonist put the word "nigger" mockingly in the mouth of a white supremacist, there were howls of protest and 1,400 canceled subscriptions and an editorial apology, even though the word was plainly being invoked against racists, not against blacks.

Faced with escalating demands of verbal absolutism, newspapers issue lists of forbidden words. The expressions "gyp" (derived from "Gypsy") and "Dutch treat" were among the dozens of terms stricken as "offensive" in a much-ridiculed (and later withdrawn) *Los Angeles Times* speech code. The University of Missouri journalism school issued a *Dictionary of Cautionary Words and Phrases*, which included "*Buxom*: Offensive reference to a woman's chest. Do not use. See 'Woman.' *Codger*: Offensive reference to a senior citizen."

As was bound to happen, purists soon discovered that chasing around after words like "gyp" or "buxom" hardly goes to the roots of the problem. As long as they remain bigoted, bigots will simply find other words. If they can't call you a kike then they will say Jewboy, Judas, or Hebe, and when all those are banned they will press words like "oven" and "lamp-shade" into their service. The vocabulary of hate is potentially as rich as your dictionary, and all you do by banning language used by cretins is to let them decide what the rest of us may say. The problem, some purists have concluded, must therefore go much deeper than laws: it must go to the deeper level of ideas. Racism, sexism, homophobia, and the rest must be built into the very structure of American society and American patterns of thought, so pervasive yet so insidious that, like water to a fish, they are both omnipresent and unseen. The mere existence of prejudice constructs a society whose very nature is prejudiced.

This line of thinking was pioneered by feminists, who argued that pornography, more than just being expressive, is an act by which men construct an oppressive society. Racial activists quickly picked up the argument. Racist expressions are themselves acts of oppression, they said. "All racist speech constructs the social reality that constrains the liberty of nonwhites because of their race," wrote Charles R. Lawrence III, then a law professor at Stanford. From the purist point of view, a society with even one racist is a racist society, because the idea itself threatens and demeans its targets. They cannot feel wholly safe or wholly welcome as long as racism is present. Pluralism says: There will always be some racists. Marginalize them, ignore them, exploit them, ridicule them, take pains to make their policies illegal, but otherwise leave them alone. Purists say: That's not enough. Society cannot be just until these pervasive and oppressive ideas are searched out and eradicated.

And so what is now under way is a growing drive to eliminate prejudice from every corner of society. I doubt that many people have noticed how far-reaching this anti-pluralist movement is becoming.

In universities: Dozens of universities have adopted codes proscribing speech or other expression that (this is from Stanford's policy, which is more or less representative) "is intended to insult or stigmatize an individual or a small number of individuals on the basis of their sex, race, color, handicap, religion, sexual orientation or national and ethnic origin." Some codes punish only persistent harassment of a targeted individual, but many, following the purist doctrine that even one racist is too many, go much further. At Penn, an administrator declared: "We at the University of Pennsylvania have guaranteed students and the community that they can live in a community free of sexism, racism, and homophobia." Here is the purism that gives "political correctness" its distinctive combination of puffy high-mindedness and authoritarian zeal.

In school curricula: "More fundamental than eliminating racial segregation has to be the removal of racist thinking, assumptions, symbols, and materials in the curriculum," writes theorist Molefi Kete Asante. In practice, the effort to "remove racist thinking" goes well beyond striking egregious references from textbooks. In many cases it becomes a kind of mental engineering in which students are encouraged to see prejudice everywhere; it includes teaching identity politics as an antidote to internalized racism; it rejects mainstream science as "white male" thinking; and it tampers with history, installing such dubious notions as that the ancient Greeks stole their culture from Africa or that an ancient carving of a bird is an example of "African experimental aeronautics."

In criminal law: Consider two crimes. In each, I am beaten brutally; in each, my jaw is smashed and my skull is split in just the same way. However, in the first crime my assailant calls me an "asshole"; in the second he calls me a "queer." In most states, in many localities, and, as of September 1994, in federal cases, these two crimes are treated differently: the crime motivated by bias—or deemed to be so motivated by prosecutors and juries—gets a stiffer punishment. "Longer prison terms for bigots," shrilled Brooklyn Democratic Congressman Charles Schumer, who introduced the federal hate-crimes legislation, and those are what the law now provides. Evidence that the assailant holds prejudiced beliefs, even if he doesn't actually express them while committing an offense, can serve to elevate the crime. Defendants in hate-crimes cases may be grilled on how many black friends they have and whether they have told racist jokes. To increase a prison sentence only because of the defendant's "prejudice" (as gauged by prosecutor and jury) is, of course, to try minds and punish beliefs. Purists say, Well, they are dangerous minds and poisonous beliefs.

In the workplace: Though government cannot constitutionally suppress bigotry directly, it is now busy doing so indirectly by requiring employers to eliminate prejudice. Since the early 1980s, courts and the Equal Employment Opportunity Commission have moved to bar workplace speech deemed to create a hostile or abusive working environment for minorities. The law, held a federal court in 1988, "does require that an employer take prompt action to prevent . . . bigots from expressing their opinions in a way that abuses or offends their co-workers," so as to achieve "the goal of eliminating prejudices and biases from our society." So it was, as UCLA law professor Eugene Volokh notes, that the EEOC charged that a manufacturer's ads using admittedly accurate depictions of samurai, kabuki, and sumo were "racist" and "offensive to people of Japanese origin"; that a Pennsylvania court found that an employer's printing Bible verses on paychecks was religious harassment of Jewish employees; that an employer had to desist using gender-based job titles like "foreman" and "draftsman" after a female employee sued.

On and on the campaign goes, darting from one outbreak of prejudice to another like a cat chasing flies. In the American Bar Association, activists demand that lawyers who express "bias or prejudice" be penalized. In the Education Department, the civil-rights office presses for a ban on computer bulletin board comments that "show hostility toward a person or group based on sex, race or color, including slurs, negative stereotypes, jokes or pranks." In its security checks for government jobs, the FBI takes to asking whether applicants are "free of biases against any class of citizens," whether, for instance, they have told racist jokes or indicated other "prejudices." Joke police! George Orwell, grasping the close relationship of jokes to dissent, said that every joke is a tiny revolution. The purists will have no such rebellions.

The purist campaign reaches, in the end, into the mind itself. In a lecture at the University of New Hampshire, a professor compared writing to sex ("You and the subject become one"); he was suspended and required to apologize, but what was most insidious was the order to undergo university-approved counseling to have his mind straightened out. At the University of Pennsylvania, a law lecturer said, "We have ex-slaves here who should know about the Thirteenth Amendment"; he was banished from campus for a year and required to make a public apology, and he, too, was compelled to attend a "sensitivity and racial awareness" session. Mandatory re-education of alleged bigots is the natural consequence of intellectual purism. Prejudice must be eliminated!

* * * "Nobody escapes," said a Rutgers University report on campus prejudice. Bias and prejudice, it found, cross every conceivable line, from sex to race to politics: "No matter who you are, no matter what the color of your skin, no matter what your gender or sexual orientation, no matter what you believe, no matter how you behave, there is somebody out there who doesn't like people of your kind." Charles Lawrence writes: "Racism is ubiquitous. We are all racists." If he means that most of us think racist thoughts of some sort at one time or another, he is right. If we are going to "eliminate prejudices and biases from our society," then the work of the prejudice police is unending. They are doomed to hunt and hunt and hunt, scour and scour and scour.

What is especially dismaying is that the purists pursue prejudice in the name of protecting minorities. In order to protect people like me (homosexual), they must pursue people like me (dissident). In order to bolster minority self-esteem, they suppress minority opinion. There are, of course, all kinds of practical and legal problems with the purists' campaign: the incursions against the First Amendment; the inevitable abuses by prosecutors and activists who define as "hateful" or "violent" whatever speech they dislike or can score points off of; the lack of any evidence that repressing prejudice eliminates rather than inflames it. But minorities, of all people, ought to remember that by definition we cannot prevail by numbers, and we generally cannot prevail by force. Against the power of ignorant mass opinion and group prejudice and superstition, we have only our voices. If you doubt that minorities' voices are powerful weapons, think of the lengths to which Southern officials went to silence the Reverend Martin Luther King, Jr. (recall that the city commissioner of Montgomery, Alabama, won a $500,000 libel suit, later overturned in *New York Times v. Sullivan* [1964], regarding an advertisement in the *Times* placed by civil-rights leaders who denounced the Montgomery police). Think of how much gay people have improved their lot over twenty-five years simply by refusing to remain silent. Recall the Michigan student who was prosecuted for saying that homosexuality is a treatable disease, and notice that he was black. Under that Michigan speech code, more than twenty blacks were charged with racist speech, while no instance of racist speech by whites was punished. In Florida, the hate-speech law was invoked against a black man who called a policeman a "white cracker"; not so surprisingly, in the first hate-crimes case to reach the Supreme Court, the victim was white and the defendant black.

In the escalating war against "prejudice," the right is already learning to play by the rules that were pioneered by the purist activists of the left. Last year leading Democrats, including the President, criticized the Republican Party for being increasingly in the thrall of the Christian right. Some of the rhetoric was harsh ("fire-breathing Christian radical right"), but it wasn't vicious or even clearly wrong. Never mind: when Democratic Representative Vic Fazio said Republicans were "being forced to the fringes by the aggressive political tactics of the religious right," the chairman of the Republican National Committee, Haley Barbour, said, "Christian-bashing" was "the left's preferred form of religious bigotry." Bigotry! Prejudice! "Christians active in politics are now on the receiving end of an extraordinary campaign of bias and prejudice," said the conservative leader William J. Bennett. One discerns, here, where the new purism leads. Eventually, any criticism of any group will be "prejudice."

DISCUSSION QUESTIONS

1. Do you agree or disagree that some groups need to be protected against offensive or hurtful ideas or speech? How do you define "hurtful" or "offensive"? What is the basis for your position? Where is the First Amendment in this debate?

2. Would a campus newspaper be justified in rejecting a paid advertisement from (a) a group or individual that denied the Holocaust had occurred; (b) a group or individual that argued against any sort of affirmative action; or (c) an environmental group that advocated violence against the property of corporations that polluted the environment? Would you support a "speech code" that prohibited someone from making these arguments on campus? Defend your answer.

Debating the Issues: Same-Sex Marriage

One of the most controversial and politically significant civil rights issues in the past few years is same-sex marriage. As of this writing, there are twelve states and the District of Columbia in which same-sex marriage is legal and ten others that recognize same-sex civil unions. In 2012, Maine, Maryland, and Washington became the first states to approve same-sex marriage through a referendum, and voters in Minnesota rejected a constitutional amendment that would have defined marriage as applying only to heterosexual couples.

Marriage has both religious and legal ramifications. As a legal matter, marriage comes with a set of rights and obligations: married couples pay a lower marginal tax rate (though two-income couples can face a "marriage penalty," in which the total tax paid for a couple filing jointly can be more than the sum of the taxes they would have paid if they were single); automatically enjoy insurance and pension benefits that are extended to families; have inheritance rights when one spouse dies; and so on. Apart from the concrete legal benefits, marriage implies a societal recognition of the legitimacy and value of a relationship. There are obligations as well, primarily from the consequences of ending a marriage through divorce.

The main argument against same-sex marriage is that it upends a longstanding and stable institution that has been central to social stability and families. Traditionalists argue that marriage has always involved one man and one woman, an arrangement that is vital for raising children. Woven into this is the view of many that homosexuality is immoral or contrary to religious tenets, and a "slippery slope" argument that recognizing same-sex marriage would inevitably lead to further redefinitions like polygamy. Supporters counter that the definition of marriage has always been evolving, and that the arguments against same-sex marriage are no different than earlier opposition to interracial marriage. Public opinion on the issue is changing rapidly. A number of public opinion polls taken in 2012 show a slight majority in favor of legalizing same-sex marriage, with the percentages supporting it ranging from about 50 percent to 54 percent (as opposed to around 35–45 percent supporting it over the previous decade). There is a huge generational difference in these views. A poll taken for the Pew Forum on Religion and Public Life found that among young people aged 18–29, 62 percent favored gay marriage, as opposed to only 32 percent of those over 65.

Ross Douthat rejects some of the standard arguments against same-sex marriage, but still argues for the ideal of marriage as being between a man and a woman. If society gives up on this ideal, he says, "we're giving up on one of the great ideas of Western civilization: the celebration of lifelong heterosexual monogamy as a unique and indispensable estate. That ideal is still worth honoring, and still worth striving to preserve." Douthat recognizes that our society has already moved away from that ideal with no-fault divorces, out-of-wedlock births, and serial monogamy, yet he believes the ideal is still important.

Justin Raimando offers a libertarian case against same-sex marriage. Libertarians believe in limited government and individual rights. In the extreme, libertarians believe that the government messes up everything that it touches. Raimando argues that same-sex marriage is no different. If the government were to endorse same-sex marriage, he says this "would not only be a setback for liberty but a disaster for those it supposedly benefits: gay people themselves." Raimando is also critical of the shift in the gay rights movement from fighting against the oppressive state, to adopting the approach of the civil rights movement and seeking the protection of the state from private sector discrimination.

Jonathan Rauch suggests two reasons why people are opposed to same-sex marriage: the simple anti-homosexual position and the not-so-simple view based on tradition. The latter is rooted in the gut-level feeling that marriage between two men or two women is simply wrong because marriage has always been between a man and a woman: no law can change this basic institution because it has roots that are deeper and older than any government or law (which comes pretty close to Douthat's view). Rauch situates this argument within the political thought of F.A. Hayek, one of the great conservative thinkers of the twentieth century. Hayek warns that changing traditions and customs may lead to social chaos. This is precisely one of the arguments made against same-sex marriage: it will undermine the institution of marriage. Rauch replies that other changes have had a far greater impact on undermining the institution of marriage, such as allowing women to own property, the abolition of arranged marriages, legalized contraception, and "no-fault" divorce law. While recognizing the legitimacy of the concerns about same-sex marriage, Rauch concludes that the fears of its negative impact are overstated and the benefits of same-sex marriage for gays and lesbians outweigh the costs for heterosexuals.

21

"The Marriage Ideal"

Ross Douthat

Here are some commonplace arguments against gay marriage: Marriage is an ancient institution that has always been defined as the union of one man and one woman, and we meddle with that definition at our peril. Lifelong heterosexual monogamy is natural; gay relationships are not. The nuclear family is the universal, time-tested path to forming families and raising children.

These have been losing arguments for decades now, as the cause of gay marriage has moved from an eccentric-seeming notion to an idea that roughly half the country supports. And they were losing arguments again last week, when California's Judge Vaughn Walker ruled that laws defining marriage as a heterosexual union are unconstitutional, irrational, and unjust.

These arguments have lost because they're wrong. What we think of as "traditional marriage" is not universal. The default family arrangement in many cultures, modern as well as ancient, has been polygamy, not monogamy. The default mode of child-rearing is often communal, rather than two parents nurturing their biological children.

Nor is lifelong heterosexual monogamy obviously natural in the way that most Americans understand the term. If "natural" is defined to mean "congruent with our biological instincts," it's arguably one of the more unnatural arrangements imaginable. In crudely Darwinian terms, it cuts against both the male impulse toward promiscuity and the female interest in mating with the highest-status male available. Hence the historic prevalence of polygamy. And hence many societies' tolerance for more flexible alternatives, from concubinage and prostitution to temporary arrangements like the "traveler's marriages" sanctioned in some parts of the Islamic world.

So what are gay marriage's opponents really defending, if not some universal, biologically inevitable institution? It's a particular vision of marriage, rooted in a particular tradition, that establishes a particular sexual ideal.

This ideal holds up the commitment to lifelong fidelity and support by two sexually different human beings—a commitment that involves the mutual surrender, arguably, of their reproductive self-interest—as a uniquely admirable kind of relationship. It holds up the domestic life that can be created only by such unions, in which children grow up in intimate contact with both of their biological parents, as a uniquely admirable approach to child-rearing. And recognizing the difficulty of achieving these goals, it surrounds wedlock with a distinctive set of rituals, sanctions, and taboos.

The point of this ideal is not that other relationships have no value, or that only nuclear families can rear children successfully. Rather, it's that lifelong heterosexual monogamy at its best can offer something distinctive and remarkable—a microcosm of civilization, and an organic connection between human generations—that makes it worthy of distinctive recognition and support.

Again, this is not how many cultures approach marriage. It's a particularly Western understanding, derived from Jewish and Christian beliefs about the order of creation, and supplemented by later ideas about romantic love, the rights of children, and the equality of the sexes.

Or at least, it *was* the Western understanding. Lately, it has come to co-exist with a less idealistic, more accommodating approach, defined by no-fault divorce, frequent out-of-wedlock births, and serial monogamy.

In this landscape, gay-marriage critics who fret about a slippery slope to polygamy miss the point. Americans already have a kind of postmodern polygamy available to them. It's just spread over the course of a lifetime, rather than concentrated in a "Big Love"-style menage.

If this newer order completely vanquishes the older marital ideal, then gay marriage will become not only acceptable but morally necessary. The lifelong commitment of a gay couple is more impressive than the serial monogamy of straights. And a culture in which weddings are optional celebrations of romantic love, only tangentially connected to procreation, has no business discriminating against the love of homosexuals.

But if we just accept this shift, we're giving up on one of the great ideas of Western civilization: the celebration of lifelong heterosexual monogamy as a unique and indispensable estate. That ideal is still worth honoring, and still worth striving to preserve. And preserving it ultimately requires some public acknowledgment that heterosexual unions and gay relationships are different: similar in emotional commitment, but distinct both in their challenges and their potential fruit.

But based on Judge Walker's logic—which suggests that any such distinction is bigoted and un-American—I don't think a society that declares gay marriage to be a fundamental right will be capable of even entertaining this idea.

22

"The Libertarian Case Against Gay Marriage"

Justin Raimondo

Opponents of same-sex marriage have marshaled all sorts of arguments to make their case, from the rather alarmist view that it would de-sanctify and ultimately destroy heterosexual marriage to the assertion that it would logically lead to polygamy and the downfall of Western civilization. None of these arguments—to my mind, at least—make the least amount of sense, and they have all been singularly ineffective in beating back the rising tide of sentiment in favor of allowing same-sex couples the "right" to marry.

The problem with these arguments is that they are all rooted in religion or in some secular concept of morality alien to American culture in the 21st century—a culture that is characterized by relativism, impiety, and a preoccupation with other matters that make this issue less pressing than it otherwise might be. Yet there is an effective conservative—or rather libertarian—case to be made against legalizing gay marriage, one that can be summarized by the old aphorism: be careful what you ask for because you just might get it.

The imposition of a legal framework on the intricate web of relationships that have previously existed in the realm of freedom—that is, outside the law and entirely dependent on the trust and compliance of the individuals involved—would not only be a setback for liberty but a disaster for those it supposedly benefits: gay people themselves.

Of course, we already have gay marriages. Just as heterosexual marriage, as an institution, preceded the invention of the state, so the homosexual version existed long before anyone thought to give it legal sanction. Extending the authority of the state into territory previously untouched by its tender ministrations, legalizing relationships that had developed and been found rewarding entirely without this imprimatur, would wreak havoc where harmony once prevailed. Imagine a relationship of some duration in which one partner, the breadwinner, had supported his or her partner without much thought about the economics of the matter: one had stayed home and tended the house, while the other had been in the workforce, bringing home the bacon. This division of labor had prevailed for many years, not requiring any written contract or threat of legal action to enforce its provisions.

Then, suddenly, they are legally married—or, in certain states, considered married under the common law. This changes the relationship, and not for the better. For now the property of the breadwinner is not his or her own: half of it belongs to the stay-at-home. Before when they argued, money was never an issue: now, when the going gets rough, the threat of divorce—and the specter of alimony—hangs over the relationship, and the mere possibility casts its dark shadow over what had once been a sunlit field.

If and when gay marriage comes to pass, its advocates will have a much harder time convincing their fellow homosexuals to exercise their "right" than they did in persuading the rest of the country to grant it. That's because they have never explained—and never could explain—why it would make sense for gays to entangle themselves in a regulatory web and risk getting into legal disputes over divorce, alimony, and the division of property.

Marriage evolved because of the existence of children: without them, the institution loses its biological, economic, and historical basis, its very reason for being. This is not to say childless couples—including gay couples—are any less worthy (or less married) than others. It means only that they are not bound by necessity to a mutual commitment involving the ongoing investment of considerable resources.

From two sets of given circumstances, two parallel traditions have evolved: one, centered around the rearing of children, is heterosexual marriage, the habits and rules of which have been recognized and formalized by the state. The reason for this recognition is simple: the welfare of the children, who must be protected from neglect and abuse.

The various childless unions and alternative relationships that are an increasing factor in modern society have evolved informally, with minimal state intervention. Rather than anchored by necessity, they are governed by the centrality of freedom.

The prospect of freedom—not only from traditional moral restraints but from legal burdens and responsibilities—is part of what made homosexuality appealing in the early days of the gay liberation movement. At any rate, society's lack of interest in formalizing the love lives of the nation's homosexuals did not result in any decrease in homosexuality or make it any less visible. Indeed, if the experience of the past thirty years means anything, quite the opposite is the case. By superimposing the legal and social constraints of heterosexual marriage on gay relationships, we will succeed only in de-eroticizing them. Are gay marriage advocates trying to take the gayness out of homosexuality?

The gay rights movement took its cues from the civil rights movement, modeling its grievances on those advanced by the moderate wing led by Dr. Martin Luther King and crafting a legislative agenda borrowed from the NAACP and allied organizations: the passage of anti-discrimination laws—covering housing, employment, and public accommodations—at the local and national level. Efforts to institutionalize gay marriage have followed this course, with "equality" as the goal.

But the civil rights paradigm never really fit: unlike most African Americans, lesbians and gay men can render their minority status invisible. Furthermore, their economic status is not analogous—indeed, there are studies that show gay men, at least, are economically better off on average than heterosexuals. They tend to be better educated, have better jobs, and these days are not at all what one could call an oppressed minority. According to GayAgenda.com, "studies show that [gay] Americans are twice as likely to have graduated from college, twice as likely to have an individual income over $60,000 and twice as likely to have a household income of $250,000 or more."

Gays an oppressed minority group? I don't think so.

The gay liberation movement started as a protest against state oppression. The earliest gay rights organizations, such as the Mattachine Society and the Daughters of Bilitis, sought to legalize homosexual activity, then illegal per se. The movement was radicalized in the 1960s over police harassment. A gay bar on New York City's Christopher Street, known as the Stonewall, was the scene of a three-day riot provoked by a police raid. Tired of being subjected to continual assault by the boys in blue, gay people fought back—and won. At the time, gay bars were under general attack from the New York State Liquor Authority, which pulled licenses as soon as a bar's reputation as a gay gathering place became apparent. Activists of that era concentrated their fire on the issues that really mattered to the gay person in the street: the legalization of homosexual conduct and the protection of gay institutions.

As gay activists grew older, however, and began to channel their political energy into the Democratic Party, they entered a new and more "moderate" phase. Instead of celebrating their unique identity and history, they undertook the arid quest for equality—which meant, in practice, battling "discrimination" in employment and housing, a marginal issue for most gay people—and finally taking up the crusade for gay marriage.

Instead of battling the state, they began to use the state against their perceived enemies. As it became fashionable and politically correct to be "pro-gay," a propaganda campaign was undertaken in the public schools, epitomized by the infamous "Rainbow Curriculum" and the equally notorious tome for tots *Heather Has Two Mommies*. For liberals, who see the state not as Nietzsche's "cold monster" but as a warm and caring therapist who is there to help, this was only natural. The Therapeutic State, after all, is meant to transform society into a liberal Utopia where no one judges anyone and everyone listens to NPR.

These legislative efforts are largely educational: once enacted, anti-discrimination ordinances in housing, for example, are meant to show that the state is taking a side and indirectly teaching citizens a lesson—that it's wrong to discriminate against gays. The reality on the ground, however, is a different matter: since there's no way to know if one is being discriminated against on account of one's presumed sexuality—and since gays have the choice not to divulge that information—it is impossible to be sure if such discrimination has occurred, short of a "No Gays Need Apply" sign on the door. Moreover, landlords, even the bigots among them, are hardly upset when a couple of gays move in, fix up the place to look like something out of *House & Garden*, and pay the rent on time. The homosexual agenda of today has little relevance to the way gay people actually live their lives.

But the legislative agenda of the modern gay rights movement is not meant to be useful to the gay person in the street: it is meant to garner support from heterosexual liberals and others with access to power. It is meant to assure the careers of aspiring gay politicos and boost the fortunes of the left wing of the Democratic Party. The gay marriage campaign is the culmination of this distancing trend, the *reductio ad absurdum* of the civil rights paradigm.

The modern gay-rights movement is all about securing the symbols of societal acceptance. It is a defensive strategy, one that attempts to define homosexuals as an officially sanctioned victim group afflicted with an inherent disability, a disadvantage that must be compensated for legislatively. But if "gay pride" means anything, it means not wanting, needing, or seeking any sort of acceptance but self-acceptance. Marriage is a social institution designed by heterosexuals for heterosexuals: Why should gay people settle for their cast-off hand-me-downs?

23

"Objections to These Unions"

Jonathan Rauch

There are only two objections to same-sex marriage that are intellectually honest and internally consistent. One is the simple anti-gay position: "It is the law's job to stigmatize and disadvantage homosexuals, and the marriage ban is a means to that end." The other is the argument from tradition—which turns out, on inspection, not to be so simple.

Many Americans may agree that there are plausible, even compelling, reasons to allow same-sex marriage, and that many of the objections to such unions are overwrought, unfair, or misguided. And yet they draw back. They have reservations that are hard to pin down but that seem not a whit less powerful for that. They may cite religion or culture, but the roots of their misgivings go even deeper. Press them, and they might say something like this:

"I understand how hard it must be to live a marriageless life, or at least I try to understand. I see that some of the objections to same-sex marriage are more about excluding gays than about defending marriage. Believe me, I am no homophobe; I want gay people to have joy and comfort. I respect their relationships and their love, even if they are not what I would want for myself.

"But look. No matter how I come at this question, I keep bumping into the same wall. For the entire history of civilization, marriage has been between men and women. In every religion, every culture, every society—maybe with some minor and rare exceptions, none of them part of our own heritage—marriage has been reserved for the union of male and female. All the words in the world cannot change that. Same-sex marriage would not be an incremental tweak but a radical reform, a break with all of Western history.

"I'm sorry. I am not prepared to take that step, not when we are talking about civilization's bedrock institution. I don't know that I can even give you good reasons. It is just that what you are asking for is too much."

Perhaps it doesn't matter what marriage is for, or perhaps we can't know exactly what marriage is for. Perhaps it is enough simply to say that marriage is as it is, and you can't just make it something else. I call this the Hayekian argument, for Friedrich August von Hayek, one of the 20th century's great economists and philosophers.

Hayek the Conservative?

Hayek—Austrian by birth, British by adoption, winner of the 1974 Nobel Memorial Prize in Economic Sciences—is generally known as one of the leading theoreticians of free market economics and, more broadly, of libertarian (he always said "liberal") social thought. He was eloquent in his defense of the dynamic change that markets bring, but many people are less aware of a deeply traditionalist, conservative strand in his thinking, a strand that traces its lineage back at least to Edmund Burke, the 18th-century English philosopher and politician. Burke famously poured scorn on the French Revolution and its claims to be inventing a new and enlightened social order. The attempt to reinvent society on abstract principles would result not in Utopia, he contended, but in tyranny. For Burke, the existing order might be flawed, even in some respects evil, but it had an organic sense to it; throwing the whole system out the window would bring greater flaws and larger evils.

Outside Britain and America, few people listened. The French Revolution inspired generations of reformers to propose their own Utopian social experiments. Communism was one such, fascism another; today, radical Islamism (the political philosophy, not the religion) is yet one more. "The attempt to make heaven on earth invariably produces hell," wrote Karl Popper, another great Austrian-British philosopher, in 1945, when the totalitarian night looked darkest. He and Hayek came of age in the same intellectual climate, when not only Marxists and fascists but many mainstream Western intellectuals took for granted that a handful of smart people could make better social decisions than could chaotic markets, blind traditions, or crude majorities.

It was in opposition to this "fatal conceit," as he called it, that Hayek organized much of his career. He vigorously argued the case for the dynamism and "spontaneous order" of free markets, but he asserted just as vigorously that the dynamism and freedom of constant change were possible only within a restraining framework of rules and customs and institutions that, for the most part, do not change, or change at a speed they themselves set. No expert or political leader can possibly have enough knowledge to get up every morning and order the world from scratch; decide whether to wear clothing, which side of the street to drive on, what counts as mine and what as yours. "Every man growing up in a given culture will find in himself rules, or may discover that he acts in accordance with rules and will similarly recognize the actions of others as conforming or not conforming to various rules," Hayek wrote in *Law, Legislation, and Liberty*. The rules, he added, are not necessarily innate or unchangeable, but "they are part of a cultural heritage which is likely to be fairly constant, especially so long as they are not articulated in words and therefore also are not discussed or consciously examined."

Tradition Over Reason

Hayek the economist is famous for the insight that, in a market system, the prices generated by impersonal forces may not make sense from any one person's point of view, but they encode far more economic information than even the cleverest person or the most powerful computer could ever hope to organize. In a similar fashion, Hayek the social philosopher wrote that human societies' complicated web of culture, traditions, and institutions embodies far more cultural knowledge than any one person could master. Like prices, the customs generated by societies over time may seem irrational or arbitrary. But the very fact that these customs have evolved and survived to come down to us implies that a practical logic may be embedded in them that might not be apparent from even a sophisticated analysis. And the web of custom cannot be torn apart and reordered at will, because once its internal logic is violated it may fall apart.

It was on this point that Hayek was particularly outspoken: Intellectuals and visionaries who seek to deconstruct and rationally rebuild social traditions will produce not a better order but chaos. In his 1952 book *The Counter-Revolution of Science: Studies in the Abuse of Reason*, Hayek made a statement that demands to be quoted in full and read at least twice:

It may indeed prove to be far the most difficult and not the least important task for human reason rationally to comprehend its own limitations. It is essential for the growth of reason that as individuals we should bow to forces and obey principles which we cannot hope fully to understand, yet on which the advance and even the preservation of civilization depends. Historically this has been achieved by the influence of the various religious creeds and by traditions and superstitions which made man submit to those forces by an appeal to his emotions rather than to his reason. The most dangerous stage in the growth of civilization may well be that in which man has come to regard all these beliefs as superstitions and refuses to accept or to submit to anything which he does not rationally understand. The rationalist whose reason is not sufficient to teach him those limitations of the powers of conscious reason, and who despises all the institutions and customs which have not been consciously designed, would thus become the destroyer of the civilization built upon them. This may well prove a hurdle which man will repeatedly reach, only to be thrown back into barbarism.

For secular intellectuals who are unhappy with the evolved framework of marriage and who are excluded from it—in other words, for people like me—the Hayekian argument is very challenging. The age-old stigmas attached to illegitimacy and out-of-wedlock pregnancy were crude and unfair to women and children. On the male side, shotgun marriages were coercive and intrusive and often made poor matches. The shame associated with divorce seemed to make no sense at all. But when modern societies abolished the stigmas on illegitimacy, divorce, and all the rest, whole portions of the social structure just caved in.

Not long ago I had dinner with a friend who is a devout Christian. He has a heart of gold, knows and likes gay people, and has warmed to the idea of civil unions. But when I asked him about gay marriage, he replied with a firm no. I asked if he imagined there was anything I could say that might budge him. He thought for a moment and then said no again. Why? Because, he said, male-female marriage is a sacrament from God. It predates the Constitution and every other law of man. We could not, in that sense, change it even if we wanted to. I asked if it might alter his conclusion to reflect that legal marriage is a secular institution, that the separation of church and state requires us to distinguish God's law from civil law, and that we must refrain from using law to impose one group's religious precepts on the rest of society. He shook his head. No, he said. This is bigger than that.

I felt he had not answered my argument. His God is not mine, and in a secular country, law can and should be influenced by religious teachings but must not enforce them. Yet in a deeper way, it was I who had not answered his argument. No doubt the government has the right to set the law of marriage without kowtowing to, say, the Vatican. But that does not make it wise for the government to disregard the centuries of tradition—of accumulated social knowledge—that the teachings of the world's great religions embody. None of those religions sanctions same-sex marriage.

My friend understood the church-state distinction perfectly well. He was saying there are traditions and traditions. Male-female marriage is one of the most hallowed. Whether you call it a sacrament from God or part of Western civilization's cultural DNA, you are saying essentially the same thing: that for many people a same-sex union, whatever else it may be, can never be a marriage, and that no judge or legislature can change this fact.

Here the advocates of same-sex marriage face peril coming from two directions. On the one side, the Hayekian argument warns of unintended and perhaps grave social consequences if, thinking we're smarter than our customs, we decide to rearrange the core elements of marriage. The current rules for marriage may not be the best ones, and they may even be unfair. But they are all we have, and you cannot reengineer the formula without causing unforeseen results, possibly including the implosion of the institution itself. On the other side, political realism warns that we could do serious damage to the legitimacy of marital law if we rewrote it with disregard for what a large share of Americans recognize as marriage.

If some state passed a law allowing you to marry a Volkswagen, the result would be to make a joke of the law. Certainly legal gay marriage would not seem so silly, but people who found it offensive or illegitimate might just ignore it or, in effect, boycott it. Civil and social marriage would fall out of step. That might not be the end of the world—the vast majority of marriages would be just as they were before—but it could not do marriage, or the law any good either. In such an environment, same-sex marriage would offer little beyond legal arrangements that could be provided just as well through civil unions, and it would come at a price in diminished respect for the law.

Call those, then, the problem of unintended consequences and the problem of legitimacy. They are the toughest problems same-sex marriage has to contend with. But they are not intractable.

The Decoy of Traditional Marriage

The Hayekian position really comes in two quite different versions, one much more sweeping than the other. In its strong version, the Hayekian argument implies that no reforms of longstanding institutions or customs should ever be undertaken, because any legal or political meddling would interfere with the natural evolution of social mores. One would thus have had to say, a century and a half ago, that slavery should not be abolished, because it was customary in almost all human societies. More recently, one would have had to say that the federal government was wrong to step in and end racial segregation instead of letting it evolve at its own pace.

Obviously, neither Hayek nor any reputable follower of his would defend every cultural practice simply on the grounds that it must exist for a reason.

Hayekians would point out that slavery violated a fundamental tenet of justice and was intolerably cruel. In calling for slavery's abolition, they would do what they must do to be human: They would establish a moral standpoint from which to judge social rules and reforms. They thus would acknowledge that sometimes society must make changes in the name of fairness or decency, even if there are bound to be hidden costs.

If the ban on same-sex marriage were only mildly unfair or if the costs of lifting it were certain to be catastrophic, then the ban could stand on Hayekian grounds. But if there is any social policy today that has a claim to being scaldingly inhumane, it is the ban on gay marriage. Marriage, after all, is the most fundamental institution of society and, for most people, an indispensable element of the pursuit of happiness. For the same reason that tinkering with marriage should not be undertaken lightly (marriage is important to personal and social well-being), barring a whole class of people from marrying imposes an extraordinary deprivation. Not so long ago, it was illegal in certain parts of the United States for blacks to marry whites; no one would call this a trivial disfranchisement. For many years, the champions of women's suffrage were patted on the head and told, "Your rallies and petitions are all very charming, but you don't really need to vote, do you?" It didn't wash. The strong Hayekian argument has traction only against a weak moral claim.

To rule out a moral and emotional claim as powerful as the right to marry for love, saying that bad things might happen is not enough. Bad things always might happen. People predicted that bad things would happen if contraception became legal and widespread, and indeed bad things did happen, but that did not make legalizing contraception the wrong thing to do; and, in any case, good things happened too. Unintended consequences can also be positive, after all.

Besides, by now the traditional understanding of marriage, however you define it, has been tampered with in all kinds of ways, some of them more consequential than gay marriage is likely to be. No-fault divorce dealt a severe blow to, "till death do us part," which was certainly an essential element of the traditional meaning of marriage.

It is hard to think of a bigger affront to tradition than allowing married women to own property independently of their husbands. In *What Is Marriage For?*, her history of marriage, the journalist E. J. Graff quotes a 19th-century New York legislator as saying that allowing wives to own property would affront both God and nature, "degrading the holy bonds of matrimony [and] striking at the root of those divinely ordained principles upon which is built the superstructure of our society." In 1844 a New York legislative committee said that permitting married women to control their own property would lead to "infidelity in the marriage bed, a high rate of divorce, and increased female criminality" and would turn marriage "from its high and holy purpose" into something arranged for "convenience and sensuality." A British parliamentarian denounced the proposal as "contrary not only to the law of England but to the law of God."

Graff assembles other quotations in the same vein, and goes on to add, wryly, "The funny thing, of course, is that those jeremiads were right." Allowing married women to control their economic destinies did indeed open the door to today's high divorce rates; but it also transformed marriage into something less like servitude for women and more in keeping with liberal principles of equality in personhood and citizenship.

An off-the-cuff list of fundamental changes to marriage would include not only divorce and property reform but also the abolition of polygamy, the fading of dowries, the abolition of childhood betrothals, the elimination of parents' right to choose mates for their children or to veto their children's choices, the legalization of interracial marriage, the legalization of contraception, the criminalization of marital rape (an offense that wasn't even recognized until recently), and of course the very concept of civil marriage. Surely it is unfair to say that marriage may be reformed for the sake of anyone and everyone except homosexuals, who must respect the dictates of tradition.

Some people will argue that permitting same-sex marriage would be a more fundamental change than any of the earlier ones. Perhaps so; but equally possible is that we forget today just how unnatural and destabilizing and contrary to the meaning of marriage it once seemed, for example, to put the wife on a par, legally, with the husband. Anyway, even if it is true that gay marriage constitutes a more radical definitional change than earlier innovations, in an important respect it stands out as one of the narrowest of reforms. All the earlier alterations directly affected many or all married couples, whereas same-sex marriage would directly pertain to only a small minority. It isn't certain that allowing same-sex couples to marry would have any noticeable effect on heterosexual marriage at all.

True, you never know what might happen when you tinker with tradition. A catastrophe cannot be ruled out. It is worth bearing in mind, though, that predictions of disaster if open homosexuals are integrated into traditionally straight institutions have a perfect track record: They are always wrong. When openly gay couples began making homes together in suburban neighborhoods, the result was not Sodom on every street corner; when openly gay executives began turning up in corporate jobs, stud collars did not replace neckties. I vividly remember, when I lived in London in 1995, the forecasts of morale and unit cohesion crumbling if open homosexuals were allowed to serve in the British armed forces. But when integration came (under court order), the whole thing turned out to be a nonevent. Again and again, the homosexual threat turns out to be imaginary; straights have far less to fear from gay inclusion than gays do from exclusion.

Jeopardizing Marriage's Universality

So the extreme Hayekian position—never reform anything—is untenable. And that point was made resoundingly by no less an authority than F. A. Hayek himself. In a 1960 essay called "Why I Am Not a Conservative," he took pains to argue that his position was as far from that of reactionary traditionalists as from that of utopian rationalists. "Though there is a need for a 'brake on the vehicle of progress,'" he said, "I personally cannot be content with simply helping to apply the brake." Classical liberalism, he writes, "has never been a backward-looking doctrine." To the contrary, it recognizes, as reactionary conservatism often fails to, that change is a constant and the world cannot be stopped in its tracks.

His own liberalism, Hayek wrote, "shares with conservatism a distrust of reason to the extent that the liberal is very much aware that we do not know all the answers," but the liberal, unlike the reactionary conservative, does not imagine that simply clinging to the past or "claiming the authority of supernatural sources of knowledge" is any kind of answer. We must move ahead, but humbly and with respect for our own fallibility.

And there are times, Hayek said (in *Law, Legislation, and Liberty*), when what he called "grown law" requires correction by legislation. "It may be due simply to the recognition that some past development was based on error or that it produced consequences later recognized as unjust," he wrote. "But the most frequent cause is probably that the development of the law has lain in the hands of members of a particular class whose traditional views made them regard as just what could not meet the more general requirements of justice. . . . Such occasions when it is recognized that some hereto accepted rules are unjust in the light of more general principles of justice may well require the revision not only of single rules but of whole sections of the established system of case law."

That passage, I think, could have been written with gay marriage in mind. The old view that homosexuals were heterosexuals who needed punishment or prayer or treatment has been exposed as an error. What homosexuals need is the love of another homosexual. The ban on same-sex marriage, hallowed though it is, no longer accords with liberal justice or the meaning of marriage as it is practiced today. Something has to give. Standing still is not an option.

Hayek himself, then, was a partisan of the milder version of Hayekianism. This version is not so much a prescription as an attitude. Respect tradition. Reject utopianism. Plan for mistakes rather than for perfection. If reform is needed, look for paths that follow the terrain of custom, if possible. If someone promises to remake society on rational or supernatural or theological principles, run in the opposite direction. In sum: Move ahead, but be careful.

Good advice. But not advice, particularly, against gay marriage. Remember Hayek's admonition against dogmatic conservatism. In a shifting current, holding your course can be just as dangerous as oversteering. Conservatives, in their panic to stop same-sex marriage, jeopardize marriage's universality and ultimately its legitimacy. They are taking risks, and big ones, and unnecessary ones. The liberal tradition and the *Declaration of Independence* are not currents you want to set marriage against.

It is worth recalling that Burke, the patron saint of social conservatism and the scourge of the French Revolution, supported the American Revolution. He distinguished between a revolt that aimed to overthrow established rights and principles and a revolt that aimed to restore them. Many of the American founders, incidentally, made exactly the same distinction. Whatever else they may have been, they were not Utopian social engineers. Whether a modern-day Burke or Jefferson would support gay marriage, I cannot begin to say; but I am confident they would, at least, have understood and carefully weighed the possibility that to preserve the liberal foundation of civil marriage, we may find it necessary to adjust its boundaries.

Discussion Questions

1. What do you make of the "slippery slope" argument that if we expand the definition of marriage beyond one man and one woman, there is no principled way to oppose further redefinition to include polygamy or other forms of marriage? Or is Douthat correct that we're already there, having replaced traditional marriage with "serial monogamy?"

2. To what extent should laws reflect a particular view of morality? Are there concrete reasons to oppose same-sex marriage, or are they rooted primarily in a moral view about what is proper?

3. If same-sex marriage becomes legal, should it be done through the courts (which would presumably invalidate state statutes or override state constitutional prohibitions as invalid under the U.S. Constitution), or through legislatures or initiatives?

4. Do you agree with Raimondo's argument that state recognition of same-sex marriage would actually make gay people worse off? If this libertarian argument is correct, should it be applied to heterosexual marriage as well?

PART II

Institutions

CHAPTER 5

Congress: The First Branch

24

From *Congress: The Electoral Connection*

David R. Mayhew

Are members of Congress motivated by the desire to make good public policy that will best serve the public and national interest? Are they willing to go against their constituents' opinions when they think it is the right thing to do? The political scientist David Mayhew argues the motivation is not so idealistic or complex. Members of Congress simply want to be reelected, and most of their behavior—advertising, credit claiming, and position taking—is designed to make reelection easier. Further, Mayhew argues that the structure of Congress is ideally suited to facilitate the reelection pursuit. Congressional offices and staff advertise member accomplishments, committees allow for the specialization necessary to claim credit for particularistic benefits provided to the district, and the political parties in Congress do not demand loyalty when constituent interests run counter to the party line.

Mayhew's argument is not universally accepted. Many political scientists accept his underlying premise as a given: elected officials are self-interested, and this is manifest in their constant pursuit of reelection. But others disagree with the premise. Motivations, they argue, are far more complex than allowed for by such a simple statement or theory. People often act unselfishly, and members of Congress have been known to vote with their consciences even if it means losing an election. Others have pointed out that parties now put stronger constraints on congressional behavior than they did when Mayhew was writing in the early 1970s.

[1.] The organization of Congress meets remarkably well the electoral needs of its members. To put it another way, if a group of planners sat down and tried to design a pair of American national assemblies with the goal of serving members' electoral needs year in and year out, they would be hard pressed to improve on what exists. * * * Satisfaction of electoral needs requires remarkably little zero-sum conflict among members. That is, one member's gain is not another member's loss; to a remarkable degree members can successfully engage in electorally useful activities without denying other members the opportunity successfully to engage in them. In regard to credit claiming, this second point requires elaboration further on. Its application to advertising is perhaps obvious. The members all have different markets, so that what any one member does is not an inconvenience to any other. There are exceptions here—House members are sometimes thrown into districts together, senators have to watch the advertising of ambitious House members within their states, and senators from the same state have to keep up with each other—but the case generally holds. With position taking the point is also reasonably clear. As long as congressmen do not attack each other—and they rarely do—any member can champion the most extraordinary causes without inconveniencing any of his colleagues.

*   *   *

A scrutiny of the basic structural units of Congress will yield evidence to support both these * * * points. First, there are the 535 Capitol Hill *offices*, the small personal empires of the members. * * * The Hill office is a vitally important political unit, part campaign management firm and part political machine. The availability of its staff members for election work in and out of season gives it some of the properties of the former; its casework capabilities, some of the properties of the latter. And there is the franking privilege for use on office emanations. * * * A final comment on congressional offices is perhaps the most important one: office resources are given to all members regardless of party, seniority, or any other qualification. They come with the job.

Second among the structural units are the *committees*. * * * Committee membership can be electorally useful in a number of different ways. Some committees supply good platforms for position taking. The best example over the years is probably the House Un-American Activities Committee (now the Internal Security Committee), whose members have displayed hardly a trace of an interest in legislation. [Theodore] Lowi has a chart showing numbers of days devoted to HUAC public hearings in Congresses from the Eightieth through the Eighty-ninth. It can be read as a supply chart, showing biennial volume of position taking on subversion and related matters; by inference it can also be read as a measure of popular demand (the peak years were 1949–56). Senator Joseph McCarthy used the Senate Government Operations Committee as his investigative base in the Eighty-third Congress; later on in the 1960s Senators Abraham Ribicoff (D., Conn.) and William Proxmire (D., Wis.) used subcommittees of this same unit in catching public attention respectively on auto safety and defense waste. With membership on the Senate Foreign Relations Committee goes a license to make speeches on foreign policy. Some committees perhaps deserve to be designated "cause committees"; membership on them can confer an ostentatious identification with salient public causes. An example is the House Education and Labor Committee, whose members, in Fenno's analysis, have two "strategic premises": "to prosecute policy partisanship" and "to pursue one's individual policy preferences regardless of party." Committee members do a good deal of churning about on education, poverty, and similar matters. In recent years Education and Labor has attracted media-conscious members such as Shirley Chisholm (D., N.Y.), Herman Badillo (D., N.Y.), and Louise Day Hicks (D., Mass.).

Some committees traffic in particularized benefits.

* * *

Specifically, in giving out particularized benefits where the costs are diffuse (falling on taxpayer or consumer) and where in the long run to reward one congressman is not obviously to deprive others, the members follow a policy of universalism. That is, every member, regardless of party or seniority, has a right to his share of benefits. There is evidence of universalism in the distribution of projects on House Public Works, projects on House Interior, projects on Senate Interior, project money on House Appropriations, project money on Senate Appropriations, tax benefits on House Ways and Means, tax benefits on Senate Finance, and (by inference from the reported data) urban renewal projects on House Banking and Currency. The House Interior Committee, in Fenno's account, "takes as its major decision rule a determination to process and pass *all* requests and to do so in such a way as to maximize the chances of passage in the House. Succinctly, then, Interior's major strategic premise is: *to secure House passage of all constituency-supported, Member-sponsored bills.*"

* * *

Particularism also has its position-taking side. On occasion members capture public attention by denouncing the allocation process itself; thus in 1972 a number of liberals held up some Ways and Means "members' bills" on the House floor. But such efforts have little or no effect. Senator Douglas used to offer floor amendments to excise projects from public works appropriations bills, but he had a hard time even getting the Senate to vote on them.

Finally, and very importantly, the committee system aids congressmen simply by allowing a division of labor among members. The parceling out of legislation among small groups of congressmen by subject area has two effects. First, it creates small voting bodies in which membership may be valuable. An attentive interest group will prize more highly the favorable issue positions of members of committees pondering its fortunes than the favorable positions of the general run of congressmen. Second, it creates specialized small-group settings in which individual congressmen can make things happen and be perceived to make things happen. "I put that bill through committee." "That was my amendment." "I talked them around on that." This is the language of credit claiming. It comes easily in the committee setting and also when "expert" committee members handle bills on the floor. To attentive audiences it can be believable. Some political actors follow committee activities closely and mobilize electoral resources to support deserving members.

*   *   *

The other basic structural units in Congress are the *parties*. The case here will be that the parties, like the offices and committees, are tailored to suit members' electoral needs. They are more useful for what they are not than for what they are.

*   *   *

What is important to each congressman, and vitally so, is that he be free to take positions that serve his advantage. There is no member of either house who would not be politically injured—or at least who would not think he would be injured—by being made to toe a party line on all policies (unless of course he could determine the line). There is no congressional bloc whose members have identical position needs across all issues. Thus on the school busing issue in the Ninety-second Congress, it was vital to Detroit white liberal Democratic House members that they be free to vote one way and to Detroit black liberal Democrats that they be free to vote the other. In regard to these member needs the best service a party can supply to its congressmen is a negative one; it can leave them alone. And this in general is what the congressional parties do. Party leaders are chosen not to be program salesmen or vote mobilizers, but to be brokers, favor-doers, agenda-setters, and protectors of established institutional routines. Party "pressure" to vote one way or another is minimal. Party "whipping" hardly deserves the name. Leaders in both houses have a habit of counseling members to "vote their constituencies."

Discussion Questions

1. If members are motivated by the desire to be reelected, is this such a bad thing? After all, shouldn't members of Congress do things that will keep the voters happy? Does the constant quest for reelection have a positive or negative impact on "representation"?

2. How could the institutions of Congress (members' offices, committees, and parties) be changed so that the collective needs of the institution would take precedence over the needs of individual members? Would there be any negative consequences for making these changes?

3. Some have argued that term limits are needed to break the never-ending quest for reelection. Do you think that term limits for members of Congress are a good idea?

25

"U.S. House Members in Their Constituencies: An Exploration"

Richard F. Fenno, Jr.

Through much of the 1970s, political scientist Richard Fenno traveled with House members in their districts, "looking over their shoulders" as the politicians met with their constituents. Fenno was interested in answering the questions, "What does an elected representative see when he or she sees a constituency? And, as a natural follow-up, what consequences do these perceptions have for his or her behavior?" This approach to research, which Fenno called "soaking and poking," gave us new insight into how House members represent their constituents.

In this excerpt from his classic book Home Style: House Members in their Districts, *Fenno argues that members perceive their districts as a set of concentric circles: the geographic, reelection, primary, and personal constituencies. The outer part of the circle is the geographic constituency, which is the entire district. At the center of the circle is the personal constituency—the inner group of advisors who are central to the member's campaign and governing operations (with the reelection and primary constituencies in between). Fenno describes how each part of the constituency has a different representational relationship with the member.*

Fenno also discusses how each member develops a distinctive "home style" in dealing with their constituency, which determines the components of district representation: the allocation of resources, the presentation of self, and explaining of Washington activity. Fenno concludes by pointing out that we have an incomplete picture of how Congress operates if we only focus on what happens in Washington. He says, ". . . the more one focuses on the home activities of its members, the more one comes to appreciate the representative strengths and possibilities of Congress. Congress is the most representative of our national political institutions."

Despite a voluminous literature on the subject of representative-constituency relationships, one question central to that relationship remains underdeveloped. It is: What does an elected representative see when he or she sees a constituency? And, as a natural follow-up, what consequences do these perceptions have for his or her behavior? The key problem is that of perception. And the key assumption is that the constituency a representative reacts to is the constituency he or she sees. The corollary assumption is that the rest of us cannot understand the representative-constituency relationship until we can see the constituency through the eyes of the representative. These ideas are not new. They were first articulated for students of the United States Congress by Lewis Dexter. Their importance has been widely acknowledged and frequently repeated ever since. But despite the acceptance and reiteration of Dexter's insights, we still have not developed much coherent knowledge about the perceptions members of Congress have of their constituencies.

A major reason for this neglect is that most of our research on the representative-constituency linkage gets conducted at the wrong end of that linkage. Our interest in the constituency relations of U.S. senators and representatives has typically been a derivative interest, pursued for the light it sheds on some behavior—like roll call voting—in Washington. When we talk with our national legislators about their constituencies, we typically talk to them *in Washington* and, perforce, in the Washington context. But that is a context far removed from the one in which their constituency relationships are created, nurtured, and changed. And it is a context equally far removed from the one in which we might expect their perceptions of their constituencies to be shaped, sharpened or altered. Asking constituency-related questions on Capitol Hill, when the House member is far from the constituency itself, could well produce a distortion of perspective. Researchers might tend to conceive of a separation between the representative "here in Washington" and his or her constituency "back home," whereas the representative may picture himself or herself as a part of the constituency—me *in* the constituency, rather than me *and* the constituency. As a research strategy, therefore, it makes some sense to study our representatives' perceptions of their constituencies while they are actually in their constituencies—at the constituency end of the linkage.

Since the fall of 1970, I have been traveling with some members of the House of Representatives while they were in their districts, to see if I could figure out—by looking over their shoulders—what it is they see there. These expeditions, designed to continue through the 1976 elections, have been totally open-ended and exploratory. I have tried to observe and inquire into anything and everything the members do. Rather than assume that I already know what is interesting or what questions to ask, I have been prepared to find interesting questions emerging in the course of the experience. The same with data. The research method has been largely one of soaking and poking—or, just hanging around. This paper, therefore, conveys mostly an impressionistic feel for the subject—as befits the earliest stages of exploration and mapping.

*   *   *

Perceptions of the Constituency

The District: The Geographical Constituency.

What then do House members see when they see a constituency? One way they perceive it—the way most helpful to me so far—is as a nest of concentric circles. The largest of these circles represents the congressman's broadest view of his constituency. This is "the district" or "my district." It is the entity to which, from which, and in which he travels. It is the entity whose boundaries have been fixed by state legislative enactment or by court decision. It includes the entire population within those boundaries. Because it is a legal entity, we could refer to it as the legal constituency. It captures more of what the congressman has in mind when he conjures up "my district," however, if we label it the *geographical constituency*. We retain the idea that the district is a legally bounded space and emphasize that it is located in a particular place.

The Washington community is often described as a group of people all of whom come from somewhere else. The House of Representatives, by design, epitomizes this characteristic; and its members function with a heightened sense of their ties to place. There are, of course, constant reminders. The member's district is, after all, "the Tenth District of *California*." Inside the chamber, he is "the gentleman from *California*"; outside the chamber he is Representative X (D. *California*). So, it is not surprising that when you ask a congressman, "What kind of district do you have?", the answer often begins with, and always includes, a geographical, space-and-place, perception. Thus, the district is seen as "the largest in the state, twenty-eight counties in the southeastern corner" or "three layers of suburbs to the west of the city, a square with the northwest corner cut out." If the boundaries have been changed by a recent redistricting, the geography of "the new district" will be compared to that of "the old district."

If one essential aspect of "the geographical constituency" is seen as its location and boundaries, another is its particular internal make-up. And House members describe their districts' internal makeup using political science's most familiar demographic and political variables—socioeconomic structure, ideology, ethnicity, residential patterns, religion, partisanship, stability, diversity, etc. Every congressman, in his mind's eye, sees his geographical constituency in terms of some special configuration of such variables. For example,

> Geographically, it covers the northern one-third of the state, from the border of (state X) to the border of (state Y), along the Z river—twenty-two counties. The basic industry is agriculture—but it's a diverse district. The city makes up one-third of the population. It is dominated by the state government and education. It's an independent-minded constituency, with a strong attachment to the work ethic. A good percentage is composed of people whose families emmigrated from Germany, Scandinavia, and Czechoslovakia. I don't exactly know the figures, but over one-half the district is German. And this goes back

to the work ethic. They are a hardworking, independent people. They have a strong thought of 'keeping the government off my back, we'll do all right here.' That's especially true of my out-counties.

Some internal configurations are more complex than others. But, even at the broadest level, no congressman sees, within his district's boundaries, an undifferentiated glob. And we cannot talk about his relations with his "constituency" as if he did.

All of the demographic characteristics of the geographical constituency carry political implications. But as most Representatives make their first perceptual cut into "the district," political matters are usually left implicit. Sometimes, the question "what kind of district do you have?" turns up the answer "it's a Democratic district." But much more often, that comes later. It is as if they first want to sketch a prepolitical background against which they can later paint in the political refinements. We, of course, know—for many of the variables—just what those political refinements are likely to be. (Most political scientists would guess that the district just described is probably more Republican than Democratic—which it is.) There is no point to dwelling on the general political relevance of each variable. But one summary characterization does seem to have special usefulness as a background against which to understand political perceptions and their consequences. And that characteristic is the relative homogeneity or heterogeneity of the district.

As the following examples suggest, members of Congress do think in terms of the homogeneity or heterogeneity of their districts—though they may not always use the words.

It's geographically compact. It's all suburban—no big city in the accepted sense of the word and no rural area. It's all white. There are very few blacks, maybe 2 per cent. Spanish surnamed make up about 10 per cent. Traditionally, it's been a district with a high percentage of home ownership. . . . Economically, it's above the national average in employment . . . the people of the district are employed. It's not that it's very high income. Oh, I suppose there are a few places of some wealth, but nothing very wealthy. And no great pockets of poverty either. And it's not dominated by any one industry. The X County segment has a lot of small, clean, technical industries. I consider it very homogeneous. By almost any standard, it's homogeneous.

This district is a microcosm of the nation. We are geographically southern and politically northern. We have agriculture—mostly soy beans and corn. We have big business—like Union Carbide and General Electric. And we have unions. We have a city and we have small towns. We have some of the worst poverty in the country in A County. And we have some very wealthy sections, though not large. We have wealth in the city and some wealthy towns. We have urban poverty and rural poverty. Just about the only thing we don't have is a good-sized ghetto. Otherwise, everything you can have, we've got it right here.

Because it is a summary variable, the perceived homogeneity-heterogeneity characteristic is particularly hard to measure; and no metric is proposed here. Intuitively, both the number and the compatibility of significant interests within the district would seem to be involved. The greater the number of significant interests—as opposed to one dominant interest—the more likely it is that the district will be seen as heterogeneous. But if the several significant interests were viewed as having a single lowest common denominator and, therefore, quite compatible, the district might still be viewed as homogeneous. One indicator, therefore, might be the ease with which the congressman finds a lowest common denominator of interests for some large proportion of his geographical constituency. The basis for the denominator could be any of the prepolitical variables. We do not think of it, however, as a political characteristic—as the equivalent, for instance, of party registration or political safeness. The proportion of people in the district who have to be included would be a subjective judgment—"enough" so that the congressman saw his geographical constituency as more homogeneous than heterogeneous, or vice versa. All we can say is that the less actual or potential conflict he sees among district interests, the more likely he is to see his district as homogeneous. Another indicator might be the extent to which the geographical constituency is congruent with a natural community. Districts that are purely artificial (sometimes purely political) creations of districting practices, and which pay no attention to pre-existing communities of interest are more likely to be heterogeneous. Pre-existing communities or natural communities are more likely to have such homogenizing ties as common sources of communication, common organizations, and common traditions.

The Supporters: The Re-election Constituency.

Within his geographical constituency, each congressman perceives a smaller, explicitly political constituency. It is composed of the people he thinks vote for him. And we shall refer to it as his *re-election constituency.* As he moves about the district, a House member continually draws the distinction between those who vote for him and those who do not. "I do well here"; "I run poorly here." "This group supports me"; "this group does not." By distinguishing supporters from nonsupporters, he articulates his baseline political perception.

House members seem to use two starting points—one cross-sectional and the other longitudinal—in shaping this perception. First, by a process of inclusion and exclusion, they come to a rough approximation of the upper and lower ranges of the re-election constituency. That is to say, there are some votes a member believes he almost always gets; there are other votes he believes he almost never gets. One of the core elements of any such distinction is the perceived partisan component of the vote—party identification as revealed in registration or poll figures and party voting. "My district registers only 37 per cent Republican. They have no place else to go. My problem is, how can I get enough Democratic votes to win the general election?" Another element is the political tendencies of various demographic groupings.

> My supporters are Democrats, farmers, labor—a DFL operation—with some academic types. . . . My opposition tends to be the main street hardware dealer. I look at that kind of guy in a stable town, where the newspaper runs the community—the typical school board member in the rural part of the district—that's the kind of guy I'll never get. At the opposite end of the scale is the country club set. I'll sure as hell never get them, either.

Starting with people he sees, very generally, as his supporters, and leaving aside people he sees, equally generally, as his nonsupporters, each congressman fashions a view of the people who give him his victories at the polls.

The second starting point for thinking about the re-election constituency is the congressman's idea of who voted for him "last time." Starting with that perception, he adds or subtracts incrementally on the basis of changes that will have taken place (or could be made by him to take place) between "last time" and "next time." It helps him to think about his re-election constituency this way because that is about the only certainty he operates with—he won last time. And the process by which his desire for re-election gets translated into his perception of a re-election constituency is filled with uncertainty. At least that is my strong impression. House members see re-election uncertainty where political scientists would fail to unearth a single objective indicator of it. For one thing, their perceptions of their supporters and nonsupporters are quite diffuse. They rarely feel certain just who did vote for them last time. And even if they do feel fairly sure about that, they may perceive population shifts that threaten established calculations. In the years of my travels, moreover, the threat of redistricting has added enormous uncertainty to the make-up of some re-election constituencies. In every district, too, there is the uncertainty which follows an unforeseen external event—recession, inflation, Watergate.

Of all the many sources of uncertainty, the most constant—and usually the greatest—involves the electoral challenger. For it is the challenger who holds the most potential for altering any calculation involving those who voted for the congressman "last time." "This time's" challenger may have very different sources of political strength from "last time's" challenger. Often, one of the major off-year uncertainties is whether or not the last challenger will try again. While it is true that House members campaign all the time, "the campaign" can be said to start only when the challenger is known. At that point, a redefinition of the re-election constituency may have to take place. If the challenger is chosen by primary, for example, the congressman may inherit support from the loser. A conservative southern Republican, waiting for the Democratic primary to determine whether his challenger would be a black or a white (both liberal), wondered about the shape of his re-election constituency:

It depends on my opponent. Last time, my opponent (a white moderate) and I split many groups. Many business people who might have supported me, split up. If I have a liberal opponent, all the business community will support me. . . . If the black man is my opponent, I should get more Democratic votes than I got before. He can't do any better there than the man I beat before. Except for a smattering of liberals and radicals around the colleges, I will do better than last time with the whites. . . . The black vote is 20 per cent and they vote right down the line Democratic. I have to concede the black vote. There's nothing I can do about it. . . . [But] against a white liberal, I would get some of the black vote.

The shaping of perceptions proceeds under conditions of considerable uncertainty.

The Strongest Supporters: The Primary Constituency.

In thinking about their political condition, House members make distinctions within their re-election constituency—thus giving us a third, still smaller concentric circle. Having distinguished between their nonsupporters and their supporters, they further distinguish between their routine or temporary supporters and their very strongest supporters. Routine supporters only vote for them, often merely following party identification; but others will support them with a special degree of intensity. Temporary supporters back them as the best available alternative; but others will support them regardless of who the challenger may be. Within each re-election constituency are nested these "others"—a constituency perceived as "my strongest supporters," "my hard core support," "my loyalists," "my true believers," "my political base." We shall think of these people as the ones each congressman believes would provide his best line of electoral defense in a primary contest, and label them *the primary constituency*. It will probably include the earliest of his supporters—those who recruited him and those who tendered identifiably strong support in his first campaign—thus, providing another reason for calculating on the basis of "last time." From its ranks will most likely come the bulk of his financial help and his volunteer workers. From its ranks will least likely come an electoral challenger.

A protected congressional seat is as much one protected from primary defeat as from general election defeat. And a primary constituency is something every congressman must have.

Everybody needs some group which is strongly for him—especially in a primary. You can win a primary with 25,000 zealots. . . . The most exquisite case I can give you was in the very early war years. I had very strong support from the anti-war people. They were my strongest supporters and they made up about 5 per cent of the district.

The primary constituency, I would guess, draws a special measure of a congressman's interest; and it should, therefore, draw a special measure of ours. But it is not easy to delineate—for us or for them. Asked to describe his "very strongest supporters," one member replied, "That's the hardest question anyone has to answer." The primary constituency is more subtly shaded than the re-election constituency, where voting provides an objective membership test. Loyalty is not the most predictable of political qualities. And all politicians resist drawing invidious distinctions among their various supporters, as if it were borrowing trouble to begin classifying people according to fidelity. House members who have worried about or fought a primary recently may find it somewhat easier. So too may those with heterogeneous districts whose diverse elements invite differentiation. Despite some difficulty, most members—because it is politically prudent to do so—make some such distinction, in speech or in action or both. By talking to them and watching them, we can begin to understand what those distinctions are.

Here are two answers to the question, "who are your very strongest supporters?"

> My strongest supporters are the working class—the blacks and labor, organized labor. And the people who were in my state legislative district, of course. The fifth ward is low-income, working class and is my base of support. I grew up there; I have my law office there; and I still live there. The white businessmen who are supporting me now are late converts—very late. They support me as the least of two evils. They are not a strong base of support. They know it and I know it.

> I have a circle of strong labor supporters and another circle of strong business supporters. . . . They will 'fight, bleed and die' for me, but in different ways. Labor gives you the manpower and the workers up front. You need them just as much as you need the guy with the two-acre yard to hold a lawn party to raise money. The labor guy loses a day's pay on election day. The business guy gets his nice lawn tramped over and chewed up. Each makes a commitment to you in his own way. You need them both.

Each description reveals the working politician's penchant for inclusive thinking. Each tells us something about a primary constituency, but each leaves plenty of room for added refinements.

The best way to make such refinements is to observe the congressman as he comes in contact with the various elements of his re-election constituency. Both he and they act in ways that help delineate the "very strongest supporters." For example, the author of the second comment above drew a standing ovation when he was introduced at the Labor Temple. During his speech, he spoke directly to individuals in the audience. "Kenny, it's good to see you here. Ben, you be sure and keep in touch." Afterward, he lingered for an hour drinking beer and eating salami. At a businessman's annual Christmas luncheon the next day, he received neither an introduction nor applause when the main speaker acknowledged his presence, saying, "I see our congressman is here; and I use the term 'our' loosely." This congressman's "circle of strong labor supporters" appears to be larger than his "circle of strong business supporters." And the congressman, for his part, seemed much more at home with the first group than he did with the second.

Like other observers of American politics, I have found this idea of "at homeness" a useful one in helping me to map the relationship between politicians and constituents—in this case the perception of a primary constituency. House members sometimes talk in this language about the groups they encounter:

> I was born on the flat plains, and I feel a lot better in the plains area than in the mountain country. I don't know why it is. As much as I like Al [whom we had just lunched with in a mountain town], I'm still not comfortable with him. I'm no cowboy. But when I'm out there on that flat land with those ranchers and wheat farmers, standing around trading insults and jibes and telling stories, I feel better. That's the place where I click.

It is also the place where he wins elections—his primary constituency. "That's my strong area. I won by a big margin and offset my losses. If I win next time, that's where I'll win it—on the plains." Obviously, there is no one-to-one relationship between the groups with whom a congressman acts and feels most at home and his primary constituency. But it does provide a pretty good unobtrusive clue. So I found myself fashioning a highly subjective "at homeness index" to rank the degree to which each congressman seems to have support from and rapport with each group.

I recall, for example, watching a man whose constituency is dominantly Jewish participating in an afternoon installation-of-officers ceremony at a Young Men's Hebrew Association attended by about forty civic leaders of the local community. He drank some spiked punch, began the festivities by saying, "I'm probably the first tipsy installation officer you ever had," told an emotional story about his own dependence on the Jewish "Y," and traded banter with his friends in the audience throughout the proceedings. That evening as we prepared to meet with yet another and much larger (Democratic party) group, I asked where we were going. He said, "We're going to a shitty restaurant to have a shitty meal with a shitty organization and have a shitty time." And he did—from high to low on the "at homeness index." On the way home, after the meal, he talked about the group.

> Ethnically, most of them are with me. But I don't always support the party candidate, and they can't stand that. . . . This group and half the other party groups in the district are against me. But they don't want to be against me too strongly for fear I might go into a primary and beat them. So self-preservation wins out. . . . They know they can't beat me.

Both groups are Jewish. The evening group was a part of his re-election constituency, but not his primary constituency. The afternoon group was a part of both.

The Intimates: The Personal Constituency.

Within the primary constituency, each member perceives still a fourth, and final, concentric circle. These are the few individuals whose relationship with him is so personal and so intimate that their relevance to him cannot be captured by their inclusion in any description of "very strongest supporters." In some cases they are his closest political advisers and confidants. In other cases, they are people from whom he draws emotional sustenance for his political work. We shall think of these people as his *personal constituency.*

One Sunday afternoon, I sat in the living room of a congressman's chief district staff assistant watching an NFL football game—with the congressman, the district aide, the state assemblyman from the congressman's home county, and the district attorney of the same county. Between plays, at halftime and over beer and cheese, the four friends discussed every aspect of the congressman's campaign, listened to and commented on his taped radio spots, analyzed several newspaper reports, discussed local and national personalities, relived old political campaigns and hijinks, discussed their respective political ambitions. Ostensibly they were watching the football game; actually the congressman was exchanging political advice, information, and perspectives with three of his six or seven oldest and closest political associates.

Another congressman begins his weekends at home by having a Saturday morning 7:30 coffee and doughnut breakfast in a cafe on the main street of his home town with a small group of old friends from the Rotary Club. The morning I was there, the congressman, a retired bank manager, a hardware store owner, a high school science teacher, a retired judge, and a past president of the city council gossiped and joked about local matters—the county historian, the library, the board of education, the churches and their lawns—for an hour. "I guess you can see what an institution this is," he said as we left. "You have no idea how invaluable these meetings are for me. They keep me in touch with my home base. If you don't keep your home base, you don't have anything."

The personal constituency is, doubtless, the most idiosyncratic of the several constituencies. Not all members will open it up to the outside observer. Nine of the seventeen did, however; and in doing so, he usually revealed a side of his personality not seen by the rest of his constituencies. "I'm really very reserved, and I don't feel at home with most groups— only with five or six friends," said the congressman after the football game. The relationship probably has both political and emotional dimensions. But beyond that, it is hard to generalize, except to say that the personal constituency needs to be identified if our understanding of the congressman's view of his constituency is to be complete.

In sum, my impression is that House members perceive four constituencies—geographical, re-election, primary, and personal—each one nesting within the previous one.

Political Support and Home Style

What, then, do these perceptions have to do with a House member's behavior? Our conventional paraphrase of this question would read: what do these perceptions have to do with behavior at the other end of the line—in Washington? But the concern that disciplines the perceptions we have been talking about is neither first nor foremost a Washington-oriented concern. It is a concern for political support at home. It is a concern for the scope of that support—which decreases as one moves from the geographical to the personal constituency. It is a concern for the stability of that support—which increases as one moves from the geographical to the personal constituency. And it ultimately issues in a concern for manipulating scopes and intensities in order to win and hold a sufficient amount of support to win elections. Representatives, and prospective representatives, think about their constituencies because they seek support there. They want to get nominated and elected, then renominated and re-elected. For most members of Congress most of the time, this electoral goal is primary. It is the prerequisite for a congressional career and, hence, for the pursuit of other goals. And the electoral goal is achieved—first and last—not in Washington but at home.

Of course, House members do many things in Washington that affect their electoral support at home. Political scientists interpret a great deal of their behavior in Washington in exactly that way—particularly their roll-call votes. Obviously, a congressman's perception of his several constituencies will affect such things as his roll-call voting, and we could, if we wished, study the effect. Indeed, that is the very direction in which our conditioned research reflexes would normally carry this investigation. But my experience has turned me in another—though not, as we shall see an unrelated—direction. I have been watching House members work to maintain or enlarge their political support at home, by going to the district and doing things there.

Our Washington-centered research has caused us systematically to underestimate the proportion of their working time House members spend in their districts. As a result, we have also underestimated its perceived importance to them. In all our studies of congressional time allocation, time spent outside of Washington is left out of the analysis. So, we end up analyzing "the average work week of a congressman" by comparing the amounts of time he spends in committee work, on the floor, doing research, handling constituent problems—but all of it in Washington. Nine of my members whose appointment and travel records I have checked carefully for the year 1973—a nonelection year—averaged 28 trips to the district and spent an average of 101 working (not traveling) days in their districts that year. A survey conducted in 419 House offices covering 1973, indicates that the average number of trips home (not counting recesses) was 35 and the number of days spent in the district during 1973 (counting recesses) was 138. No fewer than 131, nearly one-third, of the 419 members went home to their districts *every single weekend*. Obviously, the direct personal cultivation of their various constituencies takes a great deal of their time; and they must think it is worth it in terms of winning and holding political support. If it is worth *their* time to go home so much, it is worth *our* time to take a commensurate degree of interest in what they do there and why.

As they cultivate their constituencies, House members display what I shall call their *home style*. When they discuss the importance of what they are doing, they are discussing the importance of *home style* to the achievement of their electoral goal. At this stage of the research, the surest generalization one can make about home style is that there are as many varieties as there are members of Congress. "Each of us has his own formula—a truth that is true for him," said one. It will take a good deal more immersion and cogitation before I can improve upon that summary comment. At this point, however, three ingredients of home style appear to be worth looking at. They are: first, the congressman's allocation of his personal resources and those of his office; second, the congressman's presentation of self; and third, the congressman's explanation of his Washington activity. Every congressman allocates, presents, and explains. The amalgam of these three activities for any given representative constitutes (for now, at least) his home style. His home style, we expect, will be affected by his perception of his four constituencies.

*   *   *

It may be, that the congressman's effectiveness in Washington is vitally influenced by the pattern of support he has developed at home and by the allocational, presentational, and explanatory styles he displays there. To put the point most strongly, perhaps we cannot understand his Washington activity without first understanding his perception of his constituencies and the home style he uses to cultivate their support.

No matter how supportive of one another their Washington and home activities may be, House members still face constant tension between them. Members cannot be in two places at once. They cannot achieve legislative competence and maintain constituency contact, both to an optimal degree. The tension is not likely to abate. The legislative workload and the demand for legislative expertise are growing. And the problems of maintaining meaningful contact with their several constituencies—which may make different demands upon them—are also growing. Years ago, House members returned home for months at a time to live with their supportive constituencies, soak up the home atmosphere, absorb local problems at first hand. Today, they race home for a day, a weekend, a week at a time. The citizen demand for access, for communication, for the establishment of trust is as great as ever. The political necessity and the representational desirability of going home is as great as ever. So members of Congress go home. But the quality of their contact has deteriorated. It is harder to sustain a genuine two-way relationship—of a policy or an extra-policy sort—than it once was. They worry about it and as they do, the strain and frustration of the job increases. Many cope; others retire.

*   *   *

Our professional neglect of the home relationship has probably contributed to a more general neglect of the representational side of Congress's institutional capabilities. At least it does seem to be the case that the more one focuses on the home activities of its members, the more one comes to appreciate the representative strengths and possibilities of Congress. Congress *is* the most representative of our national political institutions. It mirrors much of our national diversity, and its members maintain contact with a variety of constituencies at home. While its representative strengths surely contribute to its deserved reputation as our slow institution, the same representative strengths give it the potential for acquiring a reputation as our fair institution. In a period of our national life when citizen sacrifice will be called for, what we shall be needing from our political institutions are not quick decisions, but fair decisions. . . .

Members should participate in consensus building in Washington; they should accept some responsibility for the collective performance of Congress; and they should explain to their constituents what an institution that is both collective and fair requires of its individual members.

* * *

DISCUSSION QUESTIONS

1. Do you agree with Fenno that Congress is the most representative of our national political institutions? If so, does Fenno's argument help address Hibbing and Theiss-Morse's conclusion that Congress may be too responsive (see next article)?

2. Think about your own member of Congress. Does he or she have a strong presence in the district, or does your member seem more like a Washington politician?

3. What do you see as the relationship between how a member operates in Washington and what they do in the district? Should the two be closely tied together (as in Fenno's account of "explaining Washington activity"), or should they be more separate (as with an extensive district-based constituency service operation)?

26

"Too Much of a Good Thing: More Representative Is Not Necessarily Better"

John R. Hibbing and Elizabeth Theiss-Morse

David Mayhew describes an institution that should be highly responsive to voters. If members of Congress want to get reelected, they need to do what their constituents want them to do. However, John Hibbing and Elizabeth Theiss-Morse argue that having institutions that are too representative may be "too much of a good thing." That is, it may not be in the nation's interest to always do what the public wants, especially when it comes to issues of institutional reform. On questions of reform, the public is usually convinced that the only thing preventing ideal policies is that the "people in power" are serving their own interests rather than the public's interests. According to this view, the obvious—but wrong according to Hibbing and Theiss-Morse—solution is to weaken political institutions through "reforms" such as term limits, reducing the salaries of members of Congress, and requiring Congress to balance the federal budget every year. Hibbing and Theiss-Morse argue that these reforms might make people even more disillusioned when they discover that weakening Congress will not solve our nation's problems.

The authors also argue that the public generally does not have a very realistic understanding of the inherent nature of conflict in the political process. The public believes that there is substantial consensus on most issues and that only small "fringe" groups disagree on a broad range of issues. If this were true, why people are frustrated with Congress would certainly be understandable. But in reality, as the authors point out, the nation is deeply divided about the proper course of action. This makes conflict and compromise an inherent part of the legislative process and, at the same time, dims the prospects for simple reforms.

Reform sentiments are much in evidence on the American political scene as we approach the end of the [twentieth] century, and improving the way public opinion is represented in political institutions is often the major motivation of reformers. This is clear * * * from the activities of contemporary political elites, and from the mood of ordinary people. Gross dissatisfaction exists with the nature of representation perceived to be offered by the modern political system. People believe the political process has been commandeered by narrow special interests and by political parties whose sole aim is to contradict the other political party. Given the centrality of representation in the U.S. polity, the organizers and contributors to this symposium are to be commended. It is laudable to want to consider ways of improving the system and, thereby, making people happier with their government. Many of the ideas described in the accompanying essays have considerable merit.

We do, however, wish to raise two important cautions: one briefly and the second in greater detail. Perhaps these cautions are not needed; the authors of the accompanying pieces are almost certainly aware of them. Still, general debate often neglects these two points. Therefore, quite apart from whether it is a good idea or a bad idea, say, to reform campaign finance, enact term limits, or move toward proportional representation and away from single-member districts, it is important * * * to keep in mind that 1) "because the people want them" is not a good justification for adopting procedural reforms and 2) actual enactment of the reforms craved by the people will not necessarily leave us with a system that is more liked even by the people who asked for the reforms in the first place. We take each point in turn.

Ignoring the People's Voice on Process Matters Is Not Evil

It would be easy at this point to slip into a discussion of the political acumen possessed by the American public and, relatedly, of the extent to which elected officials and political institutions should listen to the people. But such a discussion has been going on at least since the time of Plato and it is unlikely we would add much to it here. Instead, we merely wish to point out that, whatever the overall talents of the rank and file, political change in the realm of process should *not* be as sensitive to the public's wishes as political change in the realm of policy.

It is one thing to maintain that in a democracy the people should get welfare reform if they want it. It is quite another to maintain that those same people should get term limits if they want them. Process needs to have some relative permanence, some "stickiness." This is the *definiens* of institutional processes. Without this trait, policy legitimacy would be compromised. The U.S. Constitution (like all constitutions) drives home this contention by including much on process (vetoes, impeachments, representational arrangements, terms of officials, minimum qualifications for holding particular offices, etc.) and precious little about policy. What policy proclamations *are* to be found in the Constitution have faced a strong likelihood of being reversed in subsequent actions (slavery and the 13th Amendment; tax policy and the 16th Amendment; prohibition and the 21st Amendment). Constitutions are written not to enshrine policy but to enshrine a system that will then make policy. These systemic structures should not be subjected lightly to popular whimsy.

The Framers took great efforts to insulate processes from the momentary fancies of the people; specifically, they made amending the Constitution difficult. It is not unusual for reformers, therefore, to run up against the Constitution and its main interpreters—the courts. Witness recent decisions undermining the ability of citizens to impose legislative term limits on members of Congress save by constitutional amendment. This uphill battle to enact procedural reform is precisely what the founders intended—and they were wise to do so.

It may be that the people's will should be reflected directly in public policy, perhaps through initiatives or, less drastically, through the actions of citizen-legislators who act as delegates rather than Burkean trustees. But this does not mean that the rules of the system themselves should change with public preferences in the same way health care policy should change with public preferences.

There may be many good reasons to change the processes of government—possibly by making government more representative—but a persuasive defense of process reforms is *not* embedded in the claim that the people are desirous of such reform. Just as the Bill of Rights does not permit a simple majority of the people to make decisions that will restrict basic rights, so the rest of the Constitution does not permit a simple majority of the people to alter willy-nilly the processes of government. There are good reasons for such arrangements.

Be Careful What You Wish For

One important reason we should be glad ordinary people are not in a position to leave their every mark on questions of political process and institutional design is the very good possibility that people will not be happy with the reforms they themselves advocate. The people generally clamor for reforms that would weaken institutions and strengthen the role of the people themselves in policy decisions. They advocate people's courts, an increased number of popular initiatives and referenda, devolution of authority to institutions "closer" to the people, term limits, staff cuts, emaciating the bureaucracy, elimination of committees, cessation of contact between interest groups and elected officials, and a weakening of political parties. These changes would clear the way for people to have greater influence on decisions, and this is what the people want, right?

Actually, our research suggests this is *not* what the people really want. The public does not desire direct democracy; it is not even clear that people desire democracy at all, although they are quite convinced they do. People want no part of a national direct democracy in which they would be asked to register their preferences, probably electronically, on important issues of the day. Proposals for such procedures are received warmly by a very small minority of citizens. Observers who notice the public's enthusiasm for virtually every populist notion sometimes go the next step of assuming the public wants direct democracy. This is simply an inaccurate assumption.

However, the public *does* want institutions to be transformed into something much closer to the people. The public sees a big disconnect between how they want representation to work and how they believe it is working. Strong support of populist government (not direct democracy) has been detected in innumerable polls conducted during the last couple of decades. That the public looks favorably upon this process agenda is beyond dispute. A national survey we conducted in 1992 found strong support for reforms that would limit the impact of the Washington scene on members of Congress. For example, seven out of 10 respondents supported a reduction in congressional salaries, eight out of 10 supported term limitations, and nine out of 10 supported a balanced-budget amendment. What ties these reforms together is the public's desire to make elected officials more like ordinary people. In focus groups we conducted at the same time as the survey, participants stated many times that elected officials in Washington had lost touch with the people. They supported reforms believed to encourage officials to start keeping in touch. Elected officials should balance the budget just like the people back home. Elected officials should live off modest salaries just like the people back home. And elected officials should face the prospect of getting a real job back home rather than staying in Washington for years and years. These reforms would force elected officials to understand the needs of their constituents rather than get swept up in the money and power that run Washington.

If these reforms were put into place, would the public suddenly love Congress? We do not think so. Certain reforms, such as campaign finance reform, may help, since they would diminish the perception that money rules politics in Washington. But the main reason the public is disgruntled with Congress and with politics in Washington is because they are dissatisfied with the processes intrinsic to the operation of a democratic political system—debates, compromises, conflicting information, inefficiency, and slowness. This argument may seem odd on its face, so in the next few paragraphs we provide our interpretation of why the public questions the need for democratic processes.

The public operates under the erroneous assumption that the majority of the American people agrees on policy matters. In focus groups we conducted in 1997, participants adamantly stated that "80 percent of the American people agree on what needs to be done [about serious societal problems], but it's the other 20 percent who have the power." This pervasive and persistent belief in the existence of popular consensus on tough policy issues is, of course, grossly mistaken. Virtually every well-worded survey question dealing with salient policy issues of the day reveals deep divisions in the American public. From welfare reform to health care; from remaining in Bosnia to the taxes-services trade-off; from a constitutional amendment on flag desecration to the situations in which abortion is believed to be properly permitted, the people are at odds with each other.

This level of popular disagreement would be quite unremarkable except for the fact that the people will not admit that the disagreement actually exists. Instead, people project their own particular views, however ill-formed, onto a clear majority of other "real" people. Those (allegedly) few people who allow it to be known that they do not hold these views are dismissed as radical and noisy fringe elements that are accorded far too much influence by polemical parties, self-serving special interests, and spineless, out-of-touch elected officials. Thus, the desire to move the locus of decision making closer to the people is based on a faulty assumption right off the bat. Many believe that if decisions emanated from the people themselves, we would get a welcome break from the fractious politics created by politicians and institutions. Pastoral, common-sensical solutions will instead quietly begin to find their way into the statute books. The artificial conflict to which we have unfortunately become accustomed will be no more and we can then begin to solve problems.

Given people's widespread belief in popular consensus, it is no wonder they despise the existing structure of governmental institutions. All that these institutions—and the people filling them—do is obscure the will of the people by making it look as though there is a great deal of divisiveness afoot. Who then can condone debate and compromise among elected officials if these processes only give disproportionate weight to nefarious fringe elements that are intent upon subverting the desires of healthy, red-blooded Americans? Who then can condone inefficiency and slowness when we all agree on what needs to be done and politicians ought just to do it? Democratic processes merely get in the way. People react positively to the idea that we ought to run government like a business—it would be efficient, frugal, and quick to respond to problems. Of course, what people tend not to realize is that it would also be undemocratic.

Too many people do not understand political conflict: they have not been taught to deal with it; they have not come to realize it is a natural part of a culture such as ours. When they are confronted with it, they conclude it is an indication something is woefully amiss and in need of correction. They jump at any solution perceived to have the potential of reducing conflict; solutions such as giving authority over to potentially autocratic and hierarchical business-like arrangements or to mythically consensual ordinary people.

Our fear is that, if the people were actually given what they want, they might soon be even more disillusioned with the political system than ever. Suppose people *were* made to feel more represented than they are now; suppose authority *were* really pushed toward the common person. The first thing people would learn is that these changes will have done nothing to eliminate political conflict. The deep policy divisions that polls now reveal among the citizenry would be of more consequence since these very views would now be more determinative of public policy. Conflict would still be pervasive. Popular discontent would not have been ameliorated. Quite likely, people would quickly grow ever more cynical about the potential for reform to accomplish what they want it to accomplish.

Instead of allowing the people to strive for the impossible—an open and inclusive democracy that is devoid of conflict—we need to educate the people about the unrealistic nature of their desires. Instead of giving the people every reform for which they agitate, we need to get them to see where their wishes, if granted, are likely to lead them. The people pay lip service to democracy but that is the extent of it. They claim to love democracy more than life itself, but they only love the concept. They do not love the actual practice of democracy because it suggests differences, because it is ponderous, because it revolves around debate (bickering) and compromise (selling out) and divisions (gridlock).

Conclusion

We hasten to point out that we are not opposed to reforms. For what it is worth, we believe the United States polity could certainly benefit from selective modifications to current institutional arrangements. But we *are* opposed to the tendency of many ordinary people to try to enact reforms intended to weaken political institutions even though these same people evince no real plan describing where that power should be transferred. It is often assumed that the people are populists and that they therefore want power in their own hands. As we have indicated, they do not in actuality want power. They only want to know that they could have this power if they wanted it. They only want to know that this power is not being exercised by those who are in a position to use it to their own advantage. They only want decisions to be made nonconflictually. And they are willing to entertain a variety of possible structures (some far from democratic) if those reforms appear to offer hope of bringing about all these somewhat contradictory desires.

Altering representational arrangements should be considered. The current system can and must be improved. The campaign finance system is an embarrassment and the dispute over drawing oddly-shaped districts for the purpose of obtaining majority-minority districts lays bare the very real problems of single member districts. But we should not jump to enact all reforms simply because people think they want them. No one said that in a democracy the people would get to shape processes however they wanted. It is not inconsistent to have democratic governmental structures that are themselves rather impervious to popular sentiments for change in those procedures. What makes the system democratic is the ability of people to influence policy, not the ability of people to influence process.

This is fortunate because the people's ideas about process are fundamentally flawed. People (understandably) think well of the American public writ large, and people (understandably) dislike conflict, so people (nonsensically) assume the two cannot go together in spite of the impressive array of factual evidence indicating that conflict and the American people—indeed any free people, as Madison so eloquently related in *Federalist* 10—go hand in hand. As a result of their misconception, the people will undoubtedly be quite dissatisfied with the actual consequences of most attempts to expand representation via campaign finance reform, term limits, or proportional representation. There may be good reasons to enact such reforms, but, we submit, neither a public likely to be suddenly pleased with the post-reform political system nor a public that is somehow deserving of a direct voice in process reform is one of them.

DISCUSSION QUESTIONS

1. In one of the more provocative claims in their article, Hibbing and Theiss-Morse say, "The public does not desire direct democracy; it is not even clear that people desire democracy at all, although they are quite convinced they do." Do you agree? What evidence do they provide to support this claim?

2. If the public had a more complex understanding of the political process, what types of reforms would it favor?

3. Is it possible to have a political system that is too responsive?

Debating the Issues: Pork-Barrel Politics

In an era of enormous budget deficits, federal spending is under intense scrutiny. One type of spending—"pork-barrel" policies that are targeted to a specific district or project—is especially controversial because it raises questions about the capacity of Congress to deal effectively with national problems and priorities. However, the debate over pork-barrel politics illustrates the difficulties of defining national interests as opposed to parochial, or local, interests and the role of Congress in policy making.

Pork may take many forms. The most common legislative vehicle for distributing pork is the "earmark," which identifies specific, targeted spending, usually as part of a larger bill. Transportation bills and water projects are two of the traditional outlets for pork-barrel spending, but in recent years even bills funding the war against terrorism, homeland security, and the wars in Iraq and Afghanistan have been full of pork. A moratorium was placed on this type of pork in both the House and Senate starting in 2011. But Citizens Against Government Waste, the leading watchdog group on this topic, identified 152 earmarks worth $3.3 billion in the 2012 fiscal year. An article in the Capitol Hill newspaper *Roll Call* entitled "Working Around Earmark Ban" explained how members continue to "bring home the bacon" to their district. Another study uncovered "stealth pork" in which members of Congress did not require spending in an earmark but "asked for it nicely," with the same effect. Finally, the compromise that led to the resolution of the "fiscal cliff' early in 2013 included billions of dollars in tax expenditures targeted at specific industries, another favorite technique of delivering benefits to constituents. Suffice it to say, member of Congress will continue to find ways to deliver benefits to their constituents and claim credit for them, despite the moratorium on earmarks.

The Cato Institute is a libertarian think tank that is highly critical of wasteful government spending. The selection from the Cato Handbook provides a general example of how special interests win over the general interests, specific instances of pork in recent years (including grants for the Shedd Aquarium in Chicago and the Rock and Roll Hall of Fame in Cleveland), and the broader implications of pork for the policy-making process. Cato's overall critique of pork is that the American taxpayer should not be funding these programs. Rather, the private sector should provide funding (if any). Pork contributes to the ballooning federal deficit and debt and is the "currency of corruption." The selection ends with a call for more transparency in pork spending and its eventual elimination (which would go beyond the current ban on earmarks).

Where Cato sees waste and abuse of the nation's resources, however, James Inhofe, a Republican senator from Oklahoma, and Jonathan

Rauch see many positive virtues. In an interview with Brian Friel, Inhofe characterizes earmark reform as a phony issue. Inhofe sees earmarks as maintaining Congress's control over spending. Otherwise, the power to decide which projects get funded would shift to unelected bureaucrats. Also, Inhofe argues that national interests can be served by allowing local interests to dip into the pork barrel.

Rauch agrees that the power of the purse should remain with Congress rather than the executive branch, but also points out that a recent bill that was criticized as being "full of pork" had less than 2 percent of the offending spending. (Overall, pork accounts for less than 1 percent of federal spending.) Furthermore, much of the accountability and transparency Cato calls for is already in place: it isn't that easy to get an earmark, and earmark sponsors are made public. Other supporters of pork have called it the "glue" of legislating. If it takes a little pork for the home district or state to get important legislation through Congress, so be it. Also, one person's pork could be another person's essential spending. Members of Congress are best able to determine that need.

27

"Corporate Welfare and Earmarks"

CATO HANDBOOK FOR POLICYMAKERS

When considering budget issues, federal policymakers are supposed to have the broad public interest in mind. Unfortunately, that is not how the federal budget process usually works in practice. Many federal programs are sustained by special-interest groups working with policymakers seeking narrow benefits at the expense of taxpayers and the general public.

*   *   *

How can special interests regularly triumph over the broad public interest in our democracy? For one thing, recipients of federal handouts have a strong incentive to create organizations to lobby Congress to keep the federal gravy train flowing. By contrast, average citizens have no strong incentive to lobby against any particular subsidy program because each program costs just a small portion of their total tax bill.

When average citizens do speak out against particular programs, they are usually outgunned by the professionals who are paid to support programs. Those professionals have an informational advantage over citizens

TABLE 1
Majority Voting Does Not Ensure That a Project's
Benefits Outweigh Costs

Legislator	Vote	Benefits Received by Constituents	Taxes Paid by Constituents
Clinton	Yea	$12	$10
Cochran	Yea	$12	$10
Collins	Yea	$12	$10
Carper	Nay	$2	$10
Coburn	Nay	$2	$10
Total	Pass	$40	$50

because the workings of most federal programs are complex. The lobby groups that defend subsidy programs are staffed by top program experts, and they are skilled at generating media support. One typical gambit is to cloak the narrow private interests of subsidy recipients in public interest clothing, and proclaim that the nation's future depends on increased funding.

Another reason it is hard to challenge spending programs is that lobby groups, congressional supporters, and federal agencies rarely admit that any program is a failure. Washington insiders become vested in the continued funding of programs because their careers, pride, and reputations are on the line, and they will battle against any cuts or reforms.

How do dubious spending programs get enacted in the first place? Table 1 shows how Congress can pass special-interest legislation in which the costs outweigh the benefits. The table assumes that legislators vote in the narrow interest of their districts. The hypothetical project shown creates benefits of $40 and costs taxpayers $50, and is thus a loser for the nation. Nonetheless, the project gains a majority vote. The program's benefits are more concentrated than its costs, and that is the key to gaining political support.

The pro-spending bias of Congress is strengthened by the complex web of vote trading, or logrolling, that often occurs. Table 2 shows that because of logrolling, projects that are net losers to society can pass even if they do not have majority support. Because Projects A and B would fail with stand alone votes, Clinton, Cochran, and Collins enter an agreement to mutually support the two projects. That is, they logroll. The result is that the two projects get approved, even though each imposes net costs on society and benefits only a minority of voters.

The popularity of logrolling means that programs that make no economic sense and have only minimal public support are enacted all the time.

*   *   *

TABLE 2

Logrolling Allows Passage of Subsidies That Benefit Minorities of Constituents

| | Project A | | Project B | | Vote on a Bill Including Projects A and B |
Legislator	Benefits Received by Constituents	Taxes Paid by Constituents	Benefits Received by Constituents	Taxes Paid by Constituents	
Clinton	$15	$10	$8	$10	Yea
Cochran	$15	$10	$8	$10	Yea
Collins	$4	$10	$20	$10	Yea
Carper	$3	$10	$2	$10	Nay
Coburn	$3	$10	$2	$10	Nay
Total	$40	$50	$40	$50	Pass

Earmarks

The federal budget practice of "earmarking" has exploded during the last fifteen years. Earmarks are line items in spending bills inserted by legislators for specific projects in their home states. Some infamous earmarks funded a $50 million indoor rain forest in Iowa and a $223 million "bridge to nowhere" in Alaska. Earmarks can provide recipients with federal grant money, contracts, loans, or other types of benefits. Earmarks are often referred to as "pork" spending.

* * * [T]he number of pork projects increased from fewer than 2,000 annually in the mid-1990s to almost 14,000 in 2005. Various scandals and the switch to Democratic control of Congress then slowed the pace of earmarking for a couple of years. But earmarking is on the rise again. The fiscal year 2008 omnibus appropriations bill was bloated with 11,610 spending projects inserted by members of Congress for their states and districts.

Earmarked projects are generally those that have not been requested by the president and have not been subject to expert review or competitive bidding. Thus, if the government had $1 billion to spend on bioterrorism research, it might be earmarked to go to laboratories in the districts of important politicians, rather than to labs chosen by a panel of scientists. Earmarking has soared in most areas of the budget, including defense, education, housing, scientific research, and transportation.

The main problem with earmarking is that most spending projects chosen by earmark are properly the responsibility of state and local governments or the private sector, not the federal government. The rise in earmarks is one manifestation of Congress's growing intrusion into state affairs, . . . Consider these earmarks from the FY08 omnibus appropriations bill:

1. $1,648,850 for the private Shedd Aquarium in Chicago, which is also awash with corporate funding;
2. $787,200 for "green design" changes at the Museum of Natural History in Minneapolis;
3. $492,000 for the Rocky Flats Cold War Museum in Arvada, Colorado;
4. $1,950,000 for a library and archives at the Charles B. Rangel Center for Public Service at the City College of New York;
5. $2,400,000 for renovations to Haddad Riverfront Park in Charleston;
6. $500,000 for upgrades to Barracks Row, a swank Capitol Hill neighborhood;
7. $742,764 for fruit fly research, partly conducted in France;
8. $188,000 for the Lobster Institute in Maine; and
9. $492,000 for fuel cell research for Rolls-Royce Group of Canton, Ohio.

Projects 1 to 3 give taxpayer money to groups that should be funding their own activities from admissions fees and charitable contributions. Interestingly, the nonprofit Shedd Aquarium has spent hundreds of thousands of dollars on lobbyists to secure federal earmarks, and its chief executive earned a huge $600,000 salary in 2006. Or consider that the Rock and Roll Hall of Fame in Cleveland has received federal grants, even though there are thousands of music industry millionaires who should be footing the bill.

Projects 4 to 6 are examples of items that state and local governments should fund locally. Unfortunately, state and local officials are increasingly asking Washington for handouts, and lobby groups such as Cassidy and Associates are helping them "mine" the federal budget for grants.

Projects 7 to 9 fund activities that should be left to the private sector. Industries should fund their own research, which is likely to be more cost-effective than government efforts. Besides, successful research leads to higher profits for private businesses, and it makes no sense for taxpayers to foot the bill for such private gains.

Earmarks' Erosion of Fiscal Responsibility

Defenders of earmarks argue that they are no big deal since they represent just a small share of overall federal spending. The problem is that earmarking has contributed to the general erosion in fiscal responsibility in Washington. Earmarks have exacerbated the parochial mindset of most members, who spend their time appeasing state and local interest groups rather than tackling issues of broad national concern. Many politicians complain about the soaring federal deficit, yet their own staff members spend most of their time trying to secure earmarks in spending bills.

The rise in earmarking has encouraged a general spendthrift attitude in Congress. Why should rank-and-file members restrain themselves when their own leaders are usually big recipients of pork? Sen. Tom Coburn (R-OK) is right that the problem with earmarks is "the hidden cost of perpetuating a culture of fiscal irresponsibility. When politicians fund pork projects they sacrifice the authority to seek cuts in any other program." Similarly, Rep. Jeff Flake (R-AZ) concludes that "earmarking . . . has become the currency of corruption in Congress. . . . Earmarks are used as inducements to get members to sign on to large spending measures."

Reforms to Increase Transparency and Downsize the Government

A first step toward eliminating earmarks, corporate welfare, and other special-interest spending is to further increase transparency in the congressional and agency spending processes. Under pressure from reformers, the government has set up a searchable database of federal grants and contracts at www.usaspending.gov. A second step is for citizens to use this website and other tools to research federal spending, and then to call their members of Congress and tell them what programs should be cut.

Citizens should also ask their members to support reforms to the budget process. One idea for cutting corporate welfare is to set up a commission akin to the successful military base–closing commissions of the 1990s. It would draw up a list of current subsidies and present it to Congress, which would vote on the cuts as a package without amendment. To make the package a political winner, all budget savings would go toward immediate tax cuts for families.

Ultimately, earmarking and corporate welfare should be abolished, and spending on activities that are legitimate federal functions should be determined by a system of competitive bidding and expert review. Of course, it will not be easy to reform the spending practices of Congress. Members often feel committed to expanding spending in their districts and on their favored programs. But taxpayers fund all those programs, and they need to do a better job of convincing their members to cut unneeded programs and pass much leaner federal budgets.

—*Prepared by Chris Edwards and Jeff Patch*

28

"Inhofe: Earmarks Are Good for Us"

Brian Friel

Sen. James Inhofe, R-Okla., the ranking member on the Senate Environment and Public Works Committee, spent the past eight years battling liberals over climate change and arguing that predictions of catastrophic global warming are a "hoax." Now Inhofe is taking on what he describes as another "phony" issue—earmark reform. But this crusade puts him at odds with fellow conservatives in his own party.

In recent years, taxpayer watchdog groups and anti-pork-barrel lawmakers—including Sens. John McCain, R-Ariz.; Jim DeMint, R-S.C.; and Inhofe's home-state colleague and fellow Republican, Tom Coburn—have turned earmarks into a dirty word. They contend that lawmakers' long-standing practice of earmarking funding for pet projects promotes waste, big spending, and corruption. The Senate foes regularly offer floor amendments attempting to strip earmarks from legislation.

Inhofe, who ranked as the most conservative senator in *National Journal*'s 2009 vote ratings, launched a campaign this week to recast earmarks as a tool that conservatives should embrace, not deride. He noted that most people took global warming as a fact eight years ago, and he contended that he has effectively shown that it is not. His earmark battle is aimed at showing that what everyone believes about earmarks is also untrue, he said.

"They're winning on the phrase," Inhofe said of anti-earmarkers, in an interview. "It's fraudulent."

Elected to the House in 1986 and to the Senate in 1994, Inhofe says that his efforts on global warming ultimately led to the recent demise of cap-and-trade climate-change legislation. To environmentalists and many congressional Democrats, he is a villain. Dan Lashof, the climate center director of the Natural Resources Defense Council, calls Inhofe "the Senate's chief spokesman for climate deniers." But the Oklahoman has become a star in conservative circles for his outspoken and often lonely fight on the issue.

Armed with those bona fides, Inhofe is planning to take his pro-earmark campaign to rank-and-file conservatives. He said he was inspired, in part, by a column that Jonathan Rauch wrote in this magazine. . . . Inhofe is slated to speak to a "tea party" group in Jacksonville, Fla., later this month, where he expects to test-drive his message. He has drafted an op-ed outlining his views on the "phony issue of earmarks." He also hopes to convince conservative talk-radio hosts that their frequent earmark-bashing misses the more important goal: reducing overall spending to ensure greater fiscal responsibility in Washington.

"You don't save anything by cutting earmarks," Inhofe said. He maintained that eliminating lawmakers' earmarks doesn't shrink the over-all budget; it just leaves it to federal agencies—currently controlled by the Democratic Obama administration—to decide how to distribute the money. "These nonelected bureaucrats are the ones who are making the decisions."

As an example, Inhofe pointed to a transportation program that pays for low-budget initiatives such as bike trails, streetscapes, and congestion mitigation. In 2008, Congress distributed the millions of dollars in program funding through earmarks that boosted 102 projects in 35 states.

The year before, when no earmarks were permitted, the Transportation Department funded projects through a grant competition in just five big cities—Miami, Minneapolis-St. Paul, New York City, San Francisco, and Seattle.

Inhofe argues that earmarks have funded many programs that conservatives support, particularly in national defense. As the second-ranking Republican on the Armed Services Committee, behind McCain, Inhofe notes that Congress has used earmarks to keep several military programs chugging along despite executive branch objections, including additional C-17 cargo planes that President Obama fought against last year. McCain offered an amendment to the Defense appropriations bill that would have nixed the funds for the extra planes, but Inhofe and 63 other senators defeated it.

Instead of imposing an earmark moratorium, Inhofe proposes a freeze in nonsecurity appropriations at fiscal 2008 levels, a move that he says would save $600 billion more than Obama's proposal in February to freeze such spending at fiscal 2010 levels. He also maintains that individual projects should be assessed on their merits, not on whether they are deemed to be earmarks.

Opponents counter, though, that earmarked congressional projects have become a symbol of what is wrong with Washington.

"I think there is a justifiable argument for earmarks, that we as legislators probably know better in some instances than bureaucrats in Washington about how money should be spent," Sen. George LeMieux, R-Fla., conceded. "But earmarks are, unfortunately, the engine that drives the train that gets us into these huge spending problems. If I put an earmark in a particular appropriations bill, and then that appropriations bill is 15 percent more than it was last year, and I say I can't support that, they'll say, well, your earmark is in there. So the earmark is what buys you into bigger spending."

While not naming names, Inhofe argues that some Republican senators use their anti-earmark credentials as a fig leaf to cover their votes to authorize massive spending programs. As examples, he cited the $700 billion bank bailout in October 2008; the Fannie Mae and Freddie Mac takeover in July 2008; and a bill the same month to increase funding for HIV/AIDS programs in Africa from $15 billion to $50 billion.

"If you look at those three things, you're well over a trillion dollars," he said. "And you look at the Republicans who voted for them. They've been able to use earmarks to distract people."

DeMint voted with Inhofe against all three measures. McCain voted for the bank bailout; and Coburn voted for both the bank bill and the AIDS legislation. DeMint, McCain, and Coburn are among the sponsors of earmark-moratorium legislation introduced last month.

Inhofe said that if Congress bans earmarks, his fallback position is that they should be defined only as projects that receive appropriations without having been previously authorized by Congress. Inhofe is a chief authorizer—for transportation programs at the Environment and Public Works Committee and for military programs at the Armed Services Committee. He and other authorizers regularly struggle for power with appropriators, who often have their own ideas about which projects to fund in their annual spending bills.

In a brief interview, McCain defended his anti-earmark stance. "My record is very clear," he said. "For 20 years I've fought against earmarks and their corruption. They breed corruption, and they've bred corruption."

McCain said he believes that the root of the problem is unauthorized appropriations. "You've got to get the definition of an earmark: that is, an unauthorized appropriation. If you authorize it, even if I disagree with it, that's the right process," he said. "What [earmarks] have done is totally circumvent what we should be doing: that is, authorizing and *then* appropriating."

Sen. Saxby Chambliss, R-Ga.—the ranking member on the Senate Agriculture, Nutrition, and Forestry Committee, another key authorizing panel—said that giving authorizers more power to say where money should be spent could be one part of earmark reform. He is a co-sponsor of the earmark moratorium. "I hope we get some sort of meaningful earmark reform as a result of continuing to stir that issue up," Chambliss said.

Inhofe's pro-earmark campaign will certainly cause a stir among his colleagues. Some House and Senate Republicans have urged the party to unilaterally adopt an earmark moratorium to paint a strong contrast to the Democrats. Inhofe counters that doing so would simply give more money to Obama to spend on liberal-supported projects and that it would distract attention from the core issues that the GOP can ride to victory in November.

"The Republican Party has the greatest issues ever in the history of politics in America—health care, cap-and-trade, closing Gitmo—that's terrorists coming into the United States, and the deficit, and the debt," Inhofe said. "Making an issue out of earmarks serves to only mislead voters by providing cover for big spenders. Railing against earmarks helps those who vote for the billion-dollar spending bills seem more conservative than they really are."

29

"Earmarks Are a Model, Not a Menace"

Jonathan Rauch

Naturally, when a gigantic omnibus appropriations bill came to the Senate floor last week, 98 percent of it got almost no attention. "Member projects—aka earmarks or 'pork'—account for less than 2 percent of spending in the $410 billion omnibus bill on the floor of the Senate this week, but they're drawing most of the opposition fire," *The Christian Science Monitor* reported. Less than 2 percent! Of course, this orgy of waste offended me for the same reason it offended everyone else: I was not getting an earmark.

I decided to get an earmark. Seemed easy enough. Just call someone in a congressional office, make a silly request—propose converting pig vomit into drywall, that sort of thing—and voila, I would have my very own "pet project."

So I called my congressman, Rep. Jim Moran, D-Va., who, handily enough, is a member of the Appropriations Committee. Imagine my shock when I got a staffer who insisted that I would have to *apply*.

Apply? For a *pet project*? Right. There was a form. As in, paperwork. The exact form would depend on which Appropriations subcommittee has jurisdiction. And I would need to meet with legislative aides to explain why my project deserved funding. And they would probably vet my request with the relevant federal agency.

Oh. But then I'm in, right?

Not quite. Moran told me he will get a thousand earmark applications this year. "It actually goes up every year." He will accept only the best hundred or so.

But *then* I'm in?

No, then the relevant Appropriations subcommittee further whittles the list. About three dozen of Moran's earmarks will get funded, he figures.

So my chances of scoring boodle were on the order of only 3 percent. I didn't fill out the form, even though it was only a page long. Down in Norfolk, Rep. Bobby Scott, D-Va., requires earmark applicants to fill out a seven-page form that looks like my tax return—and I itemize. "Please check *all* that apply:. . . This project is largely for EPA consent decree. . . . Preliminary planning and engineering design is completed." Really, it takes all the thrill out of pet projects.

Beating up on earmarks is fun. But if you interrupt the joy long enough to take a closer look, you may discover that the case against earmarks has pretty much evaporated over the past few years. In fact, reformers seem to want to hound out of existence a system that actually works better than much of what Washington does.

When former Rep. Jim Kolbe, R-Ariz., entered Congress in 1985, "there were no earmarks," he told me recently. Perhaps, you say, this was because appropriators were indifferent to how much federal money flowed to their districts? Sorry, bad guess.

In those days, according to Kolbe (an Appropriations Committee member who retired in 2007), appropriators felt little need to write earmarks into law. Instead, subcommittee chairmen and ranking members just dropped money into program accounts. Then they called up executive branch bureaucrats with advice on how to spend it.

"Most agencies didn't need to be threatened if the chairman of their subcommittee called," says Scott Lilly, a former House Appropriations Committee staff director and now a senior fellow with the Center for American Progress. Sometimes, Lilly says, "you'd increase the entire national program in order that it would have a better chance that it would spill into your state."

In the 1980s and 1990s, the once-sequestered system cracked open. The number of earmarks increased by a factor of 25 between 1991 and 2005. Earmarks were often invisible, at least until after they were enacted. "The bill would be passed before people even started digging into what was in there," Lilly says. Public outrage swelled.

On its heels, however, came reform, notably in the last couple of years. Every earmark request now must be made public before Congress votes on it. The sponsoring member, the amount and nature of the request, and the name and address of the beneficiary must all be disclosed. You can find all this stuff online. As I was miffed to discover, many congressional offices have formalized the application procedure. Getting an earmark now is a lot like applying for a grant.

As transparency has taken over, the case against earmarks has melted away. Their budgetary impact is trivial in comparison with entitlements and other large programs. Obsessing about earmarks, indeed, has the perverse, if convenient, effect of distracting the country from its real spending problems, thus substituting indignation for discipline.

Earmarks are often criticized for rewarding political clout rather than merit. If earmarks were merit-based, says Steve Ellis of the watchdog group Taxpayers for Common Sense, you wouldn't see them flowing disproportionately to Appropriations Committee members. And earmarks, he adds, reflect parochial rather than national priorities. "There's no way the Appropriations Committee is able to vet the thousands of earmarks worth billions of dollars."

Fair enough. But if you think that executive branch decisions are strictly apolitical and merit-based, I have two words for you: Karl Rove. "The idea that the only politicians in the government are in the Congress is just false," Lilly says. If you think that executive branch decision-making is transparent, I have two more words for you: Dick Cheney.

And if you think Congress is parochial, take it up with Mr. Madison. He wrote the Constitution, which says, in terms that leave no room for quibbling, that the power of the purse belongs to Congress. The Founders' notion was that accountability to local voters was the best safeguard for the people's money. "The idea that unless something is in the president's budget Congress shouldn't consider it turns the Constitution on its head," Kolbe says.

"The problem with a lot of federal programs is that they have to take a cookie-cutter approach," Moran says. Big, conventionally authorized programs, with their funding formulas and contracting rules and national purview, may be too slow to meet urgent local needs, too rigid to support innovation, too formulaic to finance a one-shot project.

Kolbe recalls an earmark that sped up an approved but languishing highway project in Arizona. "It was desperately needed; there were huge backups on the interstate," he says. "Seeing the growing need, not anticipated at the time of its initial approval, we simply jumped it up on the priority list."

Political discretion can be abused, and one would certainly not want most federal spending to be subject to it. But, provided that transparency is assured, shouldn't there be a place in government for elected officials to exercise judgment in the use of taxpayer money? In fact, if you wanted to create a nonbureaucratic, transparent system of rapid-response grants for pressing local concerns, you would come up with something very much like today's earmarking system (and you'd call it "reinventing government").

Some earmark spending is silly, but then so is some non-earmark spending, and there is a lot more of the latter. Competition for funding, combined with flexibility and local knowledge, makes earmarks "often some of the best expenditures the federal government makes in a particular area," Lilly says. "I would say, on the whole, earmarks probably provide as much value-added as non-earmarked federal spending."

And earmark spending today is, if anything, more transparent, more accountable, and more promptly disclosed than is non-earmark spending. Indeed, executive agencies could stand to emulate some of the online disclosure rules that apply to earmarks.

These days, the problem is not so much with earmarking as with Congress's and the public's obsession with it. "It just takes too damn much time," Lilly says. "Congress is spending an inordinate amount of time on 1 percent of the budget and giving the executive branch much too free a rein on the other 99 percent."

Reformers who want to ban earmarking might think again. "You're never going to abolish earmarks," Moran says. "What you'll wind up abolishing is the transparency, the accountability." If unable to earmark, legislators will inveigle executive agencies behind the scenes, fry bureaucrats at hearings, and expand or rewrite entire programs to serve parochial needs. This, of course, is the way things worked in the bad old days. "I think you'll wind up going back to that system," Kolbe cautions.

A better approach is to improve transparency and further routinize the earmarking process, as President Obama proposed on Wednesday when he signed the omnibus spending bill. But here is a reform that would help much more: Declare earmarking an ex-problem and move on. Next time you come across someone who looks at a giant federal spending bill and sees only the 2 percent that happens to be earmarked, tell that person to get over it.

Discussion Questions

1. How would you define pork-barrel projects? Are all pork projects contrary to the national interest? How do we distinguish between local projects that are in the national interest and those that are not?

2. Consider Cato's list of examples of pork. If you were a member of Congress, which of these would you clearly support? Which would you clearly oppose? Which would you want to find out more about before deciding?

3. Members of Congress face strong incentives to serve constituent needs and claim credit for delivering federal dollars. Pork-barrel projects provide the means to do just that. What changes in Congress or the political process might be made to alter legislative behavior, or to change the incentives legislators face when securing re-election? Do we want members of Congress to be focused primarily on broad national issues rather than local priorities?

CHAPTER 6

The Presidency

30

"The Power to Persuade," from *Presidential Power*

Richard Neustadt

An enduring theme in analyses of the presidency is the gap between what the public expects of the office and the president's actual powers. Neustadt, who wrote the first edition of Presidential Power *in 1960, offered a new way of looking at the office. His main point is that formal powers (the constitutional powers set out in Article II and the statutory powers that Congress grants) are not the president's most important resource. The president cannot, Neustadt concluded, expect to get his way by command—issuing orders to subordinates and other government officials with the expectation of immediate and unquestioning compliance. In a system of "separate institutions sharing power," other political actors have their own independent sources of power and therefore can refuse to comply with presidential orders. Nobody, Neustadt argues, sees things from the president's perspective (or "vantage point"). Legislators, judges, cabinet secretaries, all have their own responsibilities, constituencies, demands of office, and resources, and their interests and the president's will often differ. The key to presidential power is the power to persuade—to convince others that they should comply with the president's wishes because doing so is in their interest. Presidents persuade by bargaining: making deals, reaching compromise positions; in other words, the give and take that is part of politics.*

The limits on command suggest the structure of our government. The constitutional convention of 1787 is supposed to have created a government of "separated powers." It did nothing of the sort. Rather, it created a government of separated institutions *sharing* powers. "I am part of the legislative process," Eisenhower often said in 1959 as a reminder of his veto. Congress, the dispenser of authority and funds, is no less part of the administrative process. Federalism adds another set of separated institutions. The Bill of Rights adds others. Many public purposes can only be achieved by voluntary acts of private institutions; the press, for one, in Douglass Cater's phrase, is a "fourth branch of government." And with the coming of alliances abroad, the separate institutions of a London, or a Bonn, share in the making of American public policy.

What the Constitution separates our political parties do not combine. The parties are themselves composed of separated organizations sharing public authority. The authority consists of nominating powers. Our national parties are confederations of state and local party institutions, with a headquarters that represents the White House, more or less, if the party has a President in office. These confederacies manage presidential nominations. All other public offices depend upon electorates confined within the states. All other nominations are controlled within the states. The President and congressmen who bear one party's label are divided by dependence upon different sets of voters. The differences are sharpest at the stage of nomination. The White House has too small a share in nominating congressmen, and Congress has too little weight in nominating Presidents for party to erase their constitutional separation. Party links are stronger than is frequently supposed, but nominating processes assure the separation.

The separateness of institutions and the sharing of authority prescribe the terms on which a President persuades. When one man shares authority with another, but does not gain or lose his job upon the other's whim, his willingness to act upon the urging of the other turns on whether he conceives the action right for him. The essence of a President's persuasive task is to convince such men that what the White House wants of them is what they ought to do for their sake and on their authority.

Persuasive power, thus defined, amounts to more than charm or reasoned argument. These have their uses for a president, but these are not the whole of his resources. For the men he would induce to do what he wants done on their own responsibility will need or fear some acts by him on his responsibility. If they share his authority, he has some share in theirs. Presidential "powers" may be inconclusive when a President commands, but always remain relevant as he persuades. The status and authority inherent in his office reinforce his logic and his charm.

* * *

A president's authority and status give him great advantages in dealing with the men he would persuade. Each "power" is a vantage point for him in the degree that other men have use for his authority. From the veto to appointments, from publicity to budgeting, and so down a long list, the White House now controls the most encompassing array of vantage points in the American political system. With hardly an exception, the men who share in governing this country are aware that at some time, in some degree, the doing of *their* jobs, the furthering of *their* ambitions, may depend upon the president of the United States. Their need for presidential action, or their fear of it, is bound to be recurrent if not actually continuous. Their need or fear is his advantage.

A president's advantages are greater than mere listing of his "powers" might suggest. The men with whom he deals must deal with him until the last day of his term. Because they have continuing relationships with him, his future, while it lasts, supports his present influence. Even though there is no need or fear of him today, what he could do tomorrow may supply today's advantage. Continuing relationships may convert any "power," any aspect of his status, into vantage points in almost any case. When he induces other men to do what he wants done, a president can trade on their dependence now *and* later.

The president's advantages are checked by the advantages of others. Continuing relationships will pull in both directions. These are relationships of mutual dependence. A president depends upon the men he would persuade; he has to reckon with his need or fear of them. They too will possess status, or authority, or both, else they would be of little use to him. Their vantage points confront his own; their power tempers his.

*   *   *

The power to persuade is the power to bargain. Status and authority yield bargaining advantages. But in a government of "separated institutions sharing powers," they yield them to all sides. With the array of vantage points at his disposal, a President may be far more persuasive than his logic or his charm could make him. But outcomes are not guaranteed by his advantages. There remain the counter pressures those whom he would influence can bring to bear on him from vantage points at their disposal. Command has limited utility; persuasion becomes give-and-take. It is well that the White House holds the vantage points it does. In such a business any president may need them all—and more.

*   *   *

This view of power as akin to bargaining is one we commonly accept in the sphere of congressional relations. Every textbook states and every legislative session demonstrates that save in times like the extraordinary Hundred Days of 1933—times virtually ruled out by definition at mid-century—a president will often be unable to obtain congressional action on his terms or even to halt action he opposes. The reverse is equally accepted: Congress often is frustrated by the president. Their formal powers are so intertwined that neither will accomplish very much, for very long, without the acquiescence of the other. By the same token, though, what one demands the other can resist. The stage is set for that great game, much like collective bargaining, in which each seeks to profit from the other's needs and fears. It is a game played catch-as-catch-can, case by case. And everybody knows the game, observers and participants alike.

*   *   *

Like our governmental structure as a whole, the executive establishment consists of separated institutions sharing powers. The president heads one of these; Cabinet officers, agency administrators, and military commanders head others. Below the departmental level, virtually independent bureau chiefs head many more. Under mid-century conditions, Federal operations spill across dividing lines on organization charts; almost every policy entangles many agencies; almost every program calls for interagency collaboration. Everything somehow involves the president. But operating agencies owe their existence least of all to one another—and only in some part to him. Each has a separate statutory base; each has its statutes to administer; each deals with a different set of subcommittees at the Capitol. Each has its own peculiar set of clients, friends, and enemies outside the formal government. Each has a different set of specialized careerists inside its own bailiwick. Our Constitution gives the president the "take-care" clause and the appointive power. Our statutes give him central budgeting and a degree of personnel control. All agency administrators are responsible to him. But they *also* are responsible to Congress, to their clients, to their staffs, and to themselves. In short, they have five masters. Only after all of those do they owe any loyalty to each other.

"The members of the Cabinet," Charles G. Dawes used to remark, "are a President's natural enemies." Dawes had been Harding's Budget Director, Coolidge's Vice-President, and Hoover's Ambassador to London; he also had been General Pershing's chief assistant for supply in the First World War. The words are highly colored, but Dawes knew whereof he spoke. The men who have to serve so many masters cannot help but be somewhat the "enemy" of any one of them. By the same token, any master wanting service is in some degree the "enemy" of such a servant. A President is likely to want loyal support but not to relish trouble on his doorstep. Yet the more his Cabinet members cleave to him, the more they may need help from him in fending off the wrath of rival masters. Help, though, is synonymous with trouble. Many a Cabinet officer, with loyalty ill-rewarded by his lights and help withheld, has come to view the White House as innately hostile to department heads. Dawes's dictum can be turned around.

*   *   *

The more an officeholder's status and his "powers" stem from sources independent of the president, the stronger will be his potential pressure *on* the President. Department heads in general have more bargaining power than do most members of the White House staff; but bureau chiefs may have still more, and specialists at upper levels of established career services may have almost unlimited reserves of the enormous power which consists of sitting still. As Franklin Roosevelt once remarked:

> The Treasury is so large and far-flung and ingrained in its practices that I find it almost impossible to get the action and results I want—even with Henry [Morgenthau] there. But the Treasury is not to be compared with the State Department. You should go through the experience of trying to get any changes in the thinking, policy, and action of the career diplomats and then you'd know what a real problem was. But the Treasury and the State Department put together are nothing compared with the Na-a-vy. The admirals are really something to cope with—and I should know. To change anything in the Na-a-vy is like punching a feather bed. You punch it with your right and you punch it with your left until you are finally exhausted, and then you find the damn bed just as it was before you started punching.

*   *   *

There is a widely held belief in the United States that were it not for folly or for knavery, a reasonable president would need no power other than the logic of his argument. No less a personage than Eisenhower has subscribed to that belief in many a campaign speech and press conference remark. But faulty reasoning and bad intentions do not cause all quarrels with presidents. The best of reasoning and of intent cannot compose them all. For in the first place, what the president wants will rarely seem a trifle to the men he wants it from. And in the second place, they will be bound to judge it by the standard of their own responsibilities, not his. However logical his argument according to his lights, their judgment may not bring them to his view.

The men who share in governing this country frequently appear to act as though they were in business for themselves. So, in a real though not entire sense, they are and have to be. When Truman and MacArthur fell to quarreling, for example, the stakes were no less than the substance of American foreign policy, the risks of greater war or military stalemate, the prerogatives of presidents and field commanders, the pride of a proconsul and his place in history. Intertwined, inevitably, were other stakes, as well: political stakes for men and factions of both parties; power stakes for interest groups with which they were or wished to be affiliated. And every stake was raised by the apparent discontent in the American public mood. There is no reason to suppose that in such circumstances men of large but differing responsibilities will see all things through the same glasses. On the contrary, it is to be expected that their views of what ought to be done and what they then should do will vary with the differing perspectives their particular responsibilities evoke. Since their duties are not vested in a "team" or a "collegium" but in themselves, as individuals, one must expect that they will see things *for* themselves. Moreover, when they are responsible to many masters and when an event or policy turns loyalty against loyalty—a day-by-day occurrence in the nature of the case—

one must assume that those who have the duties to perform will choose the terms of reconciliation. This is the essence of their personal responsibility. When their own duties pull in opposite directions, who else but they can choose what they will do?

* * *

Outside the Executive Branch the situation is the same, except that loyalty to the President may often matter *less*. . . . And when one comes to congressmen who can do nothing for themselves (or their constituents) save as they are elected, term by term, in districts and through party structures *differing* from those on which a president depends, the case is very clear. An able Eisenhower aide with long congressional experience remarked to me in 1958: "The people on the Hill don't do what they might *like* to do, they do what they think they *have* to do in their own interest as *they* see it. . . ." This states the case precisely.

The essence of a president's persuasive task with congressmen and everybody else, *is to induce them to believe that what he wants of them is what their own appraisal of their own responsibilities requires them to do in their interest, not his.* Because men may differ in their views on public policy, because differences in outlook stem from differences in duty—duty to one's office, one's constituents, oneself—that task is bound to be more like collective bargaining than like a reasoned argument among philosopher kings. Overtly or implicitly, hard bargaining has characterized all illustrations offered up to now. This is the reason why: persuasion deals in the coin of self-interest with men who have some freedom to reject what they find counterfeit.

Let me introduce a case . . . : the European Recovery Program of 1948, the so-called Marshall Plan. This is perhaps the greatest exercise in policy *agreement* since the cold war began. When the then Secretary of State, George Catlett Marshall, spoke at the Harvard commencement in June of 1947, he launched one of the most creative, most imaginative ventures in the history of American foreign relations. What makes this policy most notable for present purposes, however, is that it became effective upon action by the 80th Congress, at the behest of Harry Truman, in the election year of 1948.

Eight months before Marshall spoke at Harvard, the Democrats had lost control of both Houses of Congress for the first time in fourteen years. Truman, whom the Secretary represented, had just finished his second troubled year as president-by-succession. Truman was regarded with so little warmth in his own party that in 1946 he had been urged *not* to participate in the congressional campaign. At the opening of Congress in January 1947, Senator Robert A. Taft, "Mr. Republican," had somewhat the attitude of a president-elect. This was a vision widely shared in Washington, with Truman relegated, thereby, to the role of caretaker-on-term. Moreover, within just two weeks of Marshall's commencement address,

Truman was to veto two prized accomplishments of Taft's congressional majority: the Taft-Hartley Act and tax reduction. Yet scarcely ten months later the Marshall Plan was under way on terms to satisfy its sponsors, its authorization completed, its first-year funds in sight, its administering agency in being: all managed by as thorough a display of executive-congressional cooperation as any we have seen since the Second World War. For any president at any time this would have been a great accomplishment. In years before mid-century it would have been enough to make the future reputation of his term. And for a Truman, at this time, enactment of the Marshall Plan appears almost miraculous.

How was the miracle accomplished? How did a President so situated bring it off? In answer, the first thing to note is that he did not do it by himself. Truman had help of a sort no less extraordinary than the outcome. Although each stands for something more complex, the names of Marshall, Vandenberg, . . . Bevin, Stalin, tell the story of that help.

In 1947, two years after V-J Day, General Marshall was something more than Secretary of State. He was a man venerated by the president as "the greatest living American," literally an embodiment of Truman's ideals. He was honored at the Pentagon as an architect of victory. He was thoroughly respected by the Secretary of the Navy, James V. Forrestal, who that year became the first Secretary of Defense. On Capitol Hill Marshall had an enormous fund of respect stemming from his war record as Army Chief of Staff, and in the country generally no officer had come out of the war with a higher reputation for judgment, intellect, and probity. Besides, as Secretary of State, he had behind him the first generation of matured foreign service officers produced by the reforms of the 1920s, and mingled with them, in the departmental service, were some of the ablest of the men drawn by the war from private life to Washington.

*   *   *

Taken together, these are exceptional resources for a Secretary of State. In the circumstances, they were quite as necessary as they obviously are relevant. The Marshall Plan was launched by a "lame duck" administration "scheduled" to leave office in eighteen months. Marshall's program faced a congressional leadership traditionally isolationist and currently intent upon economy. European aid was viewed with envy by a Pentagon distressed and virtually disarmed through budget cuts, and by domestic agencies intent on enlarged welfare programs. It was not viewed with liking by a Treasury intent on budget surpluses. The plan had need of every asset that could be extracted from the personal position of its nominal author and from the skills of his assistants.

Without the equally remarkable position of the senior Senator from Michigan, Arthur H. Vandenberg, it is hard to see how Marshall's assets could have been enough. Vandenberg was chairman of the Senate Foreign Relations Committee. Actually, he was much more than that. Twenty years a senator, he was the senior member of his party in the Chamber. Assiduously cultivated by F.D.R. and Truman, he was a chief Republican proponent of "bipartisanship" in foreign policy, and consciously conceived himself its living symbol to his party, to the country, and abroad. Moreover, by informal but entirely operative agreement with his colleague Taft, Vandenberg held the acknowledged lead among Senate Republicans in the whole field of international affairs. This acknowledgment meant more in 1947 than it might have meant at any other time. With confidence in the advent of a Republican administration two years hence, most of the gentlemen were in a mood to be responsive and responsible. The war was over, Roosevelt dead, Truman a caretaker, theirs the trust. That the Senator from Michigan saw matters in this light, his diaries make clear. And this was not the outlook from the Senate side alone; the attitudes of House Republicans associated with the Herter Committee and its tours abroad suggest the same mood of responsibility. Vandenberg was not the only source of help on Capitol Hill. But relatively speaking, his position there was as exceptional as Marshall's was downtown.

*   *   *

At Harvard, Marshall had voiced an idea in general terms. That this was turned into a hard program susceptible of presentation and support is due, in major part, to Ernest Bevin, the British Foreign Secretary. He well deserves the credit he has sometimes been assigned as, in effect, co-author of the Marshall Plan. For Bevin seized on Marshall's Harvard speech and organized a European response with promptness and concreteness beyond the State Department's expectations. What had been virtually a trial balloon to test reactions on both sides of the Atlantic was hailed in London as an invitation to the Europeans to send Washington a bill of particulars. This they promptly organized to do, and the American Administration then organized in turn for its reception without further argument internally about the pros and cons of issuing the "invitation" in the first place. But for Bevin there might have been trouble from the Secretary of the Treasury and others besides.

If Bevin's help was useful at that early stage, Stalin's was vital from first to last. In a mood of self-deprecation Truman once remarked that without Moscow's "crazy" moves "we would never have had our foreign policy . . . we never could have got a thing from Congress." George Kennan, among others, had deplored the anti-Soviet overtone of the case made for the Marshall Plan in Congress and the country, but there is no doubt that this clinched the argument for many segments of American opinion. There also is no doubt that Moscow made the crucial contributions to the case.

*   *   *

The crucial thing to note about this case is that despite compatibility of views on public policy, Truman got no help he did not pay for (except

Stalin's). Bevin scarcely could have seized on Marshall's words had Marshall not been plainly backed by Truman. Marshall's interest would not have comported with the exploitation of his prestige by a president who undercut him openly, or subtly, or even inadvertently, at any point. Vandenberg, presumably, could not have backed proposals by a White House which begrudged him deference and access gratifying to his fellow-partisans (and satisfying to himself). Prominent Republicans in private life would not have found it easy to promote a cause identified with Truman's claims on 1948—and neither would the prominent New Dealers then engaged in searching for a substitute.

Truman paid the price required for their services. So far as the record shows, the White House did not falter once in firm support for Marshall and the Marshall Plan. Truman backed his Secretary's gamble on an invitation to all Europe. He made the plan his own in a well-timed address to the Canadians. He lost no opportunity to widen the involvements of his own official family in the cause. Averell Harriman the Secretary of Commerce, Julius Krug the Secretary of the Interior, Edwin Nourse the Economic Council Chairman, James Webb the Director of the Budget—all were made responsible for studies and reports contributing directly to the legislative presentation. Thus these men were committed in advance. Besides, the president continually emphasized to everyone in reach that he did not have doubts, did not desire complications and would foreclose all he could. Reportedly, his emphasis was felt at the Treasury, with good effect. And Truman was at special pains to smooth the way for Vandenberg. The Senator insisted on "no politics" from the Administration side; there was none. He thought a survey of American resources and capacity essential; he got it in the Krug and Harriman reports. Vandenberg expected advance consultation; he received it, step by step, in frequent meetings with the president and weekly conferences with Marshall. He asked for an effective liaison between Congress and agencies concerned; Lovett and others gave him what he wanted. When the Senator decided on the need to change financing and administrative features of the legislation, Truman disregarded Budget Bureau grumbling and acquiesced with grace. When, finally, Vandenberg desired a Republican to head the new administering agency, his candidate, Paul Hoffman, was appointed despite the president's own preference for another. In all of these ways Truman employed the sparse advantages his "powers" and his status then accorded him to gain the sort of help he had to have.

* * *

Had Truman lacked the personal advantages his "powers" and his status gave him, or if he had been maladroit in using them, there probably would not have been a massive European aid program in 1948. . . . The President's own share in this accomplishment was vital. He made his contribution by exploiting his advantages. Truman, in effect, lent Marshall and the rest the perquisites and status of his office. In return they lent him their prestige and their own influence. The transfer multiplied *his* influence despite his limited authority in form and lack of strength politically. Without the wherewithal to make this bargain, Truman could not have contributed to European aid.

* * *

DISCUSSION QUESTIONS

1. Considering recent presidents (Barack Obama and George W. Bush), identify and discuss some examples of Neustadt's argument that presidents cannot get their way by "command" but must bargain to get what they want.

2. Can you think of any recent examples when a president was able to get what he wanted by giving a command (that is, to someone not in the military)?

3. How should a president convince a member of Congress to pass a piece of legislation that the president favors?

31

"Perspectives on the Presidency," from *The Presidency in a Separated System*

CHARLES O. JONES

Just how powerful is the president? Have the fears of some of the framers—that the president would degrade into an imperial despot—been realized, or does the separation of powers effectively check the president's ability to misuse the powers of office? Charles Jones argues that we should view the president as only one of the players in American government; the presidency exists only as one part of a set of institutions where responsibility is diffused, where the bulk of political activity takes place independent of the presidency, and where the different players and institutions learn to adjust to the others. Consider, for example, that President George W. Bush faced a Senate controlled by the Democrats for most of his first two years in office and had to work with them to achieve some of his major goals such as education reform. Or that President Barack Obama left it to Congress to work out many details of health care reform, in contrast to President Bill Clinton, who unsuccessfully attempted to get Congress to enact a major health care reform plan produced by an administration task force. Ultimately, Jones argues, the president is only a part of a larger "separated system," in which Congress, the courts, and the bureaucracy can shape policy.

The president is not the presidency. The presidency is not the government. Ours is not a presidential system.

I begin with these starkly negative themes as partial correctives to the more popular interpretations of the United States government as presidency-centered. Presidents themselves learn these refrains on the job, if they do not know them before. President Lyndon B. Johnson, who had impressive political advantages during the early years of his administration, reflected later on what was required to realize the potentialities of the office:

> Every President has to establish with the various sectors of the country what I call "the right to govern." Just being elected to the office does not guarantee him that right. Every President has to inspire the confidence of the people. Every President has to become a leader, and to be a leader he must attract people who are willing to follow him. Every President has to develop a moral underpinning to his power, or he soon discovers that he has no power at all.

To exercise influence, presidents must learn the setting within which it has bearing. [Then] president-elect Bill Clinton recognized the complexities of translating campaign promises into a legislative program during a news conference shortly after his election in 1992:

> It's all very well to say you want an investment tax credit, and quite another thing to make the 15 decisions that have to be made to shape the exact bill you want.
>
> It's all very well to say . . . that the working poor in this country . . . should be lifted out of poverty by increasing the refundable income tax credit for the working poor, and another thing to answer the five or six questions that define how you get that done.

For presidents, new or experienced, to recognize the limitations of office is commendable. Convincing others to do so is a challenge. Presidents become convenient labels for marking historical time: the Johnson years, the Nixon years, the Reagan years. Media coverage naturally focuses more on the president: there is just one at a time, executive organization is oriented in pyramidal fashion toward the Oval Office, Congress is too diffuse an institution to report on as such, and the Supreme Court leads primarily by indirection. Public interest, too, is directed toward the White House as a symbol of the government. As a result, expectations of a president often far exceed the individual's personal, political, institutional, or constitutional capacities for achievement. Performance seldom matches promise. Presidents who understand how it all works resist the inflated image of power born of high-stakes elections and seek to lower expectations. Politically savvy presidents know instinctively that it is precisely at the moment of great achievement that they must prepare themselves for the setback that will surely follow.

Focusing exclusively on the presidency can lead to a seriously distorted picture of how the national government does its work. The plain fact is that the United States does not have a presidential system. It has a *separated* system. It is odd that it is so commonly thought of as otherwise since schoolchildren learn about the separation of powers and checks and balances. As the author of *Federalist* 51 wrote, "Ambition must be made to counteract ambition." No one, least of all presidents, the Founders reasoned, can be entrusted with excessive authority. Human nature, being what it is, requires "auxiliary precautions" in the form of competing legitimacies.

The acceptance that this is a separated, not a presidential, system, prepares one to appraise how politics works, not to be simply reproachful and reformist. Thus, for example, divided (or split-party) government is accepted as a potential or even likely outcome of a separated system, rooted as it is in the separation of elections. Failure to acknowledge the authenticity of the split-party condition leaves one with little to study and much to reform in the post–World War II period, when the government has been divided more than 60 percent of the time.

Simply put, the role of the president in this separated system of governing varies substantially, depending on his resources, advantages, and strategic position. My strong interest is in how presidents place themselves in an ongoing government and are fitted in by other participants, notably those on Capitol Hill. The central purpose of this book is to explore these "fittings." In pursuing this interest, I have found little value in the presidency-centered, party government perspective, as I will explain below. As a substitute, I propose a separationist, diffused-responsibility perspective that I find more suited to the constitutional, institutional, political, and policy conditions associated with the American system of governing.

*   *   *

The Dominant Perspective

The presidency-centered perspective is consistent with a dominant and well-developed perspective that has been highly influential in evaluating the American political system. The perspective is that of party government, typically one led by a strong or aggressive president. Those advocating this perspective prefer a system in which political parties are stronger than they normally can be in a system of separated elections.

*   *   *

The party government perspective is best summarized in the recommendations made in 1946 by the Committee on Political Parties of the American Political Science Association.

> The party system that is needed must be democratic, responsible and effective. . . .
> An effective party system requires, first, that the parties are able to bring forth programs to which they commit themselves and, second, that the parties possess sufficient internal cohesion to carry out these programs. . . .
> The fundamental requirement of such accountability is a two-party system in which the opposition party acts as the critic of the party in power, developing, defining, and presenting the policy alternatives which are necessary for a true choice in reaching public decisions.

Note the language in this summary: party in power, opposition party, policy alternatives for choice, accountability, internal cohesion, programs to which parties commit themselves. As a whole, it forms a test that a separated system is bound to fail.

I know of very few contemporary advocates of the two-party responsibility model. But I know many analysts who rely on its criteria when judging the political system. One sees this reliance at work when reviewing how elections are interpreted and presidents are evaluated. By this standard, the good campaign and election have the following characteristics:

- Publicly visible issues that are debated by the candidates during the campaign.
- Clear differences between the candidates on the issues, preferably deriving from ideology.

- A substantial victory for the winning candidate, thus demonstrating public support for one set of issue positions.
- A party win accompanying the victory for the president, notably an increase in the presidential party's share of congressional seats and state-houses so that the president's win can be said to have had an impact on other races (the coattail effect).
- A greater than expected win for the victorious party, preferably at both ends of Pennsylvania Avenue.
- A postelection declaration of support and unity from the congressional leaders of the president's party.

The good president, by this perspective, is one who makes government work, one who has a program and uses his resources to get it enacted. The good president is an activist: he sets the agenda, is attentive to the prog-ress being made, and willingly accepts responsibility for what happens. He can behave in this way because he has demonstrable support.

It is not in the least surprising that the real outcomes of separated elec-tions frustrate those who prefer responsible party government. Even a cur-sory reading of the Constitution suggests that these demanding tests will be met only by coincidence. Even an election that gives one party control of the White House and both houses of Congress in no way guarantees a unified or responsible party outcome. And even when a president and his congres-sional party leaders appear to agree on policy priorities, the situation may change dramatically following midterm elections. Understandably, advo-cates of party government are led to propose constitutional reform.

*   *   *

An Alternative Perspective

The alternative perspective for understanding American national politics is bound to be anathema to party responsibility advocates. By the rendition promoted here, responsibility is not focused, it is diffused. Representation is not pure and unidirectional; it is mixed, diluted, and multidirectional. Further, the tracking of policy from inception to implementation discour-ages the most devoted advocate of responsibility theories. In a system of diffused responsibility, credit will be taken and blame will be avoided by both institutions and both parties. For the mature government (one that has achieved substantial involvement in social and economic life), much of the agenda will be self-generating, that is, resulting from programs already on the books. Thus the desire to propose new programs is often frustrated by demands to sustain existing programs, and substantial debt will constrain both.

Additionally there is the matter of who *should* be held accountable for what and when. This is not a novel issue by any means. It is a part of the common rhetoric of split-party government. Are the Democrats responsible for how Medicare has worked because it was a part of Lyndon Johnson's Great Society? Or are the Republicans responsible because their presidents accepted, administered, and revised the program? Is President Carter responsible for creating a Department of Energy or President Reagan responsible for failing to abolish it, or both? The partisan rhetoric on deficits continues to blame the Democrats for supporting spending programs and the Republicans for cutting taxes. It is noteworthy that this level of debate fails to treat more fundamental issues, such as the constitutional roadblocks to defining responsibility. In preventing the tyranny of the majority, the founders also made it difficult to specify accountability.

Diffusion of responsibility, then, is not only a likely result of a separated system but may also be a fair outcome. From what was said above, one has to doubt how reasonable it is to hold one institution or one party accountable for a program that has grown incrementally through decades of single- and split-party control. Yet reforming a government program is bound to be an occasion for holding one or the other of the branches accountable for wrongs being righted. If, however, politics allows crossing the partisan threshold to place both parties on the same side, then agreements may be reached that will permit blame avoidance, credit taking, and, potentially, significant policy change. This is not to say that both sides agree from the start about what to do, in a cabal devoted to irresponsibility (though that process is not unknown). Rather it is to suggest that diffusion of responsibility may permit policy reform that would have been much less likely if one party had to absorb all of the criticism for past performance or blame should the reforms fail when implemented.

Institutional competition is an expected outcome of the constitutional arrangements that facilitate mixed representation and variable electoral horizons. In recent decades this competition has been reinforced by Republicans settling into the White House, the Democrats comfortably occupying the House of Representatives, and, in very recent times, both parties hotly contending for majority status in the Senate. Bargains struck under these conditions have the effect of perpetuating split control by denying opposition candidates (Democratic presidential challengers, Republican congressional challengers) both the issues upon which to campaign and the means for defining accountability.

The participants in this system of mixed representation and diffused responsibility naturally accommodate their political surroundings. Put otherwise, congressional Democrats and presidential Republicans learn how to do their work. Not only does each side adjust to its political circumstances, but both may also be expected to provide themselves with the resources to participate meaningfully in policy politics.

Much of the above suggests that the political and policy strategies of presidents in dealing with Congress will depend on the advantages they have available at any one time. One cannot employ a constant model of the activist president leading a party government. Conditions may encourage the president to work at the margins of president-congressional interaction (for example, where he judges that he has an advantage, as with foreign and defense issues). He may allow members of Congress to take policy initiatives, hanging back to see how the issue develops. He may certify an issue as important, propose a program to satisfy certain group demands, but fail to expend the political capital necessary to get the program enacted. The lame-duck president requires clearer explication. The last months and years of a two-term administration may be one of congressional initiative with presidential response. The point is that having been relieved of testing the system for party responsibility, one can proceed to analyze how presidents perform under variable political and policy conditions.

* * *

In a separated system of diffused responsibility, these are the expectations:

- Presidents will enter the White House with variable personal, political, and policy advantages or resources. Presidents are not equally good at comprehending their advantages or identifying how these advantages may work best for purposes of influencing the rest of the government.
- White House and cabinet organization will be quite personal in nature, reflecting the president's assessment of strengths and weaknesses, the challenges the president faces in fitting into the ongoing government, and the political and policy changes that occur during the term of office. There is no formula for organizing the presidency, though certain models can be identified.
- Public support will be an elusive variable in analyzing presidential power. At the very least, its importance for any one president must be considered alongside other advantages. "Going public" does not necessarily carry a special bonus, though presidents with limited advantages otherwise may be forced to rely on this tactic.
- The agenda will be continuous, with many issues derived from programs already being administered. The president surely plays an important role in certifying issues and setting priorities, but Congress and the bureaucracy will also be natural participants. At the very least, therefore, the president will be required to persuade other policy actors that his choices are the right ones. They will do the same with him.
- Lawmaking will vary substantially in terms of initiative, sequence, partisan and institutional interaction, and productivity. The challenge is to comprehend the variable role of the president in a government that is designed for continuity and change.
- Reform will be an especially intricate undertaking since, by constitutional design, the governmental structure is antithetical to efficient goal achievement. Yet many, if not most, reforms seek to achieve efficiency within the basic separated structure. There are not many reforms designed to facilitate the more effective working of split-party government.

DISCUSSION QUESTIONS

1. The conventional wisdom is that presidential power increases, often dramatically, during war and other national crises. How was President Barack Obama's ability to exercise power affected by the economic and financial crises occurring as he took office?

2. How do President Obama's first two years—declining popularity, Democratic majorities in Congress, and much partisan conflict between Republicans and the president—affect your view of Jones's argument?

3. How can Jones's view of the presidency be squared with the popular view that the president is the most powerful person in the world?

Debating the Issues—Prospects, Possibilities and Perils in Obama's Second Term

After a rocky first term, with both major policy success and major controversies (at times on the same issue), Obama was reelected by a comfortable 51–47 percent margin. He became the third consecutive two-term president. What are the prospects for Obama's second term? What issues will he push, and how likely is he to succeed? Or is he destined for failure, like so many other second-term presidents?

Conventional wisdom holds that second terms are fraught with peril, a view confirmed by scandals and crises in earlier presidencies: George W. Bush suffered from extremely low popularity stemming from the Iraq War, lost control of Congress, and had no success pushing Social Security reform. Clinton was impeached, Reagan suffered through Iran-Contra, and Nixon resigned over Watergate. Is this just a sequence of coincidences, or is there a reason why presidents seem to stumble in their second terms?

There are a number of possible explanations (assuming, of course, that the underlying pattern of failure is actually true): lame-duck status, departure of key personnel after the first term, reliance on second-tier policy ideas not pushed in the first term, congressional resistance, and public weariness, to name a few.

The readings here offer different perspectives on Obama's second term. Clymer, writing in the *New York Times*, notes the pattern of second term failures (going back to FDR's disastrous proposal to pack the Supreme Court), but also points out that not all presidents suffer. Eisenhower had some notable second-term successes, particularly (in Clymer's view) his decision to send the U.S. military into Little Rock, Arkansas, to enforce a school desegregation order. Reagan got a major tax reform law passed in 1986. Clinton, who was the first Democratic president since Truman to face a Republican Congress, nevertheless achieved some notable policy successes prior to his impeachment. Even George W. Bush pushed through the Troubled Asset Relief Program in the fall of 2008.

Cavanaugh, writing in the libertarian journal *Reason*, is worried that Obama's popular-vote majority will embolden the president to push aggressively in a second term. Freed from the fear of electoral repudiation, Obama can to pursue an even grander agenda, with the result that we will have more government and less freedom.

Amar takes a middle position, arguing that second terms hold both peril and promise, and that presidents must deal with long-term shifts in public attitudes that they cannot control. He provides some basic guidelines for a second-termer—designate a successor, don't be afraid to "go bold," and seek structural reforms that make it more difficult to obstruct your agenda.

"Triumphant Obama Faces New Foe in 'Second-Term Curse'"

ADAM CLYMER

Now that President Obama has overcome Mitt Romney, "super PACs" and a sluggish economy, he faces a challenge with deep roots in political history: what historians and commentators call the "second-term curse."

It is almost a truism that second terms are less successful than first terms, especially domestically. Franklin Delano Roosevelt lost his hold on Congress with his 1937 plan to pack the Supreme Court. Ronald Reagan faced the 1986 Iran-contra scandal. Bill Clinton was impeached in 1998. Richard Nixon resigned to avoid that fate in 1974.

Even George Washington had angry mobs surrounding his house in Philadelphia to denounce him for the Jay Treaty with Britain dealing with the aftermath of the Revolutionary War; they wanted him to side with France.

But despite these and other failures, most second-term presidents also have accomplishments to be proud of, though perhaps shadowed by a tinge of failure.

Stephen Hess, a scholar at the Brookings Institution and a veteran of the Eisenhower, Nixon, Ford and Carter administrations, said there were several explanations for the second-term curse.

One is that presidents try to push their best ideas when they first take office, often leaving them, he said, without "a whole new set of ideas" for the second.

Presidents also select the best members of the White House staff or cabinet when they first take office. When the pressure cooker of Washington or better jobs lead those first choices away, their successors are often not their equals.

Roosevelt may have had the most accursed second term. The biographer Jean Edward Smith called it "a disaster." After the 1936 death of Louis Howe, his closest adviser for years, he had no one to tell him what a bad idea the court-packing scheme was. It split his party. Conservative Democrats deserted him and allied with Republicans to deny him almost all domestic legislation.

And while that hurt Roosevelt politically—Mr. Smith said he "shot himself in the foot"—he followed with an even worse decision, cutting federal spending in the belief that the Depression was conquered. That brought on a deep recession. With that decision, Mr. Smith wrote, Roosevelt "shot the country in the foot."

Overwhelming victory can often lead to second-term hubris, persuading a president that the country thinks he can do no wrong. As Lou Cannon, the Reagan biographer and Washington Post White House reporter, observed: "Landslides are dangerous to the victor." Roosevelt lost only two states in 1936; Nixon lost only Massachusetts and the District of Columbia in 1972.

Reagan lost only one state in 1984, and the next two years were "the least successful of Reagan's 16 years in office," including his years as governor of California, Mr. Cannon said. Even a narrow victory can create overconfidence. In 2004, George W. Bush won 50.7 percent of the vote, which was no landslide (even compared with his 48.3 percent share four years earlier). But he treated the victory as a huge mandate, and plunged ahead with a plan to privatize Social Security in 2005, as he had promised during his re-election campaign.

But the Social Security plan went nowhere. Republicans cringed, and Democrats eagerly united in opposition.

Second-term presidents are also lame ducks, parrying ambitious would-be successors in the opposition and in their own party. Dwight Eisenhower often complained of the recently enacted 22nd Amendment, limiting presidents to two terms. But earlier presidents faced the same problem, because tradition back to George Washington had established the same term limit, until Roosevelt ran for his third term.

But are second terms inevitably cursed?

Richard Norton Smith, a presidential scholar at George Mason University, argues for a more nuanced approach to measuring them.

Eisenhower, who easily won re-election, is his prime example. He lacked new ideas, and he lost key cabinet officers and his chief of staff, Sherman Adams. He was embarrassed when a U-2 spy plane was shot down over the Soviet Union in 1960 and Nikita Khrushchev scuttled a Paris summit meeting in response.

But Eisenhower sent troops to Little Rock in 1957 to keep Gov. Orval Faubus of Arkansas from thwarting court-ordered school desegregation. And his 1961 farewell address classically warned, "We must guard against the acquisition of unwarranted influence, whether sought or unsought, by the military industrial complex."

Most important, Eisenhower kept the peace with the Soviet Union, an accomplishment hardly predictable in the '50s.

For President Clinton, there was the first balanced budget in decades, achieved in 1997 because Republicans wanted an accomplishment that they, too, could claim. And Mr. Clinton gained international respect for forcing the Serbs to halt a genocidal campaign in Kosovo without putting NATO troops on the ground. But impeachment was a grave scar, not only for him, but for his accusers as well. Months of debate over the issue led to Democratic gains in the House in the midterm 1998 elections.

Roosevelt accomplished little domestically in his second term, beyond the appointments of Supreme Court justices who shaped the law for many years. But his oratory and cunning moved an isolationist nation and Congress to side with Britain and France against Germany. And he began rebuilding the nation's military as World War II loomed. He also made a brilliant personnel choice, bypassing senior generals to elevate Gen. George C. Marshall to the post of Army chief of staff.

President Bush failed to achieve many legislative goals—privatizing Social Security, liberalizing immigration and overhauling the tax code. But he did win a vast increase in spending on AIDS treatment and prevention in Africa and a modest stimulus measure in 2008. And his most substantial achievement was the Troubled Assets Relief Program, a $700 billion program to rescue banks caught in the subprime mortgage mess.

Nixon achieved little domestically in his foreshortened second term. But after the Paris Peace Accords were signed just after his second inauguration in 1973, American troops were withdrawn from Vietnam and prisoners of war were released. In the Middle East, Secretary of State Henry Kissinger's shuttle diplomacy that fall ended the Arab-Israeli war. Nixon also believed that the role of the United States in overthrowing President Salvador Allende of Chile was a signal success, though today it seems a grave mistake.

For Reagan, the troubles of his second term were offset by the 1986 tax law, which closed loopholes and used the savings to lower tax rates, and his arms control agreements with Mikhail S. Gorbachev of the Soviet Union.

Presidents cannot control everything in their second terms, and President Obama has a few obstacles that are special to him. The president and Congress must be willing to work together, which in a deeply partisan Washington may be difficult to accomplish in the next four years. And like other modern presidents, Mr. Obama must cope with a "snarky" news media, said Mr. Smith, the George Mason University scholar, which glare at a president, magnifying anything that looks like success, or, especially, failure.

"Beware Obama's Big Ideas"

Tim Cavanaugh

The way President Barack Obama's acolytes are calling for bold action in his second term, you'd think he had been some kind of prudent Calvin Coolidge in his first.

"A strategic second term would begin by identifying a list of necessary and achievable goals, and then pursuing them with the unyielding manipulative skill of a Lyndon Johnson," *Washington Post* columnist David Ignatius wrote after Obama's decisive victory over hapless challenger Mitt Romney in November. "Think big. Take risks. Get it done."

"Take this second chance to get it right on housing," wrote Tracy Van Slyke, director of something called the New Bottom Line, at *The Huffington Post*, "and use your mandate to help the millions of underwater homeowners across this country." *Atlantic* Associate Editor Matthew O'Brien didn't even wait for the election results to come in, calling on the president in October to unveil a bold second-term agenda that would embrace the "vision thing" by resurrecting his deep-sixed American Jobs Act.

Given that Obama won re-election largely by not talking about his record, it's probably not surprising that so many people don't seem to have noticed what happened from 2009 through 2012. To recap, Obama rammed through a massive overhaul of medical care in the Patient Protection and Affordable Care Act, a.k.a. ObamaCare. He piled another $830 billion or so onto the national debt with his American Recovery and Reinvestment Act, a.k.a. the stimulus. He also managed to push total debt over $16 trillion.

When the Affordable Care Act's most radical component, the requirement that every American be forced to purchase health insurance, came up for Supreme Court review, the president's bumbling attorneys lucked into a tortured decision in their favor, and the law was upheld by a 5-to-4 margin. Capitalizing on (though not actually solving) the financial crisis that helped him gain office, Obama in 2010 signed the Dodd-Frank Wall Street Reform and Consumer Protection Act, bringing a massive new cudgel to the financial industry (which had hardly been free of Washington oversight and protection prior to that) and creating a federal "consumer" agency whose scope is still not well understood.

Unfazed by a public rebuke in the 2010 midterm elections, Obama continued his mission through a daunting new strategy of regulatory rule making, executive orders, administration through "White House liaison officers," and recess appointments of congressionally unpopular nominees. (These last have been carried out even when Congress was not in recess.) Such tactics are necessary to patch a weakness Obama has discovered in American government: the foundational structure of checks and balances.

"When Congress refuses to act, and as a result, hurts our economy and puts our people at risk, then I have an obligation as president to do what I can without them," the president told a crowd in Shaker Heights, Ohio, in January 2011. "I've got an obligation to act on behalf of the American people. And I'm not going to stand by while a minority in the Senate puts party ideology ahead of the people that we were elected to serve. Not with so much at stake, not at this make-or-break moment for middle-class Americans. We're not going to let that happen."

Following that bold conviction, Obama launched a war in Libya without even the almost-constitutional fig leaf of a congressional authorization vote (thus making him even less deferential to Congress' war-making power than George W. Bush). This "kinetic action" seemed to be a rousing success until the U.S. ambassador was killed by terrorists in September —an episode the administration has worked tirelessly to obscure.

Obama has also claimed powers of life and death beyond Bush's wildest ambitions, granting to himself a new presidential authority to kill citizens and noncitizens alike, both on U.S. soil and abroad, while asserting that an Oval Office discussion with advisers qualifies as constitutional due process.

After all that, what would Obama fans consider an ambitious second-term agenda? I guess mandatory self-esteem boosts, universal health care for cats, and a global war on melancholy haven't been tried yet. But Obama's penchant for intervening in all aspects of American life (according to the U.S. Chamber of Commerce, he added 11,327 pages to the Code of Federal Regulations, a 7.4 percent increase, in his first three years) while overlooking constitutional niceties has produced a consistent pattern: As you get more regulation, you get less law.

For some of us, this is a problem. Law is big and clear. It applies equally to the great and small. You can usually be confident that a law has passed at least some level of civic scrutiny. Regulation, by contrast, is small and stifling. It places burdens primarily on individuals and small companies that don't have sufficient lawyerly infrastructure.

And there's no way to know which White House czar or career apparatchik composed any particular regulation. For example, who at Eric Holder's Department of Justice (DOJ) decided in 2011 that the Americans with Disabilities Act requires hotels, restaurants, and airlines to accommodate "pygmy ponies" as service animals. (And should we be glad the

DOJ is mandating horse fairness instead of giving more guns to Mexican drug cartels?)

"The best is yet to come," Obama promised in his November victory speech. And the election result gave him some justification for that promise. He won a lopsided electoral victory and, rare in modern presidential races, a popular majority. This is what makes the second term such a matter of concern.

Nearly 61 million voters have gotten to know Obama's mix of soaring rhetoric and bureaucratic reality, messianic claims and crushing mandates, cultish iconography and lawless actions, grand hopes and bland changes. And they decided they wanted more of it.

I don't expect that avoiding the "fiscal cliff" will be reward enough for those folks. Obama came into office with talk of reversing the tides, healing the earth, and "fundamentally transforming the United States of America." He has hinted at delivering big things in the security of a second term. If the first act was any indication, those things are going to suck.

34

"Second Chances"

AKHIL REED AMAR

Second terms in the White House have, in many cases, ranged from the disappointing to the disastrous. Sick of the political infighting that intensified after his reelection, George Washington could hardly wait to retire to Mount Vernon. Ulysses S. Grant's second term was plagued by political scandal and economic panic. Woodrow Wilson left office a broken man, having suffered a massive stroke during his failed crusade to persuade America to join the League of Nations. Republican Dwight D. Eisenhower was routed in his last political battle, leaving Democrats in control of the presidency, the House, the Senate, and the Supreme Court for nearly the rest of his life. More recently, Richard Nixon resigned in disgrace; Ronald Reagan was tarred by the Iran-Contra scandal; Bill Clinton was impeached; and George W. Bush watched helplessly as his opponents surged into both houses of Congress and then the White House.

Hence the legendary "second-term curse." In the early days of the republic, second-termers were by tradition discouraged from seeking another term, and nowadays, presidents are legally barred from a third term, thanks to the Twenty-Second Amendment. Popular wisdom has it that second-termers are therefore lame ducks. Unable to run again, how can a term-limited president reward his allies or restrain his adversaries? If he is seen as a fading force, won't his allies hitch themselves to the next rising star? Won't his adversaries attack relentlessly?

Fortunately for Barack Obama, the situation is not that bleak. For one thing, the idea of a second-term curse fails to account for basic probability. Most presidents fail in one way or another, and many nose-dive so fast that they never get a second term. Perhaps the "curse" is actually an example of what statisticians call "regression to the mean": those presidents who beat the political odds in term one usually cannot maintain their lucky streak in term two. Nor does the curse account for several exceptional presidents whose authority *increased* following reelection. By looking at these two-term stars more closely, we can see how and why Obama might be more blessed than cursed.

From our nation's founding to the present, politics has followed a tidal pattern. Once a party devises a new and successful electoral formula—a workable coalition that can consistently outnumber the opposition—that party tends to win, and keep winning, until eventually, the tide changes and the other party takes the lead. So far, U.S. history has seen four such reversals, each of which coincided with the election, and reelection, of an exceptional president. Yes, each of the four figures who presided over these great shifts—Thomas Jefferson, Abraham Lincoln, Franklin Roosevelt, and Ronald Reagan—had his share of second-term tribulations and catastrophes. (Lincoln, of course, died weeks after delivering his epic second inaugural address, and only days after Lee's surrender.) But thanks to his own exceptional skills, as well as the fragility of the opposition party, each man forged a new electoral coalition that kept winning long after he left office.

The first turning of the political tide occurred shortly after George Washington's death. In 1800, Jefferson's triumph over John Adams marked the beginning of the end of the Federalist era. In 1804, Jefferson won a second term, and in 1808 he transferred power to his political lieutenant. James Madison. Jefferson and Madison's Democratic-Republican Party (later renamed the Democratic Party) remained America's dominant presidential party until the Civil War era, when the tide turned a second time. Lincoln, a Republican, won, won again, and (in the election following his assassination) was succeeded by a political heir, Ulysses Grant. Republicans dominated the presidency until the Great Depression—and FDR's election and reelections—marked a third tidal shift. The Democrats' resulting New Deal/Great Society coalition generally held until it was ripped apart by the Vietnam War and the migration of white southern Democrats to the GOP. Enter Ronald Reagan, whose two terms marked a fourth turning of the electoral tide.

We have been living in the Reagan era ever since. But now, inexorable forces—the changing voting habits of women and young adults, the rising political power of nonwhites and immigrants—mean that the Reagan electoral formula, with its reliance on southern whites, tax-averse businessmen, evangelicals, and Catholics, no longer yields a working majority. The tide may be turning back to the Democrats. Obama's reelection is particularly historic given modern Democratic presidents' track record of failing to win the popular vote. He is only the second Democratic president since the Civil War to win two popular majorities—the other was FDR (who, of course, won four). Since Lincoln, in fact, only four Democrats have won even one popular-vote majority—and that tally includes Jimmy Carter, with 50.1 percent of the vote. Bill Clinton never had a popular majority.

So what lessons might Obama borrow from his successful two-term predecessors to avoid being perceived as a lame duck? First, though he cannot succeed himself in 2016, he can designate a proxy to replace him—a loyal lieutenant willing to help his friends, smite his foes, and keep his secrets long after he leaves office. Reagan fared as well as he did in part because he had designated George H. W. Bush as his wingman, and in effect won a third term when Bush became "Bush 41." By contrast, Eisenhower kept his vice president, Richard Nixon, at a distance. (When asked during the 1960 general election whether his administration had adopted any major ideas of Nixon's, Ike replied, "If you give me a week. I might think of one.") The Lewinsky scandal drove a wedge between Clinton and his wingman, Al Gore. A successor—or the lack of one—can shape not just a president's performance, but also his legacy. When George W. Bush's time was up, his party tapped John McCain, a White House outsider whose relationship with the president was feisty and rivalrous.

Second, Obama should take advantage of his relative youth, which gives him a distinct edge over most of his predecessors: Until recently, most second-term presidents were well past their prime, both physically and mentally. At age 51, Obama can remain a potent political force even in retirement; he should exploit this fact to enhance his current clout. (Only Grant and Clinton were younger than Obama at the start of their second terms—and think of how Clinton has remained relevant in recent years.)

If he's to beat the second-term curse, Obama will also need to go bold and big. Just as FDR's New Deal programs and Reagan's tax cuts won over whole generations of voters, Obama must find ways to entrench his own legacy—and in the process, his new base. Immigration reform, for example, could draw the kind of young, highly skilled workers who might be able to pay for Social Security benefits for retiring Baby Boomers. Election reform might restore the luster of American democracy—while making it easier for Democratic voters to cast ballots.

One caveat: big changes like these can't succeed unless another big change comes early in term two—Senate filibuster of reform. The signature accomplishment of Obama's first term, Obamacare, crowded out other reforms because Senate Democrats had to scrape together 60 votes to avoid a filibuster, rather than the simple majority the Constitution requires for passage of a law. If Senate reformers can tame the filibuster early in Obama's second term—and it appears that Democratic leaders are indeed serious about changing the Senate's rules this January, using a party-line vote to limit the minority party's power to slow or stop legislation—then the political picture will change dramatically.

Without filibuster reform, the 45 Republicans in the Senate can quietly block up-or-down votes, with the result being that individual senators from moderate states don't have to visibly go on record voting against popular Obama agenda items. But if the filibuster were blunted, and only 51 senators' votes were needed, many key bills would pass with or without the GOP, and some savvy Republicans would choose to swim with the larger electoral tide. Americans would begin to see Republicans and Democrats working together again in the Senate—and this could change dynamics in the House.

And if not, there's always 2014. When it comes to midterm elections, lameness, handled deftly, can be a source of strength. In 2008, Obama ran as a uniter; had he campaigned aggressively against House Republicans in either 2010 or 2012, he might have tarnished his image, and imperiled his own reelection prospects. But this time around, there's nothing to stop him from going after those who obstruct his agenda. Beware the lame duck: he can bite hard.

By then, in any case, most eyes will be turning to the 2016 campaign trail. Which brings us back to our first lesson—possibly the most important one: each previous tide-turning president was succeeded in the next presidential election by a handpicked ally. Like Reagan, Obama has a possible wingman in his vice president. Joe Biden could dutifully offer to replace him, thus safeguarding Obama's power throughout his second term and beyond. But Obama has at least one other outstanding option: just as Jefferson handed presidential power to his talented secretary of state, James Madison, Obama could do the same with Hillary Clinton.

Ultimately, nothing succeeds like succession.

DISCUSSION QUESTIONS

1. Is the "second term" curse real, or just (as Amar argues) a matter of probability? Do we remember failures more easily than we recall successes? Do you agree with the descriptions of second term failures and successes?

2. Is the political advice in these readings particular to Obama or is it broadly true for all presidents? Do you think Obama's second term will be more or less successful than his first? Why?

3. Was the Twenty-Second Amendment (which imposes a two-term limit) a mistake? How would presidents behave differently if they were eligible for additional terms?

CHAPTER 7

Bureaucracy

35

"The Study of Administration"

Woodrow Wilson

Until the late nineteenth century, almost no one paid attention to how the government actually worked. Administrative positions were generally filled by political appointees who were supporters of elected officials, and there was little that resembled "management" in the contemporary sense. However, a great deal of money was distributed at the national level, and as scandals mounted over the manner in which the money was distributed, the demand for government accountability grew.

Reformers argued that government employees should be hired on the basis of their merit, rather than because of their political allegiance to one candidate or another. Others called for reforms in the administration of public programs. Nearly thirty years before he was president, Woodrow Wilson, then a professor at Bryn Mawr College, wrote an article for Political Science Quarterly *arguing that political scientists had neglected the study of public administration—the problems involved in managing public programs. He argued that public administration should be carried out in accordance with scientific principles of management and efficiency, an argument that would recur every few decades in demands to reform and "reinvent" government.*

It is the object of administrative study to discover, first, what government can properly and successfully do, and, secondly, how it can do these proper things with the utmost possible efficiency and at the least possible cost either of money or of energy. On both these points there is obviously much need of light among us; and only careful study can supply that light.

* * *

The science of administration is the latest fruit of that study of the science of politics which was begun some twenty-two hundred years ago. It is a birth of our own century, almost of our own generation.

Why was it so late in coming? Why did it wait till this too busy century of ours to demand attention for itself? Administration is the most obvious part of government; it is government in action; it is the executive, the operative, the most visible side of government, and is of course as old as government itself. It is government in action, and one might very naturally expect to find that government in action had arrested the attention and provoked the scrutiny of writers of politics very early in the history of systematic thought.

But such was not the case. No one wrote systematically of administration as a branch of the science of government until the present century had passed its first youth and had begun to put forth its characteristic flower of systematic knowledge. Up to our own day all the political writers whom we now read had thought, argued, dogmatized only about the *constitution* of government; about the nature of the state, the essence and seat of sovereignty, popular power and kingly prerogative; about the greatest meanings lying at the heart of government, and the high ends set before the purpose of government by man's nature and man's aims. * * * The question was always: Who shall make law, and what shall that law be? The other question, how law should be administered with enlightenment, with equity, with speed, and without fiction, was put aside as "practical detail" which clerks could arrange after doctors had agreed upon principles.

* * *

[However,] if difficulties of government action are to be seen gathering in other centuries, they are to be seen culminating in our own.

This is the reason why administrative tasks have nowadays to be so studiously and systematically adjusted to carefully tested standards of policy, the reason why we are having now what we never had before, a science of administration. The weightier debates of constitutional principle are even yet by no means concluded; but they are no longer of more immediate practical moment than questions of administration. It is getting to be harder to *run* a constitution than to frame one.

* * *

There is scarcely a single duty of government which was once simple which is not now complex; government once had but a few masters; it now has scores of masters. Majorities formerly only underwent government; they now conduct government. Where government once might follow the whims of a court, it must now follow the views of a nation.

And those views are steadily widening to new conceptions of state duty; so that at the same time that the functions of government are every day becoming more complex and difficult, they are also vastly multiplying in number. Administration is everywhere putting its hands to new undertakings. * * * Seeing every day new things which the state ought to do, the next thing is to see clearly how it ought to do them.

This is why there should be a science of administration which shall seek to straighten the paths of government, to make its business less businesslike, to strengthen and purify its organization, and to crown its dutifulness. This is one reason why there is such a science.

But where has this science grown up? Surely not on this side [of] the sea. Not much impartial scientific method is to be discerned in our administrative practices. The poisonous atmosphere of city government, the crooked secrets of state administration, the confusion, sinecurism, and corruption ever and again discovered in the bureaus at Washington forbid us to believe that any clear conceptions of what constitutes good administration are as yet very widely current in the United States.

* * *

American political history has been a history, not of administrative development, but of legislative oversight—not of progress in governmental organization, but of advance in lawmaking and political criticism. Consequently, we have reached a time when administrative study and creation are imperatively necessary to the well-being of our governments saddled with the habits of a long period of constitution-making. * * * We have reached * * * the period * * * when the people have to develop administration in accordance with the constitutions they won for themselves in a previous period of struggle with absolute power.

* * *

It is harder for democracy to organize administration than for monarchy. The very completeness of our most cherished political successes in the past embarrasses us. We have enthroned public opinion; and it is forbidden us to hope during its reign for any quick schooling of the sovereign in executive expertness or in the conditions of perfect functional balance in government. The very fact that we have realized popular rule in its fullness has made the task of *organizing* that rule just so much the more difficult. * * * An individual sovereign will adopt a simple plan and carry it out directly: he will have but one opinion, and he will embody that one opinion in one command. But this other sovereign, the people, will have a score of differing opinions. They can agree upon nothing simple: advance must be made through compromise, by a compounding of differences, by a trimming of plans and a suppression of too straightforward principles. There will be a succession of resolves running through a course of years, a dropping fire of commands running through a whole gamut of modifications.

* * *

Wherever regard for public opinion is a first principle of government, practical reform must be slow and all reform must be full of compromises. For wherever public opinion exists it must rule.

*   *   *

The field of administration is a field of business. It is removed from the hurry and strife of politics; it at most points stands apart even from the debatable ground of constitutional study. It is a part of political life only as the methods of the counting-house are a part of the life of society; only as machinery is part of the manufactured product. But it is, at the same time, raised very far above the dull level of mere technical detail by the fact that through its greater principles it is directly connected with the lasting maxims of political wisdom, the permanent truths of political progress.

The object of administrative study is to rescue executive methods from the confusion and costliness of empirical experiment and set them upon foundations laid deep in stable principle.

*   *   *

[A]dministration lies outside the proper sphere of *politics*. Administrative questions are not political questions. Although politics sets the tasks for administration, it should not be suffered to manipulate its offices.

*   *   *

There is another distinction which must be worked into all our conclusions, which, though but another side of that between administration and politics, is not quite so easy to keep sight of: I mean the distinction between *constitutional* and administrative questions, between those governmental adjustments which are essential to constitutional principle and those which are merely instrumental to the possibly changing purposes of a wisely adapting convenience.

*   *   *

A clear view of the difference between the province of constitutional law and the province of administrative function ought to leave no room for misconception; and it is possible to name some roughly definite criteria upon which such a view can be built. Public administration is detailed and systematic execution of public law. Every particular application of general law is an act of administration. The assessment and raising of taxes, for instance, the hanging of a criminal, the transportation and delivery of the mails, the equipment and recruiting of the army, and navy, etc., are all obviously acts of administration; but the general laws which direct these things to be done are as obviously outside of and above administration. The broad plans of governmental action are not administrative; the detailed execution of such plans is administrative. Constitutions, therefore, properly concern themselves only with those instrumentalities of government which are to control general law. Our federal constitution observes this principle in saying nothing of even the greatest of the purely executive offices, and speaking only of that President of the Union who was to share the legislative and policy-making functions of government, only of those judges of highest jurisdiction who were to interpret and guard its principles, and not of those who were merely to give utterance to them.

* * *

There is, [however,] one point at which administrative studies trench on constitutional ground—or at least upon what seems constitutional ground. The study of administration, philosophically viewed, is closely connected with the study of the proper distribution of constitutional authority. To be efficient it must discover the simplest arrangements by which responsibility can be unmistakably fixed upon officials; the best way of dividing authority without hampering it, and responsibility without obscuring it. And this question of the distribution of authority, when taken into the sphere of the higher, the originating functions of government, is obviously a central constitutional question.

* * *

To discover the best principle for the distribution of authority is of greater importance, possibly, under a democratic system, where officials serve many masters, than under others where they serve but a few. All sovereigns are suspicious of their servants, and the sovereign people is no exception to the rule; but how is its suspicion to be allayed by *knowledge*? If that suspicion could be clarified into wise vigilance, it would be altogether salutary; if that vigilance could be aided by the unmistakable placing of responsibility, it would be altogether beneficent. Suspicion in itself is never healthful either in the private or in the public mind. *Trust is strength* in all relations of life; and, as it is the office of the constitutional reformer to create conditions of trustfulness, so it is the office of the administrative organizer to fit administration with conditions of clearcut responsibility which shall insure trustworthiness.

And let me say that large powers and unhampered discretion seem to me the indispensable conditions of responsibility. Public attention must be easily directed, in each case of good or bad administration, to just the man deserving of praise or blame. There is no danger in power, if only it be not irresponsible. If it be divided, dealt out in shares to many, it is obscured; and if it be obscured, it is made irresponsible. But if it be centered in heads of the service and in heads of branches of the service, it is easily watched and brought to book. If to keep his office a man must achieve open and honest success, and if at the same time he feels himself intrusted with large freedom of discretion, the greater his power the less likely is he to abuse it, the more is he nerved and sobered and elevated by it. The less his power, the more safely obscure and unnoticed does he feel his position to be, and the more readily does he relapse into remissness.

Just here we manifestly emerge upon the field of that still larger question—the proper relations between public opinion and administration.

To whom is official trustworthiness to be disclosed, and by whom is it to be rewarded? Is the official to look to the public for his meed of praise and his push of promotion, or only to his superior in office? Are the people to be called in to settle administrative discipline as they are called in to settle constitutional principles? These questions evidently find their root in what is undoubtedly the fundamental problem of this whole study. That problem is: What part shall public opinion take in the conduct of administration?

The right answer seems to be, that public opinion shall play the part of authoritative critic.

But the *method* by which its authority shall be made to tell? Our peculiar American difficulty in organizing administration is not the danger of losing liberty, but the danger of not being able or willing to separate its essentials from its accidents. Our success is made doubtful by that besetting error of ours, the error of trying to do too much by vote. Self-government does not consist in having a hand in everything, any more than housekeeping consists necessarily in cooking dinner with one's own hands. The cook must be trusted with a large discretion as to the management of the fires and the ovens.

*   *   *

The problem is to make public opinion efficient without suffering it to be meddlesome. Directly exercised, in the oversight of the daily details and in the choice of the daily means of government, public criticism is of course a clumsy nuisance, a rustic handling delicate machinery. But as superintending the greater forces of formative policy alike in politics and administration, public criticism is altogether safe and beneficent, altogether indispensable. Let administrative study find the best means for giving public criticism this control and for shutting it out from all other interference.

But is the whole duty of administrative study done when it has taught the people what sort of administration to desire and demand, and how to get what they demand? Ought it not to go on to drill candidates for the public service?

*   *   *

If we are to improve public opinion, which is the motive power of government, we must prepare better officials as the *apparatus* of government. * * * It will be necessary to organize democracy by sending up to the competitive examinations for the civil service men definitely prepared for standing liberal tests as to technical knowledge. A technically schooled civil service will presently have become indispensable.

I know that a corps of civil servants prepared by a special schooling and drilled, after appointment, into a perfected organization, with appropriate hierarchy and characteristic discipline, seems to a great many very thoughtful persons to contain elements which might combine to make an offensive official class—a distinct, semi-corporate body with sympathies divorced from those of a progressive, free-spirited people, and with hearts narrowed to the meanness of a bigoted officialism.

*   *   *

But to fear the creation of a domineering, illiberal officialism as a result of the studies I am here proposing is to miss altogether the principle upon which I wish most to insist. That principle is, that administration in the United States must be at all points sensitive to public opinion. A body of thoroughly trained officials serving during good behavior we must have in any case: that is a plain business necessity. But the apprehension that such a body will be anything un-American clears away the moment it is asked, What is to constitute good behavior? For that question obviously carries its own answer on its face. Steady, hearty allegiance to the policy of the government they serve will constitute good behavior. That *policy* will have no taint of officialism about it. It will not be the creation of permanent officials, but of statesmen whose responsibility to public opinion will be direct and inevitable. Bureaucracy can exist only where the whole service of the state is removed from the common political life of the people, its chiefs as well as its rank and file. Its motives, its objects, its policy, its standards, must be bureaucratic.

*   *   *

The ideal for us is a civil service cultured and self-sufficient enough to act with sense and vigor, and yet so intimately connected with the popular thought, by means of elections and constant public counsel, as to find arbitrariness or class spirit quite out of the question.

Having thus viewed in some sort the subject-matter and the objects of this study of administration, what are we to conclude as to the methods best suited to it—the points of view most advantageous for it?

Government is so near us, so much a thing of our daily familiar handling, that we can with difficulty see the need of any philosophical study of it, or the exact point of such study, should it be undertaken. We have been on our feet too long to study now the art of walking. We are a practical people, made so apt, so adept in self-government by centuries of experimental drill that we are scarcely any longer capable of perceiving the awkwardness of the particular system we may be using, just because it is so easy for us to use any system. We do not study the art of governing: we govern. But mere unschooled genius for affairs will not save us from sad blunders in administration. Though democrats by long inheritance and repeated choice, we are still rather crude democrats. Old as democracy is, its organization on a basis of modern ideas and conditions is still an unaccomplished work. The democratic state has yet to be equipped for carrying those enormous burdens of administration which the needs of this industrial and trading age are so fast accumulating.

* * *

We can borrow the science of administration [developed elsewhere] with safety and profit if only we read all fundamental differences of condition into its essential tenets. We have only to filter it through our constitutions, only to put it over a slow fire of criticism and distil away its foreign gases.

* * *

Our own politics must be the touchstone for all theories. The principles on which to base a science of administration for America must be principles which have democratic policy very much at heart. And, to suit American habit, all general theories must, as theories, keep modestly in the background, not in open argument only, but even in our own minds—lest opinions satisfactory only to the standards of the library should be dogmatically used, as if they must be quite as satisfactory to the standards of practical politics as well. Doctrinaire devices must be postponed to tested practices. Arrangements not only sanctioned by conclusive experience elsewhere but also congenial to American habit must be preferred without hesitation to theoretical perfection. In a word, steady, practical statesmanship must come first, closet doctrine second. The cosmopolitan what-to-do must always be commanded by the American how-to-do-it.

Our duty is to supply the best possible life to a *federal* organization, to systems within systems; to make town, city, county, state, and federal governments live with a like strength and an equally assured healthfulness, keeping each unquestionably its own master and yet making all interdependent and co-operative, combining independence with mutual helpfulness. The task is great and important enough to attract the best minds.

This interlacing of local self-government with federal self-government is quite a modern conception. * * * The question for us is, how shall our series of governments within governments be so administered that it shall always be to the interest of the public officer to serve, not his superior alone but the community also, with the best efforts of his talents and the soberest service of his conscience? How shall such service be made to his commonest interest by contributing abundantly to his sustenance, to his dearest interest by furthering his ambition, and to his highest interest by advancing his honor and establishing his character? And how shall this be done alike for the local part and for the national whole?

If we solve this problem we shall again pilot the world.

DISCUSSION QUESTIONS

1. Do you agree with Wilson's central proposition that politics and administration are separate things? Can you think of any examples where the two overlap? Is it possible, or even desirable, to separate politics and administration?

2. Should there be an expectation of neutral efficiency that separates politicians' policy views from the work of government agencies?

3. Should government officials be able to take into account whether someone supports an agency's goals when deciding whom to hire? Does your answer differ depending on whether the agency is involved in foreign policy, domestic policy, or national security?

36

From *Bureaucracy: What Government Agencies Do and Why They Do It*

James Q. Wilson

Woodrow Wilson was merely the first in a long line of reformers to suggest that government might be more efficient if it ran more like a business. The sentiment remains today. Perhaps a more "businesslike" government would issue our income tax refunds more promptly, protect the environment at lower cost, and impose fewer burdens on citizens. The catch is, we want all this at low cost and minimal intrusiveness in our lives, yet we want government bureaucracies to be held strictly accountable for the authority they exercise.

James Q. Wilson argues that government will never operate like a business, nor should we expect it to. His comparison of the Watertown, Massachusetts Registry of Motor Vehicles (representing any government bureaucracy) with a nearby McDonald's (representing any private profit-seeking organization) shows that the former will most likely never service its clientele as well as the latter. The problem is not bureaucratic laziness, or any of the conventional criticisms of government agencies, but is instead due to the very different characteristics of public versus private enterprises. In order to understand "what government agencies do and why they do it," Wilson argues we must first understand that government bureaucracies operate in a political marketplace, rather than an economic one. The annual revenues and personnel resources of a government agency are determined by elected officials, not by the agency's ability to meet the demands of its customers in a cost-efficient manner. The government agency's internal structure and decision-making procedures are defined by legislation, regulation, and executive orders, whereas similar decisions in a private business are made by executive officers and management within the organization. And, perhaps most critical, a government agency's goals are often vague, difficult if not impossible to measure, and even contradictory. In business, by contrast, the task is clearer. The basic goal of a private business has always been to maximize the bottom line: profit. Although suggesting we should not approach the reform of government agencies the way we might a private bureaucracy, James Q. Wilson notes in this 1980s analysis that we should nevertheless try to make government bureaucracies operate more effectively and efficiently.

By the time the office opens at 8:45 A.M., the line of people waiting to do business at the Registry of Motor Vehicles in Watertown, Massachusetts, often will be twenty-five deep. By midday, especially if it is near the end of the month, the line may extend clear around the building. Inside, motorists wait in slow-moving rows before poorly marked windows to get a driver's license or to register an automobile. When someone gets to the head of the line, he or she is often told by the clerk that it is the wrong line: "Get an application over there and then come back," or "This is only for people getting a new license; if you want to replace one you lost, you have to go to the next window." The customers grumble impatiently. The clerks act harried and sometimes speak brusquely, even rudely. What seems to be a simple transaction may take 45 minutes or even longer. By the time people are photographed for their driver's licenses, they are often scowling. The photographer valiantly tries to get people to smile, but only occasionally succeeds.

Not far away, people also wait in line at a McDonald's fast-food restaurant. There are several lines; each is short, each moves quickly. The menu is clearly displayed on attractive signs. The workers behind the counter are invariably polite. If someone's order cannot be filled immediately, he or she is asked to step aside for a moment while the food is prepared and then is brought back to the head of the line to receive the order. The atmosphere is friendly and good-natured. The room is immaculately clean.

Many people have noticed the difference between getting a driver's license and ordering a Big Mac. Most will explain it by saying that bureaucracies are different from businesses. "Bureaucracies" behave as they do because they are run by unqualified "bureaucrats" and are enmeshed in "rules" and "red tape."

But business firms are also bureaucracies, and McDonald's is a bureaucracy that regulates virtually every detail of its employees' behavior by a complex and all-encompassing set of rules. Its operations manual is six hundred pages long and weighs four pounds. In it one learns that french fries are to be nine-thirty-seconds of an inch thick and that grill workers are to place hamburger patties on the grill from left to right, six to a row for six rows. They are then to flip the third row first, followed by the fourth, fifth, and sixth rows, and finally the first and second. The amount of sauce placed on each bun is precisely specified. Every window must be washed every day. Workers must get down on their hands and knees and pick up litter as soon as it appears. These and countless other rules designed to reduce the workers to interchangeable automata were inculcated in franchise managers at Hamburger University located in a $40 million facility. There are plenty of rules governing the Registry, but they are only a small fraction of the rules that govern every detail of every operation at McDonald's. Indeed, if the DMV manager tried to impose on his employees as demanding a set of rules as those that govern the McDonald's staff, they would probably rebel and he would lose his job.

It is just as hard to explain the differences between the two organizations by reference to the quality or compensation of their employees. The Registry workers are all adults, most with at least a high-school education; the McDonald's employees are mostly teenagers, many still in school. The Registry staff is well-paid compared to the McDonald's workers, most of whom receive only the minimum wage. When labor shortages developed in Massachusetts during the mid-1980s, many McDonald's stores began hiring older people (typically housewives) of the same sort who had long worked for the Registry. They behaved just like the teenagers they replaced.

Not only are the differences between the two organizations not to be explained by reference to "rules" or "red tape" or "incompetent workers," the differences call into question many of the most frequently mentioned complaints about how government agencies are supposed to behave. For example: "Government agencies are big spenders." The Watertown office of the Registry is in a modest building that can barely handle its clientele. The teletype machine used to check information submitted by people requesting a replacement license was antiquated and prone to errors. Three or four clerks often had to wait in line to use equipment described by the office manager as "personally signed by Thomas Edison." No computers or word processors were available to handle the preparation of licenses and registrations; any error made by a clerk while manually typing a form meant starting over again on another form.

Or: "Government agencies hire people regardless of whether they are really needed." Despite the fact that the citizens of Massachusetts probably have more contact with the Registry than with any other state agency, and despite the fact that these citizens complain more about Registry service than about that of any other bureau, the Watertown branch, like all Registry offices, was seriously understaffed. In 1981, the agency lost 400 workers—about 25 percent of its work force—despite the fact that its workload was rising.

Or: "Government agencies are imperialistic, always grasping for new functions." But there is no record of the Registry doing much grasping, even though one could imagine a case being made that the state government could usefully create at Registry offices "one-stop" multi-service centers where people could not only get drivers' licenses but also pay taxes and parking fines, obtain information, and transact other official business. The Registry seemed content to provide one service.

In short, many of the popular stereotypes about government agencies and their members are either questionable or incomplete. To explain why government agencies behave as they do, it is not enough to know that they are "bureaucracies"—that is, it is not enough to know that they are big, or complex, or have rules. What is crucial is that they are *government* bureaucracies. * * * [N]ot all government bureaucracies behave the same way or suffer from the same problems. There may even be registries of motor vehicles in other states that do a better job than the one in Massachusetts. But all government agencies have in common certain characteristics that tend to make their management far more difficult than managing a McDonald's. These common characteristics are the constraints of public agencies.

The key constraints are three in number. To a much greater extent than is true of private bureaucracies, government agencies (1) cannot lawfully retain and devote to the private benefit of their members the earnings of the organization, (2) cannot allocate the factors of production in accordance with the preferences of the organization's administrators, and (3) must serve goals not of the organization's own choosing. Control over revenues, productive factors, and agency goals is all vested to an important degree in entities external to the organization—legislatures, courts, politicians, and interest groups. Given this, agency managers must attend to the demands of these external entities. As a result, government management tends to be driven by the *constraints* on the organization, not the *tasks* of the organization. To say the same thing in other words, whereas business management focuses on the "bottom line" (that is, profits), government management focuses on the "top line" (that is, constraints). Because government managers are not as strongly motivated as private ones to define the tasks of their subordinates, these tasks are often shaped by [other] factors.

* * *

Revenues and Incentives

In the days leading up to September 30, the federal government is Cinderella, courted by legions of individuals and organizations eager to get grants and contracts from the unexpended funds still at the disposal of each agency. At midnight on September 30, the government's coach turns into a pumpkin. That is the moment—the end of the fiscal year— at which every agency, with a few exceptions, must return all unexpended funds to the Treasury Department.

Except for certain quasi-independent government corporations, such as the Tennessee Valley Authority, no agency may keep any surplus revenues (that is, the difference between the funds it received from a congressional appropriation and those it needed to operate during the year). By the same token, any agency that runs out of money before the end of the fiscal year may ask Congress for more (a "supplemental appropriation") instead of being forced to deduct the deficit from any accumulated cash reserves. Because of these fiscal rules agencies do not have a material incentive to economize: Why scrimp and save if you cannot keep the results of your frugality?

Nor can individual bureaucrats lawfully capture for their personal use any revenue surpluses. When a private firm has a good year, many of its officers and workers may receive bonuses. Even if no bonus is paid, these employees may buy stock in the firm so that they can profit from any growth in earnings (and, if they sell the stock in a timely manner, profit from a drop in earnings). Should a public bureaucrat be discovered trying to do what private bureaucrats routinely do, he or she would be charged with corruption.

We take it for granted that bureaucrats should not profit from their offices and nod approvingly when a bureaucrat who has so benefited is indicted and put on trial. But why should we take this view? Once a very different view prevailed. In the seventeenth century, a French colonel would buy his commission from the king, take the king's money to run his regiment, and pocket the profit. At one time a European tax collector was paid by keeping a percentage of the taxes he collected. In this country, some prisons were once managed by giving the warden a sum of money based on how many prisoners were under his control and letting him keep the difference between what he received and what it cost him to feed the prisoners. Such behavior today would be grounds for criminal prosecution. Why? What has changed?

Mostly we the citizenry have changed. We are creatures of the Enlightenment: We believe that the nation ought not to be the property of the sovereign; that laws are intended to rationalize society and (if possible) perfect mankind; and that public service ought to be neutral and disinterested. We worry that a prison warden paid in the old way would have a strong incentive to starve his prisoners in order to maximize his income; that a regiment supported by a greedy colonel would not be properly equipped; and that a tax collector paid on a commission basis would extort excessive taxes from us. These changes reflect our desire to eliminate moral hazards—namely, creating incentives for people to act wrongly. But why should this desire rule out more carefully designed compensation plans that would pay government managers for achieving officially approved goals and would allow efficient agencies to keep any unspent part of their budget for use next year?

Part of the answer is obvious. Often we do not know whether a manager or an agency has achieved the goals we want because either the goals are vague or inconsistent, or their attainment cannot be observed, or both. Bureau chiefs in the Department of State would have to go on welfare if their pay depended on their ability to demonstrate convincingly that they had attained their bureaus' objectives.

But many government agencies have reasonably clear goals toward which progress can be measured. The Social Security Administration, the Postal Service, and the General Services Administration all come to mind. Why not let earnings depend importantly on performance? Why not let agencies keep excess revenues?

* * *

But in part it is because we know that even government agencies with clear goals and readily observable behavior only can be evaluated by making political (and thus conflict-ridden) judgments. If the Welfare Department delivers every benefit check within 24 hours after the application is received, Senator Smith may be pleased but Senator Jones will be irritated because this speedy delivery almost surely would require that the standards of eligibility be relaxed so that many ineligible clients would get money. There is no objective standard by which the trade-off between speed and accuracy in the Welfare Department can be evaluated. Thus we have been unwilling to allow welfare employees to earn large bonuses for achieving either speed or accuracy.

The inability of public managers to capture surplus revenues for their own use alters the pattern of incentives at work in government agencies. Beyond a certain point additional effort does not produce additional earnings. (In this country, Congress from time to time has authorized higher salaries for senior bureaucrats but then put a cap on actual payments to them so that the pay increases were never received. This was done to insure that no bureaucrat would earn more than members of Congress at a time when those members were unwilling to accept the political costs of raising their own salaries. As a result, the pay differential between the top bureaucratic rank and those just below it nearly vanished.) If political constraints reduce the marginal effect of money incentives, then the relative importance of other, nonmonetary incentives will increase. . . .

That bureaucratic performance in most government agencies cannot be linked to monetary benefits is not the whole explanation for the difference between public and private management. There are many examples of private organizations whose members cannot appropriate money surpluses for their own benefit. Private schools ordinarily are run on a nonprofit basis. Neither the headmaster nor the teachers share in the profit of these schools; indeed, most such schools earn no profit at all and instead struggle to keep afloat by soliciting contributions from friends and alumni. Nevertheless, the evidence is quite clear that on the average, private schools, both secular and denominational, do a better job than public ones in educating children. Moreover, as political scientists John Chubb and Terry Moe have pointed out, they do a better job while employing fewer managers. Some other factors are at work. One is the freedom an organization has to acquire and use labor and capital.

Acquiring and Using the Factors of Production

A business firm acquires capital by retaining earnings, borrowing money, or selling shares of ownership; a government agency (with some exceptions) acquires capital by persuading a legislature to appropriate it. A business firm hires, promotes, demotes, and fires personnel with considerable though not perfect freedom; a federal government agency is told by Congress how many persons it can hire and at what rate of pay, by the Office of Personnel Management (OPM) what rules it must follow in selecting and assigning personnel, by the Office of Management and Budget (OMB) how many persons of each rank it may employ, by the Merit Systems Protection Board (MSPB) what procedures it must follow in demoting or discharging personnel, and by the courts whether it has faithfully followed the rules of Congress, OPM, OMB, and MSPB. A business firm purchases goods and services by internally defined procedures (including those that allow it to buy from someone other than the lowest bidder if a more expensive vendor seems more reliable), or to skip the bidding procedure altogether in favor of direct negotiations; a government agency must purchase much of what it uses by formally advertising for bids, accepting the lowest, and keeping the vendor at arm's length. When a business firm develops a good working relationship with a contractor, it often uses that vendor repeatedly without looking for a new one; when a government agency has a satisfactory relationship with a contractor, ordinarily it cannot use the vendor again without putting a new project out for a fresh set of bids. When a business firm finds that certain offices or factories are no longer economical it will close or combine them; when a government agency wishes to shut down a local office or military base often it must get the permission of the legislature (even when formal permission is not necessary, informal consultation is). When a business firm draws up its annual budget each expenditure item can be reviewed as a discretionary amount (except for legally mandated payments of taxes to government and interest to banks and bondholders); when a government agency makes up its budget many of the detailed expenditure items are mandated by the legislature.

All these complexities of doing business in or with the government are well-known to citizens and firms. These complexities in hiring, purchasing, contracting, and budgeting often are said to be the result of the "bureaucracy's love of red tape." But few, if any, of the rules producing this complexity would have been generated by the bureaucracy if left to its own devices, and many are as cordially disliked by the bureaucrats as by their clients. These rules have been imposed on the agencies by external actors, chiefly the legislature. They are not bureaucratic rules but *political* ones. In principle the legislature could allow the Social Security Administration, the Defense Department, or the New York City public school system to follow the same rules as IBM, General Electric, or Harvard University. In practice they could not. The reason is politics, or more precisely, democratic politics.

*   *   *

Public versus Private Management

What distinguishes public from private organizations is neither their size nor their desire to "plan" (that is, control) their environments but rather the rules under which they acquire and use capital and labor. General Motors acquires capital by selling shares, issuing bonds, or retaining earnings; the Department of Defense acquires it from an annual appropriation by Congress. GM opens and closes plants, subject to certain government regulations, at its own discretion; DOD opens and closes military bases under the watchful guidance of Congress. GM pays its managers with salaries it sets and bonuses tied to its earnings; DOD pays its managers with salaries set by Congress and bonuses (if any) that have no connection with organizational performance. The number of workers in GM is determined by its level of production; the number in DOD by legislation and civil-service rules.

What all this means can be seen by returning to the Registry of Motor Vehicles and McDonald's. Suppose you were just appointed head of the Watertown office of the Registry and you wanted to improve service there so that it more nearly approximated the service at McDonald's. Better service might well require spending more money (on clerks, equipment, and buildings). Why should your political superiors give you that money? It is a cost to them if it requires either higher taxes or taking funds from another agency; offsetting these real and immediate costs are dubious and postponed benefits. If lines become shorter and clients become happier, no legislator will benefit. There may be fewer complaints, but complaints are episodic and have little effect on the career of any given legislator. By contrast, shorter lines and faster service at McDonald's means more customers can be served per hour and thus more money can be earned per hour. A McDonald's manager can estimate the marginal product of the last dollar he or she spends on improving service; the Registry manager can generate no tangible return on any expenditure he or she makes and thus cannot easily justify the expenditure.

Improving service at the Registry may require replacing slow or surly workers with quick and pleasant ones. But you, the manager, can neither hire nor fire them at will. You look enviously at the McDonald's manager who regularly and with little notice replaces poor workers with better ones. Alternatively, you may wish to mount an extensive training program (perhaps creating a Registration University to match McDonald's Hamburger University) that would imbue a culture of service in your employees. But unless the Registry were so large an agency that the legislature would neither notice nor care about funds spent for this purpose— and it is not that large—you would have a tough time convincing anybody that this was not a wasteful expenditure on a frill project.

If somehow your efforts succeed in making Registry clients happier, you can take vicarious pleasure in it; in the unlikely event a client seeks you out to thank you for those efforts, you can bask in a moment's worth of glory. Your colleague at McDonald's who manages to make customers happier may also derive some vicarious satisfaction from the improvement but in addition he or she will earn more money owing to an increase in sales.

In time it will dawn on you that if you improve service too much, clients will start coming to the Watertown office instead of going to the Boston office. As a result, the lines you succeeded in shortening will become longer again. If you wish to keep complaints down, you will have

to spend even more on the Watertown office. But if it was hard to persuade the legislature to do that in the past, it is impossible now. Why
should the taxpayer be asked to spend more on Watertown when the Boston office, fully staffed (naturally, no one was laid off when the clients
disappeared), has no lines at all? From the legislature's point of view the
correct level of expenditure is not that which makes one office better than
another but that which produces an equal amount of discontent in all
offices.

Finally, you remember that your clients have no choice: The Registry
offers a monopoly service. It and only it supplies drivers' licenses. In the
long run all that matters is that there are not "too many" complaints to the
legislature about service. Unlike McDonald's, the Registry need not fear
that its clients will take their business to Burger King or to Wendy's. Perhaps you should just relax.

If this were all there is to public management it would be an activity
that quickly and inevitably produces cynicism among its practitioners.
But this is not the whole story. For one thing, public agencies differ in the
kinds of problems they face. For another, many public managers try hard
to do a good job even though they face these difficult constraints.

DISCUSSION QUESTIONS

1. Wilson argues that McDonald's and the Registry of Motor Vehicles
   operate differently because of the inherent differences between public and private organizations. Apply his reasoning to other cases, for
   instance the U.S. Postal Service and Fed Ex, or any other area where
   the government and the private sector compete for business. Think
   about the goals of the organizations, who controls them, how you
   distinguish success from failure, and the consequences of failure.

2. What are the advantages and disadvantages of trying to run the
   government more like a business? How would you define the basic
   parameters of a "businesslike" government—such as, Who are the
   "customers"?

3. Some critics of government inefficiency argue that nearly every
   domestic government function—from schools to road building—
   could be run more efficiently if it were "privatized"—turned over to
   private contractors. Do you agree? Are there any government functions that do not lend themselves to privatization?

Debating the Issues: Privatization of Government Activity

As the James Q. Wilson reading notes, public organizations (meaning governments) have different incentives and performance measures than private organizations (meaning, in this context, private sector businesses). Another way to say this is that governments tend to be much less efficient than businesses, but this does not mean that government can be run like a business.

Nevertheless, governments today at all levels face pressure to transfer functions to the private sector, either by spinning off government functions entirely (privatization) or by contracting with private firms to provide services once provided by government employees (outsourcing). Turning over the air traffic control system or the postal service to private companies—leaving them to provide services and collect fees in a profitmaking venture—would be examples of privatization. In 2006, the state of Indiana sold the rights to the state's major highway to a private company. For $3.8 billion, the company leased the highway for 75 years, and the rights to all tolls collected over that period. In return, the company took responsibility for maintaining the road.

Using contractors to deliver services once provided by government— food service at national museums or military bases; private security forces instead of military personnel in Iraq—are examples of outsourcing.

Both outsourcing and privatization have advantages, at least as far as some see it: smaller government or more efficient government. Yet they also have some disadvantages compared to using government agencies to provide services. Compared to private firms, governments are more sensitive to problems of equity and accountability. For example, one reason the Postal Service is inefficient is that *legislators* created laws that require it to serve remote areas of the country and maintain post offices in small towns. A private company (say, something like FedEx or UPS) would most likely not find it profitable to do the same thing, and would either not provide service or charge more for it. We would purchase efficiency at the cost of equity (and your views of whether that trade-off is worth making probably depends heavily on whether you are a beneficiary of those inefficient services).

But, as the controversy over earmarks demonstrated, disputes over whether the government does something well or not are often policy disputes about whether the government should be doing something at all. The debate here involves some of the same issues. "Privatization" was written by authors at the Cato Institute, a libertarian think tank. Cato supports a significantly smaller government, and here the authors propose privatizing a wide range of government functions: the post office, air traffic control, airports, public lands, etc. They argue that these are not core government functions, and could be provided more efficiently by private companies. Shedding these functions would also make financial sense, since private companies would be willing to pay enormous sums of money for them (think of the billions of dollars the federal government earns by auctioning off portions of the electromagnetic spectrum for telecom services).

Not so fast, argues Wedel, who is critical of contracting out government functions. Wedel argues that using contractors to provide crucial government functions—intelligence, security, information technology—has a number of negative consequences, including reduced accountability, loss of vital institutional expertise, and poor supervision. The result is that the federal government has abdicated responsibility for important functions, and has substituted profit-seeking for the more difficult (but still vital) task of allocating resources in a way that meets public demands.

37

"*Federalist* No. 70: Where Does the Public Service Begin and End?"

Janine R. Wedel

Without revolution, public debate, or even much public awareness, a giant workforce has invaded Washington, D.C.—one that can undermine the public and national interest from the inside. This workforce consists of government contractors, specifically those who perform "inherently governmental" functions that the government deems so integral to its work that only federal employees should carry them out. Today, many federal government functions are conducted, and many public priorities and decisions are driven, by private companies and players instead of government agencies and officials who are duty-bound to answer to citizens and sworn to uphold the national interest.

It is hard to imagine that the founding fathers would have embraced this state of affairs. Acting as a nation—defending its security and providing for the safety of its citizens—is a bedrock concept in some of the *Federalist Papers*. For instance, John Jay writes in *Federalist* No. 2,

> As a nation we have made peace and war; as a nation we have vanquished our common enemies; as a nation we have formed alliances, and made treaties, and entered into various compacts and conventions with foreign states.

A strong sense of the value and blessings of union induced the people, at a very early period, to institute a federal government to preserve and perpetuate it.

James Madison lays out a forceful case for the separation and distribution of government powers. He cautions against "a tyrannical concentration of all the powers of government in the same hands" and outlines the importance of maintaining boundaries among the divisions of government (see *Federalist* No. 47, 48, 51). I argue that the considerable contracting out of government functions is counter to the vision espoused by these statesmen. Such contracting out potentially erodes the government's ability to operate in the public and national interest. It also creates the conditions for the intertwining of state and private power and the concentration of power in just a few hands—about which Madison warned.

The Indispensable Hand

Once, government contractors primarily sold military parts, prepared food, or printed government reports. Today, contractors routinely perform "inherently governmental" functions—activities that involve "the exercise of sovereign government authority or the establishment of procedures and processes related to the oversight of monetary transactions or entitlements." The 20 "inherently governmental" functions on the books include "command of military forces, especially the leadership of military personnel who are members of the combat, combat support, or combat service support role"; "the conduct of foreign relations and the determination of foreign policy"; "the determination of agency policy, such as determining the content and application of regulations"; "the determination of Federal program priorities or budget requests"; "the direction and control of Federal employees"; "the direction and control of intelligence and counter-intelligence operations; the selection or nonselection of individuals for Federal Government employment, including the interviewing of individuals for employment"; and "the approval of position descriptions and performance standards for Federal employees."

Government contractors are involved in many, if not all, of these arenas of government work. Consider, for instance, that contractors perform the following tasks:

- Run intelligence operations: Contractors from private security companies have been hired to help track and kill suspected militants in Afghanistan and Pakistan. At the National Security Agency (NSA), the number of contractor facilities approved for classified work jumped from 41 in 2002 to 1,265 in 2006. A full 95 percent of the workers at the very secret National Reconnaissance Office (one of the 16 intelligence agencies), which runs U.S. spy satellites and analyzes the information that they produce, are full-time contractors. In more than half of the 117 contracts let by three big agencies of the U.S. Department of Homeland

Security (DHS)—the Coast Guard, Transportation Security Administration, and Office of Procurement Operations—the Government Accountability Office (GAO) found that contractors did inherently governmental work. One company, for instance, was awarded $42.4 million to develop budget and policies for the DHS, as well as to support its information analysis, procurement operations, and infrastructure protection.

- Manage—and more—federal taxpayer monies doled out under the stimulus plans and bailouts: The government enlisted money manager BlackRock to help advise it and manage the unsuccessful attempt to rescue Bear Stearns, as well as to save AIG and Citigroup. BlackRock also won a bid to help the Federal Reserve evaluate hard-to-price assets of Freddie Mac and Fannie Mae. * * * With regard to the $700 billion bailout in the fall of 2008, known as the Troubled Asset Relief Program, the U.S. Treasury Department hired several contractors to set up a process to disburse the funds.

- Control crucial databases: In a mega-contract awarded by the DHS in 2004, Accenture LLP was granted up to $10 billion to supervise and enlarge a mammoth U.S. government project to track citizens of foreign countries as they enter and exit the United States. As the undersecretary for border and transportation security at the DHS at the time remarked, "I don't think you could overstate the impact of this responsibility in terms of the security of our nation."

- Choose other contractors: The Pentagon has employed contractors to counsel it on selecting other contractors. The General Services Administration enlisted CACI, a company based in Arlington, Virginia—some of whose employees were among those allegedly involved in the Abu Ghraib prisoner abuse scandal in Iraq, according to U.S. Department of the Army—to help the government suspend and debar other contractors. . . . (CACI itself later became the subject of possible suspension or debarment from federal contracts.)

- Oversee other contractors: The DHS is among the federal agencies that have hired contractors to select and supervise other contractors. Some of these contractors set policy and business goals and plan reorganizations. And, in the National Clandestine Service, an integral part of the Central Intelligence Agency (CIA), contractors are sometimes in charge of other contractors.

- Execute military and occupying operations: The Department of Defense is ever more dependent on contractors to supply a host of "mission-critical services," including "information technology systems, interpreters, intelligence analysts, as well as weapons system maintenance and base operation support." U.S. efforts in Afghanistan and Iraq illustrate this reliance. As of September 2009, U.S.-paid contractors far outnumbered U.S. military personnel in Afghanistan, composing nearly two-thirds of the combined contractor and military personnel work-force (approximately 104,000 Defense Department contractors com-pared with 64,000 uniformed personnel). In Iraq, contractors made up nearly half of the combined contractor and military personnel work-force (roughly 114,000 Defense Department contractors compared with 130,000 uniformed personnel). These proportions are in sharp contrast to the 1991 Persian Gulf War: The 540,000 military personnel deployed in that effort greatly outnumbered the 9,200 contractors on the scene.

- Draft official documents: Contractors have prepared congressional tes-timony for the secretary of energy. Websites of contractors working for the Department of Defense also have posted announcements of job open-ings for analysts to perform functions such as preparing the defense bud-get. One contractor boasted of having written the U.S. Army's Field Manual on "Contractors on the Battlefield."

In short, the outsourcing of many inherently governmental functions is now routine. The government is utterly dependent on private contractors to carry out many such functions. As the Acquisition Advisory Panel, a government-mandated, typically contractor-friendly task force made up of representatives from industry, government, and academe, acknowl-edged in a 2007 report that "[m]any federal agencies rely extensively on contractors in the performance of their basic missions. In some cases, contractors are solely or predominantly responsible for the performance of mission-critical functions that were traditionally performed by civil servants." This trend, the report concluded, "poses a threat to the govern-ment's long-term ability to perform its mission" and could "undermine the integrity of the government's decision making."

Contractor officials and employees are interdependent with govern-ment, involved in all aspects of governing and negotiating "over policy making, implementation, and enforcement," as one legal scholar has noted. Contractor and government employees work side by side in what has come to be called the "blended" or "embedded" workforce, often sit-ting next to each other in cubicles or sharing an office and doing the same or similar work (but typically with markedly different pay). When the GAO looked into the setup of Defense Department offices, its inves-tigation established that, in some, the percentage of contractors was in the 80s.

Yet contractors' imperatives are not necessarily the same as the govern-ment's imperatives. Contractor companies are responsible for making a profit for their shareholders; government is supposedly answerable to the public in a democracy.

Amid this environment, which is complicated by mixed motives, con-tractors are positioned to influence policy to their liking on even the most sensitive, mission-critical government functions, such as fighting wars, guarding against terrorism, and shaping economic policy. Government investigators looking into intelligence, defense, homeland security, energy, and other arenas have raised questions about who drives policy—government or contractors—and whether government has the information, expertise, institutional memory, and personnel to manage contractors—or is it the other way around? And in three government agencies that the GAO investigated, including the DOD and DHS, the GAO found that "sensitive information is not fully safeguarded and thus may remain at risk of unauthorized disclosure or misuse." The result of all of this is that the nation's safety, security, and sovereignty may be jeopardized, along with the very core of democratic society—citizens' ability to hold their government accountable and have a say in public decisions. This seems far afield from the concept of the nation expressed by, say, John Jay.

Enabling Big Government

How did this state of affairs come to be?

Ironically, the perennial American predilection to rail against "big government" is partly to blame for the creation of still bigger government—the "shadow government" of companies, consulting firms, nonprofits, think tanks, and other nongovernmental entities that contract with the government to do so much of its work. This is government for sure, but often of a less visible and accountable kind.

The necessity of making government *look* small—or at least contained—has fueled the rise of this shadow government. In an ostensible effort to limit government, caps have been put on how many civil servants government can hire. But citizens still expect government to supply all manner of services—from Medicare and Social Security to interstate highways to national defense. To avoid this conundrum, both Democratic and Republican administrations over the years have been busily enlisting more and more contractors (who, in turn, often hire subcontractors) to do the work of government. Because they are not counted as part of the federal workforce, it can appear as if the size of government is being kept in check. Like the Potemkin village of Russia, constructed to make the ruler or the foreigner think that things are rosy, the public is led to believe they have something they do not.

*   *   *

Where federal employees once executed most government work, today, upwards of three-quarters of the work of federal government, measured in terms of jobs, is contracted out. Many of the most dramatic alterations have occurred since the end of the Cold War. Contracting out accelerated and assumed new incarnations during and after the Bill Clinton administration. The advent of ever more complex technologies, which gave birth to information technologies on which society now relies and which the U.S. government largely outsources, tipped the balance even further. The shadow government, which devises and implements so much policy and forms the core of governance, is the elephant in the room.

The shadow government encompasses all of the entities that swell the ranks of contractors and entire bastions of outsourcing—neighborhoods whose high-rise office buildings house an army of contractors and "Beltway Bandits." Largely out of sight except to Washington-area dwellers, contractors and the companies they work for do not appear in government phone books. They are less likely to be dragged before congressional committees for hostile questioning. They function with less visibility and scrutiny on a regular basis than government employees would face. Most important, they are not counted as government employees, and so the fiction of limited government can be upheld, while the reality is an expanding sprawl of entities that are the government in practice.

The Elephant in the Room

While it may be the elephant in the room, we know little about the nature of the beast. A key barometer of the growth of the shadow government, driven in part by an increase in demand for military, nation-building, and homeland security services after 9/11, is the number of government employees versus contractors. Government scholar Paul C. Light has compiled the most reliable figures on contractors. The number of contract workers—compared with civil servants, uniformed military personnel, and postal service employees—increased steadily over the last two decades. In 1990, roughly three out of every five employees in the total federal labor force worked indirectly for government—in jobs created by contracts and grants, as opposed to jobs performed by civil servants, uniformed military personnel, and postal service workers. By 2002, two out of every three employees in the federal labor force worked indirectly for government, and, by 2008, the number was three out of four.

In the DHS—the mega-bureaucracy established in 2003 through the merger of 180,000 employees and 22 agencies, the creation of which entailed the largest reorganization of the federal government in more than half a century—contractors are more numerous than federal employees. The DHS estimates that it employs 188,000 workers, compared with 200,000 contractors.

In some arenas of government, contractors virtually *are* the government. The DHS, which includes the Customs Service, Coast Guard, and Transportation Security Administration, has relied substantially on contractors to fill new security needs and shore up gaps. In nine cases examined by the GAO, "decisions to contract for . . . services were largely driven by the need for staff and expertise to get DHS programs and operations up and running quickly".

*   *   *

Meanwhile, about 70 percent of the budget of the U.S. intelligence community is devoted to contracts, according to the Office of the Director of National Intelligence, which was created in 2005 and supervises 16 federal agencies. Contract employees make up an estimated one-quarter of the country's core intelligence workforce, according to the same office. The director both heads the U.S. intelligence community and serves as the main advisor to the president on national security matters.

Contractors are plentiful in other arenas of government that directly affect national and homeland security, not only the departments of defense and homeland security. For instance, nearly 90 percent of the budgets of the Department of Energy and NASA go to contracts.

Information technology (IT), which touches practically every area of government operations, is largely contracted out. Upwards of three-quarters of governmental IT is estimated to have been outsourced even before the major Iraq War-related push to contract out. For companies in search of federal business, IT is the "the new frontier," according to Thomas Burlin, who is in charge of IBM Business Consulting Services' federal practice. With ever more complex technologies always on the horizon, the outsourcing of IT only stands to grow. Although contracting out computer network services may be unproblematic or even desirable, many IT functions cannot be separated from vital operations such as logistics that are integral to an agency's mission. * * *

Contractors are so integrated into the federal workforce that proponents of insourcing acknowledge that they face an uphill battle. Yet the proliferation of contracting widens the de facto base of government in which new forms of unaccountable governance can flourish. It makes government more vulnerable to operations that fall short of the public and national interest.

Swiss-Cheese Government

In theory, contracts and contractors are overseen by government employees who would guard against abuse. But that has become less and less true as the capacity of government oversight has diminished—a lessening that seems to flow directly from the need to maintain the facade of small government. A look at trend lines is illuminating. The number of civil servants who potentially could oversee contractors fell during the Clinton administration and continued to drop during the George W. Bush administration. The contracting business boomed under Bush, while the acquisition workforce—government workers charged with the conceptualization, design, awarding, use, or quality control of contracts and contractors—remained virtually constant. * * *

The result is that government sometimes lacks the information it needs to monitor the entities that work for it. A top GAO official reported that in many cases, government decision makers scarcely supervise the companies on their payrolls. As a result, she observed, they are unable to answer simple questions about what the firms are doing, whether they have performed well or not, and whether their performance has been cost-effective.

*   *   *

A paucity of oversight is one factor that has led the GAO to identify large procurement operations as "high risk" because of "their greater susceptibility to fraud, waste, abuse, and mismanagement." The list of high-risk areas has, since 1990 or 1992 (depending on the specific area), included the large procurement operations of the Departments of Defense and Energy, as well as NASA. The DHS has been on the high-risk list since its creation in 2003, and it has been faulted for a lack of oversight in procurement. As comptroller general of the United States, David M. Walker (2003) said that he is "not confident that [high-risk] agencies have the ability to effectively manage cost, quality, and performance in contracts." He added that the current challenges to contract oversight are "unprecedented."

*   *   *

When the number of civil servants available to supervise government contracts and contractors proportionately falls, thus decreasing the government's oversight capacity, and when crucial governmental functions are outsourced, government begins to resemble Swiss cheese—full of holes. Contractors are plugging these holes. As a consequence, contractors have become the home for much information, legitimacy, expertise, institutional memory, and leadership that once resided in government.

*   *   *

Concentrating Powers

Swiss-cheese government lends itself to the kind of concentration of powers that Madison warned about. Over the past decade and a half, new institutional forms of governing have gathered force as contractors perform inherently governmental functions beyond the capacity of government to manage them; as government and contractor officials interact (or do not) in the course of projects; as chains of command among contractors and the agencies they supposedly work for have become ever more convoluted; and as contractors standing in for government are not subject to the same rules that apply to government officials. The result is that new forms of governing join the state and the private, often most visibly in intelligence, defense, and homeland security enterprises, where so much has taken place since 9/11.

Incentive structures that encourage government executives (notably intelligence and military professionals) to move to the private sector, as well as new contracting practices and a limited number of government contracting firms, are among the factors that facilitate the intertwining of state and private power. With regard to the former, not only are salaries and perks for comparable jobs typically greater in the private sector, but often, so is prestige. Many government executives, retirees, and other employees follow the money by moving to the private sector. But the landing spots that supply the big bucks—and with them, influence and stature—are often those held by former government executives. Although there are rules to address the revolving door syndrome, companies with significant government contracts often are headed by former senior officials of intelligence- and defense-related government agencies. * * *

When government contractors hire former directors of intelligence- and defense-related government agencies, they are banking on "coincidences" of interest between their hires and their hires' former (government) employers. (A coincidence of interest occurs when a player crafts an array of overlapping roles across organizations to serve his own agenda—or that of his network—above that of those of the organizations for which he works.) The result of such coincidences in the intelligence arena is that "the Intelligence Community and the contractors are so tightly intertwined at the leadership level that their interests, practically speaking, are identical," as one intelligence expert said.

Also potentially facilitating the fusion of state and private power are changes in contracting practices and the dearth of competition among and consolidation of government contracting firms, which has led to government dependence on a limited number of firms. The Clinton administration transformed contracting rules with regard to oversight, competition, and transparency under the rubric of "reinventing government." As a result, small contracts often have been replaced by bigger, and frequently open-ended, multiyear, multimillion- and even billion-dollar and potentially much more lucrative contracts with a "limited pool of contractors," as the Acquisition Advisory Panel put it. Today, most federal procurement contracts are conferred either without competition or to a limited set of contractors. A Barack Obama White House memo noted the "significant increase in the dollars awarded without full and open competition" during the period 2001–2008. Moreover, industry consolidation (defense is a case in point) has produced fewer and larger firms. * * *

The routine outsourcing of government functions, the structures of incentives, and new contracting rules and practices encourage new forms of governing in which state and private power are joined. These forms seem very far afield indeed from Madison's vision of a nation in which government powers cannot be concentrated.

Reclaiming the Soul of Government

Some authorities have sounded alarm bells about the present state of affairs. In 2007, David M. Walker, the comptroller general of the United

States and longtime head of the GAO, called for "a fundamental reexamination of when and under what circumstances we should use contractors versus civil servants or military personnel," And President Obama acknowledged the problem. Early in his term, Obama announced plans to "insource" certain jobs—transferring work back to the government—and expressed concern about the outsourcing of inherently governmental functions. While the administration has proposed some insourcing and efforts to push back or review the ever upward spiral of outsourcing, the current state of affairs cannot simply be rolled back.

It is not just that government is utterly dependent on private companies to do much of its work. The United States faces an entrenched problem that cannot be fixed simply by insourcing jobs or by hiring more government employees to oversee contractors, as some observers have suggested. A top-to-bottom rethinking of how government makes use of contractors is necessary. One particularly important issue that deserves attention is how to rebuild capacity that has been lost with the privatization of information, expertise, and institutional memory. Another set of challenges lies in reforming the contract laws and regulations that have been changed over the past decade and a half—and that have made the contracting system less transparent and accountable and more vulnerable to the influence of private and corporate agendas.

The changes that have taken place are so systemic and sweeping that a new system, in effect, is now in place. It is the ground on which any future changes will occur. A fundamental redesign of the system is necessary. In that redesign, we would do well to pay attention to the vision of the founding fathers regarding the security of the nation and safety of its citizens, as well as the dangers inherent in the consolidation of powers.

But reclaiming government is not merely a design challenge. Government must take its soul back. While it may be strange to mention "soul" and government in the same breath, linking the quintessentially personal with the quintessentially bureaucratic and impersonal, a government procurement lawyer described the current state of affairs as the "ebbing away of the soul of government." When an institution is drained of expertise, information, and institutional memory, it not only loses its edge, but also its essence.

* * *

38

"Privatization"

CATO HANDBOOK FOR POLICYMAKERS

In recent decides, governments on every continent have sold state-owned assets, such as airports, railroads, and energy utilities. The privatization revolution has overthrown the belief widely held in the 20th century that governments should own the most important industries in the economy. Privatization has generally led to reduced costs, higher-quality services, and increased innovation in formerly moribund government industries.

The presumption that government should own industry was challenged in the 1980s by British Prime Minister Margaret Thatcher and by President Ronald Reagan, who established a Commission on Privatization. But while Thatcher made enormous reforms in Britain, only a few major federal assets have been privatized in this country. Conrail, a freight railroad, was privatized in 1987 for $1.7 billion. The Alaska Power Administration was privatized in 1996. The federal helium reserve was privatized in 1996 for $1.8 billion. The Elk Hills Petroleum Reserve was sold in 1997 for $3.7 billion. The U.S. Enrichment Corporation, which provides enriched uranium to the nuclear industry, was privatized in 1998 for $3.1 billion.

There remain many federal assets that should be privatized, including businesses such as Amtrak and infrastructure such as the air traffic control system. The government also holds billions of dollars of real estate that should be sold off. The benefits to the federal budget of privatization would be modest, but the benefits to the economy would be large as newly private businesses would improve their performance and innovate.

The Office of Management and Budget has calculated that about half of all federal employees perform tasks that are not "inherently governmental." The Bush administration attempted to contract some of those activities to outside vendors, but such "competitive sourcing" is not privatization. Privatization makes an activity entirely private, with the effect of getting spending completely off the government's books, allowing for greater innovation, and preventing corruption, which is a serious pitfall of government contracting.

Privatization of federal assets makes sense for many reasons. First, sales of federal assets would cut the budget deficit. Second, privatization would reduce the responsibilities of the government so that policymakers could better focus on their core responsibilities, such as national security.

Third, there is vast foreign privatization experience that could be drawn on in pursuing U.S. reforms. Fourth, privatization would spur economic growth by opening new markets to entrepreneurs. For example, repeal of the postal monopoly could bring major innovation to the mail industry, just as the 1980s' breakup of AT&T brought innovation to the telecommunications industry.

Some policymakers think that certain activities, such as air traffic control, are "too important" to leave to the private sector. But the reality is just the opposite. The government has shown itself to be a failure at providing efficiency and high quality in services such as air traffic control. Such industries are too important to miss out on the innovations that private entrepreneurs could bring to them.

Stand-Alone Businesses

The federal government operates numerous business enterprises that should be converted into publicly traded corporations, including the U.S. Postal Service, Amtrak, and a number of electric utilities.

- **Postal services.** The mammoth 685,000-person U.S. Postal Service is facing declining mail volume and rising costs. The way ahead is to privatize the USPS and repeal the company's legal monopoly over first-class mail. Reforms in other countries show that there is no good reason for the current mail monopoly. Since 1998, New Zealand's postal market has been open to private competition, with the result that postage rates have fallen and labor productivity at New Zealand Post has risen. Germany's Deutsche Post was partly privatized in 2000, and the company has improved productivity and expanded into new businesses. Postal services have also been privatized or opened to competition in Belgium, Britain, Denmark, Finland, the Netherlands, and Sweden. Japan is moving ahead with postal service privatization, and the European Union is planning to open postal services to competition in all its 27 member nations.

- **Passenger rail.** Subsidies to Amtrak were supposed to be temporary after it was created in 1970. That has not occurred, and Amtrak has provided second-rate rail service for more than 30 years while consuming more than $30 billion in federal subsidies. It has a poor on-time record, and its infrastructure is in bad shape. Reforms elsewhere show that private passenger rail can work. Full or partial rail privatization has occurred in Argentina, Australia, Britain, Germany, Japan, New Zealand, and other countries. Privatization would allow Amtrak greater flexibility in its finances, its capital budget, and the operation of its services—free from costly meddling by Congress.

* * *

Infrastructure

Before the 20th century, transportation infrastructure was often financed and built by the private sector. For example, there were more than 2,000 companies that built private toll roads in America in the 18th and 19th centuries. Most of those roads were put out of business by the spread of the railroads. Then, during the 20th century, roads and other infrastructure came to be thought of as government activities. By the 1980s, that started to change, and governments around the world began selling off airports, highways, bridges, and other facilities.

Any service that can be supported by consumer fees can be privatized. A big advantage of privatized airports, air traffic control, highways, and other activities is that private companies can freely tap debt and equity markets for capital expansion to meet rising demand. By contrast, modernization of government infrastructure is subject to the politics and uncertainties of government budgeting processes. As a consequence, government infrastructure is often old, congested, and poorly maintained.

- **Air traffic control.** The Federal Aviation Administration has been mismanaged for decades and provides Americans with second-rate air traffic control. The FAA has struggled to expand capacity and modernize its technology, and its upgrade efforts have often fallen behind schedule and gone over budget. For example, the Government Accountability Office found one FAA technology upgrade project that was started in 1983 and was to be completed by 1996 for $2.5 billion, but the project was years late and ended up costing $7.6 billion. The GAO has had the FAA on its watch list of wasteful "high-risk" agencies for years. Air traffic control (ATC) is far too important for such government mismanagement and should be privatized.

  The good news is that a number of countries have privatized their ATC and provide good models for U.S. reforms. Canada privatized its ATC system in 1996. It set up a private, nonprofit ATC corporation, Nav Canada, which is self-supporting from charges on aviation users. The Canadian system has received high marks for sound finances, solid management, and investment in new technologies.

- **Highways.** A number of states are moving ahead with privately financed and operated highways. The Dulles Greenway in Northern Virginia is a 14-mile private highway opened in 1995 that was financed by private bond and equity issues. In the same region, Fluor-Transurban is building and mainly funding high-occupancy toll lanes on a 14-mile stretch of the Capital Beltway. Drivers will pay to use the lanes with electronic tolling, which will recoup the company's roughly $1 billion investment. Fluor-Transurban is also financing and building toll lanes running south from Washington along Interstate 95. Similar private highway projects have been completed, or are being pursued, in California, Maryland,

Minnesota, North Carolina, South Carolina, and Texas. Private-sector highway funding and operation can help pave the way toward reducing the nation's traffic congestion.

- **Airports.** Nearly all major U.S. airports are owned by state and local governments, with the federal government subsidizing airport renovation and expansion. By contrast, airports have been fully or partly privatized in many foreign cities, including Athens, Auckland, Brussels, Copenhagen, Frankfurt, London, Melbourne, Naples, Rome, Sydney, and Vienna. Britain led the way with the 1987 privatization of British Airports Authority, which owns Heathrow and other airports. To proceed with reforms in the United States, Congress should take the lead because numerous federal roadblocks make cities hesitant to privatize. For example, government-owned airports can issue tax-exempt debt, which gives them a financial advantage over potential private airports.

* * *

- **Army Corps of Engineers.** The Corps of Engineers is a federal agency that builds and maintains infrastructure for ports and waterways. Most of the agency's $5 billion annual budget goes toward dredging harbors and investing in locks and channels on rivers, such as the Mississippi. In addition, the corps is the largest owner of hydroelectric power plants in the country, manages 4,300 recreational areas, funds beach replenishment, and upgrades local water and sewer systems.

   Congress has used the corps as a pork barrel spending machine for decades. Funds are earmarked for low-value projects in the districts of important members of Congress, while higher-value projects go unfunded. Further, the corps has a history of scandals, including the levee failures in New Orleans and bogus economic studies to justify expensive projects.

   To solve these problems, the civilian activities of the corps should be transferred to state, local, or private ownership. A rough framework for reform would be to privatize port dredging, hydroelectric dams, beach replenishment, and other activities that could be supported by user fees and charges. Levees, municipal water and sewer projects, recreational areas, locks, and other waterway infrastructure could be transferred to state governments.

Federal Assets

At the end of fiscal year 2007, the federal government held $1.2 trillion in buildings and equipment, $277 billion in inventory, $919 billion in land, and $392 billion in mineral rights. The federal government owns about one-fourth of the land in the United States.

Many government assets are neglected and abused, and would likely be better cared for in the private sector. It is common to see government property in poor shape, with public housing being perhaps the most infamous government eyesore. The GAO has found that "many assets are in an alarming state of deterioration" and the watchdog agency has put federal property holdings on its list of activities at high risk for waste.

The GAO also notes that the federal government has "many assets it does not need," including billions of dollars worth of excess and vacant buildings. The federal government spends billions of dollars each year maintaining excess facilities of the Departments of Defense, Energy, and Veterans Affairs.

The solution is to sell federal assets that are excess to public needs and to better manage the smaller set of remaining holdings. For example, there are substantial maintenance backlogs on facilities of the Forest Service, Park Service, and Fish and Wildlife Service. The solution is not a larger maintenance budget, but trimming asset holdings to fit limited taxpayer resources. Another part of the solution is to scrap the Davis-Bacon rules, which require that artificially high wages be paid on federal contracts, including maintenance contracts.

Federal asset sales would help reduce the federal deficit and create budget room for improved maintenance of remaining assets. Perhaps more important, economic efficiency and growth would increase as underused assets were put into more productive private hands.

DISCUSSION QUESTIONS:

1. What is an "inherently governmental function?" The current definition in federal law is "a function so intimately related to the public interest as to require performance by Federal Government employees." But this actually provides very little useful guidance, since it is a tautology: work that must be performed by federal government employees is defined as work so important that it must be performed by federal employees. Is there an alternative definition that is both meaningful and precise? What might that be?

2. When the government outsources, is it possible to specify contractually the correct accountability and equity incentives that would apply if the functions were performed by government agencies? Can we even identify precisely what those incentives are for *government* employees?

CHAPTER 8

The Judiciary

39

The Federalist, No. 78

Alexander Hamilton

The judiciary, Hamilton wrote in The Federalist, No. 78, "will always be the least dangerous to the political rights of the Constitution; because it will be least in a capacity to annoy or injure them." The lack of danger Hamilton spoke of stems from the courts' lack of enforcement or policy power. Or as Hamilton more eloquently put it, the judiciary has "no influence over either the sword or the purse": it must rely on the executive branch and state governments to enforce its rulings, and depends on the legislature for its appropriations and rules governing its structure. Critics of "judicial activism" would likely disagree about the weakness of the judiciary relative to the other branches of government. But Hamilton saw an independent judiciary as an important check on the other branches' ability to assume too much power (the "bulwarks of a limited Constitution against legislative encroachments"). He also argued that the federal judiciary, as interpreter of the Constitution, would gain its power from the force of its judgments, which were rooted in the will of the people.

To the People of the State of New York:

We proceed now to an examination of the judiciary department of the proposed government.

In unfolding the defects of the existing Confederation, the utility and necessity of a federal judicature have been clearly pointed out. It is the less necessary to recapitulate the considerations there urged, as the propriety of the institution in the abstract is not disputed; the only questions which have been raised being relative to the manner of constituting it, and to its extent. To these points, therefore, our observations shall be confined.

The manner of constituting it seems to embrace these several objects: 1st. The mode of appointing the judges. 2d. The tenure by which they are to hold their places. 3d. The partition of the judiciary authority between different courts, and their relations to each other.

First. As to the mode of appointing the judges; this is the same with that of appointing the officers of the Union in general, and has been so fully discussed in the two last numbers, that nothing can be said here which would not be useless repetition.

Second. As to the tenure by which the judges are to hold their places: this chiefly concerns their duration in office; the provisions for their support; the precautions for their responsibility.

According to the plan of the convention, all judges who may be appointed by the United States are to hold their offices *during good behavior*; which is conformable to the most approved of the State constitutions, and among the rest, to that of this State. Its propriety having been drawn into question by the adversaries of that plan, is no light symptom of the rage for objection, which disorders their imaginations and judgments. The standard of good behavior for the continuance in office of the judicial magistracy is certainly one of the most valuable of the modern improvements in the practice of government. In a monarchy it is an excellent barrier to the despotism of the prince; in a republic it is a no less excellent barrier to the encroachments and oppressions of the representative body. And it is the best expedient which can be devised in any government to secure a steady, upright, and impartial administration of the laws.

Whoever attentively considers the different departments of power must perceive, that, in a government in which they are separated from each other, the judiciary, from the nature of its functions, will always be the least dangerous to the political rights of the Constitution; because it will be least in a capacity to annoy or injure them. The Executive not only dispenses the honors, but holds the sword of the community. The legislature not only commands the purse, but prescribes the rules by which the duties and rights of every citizen are to be regulated. The judiciary, on the contrary, has no influence over either the sword or the purse; no direction either of the strength or of the wealth of the society; and can take no active resolution whatever. It may truly be said to have neither FORCE nor WILL, but merely judgment; and must ultimately depend upon the aid of the executive arm even for the efficacy of its judgments.

This simple view of the matter suggests several important consequences. It proves incontestably that the judiciary is beyond comparison the weakest of the three departments of power that it can never attack with success either of the other two; and that all possible care is requisite to enable it to defend itself against their attacks. It equally proves that though individual oppression may now and then proceed from the courts of justice, the general liberty of the people can never be endangered from that quarter; I mean so long as the judiciary remains truly distinct from both the legislature and the Executive. For I agree, that "there is no liberty, if the power of judging be not separated from the legislative and executive powers." And it proves, in the last place, that as liberty can have nothing to fear from the judiciary alone, but would have every thing to fear from its union with either of the other departments; that as all the effects of such a union must ensue from a dependence of the former on the latter, notwithstanding a nominal and apparent separation; that as, from the natural feebleness of the judiciary it is in continual jeopardy of being overpowered, awed, or influenced by its coordinate branches; and that as nothing can contribute so much to its firmness and independence as permanency in office, this quality may therefore be justly regarded as an indispensable ingredient in its constitution, and, in a great measure, as the citadel of the public justice and the public security.

The complete independence of the courts of justice is peculiarly essential in a limited Constitution. By a limited Constitution, I understand one which contains certain specified exceptions to the legislative authority; such, for instance, as that it shall pass no bills of attainder, no *ex-post-facto* laws, and the like. Limitations of this kind can be preserved in practice no other way than through the medium of courts of justice, whose duty it must be to declare all acts contrary to the manifest tenor of the Constitution void. Without this, all the reservations of particular rights or privileges would amount to nothing.

Some perplexity respecting the rights of the courts to pronounce legislative acts void, because contrary to the constitution, has arisen from an imagination that the doctrine would imply a superiority of the judiciary to the legislative power. It is urged that the authority which can declare the acts of another void must necessarily be superior to the one whose acts may be declared void. As this doctrine is of great importance in all the American constitutions, a brief discussion of the ground on which it rests cannot be unacceptable.

There is no position which depends on clearer principles than that every act of a delegated authority, contrary to the tenor of the commission under which it is exercised, is void. No legislative act, therefore, contrary to the Constitution, can be valid. To deny this would be to affirm that the deputy is greater than his principal; that the servant is above his master; that the representatives of the people are superior to the people themselves; that men acting by virtue of powers may do not only what their powers do not authorize, but what they forbid.

If it be said that the legislative body are themselves the constitutional judges of their own powers, and that the construction they put upon them is conclusive upon the other departments, it may be answered that this cannot be the natural presumption where it is not to be collected from any particular provisions in the Constitution. It is not otherwise to be supposed that the Constitution could intend to enable the representatives of the people to substitute their *will* to that of their constituents. It is far more rational to suppose that the courts were designed to be an intermediate body between the people and the legislature, in order, among other things, to keep the latter within the limits assigned to their authority. The interpretation of the laws is the proper and peculiar province of the courts. A constitution is, in fact, and must be regarded by the judges, as a fundamental law. It therefore belongs to them to ascertain its meaning, as well as the meaning of any particular act proceeding from the legislative body. If there should happen to be an irreconcilable variance between the two, that which has the superior obligation and validity ought, of course, to be preferred; or, in other words, the Constitution ought to be preferred to the statute, the intention of the people to the intention of their agents.

Nor does this conclusion by any means suppose a superiority of the judicial to the legislative power. It only supposes that the power of the people is superior to both; and that where the will of the legislature, declared in its statutes, stands in opposition to that of the people, declared in the Constitution, the judges ought to be governed by the latter rather than the former. They ought to regulate their decisions by the fundamental laws, rather than by those which are not fundamental.

This exercise of judicial discretion, in determining between two contradictory laws, is exemplified in a familiar instance. It not uncommonly happens that there are two statutes existing at one time, clashing in whole or in part with each other, and neither of them containing any repealing clause or expression. In such a case, it is the province of the courts to liquidate and fix their meaning and operation. So far as they can, by any fair construction, be reconciled to each other, reason and law conspire to dictate that this should be done; where this is impracticable, it becomes a matter of necessity to give effect to one in exclusion of the other. The rule which has obtained in the courts for determining their relative validity is, that the last in order of time shall be preferred to the first. But this is a mere rule of construction, not derived from any positive law but from the nature and reason of the thing. It is a rule not enjoined upon the courts by legislative provision but adopted by themselves, as consonant to truth and propriety for the direction of their conduct as interpreters of the law. They thought it reasonable, that between the interfering acts of an *equal* authority, that which was the last indication of its will should have the preference.

But in regard to the interfering acts of a superior and subordinate authority, of an original and derivative power, the nature and reason of the thing indicate the converse of that rule as proper to be followed. They teach us that the prior act of a superior ought to be preferred to the subsequent act of an inferior and subordinate authority; and that accordingly, whenever a particular statute contravenes the Constitution, it will be the duty of the judicial tribunals to adhere to the latter and disregard the former.

It can be of no weight to say that the courts, on the pretence of a repugnancy, may substitute their own pleasure to the constitutional intentions of the legislature. This might as well happen in the case of two contradictory statutes; or it might as well happen in every adjudication upon any single statute. The courts must declare the sense of the law; and if they should be disposed to exercise WILL instead of JUDGMENT, the consequence would equally be the substitution of their pleasure to that of the legislative body. The observation, if it prove any thing, would prove that there ought to be no judges distinct from that body.

If, then, the courts of justice are to be considered as the bulwarks of a limited Constitution against legislative encroachments, this consideration will afford a strong argument for the permanent tenure of judicial offices, since nothing will contribute so much as this to that independent spirit in the judges which must be essential to the faithful performance of so arduous a duty.

This independence of the judges is equally requisite to guard the Constitution and the rights of individuals from the effects of those ill humors, which the arts of designing men or the influence of particular conjunctures sometimes disseminate among the people themselves; and which, though they speedily give place to better information and more deliberate reflection, have a tendency, in the meantime, to occasion dangerous innovations in the government, and serious oppressions of the minor party in the community. Though I trust the friends of the proposed Constitution will never concur with its enemies in questioning that fundamental principle of republican government, which admits the right of the people to alter or abolish the established Constitution whenever they find it inconsistent with their happiness; yet it is not to be inferred from this principle that the representatives of the people, whenever a momentary inclination happens to lay hold of a majority of their constituents, incompatible with the provisions in the existing Constitution, would, on that account, be justifiable in a violation of those provisions; or that the courts would be under a greater obligation to connive at infractions in this shape, than when they had proceeded wholly from the cabals of the representative body. Until the people have by some solemn and authoritative act annulled or changed the established form, it is binding upon themselves collectively, as well as individually; and no presumption, or even knowledge, of their sentiments, can warrant their representatives in a departure from it, prior to such an act. But it is easy to see that it would require an uncommon portion of fortitude in the judges to do their duty as faithful guardians of the Constitution, where legislative invasions of it had been instigated by the major voice of the community.

But it is not with a view to infractions of the Constitution only that the independence of the judges may be an essential safeguard against the effects of occasional ill humors in the society. These sometimes extend no farther than to the injury of the private rights of particular classes of citizens by unjust and partial laws. Here also the firmness of the judicial magistracy is of vast importance in mitigating the severity and confining the operation of such laws. It not only serves to moderate the immediate mischiefs of those which may have been passed, but it operates as a check upon the legislative body in passing them; who, perceiving that obstacles to the success of iniquitous intention are to be expected from the scruples of the courts, are in a manner compelled by the very motives of the injustice they meditate to qualify their attempts. This is a circumstance calculated to have more influence upon the character of our governments, than but few may be aware of. The benefits of the integrity and moderation of the judiciary have already been felt in more States than one; and though they may have displeased those whose sinister expectations they may have disappointed, they must have commanded the esteem and applause of all the virtuous and disinterested. Considerate men of every description ought to prize whatever will tend to beget or fortify that temper in the courts; as no man can be sure that he may not be tomorrow the victim of a spirit of injustice by which he may be a gainer today. And every man must now feel that the inevitable tendency of such a spirit is to sap the foundations of public and private confidence, and to introduce in its stead universal distrust and distress.

That inflexible and uniform adherence to the rights of the Constitution and of individuals, which we perceive to be indispensable in the courts of justice, can certainly not be expected from judges who hold their offices by a temporary commission. Periodical appointments, however regulated or by whomsoever made, would, in some way or other, be fatal to their necessary independence. If the power of making them was committed either to the Executive or legislature, there would be danger of an improper complaisance to the branch which possessed it; if to both, there would be an unwillingness to hazard the displeasure of either; if to the people or to persons chosen by them for the special purpose, there would be too great a disposition to consult popularity, to justify a reliance that nothing would be consulted but the Constitution and the laws.

There is yet a further and a weightier reason for the permanency of the judicial offices, which is deducible from the nature of the qualifications they require. It has been frequently remarked, with great propriety, that a voluminous code of laws is one of the inconveniences necessarily connected with the advantages of a free government. To avoid an arbitrary discretion in the courts, it is indispensable that they should be bound down by strict rules and precedents, which serve to define and point out their duty in every particular case that comes before them; and it will readily be conceived from the variety of controversies which grow out of the folly and wickedness of mankind, that the records of those precedents must unavoidably swell to a very considerable bulk, and must demand long and laborious study to acquire a competent knowledge of them. Hence it is, that there can be but few men in the society who will have sufficient skill in the laws to qualify them for the stations of judges. And making the proper deductions for the ordinary depravity of human nature, the number must be still smaller of those who unite the requisite integrity with the requisite knowledge. These considerations apprise us that the government can have no great option between fit character; and that a temporary duration in office, which would naturally discourage such characters from quitting a lucrative line of practice to accept a seat on the bench, would have a tendency to throw the administration of justice into hands less able, and less well qualified, to conduct it with utility and dignity. In the present circumstances of this country and in those in which it is likely to be for a long time to come, the disadvantages on this score would be greater than they may at first sight appear; but it must be confessed that they are far inferior to those which present themselves under the other aspects of the subject.

Upon the whole, there can be no room to doubt that the convention acted wisely in copying from the models of those constitutions which have established *good behavior* as the tenure of their judicial offices, in point of duration; and that so far from being blamable on this account, their plan would have been inexcusably defective if it had wanted this important feature of good government. The experience of Great Britain affords an illustrious comment on the excellence of the institution.

Publius

Discussion Questions

1. Was Hamilton correct in arguing that the judiciary is the least dangerous branch of government?

2. Critics of the Supreme Court often charge that it rules on issues that should be properly decided in the legislature, while supporters claim that the Court is often the last check against the tyranny of the majority. Who has the stronger case? Can both sides be correct?

3. Hamilton argues that the "power of the people is superior to both" the legislature and the judiciary, and that judges uphold the power of the people when they support the Constitution over a statute that runs counter to the Constitution. He asserts that the people's will is reflected in the Constitution but refers to statutes as reflecting the will of the legislators. Is it legitimate to argue that the Supreme Court is supporting the will of the people, given that it is an unelected body?

40

"The Court and American Life," from *Storm Center: The Supreme Court in American Politics*

David O'Brien

The "textbook" view of the federal judiciary is one in which judges sit in dispassionate review of complex legal questions, render decisions based on a careful reading of constitutional or statutory language, and expect their rulings to be adhered to strictly; the law is the law. This selection shows how unrealistic that picture is. O'Brien notes that the Supreme Court is very much a political institution, whose members pay more attention to the political cycle and public opinion than one might expect. O'Brien reviews the decision-making process in the famous Brown v. Board of Education of Topeka, Kansas, *in which the Court invalidated segregated public schools, as an example of how the Court fits itself into the political process. Throughout the case, justices delayed their decision, consolidated cases from around the country, and refused to set a firm timetable for implementation, relying instead on the ambiguous standard "with all deliberate speed." Far from being a purely objective arbiter of legal questions, the Court must pay close attention to its own legitimacy, and by extension the likelihood of compliance: it does no good to issue decisions that will be ignored.*

"Why does the Supreme Court pass the school desegregation case?" asked one of Chief Justice Vinson's law clerks in 1952. *Brown v. Board of Education of Topeka, Kansas* had arrived on the Court's docket in 1951, but it was carried over for oral argument the next term and then consolidated with four other cases and reargued in December 1953. The landmark ruling did not come down until May 17, 1954. "Well," Justice Frankfurter explained, "we're holding it for the election"—1952 was a presidential election year. "You're holding it for the election?" The clerk persisted in disbelief. "I thought the Supreme Court was supposed to decide cases without regard to elections." "When you have a major social political issue of this magnitude," timing and public reactions are important considerations, and, Frankfurter continued, "we do not think this is the time to decide it." Similarly, Tom Clark recalled that the Court awaited, over Douglas's dissent, additional cases from the District of Columbia and other regions, so as "to get a national coverage, rather than a sectional one." Such political considerations are by no means unique. "We often delay adjudication. It's not a question of evading at all," Clark concluded. "It's just the practicalities of life—common sense."

Denied the power of the sword or the purse, the Court must cultivate its institutional prestige. The power of the Court lies in the persuasiveness of its rulings and ultimately rests with other political institutions and public opinion. As an independent force, the Court has no chance to resolve great issues of public policy. *Dred Scott v. Sandford* (1857) and *Brown v. Board of Education* (1954) illustrate the limitations of Supreme Court policy-making. The "great folly," as Senator Henry Cabot Lodge characterized *Dred Scott*, was not the Court's interpretation of the Constitution or the unpersuasive moral position that blacks were not persons under the Constitution. Rather, "the attempt of the Court to settle the slavery question by judicial decision was simple madness." As Lodge explained:

> Slavery involved not only the great moral issue of the right of one man to hold another in bondage and to buy and sell him but it involved also the foundations of a social fabric covering half the country and caused men to feel so deeply that it finally brought them beyond the question of nullification to a point where the life of the Union was at stake and a decision could only be reached by war.

A hundred years later, political struggles within the country and, notably, presidential and congressional leadership in enforcing the Court's school desegregation ruling saved the moral appeal of *Brown* from becoming another "great folly."

Because the Court's decisions are not self-executing, public reactions inevitably weigh on the minds of the justices. Justice Stone, for one, was furious at Chief Justice Hughes's rush to hand down *Powell v. Alabama* (1932). Picketers protested the Scottsboro boys' conviction and death sentence. Stone attributed the Court's rush to judgment to Hughes's "wish to put a stop to the [public] demonstrations around the Court." Opposition to the school desegregation ruling in *Brown* led to bitter, sometimes violent confrontations. In Little Rock, Arkansas, Governor Orval Faubus encouraged disobedience by southern segregationists. The federal National Guard had to be called out to maintain order. The school board in Little Rock unsuccessfully pleaded, in *Cooper v. Aaron* (1958), for the Court's postponement of the implementation of *Brown's* mandate. In the midst of the controversy, Frankfurter worried that Chief Justice Warren's attitude had become "more like that of a fighting politician than that of a judicial statesman." In such confrontations between the Court and the country, "the transcending issue," Frankfurter reminded the brethren, remains that of preserving "the Supreme Court as the authoritative organ of what the Constitution requires." When the justices move too far or too fast in their interpretation of the Constitution, they threaten public acceptance of the Court's legitimacy.

*   *   *

When deciding major issues of public law and policy, justices must consider strategies for getting public acceptance of their rulings. When striking down the doctrine of "separate but equal" facilities in 1954 in *Brown v. Board of Education (Brown I)*, for instance, the Warren Court waited a year before issuing, in *Brown II*, its mandate for "all deliberate speed" in ending racial segregation in public education.

Resistance to the social policy announced in *Brown I* was expected. A rigid timetable for desegregation would only intensify opposition. During oral arguments on *Brown II*, devoted to the question of what kind of decree the Court should issue to enforce *Brown*, Warren confronted the hard fact of southern resistance. The attorney for South Carolina, S. Emory Rogers, pressed for an open-ended decree—one that would not specify when and how desegregation should take place. He boldly proclaimed:

> Mr. Chief Justice, to say we will conform depends on the decree handed down. I am frank to tell you, right now [in] our district I do not think that we will send—[that] the white people of the district will send their children to the Negro schools. It would be unfair to tell the Court that we are going to do that. I do not think it is. But I do think that something can be worked out. We hope so.

"It is not a question of attitude," Warren shot back, "it is a question of conforming to the decree." Their heated exchange continued as follows:

> Chief Justice Warren: But you are not willing to say here that there would be an honest attempt to conform to this decree, if we did leave it to the district court [to implement]?
> Mr. Rogers: No, I am not. Let us get the word "honest" out of there.
> Chief Justice Warren: No, leave it in.
> Mr. Rogers: No, because I would have to tell you that right now we would not conform—we would not send our white children to the Negro schools.

The exchange reinforced Warren's view "that reasonable attempts to start the integration process is [sic] all the court can expect in view of the scope of the problem, and that an order to immediately admit all negroes in white schools would be an absurdity because impossible to obey in many areas. Thus, while total immediate integration might be a reasonable order for Kansas, it would be unreasonable for Virginia, and the district judge might decide that a grade a year or three grades a year is [sic] reasonable compliance in Virginia." Six law clerks were assigned to prepare a segregation research report. They summarized available studies, discussed how school districts in different regions could be desegregated, and projected the effects and reactions to various desegregation plans.

The Court's problem, as one of Reed's law clerks put it, was to frame a decree "so as to allow such divergent results without making it so broad that evasion is encouraged." The clerks agreed that there should be a simple decree but disagreed on whether there should be guidelines for its implementation. One clerk opposed any guidelines. The others thought that their absence "smacks of indecisiveness, and gives the extremists more time to operate." The problem was how precise a guideline should be established. What would constitute "good-faith" compliance? "Although we think a 12-year gradual desegregation plan permissible," they confessed, "we are not certain that the opinion should explicitly sanction it."

At conference, Warren repeated these concerns. Black and Minton thought that a simple decree, without an opinion, was enough. As Black explained, "the less we say the better off we are." The others disagreed. A short, simple opinion seemed advisable for reaffirming *Brown I* and providing guidance for dealing with the inevitable problems of compliance. Harlan wanted *Brown II* expressly to recognize that school desegregation was a local problem to be solved by local authorities. The others also insisted on making clear that school boards and lower courts had flexibility in ending segregation. In Burton's view, "neither this Court nor district courts should act as a school board or formulate the program" for desegregation.

Agreement emerged that the Court should issue a short opinion-decree. In a memorandum, Warren summarized the main points of agreement. The opinion should simply state that *Brown I* held racially segregated public schools to be unconstitutional. *Brown II* should acknowledge that the ruling created various administrative problems, but emphasize that "local school authorities have the primary responsibility for assessing and solving these problems; [and] the courts will have to consider these problems in determining whether the efforts of local school authorities" are in good-faith compliance. The cases, he concluded, should be remanded to the lower courts "for such proceedings and decree necessary and proper to carry out this Court's decision." The justices agreed, and along these lines Warren drafted the Court's short opinion-decree.

The phrase "all deliberate speed" was borrowed from Holmes's opinion in *Virginia v. West Virginia* (1911), a case dealing with how much of the state's public debt, and when, Virginia ought to receive at the time West Virginia broke off and became a state. It was inserted in the final opinion at the suggestion of Frankfurter. Forced integration might lead to a lowering of educational standards. Immediate, court-ordered desegregation, Frankfurter warned, "would make a mockery of the Constitutional adjudication designed to vindicate a claim to equal treatment to achieve 'integrated' but lower educational standards." The Court, he insisted, "does its duty if it gets effectively under way the righting of a wrong. When the wrong is deeply rooted state policy the court does its duty if it decrees measures that reverse the direction of the unconstitutional policy so as to uproot it 'with all deliberate speed.'" As much an apology for not setting precise guidelines as a recognition of the limitations of judicial power, the phrase symbolized the Court's bold moral appeal to the country.

Ten years later, after school closings, massive resistance, and continuing litigation, Black complained. "There has been entirely too much deliberation and not enough speed" in complying with *Brown*. "The time for mere 'deliberate speed' has run out." *Brown*'s moral appeal amounted to little more than an invitation for delay.

*   *   *

Twenty years after *Brown*, some schools remained segregated. David Mathews, secretary of the Department of Health, Education, and Welfare, reported to President Ford the results of a survey of half of the nation's primary and secondary public schools, enrolling 91 percent of all students: of these, 42 percent had an "appreciable percentage" of minority students, 16 percent had undertaken desegregation plans, while 26 percent had not, and 7 percent of the school districts remained racially segregated.

For over three decades, problems of implementing and achieving compliance with *Brown* persisted. Litigation by civil rights groups forced change, but it was piecemeal, costly, and modest. The judiciary alone could not achieve desegregation. Evasion and resistance were encouraged by the reluctance of presidents and Congress to enforce the mandate. Refusing publicly to endorse *Brown*, Eisenhower would not take steps to enforce the decision until violence erupted in Little Rock, Arkansas. He then did so *"not to enforce integration but to prevent opposition by violence to orders of a court."* Later the Kennedy and Johnson administrations lacked congressional authorization and resources to take major initiatives in enforcing school desegregation. Not until 1964, when Congress passed the Civil Rights Act, did the executive branch have such authorization.

Enforcement and implementation required the cooperation and coordination of all three branches. Little progress could be made, as Assistant Attorney General Stephen Pollock has explained, "where historically there had been slavery and a long tradition of discrimination [until] all three branches of the federal government [could] be lined up in support of a movement forward or a requirement for change." The election of Nixon in 1968 then brought changes both in the policies of the executive branch and in the composition of the Court. The simplicity and flexibility of *Brown*, moreover, invited evasion. It produced a continuing struggle over measures, such as gerrymandering school district lines and busing in the 1970s and 1980s, because the mandate itself had evolved from one of ending segregation to one of securing integration in public schools. Republican and Democratic administrations in turn differed on the means and ends of their enforcement policies in promoting integration.

Almost forty years after *Brown*, over 500 school desegregation cases remained in the lower federal courts. At issue in most was whether schools had achieved integration and become free of the vestiges of past segregation. Although lower courts split over how much proof school boards had to show to demonstrate that present *de facto* racial isolation was unrelated to past *de jure* segregation, the Court declined to review major desegregation cases from the mid-1970s to the end of the 1980s. During that time the dynamics of segregation in the country changed, as did the composition and direction of the Court.

* * *

"By itself," the political scientist Robert Dahl observed, "the Court is almost powerless to affect the course of national policy." Another political scientist, Gerald Rosenberg, goes much further in claiming that "courts can *almost never* be effective producers of significant social reform." *Brown*'s failure to achieve immediate and widespread desegregation is instructive, Rosenberg contends, in developing a model of judicial policy-making on the basis of two opposing theories of judicial power. On the theory of a "Constrained Court" three institutional factors limit judicial policy-making: "[t]he limited nature of constitutional rights"; "[t]he lack of judicial independence"; and "[t]he judiciary's lack of powers of implementation." On the other hand, a "Dynamic Court" theory emphasizes the judiciary's freedom "from electoral constraints and [other] institutional arrangements that stymie change," and thus enable the courts to take on issues that other political institutions might not or cannot. But neither theory is completely satisfactory, according to Rosenberg, because occasionally courts do bring about social change. The Court may do so when the three institutional restraints identified with the "Constrained Court" theory are absent and at least one of the following conditions exist to support judicial policy-making: when other political institutions and actors offer either (a) incentives or (b) costs to induce compliance; (c) "when judicial decisions can be implemented by the market"; or (d) when the Court's ruling serves as "a shield, cover, or excuse, for persons crucial to implementation who are *willing to act*." On the historical basis of resistance and forced compliance with *Brown*'s mandate, Rosenberg concludes that "*Brown* and its progeny stand for the proposition that courts are impotent to produce significant social reform."

Brown, nonetheless, dramatically and undeniably altered the course of American life in ways and for reasons that Rosenberg underestimates. Neither Congress nor President Eisenhower would have moved to end segregated schools in the 1950s, as their reluctance for a decade to enforce *Brown* underscores. The Court lent moral force and legitimacy to the civil rights movement and to the eventual move by Congress and President Johnson to enforce compliance with *Brown*. More importantly, to argue that the Court is impotent to bring about social change overstates the case. Neither Congress nor the president, any more than the Court, could have singlehandedly dismantled racially segregated public schools. As political scientist Richard Neustadt has argued, presidential power ultimately turns on a president's power of persuasion, the Court's power depends on the persuasiveness of its rulings and the magnitude of change in social behavior mandated. The Court raises the ante in its bid for compliance when it appeals for massive social change through a prescribed course of action, in contrast to when it simply says "no" when striking down a law. The unanimous but ambiguous ruling in *Brown* reflects the justices' awareness that their decisions are not self-enforcing, especially when they deal with highly controversial issues and their rulings depend heavily on other institutions for implementation. Moreover, the ambiguity of *Brown*'s remedial decree was the price of achieving unanimity. Unanimity appeared necessary if the Court was to preserve its institutional prestige while pursuing revolutionary change in social policy. The justices sacrificed their own policy preferences for more precise guidelines, while the Court tolerated lengthy delays in recognition of the costs of open defiance, building consensus, and gaining public acceptance. But in the ensuing decades *Brown*'s mandate was also transformed from that of a simple decree for putting an end to state-imposed segregation into the more vexing one of achieving integrated public schools. With that transformation of *Brown*'s mandate the political dynamics of the desegregation controversy evolved, along with a changing Court and country.

Discussion Questions

1. In what ways does the Supreme Court take politics and public opinion into account in making decisions? Is this appropriate? What would the alternative be?

2. How does the process of appointment to the Supreme Court shape Court decisions? Should presidents make nominations based on the political views of potential justices?

3. Does O'Brien's argument confirm Hamilton's observations about the power of the Court?

4. In several states, Supreme Courts have ruled that bans on same-sex marriage violated the state's constitution. Did these courts' rulings damage their public standing by ignoring the political context (a majority of the public opposed same-sex marriage at the time of the decision and many states passed laws or constitutional amendments following these decisions to prohibit same-sex marriage in their states), or did the courts do the correct thing by supporting the basic rights of a minority group? Is there some way the courts could have finessed the issue, the way the Supreme Court did in *Brown*? Should they have?

41

The Hollow Hope: Can Courts Bring About Social Change?

Gerald N. Rosenberg

Despite Alexander Hamilton's argument that the Supreme Court would be the "least dangerous branch" because it could not accomplish much without the assistance of Congress and the president, most political observers have viewed the Court as an important agent of social change. That is, in many instances when Congress and the president have not been inclined to act, the Court has pushed the nation to change important policies. In areas such as civil rights, environmental policy, women's and reproductive rights, and political reform, the standard view is of a "dynamic court" that is a "powerful, vigorous, and potent proponent of change." Proponents of this perspective see it as almost self-evident, pointing to decisions such as Brown v. Board of Education *on school desegregation,* Roe v. Wade *on abortion, and* Baker v. Carr *on "one-person, one-vote" as examples of the Supreme Court producing important social change.*

Gerald Rosenberg says this view of the Court is simply wrong. In contrast, he presents a view of a "constrained court" that is "weak, ineffective, and powerless." Echoing Hamilton, Rosenberg points out that courts depend on political support to produce reform; that they are unlikely to produce change if they is any serious resistance because of their lack of implementation powers; and that if they lack established legal precedents they are unlikely to break new ground in a way that promotes social change. For example, following Brown v. Board of Education *there was massive resistance from southern states to implementing the ruling, so real change did not occur until Congress acted ten years later. He also argues that courts are in a weak position to change public opinion because most Americans are only vaguely aware of most landmark Supreme Court decisions.*

Rosenberg concludes that courts can only help produce significant social change when the "institutional, structural, and ideological barriers to change are weak. A court's contribution, then, is akin to officially recognizing the evolving state of affairs, more like the cutting of the ribbon on a new project than its construction."

*　*　*

In the last several decades movements and groups advocating what I will shortly define as significant social reform have turned increasingly to the courts. Starting with the famous cases brought by the civil rights movement and spreading to issues raised by women's groups, environmental groups, political reformers, and others, American courts seemingly have become important producers of political and social change. Cases such as *Brown* (school desegregation) and *Roe* (abortion) are heralded as having produced major change. Further, such litigation has often occurred, and appears to have been most successful, when the other branches of government have failed to act. While officious government officials and rigid, unchanging institutions represent a real social force which may frustrate popular opinion, this litigation activity suggests that courts can produce significant social reform even when the other branches of government are inactive or opposed. Indeed, for many, part of what makes American democracy exceptional is that it includes the world's most powerful court system, protecting minorities and defending liberty, in the face of opposition from the democratically elected branches. Americans look to activist courts, then, as fulfilling an important role in the American scheme. This view of the courts, although informed by recent historical experience, is essentially functional. It sees courts as powerful, vigorous, and potent proponents of change. I refer to this view of the role of the courts as the "Dynamic Court" view.

As attractive as the Dynamic Court view may be, one must guard against uncritical acceptance. Indeed, in a political system that gives sovereignty to the popular will and makes economic decisions through the market, it is not obvious why courts should have the effects it asserts. Maybe its attractiveness is based on something more than effects? Could it be that the self-understanding of the judiciary and legal profession leads to an overstatement of the role of the courts, a "mystification" of the judiciary? If judges see themselves as powerful; if the Bar views itself as influential, and insulated; if professional training in law schools inculcates students with such beliefs, might these factors inflate the self-importance of the judiciary? The Dynamic Court view may be supported, then, because it offers psychological payoffs to key actors by confirming self-images, not because it is correct. And when this "mystification" is added to a normative belief in the courts as the guardian of fundamental rights and liberties—what Scheingold (1974) calls the "myth of rights"—the allure of the Dynamic Court view may grow.

Further, for all its "obviousness," the Dynamic Court view has a well-established functional and historical competitor. In fact, there is a long tradition of legal scholarship that views the federal judiciary, in Alexander Hamilton's famous language, as the "least dangerous" branch of government. Here, too, there is something of a truism about this claim. Courts, we know, lack both budgetary and physical powers. Because, in Hamilton's words, they lack power over either the "sword or the purse," their ability to produce political and social change is limited. In contrast to the first view, the "least dangerous" branch can do little more than point out how actions have fallen short of constitutional or legislative requirements and hope that appropriate action is taken. The strength of this view, of course, is that it leaves Americans free to govern themselves without interference from non-elected officials. I refer to this view of the courts as weak, ineffective, and powerless as the "Constrained Court" view.

The Constrained Court view fully acknowledges the role of popular preferences and social and economic resources in shaping outcomes. Yet it seems to rely excessively on a formal-process understanding of how change occurs in American politics. But the formal process doesn't always work, for social and political forces may be overly responsive to unevenly distributed resources. Bureaucratic inertia, too, can derail orderly, processional change. There is room, then, for courts to effectively correct the pathologies of the political process. Perhaps accurate at the founding of the political system, the Constrained Court view may miss growth and change in the American political system.

Clearly, these two views, and the aspirations they represent, are in conflict on a number of different dimensions. They differ not only on both the desirability and the effectiveness of court action, but also on the nature of American democracy. The Dynamic Court view gives courts an important place in the American political system while the older view sees courts as much less powerful than other more "political" branches and activities. The conflict is more than one of mere definition, for each view captures a very different part of American democracy. We Americans want courts to protect minorities and defend liberties, *and* to defer to elected officials. We want a robust political life *and* one that is just. Most of the time, these two visions do not clash. American legislatures do not habitually threaten liberties, and courts do not regularly invalidate the acts of elected officials or require certain actions to be taken. But the most interesting and relevant cases, such as *Brown* and *Roe*, occur when activist courts overrule and invalidate the actions of elected officials, or order actions beyond what elected officials are willing to do. What happens then? Are courts effective producers of change, as the Dynamic Court view suggests, or do their decisions do little more than point the way to a brighter, but perhaps unobtainable future? Once again, this conflict between two deeply held views about the role of the courts in the American political system has an obvious normative dimension that is worth debating. But this book has a different aim. Relying heavily on empirical data, I ask under what conditions can courts produce political and social change? When does it make sense for individuals and groups pressing for such change to litigate? What do the answers mean about the nature of the American regime?

* * *

The findings show that, with the addition of the four conditions, the constraints derived from the Constrained Court view best capture the capacity of the courts to produce significant social reform. This is the case because, on the most fundamental level, courts depend on political support to produce such reform (Constraint II). For example, since the success of civil rights in fields such as voting and education depended on political action, political hostility doomed court contributions. With women's rights, lack of enforcement of existing laws, in addition to an unwillingness to extend legal protection, had a similar dampening effect. And with abortion and the environment, hostility from many political leaders created barriers to implementation. This finding appears clearly applicable to other fields.

Courts will also be ineffective in producing change, given any serious resistance because of their lack of implementation powers (Constraint III). The structural constraints of the Constrained Court view, built into the American judicial system, make courts virtually powerless to produce change. They must depend on the actions of others for their decisions to be implemented. With civil rights, little changed until the federal government became involved. With women's rights, we still lack a serious government effort, and stereotypes that constrain women's opportunities remain powerful. Similarly, the uneven availability of access to legal abortion demonstrates the point. Where there is local hostility to change, court orders will be ignored. Community pressure, violence or threats of violence, and lack of market response all serve to curtail actions to implement court decisions. This finding, too, appears applicable across fields.

Despite these constraints on change, in at least several of the movements examined major legal cases were won. The chief reason is that the remaining constraint, the lack of established legal precedents, was weak (Constraint I). That is, there were precedents for change and supportive movements within the broader legal culture. In civil rights, litigation in the 1930s and 1940s progressively battered the separate-but-equal standard, setting up the argument and decision in *Brown*. In women's rights, the progress of civil rights litigation, particularly in the expansion of the Fourteenth Amendment, laid the groundwork. In the area of abortion, notions of a sphere of privacy in sexual matters were first developed by the Supreme Court in 1965, broadened in 1972, and forcefully presented in several widely read law-review articles. And, by the date of the Supreme Court's abortion decisions, numerous lower courts had invalidated state abortion statutes on grounds that the Supreme Court came to enunciate. Without these precedents, which took decades to develop, it would have been years before even a legal victory could have been obtained. But legal victories do not automatically or even necessarily produce the desired change.

A quick comparison between civil rights and abortion illustrates these points. While both had legal precedents on which to construct a winning legal argument, little else was similar. With civil rights, there was a great deal of white hostility to blacks, especially in the South. On the whole, political leaders, particularly Southerners, were either supportive of segregation or unwilling to confront it as an important issue. In addition, court decisions required individuals and institutions hostile to civil rights to implement the changes. Until Congress acted a decade later, these two constraints remained and none of the conditions necessary for change were present. After congressional and executive actions were taken, the constraints were overcome and conditions for change were created, including the creation of incentives, costs, and the context in which courts could be used as cover. Only then did change occur. In contrast, at the time of the abortion decisions there was much public and elite support for abortion. There was an active reform movement in the states, and Congress was quiet, with no indication of the opposition that many of its members would later provide. Also, the presence of the market condition partially overcame the implementation constraint. To the extent that the abortion decisions had judicial effects, it is precisely because the constraints were weak and a condition necessary for change was present. Civil rights and abortion litigation, then, highlight the existence and force of the constraints and conditions.

Turning to the question of extra-judicial or indirect effects, courts are in a weak position to produce change. Only a minority of Americans know what the courts have done on important issues. Fewer still combine that knowledge with the belief in the Supreme Court's constitutional role, a combination that would enable the Court, and the lower courts, to legitimate behavior. This makes courts a particularly poor tool for changing opinions or for mobilization. As Peltason puts it, "litigation, by its complexity and technical nature and by its lack of dramatic moments, furnishes an ineffective peg around which to build a mass movement." Rally round the flag is one thing but rally round the brief (or opinion) is quite another! The evidence from the movements examined makes dubious any claim for important extra-judicial effects of court action. It strikes at the heart of the Dynamic Court view.

The cases examined show that when the constraints are overcome, and one of the four conditions is present, courts can help produce significant social reform. However, this means, by definition, that institutional, structural, and ideological barriers to change are weak. A court's contribution, then, is akin to officially recognizing the evolving state of affairs, more like the cutting of the ribbon on a new project than its construction. Without such change, the constraints reign. When Justice Jackson commented during oral argument in *Brown*, "I suppose that realistically this case is here for the reason that action couldn't be obtained from Congress", he identified a fundamental reason why the Court's action in the case would have little effect.

Given the constraints and the conditions, the Constrained Court view is the more accurate: U.S. courts can *almost never* be effective producers of significant social reform. At best, they can second the social reform acts of the other branches of government. Problems that are unsolvable in the political context can rarely be solved by courts. As Scheingold puts it, the "law can hardly transcend the conflicts of the political system in which it is embedded". Turning to courts to produce significant social reform substitutes the myth of America for its reality. It credits courts and judicial decisions with a power that they do not have.

*   *   *

This conclusion does not deny that courts can sometimes help social reform movements. Occasionally, though rarely, when the constraints are overcome, and one of the conditions is present, courts can make a difference. Sometimes, too, litigation can remove minor but lingering obstacles. But here litigation is often a mopping-up operation, and it is often defensive. In civil rights, for example, when opponents of the 1964 and 1965 acts went to court to invalidate them, the courts' refusal to do so allowed change to proceed. Similarly, if there had never been a *Brown* decision, a Southern school board or state wanting to avoid a federal fund cut-off in the late 1960s might have challenged its state law requiring segregation. An obliging court decision would have removed the obstacle without causing much of a stir, or wasting the scarce resources of civil rights groups. This is a very different approach to the courts than one based on using them to produce significant social reform.

Litigation can also help reform movements by providing defense services to keep the movement afloat. In civil rights, the NAACP Legal Defense and Educational Fund, Inc. (Inc. Fund) provided crucial legal service that prevented the repressive legal structures of the Southern states from totally incapacitating the movement. In springing demonstrators from jail, providing bail money, and forcing at least a semblance of due process, Inc. Fund lawyers performed crucial tasks. But again, this is a far cry from a litigation strategy for significant social reform.

*   *   *

American courts are not all-powerful institutions. They were designed with severe limitations and placed in a political system of divided powers. To ask them to produce significant social reform is to forget their history and ignore their constraints. It is to cloud our vision with a naive and romantic belief in the triumph of rights over politics. And while romance and even naiveté have their charms, they are not best exhibited in courtrooms.

DISCUSSION QUESTIONS

1. Can you think of any examples of important Supreme Court decisions that may support the view that the Court can be an important agent of social change?

2. If Rosenberg is correct, does that mean that Hamilton's argument that the Court is the "least dangerous branch" is also correct? Or are there other ways that the Court exerts influence in the political system other than promoting social change?

3. Not having read the entire book, but rather just the argument and the conclusions, you are not really in a position to evaluate the evidence. What type of evidence would you have found convincing?

Debating the Issues: Interpreting the Constitution— Originalism or Living Constitution?

Debates over the federal judiciary's role in the political process often focus on the question of how judges should interpret the Constitution. Should judges apply the document's original meaning as stated by the Framers, or should they use a framework that incorporates shifting interpretations across time? This debate intensified during Earl Warren's tenure as Chief Justice (1953–69) because of Court decisions that expanded the scope of civil liberties and criminal rights far beyond what "originalists" thought the Constitution's language authorized. The debate continues in the current, more conservative Court. The two readings in this section offer contrasting viewpoints from two sitting Supreme Court justices.

Antonin Scalia, the intellectual force behind the conservative wing of the Court, argues that justices must be bound by the original meaning of the document, because that is the only neutral principle that allows the judiciary to function as a legal body instead of a political one. The alternative is to embrace an evolving or "Living Constitution," which Scalia criticizes as allowing judges to decide cases on the basis of what seems right at the moment. He says that this "evolutionary" approach does not have any overall guiding principle and therefore "is simply not a practicable constitutional philosophy." He provides several examples of how the Living Constitution approach had produced decisions that stray from the meaning of the Constitution in the areas of abortion rights, gay rights, the right to counsel, and the right to confront one's accuser. This last example is especially provocative, given that it concerned the right of an accused child molester to confront the child who accused him of the crime. Scalia argues that there is no coherent alternative to originalism and forcefully concludes, "The worst thing about the Living Constitution is that it will destroy the Constitution."

Stephen Breyer argues for the Living Constitution approach, and places it within a broader constitutional and theoretical framework. He argues for a "consequentialist" approach that is rooted in basic constitutional purposes, the most important of which is "active liberty," which he defines as "an active and constant participation in collective power." Breyer applies this framework to a range of difficult constitutional issues, including freedom of speech in the context of campaign finance and privacy rights in the context of rapidly evolving technology. He argues that the plain language of the Constitution does not provide enough guidance to answer these difficult questions. He turns the tables on Scalia, arguing that it is the literalist or originalist position that will, ironically, lead justices to rely too heavily on their own personal views, whereas his consequentialist position is actually the view that is more likely to produce judicial restraint. Breyer goes on to criticize the originalist position as fraught with inconsistencies. It is inherently subjective, despite its attempt to emphasize the "objective" words of the Constitution. By relying on the consequentialist perspective, which emphasizes democratic participation and active liberty, justices are more likely to reach limited conclusions that apply to the facts at hand, while maximizing the positive implications for democracy.

Linda Greenhouse, an observer of the Supreme Court, summarized the debate between Scalia and Breyer in these terms: "It is a debate over text versus context. For Justice Scalia, who focuses on text, language is supreme, and the court's job is to derive and apply rules from the words chosen by the Constitution's framers or a statute's drafters. For Justice Breyer, who looks to context, language is only a starting point to an inquiry in which a law's purpose and a decision's likely consequences are the more important elements."

42

"Constitutional Interpretation the Old-Fashioned Way"

ANTONIN SCALIA

It's a pizzazzy topic: Constitutional Interpretation. It is, however, an important one. I was vividly reminded how important it was last week when the Court came out with a controversial decision in the *Roper* case. And I watched one television commentary on the case in which the host had one person defending the opinion on the ground that people should not be subjected to capital punishment for crimes they commit when they are younger than eighteen, and the other person attacked the opinion on the ground that a jury should be able to decide that a person, despite the fact he was under eighteen, given the crime, given the person involved, should be subjected to capital punishment. And it struck me how irrelevant it was, how much the point had been missed. The question wasn't whether the call was right or wrong. The important question was who should make the call. And that is essentially what I am addressing today.

I am one of a small number of judges, small number of anybody— judges, professors, lawyers—who are known as originalists. Our manner of interpreting the Constitution is to begin with the text, and to give that text the meaning that it bore when it was adopted by the people. I'm not a "strict constructionist," despite the introduction. I don't like the term "strict construction." I do not think the Constitution, or any text, should be interpreted either strictly or sloppily; it should be interpreted reasonably. Many of my interpretations do not deserve the description "strict." I do believe, however, that you give the text the meaning it had when it was adopted.

This is such a minority position in modern academia and in modern legal circles that on occasion I'm asked when I've given a talk like this a question from the back of the room—"Justice Scalia, when did you first become an originalist?"—as though it is some kind of weird affliction that seizes some people—"When did you first start eating human flesh?"

Although it is a minority view now, the reality is that, not very long ago, originalism was orthodoxy. Everybody at least *purported* to be an originalist. If you go back and read the commentaries on the Constitution by Joseph Story, he didn't think the Constitution evolved or changed. He said it means and will always mean what it meant when it was adopted.

Or consider the opinions of John Marshall in the Federal Bank case, where he says, we must not, we must always remember it is a constitution we are expounding. And since it's a constitution, he says, you have to give its provisions expansive meaning so that they will accommodate events that you do not know of which will happen in the future.

Well, if it is a constitution that changes, you wouldn't have to give it an expansive meaning. You can give it whatever meaning you want and, when future necessity arises, you simply change the meaning. But anyway, that is no longer the orthodoxy.

Oh, one other example about how not just the judges and scholars believed in originalism, but even the American people. Consider the 19th Amendment, which is the amendment that gave women the vote. It was adopted by the American people in 1920. Why did we adopt a constitutional amendment for that purpose? The Equal Protection Clause existed in 1920; it was adopted right after the Civil War. And you know that if the issue of the franchise for women came up today, we would not have to have a constitutional amendment. Someone would come to the Supreme Court and say, "Your Honors, in a democracy, what could be a greater denial of equal protection than denial of the franchise?" And the Court would say, "Yes! Even though it never meant it before, the Equal Protection Clause means that women have to have the vote." But that's not how the American people thought in 1920. In 1920, they looked at the Equal Protection Clause and said, "What does it mean?" Well, it clearly doesn't mean that you can't discriminate in the franchise—not only on the basis of sex, but on the basis of property ownership, on the basis of literacy. None of that is unconstitutional. And therefore, since it wasn't unconstitutional, and we wanted it to be, we did things the good old-fashioned way and adopted an amendment.

Now, in asserting that originalism used to be orthodoxy, I do not mean to imply that judges did not distort the Constitution now and then; of course they did. We had willful judges then, and we will have willful judges until the end of time. But the difference is that prior to the last fifty years or so, prior to the advent of the "Living Constitution," judges did their distortions the good old-fashioned way, the honest way—they lied about it. They said the Constitution means such and such, when it never meant such and such.

It's a big difference that you now no longer have to lie about it, because we are in the era of the evolving Constitution. And the judge can simply say, "Oh yes, the Constitution didn't used to mean that, but it does now." We are in the age in which not only judges, not only lawyers, but even school children have come to learn the Constitution changes. I have grammar school students come into the Court now and then, and they recite very proudly what they have been taught: "The Constitution is a living document." You know, it morphs.

Well, let me first tell you how we got to the "Living Constitution." You don't have to be a lawyer to understand it. The road is not that complicated. Initially, the Court began giving terms in the text of the Constitution a meaning they didn't have when they were adopted. For example, the First Amendment, which forbids Congress to abridge the freedom of speech. What does the freedom of speech mean? Well, it clearly did not mean that Congress or government could not impose any restrictions upon speech. Libel laws, for example, were clearly constitutional. Nobody thought the First Amendment was *carte blanche* to libel someone. But in the famous case of *New York Times v. Sullivan*, the Supreme Court said, "But the First Amendment does prevent you from suing for libel if you are a public figure and if the libel was not malicious"—that is, the person, a member of the press or otherwise, thought that what the person said was true. Well, that had never been the law. I mean, it might be a good law. And some states could amend their libel law.

It's one thing for a state to amend its libel law and say, "We think that public figures shouldn't be able to sue." That's fine. But the courts have said that the First Amendment, which never meant this before, now means that if you are a public figure, that you can't sue for libel unless it's intentional, malicious. So that's one way to do it.

Another example is the Constitution guarantees the right to be represented by counsel. That never meant the state had to pay for your counsel. But you can reinterpret it to mean that.

That was step one. Step two, I mean, that will only get you so far. There is no text in the Constitution that you could reinterpret to create a right to abortion, for example. So you need something else. The something else is called the doctrine of "Substantive Due Process." Only lawyers can walk around talking about substantive process, inasmuch as it's a contradiction in terms. If you referred to substantive process or procedural substance at a cocktail party, people would look at you funny. But, lawyers talk this way all the time.

What substantive due process is is quite simple—the Constitution has a Due Process Clause, which says that no person shall be deprived of life, liberty, or property without due process of law. Now, what does this guarantee? Does it guarantee life, liberty, or property? No, indeed! All three can be taken away. You can be fined, you can be incarcerated, you can even be executed, but not without due process of law. It's a procedural guarantee. But the Court said, and this goes way back, in the 1920s at least—in fact the first case to do it was *Dred Scott.* But it became more popular in the 1920s. The Court said there are some liberties that are so important, that no process will suffice to take them away. Hence, substantive due process.

Now, what liberties are they? The Court will tell you. Be patient. When the doctrine of substantive due process was initially announced, it was limited in this way: the Court said it embraces only those liberties that are fundamental to a democratic society and rooted in the traditions of the American people.

Then we come to step three. Step three: that limitation is eliminated. Within the last twenty years, we have found to be covered by due process the right to abortion, which was so little rooted in the traditions of the American people that it was criminal for 200 years; the right to homosexual sodomy, which was so little rooted in the traditions of the American people that it was criminal for 200 years. So it is literally true, and I don't think this is an exaggeration, that the Court has essentially liberated itself from the text of the Constitution, from the text and even from the traditions of the American people. It is up to the Court to say what is covered by substantive due process.

What are the arguments usually made in favor of the Living Constitution? As the name of it suggests, it is a very attractive philosophy, and it's hard to talk people out of it—the notion that the Constitution grows. The major argument is the Constitution is a living organism; it has to grow with the society that it governs or it will become brittle and snap.

This is the equivalent of, an anthropomorphism equivalent to, what you hear from your stockbroker, when he tells you that the stock market is resting for an assault on the 11,000 level. The stock market panting at some base camp. The stock market is not a mountain climber and the Constitution is not a living organism, for Pete's sake; it's a legal document, and like all legal documents, it says some things, and it doesn't say other things. And if you think that the aficionados of the Living Constitution want to bring you flexibility, think again.

My Constitution is a very flexible Constitution. You think the death penalty is a good idea—persuade your fellow citizens and adopt it. You think it's a bad idea—persuade them the other way and eliminate it. You want a right to abortion—create it the way most rights are created in a democratic society: persuade your fellow citizens it's a good idea and enact it. You want the opposite—persuade them the other way. That's flexibility. But to read either result into the Constitution is not to produce flexibility, it is to produce what a constitution is designed to produce—rigidity. Abortion, for example, is offstage, it is off the democratic stage; it is no use debating it; it is unconstitutional. I mean prohibiting it is unconstitutional; I mean it's no use debating it anymore—now and forever, coast to coast, I guess until we amend the Constitution, which is a difficult thing. So, for whatever reason you might like the Living Constitution, don't like it because it provides flexibility.

That's not the name of the game. Some people also seem to like it because they think it's a good liberal thing—that somehow this is a conservative/liberal battle, and conservatives like the old-fashioned originalist Constitution and liberals ought to like the Living Constitution. That's not true either. The dividing line between those who believe in the Living Constitution and those who don't is not the dividing line between conservatives and liberals.

Conservatives are willing to grow the Constitution to cover their favorite causes just as liberals are, and the best example of that is two cases we announced some years ago on the same day, the same morning. One case was *Romer v. Evans*, in which the people of Colorado had enacted an amendment to the state constitution by plebiscite, which said that neither the state nor any subdivision of the state would add to the protected statuses against which private individuals cannot discriminate. The usual ones are race, religion, age, sex, disability and so forth. Would not add sexual preference—somebody thought that was a terrible idea, and, since it was a terrible idea, it must be unconstitutional. Brought a lawsuit, it came to the Supreme Court. And the Supreme Court said, "Yes, it is unconstitutional." On the basis of—I don't know. The Sexual Preference Clause of the Bill of Rights, presumably. And the liberals loved it, and the conservatives gnashed their teeth.

The very next case we announced is a case called *BMW v. Gore*. Not the Gore you think; this is another Gore. Mr. Gore had bought a BMW, which is a car supposedly advertised at least as having a superb finish, baked seven times in ovens deep in the Alps, by dwarfs. And his BMW apparently had gotten scratched on the way over. They did not send it back to the Alps; they took a can of spray paint and fixed it. And he found out about this and was furious, and he brought a lawsuit. He got his compensatory damages, a couple of hundred dollars—the difference between a car with a better paint job and a worse paint job—plus $2 million against BMW for punitive damages for being a bad actor, which is absurd of course, so it must be unconstitutional. BMW appealed to my Court, and my Court said, "Yes, it's unconstitutional." In violation of, I assume, the Excessive Damages Clause of the Bill of Rights. And if excessive punitive damages are unconstitutional, why aren't excessive compensatory damages unconstitutional? So you have a federal question whenever you get a judgment in a civil case. Well, that one the conservatives liked, because conservatives don't like punitive damages, and the liberals gnashed their teeth.

I dissented in both cases because I say, "A pox on both their houses." It has nothing to do with what your policy preferences are; it has to do with what you think the Constitution is.

Some people are in favor of the Living Constitution because they think it always leads to greater freedom—there's just nothing to lose, the evolving Constitution will always provide greater and greater freedom, more and more rights. Why would you think that? It's a two-way street. And indeed, under the aegis of the Living Constitution, some freedoms have been taken away.

Recently, last term, we reversed a 15-year-old decision of the Court, which had held that the Confrontation Clause—which couldn't be clearer, it says, "In all criminal prosecutions, the accused shall enjoy the right . . . to be confronted with the witness against him." But a Living Constitution Court held that all that was necessary to comply with the Confrontation Clause was that the hearsay evidence which is introduced—hearsay evidence means you can't cross-examine the person who said it because he's not in the court—the hearsay evidence has to bear indicia of reliability. I'm happy to say that we reversed it last term with the votes of the two originalists on the Court. And the opinion said that the only indicium of reliability that the Confrontation Clause acknowledges is confrontation. You bring the witness in to testify and to be cross-examined. That's just one example; there are others, of eliminating liberties.

So, I think another example is the right to jury trial. In a series of cases, the Court had seemingly acknowledged that you didn't have to have trial by jury of the facts that increase your sentence. You can make the increased sentence a "sentencing factor"—you get thirty years for burglary, but if the burglary is committed with a gun, as a sentencing factor the judge can give you another ten years. And the judge will decide whether you used a gun. And he will decide it, not beyond a reasonable doubt, but whether it's more likely than not. Well, we held recently, I'm happy to say, that this violates the right to a trial by jury. The Living Constitution would not have produced that result. The Living Constitution, like the legislatures that enacted these laws, would have allowed sentencing factors to be determined by the judge because all the Living Constitution assures you is that what will happen is what the majority wants to happen. And that's not the purpose of constitutional guarantees.

Well, I've talked about some of the false virtues of the Living Constitution; let me tell you what I consider its principle vices are. Surely the greatest—you should always begin with principle—its greatest vice is its illegitimacy. The only reason federal courts sit in judgment of the constitutionality of federal legislation is not because they are explicitly authorized to do so in the Constitution. Some modern constitutions give the constitutional court explicit authority to review German legislation or French legislation for its constitutionality; our Constitution doesn't say anything like that. But John Marshall says in *Marbury v. Madison:* Look, this is lawyers' work. What you have here is an apparent conflict between the Constitution and the statute. And, all the time, lawyers and judges have to reconcile these conflicts—they try to read the two to comport with each other. If they can't, it's judges' work to decide which ones prevail. When there are two statutes, the more recent one prevails. It implicitly repeals the older one. But when the Constitution is at issue, the Constitution prevails because it is a "superstatute." I mean, that's what Marshall says: It's judges' work.

If you believe, however, that the Constitution is not a legal text, like the texts involved when judges reconcile or decide which of two statutes prevail; if you think the Constitution is some exhortation to give effect to the most fundamental values of the society as those values change from year to year; if you think that it is meant to reflect, as some of the Supreme Court cases say, particularly those involving the Eighth Amendment, if you think it is simply meant to reflect the evolving standards of decency that mark the progress of a maturing society—if that is what you think it is, then why in the world would you have it interpreted by nine lawyers? What do I know about the evolving standards of decency of American society? I'm afraid to ask.

If that is what you think the Constitution is, then *Marbury v. Madison* is wrong. It shouldn't be up to the judges, it should be up to the legislature. We should have a system like the English—whatever the legislature thinks is constitutional is constitutional. They know the evolving standards of American society, I don't. So in principle, it's incompatible with the legal regime that America has established.

Secondly, and this is the killer argument—I mean, it's the best debaters' argument—they say in politics you can't beat somebody with nobody. It's the same thing with principles of legal interpretation. If you don't believe in originalism, then you need some other principle of interpretation. Being a non-originalist is not enough. You see, I have my rules that confine me. I know what I'm looking for. When I find it—the original meaning of the Constitution—I am handcuffed. If I believe that the First Amendment meant when it was adopted that you are entitled to burn the American flag, I have to come out that way even though I don't like to come out that way. When I find that the original meaning of the jury trial guarantee is that any additional time you spend in prison which depends upon a fact must depend upon a fact found by a jury—once I find that's what the jury trial guarantee means, I am handcuffed. Though I'm a law-and-order type, I cannot do all the mean conservative things I would like to do to this society. You got me.

Now, if you're not going to control your judges that way, what other criterion are you going to place before them? What is the criterion that governs the Living Constitutional judge? What can you possibly use, besides original meaning? Think about that. Natural law? We all agree on that, don't we? The philosophy of John Rawls? That's easy. There really is nothing else. You either tell your judges, "Look, this is a law, like all laws; give it the meaning it had when it was adopted." Or, you tell your judges, "Govern us. You tell us whether people under eighteen, who committed their crimes when they were under eighteen, should be executed. You tell us whether there ought to be an unlimited right to abortion or a partial right to abortion. You make these decisions for us." I have put this question—you know I speak at law schools with some frequency just to make trouble—and I put this question to the faculty all the time, or incite the students to ask their Living Constitutional professors: "Okay professor, you are not an originalist, what is your criterion?" There is none other.

And finally, this is what I will conclude with although it is not on a happy note. The worst thing about the Living Constitution is that it will destroy the Constitution. You heard in the introduction that I was confirmed, close to nineteen years ago now, by a vote of ninety-eight to nothing. The two missing were Barry Goldwater and Jake Games, so make it one hundred. I was known at that time to be, in my political and social views, fairly conservative. But still, I was known to be a good lawyer, an honest man—somebody who could read a text and give it its fair meaning—had judicial impartiality and so forth. And so I was unanimously confirmed. Today, barely twenty years later, it is difficult to get someone confirmed to the Court of Appeals. What has happened? The American people have figured out what is going on. If we are selecting lawyers, if we are selecting people to read a text and give it the fair meaning it had when it was adopted, yes, the most important thing to do is to get a good lawyer. If on the other hand, we're picking people to draw out of their own conscience and experience a new constitution with all sorts of new values to govern our society, then we should not look principally for good lawyers. We should look principally for people who agree with us, the majority, as to whether there ought to be this right, that right and the other right. We want to pick people that would write the new constitution that we would want.

And that is why you hear in the discourse on this subject, people talking about moderate—we want moderate judges. What is a moderate interpretation of the text? Halfway between what it really means and what you'd like it to mean? There is no such thing as a moderate interpretation of the text. Would you ask a lawyer, "Draw me a moderate contract?" The only way the word has any meaning is if you are looking for someone to write a law, to write a constitution, rather than to interpret one. The moderate judge is the one who will devise the new constitution that most people would approve of. So, for example, we had a suicide case some terms ago, and the Court refused to hold that there is a constitutional right to assisted suicide. We said, "We're not yet ready to say that. Stay tuned, in a few years, the time may come, but we're not yet ready." And that was a moderate decision, because I think most people would not want—if we had gone, looked into that and created a national right to assisted suicide—that would nave been an immoderate and extremist decision.

I think the very terminology suggests where we have arrived—at the point of selecting people to write a constitution, rather than people to give us the fair meaning of one that has been democratically adopted. And when that happens, when the Senate interrogates nominees to the Supreme Court, or to the lower courts—you know, "Judge so-and-so, do you think there is a right to this in the Constitution? You don't? Well, my constituents think there ought to be, and I'm not going to appoint to the court someone who is not going to find that"—when we are in that mode, you realize, we have rendered the Constitution useless, because the Constitution will mean what the majority wants it to mean. The senators are representing the majority, and they will be selecting justices who will devise a constitution that the majority wants. And that, of course, deprives the Constitution of its principle utility. The Bill of Rights is devised to protect you and me against, who do you think? The majority. My most important function on the Supreme Court is to tell the majority to take a walk. And the notion that the justices ought to be selected because of the positions that they will take, that are favored by the majority, is a recipe for destruction of what we have had for 200 years.

To come back to the beginning, this is new—fifty years old or so—the Living Constitution stuff. We have not yet seen what the end of the road is. I think we are beginning to see. And what it is should really be troublesome to Americans who care about a Constitution that can provide protections against majoritarian rule. Thank you.

43

"Our Democratic Constitution"

STEPHEN BREYER

I shall focus upon several contemporary problems that call for governmental action and potential judicial reaction. In each instance I shall argue that, when judges interpret the Constitution, they should place greater emphasis upon the "ancient liberty," i.e., the people's right to "an active and constant participation in collective power." I believe that increased emphasis upon this active liberty will lead to better constitutional law, a law that will promote governmental solutions consistent with individual dignity and community need.

At the same time, my discussion will illustrate an approach to constitutional interpretation that places considerable weight upon consequences—consequences valued in terms of basic constitutional purposes. It disavows a contrary constitutional approach, a more "legalistic" approach that places too much weight upon language, history, tradition, and precedent alone while understating the importance of consequences. If the discussion helps to convince you that the more "consequential" approach has virtue, so much the better.

Three basic views underlie my discussion. First, the Constitution, considered as a whole, creates a framework for a certain kind of government. Its general objectives can be described abstractly as including (1) democratic self-government, (2) dispersion of power (avoiding concentration of too much power in too few hands), (3) individual dignity (through protection of individual liberties), (4) equality before the law (through equal protection of the law), and (5) the rule of law itself.

The Constitution embodies these general objectives in particular provisions. In respect to self-government, for example, Article IV guarantees a "republican Form of Government;" Article I insists that Congress meet at least once a year, that elections take place every two (or six) years, that a census take place every decade; the Fifteenth, Nineteenth, Twenty-fourth, and Twenty-sixth Amendments secure a virtually universal adult suffrage. But a general constitutional objective such as self-government plays a constitutional role beyond the interpretation of an individual provision that refers to it directly. That is because constitutional courts must consider the relation of one phrase to another. They must consider the document as a whole. And consequently the document's handful of general purposes will inform judicial interpretation of many individual provisions that do not refer directly to the general objective in question. My examples seek to show how that is so. And, as I have said, they will suggest a need for judges to pay greater attention to one of those general objectives, namely participatory democratic self-government.

Second, the Court, while always respecting language, tradition, and precedent, nonetheless has emphasized different general constitutional objectives at different periods in its history. Thus one can characterize the early nineteenth century as a period during which the Court helped to establish the authority of the federal government, including the federal judiciary. During the late nineteenth and early twentieth centuries, the Court underemphasized the Constitution's efforts to secure participation by black citizens in representative government—efforts related to the participatory "active" liberty of the ancients. At the same time, it overemphasized protection of property rights, such as an individual's freedom to contract without government interference, to the point where President Franklin Roosevelt commented that the Court's Lochner-era decisions had created a legal "no-man's land" that neither state nor federal regulatory authority had the power to enter.

The New Deal Court and the Warren Court in part reemphasized "active liberty." The former did so by dismantling various Lochner-era distinctions, thereby expanding the scope of democratic self-government. The latter did so by interpreting the Civil War Amendments in light of their purposes and to mean what they say, thereby helping African-Americans become members of the nation's community of self-governing citizens—a community that the Court expanded further in its "one person, one vote" decisions.

More recently, in my view, the Court has again underemphasized the importance of the citizen's active liberty. I will argue for a contemporary reemphasis that better combines "the liberty of the ancients" with that "freedom of governmental restraint" that Constant called "modern."

Third, the real-world consequences of a particular interpretive decision, valued in terms of basic constitutional purposes, play an important role in constitutional decision-making. To that extent, my approach differs from that of judges who would place nearly exclusive interpretive weight upon language, history, tradition and precedent. In truth, the difference is one of degree. Virtually all judges, when interpreting a constitution or a statute, refer at one time or another to language, to history, to tradition, to precedent, to purpose, and to consequences. Even those who take a more literal approach to constitutional interpretation sometimes find consequences and general purposes relevant. But the more "literalist" judge tends to ask those who cannot find an interpretive answer in language, history, tradition, and precedent alone to rethink the problem several times, before making consequences determinative. The more literal judges may hope to find in language, history, tradition, and precedent objective interpretive standards; they may seek to avoid an interpretive subjectivity that could confuse a judge's personal idea of what is good for that which the Constitution demands; and they may believe that these more "original" sources will more readily yield rules that can guide other institutions, including lower courts. These objectives are desirable, but I do not think the literal approach will achieve them, and, in any event, the constitutional price is too high. I hope that my examples will help to show you why that is so, as well as to persuade some of you why it is important to place greater weight upon constitutionally valued consequences, my consequential focus in this lecture being the effect of a court's decisions upon active liberty.

To recall the fate of Socrates is to understand that the "liberty of the ancients" is not a sufficient condition for human liberty. Nor can (or should) we replicate today the ideal represented by the Athenian agora or the New England town meeting. Nonetheless, today's citizen does participate in democratic self-governing processes. And the "active" liberty to which I refer consists of the Constitution's efforts to secure the citizen's right to do so.

To focus upon that active liberty, to understand it as one of the Constitution's handful of general objectives, will lead judges to consider the constitutionality of statutes with a certain modesty. That modesty embodies an understanding of the judges' own expertise compared, for example, with that of a legislature. It reflects the concern that a judiciary too ready to "correct" legislative error may deprive "the people" of "the political experience and the moral education that come from . . . correcting their own errors." It encompasses that doubt, caution, prudence, and concern—that state of not being "too sure" of oneself—that Learned Hand described as the "spirit of liberty." In a word, it argues for traditional "judicial restraint."

But active liberty argues for more than that. I shall suggest that increased recognition of the Constitution's general democratic participatory objectives can help courts deal more effectively with a range of specific constitutional issues. To show this I shall use examples drawn from the areas of free speech, federalism, privacy, equal protection and statutory interpretation. In each instance, I shall refer to an important modern problem of government that calls for a democratic response. I shall then describe related constitutional implications. I want to draw a picture of some of the different ways that increased judicial focus upon the Constitution's participatory objectives can have a positive effect.

*   *   *

I begin with free speech and campaign finance reform. The campaign finance problem arises out of the recent explosion in campaign costs along with a vast disparity among potential givers. * * * The upshot is a concern by some that the matter is out of hand—that too few individuals contribute too much money and that, even though money is not the only way to obtain influence, those who give large amounts of money do obtain, or appear to obtain, too much influence. The end result is a marked inequality of participation. That is one important reason why legislatures have sought to regulate the size of campaign contributions.

The basic constitutional question, as you all know, is not the desirability of reform legislation but whether, how, or the extent to which, the First Amendment permits the legislature to impose limitations or ceilings on the amounts individuals or organizations or parties can contribute to a campaign or the kinds of contributions they can make. * * *

One cannot (or, at least, I cannot) find an easy answer to the constitutional questions in language, history, or tradition. The First Amendment's language says that Congress shall not abridge "the freedom of speech." But it does not define "the freedom of speech" in any detail. The nation's Founders did not speak directly about campaign contributions. Madison, who decried faction, thought that members of Congress would fairly represent all their constituents, in part because the "electors" would not be the "rich" any "more than the poor." But this kind of statement, while modestly helpful to the campaign reform cause, is hardly determinative.

Neither can I find answers in purely conceptual arguments. Some argue, for example, that "money is speech"; others say "money is not speech." But neither contention helps much. Money is not speech, it is money. But the expenditure of money enables speech; and that expenditure is often necessary to communicate a message, particularly in a political context. A law that forbids the expenditure of money to convey a message could effectively suppress that communication.

Nor does it resolve the matter simply to point out that campaign contribution limits inhibit the political "speech opportunities" of those who wish to contribute more. Indeed, that is so. But the question is whether, in context, such a limitation abridges "the freedom of speech." And to announce that this kind of harm could never prove justified in a political context is simply to state an ultimate constitutional conclusion; it is not to explain the underlying reasons.

To refer to the Constitution's general participatory self-government objective, its protection of "active liberty" is far more helpful. That is because that constitutional goal indicates that the First Amendment's constitutional role is not simply one of protecting the individual's "negative" freedom from governmental restraint. The Amendment in context also forms a necessary part of a constitutional system designed to sustain that democratic self-government. The Amendment helps to sustain the democratic process both by encouraging the exchange of ideas needed to make sound electoral decisions and by encouraging an exchange of views among ordinary citizens necessary to encourage their informed participation in the electoral process. It thereby helps to maintain a form of government open to participation (in Constant's words "by all citizens without exception").

The relevance of this conceptual view lies in the fact that the campaign finance laws also seek to further the latter objective. They hope to democratize the influence that money can bring to bear upon the electoral process, thereby building public confidence in that process, broadening the base of a candidate's meaningful financial support, and encouraging greater public participation. They consequently seek to maintain the integrity of the political process—a process that itself translates political speech into governmental action. Seen in this way, campaign finance laws, despite the limits they impose, help to further the kind of open public political discussion that the First Amendment also seeks to encourage, not simply as an end, but also as a means to achieve a workable democracy.

For this reason, I have argued that a court should approach most campaign finance questions with the understanding that important First Amendment-related interests lie on both sides of the constitutional equation and that a First Amendment presumption hostile to government regulation, such as "strict scrutiny" is consequently out of place. Rather, the Court considering the matter without benefit of presumptions, must look realistically at the legislation's impact, both its negative impact on the ability of some to engage in as much communication as they wish and the positive impact upon the public's confidence, and consequent ability to communicate through (and participate in) the electoral process.

The basic question the Court should ask is one of proportionality. Do the statutes strike a reasonable balance between their electoral speech-restricting and speech-enhancing consequences? Or do you instead impose restrictions on that speech that are disproportionate when measured against their corresponding electoral and speech-related benefits, taking into account the kind, the importance, and the extent of those benefits, as well as the need for the restrictions in order to secure them?

The judicial modesty discussed earlier suggests that, in answering these questions, courts should defer to the legislatures' own answers insofar as those answers reflect empirical matters about which the legislature is comparatively expert, for example, the extent of the campaign finance problem, a matter that directly concerns the realities of political life. But courts cannot defer when evaluating the risk that reform legislation will defeat the very objective of participatory self-government itself, for example, where laws would set limits so low that, by elevating the reputation-related or media-related advantages of incumbency to the point where they would insulate incumbents from effective challenge.

I am not saying that focus upon active liberty will automatically answer the constitutional question in particular campaign finance cases. I argue only that such focus will help courts find a proper route for arriving at an answer. The positive constitutional goal implies a systemic role for the First Amendment; and that role, in turn, suggests a legal framework, i.e., a more particular set of questions for the Court to ask. Modesty suggests where, and how, courts should defer to legislatures in doing so. The suggested inquiry is complex. But courts both here and abroad have engaged in similarly complex inquiries where the constitutionality of electoral laws is at issue. That complexity is demanded by a Constitution that provides for judicial review of the constitutionality of electoral rules while granting Congress the effective power to secure a fair electoral system.

I next turn to a different kind of example. It focuses upon current threats to the protection of privacy, defined as "the power to control what others can come to know about you." It seeks to illustrate what active liberty is like in modern America, when we seek to arrive democratically at solutions to important technologically based problems. And it suggests a need for judicial caution and humility when certain privacy matters, such as the balance between free speech and privacy, are at issue.

First, I must describe the "privacy" problem. That problem is unusually complex. It has clearly become even more so since the terrorist attacks. For one thing, those who agree that privacy is important disagree about why. Some emphasize the need to be left alone, not bothered by others, or that privacy is important because it prevents people from being judged out of context. Some emphasize the way in which relationships of love and friendship depend upon trust, which implies a sharing of information not available to all. Others find connections between privacy and individualism, in that privacy encourages non-conformity. Still others find connections between privacy and equality, in that limitations upon the availability of individualized information lead private businesses to treat all customers alike. For some, or all, of these reasons, legal rules protecting privacy help to assure an individual's dignity.

For another thing, the law protects privacy only because of the way in which technology interacts with different laws. Some laws, such as trespass, wiretapping, eavesdropping, and search-and-seizure laws, protect particular places or sites, such as homes or telephones, from searches and monitoring. Other laws protect not places, but kinds of information, for example laws that forbid the publication of certain personal information even by a person who obtained that information legally. Taken together these laws protect privacy to different degrees depending upon place, individual status, kind of intrusion, and type of information.

Further, technological advances have changed the extent to which present laws can protect privacy. Video cameras now can monitor shopping malls, schools, parks, office buildings, city streets, and other places that present law left unprotected. Scanners and interceptors can overhear virtually any electronic conversation. Thermal imaging devices can detect activities taking place within the home. Computers can record and collate information obtained in any of these ways, or others. This technology means an ability to observe, collate and permanently record a vast amount of information about individuals that the law previously may have made available for collection but which, in practice, could not easily have been recorded and collected. The nature of the current or future privacy threat depends upon how this technological/legal fact will affect differently situated individuals.

These circumstances mean that efforts to revise privacy law to take account of the new technology will involve, in different areas of human activity, the balancing of values in light of prediction about the technological future. If, for example, businesses obtain detailed consumer purchasing information, they may create individualized customer profiles. Those profiles may invade the customer's privacy. But they may also help firms provide publicly desired products at lower cost. If, for example, medical records are placed online, patient privacy may be compromised. But the ready availability of those records may lower insurance costs or help a patient carried unconscious into an operating room. If, for example, all information about an individual's genetic make-up is completely confidential, that individual's privacy is protected, but suppose a close relative, a nephew or cousin, needs the information to assess his own cancer risk?

Nor does a "consent" requirement automatically answer the dilemmas suggested, for consent forms may be signed without understanding and, in any event, a decision by one individual to release or to deny information can affect others as well.

Legal solutions to these problems will be shaped by what is technologically possible. Should video cameras be programmed to turn off? Recorded images to self-destruct? Computers instructed to delete certain kinds of information? Should cell phones be encrypted? Should web technology, making use of an individual's privacy preferences, automatically negotiate privacy rules with distant web sites as a condition of access?

The complex nature of these problems calls for resolution through a form of participatory democracy. Ideally, that participatory process does not involve legislators, administrators, or judges imposing law from above. Rather, it involves law revision that bubbles up from below. Serious complex changes in law are often made in the context of a national conversation involving, among others, scientists, engineers, businessmen and -women, the media, along with legislators, judges, and many ordinary citizens whose lives the new technology will affect. That conversation takes place through many meetings, symposia, and discussions, through journal articles and media reports, through legislative hearings and court cases. Lawyers participate fully in this discussion, translating specialized knowledge into ordinary English, defining issues, creating consensus. Typically, administrators and legislators then make decisions, with courts later resolving any constitutional issues that those decisions raise. This "conversation" is the participatory democratic process itself.

The presence of this kind of problem and this kind of democratic process helps to explain, because it suggests a need for, judicial caution or modesty. That is why, for example, the Court's decisions so far have hesitated to preempt that process. In one recent case the Court considered a cell phone conversation that an unknown private individual had intercepted with a scanner and delivered to a radio station. A statute forbid the broadcast of that conversation, even though the radio station itself had not planned or participated in the intercept. The Court had to determine the scope of the station's First Amendment right to broadcast given the privacy interests that the statute sought to protect. The Court held that the First Amendment trumped the statute, permitting the radio station to broadcast the information. But the holding was narrow. It focused upon the particular circumstances present, explicitly leaving open broadcaster liability in other, less innocent, circumstances.

The narrowness of the holding itself serves a constitutional purpose. The privacy "conversation" is ongoing. Congress could well rewrite the statute, tailoring it more finely to current technological facts, such as the widespread availability of scanners and the possibility of protecting conversations through encryption. A broader constitutional rule might itself limit legislative options in ways now unforeseeable. And doing so is particularly dangerous where statutory protection of an important personal liberty is at issue.

By way of contrast, the Court held unconstitutional police efforts to use, without a warrant, a thermal imaging device placed on a public sidewalk. The device permitted police to identify activities taking place within a private house. The case required the Court simply to ask whether the residents had a reasonable expectation that their activities within the house would not be disclosed to the public in this way—a well established Fourth Amendment principle. Hence the case asked the Court to pour new technological wine into old bottles; it did not suggest that doing so would significantly interfere with an ongoing democratic policy conversation.

The privacy example suggests more by way of caution. It warns against adopting an overly rigid method of interpreting the constitution—placing weight upon eighteenth-century details to the point where it becomes difficult for a twenty-first-century court to apply the document's underlying values. At a minimum it suggests that courts, in determining the breadth of a constitutional holding, should look to the effect of a holding on the ongoing policy process, distinguishing, as I have suggested, between the "eavesdropping" and the "thermal heat" types of cases. And it makes clear that judicial caution in such matters does not reflect the fact that judges are mitigating their legal concerns with practical considerations. Rather, the Constitution itself is a practical document—a document that authorizes the Court to proceed practically when it examines new laws in light of the Constitution's enduring, underlying values.

My fourth example concerns equal protection and voting rights, an area that has led to considerable constitutional controversy. Some believe that the Constitution prohibits virtually any legislative effort to use race as a basis for drawing electoral district boundaries—unless, for example, the effort seeks to undo earlier invidious race-based discrimination. Others believe that the Constitution does not so severely limit the instances in which a legislature can use race to create majority-minority districts. Without describing in detail the basic argument between the two positions, I wish to point out the relevance to that argument of the Constitution's democratic objective.

That objective suggests a simple, but potentially important, constitutional difference in the electoral area between invidious discrimination, penalizing members of a racial minority, and positive discrimination, assisting members of racial minorities. The Constitution's Fifteenth Amendment prohibits the former, not simply because it violates a basic Fourteenth Amendment principle, namely that the government must treat all citizens with equal respect, but also because it denies minority citizens the opportunity to participate in the self-governing democracy that the Constitution creates. By way of contrast, affirmative discrimination ordinarily seeks to enlarge minority participation in that self-governing democracy. To that extent it is consistent with, indeed furthers, the Constitution's basic democratic objective. That consistency, along with its more benign purposes, helps to mitigate whatever lack of equal respect any such discrimination might show to any disadvantaged member of a majority group.

I am not saying that the mitigation will automatically render any particular discriminatory scheme constitutional. But the presence of this mitigating difference supports the view that courts should not apply the strong presumptions of unconstitutionality that are appropriate where invidious discrimination is at issue. My basic purpose, again, is to suggest that reference to the Constitution's "democratic" objective can help us apply a different basic objective, here that of equal protection. And in the electoral context, the reference suggests increased legislative authority to deal with multiracial issues.

The instances I have discussed encompass different areas of law—speech, federalism, privacy, equal protection, and statutory interpretation. In each instance, the discussion has focused upon a contemporary social problem—campaign finance, workplace regulation, environmental regulation, information-based technological change, race-based electoral districting, and legislative politics. In each instance, the discussion illustrates how increased focus upon the Constitution's basic democratic objective might make a difference—in refining doctrinal rules, in evaluating consequences, in applying practical cautionary principles, in interacting with other constitutional objectives, and in explicating statutory silences. In each instance, the discussion suggests how that increased focus might mean better law. And "better" in this context means both (a) better able to satisfy the Constitution's purposes and (b) better able to cope with contemporary problems. The discussion, while not proving its point purely through logic or empirical demonstration, uses example to create a pattern. The pattern suggests a need for increased judicial emphasis upon the Constitution's democratic objective.

My discussion emphasizes values underlying specific constitutional phrases, sees the Constitution itself as a single document with certain basic related objectives, and assumes that the latter can inform a judge's understanding of the former. Might that discussion persuade those who prefer to believe that the keys to constitutional interpretation instead lie in specific language, history, tradition, and precedent and who fear that a contrary approach would permit judges too often to act too subjectively?

Perhaps so, for several reasons. First, the area of interpretive disagreement is more limited than many believe. Judges can, and should, decide most cases, including constitutional cases, through the use of language, history, tradition, and precedent. Judges will often agree as to how these factors determine a provision's basic purpose and the result in a particular case. And where they differ, their differences are often differences of modest degree. Only a handful of constitutional issues—though an important handful—are as open in respect to language, history, and basic purpose as those that I have described. And even in respect to those issues, judges must find answers within the limits set by the Constitution's language. Moreover, history, tradition, and precedent remain helpful, even if not determinative.

Second, those more literalist judges who emphasize language, history, tradition, and precedent cannot justify their practices by claiming that is what the framers wanted, for the framers did not say specifically what factors judges should emphasize when seeking to interpret the Constitution's open language. Nor is it plausible to believe that those who argued about the Bill of Rights, and made clear that it did not contain an exclusive detailed list, had agreed about what school of interpretive thought should prove dominant in the centuries to come. Indeed, the Constitution itself says that the "enumeration" in the Constitution of some rights "shall not be construed to deny or disparage others retained by the people." Professor Bailyn concludes that the Framers added this language to make clear that "rights, like law itself, should never be fixed, frozen, that new dangers and needs will emerge, and that to respond to these dangers and needs, rights must be newly specified to protect the individual's integrity and inherent dignity." Instead, justification for the literalist's practice itself tends to rest upon consequences. Literalist arguments often seek to show that such an approach will have favorable results, for example, controlling judicial subjectivity.

Third, judges who reject a literalist approach deny that their decisions are subjective and point to important safeguards of objectivity. A decision that emphasizes values, no less than any other, is open to criticism based upon (1) the decision's relation to the other legal principles (precedents, rules, standards, practices, institutional understandings) that it modifies and (2) the decision's consequences, i.e., the way in which the entire bloc of decision-affected legal principles subsequently affects the world. The relevant values, by limiting interpretive possibilities and guiding interpretation, themselves constrain subjectivity, indeed the democratic values that I have emphasized themselves suggest the importance of judicial restraint. An individual constitutional judge's need for consistency over time also constrains subjectivity. That is why Justice O'Connor has explained that need in terms of a constitutional judge's initial decisions creating "footprints" that later decisions almost inevitably will follow.

Fourth, the literalist does not escape subjectivity, for his tools, language, history, and tradition, can provide little objective guidance in the comparatively small set of cases about which I have spoken. In such cases, the Constitution's language is almost always nonspecific. History and tradition are open to competing claims and rival interpretations. Nor does an emphasis upon rules embodied in precedent necessarily produce clarity, particularly in borderline areas or where rules are stated abstractly. Indeed, an emphasis upon language, history, tradition, or prior rules in such cases may simply channel subjectivity into a choice about: Which history? Which tradition? Which rules? It will then produce a decision that is no less subjective but which is far less transparent than a decision that directly addresses consequences in constitutional terms.

Finally, my examples point to offsetting consequences—at least if "literalism" tends to produce the legal doctrines (related to the First Amendment, to federalism, to statutory interpretation, to equal protection) that I have criticized. Those doctrines lead to consequences at least as harmful, from a constitutional perspective, as any increased risk of subjectivity. In the ways that I have set out, they undermine the Constitution's efforts to create a framework for democratic government—a government that, while protecting basic individual liberties, permits individual citizens to govern themselves.

To reemphasize the constitutional importance of democratic self-government may carry with it a practical bonus. We are all aware of figures that show that the public knows ever less about, and is ever less interested in, the processes of government. Foundation reports criticize the lack of high school civics education. Comedians claim that more students know the names of the Three Stooges than the three branches of government. Even law school graduates are ever less inclined to work for government—with the percentage of those entering government (or non-government public interest) work declining at one major law school from 12% to 3% over a generation. Indeed, polls show that, over that same period of time, the percentage of the public trusting the government declined at a similar rate.

This trend, however, is not irreversible. Indeed, trust in government has shown a remarkable rebound in response to last month's terrible tragedy [September 11]. Courts cannot maintain this upward momentum by themselves. But courts, as highly trusted government institutions, can help some, in part by explaining in terms the public can understand just what the Constitution is about. It is important that the public, trying to cope with the problems of nation, state, and local community, understand that the Constitution does not resolve, and was not intended to resolve, society's problems. Rather, the Constitution provides a framework for the creation of democratically determined solutions, which protect each individual's basic liberties and assures that individual equal respect by government, while securing a democratic form of government. We judges cannot insist that Americans participate in that government, but we can make clear that our Constitution depends upon it. Indeed, participation reinforces that "positive passion for the public good," that John Adams, like so many others, felt a necessary condition for "Republican Government" and any "real Liberty."

That is the democratic ideal. It is as relevant today as it was 200 or 2,000 years ago. Today it is embodied in our Constitution. Two thousand years ago, Thucydides, quoting Pericles, set forth a related ideal—relevant in his own time and, with some modifications, still appropriate to recall today. "We Athenians," said Pericles, "do not say that the man who fails to participate in politics is a man who minds his own business. We say that he is a man who has no business here."

DISCUSSION QUESTIONS

1. Critics of the originalist perspective often point to ambiguities in the language of the Constitution. Justice Breyer outlines several of these in his speech. What are some other examples of ambiguous language in the Constitution? (Look at the Bill of Rights as a start.) What alternative interpretations can you develop?

2. Critics of the Living Constitution, such as Justice Scalia, often argue that judges substitute their own reading of what they think the law should be for what the law is. Do you think it is possible for justices to avoid having their own views shape their decisions? How could they protect against this happening?

3. Should judges take public opinion or changing societal standards into account when ruling on the constitutionality of a statute or practice? If so, what evidence of public opinion or societal standards should matter? Surveys? Laws enacted in states? If not, what are the risks in doing so?

4. Consider Scalia's examples of when the Court has employed a Living Constitution approach. How would Breyer's approach of active liberty decide these decisions? Which approach do you think leads to the better outcomes?

PART III

Political Behavior: Participation

CHAPTER 9

Public Opinion and the Media

44

"Polling the Public,"
from *Public Opinion in a Democracy*

George Gallup

Assessing public opinion in a democracy of over 310 million people is no easy task. George Gallup, who is largely responsible for the development of modern opinion polling, argued in his 1939 book that public opinion polls enhance the democratic process by providing elected officials with a picture of what Americans think about current events. Despite Gallup's vigorous defense of his polling techniques and the contribution of polling to democracy, the public opinion poll remains controversial. Some critics charge that public officials pay too much attention to polls, making decisions based on fluctuations in public opinion rather than on informed, independent judgment. Others say that by urging respondents to give an opinion, even if they initially respond that they have no opinion on a question, polls may exaggerate the amount of division in American society. And some critics worry that election-related polls may affect public behavior: If a potential voter hears that her candidate is trailing in the polls, perhaps she becomes demoralized and does not vote, and the poll becomes a self-fulfilling prophecy. In effect, rather than reporting on election news, the poll itself becomes the news.

We have a national election every two years only. In a world which moves as rapidly as the modern world does, it is often desirable to know the people's will on basic policies at more frequent intervals. We cannot put issues off and say "let them be decided at the next election." World events do not wait on elections. We need to know the will of the people at all times.

If we know the collective will of the people at all times the efficiency of democracy can be increased, because we can substitute specific knowledge of public opinion for blind groping and guesswork. Statesmen who know the true state of public opinion can then formulate plans with a sure knowledge of what the voting public is thinking. They can know what degree of opposition to any proposed plan exists, and what efforts are necessary to gain public acceptance for it. The responsibility for initiating action should, as always, rest with the political leaders of the country. But the collective will or attitude of the people needs to be learned without delay.

The Will of the People

How is the will of the people to be known at all times?

Before I offer an answer to this question, I would like to examine some of the principal channels by which, at the present time, public opinion is expressed.

The most important is of course a national election. An election is the only official and binding expression of the people's judgment. But, as viewed from a strictly objective point of view, elections are a confusing and imperfect way of registering national opinion. In the first place, they come only at infrequent intervals. In the second place, as [James] Bryce pointed out in *The American Commonwealth*, it is virtually impossible to separate issues from candidates. How can we tell whether the public is voting for the man or for his platform? How can we tell whether all the candidate's views are endorsed, or whether some are favored and others opposed by the voters? Because society grows more and more complex, the tendency is to have more and more issues in an election. Some may be discussed; others not. Suppose a candidate for office takes a position on a great many public issues during the campaign. If elected, he inevitably assumes that the public has endorsed all his planks, whereas this may actually not be the case.

*   *   *

The Role of the Elected Representative

A second method by which public opinion now expresses itself is through elected representatives. The legislator is, technically speaking, supposed to represent the interests of all voters in his constituency. But under the two-party system there is a strong temptation for him to represent, and be influenced by, only the voters of his own party. He is subject to the pressure of party discipline and of wishes of party leaders back home. His very continuance in office may depend on giving way to such pressure. Under these circumstances his behavior in Congress is likely to be governed not by what he thinks the voters of his state want, but by what he thinks the leaders of his own party in that state want.

*   *   *

Even in the event that an elected representative does try to perform his duty of representing the whole people, he is confronted with the problem: What is the will of the people? Shall he judge their views by the letters they write him or the telegrams they send him? Too often such expressions of opinion come only from an articulate minority. Shall the congressman judge their views by the visitors or delegations that come to him from his home district?

Pressure Groups and the Whole Nation

Legislators are constantly subject to the influence of organized lobbies and pressure groups. Senator Tydings * * * pointed out recently that the United States is the most fertile soil on earth for the activity of pressure groups. The American people represent a conglomeration of races, all with different cultural backgrounds. Sections and groups struggle with one another to fix national and international policy. And frequently in such struggles, as Senator Tydings pointed out, "self-interest and sectionalism, rather than the promotion of national welfare, dominate the contest." Senator Tydings mentions some twenty important group interests. These include labor, agriculture, veterans, pension plan advocates, chambers of commerce, racial organizations, isolationists and internationalists, high-tariff and low-tariff groups, preparedness and disarmament groups, budget balancers and spending advocates, soft-money associations and hard-money associations, transportation groups and states righters and centralizationists.

The legislator obviously owes a duty to his home district to legislate in its best interests. But he also owes a duty to legislate in the best interests of the whole nation. In order, however, to carry out this second duty he must *know* what the nation thinks. Since he doesn't always know what the voters in his own district think, it is just that much more difficult for him to learn the views of the nation. Yet if he could know those views at all times he could legislate more often in the interest of the whole country.

* * *

The Cross-Section Survey

This effort to discover public opinion has been largely responsible for the introduction of a new instrument for determining public opinion—the cross-section or sampling survey. By means of nationwide studies taken at frequent intervals, research workers are today attempting to measure and give voice to the sentiments of the whole people on vital issues of the day.

Where does this new technique fit into the scheme of things under our form of government? Is it a useful instrument of democracy? Will it prove to be vicious and harmful, or will it contribute to the efficiency of the democratic process?

The sampling referendum is simply a procedure for sounding the opinions of a relatively small number of persons, selected in such manner as to reflect with a high degree of accuracy the views of the whole voting population. In effect such surveys canvass the opinions of a miniature electorate.

Cross-section surveys do not place their chief reliance upon numbers. The technique is based on the fact that a few thousand voters correctly selected will faithfully reflect the views of an electorate of millions of voters. The key to success in this work is the cross section—the proper selection of voters included in the sample. Elaborate precautions must be taken to secure the views of members of all political parties—of rich and poor, old and young, of men and women, farmers and city dwellers, persons of all religious faiths—in short, voters of all types living in every State in the land. And all must be included in correct proportion.

*   *   *

Reliability of Opinion Surveys

Whether opinion surveys will prove to be a useful contribution to democracy depends largely on their reliability in measuring opinion. During the last four years [1935–39] the sampling procedure, as used in measuring public opinion, has been subjected to many tests. In general these tests indicate that present techniques can attain a high degree of accuracy, and it seems reasonable to assume that with the development of this infant science, the accuracy of its measurements will be constantly improved.

The most practical way at present to measure the accuracy of the sampling referendum is to compare forecasts of elections with election results. Such a test is by no means perfect, because a preelection survey must not only measure opinion in respect to candidates but must also predict just what groups of people will actually take the trouble to cast their ballots. Add to this the problem of measuring the effect of weather on turnout, also the activities of corrupt political machines, and it can easily be seen that election results are by no means a perfect test of the accuracy of this new technique.

*   *   *

Many thoughtful students of government have asked: Why shouldn't the Government itself, rather than private organizations, conduct these sampling surveys? A few political scientists have even suggested the establishment of a permanent federal bureau for sounding public opinion, arguing that if this new technique is a contribution to democracy, the government has a duty to take it over.

The danger in this proposal, as I see it, lies in the temptation it would place in the way of the party in power to conduct surveys to prove itself right and to suppress those which proved it to be wrong. A private organization, on the other hand, must stand or fall not so much on what it reports or fails to report as on the accuracy of its results, and the impartiality of its interpretations. An important requirement in a democracy is complete and reliable news reports of the activities of all branches of the government and of the views of all leaders and parties. But few persons would argue that, for this reason, the government should take over the press, and all its news gathering associations.

*   *   *

Cloture on Debate?

It is sometimes argued that public opinion surveys impose a cloture on debate. When the advocates of one side of an issue are shown to be in the majority, so the argument runs, the other side will lose hope and abandon their cause believing that further efforts are futile.

Again let me say that there is little evidence to support this view. Every election necessarily produces a minority. In 1936 the Republicans polled less than 40 percent of the vote. Yet the fact that the Republicans were defeated badly wasn't enough to lead them to quit the battle. They continued to fight against the New Deal with as much vigor as before. An even better example is afforded by the Socialist Party. For years the Socialist candidate for President has received but a small fraction of the total popular vote, and could count on sure defeat. Yet the Socialist Party continues as a party, and continues to poll about the same number of votes.

Sampling surveys will never impose a cloture on debate so long as it is the nature of public opinion to change. The will of the people is dynamic; opinions are constantly changing. A year ago an overwhelming majority of voters were skeptical of the prospects of the Republican Party in 1940. Today, half the voters think the GOP will win. If elections themselves do not impose cloture on debate, is it likely that opinion surveys will?

Possible Effect on Representative Government

The form of government we live under is a representative form of government. What will be the effect on representative government if the will of the people is known at all times? Will legislators become mere rubber stamps, mere puppets, and the function of representation be lost?

Under a system of frequent opinion measurement, the function of representation is not lost, for two reasons. First, it is well understood that the people have not the time or the inclination to pass on all the problems that confront their leaders. They cannot be expected to express judgment on technical questions of administration and government. They can pass judgment only on basic general policies. As society grows more complex there is a greater and greater need for experts. Once the voters have indicated their approval of a general policy or plan of action, experts are required to carry it out.

Second, it is not the province of the people to initiate legislation, but to decide which of the programs offered they like best. National policies do not spring full-blown from the common people. Leaders, knowing the general will of the people, must take the initiative in forming policies that will carry out the general will and must put them into effect.

Before the advent of the sampling referendum, legislators were not isolated from their constituencies. They read the local newspapers; they toured their districts and talked with voters; they received letters from their home State; they entertained delegations who claimed to speak for large and important blocs of voters. The change that is brought about by sampling referenda is merely one which provides these legislators with a truer measure of opinion in their districts and in the nation.

*   *   *

How Wise Are the Common People?

The sampling surveys of recent years have provided much evidence concerning the wisdom of the common people. Anyone is free to examine this evidence. And I think that the person who does examine it will come away believing as I do that, collectively, the American people have a remarkably high degree of common sense. These people may not be brilliant or intellectual or particularly well read, but they possess a quality of good sense which is manifested time and again in their expressions of opinion on present-day issues.

*   *   *

It is not difficult to understand why the conception of the stupidity of the masses has so many adherents. Talk to the first hundred persons whom you happen to meet in the street about many important issues of the day, and the chances are great that you will be struck by their lack of accurate or complete knowledge on these issues. Few of them will likely have sufficient information in this particular field to express a well founded judgment.

But fortunately a democracy does not require that every voter be well informed on every issue. In fact a democracy does not depend so much on the enlightenment of each individual, as upon the quality of the collective judgment or intelligence of thousands of individuals.

*   *   *

It would of course be foolish to argue that the collective views of the common people always represent the most intelligent and most accurate answer to any question. But results of sampling referenda on hundreds of issues do indicate, in my opinion, that we can place great faith in the collective judgment or intelligence of the people.

The New England Town Meeting Restored

One of the earliest and purest forms of democracy in this country was the New England town meeting. The people gathered in one room to discuss and to vote on the questions of the community. There was a free exchange of opinions in the presence of all the members. The town meeting was a simple and effective way of articulating public opinion, and the decisions made by the meeting kept close to the public will. When a democracy thus operates on a small scale it is able to express itself swiftly and with certainty.

But as communities grew, the town meeting became unwieldy. As a result the common people became less articulate, less able to debate the vital issues in the manner of their New England forefathers. Interest in politics lagged. Opinion had to express itself by the slow and cumbersome method of election, no longer facilitated by the town meeting with its frequent give and take of ideas. The indifference and apathy of voters made it possible for vicious and corrupt political machines to take over the administration of government in many states and cities.

The New England town meeting was valuable because it provided a forum for the exchange of views among all citizens of the community and for a vote on these views. Today, the New England town meeting idea has, in a sense, been restored. The wide distribution of daily newspapers reporting the views of statesmen on issues of the day, the almost universal ownership of radios which bring the whole nation within the hearing of any voice, and now the advent of the sampling referendum which provides a means of determining quickly the response of the public to debate on issues of the day, have in effect created a town meeting on a national scale.

How nearly the goal has been achieved is indicated in the following data recently gathered by the American Institute of Public Opinion. Of the 45,000,000 persons who voted in the last presidential election [1936], approximately 40,000,000 read a daily newspaper, 40,000,000 have radios, and only 2,250,000 of the entire group of voters in the nation neither have a radio nor take a daily newspaper.

This means that the nation is literally in one great room. The newspapers and the radio conduct the debate on national issues, presenting both information and argument on both sides, just as the townsfolk did in person in the old town meeting. And finally, through the process of the sampling referendum, the people, having heard the debate on both sides of every issue, can express their will. After one hundred and fifty years we return to the town meeting. This time the whole nation is within the doors.

DISCUSSION QUESTIONS

1. What are the advantages and disadvantages of modern public opinion polling for policy making and elections?

2. Setting aside the constitutional status of such a move, how would the American political system change if polls were banned?

3. Imagine you are an elected official. How would you determine when to pay attention to public opinion polls and when to ignore them? In a representative democracy, should you as an elected official *ever* ignore public opinion as revealed in polls?

45

"Choice Words: If You Can't Understand Our Poll Questions, Then How Can We Understand Your Answers?"

Richard Morin

Although polls play a prominent role in contemporary politics, Richard Morin cautions that polls can be "risky." Morin, former director of polling for the Washington Post, *notes that minor differences in question wording can—and, during the impeachment of President Bill Clinton, did—result in dramatically different polling results. Other problems arise because people will answer questions "even if they don't really have an opinion or understand the question that has been asked." Ultimately, argues Morin, pollsters and the politicians who rely on them should be somewhat skeptical of the depth or significance of any particular response in the absence of additional survey data that establish a pattern.*

If his current government job ends abruptly, President Clinton might think about becoming a pollster. Anyone who ponders the meaning of the word *is* has precisely the right turn of mind to track public opinion in these mindless, mindful times.

Never has polling been so risky—or so much in demand. Never have so many of the rules of polling been bent or broken so cleanly, or so often. Pollsters are sampling public reaction just hours—sometimes minutes—after events occur. Interviewing periods, which traditionally last several days to secure a solid sample, have sometimes shrunk to just a few hours on a single night. Pollsters have been asking questions that were taboo until this past year. Is oral sex really sex? (Yes, said 76 percent of those interviewed in a *Newsweek* poll conducted barely a week after the scandal broke back in January.)

"No living pollster has ever had to poll in a situation like this," said Michael Kagay, the editor of news surveys at the *New York Times*. "We're in uncharted territory." After all, Andrew Johnson had to deal with political enemies, but not pollsters. And Richard Nixon's resignation before impeachment meant that pollsters didn't have a chance to ask whether the Senate should give him the boot.

Clinton has it about right: Words do have different meanings for different people, and these differences matter. At the same time, some seemingly common words and phrases have no meaning at all to many Americans; even on the eve of the impeachment vote last month, nearly a third of the country didn't know or didn't understand what *impeachment* meant.

Every pollster knows that questions with slightly different wording can produce different results. In the past year, survey researchers learned just how big and baffling those differences can be, particularly when words are used to capture public reaction to an arcane process that no living American—not even [then ninety-five-year-old Senator] Strom Thurmond—has witnessed in its entirety.

Fear of getting it wrong—coupled with astonishment over the persistent support for Clinton revealed in poll after poll—spawned a flood of novel tests by pollsters to determine precisely the right words to use in our questions.

Last month, less than a week before Clinton was impeached by the House, *The Washington Post* and its polling partner ABC News asked half of a random sampling of Americans whether Clinton should resign if he were impeached or should "fight the charges in the Senate." The other half of the sample was asked a slightly different question: Should Clinton resign if impeached or should he "remain in office and face trial in the Senate?"

The questions are essentially the same. The results were not. Nearly six in 10—59 percent—said Clinton should quit rather than fight impeachment charges in the Senate. But well under half—43 percent—said he should resign when the alternative was to "remain in office and stand trial in the Senate." What gives?

The difference appears to be the word *fight*. America is a peaceable kingdom; we hate it when our parents squabble and are willing to accept just about any alternative—including Clinton's resignation—to spare the country a partisan fight. But when the alternative is less overtly combative— stand trial in the Senate—Americans are less likely to scurry to the resignation option.

Such a fuss over a few words. But it is just more proof that people do not share the same understanding of terms, and that a pollster who ignores this occupational hazard may wind up looking for a new job.

Think I'm exaggerating? Then let's do another test. A month ago, [December 1998], how would you have answered this question: "If the full House votes to send impeachment articles to the Senate for a trial, then do you think it would be better for the country if Bill Clinton resigned from office, or not?"

And how would you have answered this question: "If the full House votes to impeach Bill Clinton, then do you think it would be better for the country if Bill Clinton resigned from office, or not?"

The questions (asked in a *New York Times*/CBS News poll in mid-December) seem virtually identical. But the differences in results were stunning: Forty-three percent said the president should quit if the House sends "impeachment articles to the Senate" while 60 percent said he should quit if the House "votes to impeach."

What's going on here? Kagay says he doesn't know. Neither do I, but here's a guess: Perhaps "impeach" alone was taken as "found guilty" and the phrase "send impeachment articles to the Senate for a trial" suggests that the case isn't over. If only we could do another wording test. . . .

Language problems have challenged pollsters from the very start of the Monica Lewinsky scandal. Among the first: How to describe Monica herself? *The Washington Post*'s first survey questions referred to her as a "21-year-old intern at the White House," as did questions asked by other news organizations. But noting her age was potentially biasing. Highlighting her youthfulness conjured up visions of innocence and victimhood that appeared inconsistent with her apparently aggressive and explicitly amorous conduct with Clinton. In subsequent *Post* poll questions, she became a "former White House intern" of indeterminate age.

Then came the hard part: How to describe what she and Bill were accused of doing in a way that didn't offend, overly titillate or otherwise stampede people into one position or the other? In these early days, details about who did what to whom and where were sketchy but salacious. It clearly wasn't a classic adulterous love affair; love had apparently little to do with it, at least on Clinton's part. Nor was it a one-night stand. It seemed more like the overheated fantasy of a 16-year-old boy or the musings of the White House's favorite pornographer, *Penthouse* magazine publisher Larry Flynt. Piled on top of the sex were the more complex and less easily understood issues of perjury and obstruction of justice. After various iterations, we and other organizations settled on simply "the Lewinsky matter"—nice and neutral, leaving exactly what that meant to the imaginations (or memories) of survey respondents.

One thing is clear, at least in hindsight: Results of hypothetical questions—those that ask what if?—did not hold up in the past 12 months, said political scientist Michael Traugott of the University of Michigan. Last January, pollsters posed questions asking whether Clinton should resign or be impeached if he lied under oath about having an affair with Lewinsky. Clear majorities said he should quit or be impeached.

Fast forward to the eve of the impeachment vote. Nearly everybody believed Clinton had lied under oath about his relationship with Lewinsky, but now healthy majorities said he should not be impeached—a tribute, perhaps, to the White House strategy of drawing out (dare we say stonewalling?) the investigation to allow the public to get used to the idea that their president was a sleazy weasel.

Fortunately, pollsters had time to work out the kinks in question wording. Demand for polling produced a flood of questions of all shades and flavors, and good wording drove out the bad. At times, it seemed even to pollsters that there may be too many questions about the scandal, said

Kathy Frankovic, director of surveys for CBS News. Through October [1998], more than 1,000 survey questions specifically mentioned Lewinsky's name—double the number of questions that have ever been asked about the Watergate scandal, Frankovic said.

Polling's new popularity has attracted a tonier class of critic. In the past, mostly assistant professors and aggrieved political operatives or their bosses trashed the public polls. Today, one of the fiercest critics of polling is syndicated columnist Arianna Huffington, the onetime Cambridge University debating champ, A-list socialite and New Age acolyte. A few weeks ago, Huffington revealed in her column that lots of people refuse to talk to pollsters, a problem that's not new (except, apparently, to Huffington).

Actually, I think Huffington has it backward. The real problem is that people are too willing to answer poll questions—dutifully responding to poll takers even if they don't really have an opinion or understand the question that has been asked.

A famous polling experiment illustrates the prevalence of pseudo-opinions: More than 20 years ago, a group of researchers at the University of Cincinnati asked a random sample of local residents whether the 1975 Public Affairs Act should be repealed. About half expressed a view one way or another.

Of course there never was a Public Affairs Act of 1975. Researchers made it up to see how willing people were to express opinions on things they knew absolutely nothing about.

I duplicated that experiment a few years ago in a national survey, and obtained about the same result: Forty-three percent expressed an opinion, with 24 percent saying it should be repealed and 19 percent saying it should not.

But enough about the problems. In hindsight, most experts say that the polls have held up remarkably well. Within a month of the first disclosure, the public moved quickly to this consensus, as captured by the polls: Clinton's a good president but a man of ghastly character who can stay in the White House—but stay away from my house, don't touch my daughter and don't pet the dog.

"It is so striking. The public figured this one out early on and stuck with it," said Thomas E. Mann, director of governmental studies at the Brookings Institution. "If anything, the only changes were these upward blips in support for Clinton in the face of some dramatic development that was certain to presage his collapse."

Mann and others argue that public opinion polls may never have played a more important role in American political life. "This last year illustrates the wisdom of George Gallup's optimism about the use of polls in democracy: to discipline the elites, to constrain the activists, to allow ordinary citizens to register sentiments on a matter of the greatest public importance," Mann said.

Well, hooray for us pollsters! Actually, there is evidence suggesting that all the attention in the past year may have improved the public's opinions of opinion polls and pollsters. And why shouldn't they? These polls have had something for everyone: While Democrats revel in Clinton's high job-approval ratings and otherwise bulletproof presidency, Republicans can point to the equally lopsided majority who think Clinton should be censured and formally reprimanded for his behavior.

A few weeks ago, as bombs fell in Baghdad and talk of impeachment roiled Washington, pollster Nancy Belden took a break from business to attend the annual holiday pageant at her 10-year-old son's school. As she left the auditorium, the steadfast Republican mother of one of her son's classmates approached Belden and clapped her on the shoulder. "Thank heavens for you pollsters," she said.

"I was stunned. I was delighted," Belden laughed. "I've spent many years being beat up on by people who complain that public opinion polling is somewhat thwarting the political process, as opposed to helping it. Suddenly, people are coming up to me at parties and saying thanks for doing what you do. What a relief!"

DISCUSSION QUESTIONS

1. Morin presents striking differences in poll results when a word or a few words in a question are changed. Does this diminish the value of public opinion polls in the democratic process?

2. How might Morin respond to the arguments that George Gallup makes in "Polling the Public"?

3. Try to think of an example where subtly different wording might lead to very different polling results. Why do you think it would have that effect? As a consumer of polls, how would you try to determine what the "true" public opinion is on that issue?

46

"News vs. Entertainment: How Increasing Media Choice Widens Gaps in Political Knowledge and Turnout"

Markus Prior

Although everyone has contact with the government nearly every day—attending a public school, driving on public roads, using government-regulated electricity, and so on—few citizens have direct contact with the policymaking process. Because of this distance between the public and policymakers, the behavior of intermediaries between the government and the governed is a significant issue in a democratic polity. The media, in particular the news media, are among the most significant of these intermediaries that tell the people what the government is doing and tell the government what the people want.

In today's media environment, information is more abundant than ever, Markus Prior notes, yet participation and knowledge levels have remained stagnant. Rather than enhancing participatory democracy, as advocates of the new media suggest is the norm, the onset of cable television and the Internet has worsened information and participation gaps between those individuals who like to follow the news and those who are more interested in entertainment. A spread of additional news choices, which sounds democratic, has had nondemocratic effects, Prior argues. Newshounds can dig ever deeper into the news, but other members of the public are increasingly able to ignore the news. Other critics have made a similar argument that new media tend to exacerbate public polarization because readers, viewers, and listeners gravitate to outlets presenting opinions they agree with and ignore those sources that would challenge their views.

The rise of new media has brought the question of audience fragmentation and selective exposure to the forefront of scholarly and popular debate. In one of the most widely discussed contributions to this debate. Sunstein has proposed that people's increasing ability to customize their political information will have a polarizing impact on democracy as media users become less likely to encounter information that challenges their partisan viewpoints. While this debate is far from settled, the issue which precedes it is equally important and often sidestepped: as choice between different media content increases, who continues to access *any type* of political information? Cable television and the Internet have increased media choice so much in recent decades that many Americans now live in a high-choice media environment. As media choice increases, the likelihood of "chance encounters" *with any political content* declines significantly for many people. Greater choice allows politically interested people to access more information and increase their political knowledge. Yet those who prefer nonpolitical content can more easily escape the news and therefore pick up less political information than they used to. In a high-choice environment, lack of motivation, not lack of skills or resources, poses the main obstacle to a widely informed electorate.

As media choice increases, content preferences thus become the key to understanding political learning and participation. In a high-choice environment, politics constantly competes with entertainment. Until recently, the impact of content preferences was limited because media users did not enjoy much choice between different content. Television quickly became the most popular mass medium in history, but for decades the networks' scheduling ruled out situations in which viewers had to choose between entertainment and news. Largely unexposed to entertainment competition, news had its place in the early evening and again before the late-night shows. Today, as both entertainment and news are available around the clock on numerous cable channels and web sites, people's content preferences determine more of what those with cable or Internet access watch, read, and hear.

Distinguishing between people who like news and take advantage of additional information and people who prefer other media content explains a puzzling empirical finding: despite the spectacular rise in available political information, mean levels of political knowledge in the population have essentially remained constant. Yet the fact that average knowledge levels did not change hides important trends: political knowledge has risen in some segments of the electorate, but declined in others. Greater media choice thus widens the "knowledge gap." [N]umerous studies have examined the diffusion of information in the population and the differences that emerge between more and less informed individuals. According to some of these studies, television works as a "knowledge leveler" because it presents information in less cognitively demanding ways. To reconcile this effect with the hypothesis that more television widens the knowledge gap, it is necessary to distinguish the effect of news exposure from the effect of the medium itself. In the low-choice broadcast environment, access to the medium and exposure to news were practically one and the same, as less politically interested television viewers had no choice but to watch the news from time to time. As media choice increases, exposure to the news may continue to work as a "knowledge leveler," but the distribution of news exposure itself has become more unequal. Access to the medium no longer implies exposure to the news. Television news narrows the knowledge gap *among its viewers*. For the population as a whole, more channels widen the gap.

The consequences of increasing media choice reach beyond a less equal distribution of political knowledge. Since political knowledge is an important predictor of turnout and since exposure to political information motivates turnout, the shift from a low-choice to a high-choice media environment implies changes in electoral participation as well. Those with a preference for news not only become more knowledgeable, but also vote at higher rates. Those with a stronger interest in other media content vote less.

This study casts doubt on the view that the socioeconomic dimension of the digital divide is the greatest obstacle to an informed and participating electorate. Many casual observers emphasize the great promise new technologies hold for democracy. They deplore current socioeconomic inequalities in access to new media, but predict increasing political knowledge and participation among currently disadvantaged people once these inequalities have been overcome. This ignores that greater media choice leads to greater *voluntary* segmentation of the electorate. The present study suggests that gaps based on socioeconomic status will be eclipsed by preference-based gaps once access to new media becomes cheaper and more widely available. Gaps created by unequal distribution of resources and skills often emerged due to circumstances outside of people's control. The preference-based gaps documented in this article are self-imposed as many people abandon the news for entertainment simply because they like it better. Inequality in political knowledge and turnout increases as a result of voluntary, not circumstantial, consumption decisions.

*   *   *

Theory

The basic premise of this analysis is that people's media environment determines the extent to which their media use is governed by content preferences. According to theories of program choice, viewers have preferences over program characteristics or program types and select the program that promises to best satisfy these preferences. The simplest models distinguish between preferences for information and entertainment. In the low-choice broadcast environment, most people watched news and learned about politics because they were reluctant to turn off the set even if the programs offered at the time did not match their preferences. One study conducted in the early 1970s showed that 40% of the respondents reported watching programs because they appeared on the channel they were already watching or because someone else wanted to see them. Audience research has proposed a two-stage model according to which people first decide to watch television and then pick the available program they like best. Klein aptly called this model the "Theory of Least Objectionable Program." If television viewers are routinely "glued to the box" and select the best available program, we can explain why so many

Americans watched television news in the 1960s and 70s despite modest political interest. Most television viewing in the broadcast era did not stem from a deliberate choice of a program, but rather was determined by convenience, availability of spare time and the decision to spend that time in front of the TV set. And since broadcast channels offered a solid block of news at the dinner hour and again after primetime, many viewers were routinely exposed to news even though they watched television primarily to be entertained.

Once exposed to television news, people learn about politics. Although a captive news audience does not exhibit the same political interest as a self-selected one and therefore may not learn as much, research on passive learning suggests that even unmotivated exposure can produce learning. Hence, even broadcast viewers who prefer entertainment programs absorb at least basic political knowledge when they happen to tune in when only news is on.

I propose that such accidental exposure should become less likely in a high-choice environment because greater horizontal diversity (the number of genres available at any particular point in time) increases the chance that viewers will find content that matches their preferences. The impact of one's preferences increases, and "indiscriminate viewing" becomes less likely. Cable subscribers' channel repertoire (the number of frequently viewed channels) is not dramatically higher than that of non-subscribers, but their repertoire reflects a set of channels that are more closely related to their genre preferences. Two-stage viewing behavior thus predicts that news audiences should decrease as more alternatives are offered on other channels. Indeed, local news audiences tend to be smaller when competing entertainment programming is scheduled. Baum and Kernell show that cable subscribers, especially the less informed among them, are less likely to watch the presidential debates than otherwise similar individuals who receive only broadcast television. According to my first hypothesis, the advent of cable TV increased the knowledge gap between people with a preference for news and people with a preference for other media content.

Internet access should contribute to an increasing knowledge gap as well. Although the two media are undoubtedly different in many respects, access to the Internet, like cable, makes media choice more efficient. Yet, while they both increase media users' content choice, cable TV and the Internet are not perfect substitutes for each other. Compared at least to dial-up Internet service, cable offers greater immediacy and more visuals. The web offers more detailed information and can be customized to a greater extent. Both media, in other words, have unique features, and access to both of them offers users the greatest flexibility. For instance, people with access to both media can watch a campaign speech on cable and then compare online how different newspapers cover the event. Depending on their needs or the issue that interests them, they can actively search a wealth of political information online or passively consume cable politics. Hence, the effects of cable TV and Internet access should be additive and the knowledge gap largest among people with access to both new media.

There are several reasons why exposure to political information increases the likelihood that an individual will cast a vote on election day. Exposure increases political knowledge, which in turn increases turnout because people know where, how, and for whom to vote. Furthermore, knowledgeable people are more likely to perceive differences between candidates and thus less likely to abstain due to indifference. Independent of learning effects, exposure to political information on cable news and political web sites is likely to increase people's campaign interest. Interest, in turn, affects turnout even when one controls for political knowledge. Entertainment fans with a cable box or Internet connection, on the other hand, will miss both the interest- and the information-based effect of broadcast news on turnout. My second hypothesis thus predicts a widening turnout gap in the current environment, as people who prefer news vote at higher rates and those with other preferences increasingly stay home from the polls.

* * *

Conclusion

When speculating about the political implications of new media, pundits and scholars tend to either praise the likely benefits for democracy in the digital age or dwell on the dangers. The optimists claim that the greater availability of political information will lead more people to learn more about politics and increase their involvement in the political process. The pessimists fear that new media will make people apolitical and provide mind-numbing entertainment that keeps citizens from fulfilling their democratic responsibilities. These two predictions are often presented as mutually exclusive. Things will either spiral upwards or spiral downwards; the circle is either virtuous or vicious. The analyses presented here show that both are true. New media do indeed increase political knowledge and involvement in the electoral process among some people, just as the optimists predict. Yet, the evidence supports the pessimists' scenario as well. Other people take advantage of greater choice and tune out of politics completely. Those with a preference for entertainment, once they gain access to new media, become less knowledgeable about politics and less likely to vote. People's media content preferences become the key to understanding the political implications of new media.

* * *

The decline in the size of news audiences over the last three decades has been identified as cause for concern by many observers who have generally interpreted it as a sign of waning political interest and a disappearing sense of civic duty. Yet changes in available content can affect news consumption and learning *even in the absence of preference changes.* People's media use may change in a modified media environment, even if their preferences (or political interest or sense of civic duty) remain constant. By this logic, the decreasing size of the news audience is not necessarily an indication of reduced political interest. Interest in politics may simply never have been as high as audience shares for evening news suggested. A combined market share for the three network newscasts of almost 90% takes on a different meaning if one considers that people had hardly any viewing alternatives. It was "politics by default," not politics by choice. Even the mediocre levels of political knowledge during the broadcast era, in other words, were partly a result of de facto restrictions of people's freedom to choose their preferred media content.

Ironically, we might have to pin our hopes of creating a reasonably evenly informed electorate on that reviled form of communication, political advertising. Large segments of the electorate in a high-choice environment do not voluntarily watch, read, or listen to political information. Their greatest chance for encounters with the political world occurs when commercials are inserted into their regular entertainment diet. And exposure to political ads can increase viewers' political knowledge. At least for the time being, before recording services like TiVo, which automatically skip the commercial breaks, or subscriber-financed premium cable channels without advertising become more widespread, political advertising is more likely than news coverage to reach these viewers.

It might seem counterintuitive that political knowledge has decreased for a substantial portion of the electorate even though the amount of political information has multiplied and is more readily available than ever before. The share of politically uninformed people has risen since we entered the so-called "information age." Television as a medium has often been denigrated as "dumb," but, helped by the features of the broadcast environment, it may have been more successful in reaching less interested segments of the population than the "encyclopedic" Internet. In contrast to the view that politics is simply too difficult and complex to understand, this study shows that motivation, not ability, is the main obstacle that stands between an abundance of political information and a well- and evenly informed public.

When differences in political knowledge and turnout arise from inequality in the distribution of resources and skills, recommendations for how to help the information have-nots are generally uncontroversial. To the extent that knowledge and turnout gaps in the new media environment arise from voluntary consumption decisions, recommendations for how to narrow them, or whether to narrow them at all, become more contestable on normative grounds. As [Anthony] Downs remarked a long time ago, "[t]he loss of freedom involved in forcing people to acquire information would probably far outweigh the benefits to be gained from a better-informed electorate." Even if a consensus emerged to reduce media choice for the public good, it would still be technically impossible, even temporarily, to put the genie back in the bottle. Avoiding politics will never again be as difficult as it was in the "golden age" of television.

* * *

DISCUSSION QUESTIONS

1. Are you concerned by the findings in Prior's study? If not, why not? If you are, can you think of any way to overcome the problem he has identified?

2. What lessons should public officials take from Prior's study? Should they pay less attention to public opinion because of the gaps in information and interest among members of the public?

3. Do you think the sharing of news and information through new social media such as Twitter and Facebook exacerbates or diminishes the trends identified by Prior?

Debating the Issues: The Future of Political Journalism

From the 1960s through the 1980s, when people thought of media and news, they thought of newspapers and the broadcast television networks (ABC, CBS, NBC). Cable news soon emerged to provide an alternative (CNN, Fox, MSNBC), but one that for the most part followed the same style in their major nightly newscasts as the big networks. Late in the 1980s, talk radio, which had been around for some time, boomed in popularity and hosts such as Rush Limbaugh became household names. Hosts gleefully tweaked the mainstream media and embraced a much more aggressive, hard-hitting style that was explicitly ideological and partisan. There was, in this new forum, no pretense to being objective but, talk-radio fans would argue, the mainstream media were also not objective—they just pretended to be. News-oriented talk shows on CNN, Fox, and MSNBC followed the same pattern.

The rise of the Internet in the 1990s was the most recent dramatic change in communications technology. Today, Twitter receives much of the attention for breaking stories, blogs are prominent in presenting wide-ranging opinion and analysis, and YouTube makes it possible for every misstep by a politician to be easily viewed by millions.

Major changes in communications technology have produced major changes in the practice of politics and the way people learn about government. Earlier technologies do not necessarily fade away, but their role changes and their dominance diminishes. Pamphlets, then newspapers, then radio, and then television all had their eras of ascendancy. All continued to play important roles when other technologies emerged. Political talk radio in the 1980s and 1990s, for example, gave new life to radio in the age of television, creating another kind of information exchange with which politicians had to become conversant. Inevitably, these technological shifts raise concerns that the new form of information dissemination will drive out some of the positive features of the previous technology.

Does the rise of new media inevitably mean that the old media must fade away? And if so, at what cost to democracy, if any? The struggles facing newspapers have received extensive attention, and for good reason. Even when Americans relied more on television than newspapers to get their news, newspaper coverage often influenced what was reported on TV. Fans of the new media argue that those media have the potential to provide a powerful check on politicians and to allow for a more participatory democracy. By combining the knowledge, memory, and energy of multitudes of contributors, blogs and new media such as Twitter can reveal faulty or absent reporting by the mainstream media. Critics, however, worry that blogs and other new media may gain increasing sway over politicians and the public while not being held to high journalistic standards, and that they are as likely to generate misleading interpretations as they are to uncover truth.

To Paul Starr, the decline of newspapers is a crisis for democracy. In his view, newspapers were uniquely able to hold government accountable and expose corruption. In large part, this was because the financial model that supported newspapers allowed extensive news staffs to be subsidized by advertisers, classified ads, and sections catering to sports and lifestyles. In the new media world, these components have become largely unbundled. News now has to be financially self-sustaining, which has proven to be a difficult task. Starr explores whether the idea that newspapers must make money has to be abandoned in favor of a model in which philanthropy subsidizes the news.

James Fallows discusses ways in which the new media and the old are mutually interdependent. In particular, Fallows focuses on concerns at Google. Because it thrives as a search engine when users find quality content, Google is concerned about the problems facing the news media, particularly newspapers. Fallows reports on Google's concerns and the ways in which the company is attempting to assist news organizations. According to company executives, there is no single big thing that will save newspapers, but lots of little things might.

47

"Goodbye to the Age of Newspapers (Hello to a New Era of Corruption)"

PAUL STARR

I.

We take newspapers for granted. They have been so integral a part of daily life in America, so central to politics and culture and business, and so powerful and profitable in their own right, that it is easy to forget what a remarkable historical invention they are. Public goods are notoriously under-produced in the marketplace, and news is a public good—and yet, since the mid-nineteenth century, newspapers have produced news in abundance at a cheap price to readers and without need of direct subsidy. More than any other medium, newspapers have been our eyes on the state, our check on private abuses, our civic alarm systems. It is true that they have often failed to perform those functions as well as they should have done. But whether they can continue to perform them at all is now in doubt.

*   *   *

II.

These developments raise practical questions for anyone concerned about the future of American democracy. * * * To answer those practical questions, it is necessary first to ponder a more theoretical one. Along with other new technology, the Internet was supposed to bring us a cornucopia of information, and in many respects it has done so. But if one of its effects is to shrink the production of professionally reported news, perhaps we need to understand the emerging framework of post-industrial society and politics somewhat differently.

*   *   *

III.

Of course, a medium that 40 percent of the public still claim to read should not be pronounced dead yet. The situation is also a bit more complicated, and more hopeful, than these trends suggest. Total readership of news that originates from newspapers has probably at least stabilized. Online, many people read news items on blogs and other sites that take items from the press, and the news junkies among us are reading more news from more papers than they did before the Internet made the sampling of multiple publications so easy. And some newspapers are clearly gaining wider reach online.

*   *   *

Some critics of the companies wonder why they cannot adjust to lower profits and make do. The trouble is that the declines in print circulation and advertising are virtually certain to continue, and if newspapers try to maintain the size and the scope of their operations, they may not be able [to] make any profit even when the recession is over. Nor is it clear that they can cut deep enough fast enough while retaining enough readers to be profitable.

*   *   *

Among many journalists as well as investors, the hope has vanished that newspapers as we have known them can make the transition to a world of hybrid print-online publication. Like network TV news and weekly newsmagazines, newspapers have been living off aging audiences that acquired their media habits in earlier decades. A few years ago, it seemed that they could rely on that aging print readership to tide them over until revenue began gushing from the Web. But online ads still account for only 8 percent of ad sales, and their growth has stalled just as earnings from print have tumbled. The result is that newspapers are shrinking not just physically or in labor power, but in the most important dimension of all—their editorial mission.

* * *

Besides cutting back foreign, national, and state coverage, newspapers are also reducing space devoted to science and the arts, and laying off science and medical reporters, music critics, and book reviewers. But there is one type of coverage that newspapers have tried to protect, at least in the early phases of cutbacks. According to the 2008 Pew survey of news executives, they have devoted more resources to local news. The case for "hyperlocalism," as it is known, is that newspapers enjoy comparative advantage as sources of information about their immediate communities. But this strategy may not work commercially if it means moving downmarket. The less coverage of the wider world and cultural life that newspapers provide, the more they stand to lose readership among the relatively affluent who have those interests, and the less attractive newspapers will be to many advertisers. Hyperlocalism may be just a short step from hollowing out the newsroom to the point where most newspapers come to resemble the free tabloids distributed at supermarkets rather than the newspapers of the past.

* * *

* * * Many of the functions that were bundled together in the newspaper are being unbundled online. But if the emerging media environment favors niche journalism, how will public-service journalism be able to reach and influence the broad public that newspapers have had? There is no going back to the way things used to be. If independent news media capable of holding government accountable are going to flourish, they are going to have to do so in the new world of the news, not the one that used to exist.

IV.

After the dot-com bust, the effusive talk about the miracles of the information revolution thankfully went out of style. But the social transformation under way—and there ought to be no doubt that one is indeed underway—is breaking up old monopolies of communication and power and creating new possibilities for free expression and democratic politics. As in any upheaval, some effects are unanticipated, and not all of them are positive, and what is perhaps most confusing, the good and bad are often intertwined.

By vastly increasing the options for diversion as well as information, the Internet has extended a process that had already begun when cable began increasing the number of TV channels. And if the political scientist Markus Prior is right, that expansion of choice is partly responsible for one of the most worrisome trends in American life: diminished attention to the news and reduced engagement in civic life among a significant part of the public.

*   *   *

The decline of newspapers and the growth of the Internet as a source of news may have a similar impact. On the one hand, there is likely to be less incidental learning among those with low political interest. Like the entertainment-oriented TV viewers who learned about the world because they had no alternative except to sit through the national network news, many people who have bought a paper for the sports, the recipes, the comics, or the crossword puzzle have nonetheless learned something about the wider world because they have been likely at least to scan the front page. Online, by contrast, they do not necessarily see what would be front-page news in their city, and so they are likely to become less informed about news and politics as the reading of newspapers drops. * * *

But there is another side to the story. As Yochai Benkler argues in his brilliant book *The Wealth of Networks: How Social Production Transforms Markets and Freedom*, the new "networked information economy" has some critical advantages for realizing democratic values. The old "industrial model" mass media have required large investments of capital and provided a platform to speak to the public for a relatively small number of people, but now the falling costs of computers and communication have "placed the material means of information and cultural production in the hands of a significant fraction of the world's population—on the order of a billion people around the globe." Instead of being confined to a passive role, ordinary people can talk back to the media or circumvent them entirely and enter the public conversation.

The new public sphere, in Benkler's view, is also developing mechanisms for filtering information for reliability and relevance, organizing it into easily navigated paths, and raising it to higher levels of public debate, contrary to critics who have worried that the Internet would be a chaotic Babel or a polarized system of "echo chambers" (as Cass Sunstein argued in his book *Republic.com*). And, unlike the old mass media, the new digital environment facilitates decentralized individual and cooperative action, often organized on an open and voluntary basis. Benkler invests a great deal of hope in this type of non-market collaborative production—the kind that has generated new social media such as Wikipedia, which, amazingly, despite being an encyclopedia, has also become an important news medium because it is so rapidly updated.

Of course, some of these innovations are mixed blessings: people can now share their misinformation as well as their knowledge. Viral email, Twitter, and social network sites can be used to spread rumors and malice through channels hidden from the wider public and insulated from criticism. Benkler is right about the many important gains from new technology, but he does not adequately balance the gains against the losses that the emerging networked economy is also bringing about—among them the problems that Prior identifies, such as the diminished share of the public following the news, and perhaps most important, the toll on the institutions of professional journalism.

*   *   *

The non-market collaborative networks on the Web celebrated by Benkler represent an alternative way of producing information as a public good. Before Wikipedia was created, hardly anyone supposed it would work as well as it has. But it has severe limitations as a source of knowledge. Its entries, including news items, are rewritten from other sources, and it does not purport to offer original research or original reporting. The blogosphere and the news aggregators are also largely parasitic: they feed off the conventional news media. Citizen journalists contribute reports from the scene of far-flung events, but the reports may just be the propaganda of self-interested parties.

Voluntary networks cannot easily duplicate certain critical advantages that large-scale and professionally run media have had—the financial wherewithal to invest in trained reporters and editors and to assign them to beats and long projects, and a well-established system of professional norms that has been a source of conscientious motivation and restraint in the reporting of news. The new social media add value when they are a supplement to professional journalism. To the extent that they supplant it, however, the wildfires of rumor and malice will be harder to check.

*   *   *

V.

And this returns us to the central problem. If newspapers are no longer able to cross-subsidize public-service journalism and if the de-centralized, non-market forms of collaboration cannot provide an adequate substitute, how is that work going to be paid for? The answer, insofar as there is one, is that we are going to need much more philanthropic support for journalism than we have ever had in the United States.

When a society requires public goods, the solution is often to use government to subsidize them or to produce them directly. But if we want a press that is independent of political control, we cannot have government sponsoring or bailing out specific papers. In the late eighteenth and nineteenth centuries, besides using printing contracts to subsidize favored party organs, the federal government supported the press in what First Amendment lawyers today would call a "viewpoint-neutral" way—through cheap postal rates that were available to all newspapers.

And since the 1960s, both the federal and state governments have aided public broadcasting, which has enabled public TV and radio stations to become important sources of news.

Public radio has been a particularly notable success. In a period when commercial radio stations have abandoned all but headline news, National Public Radio has become the last refuge of original reporting on the dial. But as Charles Lewis, a long-time leader in investigative reporting, has pointed out in the *Columbia Journalism Review*, public radio stations, for all their excellent work, have not done a lot of investigative stories. The dependence of many local stations on state government funding makes them vulnerable to political pressure and unlikely to fill the void left by the decline in newspaper coverage of the states. Virtually any proposal for government subsidies of the press today would likely fail on just these grounds: funding by the federal government or the states has too much potential for political manipulation. Elsewhere governments are subsidizing the press. In an effort to aid newspapers in France, President Nicolas Sarkozy recently announced a program to give eighteen-year-olds a free year-long subscription to a daily paper of their choice. In America this would be a joke, though depending on how many teenagers chose one of our racier tabloids, it could give added meaning to the concept of a "stimulus package."

The other standard means of supporting the production of public goods is through private non-profit organization. In fact, non-profit support of journalism has recently been increasing. But much of the discussion about non-profit journalism has failed to recognize that it can mean at least three different things. The first, though not necessarily the most relevant, is the conversion of newspapers from commercial to non-profit status as a way of preserving their public-service role. Florida's *St. Petersburg Times*, which is owned by a journalism school, the Poynter Institute for Media Studies, is often mistakenly cited as a model for this approach. In fact, the *Times* itself has been run at a profit, which has been used to build up the Poynter Institute into a major center for training in journalism. Today, however, the question is not whether to use a money-making newspaper to support philanthropy, but whether non-profit organizations can sustain newspapers that may be losing money. Britain's Guardian Media Group, owned by the Scott Trust, comes closer to present demands. The trust uses profits from its money-making media subsidiaries to ensure the survival of the daily *Guardian*, which has lost money in recent years. But the *Guardian* model depends on having profitable subsidiaries to offset losses in a daily paper.

Before stopping the presses for the last time, the owners of some declining newspapers may try to convert them into non-profits in the hope of raising contributions to keep them in operation. I would not be surprised if some papers do have a devoted core of readers who would be willing to give more in tax-deductible contributions than they currently pay in subscriptions. But no paper has yet tested whether this option could raise enough money to stay in business.

Besides full non-profit operation of a newspaper, a second approach is philanthropic support of specific kinds of journalism, available through multiple outlets, whether they are commercial or non-profit. The best-known example of this solution is ProPublica, which describes itself as "an independent, non-profit newsroom that produces investigative journalism in the public interest." Publishing online as of last June, ProPublica also works in partnership on some stories with newspapers such as the *New York Times*. The partnerships enable newspapers to keep down the costs of investigative stories, and they give ProPublica access to mass distribution as well as a check on quality. Similarly, the Kaiser Family Foundation, which focuses on health policy, announced last fall that it would begin directly employing reporters to create a health policy news service. According to Drew Altman, Kaiser's president, besides making some stories freely available to newspapers and online, the news service will establish partnerships with newspapers for specific stories, which the papers will then have the right to release first. Some other foundations that focus on specific areas of policy may follow this approach as a way to promote public awareness of their concerns.

Both the non-profit operation of newspapers and the philanthropic subsidy of particular types of reporting are aimed at fostering forms of public-service journalism that would otherwise be in jeopardy. But there is yet a third use of non-profits—and it is for underwriting new models of journalism in the online environment. A good example of this approach is the Center for Independent Media, which, according to its director David Bennahum, receives about $4 million annually from seventy funders to support online political news sites in five states as well as one for national news, The Washington Independent. Bennahum says that "the narrative voice of newspapers is not what [online] readers want" and that the sites his center finances are instead doing a kind of journalism that brings readers into dialogue.

The notion that the digital medium requires a more inclusive relationship with the "people formerly called the audience" is a common theme among online journalists. Joshua Micah Marshall, the founder of TalkingPointsMemo.com, which runs on a commercial basis, says that many of the stories on his site grow out of ideas and tips supplied by readers in thousands of emails daily. Any news operation has information flowing in and out; an online publication can productively open up this process to anyone who is able and prepared to help. Stories develop online incrementally, often through participation in a collaborative network, rather than being written behind the scenes and released only when checked and finished. This is entirely different from "citizen journalism," and has the potential to be just as rigorous as traditional journalistic practices.

In cities around the country, journalists are experimenting with a variety of strategies for building up Web-only news sites to make up for the shrinking newsrooms of local papers. MinnPost.com in Minneapolis-St.

Paul, the most substantial of these ventures, hopes to attract a wide range of readers and sponsors with news coverage of relatively broad scope, according to its CEO and editor Joel Kramer. But its annual budget of $1.3 million cannot support an operation on the scale of a metropolitan daily; with only seven full-time staff, MinnPost.com relies primarily on free-lancers, many of them journalists who have left St. Paul's *Pioneer Press* or Minneapolis's *Star-Tribune* (which in January filed for bankruptcy protection despite having cut its editorial staff by 25 percent). Another non-profit online metropolitan news site, the VoiceofSanDiego.org, developed as a response to scandals in the city and has specialized in investigative stories. Like public radio, these ventures raise money through individual membership contributions and grants from local foundations, though not from government.

Doubtful that they can ever achieve the scale of the big metros, Rosenstiel compares the Web-based city news sites to aggressive city magazines. If one major concern is keeping government accountable, that kind of aggressive reporting is certainly a valuable function and well worth supporting. But owing to their more limited economic basis, the non-profit news sites are unlikely to be able to offer the coverage, or to exert the influence, of a daily newspaper read by half the people in a city. The great metros did not emerge just because cities needed newspapers to inform citizens—after all, cities need lots of things that they are never able to develop. Newspapers flourished at the metropolitan level because their role as local market intermediaries enabled them to generate substantial advertising as well as circulation income and thereby to become strong and independent. Non-profit news sites that lack a strong advertising base depend on donors for their survival and are at risk of being destroyed by a single lawsuit, and so they are unlikely to be able to match the traditional power of the press.

Many people have been expecting the successors of newspapers to emerge on the Web. But there may be no successor, at least none like the papers we have known. The metropolitan daily may be a peculiar historical invention whose time is passing. We may be approaching not the end of newspapers, but the end of the age of newspapers—the long phase in history when newspapers published in major cities throughout the United States have been central to both the production of news and the life of their metropolitan regions.

Metropolitan newspapers have dominated news gathering, set the public agenda, served as the focal point of controversy, and credibly represented themselves as symbolizing and speaking for the cities whose names they have carried. They have tried to be everyone's source of news, appealing across the ideological spectrum, and to be comprehensive, providing their readers with whatever was of daily interest to them. Some newspapers, a smaller number than exist today, will survive the transition to the Web, but they probably will not possess the centrality, the scope, or the authoritative voice—much less the monopolies on metropolitan advertising—that newspapers have had.

* * *

For those with the skills and interest to take advantage of this new world of news, there should be much to be pleased with. Instead of being limited to a local paper, such readers already enjoy access to a broader range of publications and discussions than ever before. But without a local newspaper or even with a shrunken one, many other people will learn less about what is going on in the world. As of now, moreover, no source in any medium seems willing and able to pay for the general-interest reporting that newspapers are abandoning. Philanthropy can help to offset some of these cutbacks, but it is unlikely to make up fully for what we are losing.

News coverage is not all that newspapers have given us. They have lent the public a powerful means of leverage over the state, and this leverage is now at risk. If we take seriously the notion of newspapers as a fourth estate or a fourth branch of government, the end of the age of newspapers implies a change in our political system itself. Newspapers have helped to control corrupt tendencies in both government and business. If we are to avoid a new era of corruption, we are going to have to summon that power in other ways. Our new technologies do not retire our old responsibilities.

48

"How to Save the News"

JAMES FALLOWS

Everyone knows that Google is killing the news business. Few people know how hard Google is trying to bring it back to life, or why the company now considers journalism's survival crucial to its own prospects.

Of course this overstates Google's power to destroy, or create. The company's chief economist, Hal Varian, likes to point out that perhaps the most important measure of the newspaper industry's viability—the number of subscriptions per household—has headed straight down, not just since Google's founding in the late 1990s but ever since World War II. In 1947, each 100 U.S. households bought an average of about 140 newspapers daily. Now they buy fewer than 50, and the number has fallen nonstop through those years. If Google had never been invented, changes in commuting patterns, the coming of 24-hour TV news and online information sites that make a newspaper's information stale before it appears, the general busyness of life, and many other factors would have created major problems for newspapers. Moreover, "Google" is shorthand for an array of other Internet-based pressures on the news business, notably the draining of classified ads to the likes of Craigslist and eBay. On the other side of the balance, Google's efforts to shore up news organizations are extensive and have recently become intense but are not guaranteed to succeed.

* * *

Let's start with the diagnosis: If you are looking at the troubled ecology of news from Google's point of view, how do you define the problem to be solved? You would accept from the outset that something "historic," "epochal," "devastating," "unprecedented," "irresistible," and so on was happening to the news business—all terms I heard used in interviews to describe the challenges facing newspapers in particular and the journalism business more broadly.

"There really is no single cause," I was told by Josh Cohen, a former Web-news manager for Reuters who now directs Google's dealings with publishers and broadcasters, at his office in New York. "Rather, you could pick any single cause, and that on its own would be enough to explain the problems—except it's not on its own." The most obvious cause is that classified advertising, traditionally 30 to 40 percent of a newspaper's total revenue, is disappearing in a rush to online sites. "There are a lot of people in the business who think that in the not-too-distant future, the classified share of a paper's revenue will go to zero," Cohen said. "Stop right there. In any business, if you lose a third of your revenue, you're going to be in serious trouble."

You can't stop right there, Cohen said, and he went through the list of the other, related trends weighing on newspapers in particular, each pointing downward and each making the others worse. First, the relentless decline of circulation—"fewer people using your product," as he put it. Then, the consequent defection of advertisers from the lucrative "display" category—the big ads for cars, banks, airlines—as well as from classifieds. The typical newspaper costs much more to print and deliver than a subscriber pays. Its business rationale is as an advertising-delivery vehicle, with 80 percent of the typical paper's total revenue coming from ads. That's what's going away. In hopes of preserving that advertising model, newspapers have decided to defend their hold on the public's attention by giving away, online, the very information they were trying to sell in print. However that decision looks in the long run, for now it has created a rising generation of "customers" who are out of the habit of reading on paper and are conditioned to think that information should be free.

"It's the triple whammy," [Google CEO] Eric Schmidt said when I interviewed him. "Loss of classifieds, loss of circulation, loss of the value of display ads in print, on a per-ad basis. Online advertising is growing but has not caught up."

So far, this may sound familiar. To me, the interesting aspects of the Google diagnosis, which of course sets the stage for the proposed cure, were these:

First, it was strikingly not moralistic or mocking. This was a change, not simply from what I'd grown used to hearing at tech conferences over the past decade—the phrase "dead-tree edition" captures the tone—but also from the way Americans usually talk about distressed industries. Think of the connotations of "Big Auto" or "Rust Belt." * * *

Next in the Google assessment is the emphasis on "unbundling" as an insurmountable business problem for journalism. "Bundling" was the idea that all parts of the paper came literally in one wrapper—news, sports, comics, grocery-store coupons—and that people who bought the paper for one part implicitly subsidized all the rest. This was important not just because it boosted overall revenue but because it kept publishers from having to figure out whether enough people were reading stories from the statehouse or Mexico City to pay the costs of reporters there.

* * * The Internet has been one giant system for stripping away such cross-subsidies. Why look to the newspaper real-estate listings when you can get more up-to-date, searchable info on Zillow—or better travel deals on Orbitz, or a broader range of movie showtimes on Yahoo? Google has been the most powerful unbundling agent of all. It lets users find the one article they are looking for, rather than making them buy the entire paper that paid the reporter. It lets advertisers reach the one customer who is searching for their product, rather than making them advertise to an entire class of readers.

Next, and significantly for the company's vision of the future, nearly everyone at Google emphasized that prospects look bleak for the printed versions of newspapers—but could be bright for the news industry as a whole, including newspaper publishers. This could seem an artificial distinction, but it is fundamental to the company's view of how news organizations will support themselves.

* * *

Publishers would be overjoyed to stop buying newsprint—if the new readers they are gaining for their online editions were worth as much to advertisers as the previous ones they are losing in print. Here is a crucial part of the Google analysis: they certainly will be. The news business, in this view, is passing through an agonizing transition—bad enough, but different from dying. The difference lies in the assumption that soon readers will again pay for subscriptions, and online display ads will become valuable.

"Nothing that I see suggests the 'death of newspapers,'" Eric Schmidt told me. The problem was the high cost and plummeting popularity of their print versions. "Today you have a subscription to a print newspaper," he said. "In the future model, you'll have subscriptions to information sources that will have advertisements embedded in them, like a newspaper. You'll just leave out the print part. I am quite sure that this will happen." We'll get to the details in a moment, but the analytical point behind his conviction bears emphasis. "I observe that as print circulation falls, the growth of the online audience is dramatic," Schmidt said. "Newspapers don't have a demand problem; they have a business-model problem." Many of his company's efforts are attempts to solve this, so that newspaper companies can survive, as printed circulation withers away.

Finally, and to me most surprisingly, the Google analysis reveals something about journalism that people inside the business can't easily see about themselves. This involves a kind of inefficiency that a hard-pressed journalistic establishment may no longer be able to afford.

* * *

Except for an 18-month period when [Krishna] Bharat founded and ran Google's R&D center in Bangalore, his original hometown, he has been guiding Google News ever since. In this role, he sees more of the world's news coverage daily than practically anyone else on Earth. I asked him what he had learned about the news business.

He hesitated for a minute, as if wanting to be very careful about making a potentially offensive point. Then he said that what astonished him was the predictable and pack-like response of most of the world's news outlets to most stories. Or, more positively, how much opportunity he saw for anyone who was willing to try a different approach.

The Google News front page is a kind of air-traffic-control center for the movement of stories across the world's media, in real time. "Usually, you see essentially the same approach taken by a thousand publications at the same time," he told me. "Once something has been observed, nearly everyone says approximately the same thing." He didn't mean that the publications were linking to one another or syndicating their stories. Rather, their conventions and instincts made them all emphasize the same things. This could be reassuring, in indicating some consensus on what the "important" stories were. But Bharat said it also indicated a faddishness of coverage—when Michael Jackson dies, other things cease to matter—and a redundancy that journalism could no longer afford. "It makes you wonder, is there a better way?" he asked. "Why is it that a thousand people come up with approximately the same reading of matters? Why couldn't there be five readings? And meanwhile use that energy to observe something else, equally important, that is currently being neglected." He said this was not a purely theoretical question. "I believe the news industry is finding that it will not be able to sustain producing highly similar articles."

With the debut of Krishna Bharat's Google News in 2002, Google began its first serious interactions with news organizations. Two years later, it introduced Google Alerts, which sent e-mail or instant-message notifications to users whenever Google's relentless real-time indexing of the world's news sites found a match for a topic the user had flagged. Two years after that, in the fall of 2006, Google began scanning the paper or microfilmed archives of many leading publications so that articles from their pre-digital era could be indexed, searched for, and read online.

*   *   *

"About two years ago, we started hearing more and more talk about the decline of the press," Schmidt told me. "A set of people [inside the company] began looking at what might be the ways we could help newspapers."

Why should the company bother? Until recently, I would have thought that the answer was a combination of PR concerns and Schmidt's personal interest. * * *

Before this year, when I asked Google employees about the health of the news business, their answers often seemed dutiful. During my interviews this year, people sounded as if they meant it. Google is valuable, by the logic I repeatedly heard, because the information people find through it is valuable. If the information is uninteresting, inaccurate, or untimely, people will not want to search for it. How valuable would Google Maps be, if the directions or street listings were wrong?

Nearly everyone I spoke with made this point in some way. Nikesh Arora's version was that Google had a "deeply symbiotic relationship" with serious news organizations. "We help people find content," he told me. "We don't generate content ourselves. As long as there is great content, people will come looking for it. When there's no great content, it's very hard for people to be interested in finding it. That's what we do for a living." * * *

"For the last eight years, we mainly focused on getting the algorithms better," Krishna Bharat said, referring to the automated systems for finding and ranking items in Google News. "But lately, a lot of my time has gone into thinking about the basis on which the product"—news—"is built. A lot of our thinking now is focused on making the news sustainable."

So how can news be made sustainable? The conceptual leap in Google's vision is simply to ignore print. It's not that everyone at the company assumes "dead tree" newspapers and magazines will disappear. * * * No one I spoke with at Google went quite that far. But all of their plans for reinventing a business model for journalism involve attracting money to the Web-based news sites now available on computers, and to the portable information streams that will flow to whatever devices evolve from today's smart phones, iPods and iPads, Nooks and Kindles, and mobile devices of any other sort. This is a natural approach for Google, which is, except for its Nexus One phone, a strictly online company.

The three pillars of the new online business model, as I heard them invariably described, are distribution, engagement, and monetization. That is: getting news to more people, and more people to news-oriented sites; making the presentation of news more interesting, varied, and involving; and converting these larger and more strongly committed audiences into revenue, through both subscription fees and ads. Conveniently, each calls on areas of Google's expertise. "Not knowing as much about the news business as the newspapers do, it is unlikely that we can solve the problems better than they can," Nikesh Arora told me. "But we are willing to support any formal and informal effort that newspapers or journalists more generally want to make" to come up with new sources of money.

In practice this involves projects like the ones I'm about to describe, which share two other traits beyond the "distribution, engagement, monetization" strategy that officially unites them. One is the Google concept of "permanent beta" and continuous experimentation—learning what does work by seeing all the things that don't. "We believe that teams must be nimble and able to fail quickly," Josh Cohen told me. (I resisted making the obvious joke about the contrast with the journalism world, which believes in slow and statesmanlike failure.) "The three most important things any newspaper can do now are experiment, experiment, and experiment," Hal Varian said.

*   *   *

The other implicitly connecting theme is that an accumulation of small steps can together make a surprisingly large difference. The forces weighing down the news industry are titanic. In contrast, some of the proposed solutions may seem disappointingly small-bore. But many people at Google repeated a maxim from Clay Shirley, of New York University, in an essay last year about the future of the news: "Nothing will work, but everything might."

In all, Google teams are working with hundreds of news organizations, which range in scale from the Associated Press, the Public Broadcasting System, and *The New York Times* to local TV stations and papers. The last two efforts I'll mention are obviously different in scale and potential from all the others, but these examples give a sense of what "trying everything" means.

Living Stories

News reporting is usually incremental. Something happens in Kabul today. It's related to what happened there yesterday, plus 20 years ago, and further back. It has a bearing on what will happen a year from now. High-end news organizations reflect this continuous reality in hiring reporters and editors who (ideally) know the background of today's news and in the way they present it, usually with modest additions to the sum of established knowledge day by day.

The modest daily updating of the news—another vote in Congress, another debate among political candidates—matches the cycle of papers and broadcasts very well, but matches the Internet very poorly, in terms of both speed and popularity rankings. *The Financial Times* might have given readers better sustained coverage of European economic troubles than any other paper. But precisely because it has done so many incremental stories, no one of them might rise to the top of a Google Web search, compared with an occasional overview story somewhere else. By the standards that currently generate online revenue, better journalism gets a worse result.

This past winter, the Google News team worked with *The New York Times* and *The Washington Post* to run the Living Stories experiment, essentially a way to rig Google's search results to favor serious, sustained reporting. All articles about a big topic—the war in Afghanistan, healthcare reform—were grouped on one page that included links to all aspects of the paper's coverage (history, videos, reader comments, related articles). "It is a repository of information, rather than ephemeral information," Krishna Bharat said, explaining that it was a repository designed to prosper in what he called "today's link economy." In February, Google called off the *Times-Post* experiment—and declared it a success, by making the source code available free online, for any organization that would like to create a Living Stories feature for its site.

*   *   *

Fast Flip

The Internet is a great way to get news but often a poor way to read it. Usually the longer the item, the worse the experience; a screenful is fine, clicking through thousands of words is an ordeal. * * *

The Fast Flip project, which began last summer and has now graduated to "official" status, is an attempt to approximate the inviting aspects of leafing through a magazine. It works by loading magazine pages not as collections of text but as highly detailed photos of pages as a whole, cached in Google's system so they load almost as quickly as a (human) reader can leaf through them. "It was an experiment in giving you a preview of an article that was more than just a link to the title," Krishna Bharat said. "It gives you a sense of the graphics, the emphasis, the quality, the feel. Whether you would like to spend time with it." Spending time with an article, whether in print or online, is of course the definition of "engagement" and the behavior advertisers seek. * * *

"We're not saying we have worked out exactly the right model," Krishna Bharat said when I asked about Fast Flip details. "We just want news to be available, fast, all over the place on the Internet."

YouTube Direct

Projects like Living Stories and Fast Flip are tactical in their potential. Google's hope is that broader use of YouTube videos could substantially boost a news organization's long-term ability to engage an audience. Amateur-produced video is perhaps the most powerful new tool of the Internet era in journalism, making the whole world a potential witness to dramas, tragedies, achievements almost anywhere. The idea behind the various YouTube projects is that the same newspapers that once commanded an audience with printed reports of local news, sports, crime, and weather could re-create their central role by becoming a clearinghouse for video reports.

* * * For instance, Google offers, for free, the source code for YouTube Direct, which any publication can put on its own Web site. Readers can then easily send in their video clips, for the publication to review, censor, combine, or shorten before putting them up on its site. After a blizzard, people could send in clips of what they had seen outside. Same for a local football game, or a train wreck, or a city-council meeting, or any other event when many people would be interested in what their neighbors had seen. The advertising potential might be small, for YouTube and the local paper alike. The point would be engagement. Al Jazeera used YouTube Direct during the elections in Iraq this spring to show footage from around the country.

*   *   *

Another tool extends the lessons of the YouTube Debates during the 2008 presidential campaign, in which [Google] invited YouTube users from around the country to send in clips of brief questions for the candidates. Anderson Cooper of CNN then introduced YouTube clips of the questions CNN had chosen to use. They ranged from serious to silly and included one asking Barack Obama whether he was "black enough." YouTube has added a feature that lets users vote for the questions they want asked and has used the method effectively many times since then. . . .

Whatever comes of these experiments, two other broad initiatives are of unquestionable importance, because they address the two biggest business emergencies today's news companies face: they can no longer make enough money on display ads, and they can no longer get readers to pay. According to the Google view, these are serious situations, but temporary.

Display Ads

The idea for improving display-ad prospects begins with insignificant-sounding adjustments that have great potential payoff. For instance: Neal Mohan of Google pointed out that news organizations now typically sell their online ad space in two very different ways. Premium space—on the home page, facing certain featured articles or authors—is handled by "direct sales," through the publication's own sales staff. "Remnant" space, anything left over, is generally franchised out to a national sales network or "exchange" that digs up whatever advertisers it can. Publications decide on the division of space ahead of time, and hope the real-world results more or less fit.

One of Google's new systems does for online ad space what the airlines' dreaded "yield management" systems do for seats on a plane. Airlines constantly adjust the fares on a route, and the size of the planes that will fly it, toward the goal of making each plane as full as it can be before it takes off. The Google system does the same thing, allowing publishers to adjust the allocation of high- and low-priced space, second by second. "Your top salesperson might just have had dinner with the biggest client, who decides to run a big campaign," Mohan told me. The dynamic allocation system ensures that the publisher doesn't lose a penny of potential ad revenue to avoidable supply/demand glitches. If an advertiser wants to spend more on "premium" ads, the necessary space will be automatically redeployed from lower-value sections. * * * Yield management has allowed airlines to survive; according to Mohan, the advertising equivalent in Google's new system "has generated a lift for publishers of 130 percent, versus what they did when dividing the space themselves."

Mohan suggested a variety of other small but significant operational improvements, which together led to a proposal so revolutionary that it challenges all despairing conclusions about the economic future of the press. * * * Online display ads may not be so valuable now, he said, but that is because we're still in the drawn-out "transition" period. Sooner or later—maybe in two years, certainly in 10—display ads will, per eyeball, be worth more online than they were in print.

How could this be? In part, he said, today's discouraging ad results simply reflect a lag time. The audience has shifted dramatically from print to online. So has the accumulation of minutes people choose to spend each day reading the news. Wherever people choose to spend their time, Mohan said, they can eventually be "monetized"—the principle on which every newspaper and magazine (and television network) has survived until today.

*   *   *

* * * "The online world will be a lot more attuned to who you are and what you care about, and it will be interactive in a way it never has been before." Advertising has been around forever, Mohan said, "but until now it has always been a one-way conversation. Now your users can communicate back to you." His full argument is complex, but his conclusion is: eventually news operations will wonder why they worried so much about print display ads, since online display will be so much more attractive.

*   *   *

Designing the Paywall

The other hugely consequential effort Google is exploring involves reviving the idea of "subscriptions"—the quaint old custom of an audience paying for what it receives. Most Google people I spoke with had zero interest in the paywall question as an abstraction, because it seemed so obvious that different publications in different circumstances with different business models will make different decisions about how customers should pay.

*   *   *

"We don't want to encourage anyone to start charging for content, or not to charge for content," Chris Gaither said. "That is entirely up to them." But Google teams based in Mountain View and New York have been working with newspapers and magazines on the surprisingly complex details of making any kind of payment system work. Paywalls themselves come in a wide variety: absolute barriers to anyone who is not a subscriber, metered approaches that allow nonsubscribers a certain number of free views per day or month, "first click free" schemes to let anyone see the start of an article but reserve the full text for subscribers, and many more. Each involves twists in how the publication's results show up in Google searches and on Google News. For instance: if you are a paid subscriber to the *Financial Times*, any Web search you run should include FT results—and indeed rank them all the higher, since your status as a subscriber means you place extra value on the paper's reports. If you don't subscribe, those FT links should come lower in the search results, since you won't be able to read them—but the results should still appear, in case you decide you want them enough to subscribe. But when you run the search, how can Google tell whether or not you subscribe? How can it know that you are you, whether you're using your computer, or a friend's, or one at an Internet cafe, or an iPhone? And how can its Web crawlers index the FTs stories in the first place, if they're behind the paywall? All these questions have answers, but they're not always obvious.

"We often hear from publishers saying, 'We're thinking of this approach, and we want to understand it fully,'" Josh Cohen told me. "'We want to be sure this works the way we intend it to work. Can you give it a look?' We will tell them how their ideas would turn out with our system." Then, without giving the newspaper's name or the proprietary details of its specific plan, the Google team will also post its findings and advice on its public Web site. And for publications thinking of the "E-ZPass" approach—some automatic way to collect small per-article charges without slowing the user down or involving cumbersome forms—another Google team is working on the practicalities.

As for the very idea of paid subscriptions: How can they have a future in the Google-driven world of atomized spot information? "It is probable that unbundling has a limit," Eric Schmidt said. Something basic in human nature craves surprise and new sources of stimulation. Few people are "so monomaniacal," as he put it, that they will be interested only in a strict, predefined list of subjects. Therefore people will still want to buy subscriptions to sources of information and entertainment— "bundles," the head of the world's most powerful unbundler said—and advertisers will still want to reach them. His example:

"It's obvious that in five or 10 years, most news will be consumed on an electronic device of some sort. Something that is mobile and personal, with a nice color screen. Imagine an iPod or Kindle smart enough to show you stories that are incremental to a story it showed you yesterday, rather than just repetitive. And it knows who your friends are and what they're reading and think is hot. And it has display advertising with lots of nice color, and more personal and targeted, within the limits of creepiness. And it has a GPS and a radio network and knows what is going on around you. If you think about that, you get to an interesting answer very quickly, involving both subscriptions and ads."

This vision, which Schmidt presented as Utopian, helps illustrate the solution Google believes it will find; the problem it knows it can't solve; and another problem that goes well beyond its ambitions.

The solution is simply the idea that there can be a solution. The organization that dominates the online-advertising world says that much more online-ad money can be flowing to news organizations. The company whose standard price to consumers is zero says that subscribers can and will pay for news. The name that has symbolized disruption of established media says it sees direct self-interest in helping the struggling journalism business. In today's devastated news business, these are major and encouraging developments, all the more so for their contrast with what other tech firms are attempting.

The problem Google is aware of involves the disruption still ahead. Ten years from now, a robust and better-funded news business will be thriving. What next year means is harder to say. * * * But this is consistent with the way the news has always worked, rather than a threatening change. Fifteen years ago, Fox News did not exist. A decade ago, Jon Stewart was not known for political commentary. The news business has continually been reinvented by people in their 20s and early 30s. . . .

The challenge Google knows it has not fully coped with is a vast one, which involves the public function of the news in the broadest sense. The company views the survival of "premium content" as important to its own welfare. But Schmidt and his colleagues realize that a modernized news business might conceivably produce "enough" good content for Google's purposes even if no one has fully figured out how to pay for the bureau in Baghdad, or even at the statehouse. This is the next challenge, and a profound one, for a reinvented journalistic culture. The fluid history of the news business, along with today's technological pattern of

Google-style continuous experimentation, suggests that there will be no one big solution but a range of partial remedies. Google's efforts may have bought time for a panicked, transitional news business to see a future for itself and begin discovering those new remedies and roles.

DISCUSSION QUESTIONS

1. Which part or parts of the news media—newspapers, television, websites, blogs, radio, social networks, Twitter—do you rely on most? Which would you say you trust the most? Should all news-oriented media, whether new or old, use the same journalistic standards in determining what to broadcast or publish?

2. Imagine you are a blogger and you have come across some damaging information about a presidential candidate. Do you blog it? On one hand, it might not be true. On the other, if it is true, it is critical information that voters should know. Do you put the information into the blogosphere and trust it will be filtered and proven true or false by other media? Or do you approach it as mainstream media journalists traditionally would, requiring more corroboration for the story—which can take time to obtain—before presenting it to the public? Would your answer depend on how late in the campaign it is? Now imagine the same scenario, except that the office in question is an elected position in your hometown, where people know you. Would you handle this situation differently?

3. Both articles express concerns about the fate of newspapers. What are the key concerns? Do you share them? Why or why not?

4. What do you see as the strengths and weaknesses of the solutions described by Starr and Fallows for the problems facing newspapers?

CHAPTER 10

Elections and Voting

49

"The Voice of the People: An Echo," from *The Responsible Electorate*

V. O. KEY, JR.

The votes are cast, the tallies are in, the winning candidate claims victory and a mandate to govern—the people have spoken! But what exactly have the people said when they cast a plurality of the votes for one candidate? The political scientist V. O. Key, Jr., argued that the voice of the people was an echo of the cacophony and hubbub of candidates and parties scrambling for popular support. "Even the most discriminating popular judgment," wrote Key, "can reflect only ambiguity, uncertainty, or even foolishness if those are the qualities of the input into the echo chamber."

So what was the logic of the voting decision? Key argued that the effort among social scientists to develop theories for understanding the voting decision was important because of the ways political candidates and political leaders would respond to them. If research demonstrates that voters are influenced by "images and cultivation of style," rather than the "substance of politics," then that is what candidates will offer the voters. If the people receive only images and style as the input to the echo chamber, then eventually that is all they will come to expect. However, Key argues that contrary to the picture of voters held by many politicians and some academic research of his day, the "voters are not fools" who are easily manipulated by campaign tactics or who vote predictably according to the social groups they are in. Individual voters may behave oddly, he concedes, but "in the large, the electorate behaves about as rationally and responsibly as we should expect." His analysis of presidential elections convinced him that the electorate made sensible decisions based upon a concern for public policy, the performance of government, and the personalities of the candidates.

In his reflective moments even the most experienced politician senses a nagging curiosity about why people vote as they do. His power and his position depend upon the outcome of the mysterious rites we perform as opposing candidates harangue the multitudes who finally march to the polls to prolong the rule of their champion, to thrust him, ungratefully, back into the void of private life, or to raise to eminence a new tribune of the people. What kinds of appeals enable a candidate to win the favor of the great god, The People? What circumstances move voters to shift their preferences in this direction or that? What clever propaganda tactic or slogan led to this result? What mannerism of oratory or style of rhetoric produced another outcome? What band of electors rallied to this candidate to save the day for him? What policy of state attracted the devotion of another bloc of voters? What action repelled a third sector of the electorate?

The victorious candidate may claim with assurance that he has the answers to all such questions. He may regard his success as vindication of his beliefs about why voters vote as they do. And he may regard the swing of the vote to him as indubitably a response to the campaign positions he took, as an indication of the acuteness of his intuitive estimates of the mood of the people, and as a ringing manifestation of the esteem in which he is held by a discriminating public. This narcissism assumes its most repulsive form among election winners who have championed intolerance, who have stirred the passions and hatreds of people, or who have advocated causes known by decent men to be outrageous or dangerous in their long-run consequences. No functionary is more repugnant or more arrogant than the unjust man who asserts, with a color of truth, that he speaks from a pedestal of popular approbation.

It thus can be a mischievous error to assume, because a candidate wins, that a majority of the electorate shares his views on public questions, approves his past actions, or has specific expectations about his future conduct. Nor does victory establish that the candidate's campaign strategy, his image, his television style, or his fearless stand against cancer and polio turned the trick. The election returns establish only that the winner attracted a majority of the votes—assuming the existence of a modicum of rectitude in election administration. They tell us precious little about why the plurality was his.

For a glaringly obvious reason, electoral victory cannot be regarded as necessarily a popular ratification of a candidate's outlook. The voice of the people is but an echo. The output of an echo chamber bears an inevitable and invariable relation to the input. As candidates and parties clamor for attention and vie for popular support, the people's verdict can be no more than a selective reflection from among the alternatives and outlooks presented to them. Even the most discriminating popular judgment can reflect only ambiguity, uncertainty, or even foolishness if those are the qualities of the input into the echo chamber. A candidate may win despite his tactics and appeals rather than because of them. If the people can choose only from among rascals, they are certain to choose a rascal.

Scholars, though they have less at stake than do politicians, also have an abiding curiosity about why voters act as they do. In the past quarter of a century [since the 1940s] they have vastly enlarged their capacity to check the hunches born of their curiosities. The invention of the sample survey—the most widely known example of which is the Gallup poll—enabled them to make fairly trustworthy estimates of the characteristics and behaviors of large human populations. This method of mass observation revolutionized the study of politics—as well as the management of political campaigns. The new technique permitted large-scale tests to check the validity of old psychological and sociological theories of human behavior. These tests led to new hunches and new theories about voting behavior, which could, in turn, be checked and which thereby contributed to the extraordinary ferment in the social sciences during recent decades.

The studies of electoral behavior by survey methods cumulate into an imposing body of knowledge which conveys a vivid impression of the variety and subtlety of factors that enter into individual voting decisions. In their first stages in the 1930s the new electoral studies chiefly lent precision and verification to the working maxims of practicing politicians and to some of the crude theories of political speculators. Thus, sample surveys established that people did, indeed, appear to vote their pocketbooks. Yet the demonstration created its embarrassments because it also established that exceptions to the rule were numerous. Not all factory workers, for example, voted alike. How was the behavior of the deviants from "group interest" to be explained? Refinement after refinement of theory and analysis added complexity to the original simple explanation. By introducing a bit of psychological theory it could be demonstrated that factory workers with optimistic expectations tended less to be governed by pocketbook considerations than did those whose outlook was gloomy. When a little social psychology was stirred into the analysis, it could be established that identifications formed early in life, such as attachments to political parties, also reinforced or resisted the pull of the interest of the moment. A sociologist, bringing to play the conceptual tools of his trade, then could show that those factory workers who associate intimately with like-minded persons on the average vote with greater solidarity than do social isolates. Inquiries conducted with great ingenuity along many such lines have enormously broadened our knowledge of the factors associated with the responses of people to the stimuli presented to them by political campaigns.

Yet, by and large, the picture of the voter that emerges from a combination of the folklore of practical politics and the findings of the new electoral studies is not a pretty one. It is not a portrait of citizens moving to considered decision as they play their solemn role of making and unmaking governments. The older tradition from practical politics may regard the voter as an erratic and irrational fellow susceptible to manipulation by skilled humbugs. One need not live through many campaigns to observe politicians, even successful politicians, who act as though they regarded the people as manageable fools. Nor does a heroic conception of the voter emerge from the new analyses of electoral behavior. They can be added up to a conception of voting not as a civic decision but as an almost purely deterministic act. Given knowledge of certain characteristics of a voter—his occupation, his residence, his religion, his national origin, and perhaps certain of his attitudes—one can predict with a high probability the direction of his vote. The actions of persons are made to appear to be only predictable and automatic responses to campaign stimuli.

*   *   *

Conceptions and theories of the way voters behave do not raise solely arcane problems to be disputed among the democratic and antidemocratic theorists or questions to be settled by the elegant techniques of the analysts of electoral behavior. Rather, they touch upon profound issues at the heart of the problem of the nature and workability of systems of popular government. Obviously the perceptions of the behavior of the electorate held by political leaders, agitators, and activists condition, if they do not fix, the types of appeals politicians employ as they seek popular support. These perceptions—or theories—affect the nature of the input to the echo chamber, if we may revert to our earlier figure, and thereby control its output. They may govern, too, the kinds of actions that governments take as they look forward to the next election. If politicians perceive the electorate as responsive to father images, they will give it father images. If they see voters as most certainly responsive to nonsense, they will give them nonsense. If they see voters as susceptible to delusion, they will delude them. If they see an electorate receptive to the cold, hard realities, they will give it the cold, hard realities.

In short, theories of how voters behave acquire importance not because of their effects on voters, who may proceed blithely unaware of them. They gain significance because of their effects, both potentially and in reality, on candidates and other political leaders. If leaders believe the route to victory is by projection of images and cultivation of styles rather than by advocacy of policies to cope with the problems of the country, they will project images and cultivate styles to the neglect of the substance of politics. They will abdicate their prime function in a democratic system, which amounts, in essence, to the assumption of the risk of trying to persuade us to lift ourselves by our bootstraps.

Among the literary experts on politics there are those who contend that, because of the development of tricks for the manipulation of the masses, practices of political leadership in the management of voters have moved far toward the conversion of election campaigns into obscene parodies of the models set up by democratic idealists. They point to the good old days when politicians were deep thinkers, eloquent orators, and farsighted statesmen. Such estimates of the course of change in social institutions must be regarded with reserve. They may be only manifestations of the inverted optimism of aged and melancholy men who, estopped from hope for the future, see in the past a satisfaction of their yearning for greatness in our political life.

Whatever the trends may have been, the perceptions that leadership elements of democracies hold of the modes of response of the electorate must always be a matter of fundamental significance. Those perceptions determine the nature of the voice of the people, for they determine the character of the input into the echo chamber. While the output may be governed by the nature of the input, over the longer run the properties of the echo chamber may themselves be altered. Fed a steady diet of buncombe [bunkum], the people may come to expect and to respond with highest predictability to buncombe. And those leaders most skilled in the propagation of buncombe may gain lasting advantage in the recurring struggles for popular favor.

The perverse and unorthodox argument of this little book is that voters are not fools. To be sure, many individual voters act in odd ways indeed; yet in the large the electorate behaves about as rationally and responsibly as we should expect, given the clarity of the alternatives presented to it and the character of the information available to it. In American presidential campaigns of recent decades the portrait of the American electorate that develops from the data is not one of an electorate straitjacketed by social determinants or moved by subconscious urges triggered by devilishly skillful propagandists. It is rather one of an electorate moved by concern about central and relevant questions of public policy, of governmental performance, and of executive personality. Propositions so uncompromisingly stated inevitably represent overstatements. Yet to the extent that they can be shown to resemble the reality, they are propositions of basic importance for both the theory and the practice of democracy.

To check the validity of this broad interpretation of the behavior of voters, attention will center on the movements of voters across party lines as they reacted to the issues, events, and candidates of presidential campaigns between 1936 and 1960. Some Democratic voters of one election turned Republican at the next; others stood pat. Some Republicans of one presidential season voted Democratic four years later; others remained loyal Republicans. What motivated these shifts, sometimes large and sometimes small, in voter affection? How did the standpatters differ from the switchers? What led them to stand firmly by their party preference of four years earlier? Were these actions governed by images, moods, and other irrelevancies; or were they expressions of judgments about the sorts of questions that, hopefully, voters will weigh as they responsibly cast their ballots? On these matters evidence is available that is impressive in volume, if not always so complete or so precisely relevant as hindsight would wish. If one perseveres through the analysis of this extensive body of information, the proposition that the voter is not so irrational a fellow after all may become credible.

Discussion Questions

1. When you cast your vote, how do you decide whom to vote for? Is your decision process affected by the nature of the political campaign that has just been completed, or does the campaign have little effect?

2. Do the 2010 and 2012 midterm and presidential elections support Key's view of the electoral process? How would he explain the differing results in the two elections?

50

"The Unpolitical Animal: How Political Science Understands Voters"

Louis Menand

How well do Americans measure up to the ideal of highly informed, engaged, atten-
tive, involved citizens? V. O. Key argued that Americans, on the whole, do reason-
ably well in making sound collective judgments. Writing around the same time as
Key, another political scientist, Philip Converse, reached a gloomier conclusion.
Most Americans couldn't be "ideal" citizens because most had minimal and incon-
sistent political belief systems. To a large degree, he concluded, Americans had many
top-of-the-head opinions that had no strong connection to a set of principles. Louis
Menand revisits the question addressed by V. O. Key: do elections represent the will
of the people? Menand reviews Converse's conclusions and then discusses three
theories that attempt to make some sense of Americans' failure to behave as ideal
citizens. One theory declares that elections are more or less random events in
which a large bloc of voters responds to "slogans, misinformation, 'fire alarms'
(sensational news), 'October surprises' (last-minute sensational news), random
personal associations, and 'gotchas.' " Another theory posits that voter decisions
are guided not simply by random events and information, but by elite opinion.
Elites do understand the issues and work within ideological frameworks and they
find ways to pitch ideas to voters so they gain a governing majority. Elections are
thus primarily about the interests and beliefs of rival elite factions. The third theory
in part rescues the voter from these unflattering portraits. Here, voters use informa-
tion shortcuts, especially but not only political party labels, to render verdicts that
are substantively meaningful. "People use shortcuts—the social–scientific term is
'heuristics'—to reach judgments about political candidates, and, on the whole, these
shortcuts are as good as the long and winding road of reading party platforms, lis-
tening to candidate debates, and all the other elements of civic duty." Menand con-
cludes in this 2004 article that voter decisions may be based on shortcuts that make
sense to them—such as which candidate is more optimistic—rather than the weigh-
ing and balancing of principles and policy positions that ideologues would prefer.

In every presidential-election year, there are news stories about undecided voters, people who say that they are perplexed about which candidate's positions make the most sense. They tell reporters things like "I'd
like to know more about Bush's plan for education," or "I'm worried that
Kerry's ideas about Social Security don't add up." They say that they are

thinking about issues like "trust," and whether the candidate cares about people like them. To voters who identify strongly with a political party, the undecided voter is almost an alien life form. For them, a vote for Bush is a vote for a whole philosophy of governance and a vote for Kerry is a vote for a distinctly different philosophy. The difference is obvious to them, and they don't understand how others can't see it, or can decide whom to vote for on the basis of a candidate's personal traits or whether his or her position on a particular issue "makes sense." To an undecided voter, on the other hand, the person who always votes for the Democrat or the Republican, no matter what, must seem like a dangerous fanatic. Which voter is behaving more rationally and responsibly?

If you look to the political professionals, the people whose job it is to know what makes the fish bite, it is clear that, in their view, political philosophy is not the fattest worm. *Winning Elections: Political Campaign Management, Strategy & Tactics . . .* is a collection of articles drawn from the pages of *Campaigns & Elections: The Magazine for People in Politics.* The advice [of] the political professionals is: Don't assume that your candidate's positions are going to make the difference. "In a competitive political climate," as one article explains, "informed citizens may vote for a candidate based on issues. However, uninformed or undecided voters will often choose the candidate whose name and packaging are most memorable. To make sure your candidate has that 'top-of-mind' voter awareness, a powerful logo is the best place to start." You want to present your candidate in language that voters will understand. They understand colors. "Blue is a positive color for men, signaling authority and control," another article advises. "But it's a negative color for women, who perceive it as distant, cold and aloof. Red is a warm, sentimental color for women—and a sign of danger or anger to men. If you use the wrong colors to the wrong audience, you're sending a mixed message."

It can't be the case, though, that electoral outcomes turn on things like the color of the buttons. Can it? When citizens stand in the privacy of the booth and contemplate the list of those who bid to serve, do they really think, That's the guy with the red logo. A lot of anger there. I'll take my chances with the other one? In Civics 101, the model voter is a citizen vested with the ability to understand the consequences of his or her choice; when these individual rational choices are added up, we know the will of the people. How accurate is this picture?

Skepticism about the competence of the masses to govern themselves is as old as mass self-government. Even so, when that competence began to be measured statistically, around the end of the Second World War, the numbers startled almost everyone. The data were interpreted most powerfully by the political scientist Philip Converse, in an article on "The Nature of Belief Systems in Mass Publics," published in 1964. Forty years later, Converse's conclusions are still the bones at which the science of voting behavior picks.

Converse claimed that only around ten per cent of the public has what can be called, even generously, a political belief system. He named these people "ideologues," by which he meant not that they are fanatics but that they have a reasonable grasp of "what goes with what"—of how a set of opinions adds up to a coherent political philosophy. Non-ideologues may use terms like "liberal" and "conservative," but Converse thought that they basically don't know what they're talking about, and that their beliefs are characterized by what he termed a lack of "constraint": they can't see how one opinion (that taxes should be lower, for example) logically ought to rule out other opinions (such as the belief that there should be more government programs). About forty-two per cent of voters, according to Converse's interpretation of surveys of the 1956 electorate, vote on the basis not of ideology but of perceived self-interest. The rest form political preferences either from their sense of whether times are good or bad (about twenty-five per cent) or from factors that have no discernible "issue content" whatever. Converse put twenty-two per cent of the electorate in this last category. In other words, about twice as many people have no political views as have a coherent political belief system.

Just because someone's opinions don't square with what a political scientist recognizes as a political ideology doesn't mean that those opinions aren't coherent by the lights of some more personal system of beliefs. But Converse found reason to doubt this possibility. When pollsters ask people for their opinion about an issue, people generally feel obliged to have one. Their answer is duly recorded, and it becomes a datum in a report on "public opinion." But, after analyzing the results of surveys conducted over time, in which people tended to give different and randomly inconsistent answers to the same questions, Converse concluded that "very substantial portions of the public" hold opinions that are essentially meaningless—off-the-top-of-the-head responses to questions they have never thought about, derived from no underlying set of principles. These people might as well base their political choices on the weather. And, in fact, many of them do.

Findings about the influence of the weather on voter behavior are among the many surveys and studies that confirm Converse's sense of the inattention of the American electorate. In election years from 1952 to 2000, when people were asked whether they cared who won the presidential election, between twenty-two and forty-four per cent answered "don't care" or "don't know." In 2000, eighteen per cent said that they decided which presidential candidate to vote for only in the last two weeks of the campaign; five per cent, enough to swing most elections, decided the day they voted.

Seventy per cent of Americans cannot name their senators or their congressman. Forty-nine per cent believe that the President has the power to suspend the Constitution. Only about thirty per cent name an issue when they explain why they voted the way they did, and only a fifth hold consistent opinions on issues over time. Rephrasing poll questions reveals that many people don't understand the issues that they have just offered an opinion on. According to polls conducted in 1987 and 1989, for example, between twenty and twenty-five per cent of the public thinks that too little is being spent on welfare, and between sixty-three and sixty-five per cent feels that too little is being spent on assistance to the poor. And voters apparently do punish politicians for acts of God. In a paper written in 2004, the Princeton political scientists Christopher Achen and Larry Bartels estimate that "2.8 million people voted against Al Gore in 2000 because their states were too dry or too wet" as a consequence of that year's weather patterns. Achen and Bartels think that these voters cost Gore seven states, any one of which would have given him the election.

All political systems make their claim to legitimacy by some theory, whether it's the divine right of kings or the iron law of history. Divine rights and iron laws are not subject to empirical confirmation, which is one reason that democracy's claims have always seemed superior. What polls and surveys suggest, though, is that the belief that elections express the true preferences of the people may be nearly as imaginary. When you move downward through what Converse called the public's "belief strata," candidates are quickly separated from ideology and issues, and they become attached, in voters' minds, to idiosyncratic clusters of ideas and attitudes. The most widely known fact about George H. W. Bush in the 1992 election was that he hated broccoli. Eighty-six per cent of likely voters in that election knew that the Bushes' dog's name was Millie; only fifteen per cent knew that Bush and Clinton both favored the death penalty. It's not that people know nothing. It's just that politics is not what they know.

In the face of this evidence, three theories have arisen. The first is that electoral outcomes, as far as "the will of the people" is concerned, are essentially arbitrary. The fraction of the electorate that responds to substantive political arguments is hugely outweighed by the fraction that responds to slogans, misinformation, "fire alarms" (sensational news), "October surprises" (last-minute sensational news), random personal associations, and "gotchas." Even when people think that they are thinking in political terms, even when they believe that they are analyzing candidates on the basis of their positions on issues, they are usually operating behind a veil of political ignorance. They simply don't understand, as a practical matter, what it means to be "fiscally conservative," or to have "faith in the private sector," or to pursue an "interventionist foreign policy." They can't hook up positions with policies. From the point of view of democratic theory, American political history is just a random walk through a series of electoral options. Some years, things turn up red; some years, they turn up blue.

A second theory is that although people may not be working with a full deck of information and beliefs, their preferences are dictated by something, and that something is elite opinion. Political campaigns, on this theory, are essentially struggles among the elite, the fraction of a fraction of voters who have the knowledge and the ideological chops to understand the substantive differences between the candidates and to argue their policy implications. These voters communicate their preferences to the rest of the electorate by various cues, low-content phrases and images (warm colors, for instance) to which voters can relate, and these cues determine the outcome of the race. Democracies are really oligarchies with a populist face.

The third theory of democratic politics is the theory that the cues to which most voters respond are, in fact, adequate bases on which to form political preferences. People use shortcuts—the social-scientific term is "heuristics"—to reach judgments about political candidates, and, on the whole, these shortcuts are as good as the long and winding road of reading party platforms, listening to candidate debates, and all the other elements of civic duty. Voters use what Samuel Popkin, one of the proponents of this third theory, calls "low-information rationality"—in other words, gut reasoning—to reach political decisions; and this intuitive form of judgment proves a good enough substitute for its high-information counterpart in reflecting what people want.

An analogy (though one that Popkin is careful to dissociate himself from) would be to buying an expensive item like a house or a stereo system. A tiny fraction of consumers has the knowledge to discriminate among the entire range of available stereo components, and to make an informed choice based on assessments of cost and performance. Most of us rely on the advice of two or three friends who have recently made serious stereo-system purchases, possibly some online screen shopping, and the pitch of the salesman at J&R Music World. We eyeball the product, associate idiosyncratically with the brand name, and choose from the gut. When we ask "experts" for their wisdom, mostly we are hoping for an "objective" ratification of our instinctive desire to buy the coolest-looking stuff. Usually, we're O.K. Our tacit calculation is that the marginal utility of more research is smaller than the benefit of immediate ownership.

On the theory of heuristics, it's roughly the same with candidates: voters don't have the time or the inclination to assess them in depth, so they rely on the advice of experts—television commentators, political activists, Uncle Charlie—combined with their own hunches, to reach a decision. Usually (they feel), they're O.K. If they had spent the time needed for a top-to-toe vetting, they would probably not have chosen differently. Some voters might get it wrong in one direction, choosing the liberal candidate when they in fact preferred a conservative one, but their error is cancelled out by the voters who mistakenly choose the conservative. The will of the people may not be terribly articulate, but it comes out in the wash.

This theory is the most attractive of the three, since it does the most to salvage democratic values from the electoral wreckage Converse described.

It gives the mass of voters credit for their decisions by suggesting not only that they can interpret the cues given by the campaigns and the elite opinion-makers but that the other heuristics they use—the candidate seems likable, times are not as good as they were—are actually defensible replacements for informed, logical reasoning. Popkin begins his well-regarded book on the subject, *The Reasoning Voter*, with an example from Gerald Ford's primary campaign against Ronald Reagan in 1976. Visiting a Mexican-American community in Texas, Ford (never a gaffe-free politician) made the mistake of trying to eat a tamale with the corn husk, in which it is traditionally served, still on it. This ethnic misprision made the papers, and when he was asked, after losing to Jimmy Carter in the general election, what the lesson of his defeat was, Ford answered, "Always shuck your tamales." Popkin argues that although familiarity with Mexican-American cuisine is not a prerequisite for favoring policies friendly to Mexican-Americans, Mexican-Americans were justified in concluding that a man who did not know how to eat a tamale was not a man predisposed to put their needs high on his list. The reasoning is illogical: Ford was not running for chef, and it was possible to extrapolate, from his positions, the real difference it would make for Mexican-Americans if he were President rather than Reagan or Carter. But Mexican-Americans, and their sympathizers, felt "in their gut" that Ford was not their man, and that was enough.

The principal shortcut that people use in deciding which candidates to vote for is, of course, the political party. The party is the ultimate Uncle Charlie in American politics. Even elite voters use it when they are confronted, in the voting booth, with candidates whose names they have never seen before. There is nothing in the Constitution requiring candidates to be listed on the ballot with their party affiliations, and, if you think about it, the custom of doing so is vaguely undemocratic. It makes elections a monopoly of the major parties, by giving their candidates an enormous advantage—the advantage of an endorsement right there on the ballot—over everyone else who runs. It is easy to imagine a constitutional challenge to the practice of identifying candidates by party, but it is also easy to imagine how wild the effects would be if voters were confronted by a simple list of names with no identifying tags. Every election would be like an election for student-body president: pure name recognition.

Any time information is lacking or uncertain, a shortcut is generally better than nothing. But the shortcut itself is not a faster way of doing the math; it's a way of skipping the math altogether. My hunch that the coolest-looking stereo component is the best value simply does not reflect an intuitive grasp of electronics. My interest in a stereo is best served if I choose the finest sound for the money, as my interest in an election is best served if I choose the candidate whose policies are most likely to benefit me or the people I care about. But almost no one calculates in so abstract a fashion. Even voters who supported Michael Dukakis in 1988 agreed that he looked ridiculous wearing a weird helmet when he went for a ride in a tank, and a lot of those people felt that, taken together with other evidence of his manner and style of self-expression, the image was not irrelevant to the substance of his campaign. George H. W. Bush underwent a similar moment in 1992, when he was caught showing astonishment at the existence of scanners at supermarket checkout counters. Ideologues opposed to Bush were pleased to propose this as what psychologists call a "fast and frugal" means of assessing the likely effects of his economic policies.

When political scientists interpret these seat-of-the-pants responses as signs that voters are choosing rationally, and that representative government therefore really does reflect the will of the people, they are, in effect, making a heuristic of heuristics. They are not doing the math. Doing the math would mean demonstrating that the voters' intuitive judgments are roughly what they would get if they analyzed the likely effects of candidates' policies, and this is a difficult calculation to perform. One shortcut that voters take, and that generally receives approval from the elite, is pocketbook voting. If they are feeling flush, they vote for the incumbent; if they are feeling strapped, they vote for a change. But, as Larry Bartels, the co-author of the paper on Gore and the weather, has pointed out, pocketbook voting would be rational only if it could be shown that replacing the incumbent did lead, on average, to better economic times. Without such a demonstration, a vote based on the condition of one's pocketbook is no more rational than a vote based on the condition of one's lawn. It's a hunch.

Bartels has also found that when people do focus on specific policies they are often unable to distinguish their own interests. His work, which he summed up in a recent article for *The American Prospect*, concerned public opinion about the estate tax. When people are asked whether they favor Bush's policy of repealing the estate tax, two-thirds say yes—even though the estate tax affects only the wealthiest one or two per cent of the population. Ninety-eight per cent of Americans do not leave estates large enough for the tax to kick in. But people have some notion—Bartels refers to it as "unenlightened self-interest"—that they will be better off if the tax is repealed. What is most remarkable about this opinion is that it is unconstrained by other beliefs. Repeal is supported by sixty-six per cent of people who believe that the income gap between the richest and the poorest Americans has increased in recent decades, and that this is a bad thing. And it's supported by sixty-eight per cent of people who say that the rich pay too little in taxes. Most Americans simply do not make a connection between tax policy and the overall economic condition of the country. Whatever heuristic they are using, it is definitely not doing the math for them. This helps make sense of the fact that the world's greatest democracy has an electorate that continually "chooses" to transfer more and more wealth to a smaller and smaller fraction of itself.

But who *ever* does the math? As Popkin points out, everybody uses heuristics, including the elite. Most of the debate among opinion-makers is conducted in shorthand, and even well-informed voters rely on endorsements and party affiliations to make their choices. The very essence of being an ideologue lies in trusting the label—liberal or conservative, Republican or Democrat. Those are "bundling" terms: they pull together a dozen positions on individual issues under a single handy rubric. They do the work of assessment for you.

It is widely assumed that the upcoming [2004] Presidential election will be decided by an electorate that is far more ideological than has historically been the case. Polls indicate much less volatility than usual, supporting the view that the public is divided into starkly antagonistic camps—the "red state-blue state" paradigm. If this is so, it suggests that we have at last moved past Converse's picture of an electoral iceberg, in which ninety per cent of the population is politically underwater. But Morris Fiorina, a political scientist at Stanford, thinks that it is not so, and that the polarized electorate is a product of elite opinion. "The simple truth is that there is no culture war in the United States—no battle for the soul of America rages, at least none that most Americans are aware of," he says in his short book *Culture War? The Myth of a Polarized America. . . .* Public-opinion polls, he argues, show that on most hot-button issues voters in so-called red states do not differ significantly from voters in so-called blue states. Most people identify themselves as moderates, and their responses to survey questions seem to substantiate this self-description. What has become polarized, Fiorina argues, is the elite. The chatter—among political activists, commentators, lobbyists, movie stars, and so on—has become highly ideological. It's a non-stop *Crossfire*, and this means that the candidates themselves come wrapped in more extreme ideological coloring. But Fiorina points out that the ideological position of a candidate is not identical to the position of the people who vote for him or her. He suggests that people generally vote for the candidate whose views strike them as closest to their own, and "closest" is a relative term. With any two candidates, no matter how far out, one will always be "closer" than the other.

Of course, if Converse is correct, and most voters really don't have meaningful political beliefs, even ideological "closeness" is an artifact of survey anxiety, of people's felt need, when they are asked for an opinion, to have one. This absence of "real opinions" is not from lack of brains; it's from lack of interest. "The typical citizen drops down to a lower level of mental performance as soon as he enters the political field," the economic theorist Joseph Schumpeter wrote, in 1942. "He argues and analyzes in a way which he would readily recognize as infantile within the sphere of his real interests. He becomes a primitive again. His thinking is associative and affective." And Fiorina quotes a passage from the political scientist Robert Putnam: "Most men are not political animals. The world of public affairs is not their world. It is alien to them—possibly benevolent, more probably threatening, but nearly always alien. Most men are not interested in politics. Most do not participate in politics."

Man may not be a political animal, but he is certainly a social animal. Voters do respond to the cues of commentators and campaigners, but only when they can match those cues up with the buzz of their own social group. Individual voters are not rational calculators of self-interest (nobody truly is), and may not be very consistent users of heuristic shortcuts, either. But they are not just random particles bouncing off the walls of the voting booth. Voters go into the booth carrying the imprint of the hopes and fears, the prejudices and assumptions of their family, their friends, and their neighbors. For most people, voting may be more meaningful and more understandable as a social act than as a political act.

That it is hard to persuade some people with ideological arguments does not mean that those people cannot be persuaded, but the things that help to convince them are likely to make ideologues sick—things like which candidate is more optimistic. For many liberals, it may have been dismaying to listen to John Kerry and John Edwards, in their speeches at the Democratic National Convention, utter impassioned bromides about how "the sun is rising" and "our best days are still to come." But that is what a very large number of voters want to hear. If they believe it, then Kerry and Edwards will get their votes. The ideas won't matter, and neither will the color of the buttons.

DISCUSSION QUESTIONS

1. What information shortcuts do you think would be reasonable to use when making voting decisions?

2. Menand is concerned that voters' heuristics might not be reliable if voters actually "did the math." What heuristics do you think might be particularly unreliable guides to voting choices?

3. What, if any, risks are posed to the American political system if voters base their decisions on information shortcuts? Which of the three theories discussed by Menand would be the most troubling for democracy, in your view?

51

"Telling Americans to Vote, or Else"

William Galston

Observers of American politics have long lamented the relatively low rate of election turnout in the United States. Nationally, turnout in presidential elections dropped gradually after 1960 before ticking up in 2004 and 2008. Depending on the measure used, the rate in those two elections ranged from about 55 percent to 62 percent—higher in some states, lower in others. Turnout dropped in 2012. Midterm congressional races and most state-level elections and local contests see even lower turnout. Many propositions have been put forward to explain low turnout, and more have been offered as ways to increase turnout. Among others, these include making voter registration easier, allowing registration on the day of the election, offering more absentee voting or early in-person voting options, extending voting hours on Election Day, and making Election Day a national holiday. William Galston contends that another option should be considered: mandatory voting. Galston reports that mandatory voting is employed in over thirty countries, about half with an enforcement mechanism such as a small fine. The results on turnout, he states, have been positive and significant. Writing in 2011, he argues that mandatory voting has three advantages: it would strengthen the concept of citizenship by reminding citizens that there are responsibilities that go along with rights; it would reduce the skews in turnout across groups, so that the electorate on Election Day better reflected the composition of the population; and it would reduce polarization in American politics by enticing middle-of-the-road voters back to the voting booth. Despite the advantages he claims for mandatory voting, Galston recognizes that America's individualistic and libertarian ways of thinking make the concept a difficult one to sell in the United States.

Jury duty is mandatory; why not voting? The idea seems vaguely un-American. Maybe so, but it's neither unusual nor undemocratic. And it would ease the intense partisan polarization that weakens our capacity for self-government and public trust in our governing institutions.

Thirty-one countries have some form of mandatory voting, according to the International Institute for Democracy and Electoral Assistance. The list includes nine members of the Organization for Economic Cooperation and Development and two-thirds of the Latin American nations. More than half back up the legal requirement with an enforcement mechanism, while the rest are content to rely on the moral force of the law.

Despite the prevalence of mandatory voting in so many democracies, it's easy to dismiss the practice as a form of statism that couldn't work in America's individualistic and libertarian political culture. But consider Australia, whose political culture is closer to that of the United States than that of any other English-speaking country. Alarmed by a decline in voter turnout to less than 60 percent in 1922, Australia adopted mandatory voting in 1924, backed by small fines (roughly the size of traffic tickets) for nonvoting, rising with repeated acts of nonparticipation. The law established permissible reasons for not voting, like illness and foreign travel, and allows citizens who faced fines for not voting to defend themselves.

The results were remarkable. In the 1925 election, the first held under the new law, turnout soared to 91 percent. In recent elections, it has hovered around 95 percent. The law also changed civic norms. Australians are more likely than before to see voting as an obligation. The negative side effects many feared did not materialize. For example, the percentage of ballots intentionally spoiled or completed randomly as acts of resistance remained on the order of 2 to 3 percent.

Proponents offer three reasons in favor of mandatory voting. The first is straightforwardly civic. A democracy can't be strong if its citizenship is weak. And right now American citizenship is attenuated—strong on rights, weak on responsibilities. There is less and less that being a citizen requires of us, especially after the abolition of the draft. Requiring people to vote in national elections once every two years would reinforce the principle of reciprocity at the heart of citizenship.

The second argument for mandatory voting is democratic. Ideally, a democracy will take into account the interests and views of all citizens. But if some regularly vote while others don't, officials are likely to give greater weight to participants. This might not matter much if nonparticipants were evenly distributed through the population. But political scientists have long known that they aren't. People with lower levels of income and education are less likely to vote, as are young adults and recent first-generation immigrants.

Changes in our political system have magnified these disparities. During the 1950s and '60s, when turnout rates were much higher, political parties reached out to citizens year-round. At the local level these parties, which reformers often criticized as "machines," connected even citizens of modest means and limited education with neighborhood institutions and gave them a sense of participation in national politics as well. (In its heyday, organized labor reinforced these effects.) But in the absence of these more organic forms of political mobilization, the second-best option is a top-down mechanism of universal mobilization.

Mandatory voting would tend to even out disparities stemming from income, education and age, enhancing our system's inclusiveness. It is true, as some object, that an enforcement mechanism would impose greater burdens on those with fewer resources. But this makes it all the more likely that these citizens would respond by going to the polls, and they would stand to gain far more than the cost of a traffic ticket.

The third argument for mandatory voting goes to the heart of our current ills. Our low turnout rate pushes American politics toward increased polarization. The reason is that hardcore partisans are more likely to dominate lower-turnout elections, while those who are less fervent about specific issues and less attached to political organizations tend not to participate at levels proportional to their share of the electorate.

A distinctive feature of our constitutional system—elections that are quadrennial for president but biennial for the House of Representatives—magnifies these effects. It's bad enough that only three-fifths of the electorate turns out to determine the next president, but much worse that only two-fifths of our citizens vote in House elections two years later. If events combine to energize one part of the political spectrum and dishearten the other, a relatively small portion of the electorate can shift the system out of all proportion to its numbers.

Some observers are comfortable with this asymmetry. But if you think that today's intensely polarized politics impedes governance and exacerbates mistrust—and that is what most Americans firmly (and in my view rightly) believe—then you should be willing to consider reforms that, would strengthen the forces of conciliation.

Imagine our politics with laws and civic norms that yield near-universal voting. Campaigns could devote far less money to costly, labor-intensive get-out-the-vote efforts. Media gurus wouldn't have the same incentive to drive down turnout with negative advertising. Candidates would know that they must do more than mobilize their bases with red-meat rhetoric on hot-button issues. Such a system would improve not only electoral politics but also the legislative process. Rather than focusing on symbolic gestures whose major purpose is to agitate partisans, Congress might actually roll up its sleeves and tackle the serious, complex issues it ignores.

The United States is not Australia, of course, and there's no guarantee that the similarity of our political cultures would produce equivalent political results. For example, reforms of general elections would leave untouched the distortions generated by party primaries in which small numbers of voters can shape the choices for the entire electorate. And the United States Constitution gives the states enormous power over voting procedures. Mandating voting nationwide would go counter to our traditions (and perhaps our Constitution) and would encounter strong state opposition. Instead, a half-dozen states from parts of the country with different civic traditions should experiment with the practice, and observers—journalists, social scientists, citizens' groups and elected officials—would monitor the consequences.

We don't know what the outcome would be. But one thing is clear: If we do nothing and allow a politics of passion to define the bounds of the electorate, as it has for much of the last four decades, the prospect for a less polarized, more effective political system that enjoys the trust and confidence of the people is not bright.

Discussion Questions

1. How convinced are you that mandatory voting would have the benefits identified by Galston? Are there other benefits that might result?

2. Would mandatory voting create problems? If so, what might these be?

3. Should voting be considered a responsibility in the same sense that jury duty is considered a responsibility?

Debating the Issues: Voter Identification

Recent national elections have raised many concerns about the voting system and the standards for administering elections in the United States. Charges of impropriety in voting procedures and vote counting, as well as complaints that certain voting technologies were systematically likely to produce more voter error or not accurately record voter choices, were legion. Massive voter mobilization campaigns on both the political left and right registered millions of new voters. Huge sums were poured into campaign advertising, further stoking the interest of these newly registered voters and the public in general. In such a charged political environment, concerns about the integrity of the process took on a particular urgency. One issue on which battle lines are frequently drawn is voter identification, especially requiring voters to show a photo ID. In 2012, thirty states required some form of identification, with eleven of those states requiring photo ID. Several other states had photo ID laws that were on hold pending legal challenges and U.S. Department of Justice investigations.

One argument, presented here by Chandler Davidson, contends that these complaints about fraud are part of a strategy to discourage or scare away potential voters. Voter ID laws are most likely to restrict turnout among minorities and the elderly, and the threat of fraud is minimal. To Davidson, voter ID laws are intended to promote the fortunes of the Republican Party and are little different from other attempts to suppress voter turnout, such as the poll tax.

The opposing argument, presented here by Hans von Spakovsky, is that voter fraud is a reality. He points to voters registered in multiple locations, voting more than once, illegally registered, paid an inducement to vote, and to felons voting as symptomatic of the lack of control over the voting process. Spakovsky supports voter-ID laws and rejects the idea that they will systematically discriminate against minorities or other groups.

Edward Foley argues that conservatives and liberals both have valid points. Even if voting fraud is minimal, he writes, it is real and should be a concern, as conservatives argue. Similarly, liberals are right to be concerned that the cost of obtaining a photo ID might discourage some citizens from voting. Foley suggests the solution is to delink the photo ID from voting. Instead, potential voters would be able to get free digital photos from government offices if they do not have one. They would have to show this photo when they register to vote. When a voter arrives at the polls to vote, poll workers could pull up an electronic file of the photo and match it to the person standing in front of them. This solution, Foley argues, ensures that anyone who wants to register can, while also guaranteeing that the person voting at the polling place is the same person who is registered under that name.

52

"The Historical Context of Voter Photo-ID Laws"

Chandler Davidson

The issue before the U.S. Supreme Court in the *Crawford* case (*Crawford v. Marion County Election Bd.* 2008) was whether a law (Indiana Senate Enrolled Act No. 483) passed by the Indiana legislature requiring most voters to show a photo ID in order to cast a ballot violates the First and Fourteenth Amendments. Plaintiffs argued that it works an unfair hardship on many people who do not have the government-issued documents that count as a legitimate ID. They argued that the law, in effect, constitutes a poll tax, inasmuch as there are costs to obtain the right kind of photo ID, costs that unduly burden many eligible citizens wanting to exercise their right to vote.

Given the long history of legally sanctioned disfranchisement of large and disparate groups of citizens, from the founding of the Republic to the recent past, the case raised important questions to scholars of voting rights. Indeed, Indiana's new law brought to mind events during the half-century following the Civil War, when the language of "progressive reform" cloaked the disfranchisement of blacks and poor whites in the South—those most likely to vote for Republican or Populist candidates. Actually adopted for partisan and racially discriminatory purposes, these laws were often presented as high-minded attacks on fraud—efforts to "purify" the electorate that would only inconvenience "vote sellers" or the ignorant and "shiftless."

To be sure, unlike today, when proponents of voter identification must strain mightily to find the rarest examples of fraud, particularly in-person voter fraud at the polls, in the nineteenth century there was widespread and readily admitted fraud. However, this was often committed against African Americans and the Republican Party to which they then overwhelmingly adhered. Louisiana senator and former governor Samuel D. McEnery stated in 1898 that his state's 1882 election law "was intended to make it the duty of the governor to treat the law as a formality and count in the Democrats." A leader of the 1890 Mississippi constitutional convention admitted that "it is no secret that there has not been a full vote and a fair count in Mississippi since 1875," which was the last year until 1967 in which blacks voted at all freely in the state. Nonetheless, these same Democrats invoked the language of reform in calling for a wide range of restrictions on the suffrage: registration acts, poll taxes, literacy and property tests, "understanding" qualifications, and white primaries, among others.

Between 1889 and 1913, for example, nine states outside the South made the ability to read English a prerequisite for voting. Literacy tests were said to reduce the influence of immigrants or African Americans who supported "bosses" and "demagogues." Moreover, between 1890 and 1908, seven of the 11 ex-Confederate states adopted state constitutional amendments allowing only literate voters or those with a certain amount of property to vote. There were sometimes loopholes like "understanding" qualifications or "grandfather" clauses that allowed some whites to vote who could not meet literacy or property tests. Shortly after passage of these amendments, less than 10% of African Americans managed to register to vote in most states, and no more than 15% in any.

The poll tax was one of the most notorious disfranchising mechanisms of its day. The current debate over the Indiana photo-ID requirement—as well as similar laws in other states—has led to claims that they are a "modern-day poll tax." This implies that the new Indiana law, too, falls within the ignominious American tradition of disfranchising laws passed under the guise of "good government" reform.

Frederick Ogden, perhaps the foremost scholar of the poll tax, wrote in the 1950s: "While critics of legalized restrictions on Negro voting may find it hard to discover any high moral tone in such activities, these restrictions reflected a movement for purifying the electoral process in southern states." Ogden quotes the editor of the *San Antonio Express* writing in 1902: "By requiring a poll tax receipt, secured six months previous to an election, fraudulent elections can be prevented almost entirely."

Other essays in this symposium address the nature and extent of burdens imposed on various subsets of Indiana citizens by the photo-ID law, and I shall forgo discussing them. Suffice it to say that the most accessible photo-ID in Indiana consists either of the state's driver's license or a state-issued ID card. Obtaining one or the other has been shown to be a good deal more difficult for some people than it might seem at first glance. At least 43,000 persons of voting age in Indiana are estimated to have neither.

The demographic characteristics of persons lacking the requisite ID are suggested by a November 2006 telephone survey of 987 randomly selected voting-age American citizens by the independent Opinion Research Corporation conducted for the Brennan Center for Justice at NYU School of Law: 11% did not have valid government-issued photo ID, while 18% of citizens 65 years of age or older lacked it, as did 25% of African Americans. The latter two demographic groups, the elderly and African Americans, are more likely to self-identify as Democrats—African-Americans disproportionately so. Elderly African Americans, who are even more unlikely than members of their ethnic group in general to have a photo

ID, would be strongly predisposed to vote Democratic. In close elections, the additional burdens placed on both the elderly and African Americans by the photo-ID law could help elect Republican candidates. There is no reason to believe this national pattern is much different from that in Indiana.

Nonetheless, it is often asserted that such barriers should not prevent a truly motivated citizen from voting. In a classic article by Kelley, Ayres, and Bowen attempting to measure determinants of voter turnout, the authors make the following observation:

> A frequent objection to such efforts [to get out the vote] is that voters not interested enough to vote are not apt to vote wisely and so should be left alone. This view recalls the statement of a New York voter regarding the adequacy of the facilities for registering in New York City in 1964: "I sure do want to vote against that man . . . but I don't think I hate him enough to stand on that line all day long." How much interest should a voter have to qualify him for voting? Enough to stand in line all day? For half a day? For two days? We cannot say, but those who think voting should be limited to the "interested" ought to be prepared to do so.

Their question, posed in terms of the burden of time alone, can also be posed with regard to money: particularly concerning the least well off, how large a monetary imposition should be placed on the right to vote before it becomes the functional equivalent of a poll tax? Regarding these twin burdens, two questions may be posed to help determine whether the Indiana photo-ID law should be interpreted according to the good-government language of its proponents: First, how will the application of the law help shape the Indiana electorate "to a size and composition deemed desirable by those in power," as Kelley, Ayres, and Bowen put it? In other words, to what extent is the law motivated by partisan efforts to disfranchise voters who are undesirable to Republicans and thus increase their chances of winning elections? Second, did supporters of the law demonstrate a significant degree of fraud of the kind the law was fashioned to prevent? Let us consider each question in turn.

While it is impossible to know the motives of those lawmakers who favored the photo-ID bill under consideration by the Indiana legislature in April 2005, we can ascertain whether it was passed by a partisan vote. Significantly, Indiana's photo-ID bill was one of at least 10 bills introduced by Republicans in state legislatures between 2005 and 2007 requiring voters to show a photo ID at the polls. Two of these states' bills were initially enjoined, and a second bill was introduced in one state. (Besides Indiana, the other states included Georgia, Florida, Missouri, Kansas, New Hampshire, Pennsylvania, Texas, and Wisconsin.) If the House and Senate votes for all 10 proposals are combined, 95.3% of the 1,222 Republicans voting and 2.1% of the 796 Democrats voting supported the bills. Moreover, in the five cases in which both houses passed a bill and a Republican was governor, he signed it. In the three cases in which both houses passed a bill and a Democrat was governor, he vetoed it. (In two cases, only one house passed a bill.) The Indiana vote was part of this pattern, although even more extreme. In the vote on Senate Bill 483, 85 Republicans voted for it and none against; 62 Democrats voted against it and none in favor. The Republican governor signed the bill into law.

Did supporters of the law demonstrate that there is a significant degree of fraud of the kind the law was fashioned to prevent? The debate over the extent and kind of vote fraud that exists in the United States today has been widespread and acerbic at least since the 2000 presidential election, and it shows no signs of abating. There are numerous kinds of vote fraud, and distinctions among them—which are necessary to determine the most effective means of their prevention—are often lost in popular debate. As critics of the Indiana law have asserted, the photo-ID requirement was implemented to prevent one type of fraud: voter impersonation at the polls on Election Day. Among the many kinds it does not prevent is that involving mail-in ballots, which some believe to be more common than impersonation at the polls. What makes the statute particularly suspect in the case of Indiana is the fact that there has not been a single prosecution for in-person vote fraud in the history of the state—a fact that Richard Posner, judge on the U.S. Court of Appeals for the Seventh Circuit and author of that court's split decision favoring Indiana, attributed to lax law enforcement.

Recent events in Texas are relevant in this regard. In both 2005 and 2007 Republicans in the legislature introduced photo-ID bills less restrictive than that in Indiana. In 2007, according to a newspaper reporter: "Republicans like the voter ID bill because they believe it will weaken Democrats, but can argue that it is a reasonable requirement" because it would prevent vote fraud. Not all Republicans, however, shared the belief that it would curtail fraud. Royal Masset, former political director of the Texas Republican Party, was one. He told the reporter he agreed that among his fellow Republicans it was "an article of religious faith that voter fraud is causing us to lose elections." He was not convinced. He did believe, however, that requiring photo IDs could cause enough of a drop-off in legitimate Democratic voting to add 3% to the Republican vote.

In January 2006, after his party's first failure to pass a photo-ID bill, Greg Abbott, the Republican attorney general of Texas, announced a "training initiative to identify, prosecute [and] prevent voter fraud." This was the most ambitious and costly effort in recent Texas history—perhaps ever—by the state's government to attack the alleged problem. "Vote fraud has been an epidemic in Texas for years, but it hasn't been treated like one," Abbott said. "It's time for that to change." He promised that his newly created Special Investigations Unit (SIU) would "help police departments, sheriff's offices, and district and county attorneys successfully identify, investigate and prosecute various types of voter fraud offences." Established with a $1.5 million grant from the governor's office, the SIU would have as one of its prime responsibilities investigating voter-fraud allegations, he said. Abbott targeted 44 counties containing 78% of registered voters in the state. According to the *Austin American-Statesman,* "Complaints originate from voting officials, district attorneys or citizens and are sent to the secretary of state or the attorney general. Each complaint is evaluated by a professional employee to determine whether the complaint is legitimate and warrants further investigation."

Such an initiative would seem to constitute a model of the aggressive, responsible, multi-level law-enforcement effort that Judge Posner seemed to believe had been lacking in Indiana. Moreover, given Republicans' desire to provide evidence of widespread voter fraud in order to justify new statutes criticized by Democrats and some media sources, one would expect Abbott to have conducted the effort with enthusiasm. What has been the result?

Texas is a large state, with thousands of elections occurring in a four-year period in its numerous governmental units. In 2006, there were 16.6 million persons of voting age, and of those, 13.1 million were registered to vote. An anti-immigration organization estimated that 1.7 million Texas inhabitants resided there illegally in 2007. Given these facts, one would expect an aggressive, centralized vote-fraud initiative by the state's highest law-enforcement officer to yield a sizable number of indictments during the more than 21 months of its existence if, in fact, vote fraud had reached "epidemic" proportions.

The data presented by Attorney General Abbot on his Web site told a different story. In the almost two years between the day the initiative was announced in late January 2006 and October 2007, 13 persons had either been indicted, found guilty, or sentenced for vote fraud, six on misdemeanor counts typically involving helping others with mail-in ballots. Of the 13, five were accused of having committed fraud before 2006, the year the initiative was announced, and the remaining eight in 2006. A total of 4.4 million Texans voted in the general elections for governor or U.S. senator that year, in addition to those who voted in primaries and local nonpartisan elections. At that point, six of the 13 persons mentioned above had not yet been found guilty. This, then, is the extent of vote fraud in Texas that has been uncovered after the announcement and implementation of the $1.5 million vote-fraud initiative. Moreover, of the seven found guilty and the six remaining under indictment, *none of the types of fraud they had been charged with would have been prevented by the photo-ID requirement advocated by Republicans in the 2007 legislative session.* That is to say, none involved voter impersonation at the polls. Most either involved political officials who were charged with engaging in illegal efforts to affect the election outcome, or persons who helped elderly or disabled friends with their mail-in ballots, apparently unaware of a law passed in 2003 requiring them to sign the envelope containing the friend's ballot before mailing it.

These data do not appear to be anomalous. A survey of the director or deputy director of all 88 Ohio boards of election in June 2005 found that a total of only four votes cast in the state's general elections in 2002 and 2004 (in which over nine million votes were cast) were judged ineligible and thus likely constituted actual voter fraud. Interviews by *New York Times* reporters with election-law-enforcement officials and academic experts suggest that the pattern in Ohio is not anomalous. Professor Richard L. Hasen, an election law expert at Loyola Law School, summed up knowledgeable opinion about vote fraud to the reporters as follows: "what we see is isolated, small-scale activities that often have not shown any kind of criminal intent."

While it is possible, as Judge Posner implied in his Seventh Circuit decision, that aggressive vote-fraud enforcement in Indiana might uncover its existence in the state, the Texas investigation suggests otherwise, and the burden of proof rests on those who allege that vote fraud there is widespread and of the kind that is deterred by a photo-ID requirement. Until that burden is responsibly shouldered by state authorities, the question of whether the Indiana voter-ID law has accomplished its ostensible purpose must be answered in the negative. When this conclusion is placed alongside our earlier findings that the legislative vote for the law was strictly along partisan lines and that the people most likely to be disfranchised by it are Democratic voters—particularly African Americans—Indiana's law appears to fit comfortably within the long and unsavory history of those in positions of power disfranchising blacks and less-well-off whites for partisan gain. Moreover, Indiana's attempt to justify its new law with claims of voter fraud is as dubious as those that justified the now unconstitutional poll tax.

A great deal of progress has been made over the past 50 years in combating racial discrimination in politics, thanks in part to such epochal events as passage of the Twenty-Fourth Amendment and the Voting Rights Act. However, race, class, and partisanship continue to be inextricably intertwined in the United States, just as they were from the end of Reconstruction to the Civil Rights Era. The 2005 Indiana voter-ID law, if the above analysis is correct, is an excellent example of this fact.

53

"Requiring Identification by Voters"

Hans von Spakovsky

Testimony Before the Texas Senate
Delivered March 10, 2009

I appreciate the invitation to be here today to discuss the importance of states such as Texas requiring individuals to authenticate their identity at the polls through photo and other forms of identification.

By way of background, I have extensive experience in voting matters, including both the administration of elections and the enforcement of federal voting rights laws. Prior to becoming a Legal Scholar at the Heritage Foundation, I was a member for two years of the Federal Election Commission. I spent four years at the Department of Justice as a career lawyer, including as Counsel to the Assistant Attorney General for Civil Rights. I also spent five years in Atlanta, Georgia, on the Fulton County Board of Registration and Elections, which is responsible for administering elections in the largest county in Georgia, a county that is almost half African American. I have published extensively on election and voting issues, including on the subject of voter ID.

Guaranteeing the integrity of elections requires having security throughout the entire election process, from voter registration to the casting of votes to the counting of ballots at the end of the day when the polls have closed. For example, jurisdictions that use paper ballots seal their ballot boxes when all of the ballots have been deposited, and election officials have step-by-step procedures for securing election ballots and other materials throughout the election process.

I doubt any of you think that it would be a good idea for a county to allow world wide Internet access to the computer it uses in its election headquarters to tabulate ballots and count votes—we are today a computer-literate generation and you understand that allowing that kind of outside access to the software used for counting votes would imperil the integrity of the election.

Requiring voters to authenticate their identity at the polling place is part and parcel of the same kind of security necessary to protect the integrity of elections. Every illegal vote steals the vote of a legitimate voter. Voter ID can prevent:

- impersonation fraud at the polls;
- voting under fictitious voter registrations;
- double voting by individuals registered in more than one state or locality; and
- voting by illegal aliens.

As the Commission on Federal Election Reform headed by President Jimmy Carter and Secretary of State James Baker said in 2005:

> The electoral system cannot inspire public confidence if no safeguards exist to deter or detect fraud or to confirm the identity of voters. Photo identification cards currently are needed to board a plane, enter federal buildings, and cash a check. Voting is equally important.

Voter fraud does exist, and criminal penalties imposed after the fact are an insufficient deterrent to protect against it. In the Supreme Court's voter ID case decided last year, the Court said that despite such criminal penalties:

> It remains true, however, that flagrant examples of such fraud in other parts of the country have been documented throughout this Nation's history by respected historians and journalists, that occasional examples have surfaced in recent years, and that [they] demonstrate that not only is the risk of voter fraud real but that it could affect the outcome of a close election.

The relative rarity of voter fraud prosecutions for impersonation fraud at the polls, as the Seventh Circuit Court of Appeals pointed out in the Indiana case, can be explained in part because the fraud cannot be detected without the tools—a voter ID—available to detect it. However, as I pointed out in a paper published by the Heritage Foundation last year, a grand jury in New York released a report in the mid-1980s detailing a widespread voter fraud conspiracy involving impersonation fraud at the polls that operated successfully for 14 years in Brooklyn without detection. That fraud resulted in thousands of fraudulent votes being cast in state and congressional elections and involved not only impersonation of legitimate voters at the polls, but voting under fictitious names that had been successfully registered without detection by local election officials. This fraud could have been easily stopped and detected if New York had required voters to authenticate their identity at the polls. According to the grand jury, the advent of mail-in registration was also a key factor in perpetrating the fraud. In recent elections, thousands of fraudulent voter registration forms have been detected by election officials. But given the minimal to nonexistent screening efforts engaged in by most election jurisdictions, there is no way to know how many others slipped through. In states without identification requirements, election officials have no way to prevent bogus votes from being cast by unscrupulous individuals based on fictitious voter registrations.

The problem of possible double voting by someone who is registered in two states is illustrated by one of the Indiana voters who was highlighted by the League of Women Voters in their amicus brief before the Supreme Court in the Indiana case. After an Indiana newspaper interviewed her, it turned out that the problems she encountered voting in Indiana stemmed from her trying to use a Florida driver's license to vote in Indiana. Not only did she have a Florida driver's license, but she was also registered to vote in Florida where she owned a second home. In fact, she had claimed residency in Florida by claiming a homestead exemption on her property taxes, which as you know is normally only available to residents. So the Indiana law worked perfectly as intended to prevent someone who could have illegally voted twice without detection.

I don't want to single out Texas, but just like Indiana, New York, and Illinois, Texas has a long and unfortunate history of voter fraud. In the late 1800s, for example, Harrison County was so infamous for its massive election fraud that the phrase "Harrison County Methods" became synonymous with election fraud. From Ballot Box 13 in Lyndon Johnson's 1948 Senate race, to recent reports of voting by illegal aliens in Bexar County, Texas does have individuals who are willing to risk criminal prosecution in order to win elections. I do not claim that there is massive voter fraud in Texas or anywhere else. In fact, as a former election official, I think we do a good job overall in administering our elections. But the potential for abuse exists, and there are many close elections that could turn on a very small number of votes. There are enough incidents of voter fraud to make it very clear that we must take the steps necessary to make it hard to commit. Requiring voter ID is just one such common sense step.

Not only does voter ID help prevent fraudulent voting, but where it has been implemented, it has not reduced turnout. There is no evidence that voter ID decreases the turnout of voters or has a disparate impact on minority voters, the poor, or the elderly—the overwhelming majority of Americans have photo ID or can easily obtain one.

Numerous studies have borne this out. A study by a University of Missouri professor of turnout in Indiana showed that turnout actually increased by about two percentage points overall in Indiana after the voter ID law went into effect. There was no evidence that counties with higher percentages of minority, poor, elderly or less-educated populations suffered any reduction in voter turnout. In fact, "the only consistent and statistically significant impact of photo ID in Indiana is to increase voter turnout in counties with a greater percentage of Democrats relative to other counties."

The Heritage Foundation released a study in September of 2007 that analyzed 2004 election turnout data for all states. It found that voter ID laws do not reduce the turnout of voters, including African Americans and Hispanics—such voters were just as likely to vote in states with ID as in states where just their name was asked at the polling place.

A study by professors at the Universities of Delaware and Nebraska–Lincoln examined data from the 2000, 2002, 2004, and 2006 elections. At both the aggregate and individual levels, the study found that voter ID laws do not affect turnout including across racial/ethnic/socioeconomic lines. The study concluded that "concerns about voter identification laws affecting turnout are much ado about nothing."

In 2007 as part of the MIT/CalTech Voter Project, an MIT professor did an extensive national survey of 36,500 individuals about Election Day practices. The survey found:

- overwhelming support for photo ID requirements across ethnic and racial lines with "over 70% of Whites, Hispanics and Blacks support[ing] the requirement"; and
- Only twenty-three people out of the entire 36,500 person sample said that they were not allowed to vote because of voter ID, although the survey did not indicate whether they were even eligible to vote or used provisional ballots.

A similar study by John Lott in 2006 also found no effect on voter turnout, and in fact, found an indication that efforts to reduce voter fraud such as voter ID may have a positive impact on voter turnout. That is certainly true in a case study of voter fraud in Greene County, Alabama that I wrote about recently for the Heritage Foundation. In that county, voter turnout went up after several successful voter fraud prosecutions instilled new confidence in local voters in the integrity of the election process.

Recent election results in Georgia and Indiana also confirm that the suppositions that voter ID will hurt minority turnout are incorrect. Turnout in both states went up dramatically in 2008 in both the presidential preference primary and the general election.

In Georgia, there was record turnout in the 2008 presidential primary election—over 2 million voters, more than twice as much as in 2004 when the voter photo ID law was not in effect. The number of African-Americans voting in the 2008 primary also doubled from 2004. In fact, there were 100,000 more votes in the Democratic Primary than in the Republican Primary. And the number of individuals who had to vote with a provisional ballot because they had not gotten the free photo ID available from the state was less that 0.01%.

In the general election, Georgia, with one of the strictest voter ID laws in the nation, had the largest turnout in its history—more than 4 million voters. Democratic turnout was up an astonishing 6.1 percentage points from the 2004 election. Overall turnout in Georgia went up 6.7 percentage points, the second highest increase of any state in the country. The black share of the statewide vote increased from 25% in 2004 to 30% in 2008. By contrast, the Democratic turnout in the nearby state of Mississippi, also a state with a high percentage of black voters but without a voter ID requirement, increased by only 2.35 percentage points.

I should point out that the Georgia voter ID law was upheld in final orders issued by every state and federal court in Georgia that reviewed the law, including most recently by the Eleventh Circuit Court of Appeals. Just as in Texas, various organizations in Georgia made the specious claims that there were hundreds of thousands of Georgians without photo ID. Yet when the federal district court dismissed all of their claims, the court pointed out that after two years of litigation, none of the plaintiff organizations like the NAACP had been able to produce a single individual or member who did not have a photo ID or could not easily obtain one. The district court judge concluded that this "failure to identify those individuals is particularly acute in light of the Plaintiffs' contention that a large number of Georgia voters lack acceptable Photo ID . . . the fact that Plaintiffs, in spite of their efforts, have failed to uncover anyone who can attest to the fact that he/she will be prevented from voting provides significant support for a conclusion that the photo ID requirement does not unduly burden the right to vote."

In Indiana, which the Supreme Court said has the strictest voter ID law in the country, turnout in the Democratic presidential preference primary in 2008 quadrupled from the 2004 election when the photo ID law was not in effect—in fact, there were 862,000 more votes cast in the Democratic primary than the Republican primary. In the general election in November, the turnout of Democratic voters increased by 8.32 percentage points from 2004, the largest increase in Democratic turnout of any state in the nation. The neighboring state of Illinois, with no photo ID requirement and President Obama's home state, had an increase in Democratic turnout of only 4.4 percentage points—nearly half of Indiana's increase.

Just as in the federal case in Georgia, the federal court in Indiana noted the complete inability of the plaintiffs in that case to produce anyone who would not be able to vote because of the photo ID law:

> Despite apocalyptic assertions of wholesale vote disenfranchisement, Plaintiffs have produced not a single piece of evidence of any identifiable registered voter who would be prevented from voting pursuant to [the photo ID law] because of his or her inability to obtain the necessary photo identification.

One final point on the claims that requiring an ID, even when it is free, is a "poll tax" because of the incidental costs like possible travel to a registrar's office or obtaining a birth certificate that may be involved. That claim was also raised in Georgia. The federal court dismissed this claim, pointing out that such an "argument represents a dramatic overstatement of what fairly constitutes a 'poll tax'. Thus, the imposition of tangential burdens does not transform a regulation into a poll tax. Moreover, the cost of time and transportation cannot plausibly qualify as a prohibited poll tax because those same 'costs' also result from voter registration and in-person voting requirements, which one would not reasonably construe as a poll tax."

We are [the only] one of about one hundred democracies that do not uniformly require voters to present photo ID when they vote. All of those countries administer that law without any problems and without any reports that their citizens are in any way unable to vote because of that requirement. In fact, our southern neighbor Mexico, which has a much larger population in poverty than Texas or the United States, requires both a photo ID and a thumbprint to vote—and turnout has increased in their elections since this requirement went into effect in the 1990s.

Requiring voters to authenticate their identity is a perfectly reasonable and easily met requirement. It is supported by the vast majority of voters of all races and ethnic backgrounds. As the Supreme Court said, voter ID protects the integrity and reliability of the electoral process. Texas has a valid and legitimate state interest not only in deterring and detecting voter fraud, but in maintaining the confidence of its citizens in the security of its elections.

54

"Is There a Middle Ground in the Voter ID Debate?"

Edward B. Foley

The left and the right are increasingly trading accusations in the debate over new voter ID laws, and the rhetoric is heating up. Georgia's new law has been called the new "Jim Crow," although similar measures have recently been enacted in non-Southern states like Arizona and Indiana. Defenders of such measures say opponents are willfully blind to the possibility of fraud unless a photo ID requirement is imposed.

Given that heels are digging in, it might seem naïve to search for a compromise. Yet it is imperative to do so. Election laws cannot serve their intended function unless they are accepted by both the left and the right as fair means for conducting the competition between these two political camps to win approval from the citizenry. If the right insists that a voter ID law is necessary to make the electoral process legitimate, while the left simultaneously says that the same ID law makes the electoral process illegitimate, then it becomes impossible for our society to settle upon rules of procedure for a fair contest between opposing political forces.

With that observation in mind, it is worth searching for a middle position on the voter ID issue, even if at the outset a successful conclusion to this endeavor is far from assured.

In principle, some form of identification requirement should not be objectionable to liberals. Voting is an activity that only the eligible are entitled to engage in, and so it is not unreasonable to ask citizens for some information to demonstrate their eligibility. For example, liberals do not generally object to the traditional requirements that voters provide their names, addresses, and signatures before casting their ballots.

Conservatives, however, say that these traditional requirements no longer suffice because an imposter easily could forge a signature and, in contemporary society, poll workers are unlikely to distinguish eligible from ineligible voters simply by looking at their visages. Therefore, according to these conservatives, a photo ID is necessary to show the voter's eligibility. The picture will show that the person standing before the poll worker is the same one who, according to the poll book, is registered to vote under that particular name and address.

Liberals object, however, to a photo ID requirement on the ground that it is burdensome to citizens who do not have a driver's license, passport, or comparable document. Part of the burden is cost, which can be addressed by making a valid photo ID free of charge. Another part of the burden is the difficulty of accessing locations where no-charge IDs may be obtained. That problem could be remedied by making them available at any post office, public library, or public school, as well as other social service agencies (hospitals, police stations, and so forth).

But a remaining concern of liberals is that, even if photo IDs are easily obtained, many voters will fail to bring them to the polls on Election Day. Public reminders may be issued, including public service announcements on TV. Still, some voters are forgetful, perhaps senior citizens more so than younger adults, and thus the obligation to carry an ID to the polls might serve as a barrier for these eligible citizens.

A potential solution to this problem is to break the connection with the photo requirement and the obligation to produce identification at the polls. Eligible citizens could be required to provide a photograph at the time they *register* to vote, and poll workers would match this photograph with the image of the person standing in front of them. Given the availability of digital photography, the photos of registered voters could be stored in electronic poll books and easily "pulled up" with a click of a computer mouse when voters sign in to vote.

These electronic photos should satisfy the anti-fraud concerns of conservatives as much as printed photos that citizens would be required to bring to the polls. After all, the purpose of a *photo* ID requirement—beyond the traditional requirement of providing one's name, address, and signature—is to compare the likeness of the person seeking to vote with the photograph that is linked to the name and address of the registered voter (whom the flesh-and-blood person purports to be). This function can just as easily occur by comparing the likeness of the person with the computerized photo in the electronic poll book, which was linked to the name and address of the registered voter at time of registration.

Of course, to satisfy the concerns of liberals, a requirement to provide a digital photograph at time of registration would have to address the cost and accessibility issues identified earlier. But, again, a system in which citizens could go to a wide variety of public offices (including post offices, libraries, and schools), where clerical officials would be authorized to take a digital photo of the citizen and then email it to the applicable board of election, without any cost to the citizen, would satisfactorily address these concerns. In addition, for those citizens seeking to register by mail, they could be permitted to email their own digital photos of themselves, if they conform to "passport style" specifications. In this way, nursing homes and other senior citizens centers could take "at home" digital photos of their elderly residents and email them to the board of election, without requiring these elderly citizens to travel to a post office, library, or other public building. (Another comparable approach would be to permit individuals to become a kind of "deputized notary public," trained to take the right sort of digital photo, so that other citizens could meet with any of these designated individuals whenever and wherever it would be convenient.) Moreover, as an alternative, those citizens who do not submit a digital photo at time of registration could provide the more conventional form of photo ID (like a driver's license) at time of voting, making either approach an equally available option, depending solely on which the particular citizen prefers.

Liberals might still complain that any form of photo ID requirement is unnecessary to reduce the risk of fraud and, in any event, will be ineffective if inapplicable to absentee voting. The point about absentee voting is surely a valid one. (For this reason, one wonders whether it is wise to expand the availability of at-home voting, as many states are doing.) If individuals sitting at home can vote without providing any form of photo ID, the opportunity for fraud exists even if voters who go to the polls are subject to a photograph requirement. One way around this discrepancy would be to require absentee voters to submit a photocopy of their photo ID when they mail in their absentee ballot. Or, if the digital photo proposal is adopted, absentee voters could mail with their ballot a printed copy of the digital photo they submitted as part of their registration. In the future, absentee voters might simply email a second copy of their digital photo when emailing their absentee ballots.

A liberal objection to any form of photo ID requirement is more difficult to sustain, particularly if the goal is a compromise acceptable to both sides. To be sure, the frequency of fraud at polling places that would be preventable by a photo ID requirement may be fairly low—there is clearly a debate between conservatives and liberals on this factual point—but it is not non-existent. Liberals acknowledge the possibility of fraudulent absentee voting, saying that its risk is greater than polling place voting. But if an imposter can obtain and submit an absentee ballot, he or she can show up at a polling place purporting to be someone else. Even if the latter is more difficult, the lack of a photo ID requirement makes this deceit easier than it otherwise would be.

Thus, an acceptable compromise must take the form of a photo ID requirement that is not unduly onerous. The proposal here, to permit voters to submit an easily obtainable and no-charge digital photo at the time they register, as an alternative to having to produce a driver's license or comparable photo ID when they go to the polls on Election Day, satisfies this objective. Pursuing this proposal would enable both sides to move beyond the vituperative rhetoric that increasingly, and unfortunately, is clouding the policy debate on this topic.

Discussion Questions

1. Would you approve of a proposal that all voters had to show photo identification at polling places? Do you think it would decrease turnout? If so, is that a reasonable cost to pay to ensure that people cannot vote using another person's name? Or should turnout be prioritized and the risk that some people will vote inappropriately be accepted as a reasonable risk?

2. Would you have any concerns with having voting conducted over the Internet or by mail (as is done in Washington and Oregon)? Are there benefits that outweigh these concerns?

3. What might be some possible objections raised against Foley's proposal by the two sides in the voter-ID debate?

4. As a general matter, do you believe there is a trade-off between maximizing turnout and minimizing fraud? Or are these goals compatible? Why?

CHAPTER 11

Political Parties

55

"The Decline of Collective Responsibility in American Politics"

Morris P. Fiorina

For more than three decades, political scientists have studied the changing status of American political parties. Morris Fiorina suggests that political parties provide many benefits for American democracy, in particular by clarifying policy alternatives and letting citizens know whom to hold accountable when they are dissatisfied with government performance. Writing in the early 1980s, he sees decline in all the key areas of political-party activity: in the electorate, in government, and in party organizations. He argues that the decline eliminates the motivation for elected members of the parties to define broad policy objectives, leading to diminished political participation and a rise in alienation. Policies are aimed at serving the narrow interests of the various single-issue groups that dominate politics rather than the broad constituencies represented by parties. Without strong political parties to provide electoral accountability, American politics has suffered a "decline in collective responsibility" in Fiorina's view. In the effort to reform the often-corrupt political parties of the late 1800s—commonly referred to as "machines" led by "bosses"—Fiorina asks us to consider whether Americans have overly weakened the best institutional device available to hold elected officials accountable at the ballot box.

Though the Founding Fathers believed in the necessity of establishing a genuinely national government, they took great pains to design one that could not lightly do things *to* its citizens; what government might do *for* its citizens was to be limited to the functions of what we know now as the "watchman state."

* * *

Given the historical record faced by the Founders, their emphasis on constraining government is understandable. But we face a later historical record, one that shows two hundred years of increasing demands for government to act positively. Moreover, developments unforeseen by the Founders increasingly raise the likelihood that the uncoordinated actions of individuals and groups will inflict serious damage on the nation as a whole. The by-products of the industrial and technological revolutions impose physical risks not only on us, but on future generations as well. Resource shortages and international cartels raise the spectre of economic ruin. And the simple proliferation of special interests with their intense, particularistic demands threatens to render us politically incapable of taking actions that might either advance the state of society or prevent foreseeable deteriorations in that state. None of this is to suggest that we should forget about what government can do *to* us—the contemporary concern with the proper scope and methods of government intervention in the social and economic orders is long overdue. But the modern age demands as well that we worry about our ability to make government work *for* us. The problem is that we are gradually losing that ability, and a principal reason for this loss is the steady erosion of *responsibility* in American politics.

*   *   *

Unfortunately, the importance of responsibility in a democracy is matched by the difficulty of attaining it. In an autocracy, individual responsibility suffices; the location of power in a single individual locates responsibility in that individual as well. But individual responsibility is insufficient whenever more than one person shares governmental authority. We can hold a particular congressman individually responsible for a personal transgression such as bribe-taking. We can even hold a president individually responsible for military moves where he presents Congress and the citizenry with a *fait accompli*. But on most national issues individual responsibility is difficult to assess. If one were to go to Washington, randomly accost a Democratic congressman, and berate him about a 20-percent rate of inflation, imagine the response. More than likely it would run, "Don't blame me. If 'they' had done what I've advocated for *x* years, things would be fine today."

*   *   *

American institutional structure makes this kind of game-playing all too easy. In order to overcome it we must lay the credit or blame for national conditions on all those who had any hand in bringing them about: some form of *collective responsibility* is essential.

The only way collective responsibility has ever existed, and can exist given our institutions, is through the agency of the political party; in American politics, responsibility requires cohesive parties. This is an old claim to be sure, but its age does not detract from its present relevance. In fact, the continuing decline in public esteem for the parties and continuing efforts to "reform" them out of the political process suggest that old arguments for party responsibility have not been made often enough or, at least, convincingly enough, so I will make these arguments once again in this essay.

A strong political party can generate collective responsibility by creating incentive for leaders, followers, and popular supporters to think and act in collective terms. First, by providing party leaders with the capability (e.g., control of institutional patronage, nominations, and so on) to discipline party members, genuine leadership becomes possible. Legislative output is less likely to be a least common denominator—a residue of myriad conflicting proposals—and more likely to consist of a program actually intended to solve a problem or move the nation in a particular direction. Second, the subordination of individual officeholders to the party lessens their ability to separate themselves from party actions. Like it or not, their performance becomes identified with the performance of the collectivity to which they belong. Third, with individual candidate variation greatly reduced, voters have less incentive to support individuals and more incentive to support or oppose the party as a whole. And fourth, the circle closes as party-line voting in the electorate provides party leaders with the incentive to propose policies that will earn the support of a national majority, and party back-benchers* with the personal incentive to cooperate with leaders in the attempt to compile a good record for the party as a whole.

In the American context, strong parties have traditionally clarified politics in two ways. First, they allow citizens to assess responsibility easily, at least when the government is unified, which it more often was in earlier eras when party meant more than it does today. Citizens need only evaluate the social, economic, and international conditions they observe and make a simple decision for or against change. They do not need to decide whether the energy, inflation, urban, and defense policies advocated by their congressman would be superior to those advocated by [the president]—were any of them to be enacted!

The second way in which strong parties clarify American politics follows from the first. When citizens assess responsibility on the party as a whole, party members have personal incentives to see the party evaluated favorably. They have little to gain from gutting their president's program one day and attacking him for lack of leadership the next, since they share in the president's fate when voters do not differentiate within the party. Put simply, party responsibility provides party members with a personal stake in their collective performance.

---

*Back-benchers are junior members of the British Parliament, who sit in the rear benches of the House of Commons. Here, the term refers to junior members of political parties [*Editors*].

Admittedly, party responsibility is a blunt instrument. The objection immediately arises that party responsibility condemns junior Democratic representatives to suffer electorally for an inflation they could do little to affect. An unhappy situation, true, but unless we accept it, Congress as a whole escapes electoral retribution for an inflation they *could* have done something to affect. Responsibility requires acceptance of both conditions. The choice is between a blunt instrument or none at all.

* * *

In earlier times, when citizens voted for the party, not the person, parties had incentives to nominate good candidates, because poor ones could have harmful fallout on the ticket as a whole. In particular, the existence of presidential coattails (positive and negative) provided an inducement to avoid the nomination of narrowly based candidates, no matter how committed their supporters. And, once in office, the existence of party voting in the electorate provided party members with the incentive to compile a good *party* record. In particular, the tendency of national midterm elections to serve as referenda on the performance of the president provided a clear inducement for congressmen to do what they could to see that their president was perceived as a solid performer. By stimulating electoral phenomena such as coattail effects and mid-term referenda, party transformed some degree of personal ambition into concern with collective performance.

* * *

The Continuing Decline of Party in the United States

Party Organizations

In the United States, party organization has traditionally meant state and local party organization. The national party generally has been a loose confederacy of subnational units that swings into action for a brief period every four years. This characterization remains true today, despite the somewhat greater influence and augmented functions of the national organizations. Though such things are difficult to measure precisely, there is general agreement that the formal party organizations have undergone a secular decline since their peak at the end of the nineteenth century. The prototype of the old-style organization was the urban machine, a form approximated today only in Chicago.

* * *

[*Fiorina discusses the reforms of the late nineteenth and early twentieth century.*]
    In the 1970s two series of reforms further weakened the influence of organized parties in American national politics. The first was a series of legal changes deliberately intended to lessen organized party influence in the presidential nominating process. In the Democratic party, "New Poli-

tics" activists captured the national party apparatus and imposed a series of rules changes designed to "open up" the politics of presidential nominations. The Republican party—long more amateur and open than the Democratic party—adopted weaker versions of the Democratic rules changes. In addition, modifications of state electoral laws to conform to the Democratic rules changes (enforced by the federal courts) stimulated Republican rules changes as well.

*   *   *

A second series of 1970s reforms lessened the role of formal party organizations in the conduct of political campaigns. These are financing regulations growing out of the Federal Election Campaign Act of 1971 as amended in 1974 and 1976. In this case the reforms were aimed at cleaning up corruption in the financing of campaigns; their effects on the parties were a by-product, though many individuals accurately predicted its nature. Serious presidential candidates are now publicly financed. Though the law permits the national party to spend two cents per eligible voter on behalf of the nominee, it also obliges the candidate to set up a finance committee separate from the national party. Between this legally mandated separation and fear of violating spending limits or accounting regulations, for example, the law has the effect of encouraging the candidate to keep his party at arm's length.

*   *   *

The ultimate results of such reforms are easy to predict. A lesser party role in the nominating and financing of candidates encourages candidates to organize and conduct independent campaigns, which further weakens the role of parties. . . . [I]f parties do not grant nominations, fund their choices, and work for them, why should those choices feel any commitment to their party?

Party in the Electorate

In the citizenry at large, party takes the form of a psychological attachment. The typical American traditionally has been likely to identify with one or the other of the two major parties. Such identifications are transmitted across generations to some degree, and within the individual they tend to be fairly stable. But there is mounting evidence that the basis of identification lies in the individual's experiences (direct and vicarious, through family and social groups) with the parties in the past. Our current party system, of course, is based on the dislocations of the Depression period and the New Deal attempts to alleviate them. Though only a small proportion of those who experienced the Depression directly are active voters today, the general outlines of citizen party identifications much resemble those established at that time.

Again, there is reason to believe that the extent of citizen attachments to parties has undergone a long-term decline from a nineteenth-century high. And again, the New Deal appears to have been a period during which the decline was arrested, even temporarily reversed. But again, the decline of party has reasserted itself in the 1970s.

* * *

As the 1960s wore on, the heretofore stable distribution of citizen party identifications began to change in the general direction of weakened attachments to the parties. Between 1960 and 1976, independents, broadly defined, increased from less than a quarter to more than a third of the voting-age population. Strong identifiers declined from slightly more than a third to about a quarter of the population.

* * *

Indisputably, party in the electorate has declined in recent years. Why? To some extent the electoral decline results from the organizational decline. Few party organizations any longer have the tangible incentives to turn out the faithful and assure their loyalty. Candidates run independent campaigns and deemphasize their partisan ties whenever they see any short-term electoral gain in doing so. If party is increasingly less important in the nomination and election of candidates, it is not surprising that such diminished importance is reflected in the attitudes and behavior of the voter.

Certain long-term sociological and technological trends also appear to work against party in the electorate. The population is younger, and younger citizens traditionally are less attached to the parties than their elders. The population is more highly educated; fewer voters need some means of simplifying the choices they face in the political arena, and party, of course, has been the principal means of simplification. And the media revolution has vastly expanded the amount of information easily available to the citizenry. Candidates would have little incentive to operate campaigns independent of the parties if there were no means to apprise the citizenry of their independence. The media provide the means.

Finally, our present party system is an old one. For increasing numbers of citizens, party attachments based on the Great Depression seem lacking in relevance to the problems of the late twentieth century. Beginning with the racial issue in the 1960s, proceeding to the social issue of the 1970s, and to the energy, environment, and inflation issues of today, the parties have been rent by internal dissension. Sometimes they failed to take stands, at other times they took the wrong ones from the standpoint of the rank and file, and at most times they have failed to solve the new problems in any genuine sense. Since 1965 the parties have done little or nothing to earn the loyalties of modern Americans.

Party in Government

If the organizational capabilities of the parties have weakened, and their psychological ties to the voters have loosened, one would expect predictable consequences for the party in government. In particular, one would expect to see an increasing degree of split party control within and across the levels of American government. The evidence on this point is overwhelming.

*   *   *

The increased fragmentation of the party in government makes it more difficult for government officeholders to work together than in times past (not that it has ever been terribly easy). Voters meanwhile have a more difficult time attributing responsibility for government performance, and this only further fragments party control. The result is lessened collective responsibility in the system.

What has taken up the slack left by the weakening of the traditional [party] determinants of congressional voting? It appears that a variety of personal and local influences now play a major role in citizen evaluations of their representatives. Along with the expansion of the federal presence in American life, the traditional role of the congressman as an all-purpose ombudsman has greatly expanded. Tens of millions of citizens now are directly affected by federal decisions. Myriad programs provide opportunities to profit from government largesse, and myriad regulations impose costs and/or constraints on citizen activities. And, whether seeking to gain profit or avoid costs, citizens seek the aid of their congressmen. When a court imposes a desegregation plan on an urban school board, the congressional offices immediately are contacted for aid in safeguarding existing sources of funding and in determining eligibility for new ones. When a major employer announces plans to quit an area, the congressional offices immediately are contacted to explore possibilities for using federal programs to persuade the employer to reconsider. Contractors appreciate a good congressional word with DOD [Department of Defense] procurement officers. Local artistic groups cannot survive without NEA [National Endowment for the Arts] funding. And, of course, there are the major individual programs such as social security and veterans' benefits that create a steady demand for congressional information and aid services. Such activities are nonpartisan, nonideological, and, most important, noncontroversial. Moreover, the contribution of the congressman in the realm of district service appears considerably greater than the impact of his or her single vote on major national issues. Constituents respond rationally to this modern state of affairs by weighing nonprogrammatic constituency service heavily when casting their congressional votes. And this emphasis on the part of constituents provides the means for incumbents to solidify their hold on the office. Even if elected by a narrow margin, diligent service activities enable a congressman to neutralize or even convert a portion of those who would otherwise oppose him on policy or ideological grounds. Emphasis on local, nonpartisan factors in congressional voting enables the modern congressman to withstand national swings, whereas yesteryear's uninsulated congressmen were more dependent on preventing the occurrence of the swings.

*   *   *

[*The result is the insulation of the modern congressional member from national forces altogether.*]

The withering away of the party organizations and the weakening of party in the electorate have begun to show up as disarray in the party in government. As the electoral fates of congressmen and the president have diverged, their incentives to cooperate have diverged as well. Congressmen have little personal incentive to bear any risk in their president's behalf, since they no longer expect to gain much from his successes or suffer much from his failures. Only those who personally agree with the president's program and/or those who find that program well suited for their particular district support the president. And there are not enough of these to construct the coalitions necessary for action on the major issues now facing the country. By holding only the president responsible for national conditions, the electorate enables officialdom as a whole to escape responsibility. This situation lies at the root of many of the problems that now plague American public life.

Some Consequences of the Decline of Collective Responsibility

The weakening of party has contributed directly to the severity of several of the important problems the nation faces. For some of these, such as the government's inability to deal with inflation and energy, the connections are obvious. But for other problems, such as the growing importance of single-issue politics and the growing alienation of the American citizenry, the connections are more subtle.

Immobilism

As the electoral interdependence of the party in government declines, its ability to act also declines. If responsibility can be shifted to another level or to another officeholder, there is less incentive to stick one's neck out in an attempt to solve a given problem. Leadership becomes more difficult, the ever-present bias toward the short-term solution becomes more pronounced, and the possibility of solving any given problem lessens.

. . . [P]olitical inability to take actions that entail short-run costs ordinarily will result in much higher costs in the long run—we cannot continually depend on the technological fix. So the present American immobilism cannot be dismissed lightly. The sad thing is that the American people appear to understand the depth of our present problems and, at least in principle, appear prepared to sacrifice in furtherance of the long-run good. But they will not have an opportunity to choose between two or more such long-term plans. Although both parties promise tough, equitable policies, in the present state of our politics, neither can deliver.

Single-Issue Politics

In recent years both political analysts and politicians have decried the increased importance of single-issue groups in American politics. Some in fact would claim that the present immobilism in our politics owes more to the rise of single-issue groups than to the decline of party. A little thought, however, should reveal that the two trends are connected. Is single-issue politics a recent phenomenon? The contention is doubtful; such groups have always been active participants in American politics. The gun lobby already was a classic example at the time of President Kennedy's assassination. And however impressive the antiabortionists appear today, remember the temperance movement, which succeeded in getting its constitutional amendment. American history contains numerous forerunners of today's groups, from anti-Masons to abolitionists to the Klan—singularity of purpose is by no means a modern phenomenon. Why, then, do we hear all the contemporary hoopla about single-issue groups? Probably because politicians fear them now more than before and thus allow them to play a larger role in our politics. Why should this be so? Simply because the parties are too weak to protect their members and thus to contain single-issue politics.

In earlier times single-issue groups were under greater pressures to reach accommodations with the parties. After all, the parties nominated candidates, financed candidates, worked for candidates, and, perhaps most important, party voting protected candidates. When a contemporary single-issue group threatens to "get" an officeholder, the threat must be taken seriously.

* * *

Not only did the party organization have greater ability to resist single-issue pressures at the electoral level, but the party in government had greater ability to control the agenda, and thereby contain single-issue pressures at the policy-making level. Today we seem condemned to go through an annual agony over federal abortion funding. There is little doubt that politicians on both sides would prefer to reach some reasonable compromise at the committee level and settle the issue. But in today's decentralized Congress there is no way to put the lid on. In contrast, historians tell us that in the late nineteenth century a large portion of the Republican constituency was far less interested in the tariff and other questions of national economic development than in whether German immigrants should be permitted to teach their native language in their local schools, and whether Catholics and "liturgical Protestants" should be permitted to consume alcohol. Interestingly, however, the national agenda of the period is devoid of such issues. And when they do show up on the state level, the exceptions prove the rule; they produce party splits and striking defeats for the party that allowed them to surface.

In sum, a strong party that is held accountable for the government of a nation-state has both the ability and the incentive to contain particularistic pressures. It controls nominations, elections, and the agenda, and it collectively realizes that small minorities are small minorities no matter how intense they are. But as the parties decline they lose control over nominations and campaigns, they lose the loyalty of the voters, and they lose control of the agenda. Party officeholders cease to be held collectively accountable for party performance, but they become individually exposed to the political pressure of myriad interest groups. The decline of party permits interest groups to wield greater influence, their success encourages the formation of still more interest groups, politics becomes increasingly fragmented, and collective responsibility becomes still more elusive.

Popular Alienation from Government

For at least a decade political analysts have pondered the significance of survey data indicative of a steady increase in the alienation of the American public from the political process. . . . The American public is in a nasty mood, a cynical, distrusting, and resentful mood. The question is, Why?

If the same national problems not only persist but worsen while ever-greater amounts of revenue are directed at them, why shouldn't the typical citizen conclude that most of the money must be wasted by incompetent officials? If narrowly based interest groups increasingly affect our politics, why shouldn't citizens increasingly conclude that the interests run the government? For fifteen years the citizenry has listened to a steady stream of promises but has seen very little in the way of follow-through. An increasing proportion of the electorate does not believe that elections make a difference, a fact that largely explains the much-discussed post-1960 decline in voting turnout.

Continued public disillusionment with the political process poses several real dangers. For one thing, disillusionment begets further disillusionment. Leadership becomes more difficult if citizens do not trust their leaders and will not give them the benefit of a doubt. Policy failure becomes more likely if citizens expect the policy to fail. Waste increases and government competence decreases as citizens' disrespect for politics encourages a lesser breed of person to make careers in government. And "government by a few big interests" becomes more than a cliché if citizens increasingly decide the cliché is true and cease participating for that reason.

Finally, there is the real danger that continued disappointment with particular government officials ultimately metamorphoses into disillusionment with government per se. Increasing numbers of citizens believe that government is not simply overextended but perhaps incapable of any further bettering of the world. Yes, government is overextended, inefficiency is pervasive, and ineffectiveness is all too common. But government is one of the few instruments of collective action we have, and even those committed to selective pruning of government programs cannot blithely allow the concept of an activist government to fall into disrepute.

Of late, however, some political commentators have begun to wonder whether contemporary thought places sufficient emphasis on government *for* the people. In stressing participation have we lost sight of *accountability*? Surely, we should be as concerned with what government produces as with how many participate. What good is participation if the citizenry is unable to determine who merits their support?

Participation and responsibility are not logically incompatible, but there is a degree of tension between the two, and the quest for either may be carried to extremes. Participation maximizers find themselves involved with quotas and virtual representation schemes, while responsibility maximizers can find themselves with a closed shop under boss rule. Moreover, both qualities can weaken the democracy they supposedly underpin. Unfettered participation produces Hyde Amendments* and immobilism. Responsible parties can use agenda power to thwart democratic decision—for more than a century the Democratic party used what power it had to suppress the racial issue. Neither participation nor responsibility should be pursued at the expense of all other values, but that is what has happened with participation over the course of the past two decades, and we now reap the consequences in our politics.

DISCUSSION QUESTIONS

1. How do political parties provide "collective responsibility" and improve the quality of democracy? Do you believe the complaints raised by Fiorina thirty years ago remain persuasive?

2. Are strong parties in the interest of individual politicians? What might be some reasons that members of Congress would agree to strong parties? What would make them distance themselves from their party's leadership?

---

*The Hyde Amendment, passed in 1976 (three years after *Roe v. Wade*), prohibited using Medicaid funds for abortion [*Editors*].

56

"Be Careful What You Wish For: The Rise of Responsible Parties in American National Politics"

Nicol Rae

Writing about twenty-five years after Morris Fiorina, Nicol Rae sees significant changes in American political parties. To Rae, American parties had developed in the ways preferred by many reformers who wanted parties to be more cohesive, policy-focused, determined to implement their agendas, and active in elections. Parties in Congress have become more unified and more determined to exercise their authority. The party national committees have become highly involved in candidate recruitment and training, fundraising, and advertising. Presidential nomination rules have been adjusted to make it more difficult for outsider candidates to triumph over those preferred by party insiders. The nomination system works to produce candidates satisfactory to the middle of the party rather than the middle of the nation. Among voters, partisanship appeared to be on the rise and the proportion of split-ticket voters was decreasing. His diagnosis is that "American national parties appear very healthy in all aspects compared to their condition thirty years ago."

The results, he suggests, have not been as beneficial for democracy as many scholars assumed they would be. Pointing to partisan conflict, especially in Congress, he writes that "it is hard to argue that the strengthening of America's parties has improved the governmental process and enhanced the quality of America's representative democracy." Rae argues that the parties have increasingly become defined by interests that attach themselves to one party or the other rather than truly straddling the two parties. The parties, in turn, must become more vigilant in defending those interests that attach to them, leaving little room to work with members of the other party to solve problems.

Despite all these changes, Rae concludes that American parties have not become "responsible parties" in the sense advocated by many reformers. They may be doing a better job of pursuing coherent agendas—though not to the degree seen in other countries—but the nature of the U.S. system of separated, divided, and federal powers makes truly responsible parties highly unlikely. Responsible parties would be able to implement their promises and agendas without obstruction from the other party, a situation that Rae argues appears only rarely in American politics.

In the comparative study of political parties in twentieth-century advanced democracies, the United States has always been something of a problematic outlier owing to the absence of organized, disciplined, and ideological mass political parties. Almost all other advanced democracies are parliamentary political systems characterized by what [political scientist J. Austin] Ranney termed "responsible party government," in which a party or coalition of parties forms a cabinet responsible to the lower house of the legislature. Legislators from the governing party or coalition thus have powerful incentives in terms of re-election, career, and policy goals to sustain the government in office, and at election time the government is ultimately held accountable as voters vote for or against the candidates of the governing party (or parties).

From its very beginning, however, the U.S. political system has remained conspicuously resistant to strong mass political parties, and responsible party government has found little enthusiasm among Americans outside the academy. The framers of the U.S. Constitution equated parties with interest groups ("factions"), which they regarded as the greatest danger to republican virtue and future government stability in the United States. The constitutional separation of the branches of the federal government— with separated elections and staggered terms for the executive and legislatures—places formidable obstacles in the way of responsible party government by comparison with parliamentary systems where the two branches are fused by cabinet governments. American federalism—with significant governmental powers reserved to the states—has also presented a barrier to responsible party government. Beyond the constitutional impediments to party government, the notion of strong, centralized governing parties is also antithetical to America's political culture. The individualism and suspicion of government ingrained in the American political psyche since colonial times has militated against large concentrations of private power with influence over government. Finally, unlike in Europe, mass political parties failed to develop in the United States, and so the American parties never developed the mass ideological loyalty and organizational apparatus necessary for them to serve as channels of accountability in a responsible party government model.

The United States has nevertheless had national political parties of a sort and party conflict since the 1790s, and no representative democracy of any significance has been able to operate without them. Without such intermediary political institutions to structure political choices, mass representative democracy would surely be rendered meaningless. So although Americans have never had much love for national political parties, they have not been able to devise a political system in which parties do not play a significant role. The 1950 APSA [American Political Science Association] report reflected the consensus among American political scientists of the New Deal generation that the American parties were too weak to perform their necessary role in channeling democratic choices for Americans and suggested a number of methods by which they might be strengthened and made more nearly "responsible" on the European model.

In America, by comparison, the parties were too outdated and ramshackle to play what the party scholars saw as their appropriate role in the world's leading representative democracy. This was seen as an issue that needed to be addressed by the political science profession as a whole—hence the APSA committee on the state of the parties, headed by the most distinguished American parties scholar of the day—E.E. Schattschneider. The Foreword succinctly summarized the consensus among contemporary American party scholars:

> Historical and other factors have caused the American two-party system to operate as two loose associations of state and local organizations, with very little national machinery and very little national cohesion. As a result, either major party, when in power, is ill-equipped to organize its members in the legislative and executive branches into a government held together and guided by a party program. Party responsibility at the polls thus tends to vanish. This is a very serious matter, for it affects the very heartbeat of American democracy.

Part I of the report developed the argument for greater party responsibility and illustrated how the contemporary American national parties were simply not living up to the role. Part II consisted of a set of concrete proposals by the committee to make the parties more responsible, e.g., enhance the role of the national party committees; create an elite 50-member national party body or "party council" to coordinate the national state and local party organizations, draft the platform, and generally set party policy; strengthen the party organizations in Congress; encourage intraparty participation (particularly in the presidential nominating process), including the creation of a formal "party membership"; and, finally, expand the research capacity of the parties.

*　*　*

If the Parties Are Dead, How Did American Politics Get to Be So Partisan?

Thirty years on, a contemporary analysis of American politics would not regard the weakness of the political parties as primarily responsible for the ills of the political system. There does now appear to be some real evidence that in several important aspects the parties are beginning to resemble those advocated by the 1950 APSA report, yet it is by no means clear that the quality of American democracy has been enhanced by this development in the manner envisaged by the party theorists. If anything, it is the apparent strength and ideological coherence of the parties and the apparent polarization between them that is now seen as problematic. Moreover, the rise of partisanship and polarization in a separated system of government appears only to have enhanced policy gridlock and increased popular frustration with government. This might seem to imply that the prescriptions of the "responsible party government" theorists were always flawed in their application to the American context. * * *

Some signs of party revival in the United States were already evident during the 1970s, but it took some time for party scholars to recognize the trend. The area where political scientists first began to notice party renewal was the new role of the national party committees. Traditionally, the national party committees had no control over the state parties, and their duties were largely confined to organizing the quadrennial national party nominating convention and conducting presidential election campaigns. The Democrats' reform of the presidential nominating process after 1968 gave the Democratic National Committee sovereignty over the state parties in issues regarding presidential delegate selection. This authority was confirmed by the 1975 Supreme Court decision in the case of *Cousins v. Wigoda.*

Perhaps more significant, however, was the transformation of the Republican National Committee following the Watergate debacle. Under a series of national chairmen beginning with William Brock (1977–1981), the committee began to transform itself into a major fundraising and campaign service organization for GOP candidates right down to the state legislative level. The Republican National Committee developed a formidable national small-donor fundraising base, established training programs for candidates and campaign managers at all levels, played a greater role in candidate recruitment, and coordinated national Republican media campaigns in election years. The Democratic National Committee began to play a similar role in the 1980s and 1990s, although their fundraising prowess has lagged behind that of their Republican counterparts. This evolution of what Aldrich has termed "the party in service" has greatly heightened the visibility and electoral role of national party committees and helped create a genuine national party identity. To the extent that the national parties have worked with Republican and Democratic candidates, their heightened level of activity—combined with the increasing ideological homogeneity of party candidates—has surely enhanced national party solidarity since the APSA report was issued.

Congress provides the clearest example of the revival of party in the United States over the past quarter century. Congressional scholars first became aware of what was happening when they noticed that party unity scores in Congress had risen significantly during the 1980s and early 1990s. [David] Rohde noted that southern Democrats, traditionally at least as conservative as Republicans in their voting, were now voting much more in line with their liberal national party colleagues. The 1960s civil rights revolution had finally unraveled the ideologically incoherent parties of the post–New Deal era that had so exasperated President Roosevelt. With southern blacks enfranchised and voting Democratic, southern

Democratic candidates now had to pay attention to their political demands, which did not differ greatly from those of their liberal northern counterparts. Similarly, genuinely conservative southern whites now found a more ideologically congenial home in the rising southern GOP. Liberal Democratic and conservative Republican growth in the South paralleled each other, and the effect on the national Republican and Democratic parties was to make them more broadly conservative and liberal (respectively) in the ideological sense. This process was already under way during the 1970s but was generally overlooked in the general consensus of pessimism regarding the future of the parties. The decline in the number and influence of conservative Democrats as the Republican Party grew in the South was also paralleled by a decline in the number of liberal or progressive Republicans as the Democrats gradually grew stronger in the Northeastern states. In retrospect, then, the civil rights revolution was an absolutely critical development in the emergence of modern American political parties.

Rohde and [Barbara] Sinclair also noted that the growth in party coherence and unity on Capitol Hill was accompanied by dramatic growth in the power of the party leadership in both chambers of Congress. During the 1970s, the growing number of northern liberal Democrats in the House Democratic caucus finally revolted against the dominance of largely southern conservative Democratic committee chairs. The Democrats introduced new rules providing for elections of committee chairs and reduced the chairs' control over committee personnel and agendas. At the same time, they empowered the party caucus and the party leadership. Party leaders gained a much greater role in committee assignments and, since the Speaker gained control over the membership of the powerful House Rules committee, de facto control over the schedule of legislation.

Commentary on these rules changes initially focused on the great power given to subcommittees and individual members by the reductions in chairs' powers, but the most important long-term effect was the dramatic strengthening of the congressional party leadership that occurred once party leaders started to take advantage of the new opportunities provided by the reforms. With more ideologically homogeneous congressional parties, it is logical to expect that individual members would seek to empower the party leadership to ensure implementation of common policy goals. In what Sinclair describes as a "principal-agent" relationship, members have indeed empowered leaders to perform legislative tasks in line with those goals. [John] Aldrich and Rohde go further, describing the emergence of a system of "conditional party government" in Congress: If there is a sufficient consensus on policy objectives within the majority party, members will empower party leaders to deliver those objectives. The ideological congressional party realignment engendered by the civil rights revolution has, according to Aldrich and Rohde, created the perfect environment for stronger partisanship and party leadership on Capitol Hill. The accuracy of this analysis is also borne out by the experience of the U.S. Senate, where, despite the absence of such explicit reforms as in the House, the same pattern of growing party unity and enhanced leadership influence can be observed.

While the Democrats were acting like a more coherent majority party during the 1980s, the Republican minority arguably went even farther in an ideological and partisan direction. The reassertion of control by the Democratic Party leadership led to a loss of influence on the part of the Republican minority—particularly in the House of Representatives. During the era of the conservative coalition, the Republicans had considerable leverage over legislation through their alliance with the conservative southern Democrats, both on the House and Senate floors and in committee. In the postreform House of the 1980s, the Republicans found themselves shut out of the policy-making process by a reassertive Democratic leadership. In reaction, the Republican minority became increasingly vocal, ideological, and partisan, as demonstrated by the rise of the Georgia firebrand Newt Gingrich to a position of party leadership by the late 1980s.

In presidential politics the case for party revival appears somewhat less evident. Even before the establishment of the primary nominating system, candidate organizations and the news media were becoming more important players in nominating politics at the expense of traditional state and local party bosses. The primary system confirmed this development and rendered the national party conventions purely ceremonial occasions to ratify the winners of the primary election campaign. Performance in early caucuses and primary contests (particularly in the relatively small states of Iowa and New Hampshire), fundraising ability, and the impact of media expectations and coverage have become the crucial determinants of presidential success, with no significant role for party officeholders in the process. Indeed, the reformed process allowed rank outsiders who would never have gained the support of traditional party leaders—such as George McGovern and Jimmy Carter—to secure presidential nominations.

Although the fundamentals of the nominating system have not changed in the decades since, modifications in the primary calendar have diluted the chances of outsider candidates and to some extent increased the influence of party elites. The tendency toward "frontloading" of the primary calendar, with more and more major states with large numbers of delegates voting at an earlier stage in the process, has considerably diluted the potential impact of an outsider candidate's unexpectedly strong showing in Iowa and New Hampshire. In a frontloaded calendar, with more than 50 percent of the delegates being chosen in a one-month period and dozens of simultaneous campaigns in some of the country's biggest and most expensive media markets, the advantages of nationally known candidates able to raise large sums of money have increased considerably. These are likely to be candidates "anointed" by the contemporary party "establishment"—large fundraisers and leaders of political action committees, or 527 committees. Though not on the ideological fringe of either party, these elites are not going to back candidates who are outside the mainstream of national party ideology; after all, that ideology is largely determined by the very interest groups that provide the money for the party. All presidential nominees since 1984 have been the candidates closest to this fundraising party establishment. In a clear example of the advantages of the present system, Arizona Senator John McCain won the New Hampshire primary easily in 2000, but because he lacked support among the Republican allied interests and fundraisers, McCain was overtaken by the establishment favorite George W. Bush, whose fundraising and organizational prowess proved decisive in the multistate primaries that followed shortly thereafter.

The impact of money and organization on presidential nominating politics thus also has the effect of driving the candidates toward the ideological center of the party rather than that of the nation. Interest groups and large donors contribute to the candidate who holds issue positions that they approve of but who they also bet can defeat the other party's candidate in the general election. The outcome in primary politics is to drive candidates toward their party's ideological agenda and single-issue interest group supporters. The overall effect is a polarization of party candidates that mirrors the increased partisanship in Congress. Informally, the donors of primary campaign money have become a de facto party elite, although far removed from the background and motivation of traditional party bosses.

We must finally consider the evidence of party revival in the electorate. The 1970s theory of dealignment was based on the apparent alienation of the American electorate from the major political parties. This was evident in declining levels of partisan affiliation, growth in the number of self-described independents in the electorate, increased electoral volatility, declining turnout, and increased levels of split-ticket voting. All of these phenomena were more pronounced among the younger voters of the baby boom generation, who came of age politically during the 1960s. It was their electoral disaffection from the parties that provided the strongest evidence of dealignment, with some scholars tracing a long-term pattern of electoral disaggregation set in train by the reforms of the progressive era.

In the succeeding decades, however, the worst fears of the dealignment theorists have not been borne out. The surge toward independent affiliation appears to have crested in the 1970s, and partisanship in the electorate has experienced something of a revival. Partisans have held their own and there is evidence that the intensity of partisanship has increased. The 2004 election, the most partisan election in recent history, also witnessed marked increases in voter turnout. The electoral volatility of the 1960s and 1970s appears to have been a temporary phenomenon; recent American elections have been exceedingly close and competitive, with relatively small margins separating the parties' national totals in both presidential and congressional races, and a markedly stable pattern in the geographic distribution of the vote. Finally, split-ticket voting, which peaked in the 1970s, has also gone into a marked decline, with far fewer split party outcomes between presidential and congressional candidates at the state and district levels. In fact, the 2004 election had the fewest in decades.

In summary, American national parties appear very healthy in all aspects compared to their condition thirty years ago. They are more ideologically coherent, maintain viable and significant national organizations, are much stronger in Congress, and enjoy a stronger and more committed mass base of support. It would appear that the parties have gone at least some way toward the model envisaged by the authors of the 1950 report. Yet this enhanced partisanship has not produced entirely positive results. On the contrary, it is argued today that the country is too partisan and too polarized, and that this polarization and partisanship has led to an unhealthy degree of bitterness and invective in national political debate. Party polarization in Congress and between Congress and the White House has also impeded the smooth working of a legislative process devised by the framers to generate compromise. In short, it is hard to argue that the strengthening of America's parties has improved the governmental process and enhanced the quality of America's representative democracy.

*　*　*

American Parties in the Twenty-First Century

What are we to make of American parties at the dawn of the twenty-first century? Certainly American parties today look more like political parties in other democracies than they did when Duverger was writing in the late 1940s. The impact of the 1960s civil rights revolution has been to create two more ideologically coherent parties: a generally liberal or center-left party and a conservative party. The national party organizations, though not in direct control of the party machinery in the states and locales as in other democratic systems, now play a major part in electoral campaigning at all levels. Party unity and the power of the party leadership in Congress is at its highest levels since the Gilded Age. In presidential politics, the new party elite of fundraisers, political action committees, and 527 organizations uses the frontloaded nominating system to nominate established political figures in the ideological mainstream of the party rather than mavericks. Finally, the electorate is more inclined to behave in a partisan fashion than it was in the 1960s and 1970s. We can say conclusively that dealignment is over and that American parties are more serious political institutions and more significant in the governing process than they were 30 years ago, or even when the APSA committee issued its report in 1950.

*   *   *

Contemporary American parties are alliances of interest groups. In some sense they always have been, although in the traditional party these interests were defined geographically or locally. In modern America, interests are primarily national in scope. Very few national interests today are genuinely bipartisan, and most associate with one political party or the other—labor, teachers, environmentalists, trial lawyers, the entertainment industry, and national organizations that campaign on behalf of women, minorities, and gays tend to cleave to the Democratic party, while the Republicans are supported by corporate and financial interests, conservative religious organizations, and gun owners. Dislike of the opposing coalition is the glue that keeps each interest alliance together. These groups fund the party campaigns at all levels and provide the activists and other critical resources. Their endorsements are eagerly sought by party candidates, and they generally play a critical role in primary elections. Of course this means that successful candidates must adhere closely to the groups' positions to get nominated. Once in office, their political objectives are logically in line with those of the groups that support them. Since groups on opposite sides of the party divide generally hold opposing positions on issues, the overall effect has been to pull both parties away from the center ground on most issues and closer to the positions of their interest group allies.

Several other factors operate to maximize the influence of the interest group activists over party politics. One of the most obvious is legislative redistricting. In recent decades, the cumulative effect of state legislatures drawing electoral district boundaries for themselves—and for the U.S. House—combined with post–1965 federal voting rights legislation, federal court rulings, and modern computer technology has been to create legislative districts that are usually "safe" for one major party or the other. With the overwhelming majority of legislative districts now being deliberately configured to produce a partisan outcome, the key contest becomes the primary election—invariably low in turnout and with an electorate disproportionately composed of the most committed interest group and party activists. The overall effect has been to homogenize party candidates' ideology, increase party unity, and bolster the party leadership as the agent that has to produce legislative outcomes satisfactory to the groups that support the party and thereby help insure incumbents' re-election.

The nature of contemporary news media also encourages the more polarized tone of American politics. Cable news media and radio talk shows are the province of the party activists and tend to cover politics in an adversarial fashion. The further "narrowcasting" created by the Internet has tended to encourage discussions among the like-minded rather than a nuanced consideration of the issues. All these news sources tend to encourage partisanship and adversarial politics. It certainly cannot be argued—as it was in the 1950 report—that the contemporary American voter is denied a debate between clear-cut choices on the issues.

Conclusion

None of the factors encouraging polarization seems likely to change in the short term. Although mass party development or responsible party government still seem highly unlikely, there has undoubtedly been a revival of parties and partisanship in the United States in the past quarter century, primarily due to three factors: (a) the civil rights revolution; (b) the capture of the party labels by coalitions of single-issue and ideological elite interests who see those labels as instruments to achieve their ends; and (c) the development of political communications media that encourage rhetorical and political conflict.

Despite these changes, American political parties are likely to remain outliers in the study of comparative parties because America itself is an outlier on so many political indices. Relative to European parties, the American parties are still generally less ideological, far less well-organized, less cohesive, less centralized, and less critical to the day-to-day business of government. * * * Despite the wishes of the APSA committee, the U.S. Constitution and American political culture effectively preclude responsible party government from developing in the United States except during intermittent periods when one party controls all the branches of the federal government.

*   *   *

The party scholars behind the 1950 report would certainly be pleased to see the development of more coherent and effective parties in the United States and the end of the organizationally ramshackle and ideologically incoherent parties of the post–New Deal era. Whether they would be pleased by the degree of polarization and conflict in contemporary American party politics is a different matter. Implicit in the concept of responsible party government was the notion that in addition to presenting distinct choices to the electorate and enabling voters to hold the government to account at election time, political parties were also the most effective agents for containing and resolving conflict in society. The assumption was that party elites would have sufficient consensus on the fundamentals of political debate to prevent political conflict from getting out of hand. If parties are merely vehicles of polarized political elites, however, they are more likely to magnify such conflict than to contain it.

The irony may be that having finally witnessed the development of ideologically coherent parties that make sense to external observers, political scientists have also become more aware of the potentially unhealthy side effects—partisan rancor, political polarization, policy stasis in a separated national governing system—that may attend such a development.

Discussion questions

1. Is it more of a problem for American democracy that parties have become more cohesive, unified, and determined to implement their views, or is it more of a problem that the structure of American government makes it difficult for parties to implement their plans?

2. Rae details several ways in which American parties have changed. Are all of these changes for the worse in your view? If so, explain why. If not, explain which changes you see as positive and which you see as problems.

Debating the Issues: Red America versus Blue America—Are We Polarized?

In 1992, presidential nominee contender Patrick Buchanan famously stated at the Republican National Convention that the United States was in the midst of a culture war that posited traditional, conservative social values against liberal, secular values. Bill Clinton's defeat of President George H. W. Bush seemed to defuse that idea: Clinton was a southern Democrat who had pushed his party toward the ideological center and, although garnering only 43 percent of the vote, he won states in all regions of the country. His 1996 victory was broader, adding some states he had lost in 1992. In the 2000 presidential election, however, a striking regional pattern emerged in the results. Al Gore, the Democratic candidate, did well on the coasts and in the upper Midwest, while George W. Bush, the Republican candidate, picked up the remaining states. Many analysts were struck by this "red state/blue state" pattern—named after the coloring of the states on post-election maps—and suggested that it told us something more fundamental about American politics. Indeed, these analysts argued, Patrick Buchanan was in large measure right: the American public was deeply divided and polarized and in many respects living in two different worlds culturally. This polarization showed up not only in voting, but in presidential approval ratings, with the partisan gap in evaluations of Bill Clinton and George W. Bush being larger than for any previous presidents. The 2004 presidential election looked very much like 2000: with a few exceptions, the red states stayed red and the blue states stayed blue. Eighty-five percent of conservatives voted for Bush; the same percentage of liberals voted for Kerry; and moderates split 54–45 percent for Kerry.

In 2008, Barack Obama campaigned on the idea of practicing a new kind of politics that set aside red-America/blue-America distinctions. His victory scattered the red/blue map, as he picked up nine states Bush had won in 2004. Shortly into his presidency, however, Obama's policy plans became engulfed in deep partisan and ideological strife. Like those of Clinton and Bush before him, President Obama's approval ratings were sharply different among Democrats and Republicans. And like those two presidents, Obama invigorated his opponents. Where the Bush presidency played a major role in galvanizing the liberal blogosphere, Obama's contributed to the rise of the Tea Party, a political movement deeply skeptical about the effectiveness and growing size of American government. Victorious in the 2010 election, the Tea Party suffered a set back in 2012 when President Obama was reelected.

Is America deeply polarized along partisan lines? Is there a culture war? Is the red-America/blue-America split real? Is there division on certain highly charged issues but not on most others? Are the divisions just artifacts of the way that survey questions are worded? In this debate, the political scientists James Q. Wilson and Morris Fiorina agree that the political elite—elected leaders, the news media, and interest groups—are polarized, but they disagree on the answers to the rest of the questions. Wilson argues that the cultural split is deep and is reflected in party competition and the public opinion of partisans within and across the red and blue states. Fiorina counters that the idea of a culture war is vastly exaggerated—there might be a skirmish, but there is no war.

John Judis aligns more with Wilson. Although not a fan of the Tea Party, Judis nonetheless argues that it is a real movement with the potential for lasting influence. Its issues, anxieties, and ideological orientation, he states, draw on a deep populist tradition in American politics. As with other populist movements, supporters see the Tea Party as engaged in a struggle to define America, a struggle between "the people" and "the elites."

57

"*What* Culture Wars? Debunking the Myth of a Polarized America"

MORRIS P. FIORINA

"There is a religious war going on in this country, a cultural war as critical to the kind of nation we shall be as the Cold War itself, for this war is for the soul of America."

With those ringing words insurgent candidate Pat Buchanan fired up his supporters at the 1992 Republican National Convention. To be sure, not all delegates cheered Buchanan's call to arms, which was at odds with the "kinder, gentler" image that George H.W. Bush had attempted to project. Election analysts later included Buchanan's fiery words among the factors contributing to the defeat of President Bush, albeit one of lesser importance than the slow economy and the repudiation of his "Read my lips, no new taxes" pledge.

In the years since Buchanan's declaration of cultural war, the idea of a clash of cultures has become a common theme in discussions of American politics. The culture war metaphor refers to a displacement of the classic economic conflicts that animated twentieth-century politics in the advanced democracies by newly emergent moral and cultural ones. The literature generally attributes Buchanan's inspiration to a 1991 book, *Culture Wars,* by sociologist James Davison Hunter, who divided Americans into the culturally "orthodox" and the culturally "progressive" and argued that increasing conflict was inevitable.

No one has embraced the concept of the culture war more enthusiastically than journalists, ever alert for subjects that have "news value." Conflict is high in news value. Disagreement, division, polarization, battles, and war make good copy. Agreement, consensus, moderation, compromise, and peace do not. Thus, the notion of a culture war fits well with the news sense of journalists who cover politics. Their reports tell us that contemporary voters are sharply divided on moral issues. As David Broder wrote in the *Washington Post* in November 2000, "The divide went deeper than politics. It reached into the nation's psyche. . . . It was the moral dimension that kept Bush in the race."

Additionally, it is said that close elections do not reflect indifferent or ambivalent voters; rather, such elections reflect evenly matched blocs of deeply committed partisans. According to a February 2002 report in *USA Today*, "When George W. Bush took office, half the country cheered and the other half seethed"; some months later the *Economist* wrote that "such political divisions cannot easily be shifted by any president, let alone in two years, because they reflect deep demographic divisions. . . . The 50-50 nation appears to be made up of two big, separate voting blocks, with only a small number of swing voters in the middle."

The 2000 election brought us the familiar pictorial representation of the culture war in the form of the "red" and "blue" map of the United States. Vast areas of the heartland appeared as Republican red, while coastal and Great Lakes states took on a Democratic blue hue. Pundits reified the colors on the map, treating them as prima facie evidence of deep cultural divisions: Thus "Bush knew that the landslide he had wished for in 2000 . . . had vanished into the values chasm separating the blue states from the red ones" (John Kenneth White, in *The Values Divide*). In the same vein, the *Boston Herald* reported Clinton adviser Paul Begala as saying, on November 18, 2000, that "tens of millions of good people in Middle America voted Republican. But if you look closely at that map you see a more complex picture. You see the state where James Byrd was lynched—dragged behind a pickup truck until his body came apart—it's red. You see the state where Matthew Shepard was crucified on a split-rail fence for the crime of being gay—it's red. You see the state where right-wing extremists blew up a federal office building and murdered scores of federal employees—it's red."

Claims of bitter national division were standard fare after the 2000 elections, and few commentators publicly challenged them. On the contrary, the belief in a fractured nation was expressed even by high-level political operatives. Republican pollster Bill McInturff commented to the *Economist* in January 2001 that "we have two massive colliding forces. One is rural, Christian, religiously conservative. [The other] is socially tolerant, pro-choice, secular, living in New England and the Pacific Coast." And

Matthew Dowd, a Bush re-election strategist, explained to the *Los Angeles Times* why Bush has not tried to expand his electoral base: "You've got 80 to 90 percent of the country that look at each other like they are on separate planets."

The journalistic drumbeat continues unabated. A November 2003 report from the Pew Research Center led E. J. Dionne Jr. of the *Washington Post* to comment: "The red states get redder, the blue states get bluer, and the political map of the United States takes on the coloration of the Civil War."

And as the 2004 election approaches, commentators see a continuation, if not an intensification, of the culture war. *Newsweek*'s Howard Fineman wrote in October 2003, "The culture war between the Red and Blue Nations has erupted again—big time—and will last until Election Day next year. Front lines are all over, from the Senate to the Pentagon to Florida to the Virginia suburbs where, at the Bush-Cheney 2004 headquarters, they are blunt about the shape of the battle: 'The country's split 50–50 again,' a top aide told me, 'just as it was in 2000.' "

In sum, observers of contemporary American politics have apparently reached a new consensus around the proposition that old disagreements about economics now pale in comparison to new divisions based on sexuality, morality, and religion, divisions so deep and bitter as to justify talk of war in describing them.

Yet research indicates otherwise. Publicly available databases show that the culture war script embraced by journalists and politicos lies somewhere between simple exaggeration and sheer nonsense. There is no culture war in the United States; no battle for the soul of America rages, at least none that most Americans are aware of.

Certainly, one can find a few warriors who engage in noisy skirmishes. Many of the activists in the political parties and the various cause groups do hate each other and regard themselves as combatants in a war. But their hatreds and battles are not shared by the great mass of Americans—certainly nowhere near "80–90 percent of the country"—who are for the most part moderate in their views and tolerant in their manner. A case in point: To their embarrassment, some GOP senators recently learned that ordinary Americans view gay marriage in somewhat less apocalyptic terms than do the activists in the Republican base.

If swing voters have disappeared, how did the six blue states in which George Bush ran most poorly in 2000 all elect Republican governors in 2002 (and how did Arnold Schwarzenegger run away with the 2003 recall in blue California)? If almost all voters have already made up their minds about their 2004 votes, then why did John Kerry surge to a 14-point trial-heat lead when polls offered voters the prospect of a Kerry-McCain ticket? If voter partisanship has hardened into concrete, why do virtually identical majorities in both red and blue states favor divided control of the presidency and Congress, rather than unified control by their party? Finally, and ironically, if voter positions have become so uncompromising, why did a recent CBS story titled "Polarization in America" report that 76 percent of Republicans, 87 percent of Democrats, and 86 percent of Independents would like to see elected officials compromise more rather than stick to their principles?

Still, how does one account for reports that have almost 90 percent of Republicans planning to vote for Bush and similarly high numbers of Democrats planning to vote for Kerry? The answer is that while voter *positions* have not polarized, their *choices* have. There is no contradiction here; positions and choices are not the same thing. Voter choices are functions of their positions and the positions and actions of the candidates they choose between.

Republican and Democratic elites unquestionably have polarized. But it is a mistake to assume that such elite polarization is equally present in the broader public. It is not. However much they may claim that they are responding to the public, political elites do not take extreme positions because *voters* make them. Rather, by presenting them with polarizing alternatives, elites make voters appear polarized, but the reality shows through clearly when voters have a choice of more moderate alternatives— as with the aforementioned Republican governors.

Republican strategists have bet the Bush presidency on a high-risk gamble. Reports and observation indicate that they are attempting to win in 2004 by getting out the votes of a few million Republican-leaning evangelicals who did not vote in 2000, rather than by attracting some modest proportion of 95 million other non-voting Americans, most of them moderates, not to mention moderate Democratic voters who could have been persuaded to back a genuinely compassionate conservative. Such a strategy leaves no cushion against a negative turn of events and renders the administration vulnerable to a credible Democratic move toward the center. Whether the Democrats can capitalize on their opportunity remains to be seen.

58

"How Divided Are We?"

James Q. Wilson

The 2004 election left our country deeply divided over whether our country is deeply divided. For some, America is indeed a polarized nation, perhaps more so today than at any time in living memory. In this view, yesterday's split over Bill Clinton has given way to today's even more acrimonious split between Americans who detest George Bush and

Americans who detest John Kerry, and similar divisions will persist as long as angry liberals and angry conservatives continue to confront each other across the political abyss. Others, however, believe that most Americans are moderate centrists, who, although disagreeing over partisan issues in 2004, harbor no deep ideological hostility. I take the former view.

By polarization I do not have in mind partisan disagreements alone. These have always been with us. Since popular voting began in the 19th century, scarcely any winning candidate has received more than 60 percent of the vote, and very few losers have received less than 40 percent. Inevitably, Americans will differ over who should be in the White House. But this does not necessarily mean they are polarized.

By polarization I mean something else: an intense commitment to a candidate, a culture, or an ideology that sets people in one group definitively apart from people in another, rival group. Such a condition is revealed when a candidate for public office is regarded by a competitor and his supporters not simply as wrong but as corrupt or wicked; when one way of thinking about the world is assumed to be morally superior to any other way; when one set of political beliefs is considered to be entirely correct and a rival set wholly wrong. In extreme form, as defined by Richard Hofstadter in *The Paranoid Style in American Politics* (1965), polarization can entail the belief that the other side is in thrall to a secret conspiracy that is using devious means to obtain control over society. Today's versions might go like this: "Liberals employ their dominance of the media, the universities, and Hollywood to enforce a radically secular agenda"; or, "conservatives, working through the religious Right and the big corporations, conspired with their hired neocon advisers to invade Iraq for the sake of oil."

Polarization is not new to this country. It is hard to imagine a society more divided than ours was in 1800, when pro-British, pro-commerce New Englanders supported John Adams for the presidency while pro-French, pro-agriculture Southerners backed Thomas Jefferson. One sign of this hostility was the passage of the Alien and Sedition Acts in 1798; another was that in 1800, just as in 2000, an extremely close election was settled by a struggle in one state (New York in 1800, Florida in 2000).

The fierce contest between Abraham Lincoln and George McClellan in 1864 signaled another national division, this one over the conduct of the Civil War. But thereafter, until recently, the nation ceased to be polarized in that sense. Even in the half-century from 1948 to (roughly) 1996, marked as it was by sometimes strong expressions of feeling over whether the presidency should go to Harry Truman or Thomas Dewey, to Dwight Eisenhower or Adlai Stevenson, to John F. Kennedy or Richard Nixon, to Nixon or Hubert Humphrey, and so forth, opinion surveys do not indicate widespread detestation of one candidate or the other, or of the people who supported him.

Now they do. Today, many Americans and much of the press regularly speak of the president as a dimwit, a charlatan, or a knave. A former

Democratic presidential candidate has asserted that Bush "betrayed" America by launching a war designed to benefit his friends and corporate backers. A senior Democratic Senator has characterized administration policy as a series of "lies, lies, and more lies" and has accused Bush of plotting a "mindless, needless, senseless, and reckless" war. From the other direction, similar expressions of popular disdain have been directed at Senator John Kerry (and before him at President Bill Clinton); if you have not heard them, that may be because (unlike many of my relatives) you do not live in Arkansas or Texas or other locales where the *New York Times* is not read. In these places, Kerry is widely spoken of as a scoundrel.

In the 2004 presidential election, over two-thirds of Kerry voters said they were motivated explicitly by the desire to defeat Bush. By early 2005, President Bush's approval rating, which stood at 94 percent among Republicans, was only 18 percent among Democrats—the largest such gap in the history of the Gallup poll. These data, moreover, were said to reflect a mutual revulsion between whole geographical sections of the country, the so-called Red (Republican) states versus the so-called Blue (Democratic) states. As summed up by the distinguished social scientist who writes humor columns under the name of Dave Barry, residents of Red states are "ignorant racist fascist knuckle-dragging NASCAR-obsessed cousin-marrying roadkill-eating tobacco-juice-dribbling gun-fondling religious fanatic rednecks," while Blue-state residents are "godless unpatriotic pierced-nose Volvo-driving France-loving leftwing Communist latte-sucking tofu-chomping holistic-wacko neurotic vegan weenie perverts."

To be sure, other scholars differ with Dr. Barry. To them, polarization, although a real enough phenomenon, is almost entirely confined to a small number of political elites and members of Congress. In *Culture War?*, which bears the subtitle "The Myth of a Polarized America," Morris Fiorina of Stanford argues that policy differences between voters in Red and Blue states are really quite small, and that most are in general agreement even on issues like abortion and homosexuality.

But the extent of polarization cannot properly be measured by the voting results in Red and Blue states. Many of these states are in fact deeply divided internally between liberal and conservative areas, and gave the nod to one candidate or the other by only a narrow margin. Inferring the views of individual citizens from the gross results of presidential balloting is a questionable procedure.

Nor does Fiorina's analysis capture the very real and very deep division over an issue like abortion. Between 1973, when *Roe v. Wade* was decided, and now, he writes, there has been no change in the degree to which people will or will not accept any one of six reasons to justify an abortion: (1) the woman's health is endangered; (2) she became pregnant because of a rape; (3) there is a strong chance of a fetal defect; (4) the family has a low income; (5) the woman is not married; and (6) the woman simply wants no more children. Fiorina may be right about that. Nevertheless, only about 40 percent of all Americans will support abortion for any of the last three reasons in his series, while over 80 percent will support it for one or another of the first three.

In other words, almost all Americans are for abortion in the case of maternal emergency, but fewer than half if it is simply a matter of the mother's preference. That split—a profoundly important one—has remained in place for over three decades, and it affects how people vote. In 2000 and again in 2004, 70 percent of those who thought abortion should always be legal voted for Al Gore or John Kerry, while over 70 percent of those who thought it should always be illegal voted for George Bush.

Division is just as great over other high-profile issues. Polarization over the war in Iraq, for example, is more pronounced than any war-related controversy in at least a half-century. In the fall of 2005, according to Gallup, 81 percent of Democrats but only 20 percent of Republicans thought the war in Iraq was a mistake. During the Vietnam war, by contrast, itself a famously contentious cause, there was more unanimity across party lines, whether for or against: in late 1968 and early 1969, about equal numbers of Democrats and Republicans thought the intervention there was a mistake. Pretty much the same was true of Korea: in early 1951, 44 percent of Democrats and 61 percent of Republicans thought the war was a mistake—a partisan split, but nowhere near as large as the one over our present campaign in Iraq.

Polarization, then, is real. But what explains its growth? And has it spread beyond the political elites to influence the opinions and attitudes of ordinary Americans?

The answer to the first question, I suspect, can be found in the changing politics of Congress, the new competitiveness of the mass media, and the rise of new interest groups.

That Congress is polarized seems beyond question. When, in 1998, the House deliberated whether to impeach President Clinton, all but four Republican members voted for at least one of the impeachment articles, while only five Democrats voted for even one. In the Senate, 91 percent of Republicans voted to convict on at least one article; every single Democrat voted for acquittal.

The impeachment issue was not an isolated case. In 1993, President Clinton's budget passed both the House and the Senate without a single Republican vote in favor. The same deep partisan split occurred over taxes and supplemental appropriations. Nor was this a blip: since 1950, there has been a steady increase in the percentage of votes in Congress pitting most Democrats against most Republicans.

In the midst of the struggle to pacify Iraq, Howard Dean, the chairman of the Democratic National Committee, said the war could not be won and Nancy Pelosi, the leader of the House Democrats, endorsed the view that American forces should be brought home as soon as possible. By contrast, although there was congressional grumbling (mostly by Republicans) about Korea and complaints (mostly by Democrats) about Vietnam, and although Senator George Aiken of Vermont famously proposed that we declare victory and withdraw, I cannot remember party leaders calling for unconditional surrender.

The reasons for the widening fissures in Congress are not far to seek. Each of the political parties was once a coalition of dissimilar forces: liberal Northern Democrats and conservative Southern Democrats, liberal coastal Republicans and conservative Midwestern Republicans. No longer; the realignments of the South (now overwhelmingly Republican) and of New England (now strongly Democratic) have all but eliminated legislators who deviate from the party's leadership. Conservative Democrats and liberal Republicans are endangered species now approaching extinction. At the same time, the ideological gap between the parties is growing: if there was once a large overlap between Democrats and Republicans—remember "Tweedledum and Tweedledee"?—today that congruence has almost disappeared. By the late 1990s, virtually every Democrat was more liberal than virtually every Republican.

The result has been not only intense partisanship but a sharp rise in congressional incivility. In 1995, a Republican-controlled Senate passed a budget that President Clinton proceeded to veto; in the loggerhead that followed, many federal agencies shut down (in a move that backfired on the Republicans). Congressional debates have seen an increase not only in heated exchanges but in the number of times a representative's words are either ruled out of order or "taken down" (that is, written by the clerk and then read aloud, with the offending member being asked if he or she wishes to withdraw them).

It has been suggested that congressional polarization is exacerbated by new districting arrangements that make each House seat safe for either a Democratic or a Republican incumbent. If only these seats were truly competitive, it is said, more centrist legislators would be elected. That seems plausible, but David C. King of Harvard has shown that it is wrong: in the House, the more competitive the district, the more extreme the views of the winner. This odd finding is apparently the consequence of a nomination process dominated by party activists. In primary races, where turnout is low (and seems to be getting lower), the ideologically motivated tend to exercise a preponderance of influence.

All this suggests a situation very unlike the half-century before the 1990s, if perhaps closer to certain periods in the eighteenth and nineteenth centuries. Then, too, incivility was common in Congress, with members not only passing the most scandalous remarks about each other but on occasion striking their rivals with canes or fists. Such partisan feeling ran highest when Congress was deeply divided over slavery before the Civil War and over Reconstruction after it. Today the issues are different, but the emotions are not dissimilar.

Next, the mass media: Not only are they themselves increasingly polarized, but consumers are well aware of it and act on that awareness. Fewer people now subscribe to newspapers or watch the network evening news. Although some of this decline may be explained by a preference for entertainment over news, some undoubtedly reflects the growing conviction that the mainstream press generally does not tell the truth, or at least not the whole truth.

In part, media bias feeds into, and off, an increase in business competition. In the 1950s, television news amounted to a brief 30-minute interlude in the day's programming, and not a very profitable one at that; for the rest of the time, the three networks supplied us with westerns and situation comedies. Today, television news is a vast, growing, and very profitable venture by the many broadcast and cable outlets that supply news twenty-four hours a day, seven days a week.

The news we get is not only more omnipresent, it is also more competitive and hence often more adversarial. When there were only three television networks, and radio stations were forbidden by the fairness doctrine from broadcasting controversial views, the media gravitated toward the middle of the ideological spectrum, where the large markets could be found. But now that technology has created cable news and the Internet, and now that the fairness doctrine has by and large been repealed, many media outlets find their markets at the ideological extremes.

Here is where the sharper antagonism among political leaders and their advisers and associates comes in. As one journalist has remarked about the change in his profession, "We don't deal in facts [any longer], but in attributed opinions." Or, these days, in unattributed opinions. And those opinions are more intensely rivalrous than was once the case.

The result is that, through commercial as well as ideological self-interest, the media contribute heavily to polarization. Broadcasters are eager for stories to fill their round-the-clock schedules, and at the same time reluctant to trust the government as a source for those stories. Many media outlets are clearly liberal in their orientation; with the arrival of Fox News and the growth of talk radio, many are now just as clearly conservative.

The evidence of liberal bias in the mainstream media is very strong. The Center for Media and Public Affairs (CMPA) has been systematically studying television broadcasts for a quarter-century. In the 2004 presidential campaign, John Kerry received more favorable mentions than any presidential candidate in CMPA's history, especially during the month before election day. This is not new: since 1980 (and setting aside the recent advent of Fox News), the Democratic candidate has received more favorable mentions than the Republican candidate in every race except the 1988 contest between Michael Dukakis and George H. W. Bush. A similarly clear orientation characterizes weekly newsmagazines like *Time* and *Newsweek*.

For its part, talk radio is listened to by about one-sixth of the adult public, and that one-sixth is made up mostly of conservatives. National Public Radio has an audience of about the same size; it is disproportionately liberal. The same breakdown affects cable-television news, where the rivalry is between CNN (and MSNBC) and Fox News. Those who watch CNN are more likely to be Democrats than Republicans; the reverse is emphatically true of Fox. As for news and opinion on the Internet, which has become an important source for college graduates in particular, it, too, is largely polarized along political and ideological lines, emphasized even more by the culture that has grown up around news blogs.

At one time, our culture was only weakly affected by the media because news organizations had only a few points of access to us and were largely moderate and audience-maximizing enterprises. Today the media have many lines of access, and reflect both the maximization of controversy and the cultivation of niche markets. Once the media talked to us; now they shout at us.

And then there are the interest groups. In the past, the major ones—the National Association of Manufacturers, the Chamber of Commerce, and labor organizations like the AFL-CIO—were concerned with their own material interests. They are still active, but the loudest messages today come from very different sources and have a very different cast to them. They are issued by groups concerned with social and cultural matters like civil rights, managing the environment, alternatives to the public schools, the role of women, access to firearms, and so forth, and they directly influence the way people view politics.

Interest groups preoccupied with material concerns can readily find ways to arrive at compromise solutions to their differences; interest groups divided by issues of rights or morality find compromise very difficult. The positions taken by many of these groups and their supporters, often operating within the two political parties, profoundly affect the selection of candidates for office. In brief, it is hard to imagine someone opposed to abortion receiving the Democratic nomination for President, or someone in favor of it receiving the Republican nomination.

Outside the realm of party politics, interest groups also file briefs in important court cases and can benefit from decisions that in turn help shape the political debate. Abortion became a hot controversy in the 1970s not because the American people were already polarized on the matter but because their (mainly centrist) views were not consulted; instead, national policy was determined by the Supreme Court in a decision, *Roe v. Wade*, that itself reflected a definition of "rights" vigorously promoted by certain well-defined interest groups.

Polarization not only is real and has increased, but it has also spread to rank-and-file voters through elite influence.

In *The Nature and Origins of Mass Opinion* . . . , John R. Zaller of UCLA listed a number of contemporary issues—homosexuality, a nuclear freeze, the war in Vietnam, busing for school integration, the 1990–91 war to expel Iraq from Kuwait—and measured the views held about them by politically aware citizens. (By "politically aware," Zaller meant people who did well answering neutral factual questions about politics.) His findings were illuminating.

Take the Persian Gulf war. Iraq had invaded Kuwait in August 1990. From that point through the congressional elections in November 1990, scarcely any elite voices were raised to warn against anything the United States might contemplate doing in response. Two days after the mid-term elections, however, President George H. W. Bush announced that he was sending many more troops to the Persian Gulf. This provoked strong criticism from some members of Congress, especially Democrats.

As it happens, a major public-opinion survey was under way just as these events were unfolding. Before criticism began to be voiced in Congress, both registered Democrats and registered Republicans had supported Bush's vaguely announced intention of coming to the aid of Kuwait; the more politically aware they were, the greater their support. After the onset of elite criticism, the support of Republican voters went up, but Democratic support flattened out. As Bush became more vigorous in indicating his aims, politically aware voters began to differ sharply, with Democratic support declining and Republican support increasing further.

Much the same pattern can be seen in popular attitudes toward the other issues studied by Zaller. As political awareness increases, attitudes split apart, with, for example, highly aware liberals favoring busing and job guarantees and opposing the war in Vietnam, and highly aware conservatives opposing busing and job guarantees and supporting the war in Vietnam.

But why should this be surprising? To imagine that extremist politics has been confined to the chattering classes is to believe that Congress, the media, and American interest groups operate in an ideological vacuum. I find that assumption implausible.

As for the extent to which these extremist views have spread, that is probably best assessed by looking not at specific issues but at enduring political values and party preferences. In 2004, only 12 percent of Democrats approved of George Bush; at earlier periods, by contrast, three to four times as many Democrats approved of Ronald Reagan, Gerald Ford, Richard Nixon, and Dwight D. Eisenhower. Over the course of about two decades, in other words, party affiliation had come to exercise a critical influence over what people thought about a sitting President.

The same change can be seen in the public's view of military power. Since the late 1980s, Republicans have been more willing than Democrats to say that "the best way to ensure peace is through military strength." By the late 1990s and on into 2003, well over two-thirds of all Republicans agreed with this view, but far fewer than half of all Democrats did. In 2005, three-fourths of all Democrats but fewer than a third of all Republicans told pollsters that good diplomacy was the best way to ensure peace. In the same survey, two-thirds of all Republicans but only one fourth of all Democrats said they would fight for this country "whether it is right or wrong."

Unlike in earlier years, the parties are no longer seen as Tweedledum and Tweedledee. To the contrary, as they sharpen their ideological differences, attentive voters have sharpened their ideological differences. They now like either the Democrats or the Republicans more than they once did, and are less apt to feel neutral toward either one.

How deep does this polarization reach? As measured by opinion polls, the gap between Democrats and Republicans was twice as great in 2004 as in 1972. In fact, rank-and-file Americans disagree more strongly today than did politically active Americans in 1972.

To be sure, this mass polarization involves only a minority of all voters, but the minority is sizable, and a significant part of it is made up of the college-educated. As Marc Hetherington of Vanderbilt puts it: "people with the greatest ability to assimilate new information, those with more formal education, are most affected by elite polarization." And that cohort has undeniably grown.

In 1900, only 10 percent of all young Americans went to high school. My father, in common with many men his age in the early twentieth century, dropped out of school after the eighth grade. Even when I graduated from college, the first in my family to do so, fewer than one-tenth of all Americans over the age of twenty-five had gone that far. Today [2006], 84 percent of adult Americans have graduated from high school and nearly 27 percent have graduated from college. This extraordinary growth in schooling has produced an ever larger audience for political agitation.

Ideologically, an even greater dividing line than undergraduate education is postgraduate education. People who have proceeded beyond college seem to be very different from those who stop with a high-school or college diploma. Thus, about a sixth of all voters describe themselves as liberals, but the figure for those with a postgraduate degree is well over a quarter. In mid-2004, about half of all voters trusted George Bush; less than a third of those with a postgraduate education did. In November of the same year, when over half of all college graduates voted for Bush, well over half of the smaller cohort who had done postgraduate work voted for Kerry. According to the Pew Center for Research on the People and the Press, more than half of all Democrats with a postgraduate education supported the antiwar candidacy of Howard Dean.

The effect of postgraduate education is reinforced by being in a profession. Between 1900 and 1960, write John B. Judis and Ruy Teixeira in *The Emerging Democratic Majority* . . . , professionals voted pretty much the same way as business managers; by 1988, the former began supporting Democrats while the latter supported Republicans. On the other hand, the effect of postgraduate education seems to outweigh the effect of affluence. For most voters, including college graduates, having higher incomes means becoming more conservative; not so for those with a postgraduate education, whose liberal predilections are immune to the wealth effect.

The results of this linkage between ideology, on the one hand, and congressional polarization, media influence, interest-group demands, and education on the other are easily read in the commentary surrounding the 2004 election. In their zeal to denigrate the President, liberals, pronounced one conservative pundit, had "gone quite around the twist." According to liberal spokesmen, conservatives with their "religious intolerance" and their determination to rewrite the Constitution had so befuddled their fellow Americans that a "great nation was felled by a poisonous nut."

If such wholesale slurs are not signs of polarization, then the word has no meaning. To a degree that we cannot precisely measure, and over issues that we cannot exactly list, polarization has seeped down into the public, where it has assumed the form of a culture war. The sociologist James Davison Hunter, who has written about this phenomenon in a mainly religious context, defines culture war as "political and social hostility rooted in different systems of moral understanding." Such conflicts, he writes, which can involve "fundamental ideas about who we are as Americans," are waged both across the religious/secular divide and within religions themselves, where those with an "orthodox" view of moral authority square off against those with a "progressive" view.

To some degree, this terminology is appropriate to today's political situation as well. We are indeed in a culture war in Hunter's sense, though I believe this war is itself but another component, or another symptom, of the larger ideological polarization that has us in its grip. Conservative thinking on political issues has religious roots, but it also has roots that are fully as secular as anything on the Left. By the same token, the liberal attack on conservatives derives in part from an explicitly "progressive" religious orientation—liberal Protestantism or Catholicism, or Reform Judaism—but in part from the same secular sources shared by many conservatives.

But what, one might ask, is wrong with having well-defined parties arguing vigorously about the issues that matter? Is it possible that polarized politics is a good thing, encouraging sharp debate and clear positions? Perhaps that is true on those issues where reasonable compromises can be devised. But there are two limits to such an arrangement.

First, many Americans believe that unbridgeable political differences have prevented leaders from addressing the problems they were elected to address. As a result, distrust of government mounts, leading to an alienation from politics altogether. The steep decline in popular approval of our national officials has many causes, but surely one of them is that ordinary voters agree among themselves more than political elites agree with each other—and the elites are far more numerous than they once were.

In the 1950s, a committee of the American Political Science Association (APSA) argued the case for a "responsible" two-party system. The model the APSA had in mind was the more ideological and therefore more "coherent" party system of Great Britain. At the time, scarcely anyone thought our parties could be transformed in such a supposedly salutary direction. Instead, as Governor George Wallace of Alabama put it in his failed third-party bid for the presidency, there was not a "dime's worth of difference" between Democrats and Republicans.

What Wallace forgot was that, however alike the parties were, the public liked them that way. A half-century ago, Tweedledum and Tweedledee enjoyed the support of the American people; the more different they have become, the greater has been the drop in popular confidence in both them and the federal government.

A final drawback of polarization is more profound. Sharpened debate is arguably helpful with respect to domestic issues, but not for the management of important foreign and military matters. The United States, an unrivaled superpower with unparalleled responsibilities for protecting the peace and defeating terrorists, is now forced to discharge those duties with its own political house in disarray.

We fought World War II as a united nation, even against two enemies (Germany and Italy) that had not attacked us. We began the wars in Korea and Vietnam with some degree of unity, too, although it was eventually whittled away. By the early 1990s, when we expelled Iraq from Kuwait, we had to do so over the objections of congressional critics; the first President Bush avoided putting the issue to Congress altogether. In 2003 we toppled Saddam Hussein in the face of catcalls from many domestic leaders and opinion-makers. Now, in stabilizing Iraq and helping that country create a new free government, we have proceeded despite intense and mounting criticism, much of it voiced by politicians who before the war agreed that Saddam Hussein was an evil menace in possession of weapons of mass destruction and that we had to remove him.

Denmark or Luxembourg can afford to exhibit domestic anguish and uncertainty over military policy; the United States cannot. A divided America encourages our enemies, disheartens our allies, and saps our resolve—potentially to fatal effect. What General Giap of North Vietnam once said of us is even truer today. America cannot be defeated on the battlefield, but it can be defeated at home. Polarization is a force that can defeat us.

"Polarized America?"

February 21, 2006

To the editor:

James Q. Wilson (February) takes issue with my demonstration in *Culture War? The Myth of a Polarized America* (with Samuel Abrams and Jeremy Pope) that the polarization evident among the members of the American political class has only a faint reflection in the American public. As a long-time admirer of Wilson's work I am naturally concerned when his take on some aspect of American politics differs from mine. But I believe that his criticisms are a result of misunderstanding. I would like to address two of them.

First, Wilson discounts our red state-blue state comparisons with the comment that "Inferring the views of individual citizens from the gross results of presidential balloting is a questionable procedure." Indeed it is, which is why we did not do that. As we wrote in the book, inferring polarization from close elections is precisely what pundits have done and why their conclusions have been wrong. In contrast, we report detailed analyses of the policy views expressed by voters in 2000 and 2004 and contrary to the claims of Garry Wills, Maureen Dowd, and other op-ed columnists, we find surprisingly small differences between the denizens of the blue states and the red states. As we show in the book and emphasize repeatedly, people's *choices* (as expressed, say, in presidential balloting) can be polarized while their *positions* are not, and the evidence strongly indicates that this is the case.

Moreover, we report that not only are red and blue state citizens surprisingly similar in their views, but other studies find little evidence of growing polarization no matter how one slices and dices the population—affluent v. poor, white v. black v. brown, old v. young, well educated v. the less educated, men v. women, and so on. Like many before him, Wilson confuses partisan *sorting* with polarization—the Democrats have largely shed their conservative southern wing while Republicans have largely shed their liberal Rockefeller wing, resulting in more distinct parties, even while the aggregate distribution of ideology and issue stances among the citizenry remains much the same as in the past.

Second, Wilson criticizes our analysis of Americans' views on the specific issue of abortion, contending that the small numerical differences expressed by people on a General Social Survey scale constitute a significantly larger substantive difference. Although we disagree, even if one accepted Wilson's contention, it would not apply to our supporting analysis of a differently-worded Gallup survey item that yields the same conclusions, or to numerous other survey items that clearly show that most Americans are "pro-choice, buts."

For example, Wilson notes that "70 percent of those who thought abortion should always be legal voted for Al Gore or John Kerry, while over 70 percent of those who thought it should always be illegal voted for George Bush." True enough, but he does not mention that Gallup repeatedly finds that a majority of the American people place themselves between those polar categories—they think abortion should be "legal only under certain circumstances." Even limiting the analysis to avowed partisans, in 2005 only 30 percent of Democrats thought abortion should always be legal, and fewer than 30 percent of Republicans thought it should always be illegal. One can raise questions about every survey item that has ever been asked, but the cumulative weight of the evidence on Americans' abortion views is overwhelming. Contrary to the wishes of the activists on both sides, the American people prefer a middle ground on abortion, period.

Wilson approvingly cites James Davison Hunter, whose book, *Culture War*, inspired Patrick Buchanan's 1992 speech at the Republican National Convention. In a forthcoming Brookings Institution volume, Hunter now limits his thesis to "somewhere between 10 and 15 percent who occupy these opposing moral and ideological universes." That leaves more than 80 percent of the American public not engaged in the moral and ideological battles reveled in by the political class. Note that Wilson's examples of incivil discourse reference "the press," "a former Democratic presidential candidate," "a senior Democratic Senator," "liberal spokesmen," and "one conservative pundit." Absent from this list are well-intentioned, ordinary working Americans not given to the kind of incendiary remarks that get quoted by journalists.

I share Wilson's concern with the potentially harmful consequences of polarization. But the first step in addressing those concerns is to get the facts correct. I remain convinced that we have done that. If Americans are offered competent, pragmatic candidates with a problem-solving orientation, the shallow popular roots of political polarization will be exposed for all to see.

Morris P. Fiorina
Stanford, California

59

"Tea Minus Zero"

John B. Judis

Liberals have responded to the Tea Party movement by reaching a comforting conclusion: that there is no way these guys can possibly be for real. The movement has variously been described as a "front group for the Republican party" and a "media creation"; Paul Krugman has called Tea Party rallies "AstroTurf (fake grass roots) events, manufactured by the usual suspects."

I can understand why liberals would want to dismiss the Tea Party movement as an inauthentic phenomenon; it would certainly be welcome news if it were. The sentiments on display at Tea Party rallies go beyond run-of-the-mill anti-tax, anti-spending conservatism and into territory that rightly strikes liberals as truly disturbing. Among the signs I saw at an April 15 protest in Washington: "IF IT SOUNDS LIKE MARX AND ACTS LIKE STALIN IT MUST BE OBAMA," "STOP OBAMA'S BROWN-SHIRT INFILTRAITORS," and "OBAMA BIN LYIN," which was accompanied by an illustration of the president looking like a monkey.

But the Tea Party movement is not inauthentic, and—contrary to the impression its rallies give off—it isn't a fringe faction either. It is a genuine popular movement, one that has managed to unite a number of ideological strains from U.S. history—some recent, some older. These strains can be described as many things, but they cannot be dismissed as passing phenomena. Much as liberals would like to believe otherwise, there is good reason to think the Tea Party movement could exercise considerable influence over our politics in the coming years.

The movement essentially began on February 19, 2009, when CNBC commentator Rick Santelli, speaking from the floor of the Chicago Mercantile Exchange, let loose against the Obama administration's plan to help homeowners who could no longer pay their mortgages. "This is America!" Santelli exclaimed. "How many of you people want to pay for your neighbors' mortgage that has an extra bathroom and can't pay their bills?" Santelli called for a "Chicago Tea Party" to protest the administration's plan.

Santelli's appeal was answered by a small group of bloggers, policy wonks, and Washington politicos who were primarily drawn from the libertarian wing of the conservative movement. They included John O'Hara from the Illinois Policy Institute (who has written a history of the movement, titled *A New American Tea Party*); Brendan Steinhauser of

FreedomWorks, a Washington lobbying group run by former Representative Dick Armey; and blogger Michael Patrick Leahy, a founder of Top Conservatives on Twitter. The initial round of Tea Party protests took place at the end of February in over 30 cities. There were more protests in April, and, by the time of the massive September 12 protest last year, the Tea Party movement had officially arrived as a political force.

Like many American movements, the Tea Parties are not tightly organized from above. They are a network of local groups and national ones (Tea Party Patriots, Tea Party Express, Tea Party Nation), Washington lobbies and quasi-think tanks (FreedomWorks, Americans for Prosperity), bloggers, and talk-show hosts. There are no national membership lists, but extensive polls done by Quinnipiac, the Winston Group, and Economist/YouGov suggest that the movement commands the active allegiance of between 13 percent and 15 percent of the electorate. That is a formidable number, and, judging from other polls that ask whether someone has a "favorable" view of the Tea Parties, the movement gets a sympathetic hearing from as much as 40 percent of the electorate.

Tea Partiers' favorite politician is undoubtedly Sarah Palin—according to the Economist/YouGov poll, 71 percent of Tea Partiers think Palin "is more qualified to be president than Barack Obama" (and another 15 percent are "not sure")—but, more than anyone else, the movement takes its cues from Glenn Beck. Unlike fellow talkers Rush Limbaugh and Sean Hannity, Beck has never been a conventional Republican; he calls himself a conservative rather than a member of the GOP. While Limbaugh has attempted to soft-pedal his personal failings, the baby-faced Beck makes his into a story of redemption. He is, in his own words, an "average, everyday person." You need to have followed Beck's conspiratorial meanderings to understand what preoccupies many members of the Tea Party movement. At the Washington demonstration in April, for instance, there were people holding signs attacking Frances Fox Piven and Richard Cloward, two 1960s-era Columbia University sociologists who, Beck claims, were the brains behind both the community group ACORN and Obama's attempt to destroy capitalism by bankrupting the government through national health care reform.

In the last year, the movement's focus has shifted from demonstrations to elections. Currently, Tea Party groups are backing Republican Senate candidates in Kentucky, Utah, and Florida, while trying to knock off Democratic Senators Harry Reid in Nevada and Arlen Specter in Pennsylvania. In some places, Tea Party organizations have begun to displace the state GOP. Last month, Action is Brewing, the northern Nevada Tea Party affiliate, hosted a televised debate for the Republican gubernatorial and senatorial candidates. In addition, numerous candidates are running for Congress as Tea Party supporters.

The Tea Parties are the descendants of a number of conservative insurgencies from the past two generations: the anti-tax rebellion of the late

'70s, the Moral Majority and Christian Coalition of the '80s and '90s, and Pat Buchanan's presidential runs. Like the Tea Partiers I saw in Washington—and the picture of the Tea Partiers put forward by the Winston and Quinnipiac polls—these movements have been almost entirely white, disproportionately middle-aged or older, and more male than female (though parts of the Christian right are an exception on this count). A majority of their adherents generally are not college-educated, with incomes in the middle range—attributes that also closely match the Tea Party movement's demographic profile. (A misleading picture of Tea Partiers as college-educated and affluent came from a *New York Times*/CBS poll of people who merely "support," but don't necessarily have anything to do with, the Tea Party movement. The other polls surveyed people who say they are "part of" the movement.)

Sociologists who have studied these earlier movements describe their followers as coming from the "marginal segments of the middle class." That's a sociological, but also a political, fact. These men and women look uneasily upward at corporate CEOs and investment bankers, and downward at low-wage service workers and laborers, many of whom are minorities. And their political outlook is defined by whether they primarily blame those below or above for the social and economic anxieties they feel. In the late nineteenth and early twentieth century, the marginal middle class was the breeding ground for left-wing attacks against Wall Street. For the last half-century, it has nourished right-wing complaints about blacks, illegal immigrants, and the poor.

It isn't just demography that the Tea Parties have in common with recent conservative movements; it's also politics. To be sure, some of the original Tea Party organizers were young libertarians, many of whom, like Brendan Steinhauser, voted for Ron Paul in 2008 and have rediscovered Ayn Rand's ethic of rational selfishness. They remain part of the movement—one sign I saw at the Washington rally read, "WE ARE JOHN GALT," referring to the hero of *Atlas Shrugged*—but, as the movement has grown, its adherents have become more conventionally conservative. As Grover Norquist likes to point out, what distinguishes one conservative group from another is not their members' overall views, but what "moves" them to demonstrate or to vote. The Christian right, for instance, went to the barricades over abortion and gay marriage, yet most members also hold conservative economic views. Likewise, the Tea Partiers have been moved to action by economic issues, but they share the outlook of social conservatives. According to the Economist/YouGov poll, 74 percent of Tea Party members think abortion is "murder," and 81 percent are against gay marriage. Sixty-three percent are in favor of public school students learning that "the Book of Genesis in the Bible explains how God created the world"; 62 percent think that "the only way to Heaven is through Jesus Christ." These beliefs are on display at rallies: In Washington, one demonstrator in clerical garb held a sign saying, "GOD HATES TAXES." Moreover, aside from the followers of Ron Paul, Tea Party members also share the post-September 11 national security views of the GOP. When Tea Partiers were asked to name the "most important issue" to them, terrorism came in third out of ten, behind only the economy and the budget deficit.

If you look at the people who are running as pro–Tea Party candidates, you discover that some of them have simply graduated from one stage of the conservative movement to another. Jason Meade, who is running for Congress in Ohio, was just out of school, working in his father's business and playing music, when he "returned to the church and left the music world behind." Now 38, he sees his participation in Tea Party politics as a continuation of his twelve subsequent years in ministry school. "I decided to try and minister in a new way; by trying to be involved in the protection of the freedoms and liberty that God has given us and that have been woven into the fabric of our country," he wrote on his Web site. Jason Sager, 36, who is running in a Republican congressional primary northeast of Tampa, got into conservative politics in the wake of September 11. A Navy veteran, he joined a group called Protest Warrior that staged counter-demonstrations at antiwar rallies, and he was a volun-teer in George W. Bush's 2004 campaign. After Obama's election, he got involved with Glenn Beck's 912 Project and, then, with the local Tea Parties.

But the Tea Parties' roots in U.S. history go back much further than the conservative movements of recent decades. The Tea Parties are defined by three general ideas that have played a key role in U.S. politics since the country's early days. The first is an obsession with decline. This idea, which traces back to the outlook of New England Puritans during the seventeenth century, consists of a belief that a golden age occurred some time ago; that we are now in a period of severe social, economic, or moral decay; that evil forces and individuals are the cause of this situation; that the goal of politics is to restore the earlier period; and that the key to doing so is heeding a special text that can serve as a guidebook for the journey backward. (The main difference between the far right and far left is that the left locates the golden age in the future.) The Puritans were trying to reproduce the circumstances of early Christianity in New England, using the Bible as their guiding text. Their enemies were Catholics and the Church of England, who they believed had corrupted the religion. For the Tea Partiers, the golden age is the time of the Founders, and adherence to the Constitution is the means to restore this period in the face of challenges from secular humanism, radical Islam, and especially socialism.

Beck has been instrumental in sacralizing the Constitution. He has touted the works of the late W. Cleon Skousen, a John Birch Society defender who projected his ultraconservative views back onto the Founding Fathers. In *The 5000 Year Leap*, which has been reissued with a foreword by Beck, Skousen claimed that the Founders "warned against the 'welfare state'" and against "the drift toward the collectivist left."

In Arizona, Tea Party members hand out copies of the Constitution at political meetings the way a missionary group might hand out Bibles. The San Antonio Tea Party group has demanded that politicians sign a "contract with the Constitution." In speeches, Tea Partiers cite articles and amendments from the Constitution the same way that clerics cite Biblical verses. Speaking at the Lakeland Tea Party rally on tax day, Jason Sager said, "You are now able to see the most pressing issue that faces our nation and our society. Do you know what that issue is? We are now witnessing the fundamental breakdown of the republican form of government that we are guaranteed in Article Four, Section Four of our Constitution." In typical fashion, Sager did not go on to explain what Article Four, Section Four was. (You can look it up. I had to.)

Just as the Puritans believed Catholics and the Church of England were undermining Christianity, the Tea Partiers have fixated on nefarious individuals and groups—Saul Alinsky, ACORN, and, of course, Obama himself—who they believe are destroying the country. (According to the Economist/YouGov poll, 52 percent of Tea Party members think ACORN stole the 2008 election from John McCain; another 24 percent are still not sure.) "America has let thieves into her home," writes Beck, "and that nagging in your gut is a final warning that our country is about to be stolen." Their determination to locate the threat outside the United States accounts for their emphasis on Obama being a socialist, Marxist, communist, or even fascist—all of which are foreign faiths—rather than what he is: a conventional American liberal. It also helps explain the repeated references to Obama's African father. And it explains why some Tea Partiers continue to believe, in the face of incontrovertible evidence, that Obama was born outside the United States. The Economist/YouGov poll found that 34 percent of Tea Party members think he was not born in the United States, and another 34 percent are not sure.

But how could a movement that cultivates such crazy, conspiratorial views be regarded favorably by as much as 40 percent of the electorate? That is where the Tea Party movement's second link to early U.S. history comes in. The Tea Partiers may share the Puritans' fear of decline, but it is what they share with Thomas Jefferson that has far broader appeal: a staunch anti-statism. What began as a sentiment of the left—a rejection of state monopolies—became, after the industrial revolution and the rise of the labor movement, a weapon against progressive reforms. The basic idea—that government is a "necessary evil"—has retained its power, and, when the economy has faltered, Americans have been quick to blame Washington, perhaps even before they looked at Wall Street or big corporations. It happened in the late '70s under Jimmy Carter and in the early '90s under George H. W. Bush; and it has happened again during Obama's first 18 months in office. According to a Pew poll, the percentage of Americans "angry" with government has risen from 10 percent in February 2000 to 21 percent today, while another 56 percent are "frustrated" with government.

Of course, during Franklin Roosevelt's first term, most voters didn't blame the incumbent administration for the Great Depression. Roosevelt was able to deflect blame for the depression back onto the Hoover administration and the "economic royalists" of Wall Street and corporate America. But Roosevelt took office at the nadir of the Great Depression, and his policies achieved dramatic improvements in unemployment and economic growth during his first term. Obama took office barely four months after the financial crisis visibly hit, and he has had to preside over growing unemployment.

Simmering economic frustration also accounts for the final historical strain that defines the Tea Parties: They are part of a tradition of producerism that dates to Andrew Jackson. Jacksonian Democrats believed that workers should enjoy the fruits of what they produce and not have to share them with the merchants and bankers who didn't actually create anything. The Populists of the late nineteenth century invoked this ethic in denouncing the Eastern bankers who held their farms hostage. Producerism also underlay Roosevelt's broadsides against economic royalists and Bill Clinton's promise to give priority to those who "work hard and play by the rules."

During the 1970s, conservatives began invoking producerism to justify their attacks on the welfare state, and it was at the core of the conservative tax revolt. While the Jacksonians and Populists had largely directed their anger upward, conservatives directed their ire at the people below who were beneficiaries of state programs—from the "welfare queens" of the ghetto to the "illegal aliens" of the barrio. Like the attack against "big government," this conservative producerism has most deeply resonated during economic downturns. And the Tea Parties have clearly built their movement around it.

Producerism was at the heart of Santelli's rant against government forcing the responsible middle class to subsidize those who bought homes they couldn't afford. In his history of the Tea Party movement, O'Hara described an America divided between "moochers, big and small, corporate and individual, trampling over themselves with their hands out demanding endless bailouts" and "disgusted, hardworking citizens getting sick of being played for chumps and punished for practicing personal responsibility." The same theme recurs in the Tea Partiers' rejection of liberal legislation. Beck dismissed Obama's health care reform plan as "good old socialism . . . raping the pocketbooks of the rich to give to the poor." Speaking to cheers at the April 15 rally in Washington, Armey denounced the progressive income tax in the same terms. "I can't steal your money and give it to this guy," he declared. "Therefore, I shouldn't use the power of the state to steal your money and give it to this guy."

The Tea Parties are not managed by the Republican National Committee, and they are not really a wing of the GOP. It is telling that Beck devoted his February speech at the Conservative Political Action Conference to bashing Republicans—and that, in a survey of 50 Tea Party leaders, the Sam Adams Alliance found that 28 percent identify themselves as Independents and 11 percent as Tea Party members rather than Republicans. Still, the Tea Partiers' political objective is clearly to push the GOP to the right. They agitated last summer for a Republican party-line vote against health care reform and are now arguing that states have a constitutional right to refuse to comply with it. They have been calling the offices of Republican senators to demand that they oppose a bipartisan compromise on financial regulatory reform. In South Carolina, they have attacked Senator Lindsey Graham, who is also a favorite Beck target, for backing a cap-and-trade [environmental] bill. The Arizona Tea Party pressured Governor Jan Brewer to sign the now-infamous bill targeting illegal immigrants. And Tea Party Nation has issued a "Red Alert" to prevent Congress from adopting "amnesty" legislation.

If the GOP wins back at least one house of Congress in November, the Tea Parties will be able to claim victory and demand a say in Republican congressional policies. That could lead to a replay of the Newt Gingrich Congress of 1995–1996, from which the country was lucky to escape relatively unscathed. But, beyond this, it's hard to say what will become of the movement. If the economy improves in a significant way next year, it is likely to fade. That is what happened to the tax revolt, which peaked from 1978 to 1982 and then subsided. But, if the economy limps along—say, in the manner of Japan over the last 15 years—then the Tea Parties will likely remain strong, and may even become a bigger force in U.S. politics than they are now.

For all of its similarities to previous insurgencies, the Tea Party movement differs in one key respect from the most prominent conservative movement of recent years, the Christian right: The Tea Parties do not have the same built-in impediments to growth. The Christian right looked like it was going to expand in the early '90s, but it ran up against the limit of its politics, which were grounded ultimately in an esoteric theology and a network of churches. If it strayed too far from the implications of that theology, it risked splitting its membership. But, if it articulated it—as Pat Robertson and others did at various inopportune moments—then it risked alienating the bulk of Americans. The Tea Parties do not have the same problem. They have their own crazy conspiracy theories, but even the wackiest Tea Partiers wouldn't demand that a candidate seeking their endorsement agree that ACORN fixed the election or that Obama is foreign-born. And their core appeal on government and spending will continue to resonate as long as the economy sputters. None of this is what liberals want to hear, but we might as well face reality: The Tea Party movement—firmly grounded in a number of durable U.S. political traditions and well-positioned for a time of economic uncertainty—could be around for a while.

DISCUSSION QUESTIONS

1. According to Wilson and Judis, what are the chief factors contributing to polarization and cultural division in the United States? Are these factors likely to change any time soon? What part, if any, of Wilson's and Judis's arguments would Fiorina agree with?

2. Based on the articles and other information you might have, do you think Fiorina is right that the American public is not deeply split on a range of issues and that they tend to favor more moderate solutions to problems? Can you think of issues for which this would be true?

3. If you were an adviser for one of the two major parties, how would you advise them to address the issue of polarization or culture war? Should they emphasize issues where broader consensus might be possible? Or is it the job of political parties to emphasize precisely those issues that might be the most divisive in order to appeal to their strongest supporters? Which is better for voters—a focus on consensus or on contrasts?

4. Party strategists often talk about changing a party's public image. In your view, what would a party have to do to change its public image significantly? What would convince you that a party had changed?

CHAPTER 12

Groups and Interests

60

"Political Association in the United States," from *Democracy in America*

Alexis de Tocqueville

The right of political association—joining together—has long been a cornerstone of American democracy. Alexis de Tocqueville, a French citizen who studied early nineteenth-century American society, argued that the right to associate provides an important check on a majority's power to suppress a political minority. Tocqueville pointed out that allowing citizens to associate in a variety of groups with a variety of interests provides a political outlet for all types of political perspectives to be heard. It also enables compromises to be reached as each interest group attempts to build support among shifting coalitions on individual issues. "There is a place for individual independence," Tocqueville argued, in the American system of government. "[A]s in society, all the members are advancing at the same time toward the same goal, but they are not obliged to follow exactly the same path."

Better use has been made of association and this powerful instrument of action has been applied to more varied aims in America than anywhere else in the world.

*   *   *

The inhabitant of the United States learns from birth that he must rely on himself to combat the ills and trials of life; he is restless and defiant in his outlook toward the authority of society and appeals to its power only when he cannot do without it. The beginnings of this attitude first appear at school, where the children, even in their games, submit to rules settled by themselves and punish offenses which they have defined themselves. The same attitude turns up again in all the affairs of social life. If some obstacle blocks the public road halting the circulation of traffic, the neighbors at once form a deliberative body; this improvised assembly produces an executive authority which remedies the trouble before anyone has thought of the possibility of some previously constituted authority beyond that of those concerned. Where enjoyment is concerned, people associate to make festivities grander and more orderly. Finally, associations are formed to combat exclusively moral troubles: intemperance is fought in common. Public security, trade and industry, and morals and religion all provide the aims for associations in the United States. There is no end which the human will despairs of attaining by the free action of the collective power of individuals.

* * *

The right of association being recognized, citizens can use it in different ways. An association simply consists in the public and formal support of specific doctrines by a certain number of individuals who have undertaken to cooperate in a stated way in order to make these doctrines prevail. Thus the right of association can almost be identified with freedom to write, but already associations are more powerful than the press. When some view is represented by an association, it must take clearer and more precise shape. It counts its supporters and involves them in its cause; these supporters get to know one another, and numbers increase zeal. An association unites the energies of divergent minds and vigorously directs them toward a clearly indicated goal.

Freedom of assembly marks the second stage in the use made of the right of association. When a political association is allowed to form centers of action at certain important places in the country, its activity becomes greater and its influence more widespread. There men meet, active measures are planned, and opinions are expressed with that strength and warmth which the written word can never attain.

But the final stage is the use of association in the sphere of politics. The supporters of an agreed view may meet in electoral colleges and appoint mandatories to represent them in a central assembly. That is, properly speaking, the application of the representative system to one party.

* * *

In our own day freedom of association has become a necessary guarantee against the tyranny of the majority. In the United States, once a party has become predominant, all public power passes into its hands; its close supporters occupy all offices and have control of all organized forces. The most distinguished men of the opposite party, unable to cross the barrier keeping them from power, must be able to establish themselves outside it; the minority must use the whole of its moral authority to oppose the physical power oppressing it. Thus the one danger has to be balanced against a more formidable one.

The omnipotence of the majority seems to me such a danger to the American republics that the dangerous expedient used to curb it is actually something good.

Here I would repeat something which I have put in other words when speaking of municipal freedom: no countries need associations more—to prevent either despotism of parties or the arbitrary rule of a prince—than those with a democratic social state. In aristocratic nations secondary bodies form natural associations which hold abuses of power in check. In countries where such associations do not exist, if private people did not artificially and temporarily create something like them, I see no other dike to hold back tyranny of whatever sort, and a great nation might with impunity be oppressed by some tiny faction or by a single man.

*   *   *

In America the citizens who form the minority associate in the first place to show their numbers and to lessen the moral authority of the majority, and secondly, by stimulating competition, to discover the arguments most likely to make an impression on the majority, for they always hope to draw the majority over to their side and then to exercise power in its name.

Political associations in the United States are therefore peaceful in their objects and legal in the means used; and when they say that they only wish to prevail legally, in general they are telling the truth.

*   *   *

The Americans * * * have provided a form of government within their associations, but it is, if I may put it so, a civil government. There is a place for individual independence there; as in society, all the members are advancing at the same time toward the same goal, but they are not obliged to follow exactly the same path. There has been no sacrifice of will or of reason, but rather will and reason are applied to bring success to a common enterprise.

DISCUSSION QUESTIONS

1. Tocqueville argues that "freedom of association has become a necessary guarantee against the tyranny of the majority." Although freedom of association is a central part of any free society, would you place limits on this freedom? What if an American sought to offer nonviolent assistance to a foreign terrorist group? In your view, what activities would be acceptable and which would be unacceptable for this individual?

2. The Constitution guarantees the people the right to assemble and to petition government regarding their grievances. It also guarantees freedom of speech. All these are the essence of interest-group activ-

ity. Nonetheless, many Americans are uneasy with the influence wielded by organized interest groups. What, if any, restrictions on interest-group activity would you be comfortable with? Would you support limits on what interest groups could spend to lobby government officials? To communicate with the public? To run advertisements that support or criticize candidates? How, if at all, can these restrictions be made consistent with the constitutional guarantee of freedom to associate, organize, and petition government, and the guarantee of free speech?

61

"The Alleged Mischiefs of Faction," from *The Governmental Process*

David B. Truman

At various times in U.S. history, the public has become especially concerned with the power of interest groups in politics and seeks to limit their activities. One political scientist refers to this as the "ideals vs. institutions" gap—there are times when "what is" is so different from what Americans believe "should be," that pressure mounts to reform lobbying laws, campaign regulations, business practices, and so on. Going back to James Madison in his famous Federalist 10, *however, the argument that encouraging competition between interests should be encouraged has also been powerful in American political thought. The claim in this school of thought, known as pluralist theory, is that the competition among groups in society for political power produces the best approximation of the overall public good. In the following excerpt from* The Governmental Process, *David Truman argues that such groups have been a common and inevitable feature of American politics. Groups form to give individuals a means of self-expression and to help individuals find security in an uncertain world. In fact, the uncertainty of the social environment, and the resulting threat to one's interests, is a chief motivation for groups to form, and "taming" this environment is a central concern for group members. Rather than leading to a system rigidly ruled by a few dominant powers, Truman, writing in the 1950s, suggests the reality is more dynamic. What the critics of group influence fail to recognize is the fact that people have "multiple or overlapping membership" in groups so that "no tolerably normal person is totally absorbed in any group in which he participates." There is balance, in other words, to the views any one member brings to the organization and ultimately to the political process. Further, the potential for a group to form is always present, and "[s]ometimes it may be this possibility of organization that alone gives the potential group a minimum of influence in the political process." These features of the interest group system push toward compromise and balance in public policy.*

Most accounts of American legislative sessions—national, state, or local—are full of references to the maneuverings and iniquities of various organized groups. Newspaper stories report that a legislative proposal is being promoted by groups of business men or school teachers or farmers or consumers or labor unions or other aggregations of citizens. Cartoonists picture the legislature as completely under the control of sinister, portly, cigar-smoking individuals labeled "special interests," while a diminutive John Q. Public is pushed aside to sulk in futile anger and pathetic frustrations. A member of the legislature rises in righteous anger on the floor of the house or in a press conference to declare that the bill under discussion is being forced through by the "interests," by the most unscrupulous high-pressure "lobby" he has seen in all his years of public life. An investigating committee denounces the activities of a group as deceptive, immoral, and destructive of our constitutional methods and ideals. A chief executive attacks a "lobby" or "pressure group" as the agency responsible for obstructing or emasculating a piece of legislation that he has recommended "in the public interest."

*   *   *

Such events are familiar even to the casual student of day-to-day politics, if only because they make diverting reading and appear to give the citizen the "low-down" on his government. He tends, along with many of his more sophisticated fellow citizens, to take these things more or less for granted, possibly because they merely confirm his conviction that "as everybody knows, politics is a dirty business." Yet at the same time he is likely to regard the activities of organized groups in political life as somehow outside the proper and normal processes of government, as the lapses of his weak contemporaries whose moral fiber is insufficient to prevent their defaulting on the great traditions of the Founding Fathers. These events appear to be a modern pathology.

Group Pressure and the Founding Fathers

Group pressures, whatever we may wish to call them, are not new in America. One of the earliest pieces of testimony to this effect is essay number 10 of *The Federalist*, which contains James Madison's classic statement of the impact of divergent groups upon government and the reasons for their development. He was arguing the virtues of the proposed Union as a means to "break and control the violence of faction," having in mind, no doubt, the groups involved in such actions of the debtor or propertyless segment of the population as Shays's Rebellion. He defined faction in broader terms, however, as "a number of citizens, whether amounting to a majority or minority of the whole, who are united and actuated by some common impulse of passion, or of interest. . . ."

*   *   *

[Madison's] analysis is not just the brilliant generalization of an armchair philosopher or pamphleteer; it represents as well the distillation from Madison's years of acquaintance with contemporary politics as a member of the Virginia Assembly and of [the Continental] Congress. Using the words "party" and "faction" almost interchangeably, since the political party as we know it had not yet developed, he saw the struggles of such groups as the essence of the political process. One need not concur in all his judgments to agree that the process he described had strong similarities to that of our own day.

The entire effort of which *The Federalist* was a part was one of the most skillful and important examples of pressure group activity in American history. The State ratifying conventions were handled by the Federalists with a skill that might well be the envy of a modern lobbyist. It is easy to overlook the fact that "unless the Federalists had been shrewd in manipulation as they were sound in theory, their arguments could not have prevailed."

* * *

Alexis de Tocqueville, perhaps the keenest foreign student ever to write on American institutions, noted as one of the most striking characteristics of the nation the penchant for promoting a bewildering array of projects through organized societies, among them those using political means. "In no country in the world," he observed, "has the principle of association been more successfully used or applied to a greater multitude of objects than in America." Tocqueville was impressed by the organization of such groups and by their tendency to operate sometimes upon and sometimes parallel to the formal institutions of government. Speaking of the similarity between the representatives of such groups and the members of legislatures, he stated: "It is true that they [delegates of these societies] have not the right, like the others, of making the laws; but they have the power of attacking those which are in force and of drawing up beforehand those which ought to be enacted."

Since the modern political party was, in the Jackson period, just taking the form that we would recognize today, Tocqueville does not always distinguish sharply between it and other types of political interest groups. In his discussion of "political associations," however, he gives an account of the antitariff convention held in Philadelphia in October of 1831, the form of which might well have come from the proceedings of a group meeting in an American city today:

> Its debates were public, and they at once assumed a legislative character; the extent of the powers of Congress, the theories of free trade, and the different provisions of the tariff were discussed. At the end of ten days the Convention broke up, having drawn up an address to the American people in which it declared: (1) that Congress had not the right of making a tariff, and that the existing tariff was unconstitutional; (2) that the prohibition of free trade was prejudicial to the interests of any nation, and to those of the American people especially.

Additional evidence might be cited from many quarters to illustrate the long history of group politics in this country. Organized pressures supporting or attacking the charter of the Bank of the United States in

Jackson's administration, the peculations surrounding Pendleton's "Palace of Fortune" in the pre–Civil War period, the operations of the railroads and other interests in both national and state legislatures in the latter half of the last century, the political activities of farm groups such as the Grange in the same period—these and others indicate that at no time have the activities of organized political interests not been a part of American politics. Whether they indicate pathology or not, they are certainly not new.

*   *   *

The political interest group is neither a fleeting, transitory newcomer to the political arena nor a localized phenomenon peculiar to one member of the family of nations. The persistence and the dispersion of such organizations indicate rather that we are dealing with a characteristic aspect of our society. That such groups are receiving an increasing measure of popular and technical attention suggests the hypothesis that they are appreciably more significant in the complex and interdependent society of our own day than they were in the simpler, less highly developed community for which our constitutional arrangements were originally designed.

Many people are quite willing to acknowledge the accuracy of these propositions about political groups, but they are worried nevertheless. They are still concerned over the meaning of what they see and read of the activities of such organizations. They observe, for example, that certain farm groups apparently can induce the Government to spend hundreds of millions of dollars to maintain the price of food and to take "surplus" agricultural produce off the market while any urban residents are encountering painful difficulty in stretching their food budgets to provide adequately for their families. They observe that various labor organizations seem to be able to prevent the introduction of cheaper methods into building codes, although the cost of new housing is already beyond the reach of many. Real estate and contractors' trade associations apparently have the power to obstruct various governmental projects for slum clearance and low-cost housing. Veterans' organizations seem able to secure and protect increases in pensions and other benefits almost at will. A church apparently can prevent the appropriation of Federal funds to public schools unless such funds are also given to the schools it operates in competition with the public systems. The Government has declared that stable and friendly European governments cannot be maintained unless Americans buy more goods and services abroad. Yet American shipowners and seamen's unions can secure a statutory requirement that a large proportion of the goods purchased by European countries under the Marshall Plan* must be carried in American ships. Other industries

---

*The Marshall Plan was the U.S. European Recovery Plan after World War II [*Editors*].

and trade associations can prevent the revision of tariff rates and customs regulations that restrict imports from abroad.

In all these situations the fairly observant citizen sees various groups slugging it out with one another in pursuit of advantages from the Government. Or he sees some of them co-operating with one another to their mutual benefit. He reads of "swarms" of lobbyists "putting pressure on" congressmen and administrators. He has the impression that any group can get what it wants in Washington by deluging officials with mail and telegrams. He may then begin to wonder whether a governmental system like this can survive, whether it can carry its responsibilities in the world and meet the challenges presented by a ruthless dictatorship. He wants to see these external threats effectively met. The sentimental nonsense of the commercial advertisements aside, he values free speech, free elections, representative government, and all that these imply. He fears and resents practices and privileges that seem to place these values in jeopardy.

A common reaction to revelations concerning the more lurid activities of political groups is one of righteous indignation. Such indignation is entirely natural. It is likely, however, to be more comforting than constructive. What we seek are correctives, protections, or controls that will strengthen the practices essential in what we call democracy and that will weaken or eliminate those that really threaten that system. Uncritical anger may do little to achieve that objective, largely because it is likely to be based upon a picture of the governmental process that is a composite of myth and fiction as well as of fact. We shall not begin to achieve control until we have arrived at a conception of politics that adequately accounts for the operations of political groups. We need to know what regular patterns are shown by group politics before we can predict its consequences and prescribe for its lapses. We need to re-examine our notions of how representative government operates in the United States before we can be confident of our statements about the effects of group activities upon it. Just as we should not know how to protect a farm house from lightning unless we knew something of the behavior of electricity, so we cannot hope to protect a governmental system from the results of group organization unless we have an adequate understanding of the political process of which these groups are a part.

*   *   *

There are two elements in this conception of the political process in the United States that are of crucial significance and that require special emphasis. These are, first, the notion of multiple or overlapping membership and, second, the function of unorganized interests, or potential interest groups.

The idea of overlapping membership stems from the conception of a group as a standardized pattern of interactions rather than as a collection of human units. Although the former may appear to be a rather misty abstraction, it is actually far closer to complex reality than the latter notion. The view of a group as an aggregation of individuals abstracts from the observable fact that in any society, and especially a complex one, no single group affiliation accounts for all of the attitudes or interests of any individual except a fanatic or a compulsive neurotic. No tolerably normal person is totally absorbed in any group in which he participates. The diversity of an individual's activities and his attendant interests involve him in a variety of actual and potential groups. Moreover, the fact that the genetic experiences of no two individuals are identical and the consequent fact that the spectra of their attitudes are in varying degrees dissimilar means that the members of a single group will perceive the group's claims in terms of a diversity of frames of reference. Such heterogeneity may be of little significance until such time as these multiple memberships conflict. Then the cohesion and influence of the affected group depend upon the incorporation or accommodation of the conflicting loyalties of any significant segment of the group, an accommodation that may result in altering the original claims. Thus the leaders of a Parent-Teacher Association must take some account of the fact that their proposals must be acceptable to members who also belong to the local taxpayers' league, to the local chamber of commerce, and to the Catholic Church.

* * *

We cannot account of an established American political system without the second crucial element in our conception of the political process, the concept of the unorganized interest, or potential interest group. Despite the tremendous number of interest groups existing in the United States, not all interests are organized. If we recall the definition of an interest as a shared attitude, it becomes obvious that continuing interaction resulting in claims upon other groups does not take place on the basis of all such attitudes. One of the commonest interest groups forms, the association, emerges out of severe or prolonged disturbances in the expected relationships of individuals in similar institutionalized groups. An association continues to function as long as it succeeds in ordering these disturbed relationships, as a labor union orders the relationships between management and workers. Not all such expected relationships are simultaneously or in a given short period sufficiently disturbed to produce organization. Therefore only a portion of the interests or attitudes involved in such expectations are represented by organized groups. Similarly, many organized groups—families, businesses, or churches, for example—do not operate continuously as interest groups or as political interest groups.

Any mutual interest, however, any shared attitude, is a potential group. A disturbance in established relationships and expectations anywhere in the society may produce new patterns of interaction aimed at restricting or eliminating the disturbance. Sometimes it may be this possibility of organization that alone gives the potential group a minimum of influence in the political process. Thus . . . the Delta planters in Mississippi "must speak for their Negroes in such programs as health and education," although the latter are virtually unorganized and are denied the means of active political participation.*

* * *

Obstacles to the development of organized groups from potential ones may be presented by inertia or by the activities of opposed groups, but the possibility that severe disturbances will be created if these submerged, potential interests should organize necessitates some recognition of the existence of these interests and gives them at least a minimum of influence.

More important for present purposes than the potential groups representing separate minority elements are those interests or expectations that are so widely held in the society and are so reflected in the behavior of almost all citizens that they are, so to speak, taken for granted. Such "majority" interests are significant not only because they may become the basis for organized interest groups overlaps extensively the memberships of the various organized interest groups. The resolution of conflicts between the claims of such unorganized interests and those of organized interest groups must grant recognition to the former not only because affected individuals may feel strongly attached to them but even more certainly because these interests are widely shared and are a part of many established patterns of behavior the disturbance of which would be difficult and painful. They are likely to be highly valued.

* * *

It is thus multiple memberships in potential groups based on widely held and accepted interests that serve as a balance wheel in a going political system like that of the United States. To some people this observation may appear to be a truism and to others a somewhat mystical notion. It is neither. In the first place, neglect of this function of multiple memberships in most discussions of organized interest groups indicates that the observation is not altogether commonplace. Secondly, the statement has no mystical quality; the effective operation of these widely held interests is to be inferred directly from verbal and other behavior in the political sphere. Without the notion of multiple memberships in potential groups it is literally impossible to account for the existence of a viable polity such as that in the United States or to develop a coherent conception of the political process. The strength of these widely held but largely unorganized interests explains the vigor with which propagandists for organized groups

*Until the 1960s, most Southern blacks were denied the right to vote [Editors].

attempt to change other attitudes by invoking such interests. Their importance is further evidenced in the recognized function of the means of mass communication, notably the press, in reinforcing widely accepted norms of "public morality."

* * *

Thus it is only as the effects of overlapping memberships and the functions of unorganized interests and potential groups are included in the equation that it is accurate to speak of governmental activity as the product or resultant of interest group activity. As [political scientist Arthur F.] Bentley has put it:

> There are limits to the technique of the struggle, this involving also limits to the group demands, all of which is solely a matter of empirical observation. . . . Or, in other words, when the struggle proceeds too harshly at any point there will become insistent in the society a group more powerful than either of those involved which tends to suppress the extreme and annoying methods of the groups in the primary struggle. It is within the embrace of these great lines of activity that the smaller struggles proceed, and the very word struggle has meaning only with reference to its limitations.

To assert that the organization and activity of powerful interest groups constitutes a threat to representative government without measuring their relation to and effects upon the widespread potential groups is to generalize from insufficient data and upon an incomplete conception of the political process. Such an analysis would be as faulty as one that ignoring differences in national systems, predicted identical responses to a given technological change in the United States, Japan, and the Soviet Union.

Discussion Questions

1. Even if you are not a member of an organized interest group, can you think of any such groups that speak for you?

2. Is Truman right that new organizations emerge in important policy debates, leaving most views well represented? Can you think of instances in which, counter to Truman's viewpoint, a new organization did not emerge, leaving a group unrepresented?

3. Among the many forms of interest group activity, campaign contributions seem to provoke some of the harshest criticisms. Is this reasonable? Is there any reason to be more concerned about campaign contributions than about lobbying, lawsuits, funding research, or any other activities groups employ to pursue their cause? How would Truman answer this question?

62

"The Logic of Collective Action," from *Rise and Decline of Nations*

Mancur Olson

Americans organize at a tremendous rate to pursue common interests in the political arena. Yet not all groups are created equal, and some types of political organizations are much more common than others. In particular, it is far easier to organize groups around narrow economic interests than it is to organize around broad "public goods" interests. Why do some groups organize while others do not?

The nature of collective goods, according to the economist Mancur Olson, explains this phenomenon. When a collective good is provided to a group, no member of the group can be denied the benefits of the good. For example, if Congress passes a law that offers subsidies for a new kind of energy technology, any company that produces that technology will benefit from the subsidy. The catch is, any company will benefit even if they did not participate in the collective effort to win the subsidy. Olson argues that "the larger the number of individuals or firms that would benefit from a collective good, the smaller the share of the gains . . . that will accrue to the individual or firm." Hence, the less likely any one member of the group will contribute to the collective effort to secure the collective benefit. For smaller groups, any one member's share of the collective good is larger and more meaningful; thus it is more likely any one member of the group will be willing to make an individual sacrifice to provide a benefit shared by the entire group. An additional distinction is that in a large group, there is often a tendency to assume someone else will take care of the problem—this is known as the "free rider" problem or, as Olson puts it, "let George do it." This is less likely to happen in smaller groups.

The logic helps to explain the greater difficulty so-called "public interest groups" have in organizing and staying organized to pursue such collective goods as air pollution control and consumer product safety. These goods benefit large numbers of people, but the benefit to any one person, Olson would argue, is not sufficient for them to sacrifice time or money for the effort to succeed, especially if the individual believes that he or she will benefit from the collective good even if they do not contribute. Olson identifies "selective incentives" as one way in which these larger groups are able to overcome the incentive to free ride.

The Logic

The argument of this book begins with a paradox in the behavior of groups. It has often been taken for granted that if everyone in a group of individuals or firms had some interest in common, then there would be a tendency for the group to seek to further this interest. Thus many students of politics in the United States for a long time supposed that citizens with a common political interest would organize and lobby to serve that interest. Each individual in the population would be in one or more groups and the vector of pressures of these competing groups explained the outcomes of the political process. Similarly, it was often supposed that if workers, farmers, or consumers faced monopolies harmful to their interests, they would eventually attain countervailing power through organizations such as labor unions or farm organizations that obtained market power and protective government action. On a larger scale, huge social classes are often expected to act in the interest of their members; the unalloyed form of this belief is, of course, the Marxian contention that in capitalist societies the bourgeois class runs the government to serve its own interests, and that once the exploitation of the proletariat goes far enough and "false consciousness" has disappeared, the working class will in its own interest revolt and establish a dictatorship of the proletariat. In general, if the individuals in some category or class had a sufficient degree of self-interest and if they all agreed on some common interest, then the group would to some extent also act in a self-interested or group-interested manner.

If we ponder the logic of the familiar assumption described in the preceding paragraph, we can see that it is fundamentally and indisputably faulty. Consider those consumers who agree that they pay higher prices for a product because of some objectionable monopoly or tariff, or those workers who agree that their skill deserves a higher wage. Let us now ask what would be the expedient course of action for an individual consumer who would like to see a boycott to combat a monopoly or a lobby to repeal the tariff, or for an individual worker who would like a strike threat or a minimum wage law that could bring higher wages. If the consumer or worker contributes a few days and a few dollars to organize a boycott or a union or to lobby for favorable legislation, he or she will have sacrificed time and money. What will this sacrifice obtain? The individual will at best succeed in advancing the cause to a small (often imperceptible) degree. In any case he will get only a minute share of the gain from his action. The very fact that the objective or interest is common to or shared by the group entails that the gain from any sacrifice an individual makes to serve this common purpose is shared with everyone in the group. The successful boycott or strike or lobbying action will bring the better price or wage for everyone in the relevant category, so the individual in any large group with a common interest will reap only a minute share of the gains from whatever sacrifices the individual makes to achieve this common interest. Since any gain goes to everyone in the group, those who contribute nothing to the effort will get just as much as those who made a contribution. It pays to "let George do it," but George has little or no incentive to do anything in the group interest either, so (in the absence of factors that are completely left out of the conceptions mentioned in the first paragraph) there will be little, if any, group action. The paradox, then, is that (in the absence of special arrangements or circumstances to which we shall turn later) large groups, at least if they are composed of rational individuals, will *not* act in their group interest.

This paradox is elaborated and set out in a way that lets the reader check every step of the logic in a book I wrote entitled *The Logic of Collective Action.*

*   *   *

Organizations that provide collective goods to their client groups through political or market action * * * are * * * not supported because of the collective goods they provide, but rather because they have been fortunate enough to find what I have called *selective incentives*. A selective incentive is one that applies selectively to the individuals depending on whether they do or do not contribute to the provision of the collective good.

A selective incentive can be either negative or positive; it can, for example, be a loss or punishment imposed only on those who do *not* help provide the collective good. Tax payments are, of course, obtained with the help of negative selective incentives, since those who are found not to have paid their taxes must then suffer both taxes and penalties. The best-known type of organized interest group in modern democratic societies, the labor union, is also usually supported, in part, through negative selective incentives. Most of the dues in strong unions are obtained through union shop, closed shop, or agency shop arrangements which make dues paying more or less compulsory and automatic. There are often also informal arrangements with the same effect; David McDonald, former president of the United Steel Workers of America, describes one of these arrangements used in the early history of that union. It was, he writes, a technique

> which we called . . . visual education, which was a high-sounding label for a practice much more accurately described as dues picketing. It worked very simply. A group of dues-paying members, selected by the district director (usually more for their size than their tact) would stand at the plant gate with pick handles or baseball bats in hand and confront each worker as he arrived for his shift.

As McDonald's "dues picketing" analogy suggests, picketing during strikes is another negative selective incentive that unions sometimes need; although picketing in industries with established and stable unions is usually peaceful, this is because the union's capacity to close down an enterprise against which it has called a strike is clear to all; the early phase of unionization often involves a great deal of violence on the part of both unions and anti-union employers and scabs.

* * *

Positive selective incentives, although easily overlooked, are also commonplace, as diverse examples in *The Logic* demonstrate. American farm organizations offer prototypical examples. Many of the members of the stronger American farm organizations are members because their dues payments are automatically deducted from the "patronage dividends" of farm cooperatives or are included in the insurance premiums paid to mutual insurance companies associated with the farm organizations. Any number of organizations with urban clients also provide similar positive selective incentives in the form of insurance policies, publications, group air fares, and other private goods made available only to members. The grievance procedures of labor unions usually also offer selective incentives, since the grievances of active members often get most of the attention. The symbiosis between the political power of a lobbying organization and the business institutions associated with it often yields tax or other advantages for the business institution, and the publicity and other information flowing out of the political arm of a movement often generates patterns of preference or trust that make the business activities of the movement more remunerative. The surpluses obtained in such ways in turn provide positive selective incentives that recruit participants for the lobbying efforts.

Small groups, or occasionally large "federal" groups that are made up of many small groups of socially interactive members, have an additional source of both negative and positive selective incentives. Clearly most people value the companionship and respect of those with whom they interact. In modern societies solitary confinement is, apart from the rare death penalty, the harshest legal punishment. The censure or even ostracism of those who fail to bear a share of the burdens of collective action can sometimes be an important selective incentive. An extreme example of this occurs when British unionists refuse to speak to uncooperative colleagues, that is, "send them to Coventry." Similarly, those in a socially interactive group seeking a collective good can give special respect or honor to those who distinguish themselves by their sacrifices in the interest of the group and thereby offer them a positive selective incentive. Since most people apparently prefer relatively like-minded or agreeable and respectable company, and often prefer to associate with those whom they especially admire, they may find it costless to shun those who shirk the collective action and to favor those who over-subscribe.

Social selective incentives can be powerful and inexpensive, but they are available only in certain situations. As I have already indicated, they have little applicability to large groups, except in those cases in which the large groups can be federations of small groups that are capable of social interaction. It also is not possible to organize most large groups in need of a collective good into small, socially interactive subgroups, since most individuals do not have the time needed to maintain a huge number of friends and acquaintances.

The availability of social selective incentives is also limited by the social heterogeneity of some of the groups or categories that would benefit from a collective good. Everyday observation reveals that most socially interactive groups are fairly homogeneous and that many people resist extensive social interaction with those they deem to have lower status or greatly different tastes. Even Bohemian or other nonconformist groups often are made up of individuals who are similar to one another, however much they differ from the rest of society. Since some of the categories of individuals who would benefit from a collective good are socially heterogeneous, the social interaction needed for selective incentives sometimes cannot be arranged even when the number of individuals involved is small.

*   *   *

In short, the political entrepreneurs who attempt to organize collective action will accordingly be more likely to succeed if they strive to organize relatively homogeneous groups. The political managers whose task it is to maintain organized or collusive action similarly will be motivated to use indoctrination and selective recruitment to increase the homogeneity of their client groups. This is true in part because social selective incentives are more likely to be available to the more nearly homogeneous groups, and in part because homogeneity will help achieve consensus.

Information and calculation about a collective good is often itself a collective good. Consider a typical member of a large organization who is deciding how much time to devote to studying the policies or leadership of the organization. The more time the member devotes to this matter, the greater the likelihood that his or her voting and advocacy will favor effective policies and leadership for the organization. This typical member will, however, get only a small share of the gain from the more effective policies and leadership: in the aggregate, the other members will get almost all the gains, so that the individual member does not have an incentive to devote nearly as much time to fact-finding and thinking about the organization as would be in the group interest. Each of the members of the group would be better off if they all could be coerced into spending more time finding out how to vote to make the organization best further their interests. This is dramatically evident in the case of the typical voter in a national election in a large country. The gain to such a voter from studying issues and candidates until it is clear what vote is truly in his or her interest is given by the difference in the value to the individual of the "right" election outcome as compared with the "wrong" outcome, *multiplied by the probability a change in the individual's vote will alter the outcome of the election*. Since the probability that a typical voter will change the outcome of the election is vanishingly small, the typical citizen is usually "rationally ignorant" about public affairs. Often, information about public affairs is so interesting or entertaining that it pays to acquire it for these reasons alone—this appears to be the single most important source of exceptions to the generalization that *typical* citizens are rationally ignorant about public affairs.

Individuals in a few special vocations can receive considerable rewards in private goods if they acquire exceptional knowledge of public goods. Politicians, lobbyists, journalists, and social scientists, for example, may earn more money, power, or prestige from knowledge of this or that public business. Occasionally, exceptional knowledge of public policy can generate exceptional profits in stock exchanges or other markets. Withal, the typical citizen will find that his or her income and life chances will not be improved by zealous study of public affairs, or even of any single collective good.

The limited knowledge of public affairs is in turn necessary to explain the effectiveness of lobbying. If all citizens had obtained and digested all pertinent information, they could not then be swayed by advertising or other persuasion. With perfectly informed citizens, elected officials would not be subject to the blandishments of lobbyists, since the constituents would then know if their interests were betrayed and defeat the unfaithful representative at the next election. Just as lobbies provide collective goods to special-interest groups, so their effectiveness is explained by the imperfect knowledge of citizens, and this in turn is due mainly to the fact that information and calculation about collective goods is also a collective good.

* * *

The fact that the typical individual does not have an incentive to spend much time studying many of his choices concerning collective goods also helps to explain some otherwise inexplicable individual contributions toward the provision of collective goods. The logic of collective action that has been described in this chapter is not immediately apparent to those who have never studied it; if it were, there would be nothing paradoxical in the argument with which this chapter opened, and students to whom the argument is explained would not react with initial skepticism. No doubt the practical implications of this logic for the individual's own choices were often discerned before the logic was ever set out in print, but this does not mean that they were always understood even at the intuitive and practical level. In particular, when the costs of individual contributions to collective action are very small, the individual has little incentive to investigate whether or not to make a contribution or even to exercise intuition. If the individual knows the costs of a contribution to collective action in the interest of a group of which he is a part are trivially small, he may rationally not take the trouble to consider whether the gains are smaller still. This is particularly the case since the size of these gains and the policies that would maximize them are matters about which it is usually not rational for him to investigate.

This consideration of the costs and benefits of calculation about public goods leads to the testable prediction that voluntary contributions toward the provision of collective goods for large groups without selective incentives will often occur when the costs of the individual contributions are negligible, but that they will *not* often occur when the costs of the individual contributions are considerable. In other words, when the costs of individual action to help to obtain a desired collective good are small enough, the result is indeterminate and sometimes goes one way and sometimes the other, but when the costs get larger this indeterminacy disappears. We should accordingly find that more than a few people are willing to take the moment of time needed to sign petitions for causes they support, or to express their opinions in the course of discussion, or to vote for the candidate or party they prefer. Similarly, if the argument here is correct, we should not find many instances where individuals voluntarily contribute substantial sums of resources year after year for the purpose of obtaining some collective good for some large group of which they are a part. Before parting with a large amount of money or time, and particularly before doing so repeatedly, the rational individual will reflect on what this considerable sacrifice will accomplish. If the individual is a typical individual in a large group that would benefit from a collective good, his contribution will not make a perceptible difference in the amount that is provided. The theory here predicts that such contributions become less likely the larger the contribution at issue.

Even when contributions are costly enough to elicit rational calculation, there is still one set of circumstances in which collective action can occur without selective incentives. This set of circumstances becomes evident the moment we think of situations in which there are only a few individuals or firms that would benefit from collective action. Suppose there are two firms of equal size in an industry and no other firms can enter the industry. It still will be the case that a higher price for the industry's product will benefit both firms and that legislation favorable to the industry will help both firms. The higher price and the favorable legislation are then collective goods to this "oligopolistic" industry, even though there are only two in the group that benefit from the collective goods. Obviously, each of the oligopolists is in a situation in which if it restricts output to raise the industry price, or lobbies for favorable legislation for the industry, it will tend to get half of the benefit. And the cost-benefit ratio of action in the common interest easily could be so favorable that, even though a firm bears the whole cost of its action and gets only half the benefit of this action, it could still profit from acting in the common interest. Thus if the group that would benefit from collective action is sufficiently small and the cost-benefit ratio of collective action for the group sufficiently favorable, there may well be calculated action in the collective interest even without selective incentives.

*   *   *

Untypical as my example of equal-sized firms may be, it makes the general point intuitively obvious: other things being equal, *the larger the number of individuals or firms that would benefit from a collective good, the smaller the share of the gains from action in the group interest that will accrue to the individual or firm that undertakes the action. Thus, in the absence of selective incentives, the incentive for group action diminishes as group size increases, so that large groups are less able to act in their common interest than small ones.* If an additional individual or firm that would value the collective good enters the scene, then the share of the gains from group-oriented action that anyone already in the group might take must diminish. This holds true whatever the relative sizes or valuations of the collective good in the group.

*   *   *

The significance of the logic that has just been set out can best be seen by comparing groups that would have the same net gain from collective action, if they could engage in it, but that vary in size. Suppose there are a million individuals who would gain a thousand dollars each, or a billion in the aggregate, if they were to organize effectively and engage in collective action that had a total cost of a hundred million. If the logic set out above is right, they could not organize or engage in effective collective action without selective incentives. Now suppose that, although the total gain of a billion dollars from collective action and the aggregate cost of a hundred million remain the same, the group is composed instead of five big corporations or five organized municipalities, each of which would gain two hundred million. Collective action is not an absolute certainty even in this case, since each of the five could conceivably expect others to put up the hundred million and hope to gain the collective good worth two hundred million at no cost at all. Yet collective action, perhaps after some delays due to bargaining, seems very likely indeed. In this case any one of the five would gain a hundred million from providing the collective good even if it had to pay the whole cost itself; and the costs of bargaining among five would not be great, so they would sooner or later probably work out an agreement providing for the collective action. The numbers in this example are arbitrary, but roughly similar situations occur often in reality, and the contrast between "small" and "large" groups could be illustrated with an infinite number of diverse examples.

The significance of this argument shows up in a second way if one compares the operations of lobbies or cartels within jurisdictions of vastly different scale, such as a modest municipality on the one hand and a big country on the other. Within the town, the mayor or city council may be influenced by, say, a score of petitioners or a lobbying budget of a thousand dollars. A particular line of business may be in the hands of only a few firms, and if the town is distant enough from other markets only these few would need to agree to create a cartel. In a big country, the resources needed to influence the national government are likely to be much more substantial, and unless the firms are (as they sometimes are) gigantic, many of them would have to cooperate to create an effective cartel. Now suppose that the million individuals in our large group in the previous paragraph were spread out over a hundred thousand towns or jurisdictions, so that each jurisdiction had ten of them, along with the same proportion of citizens in other categories as before. Suppose also that the cost-benefit ratios remained the same, so that there was still a billion dollars to gain across all jurisdictions or ten thousand in each, and that it would still cost a hundred million dollars across all jurisdictions or a thousand in each. It no longer seems out of the question that in many jurisdictions the groups of ten, or subsets of them, would put up the thousand-dollar total needed to get the thousand for each individual. Thus we see that, if all else were equal, small jurisdictions would have more collective action per capita than large ones.

Differences in intensities of preference generate a third type of illustration of the logic at issue. A small number of zealots anxious for a particular collective good are more likely to act collectively to obtain that good than a larger number with the same aggregate willingness to pay. Suppose there are twenty-five individuals, each of whom finds a given collective good worth a thousand dollars in one case, whereas in another there are five thousand, each of whom finds the collective good worth five dollars. Obviously, the argument indicates that there would be a greater likelihood of collective action in the former case than in the latter, even though the aggregate demand for the collective good is the same in both. The great historical significance of small groups of fanatics no doubt owes something to this consideration.

The argument in this chapter predicts that those groups that have access to selective incentives will be more likely to act collectively to obtain collective goods than those that do not, and that smaller groups will have a greater likelihood of engaging in collective action than larger ones. The empirical portions of *The Logic* show that this prediction has been correct for the United States.

* * *

Discussion Questions

1. Besides the size of a group, what other considerations do you think would play a role in people's decision to join a collective endeavor? Are you convinced that the size of a group is as important as Olson argues?

2. Think of your own decisions to join or not join a group. Have you ever been a "free rider?" For example, have there been protests against tuition increases at your school that you supported but did not participate in? If so, what would it have taken to get you to join?

3. If Olson is right, would Tocqueville's view (see article 60 in this book) about the role of groups in overcoming the potential tyranny of the majority need to be modified?

Debating the Issues: Corporate and Labor Spending in Campaigns

The First Amendment of the U.S. Constitution says that "Congress shall make no law . . . abridging the freedom of speech." The Supreme Court must define the boundaries of what that broad prohibition means. Does it apply to pornography? To commercial speech? To speech that advocates the overthrow of the government or incites violence? Political advertising and campaign spending similarly generate a difficult set of questions. In its rulings, the Court has equated the use of money in campaigns with speech. In other words, money facilitates the making and spreading of messages. Supporting a candidate with a contribution is making a statement, and is thus speech, and the money itself helps the candidate speak through advertisements and other means. Spending independently to promote a candidate or message and not giving the money to a candidate is similarly a kind of speech—spending the money allows you to distribute the message. The Court has recognized a government interest in promoting fair elections that are free from corruption, so it has determined that some regulation of campaign finance is warranted. But the question is where to draw the line between activity that is permissible and that which is prohibited.

In its January 2010 decision in *Citizens United v. Federal Election Commission* (FEC), the Supreme Court decided that the First Amendment protects the right of non-profit and for-profit corporations and labor unions to spend directly to run ads calling for the election or defeat of a candidate in political campaigns, rather than having to set up political action committees (PACs). Political action committees must raise donations that they then either contribute directly to candidates and parties or spend independently to send a campaign message. The Court decision said that corporations and unions could bypass PACs and spend directly from their treasuries to speak on matters of interest to their organizations, including who they believe would be preferable candidates to elect. The amounts they could spend to support these messages, so long as they were not giving the money directly to a candidate or party, was not limited. The premise in the Court's decision was that the risk of the corrupting influence of money is most powerful when the money is going directly to a candidate or party's campaign coffers, not when an organization is spending money to transmit a message independently. *Citizens United* and subsequent lower court rulings and Federal Election Commission decisions also paved the way for so-called Super PACs, which could collect unlimited donations so long as they spent the money independently—for example, on TV ads—and did not contribute it to a candidate or party.

Ronald Dworkin, a law professor at New York University, says *Citizens United* "threatens democracy" because it will create "an avalanche of negative political commercials financed by huge corporate wealth." He also is concerned that the decision has "generated open hostilities among the three branches of our government," pointing to comments from President Barack Obama in his 2010 State of the Union message and the subsequent negative reaction from Supreme Court Justices Samuel Alito and John Roberts. Dworkin argues that this radical a decision cannot be grounded in any theory of the First Amendment, ignored relevant precedent despite the conservative majority's avowed belief in judicial restraint, and opened American electoral campaigns to influence from foreign corporations. Dworkin concludes with a plea for stronger disclosure laws and public financing for congressional elections.

Bradley Smith, a law professor and former chair of the Federal Election Commission, strongly disagrees. He calls the decision a "wonderful affirmation of the primacy of political speech in First Amendment jurisprudence." Furthermore, he says, the impact of the decision is almost certainly overstated: over half the states already allowed corporations to advertise in state elections at the time of the ruling, and most large corporations are unlikely to start spending huge amounts of money because they prefer lobbying to spending money in elections. Also, he notes the decision empowers not only corporations but also labor unions, which are more likely to want to spend in elections.

Matt Bai agrees with Smith that critics have overstated the impact of *Citizens United* and that much of what has happened in elections since the ruling was already happening before it. Bai argues that criticizing the Court's decision is a useful organizing device by liberal politicians because they know fellow liberals strongly disapprove of the ruling. But Bai doubts the ruling has had anywhere near the effects claimed by critics. Instead, he suggests that the surge of money in recent elections can be attributed to two factors. First, the Bipartisan Campaign Reform Act of 2002 made it more difficult to give money to political parties, which resulted in a rise in independent campaign spending. Second, the major issues under discussion in the Bush and Obama presidencies naturally led citizens with strong views on these issues, including but not exclusively, wealthy individuals, to attempt to have some influence on the direction of the country through campaign-related messages.

63

"The Decision That Threatens Democracy"

Ronald Dworkin

No Supreme Court decision in decades has generated such open hostilities among the three branches of our government as has the Court's 5–4 decision in *Citizens United v. FEC* in January 2010. The five conservative justices, on their own initiative, at the request of no party to the suit, declared that corporations and unions have a constitutional right to spend as much as they wish on television election commercials specifically supporting or targeting particular candidates. President Obama immediately denounced the decision as a catastrophe for American democracy and then, in a highly unusual act, repeated his denunciation in his State of the Union address with six of the justices sitting before him.

"With all due deference to separation of powers," he said, "last week the Supreme Court reversed a century of law that I believe will open the floodgates for special interests—including foreign corporations—to spend without limit in our elections." As he spoke one of the conservative justices, Samuel Alito, in an obvious breach of decorum, mouthed a denial, and a short time later Chief Justice John Roberts publicly chastised the President for expressing that opinion on that occasion. The White House press secretary, Robert Gibbs, then explained Obama's remarks: "The President has long been committed to reducing the undue influence of special interests and their lobbyists over government. That is why he spoke out to condemn the decision and is working with Congress on a legislative response." Democrats in Congress have indeed called for a constitutional amendment to repeal the decision and several of them, more realistically, have proposed statutes to mitigate its damage.

The history of the Court's decision is as extraordinary as its reception. At least since 1907, when Congress passed the Tillman Act at the request of President Theodore Roosevelt, it had been accepted by the nation and the Court that corporations, which are only fictitious persons created by law, do not have the same First Amendment rights to political activity as real people do. In 1990, in *Austin v. Michigan Chamber of Commerce*, the Court firmly upheld that principle. In 2002, Congress passed the Bipartisan Campaign Reform Act (BCRA) sponsored by Senators John McCain and Russell Feingold, which forbade corporations to engage in television electioneering for a period of thirty days before a primary for federal office and sixty days before an election. In 2003, in *McConnell v. Federal*

Election Commission (FEC), the Court upheld the constitutionality of that prohibition.

In the 2008 presidential primary season a small corporation, Citizens United, financed to a minor extent by corporate contributions, tried to broadcast a derogatory movie about Hillary Clinton. The FEC declared the broadcast illegal under the BCRA. Citizens United then asked the Supreme Court to declare it exempt from that statute on the ground, among others, that it proposed to broadcast its movie only on a pay-per-view channel. It did not challenge the constitutionality of the act. But the five conservative justices—Chief Justice Roberts and Justices Samuel Alito, Anthony Kennedy, Antonin Scalia, and Clarence Thomas—decided on their own initiative, after a rehearing they themselves called for, that they wanted to declare the act unconstitutional anyway.

They said that the BCRA violated the First Amendment, which declares that Congress shall make no law infringing the freedom of speech. They agreed that their decision was contrary to the *Austin* and *McConnell* precedents; they therefore overruled those decisions as well as repealing a century of American history and tradition. Their decision threatens an avalanche of negative political commercials financed by huge corporate wealth, beginning in this year's midterm elections. Overall these commercials can be expected to benefit Republican candidates and to injure candidates whose records dissatisfy powerful industries. The decision gives corporate lobbyists, already much too influential in our political system, an immensely powerful weapon. It is important to study in some detail a ruling so damaging to democracy.

The First Amendment, like many of the Constitution's most important provisions, is drafted in the abstract language of political morality: it guarantees a "right" of free speech but does not specify the dimensions of that right—whether it includes a right of cigarette manufacturers to advertise their product on television, for instance, or a right of a Ku Klux Klan chapter publicly to insult and defame blacks or Jews, or a right of foreign governments to broadcast political advice in American elections. Decisions on these and a hundred other issues require interpretation and if any justice's interpretation is not to be arbitrary or purely partisan, it must be guided by principle—by some theory of why speech deserves exemption from government regulation in principle. Otherwise the Constitution's language becomes only a meaningless mantra to be incanted whenever a judge wants for any reason to protect some form of communication. Precedent—how the First Amendment has been interpreted and applied by the Supreme Court in the past—must also be respected. But since the meaning of past decisions is also a matter of interpretation, that, too, must be guided by a principled account of the First Amendment's point.

A First Amendment theory is therefore indispensible to responsible adjudication of free speech issues. Many such theories have been offered by justices, lawyers, constitutional scholars, and philosophers, and most of them assign particular importance to the protection of political speech—speech about candidates for public office and about issues that are or might be topics of partisan political debate. But none of these theories—absolutely none of them—justifies the damage the five conservative justices have just inflicted on our politics.

The most popular of these theories appeals to the need for an informed electorate. Freedom of political speech is an essential condition of an effective democracy because it ensures that voters have access to as wide and diverse a range of information and political opinion as possible. Oliver Wendell Holmes Jr., Learned Hand, and other great judges and scholars argued that citizens are more likely to reach good decisions if no ideas, however radical, are censored. But even if that is not so, the basic justification of majoritarian democracy—that it gives power to the informed and settled opinions of the largest number of people—nevertheless requires what Holmes called a "free marketplace of ideas."

Kennedy, who wrote the Court's opinion in *Citizens United* on behalf of the five conservatives, appealed to the "informed electorate" theory. But he offered no reason for supposing that allowing rich corporations to swamp elections with money will in fact produce a better-informed public—and there are many reasons to think it will produce a worse-informed one. Corporations have no ideas of their own. Their ads will promote the opinions of their managers, who could publish or broadcast those opinions on their own or with others of like mind through political action committees (PACs) or other organizations financed through voluntary individual contributions. So though allowing them to use their stockholders' money rather than their own will increase the volume of advertising, it will not add to the diversity of ideas offered to voters.

Corporate advertising will mislead the public, moreover, because its volume will suggest more public support than there actually is for the opinions the ads express. Many of the shareholders who will actually pay for the ads, who in many cases are members of pension and union funds, will hate the opinions they pay to advertise. Obama raised a great deal of money on the Internet, mostly from small contributors, to finance his presidential campaign, and we can expect political parties, candidates, and PACs to tap that source much more effectively in the future. But these contributions are made voluntarily by supporters, not by managers using the money of people who may well be opposed to their opinions. Corporate advertising is misleading in another way as well. It purports to offer opinions about the public interest, but in fact managers are legally required to spend corporate funds only to promote their corporation's own financial interests, which may very well be different.

There is, however, a much more important flaw in the conservative justices' argument. If corporations exercise the power that the Court has now given them, and buy an extremely large share of the television time available for political ads, their electioneering will undermine rather than improve the public's political education. Kennedy declared that speech may not be restricted just to make candidates more equal in their financial resources. But he misunderstood why other nations limit campaign expenditures. This is not just to be fair to all candidates, like requiring a single starting line for runners in a race, but to create the best conditions for the public to make an informed decision when it votes—the main purpose of the First Amendment, according to the marketplace theory. The Supreme Court of Canada understands the difference between these different goals. Creating "a level playing field for those who wish to engage in the electoral discourse," it said, ". . . enables voters to be better informed; no one voice is overwhelmed by another."

Monopolies and near monopolies are just as destructive to the marketplace of ideas as they are to any other market. A public debate about climate change, for instance, would not do much to improve the understanding of its audience if speaking time were auctioned so that energy companies were able to buy vastly more time than academic scientists. The great mass of voters is already very much more aware of electoral advertising spots constantly repeated, like beer ads, in popular dramatic series or major sports telecasts than of opinions reported mainly on public broadcasting news programs. Unlimited corporate advertising will make that distortion much greater.

The difference between the two goals I distinguished—aiming at electoral equality for its own sake and reducing inequality in order to protect the integrity of political debate—is real and important. If a nation capped permissible electoral expenditure at a very low level, it would achieve the greatest possible financial equality. But it would damage the quality of political debate by not permitting enough discussion and by preventing advocates of novel or unfamiliar opinion from spending enough funds to attract any public attention. Delicate judgment is needed to determine how much inequality must be permitted in order to ensure robust debate and an informed population. But allowing corporations to spend their corporate treasure on television ads conspicuously fails that test. Judged from the perspective of this theory of the First Amendment's purpose—that it aims at a better-educated populace—the conservatives' decision is all loss and no gain.

A second popular theory focuses on the importance of free speech not to educate the public at large but to protect the status, dignity, and moral development of individual citizens as equal partners in the political process. Justice John Paul Stevens summarized this theory in the course of his very long but irresistibly powerful dissenting opinion in *Citizens United*. Speaking for himself and Justices Stephen Breyer, Ruth Ginsburg, and Sonia Sotomayor, he said that "one fundamental concern of the First Amendment is to 'protec[t] the individual's interest in self-expression.'" Kennedy tried to appeal to this understanding of the First Amendment to justify free speech for corporations. "By taking the right to speak from some and giving it to others," he stated, "the Government deprives the disadvantaged person or class of the right to use speech to strive to establish worth, standing, and respect for the speaker's voice." But this is bizarre. The interests the First Amendment protects, on this second theory, are only the moral interests of individuals who would suffer frustration and indignity if they were censored. Only real human beings can have those emotions or suffer those insults. Corporations, which are only artificial legal inventions, cannot. The right to vote is surely at least as important a badge of equal citizenship as the right to speak, but not even the conservative justices have suggested that every corporation should have a ballot.

A third widely accepted purpose of the First Amendment lies in its contribution to honesty and transparency in government. If government were free to censor its critics, or to curtail the right to a free press guaranteed in a separate phrase of the First Amendment, then it would be harder for the public to discover official corruption. The Court's *Citizens United* decision does nothing to serve that further purpose. Corporations do not need to run television ads in the run-up to an election urging votes against particular candidates in order to report discoveries they may make about official dishonesty, or in order to defend themselves against any accusation of dishonesty made against them. And of course they have everyone else's access to print and television reporters.

Though the Court's decision will do nothing to deter corruption in that way, it will do a great deal to encourage one particularly dangerous form of it. It will sharply increase the opportunity of corporations to tempt or intimidate congressmen facing reelection campaigns. Obama and Speaker Nancy Pelosi had great difficulty persuading some members of the House of Representatives to vote for the health care reform bill, which finally passed with a dangerously thin majority, because those members feared they were risking their seats in the coming midterm elections. They knew, after the Court's decision, that they might face not just another party and candidate but a tidal wave of negative ads financed by health insurance companies with enormous sums of their shareholders' money to spend.

Kennedy wrote that there is no substantial risk of such corrupting influence so long as corporations do not "coordinate" their electioneering with any candidate's formal campaign. That seems particularly naive. Few congressmen would be unaware of or indifferent to the likelihood of a heavily financed advertising campaign urging voters to vote for him, if he worked in a corporation's interests, or against him if he did not. No coordination—no role of any candidate or his agents in the design of the ads—would be necessary.

Kennedy's naiveté seems even stranger when we notice the very substantial record of undue corporate influence laid before Congress when it adopted the BCRA. Before that act, corporations and other organizations were free to broadcast "issue" ads that did not explicitly endorse or oppose any candidates. The district court judge who first heard the *Citizens United* case found that, according to testimony of lobbyists and political consultants, at least some "Members of Congress are particularly grateful when negative issue advertisements are run by these organizations . . . [that] . . . use issue advocacy as a means to influence various Members of Congress." That influence can be expected to be even greater now that the Court has permitted explicit political endorsements or opposition as well. Kennedy's optimism went further: he denied that heavy corporate spending would lead the public to suspect that form of corruption. But the district court judge had reported that

> eighty percent of Americans polled are of the view that corporations and other organizations that engage in electioneering communications, which benefit specific elected officials, receive special consideration from those officials when matters arise that affect these corporations and organizations.

So the radical decision of the five conservative justices is not only not supported by any plausible First Amendment theory but is condemned by them all. Was their decision nevertheless required by the best reading of past Supreme Court decisions? That seems initially unlikely because, as I said, the decision overruled the two most plainly pertinent such decisions: *Austin* and *McConnell*. Nothing had happened to the country, or through further legislation, that cast any doubt on those decisions. The change that made the difference was simply Justice Sandra Day O'Connor's resignation in 2006 and President George W. Bush's appointment of Alito to replace her.

Overruling these decisions is itself remarkable, particularly for Roberts and Alito, who promised to respect precedent in their Senate confirmation hearings. One of the reasons that Kennedy offered to justify his decision is alarming. He said that since the conservative justices who dissented in those past cases and who remain on the Court had continued to complain about them, the decisions were only weak precedents. "The simple fact that one of our decisions remains controversial," he announced, "is, of course, insufficient to justify overruling it. But it does undermine the precedent's ability to contribute to the stable and orderly development of the law." In other words, if the four more liberal justices who dissented in this case continue to express their dissatisfaction with it, they would be free to overrule it if the balance of the Court shifts again. That novel view would mean the effective end of the doctrine of precedent on the Supreme Court.

*   *   *

* * * [T]he central issue in *Citizens United* * * * is whether corporations are entitled to the First Amendment protection that individuals and groups of individuals have. We have already noticed a variety of arguments that they do not. Very few individuals have anything like the capital accumulation of any of the Fortune 500 corporations, the smallest of which had revenues of $5 billion (the top of the list—Exxon Mobil—had $443 billion) in 2008. Individuals speak and spend for themselves, together or in association with other individuals, while corporations speak for their commercial interests and spend other people's money, not their own. Individuals have rights, on which their dignity and standing depend, to play a part in the nation's government; corporations do not. No one thinks corporations should vote, and their rights to speak as institutions have been limited for over a century. * * *

*   *   *

Two Democrats—Senator Charles Schumer of New York and Representative Chris Van Hollen of Maryland—have announced proposals for legislation to protect the country from the Court's ruling. The Court might reject some of their proposals—forbidding corporate advertising by TARP recipients who have not paid back the government's loan, for example—as unconstitutional attempts to ban speech according to the speaker's identity. Kennedy left open the possibility, however, that Congress might constitutionally accept another of their proposals: banning electioneering by corporations controlled by foreigners.

He also explicitly recognized the constitutionality of another of the Democrats' proposals: he said that Congress might require public disclosure of a corporation's expenses for electioneering. (Thomas dissented from that part of Kennedy's ruling.) Congress should require prompt disclosures on the Internet so that the information could be made quickly available to voters. It would be even more important for Congress to provide for ample disclosure within a television advertisement itself. The disclosure should name not only fronting organizations, like Citizens United, but also at least the major corporate contributors to that organization. Congress should also require that any corporation that wished to engage in electioneering obtain at least the annual consent of its stockholders to that activity and to a proposed budget for it, and that the required disclosure in an ad report the percentage of stockholders who have refused that blanket consent. Finally, Congress should require that the CEO of the major corporate contributor to any ad appear in that ad to state that he or she believes that broadcasting it is in the corporation's own financial interests.

The conservative justices might object that such disclosure requirements would unduly burden corporate speech and impermissibly target one type of speaker for special restriction. They might say, to use one of Kennedy's favorite terms, that these requirements would "chill" corporate speech. But we must distinguish measures designed to deter speech from those designed to guard against deception. The in-ad disclosures I describe need not take significantly more broadcast time than the "Stand By My Ad" rule that now requires a candidate to declare in his campaign's ad that he approves it. If several corporations finance an ad together, much of the required information—the amount of shareholder dissent, for instance—could be disclosed as an aggregate figure. If these requirements discourage a corporation's speech not because of the expense but for the different reason that managers are unwilling to report shareholder opposition or to acknowledge their fiduciary duty to act only in the financial interests of their own company, then their fear only shows the pertinence of Kennedy's own claim that "shareholder democracy" is the right remedy to protect shareholders who oppose a corporation's politics.

* * *

The Supreme Court's conservative phalanx has demonstrated once again its power and will to reverse America's drive to greater equality and more genuine democracy. It threatens a step-by-step return to a constitutional stone age of right-wing ideology. Once again it offers justifications that are untenable in both constitutional theory and legal precedent. Stevens's remarkable dissent in this case shows how much we will lose when he soon retires. We must hope that Obama nominates a progressive replacement who not only is young enough to endure the bad days ahead but has enough intellectual firepower to help construct a rival and more attractive vision of what our Constitution really means.

64

"Citizens United We Stand"

Bradley A. Smith

March 24, 2009, was a turning point in the long-running battle to restrict political speech, aka "campaign finance reform." On that day, the Supreme Court heard oral argument in *Citizens United v. Federal Election Commission*, in which the conservative activist group Citizens United challenged the provisions of the McCain-Feingold law that had prohibited it from airing a documentary film, *Hillary: The Movie*, through video on demand within 30 days of any 2008 Democratic presidential primary.

In the course of the argument, Deputy Solicitor General Malcolm Stewart, an experienced Supreme Court litigator, argued that a 1990 precedent, *Austin v. Michigan Chamber of Commerce*, gave the government the power to limit any political communication funded by a corporation, even a nonprofit such as Citizens United. Justice Samuel Alito asked Stewart if that power would extend to censoring political books published by corporations. Stewart responded—consistent with the government's position at all stages of the case—that yes, it would. There was an audible hush—if such a thing is possible—in the court. Then Justice Alito, appearing to speak for the room, merely said, "I find that pretty incredible."

Incredible or not, that was, and had been for many years, the position of the U.S. government. But until that moment, it seemed to have never quite sunken in with the justices. Americans are willing to accept far more abridgements of free speech than we sometimes like to believe, but the idea of banning books strikes an emotional chord that something described simply as "prohibitions and limits on campaign spending" does not. Americans may not always live up to the Bill of Rights, but Americans do not ban books. A stunned Court eventually asked the parties to reargue the case, to consider whether *Austin* should be overruled.

On reargument last September, Solicitor General Elena Kagan tried to control the damage, arguing that the government never actually had tried to censor books, even as she reaffirmed its claimed authority to do just that. She also stated that "pamphlets," unlike books, were clearly fair game for government censorship. (Former Federal Election Commissioner Hans von Spakovksy has noted that in fact the FEC has conducted lengthy investigations into whether certain books violated campaign finance laws, though it has not yet held that a book publisher violated the law through publication. And the FEC has attempted to penalize publishers of magazines and financial newsletters, only to be frustrated by the courts.) With the endgame of "campaign finance reform" finally laid out plainly, the Supreme Court's decision seemed a foregone conclusion. Sure enough, in January, the Court ruled that corporations, as associations of natural persons, have a right to spend funds from their general treasuries to support or oppose political candidates and causes—including through the publication or distribution of books and movies.

Though this ruling is obviously a correct interpretation of the First Amendment, reaction to the Court's decision in *Citizens United* has been loud, often disingenuous, and in some cases nearly hysterical. President Obama used his State of the Union address to publicly scold the Court, in the process so mischaracterizing the Court's decision that he prompted Judge Alito's now famous, spontaneous rejoinder, "Not true."

Meanwhile, Democrats in Congress and the states have been working overtime to come up with "fixes," ranging from the absurd (a Vermont legislator proposed forcing corporate sponsors to be identified every five seconds during any broadcast ad), to the merely pernicious (such as proposals that seek to immobilize corporate speech by forcing corporations to hold a majority vote of shareholders before each and every expenditure). The fact that virtually all of these proposed "fixes" have been sponsored by Democrats, with the aim of silencing what they perceive to be the pro-Republican voices of the business community, merely illustrates once again the basic problem with campaign finance reform that *Citizens*

United sought to alleviate: the desire to manipulate the law for partisan purposes.

Citizens United is at once both a potential game-changer and a decision whose "radicalism" has been widely overstated. Why overstated? Well, to start, one would never guess from the left's hysteria that even prior to *Citizens United*, 28 states, representing roughly 60 percent of the U.S. population, already allowed corporations and unions to make expenditures promoting or opposing candidates for office in state elections; in 26 states, such corporate and union expenditures were unlimited. Moreover, while the first bans on corporate spending were enacted more than a century ago, prior to the 1990 *Austin* decision, the Supreme Court had never upheld a ban, or even a limitation, on independent expenditures supporting or opposing a political candidate. It was the misleading contention that the decision overturned "100 years of law and precedent," that appears to have evoked Justice Alito's "not true" response to the president's State of the Union comments.

The president also stated, again misleadingly, that the decision would open the door for foreign corporations to spend unlimited sums in American elections. In fact, another provision of federal law, not at issue in the case, already prohibits any foreign national, including foreign corporations, from spending money in any federal campaign. FEC regulations, which have the force of the law, further prohibit any foreign national from playing any role in the political spending decisions of any U.S. corporation, political action committee, or association. And the Court specifically stated that *Citizens United* was not addressing these laws at all. So while some states may tweak their state rules in the wake of *Citizens United* to limit the ability of U.S. incorporated and headquartered subsidiaries of foreign corporations to spend money in campaigns, the "foreign corporation" bogeyman is little more than leftist demagoguery.

What is much more alarming than the prospect of U.S. corporations with some foreign ownership participating in campaigns is the fact that the four most liberal justices on the Supreme Court would have upheld the *Austin* precedent, and with it the authority of the federal government to censor books and movies published, produced, or distributed by U.S. corporations. But by affirming the rights of citizens to speak out on political issues, even when organized through the corporate form, the Supreme Court quite rightly put political speech back at the core of the First Amendment.

After four decades in which the Court had given greater First Amendment protection to such activities as topless dancing, simulated child pornography, Internet porn, flag burning, and the transfer of stolen information than to political speech, *Citizens United* is a wonderful reaffirmation of the primacy of political speech in the First Amendment jurisprudence. In that respect, the case has already been a constitutional game-changer.

Future litigation is sure to follow, building on the success of *Citizens United* to free up the political system and strike down the still extensive web of regulation that envelops political speech.

Some of these challenges are already well under way. For example, under current federal law, an individual such as George Soros is free to spend $20 million to promote his favored candidates, but if two or more individuals get together to do the same thing, neither can contribute more than $5,000 to the effort. It is hard to see what anti-corruption purpose such a dichotomy serves, and in *SpeechNow.org v. FEC*, argued before the U.S. Court of Appeals for the District of Columbia Circuit in January, plain-tiffs argue that if it is not corrupting for one person to spend unlimited sums on independent expenditures, it is not corrupting if two or more people combine their resources to promote the candidates of their choice. A decision is expected soon. Expect, too, legal challenges to the federal prohibition on contributions by corporations directly to candidates—if a $2,300 contribution from a corporate CEO or PAC is not corrupting, it is hard to see how a $2,300 contribution directly from a corporate treasury is corrupting.

Much less clear is whether *Citizens United* will be a game-changer in elec-toral politics. The general consensus is that *Citizens United* favors Republi-cans, based on the widely held perception that corporations are more likely to support Republicans than Democrats. But this perception may not be true. Even before *Citizens United*, the federal government and most states also allowed corporations to operate political action committees (PACs), which could then solicit the corporation's managers and share-holders for voluntary contributions to the PAC, which in turn could con-tribute limited amounts to candidates or make independent expenditures to support candidates. But whereas corporate PACs typically gave about two-thirds of their contributions to Republicans during the 1990s and the first part of the last decade, peaking in the 2004 cycle at nearly 10 to 1 for the GOP, over the past three years corporate PACs have devoted a slim majority of the contributions to Democrats.

More importantly, there is good reason to doubt that *Fortune* 500 com-panies are going to start making large expenditures in political cam-paigns. As noted, even before *Citizens United*, 28 states allowed corporate and union spending on state and local political races, yet large-scale cor-porate spending was very rare in those states. Another sign that corpora-tions are not eager to jump headfirst into political spending comes from the relatively low level of activity by corporate PACs. Among the *Fortune* 500—huge corporations that are all heavily regulated by the government—only about 60 percent actually maintained PACs.

These PACs are subject to extensive regulation, which runs up operat-ing costs to the point that the operating costs of PACs often total more than half of their total revenue. Corporations can, however, pay these operating costs directly from their corporate treasuries. Yet roughly half of these PACs' operating expenses were paid not by the corporations that established them, but out of funds donated to the PACs. In other words, even before *Citizens United*, corporate America could have roughly doubled the amount of money available in their PACs to use for political expenditures simply by paying the administrative and legal costs of operating the PAC from their general treasuries. Yet they did not. And only about 10 percent of PACs contributed the maximum legal amount in any election. All this suggests a lack of interest in political participation.

The truth is, the *Fortune* 500 prefer lobbying to campaigning. Even prior to McCain-Feingold, when corporations could support parties with "soft money," the *Fortune* 500 spent roughly 10 times as much money on lobbying as on political expenditures. As Edward Kangas, former chairman of Deloitte Touche Tohmatsu and of the Committee for Economic Development said in the *New York Times*, explaining his support for McCain-Feingold, "We have lobbyists."

But if large corporations may be reluctant to spend on political races, Big Labor is not. Labor unions also benefit from the *Citizens United* decision, and have historically been much more partisan in their political activity than has big business. The relatively small number of unions makes it easier for them to coordinate their activity. Add in the lack of any need to avoid offending a portion of their customer base, and unions are well positioned to take advantage of *Citizens United*. Indeed, within weeks of the *Citizens United* decision, three unions pledged to spend $1 million each to try to defeat U.S. senator Blanche Lincoln in the Democratic primary in Arkansas, finding her insufficiently dedicated to Big Labor's agenda.

Thus, if *Citizens United* ultimately works to favor conservatives, it may be less due to the *Fortune* 500 than to the small business community. These small and midsized companies usually cannot afford the high administrative costs of maintaining a PAC, and often don't have enough employees eligible for solicitation to make forming a PAC worthwhile in any case. Moreover, unlike *Fortune* 500 companies, small businesses typically do not maintain permanent large lobbying operations in Washington, and because they are less likely to be heavily regulated or engaged in government contracting, their contact with Washington is likely to be more sporadic. For these companies, the ability to speak directly to the public is potentially a great benefit.

This small business community is generally much more conservative in its politics than is the *Fortune* 500, and in particular much more hostile to government regulation. But these small companies are unlikely to undertake major campaigns on their own. Thus it may be up to trade associations and business groups, such as chambers of commerce, to organize business efforts.

Meanwhile, managers and executives, particularly of large, publicly traded companies, will need to do some serious rethinking about their obligations to shareholders. Do they have an obligation to their shareholders to try to maximize long-term value by opposing tax and spend, pro-regulatory politicians, and working to elect officials who appreciate pro-growth policies? Or do they play it safe, avoid political activity, and hope that the regulators will eat them last? The decisions they make may ultimately determine the real importance of *Citizens United*.

65

"How Much Has *Citizens United* Changed the Political Game?"

Matt Bai

"A hundred million dollars is nothing," the venture capitalist Andy Rappaport told me back in the summer of 2004. This was at a moment when wealthy liberals like George Soros and Peter Lewis were looking to influence national politics by financing their own voter-turnout machine and TV ads and by creating an investment fund for start-ups. Rappaport's statement struck me as an expression of supreme hubris. In American politics at that time, $100 million really meant something.

Eight years later, of course, his pronouncement seems quaint. Conservative groups alone, including a super PAC led by Karl Rove and another group backed by the brothers Charles and David Koch, will likely spend more than a billion dollars trying to take down Barack Obama by the time November rolls around.

The reason for this exponential leap in political spending, if you talk to most Democrats or read most news reports, comes down to two words: Citizens United. The term is shorthand for a Supreme Court decision that gave corporations much of the same right to political speech as individuals have, thus removing virtually any restriction on corporate money in politics. The oft-repeated narrative of 2012 goes like this: Citizens United unleashed a torrent of money from businesses and the multimillionaires who run them, and as a result we are now seeing the corporate takeover of American politics.

As a matter of political strategy, this is a useful story to tell, appealing to liberals and independent voters who aren't necessarily enthusiastic about the administration but who are concerned about societal inequality, which is why President Obama has made it a rallying cry almost from the moment the Citizens United ruling was made. But if you're trying to understand what's really going on with politics and money, the accepted narrative around Citizens United is, at best, overly simplistic. And in some respects, it's just plain wrong.

It helps first to understand what Citizens United did and didn't do to change the opaque rules governing outside money. Go back to, say, 2007, and pretend you're a conservative donor. At this moment, you would still have been free to write a check for any amount to a 527—so named because of the shadowy provision in the tax code that made such groups legal. (America Coming Together and the infamous Swift Boat Veterans for Truth were both 527s.) Even corporations, though they couldn't contribute to a candidate or a party, were free to write unlimited checks to something called a social-welfare group, whose principal purpose, ostensibly, is issue advocacy rather than political activity. The anti-tax Club for Growth, for instance, is a social-welfare group. So, remarkably, are the Koch brothers' Americans for Prosperity and Karl Rove's Crossroads GPS.

There were, however, a few caveats when it came to the way these groups could spend their money. Neither a 527 nor a social-welfare group could engage in "express advocacy"—that is, overtly making the case for one candidate over another. Nor could they use corporate money for "electioneering communications"—a category defined as radio or television advertising that even mentions a candidate's name within 30 days of a primary or 60 days of a general election. So under the old rules, the Club for Growth couldn't broadcast an ad that said "Vote Against Barack Obama," but it could spend that money on as many ads as it wanted that said "Barack Obama has ruined America—call and tell him to stop!" as long as it did so more than 60 days before an election. (The distinction between those two ads may sound silly and arcane to you, but that's why you don't sit on the Federal Election Commission.)

Citizens United and a couple of related court decisions changed all of this in two essential ways, and each of them was more incremental than transformational. First, the Supreme Court wiped away much of the rigmarole about "express advocacy" and "electioneering." Now any outside group can use corporate money to make a direct case for who deserves your vote and why, and they can do so right up to Election Day. The second change is that the old 527s have now been made effectively obsolete, replaced by the super PAC. The main difference between a super PAC and a social-welfare group, practically speaking, is that a super PAC has to disclose the identity of its donors, while social-welfare groups generally do not.

Those who criticize the effect of Citizens United look at these very technical changes and see an obvious causal relationship. The high court says outside groups are allowed to use corporate dollars to expressly support candidates, and suddenly we have this tidal wave of money threatening to overwhelm the airways. One must have led to the other, right?

Well, not necessarily. Legally speaking, zillionaires were no less able to write fat checks four years ago than they are today. And while it is true that corporations can now give money for specific purposes that were prohibited before, it seems they aren't, or at least not at a level that accounts for anything like the sudden influx of money into the system. According to a brief filed by Mitch McConnell, the Senate minority leader, and Floyd Abrams, the First Amendment lawyer, in a Montana case on which the Supreme Court ruled last month, not a single Fortune 100 company contributed to a candidate's super PAC during this year's Republican primaries. Of the $96 million or more raised by these super PACs, only about 13 percent came from privately held corporations, and less than 1 percent came from publicly traded corporations.

This only tells part of the story. The general election has just begun, and big energy and health care companies may still be pouring money into social-welfare groups that don't have to disclose their donors. The watchdog group Citizens for Responsibility and Ethics in Washington reported last month, for instance, that Aetna anonymously contributed more than $7 million to two such groups. We may never know precisely how much money is coming from similar companies, which should alarm anyone who cares about the integrity and transparency of government.

But the best anecdotal evidence suggests that this kind of thing isn't happening in nearly the proportions you might expect. Kenneth Gross, an election lawyer who represents an array of large corporations, told me that few of his clients have contributed to the social-welfare groups engaged in political activity this year. They know those contributions might become public at some point, and no company that sells a product wants to risk the kind of consumer reaction that engulfed Target in 2010, after it contributed $150,000 to a Minnesota group backing a conservative candidate opposing gay marriage. "If you've got a bank on every corner, if you've got stores in every strip mall, you don't want to be associated with a social cause," Gross told me.

None of this is to say that Citizens United hasn't had an impact. Gross and others point out that in the era before Citizens United, while individuals and companies could still contribute huge sums to outside groups, they were to some extent deterred by the confusing web of rules and the liability they might incur for violations. What the new rulings did, as the experts like to put it, was to "lift the cloud of uncertainty" that hung over such expenditures, and the effect of this psychological shift should not be underestimated. It almost certainly accounts for some rise in political money this year, both from individuals and companies.

Even so, the Supreme Court's ruling really wasn't the sort of tectonic event that Obama and his allies would have you believe it was. "I'd go so far as to call it a liberal delusion," Ira Glasser, the former executive director of the ACLU and a liberal dissenter on Citizens United, told me. Which leads to an obvious question: If Citizens United doesn't explain this billion-dollar blast of outside money, then what does?

You may remember that back in the '90s, the most nefarious influence in politics emanated from what was then called "soft money"—basically, unlimited contributions from rich people, corporations, and labor unions to both major parties. According to data from the Center for Responsive Politics, in 2000, the last presidential year in which soft money was legal, the two parties raised more than $450 million of it, divided almost equally between them. Only 38 percent of that came from individuals.

That all changed with the passage of the Bipartisan Campaign Reform Act of 2002, popularly known as the McCain-Feingold law. The new law stamped out soft money for good, but it also created a vacuum in political fund-raising. The parties could no longer tap an endless stream of soft money, but thanks to the advent of the 527, rich ideologues with their own agendas could write massive checks for the purpose of building what were, essentially, shadow parties—independent groups with their own turnout and advertising campaigns, limited in what they could say but accountable to no candidate or party boss. Wealthy liberals like Soros and Lewis, along with groups like MoveOn.org, were the first to spot the opportunity. All told, wealthy liberals spent something close to $200 million in an effort to oust George W. Bush in 2004, setting an entirely new standard for outside spending.

Richard L. Hasen, an expert on campaign finance at the University of California at Irvine, recently wrote an article for Slate titled, "The Numbers Don't Lie," in which he showed that total outside spending, as measured through March 8 of every election season, seemed to explode after the Citizens United decision, reaching about $15.9 million in 2010 (compared with $1.8 million in the previous midterm cycle) and $88 million this year (compared with $37.5 million at the same point in 2008). "If this was not caused by Citizens United," he wrote, "we have a mighty big coincidence on our hands."

But there are alternate ways to interpret this data. The level of outside money increased 164 percent from 2004 to 2008. Then it rose 135 percent from 2008 to 2012. In other words, while the sheer amount of dollars seems considerably more ominous after Citizens United, the percentage of change from one presidential election to the next has remained pretty consistent since the passage of McCain-Feingold. And this suggests that the rising amount of outside money was probably bound to reach ever more staggering levels with or without Citizens United. The unintended consequence of McCain-Feingold was to begin a gradual migration of political might from inside the party structure to outside it.

And in his examination of raw numbers, Hasen managed to ignore what is probably the most relevant bit of data during this period: 2010 and 2012 were the first election cycles since the enactment of McCain-Feingold in which a Democrat occupied the White House. Rich conservatives weren't inspired to invest their fortunes in 2004, when Bush ran for the second time while waging an unpopular war, or in 2008, when they were forced to endure the nomination of McCain. But now there's a president and a legislative agenda they bitterly despise (much as Soros and his friends saw the Bush presidency as an existential threat to the country), so it's not surprising that outside spending by Republicans in 2010 and 2012 would dwarf everything that came before. What we are seeing—what we almost certainly would have seen even without the court's ruling in Citizens United—is the full force of conservative wealth in America, mobilized by a common enemy for the first time since the fall of party monopolies.

A consequence of McCain-Feingold has been to flip on its head an old truism of politics, which is that incumbency comes with a fixed financial advantage. In the era of soft money, controlling the White House meant that a party could almost always leverage its considerable resources to dominate fund-raising. But today it's much easier to tap into the fury and anxiety of out-of-power millionaires than it is to amass contributions in defense of the status quo. This dynamic probably explains why wealthy Democrats who pioneered the idea of outside money during the Bush years have largely stood down this year, even while conservative fund-raising has soared. It isn't that liberals don't like Obama or grow queasy at the mention of super PACs. It's a function of human nature: nobody really gets pumped up to write a $10 million check just to keep things more or less as they are.

If you're a Democrat, there's some good news here. One persistent fear you hear from liberals is that Citizens United altered the balance between the parties in a permanent way—that corporate money will give Republicans a structural advantage that can never be overcome. What's more likely is that the boom in outside money will prove to be cyclical, with the momentum swinging toward whoever feels shut out and persecuted at the moment. Liberals dominated outside spending in 2004 and 2006. And should Romney become president, they'll most likely do so again.

It's worth asking just how much an advantage all of this outside money actually confers. The greatest impact of this year's imbalance in outside money will be felt on the state level, where a lot of House seats and control of the Senate hang in the balance, and where a sharp gust of advertising can often blow the results in one direction or another. But a presidential campaign is different, focusing as it does on a dozen or so pivotal states and a limited number of advertising markets. There's probably a limit to how many 30-second spots all of these groups can cram onto cable stations during late-night showings of *Turner & Hooch*.

I recently called Carter Eskew, a longtime Democratic adman and strategist whose clients included Al Gore in 2000, and asked him a simple question: How much did he think he would really need for a candidate today, if he could have an unlimited budget to run a national ad campaign, including all the outside money? Eskew paused before giving a declarative answer: $500 million. Anything beyond that, he said, was probably overkill.

In other words, there's a threshold below which a presidential candidate can't really compete effectively, and that number—whether it's $500 million or something less—is outlandish enough that it should give us pause. But beyond that number, it's not clear that spending an extra $200 million or $500 million will really make all that much of a difference on Election Day. More likely, the two ideological factions are now like rivals of the nuclear age, stockpiling enough bombs to destroy the same cities over and over again, when one would do the job.

You could even argue that whatever benefit a campaign derives from all this money is balanced, somewhat, by the threat it poses. Back in the days of soft money, a candidate had ownership of his party's national apparatus and the accusations it hurled on prime-time TV. He was responsible for the integrity of his argument, and his advisers ultimately controlled it. What the reform-minded architects of McCain-Feingold inadvertently unleashed, what Citizens United intensified but by no means created, is a world in which a big part of the money in a presidential campaign is spent by political entrepreneurs and strategists who are unanswerable to any institution. Candidates and parties who become the vehicles of angry outsiders, as Mitt Romney is now, don't really have control of their own campaigns anymore; to a large extent, they are the instruments of volatile forces beyond their own reckoning.

Maybe that makes for a cleaner and more democratic system than the one we had before, in the way the campaign-finance reformers intended. Standing here in 2012, it's just hard to see how.

Discussion Questions

1. The actions of public officials affect corporate entities, including labor unions. Should these entities thus be free to express their views on candidates by spending independently on campaign ads in elections (i.e., not donating directly to candidates)? If so, what concerns if any would you have about the impact of this spending on democracy? If not, why is it acceptable for government officials to take actions that affect these organizations but not acceptable for these organizations to spend money to try to influence who the government officials should be?

2. Do you agree with Dworkin's argument that none of the five theories of the First Amendment apply to corporate speech? Which of the five would have the strongest basis for justifying a First Amendment protection for corporate speech?

3. Should corporations be treated as people for purposes of political speech? If yes, why isn't it sufficient that the individuals who work for the corporations can spend their own money independently in elections? If not, why should individuals give up their free speech

rights just because they incorporate as a group that shares common concerns?

4. Whose arguments about the implications of *Citizens United* do you find more compelling? Do you agree with Dworkin, who sees it as a threat to democracy? Smith, who thinks the decision promotes freedom of speech? Or Bai, who believes the decision was mildly consequential but who appears to have some concerns about the amount of spending in politics?

5. The *Citizens United* ruling applies to many forms of corporate entities, including for-profit corporations, many non-profits, and labor unions. Whether you support or oppose the decision, does this wide reach increase or decrease your support or opposition?

PART IV

Public Policy

CHAPTER 13

Government and the Economy

66

"Call for Federal Responsibility"

FRANKLIN ROOSEVELT

The national government has always played a role in the economy. Since the late 1700s, the government has provided property for private development, enforced contracts and prohibited the theft of private property, provided subsidies to encourage the growth of particular industries, developed the infrastructure of the growing country, and regulated trade. The question that commands the attention of political leaders and citizens alike today is what the limits of government involvement in the economy ought to be. To what extent should the free market make most economic decisions to maximize efficiency and productivity? Should the government regulate markets in the pursuit of other goals, such as equality, and to address market failures, such as monopolies and public goods that are underprovided by the market (such as education and environmental protection)?

This debate reached a peak during the Great Depression, as the nation struggled to define the government's role in reviving the economy, and played a critical role in the 1932 presidential election between the Democratic candidate, Franklin Roosevelt, and the Republican president, Herbert Hoover. In the campaign speech printed here, FDR argued that the federal government should play a role in unemployment insurance, housing for the poor, and public-works programs to compensate for the hardship of the Great Depression. Hoover, on the other hand, was very much opposed to altering the relationship between government and the private sector, which was "built up by 150 years of toil of our fathers." It was the extension of freedom and the exercise of individual initiative, Hoover claimed, that made the American economic system strong and that would gradually bring about economic recovery. Roosevelt prevailed, and the resulting New Deal changed the face of government. Although the federal government adopted a much more active role in regulating the economy and providing social safety, the central issues discussed by Roosevelt and Hoover are still being debated today.

The first principle I would lay down is that the primary duty rests on the community, through local government and private agencies, to take care of the relief of unemployment. But we then come to a situation where there are so many people out of work that local funds are insufficient.

It seems clear to me that the organized society known as the State comes into the picture at this point. In other words, the obligation of government is extended to the next higher unit.

I [practice] what I preach. In 1930 the state of New York greatly increased its employment service and kept in close touch with the ability of localities to take care of their own unemployed. But by the summer of 1931 it became apparent to me that actual state funds and a state-supervised system were imperative.

I called a special session of the legislature, and they appropriated a fund of $20 million for unemployment relief, this fund to be reimbursed to the state through the doubling of our income taxes. Thus the state of New York became the first among all the states to accept the definite obligation of supplementing local funds where these local funds were insufficient.

The administration of this great work has become a model for the rest of the country. Without setting up any complex machinery or any large overhead, the state of New York is working successfully through local agencies, and, in spite of the fact that over a million people are out of work and in need of aid in this one state alone, we have so far met at least the bare necessities of the case.

This past spring the legislature appropriated another $5 million, and on November 8 the voters will pass on a $30 million bond issue to tide us over this winter and at least up to next summer.

*   *   *

I am very certain that the obligation extends beyond the states and to the federal government itself, if and when it becomes apparent that states and communities are unable to take care of the necessary relief work.

It may interest you to have me read a short quotation from my message to the legislature in 1931:

> What is the State? It is the duly constituted representative of an organized society of human beings, created by them for their mutual protection and well-being. One of the duties of the State is that of caring for those of its citizens who find themselves the victims of such adverse circumstances as make them unable to obtain even the necessities of mere existence without the aid of others.
>
> In broad terms, I assert that modern society, acting through its government, owes the definite obligation to prevent the starvation or the dire want of any of its fellowmen and women who try to maintain themselves but cannot. To these unfortunate citizens aid must be extended by the government, not as a matter of charity but as a matter of social duty.

That principle which I laid down in 1931, I reaffirm. I not only reaffirm it, I go a step further and say that where the State itself is unable successfully to fulfill this obligation which lies upon it, it then becomes the positive duty of the federal government to step in to help.

In the words of our Democratic national platform, the federal government has a "continuous responsibility for human welfare, especially for the protection of children." That duty and responsibility the federal government should carry out promptly, fearlessly, and generously.

It took the present Republican administration in Washington almost three years to recognize this principle. I have recounted to you in other speeches, and it is a matter of general information, that for at least two years after the crash, the only efforts made by the national administration to cope with the distress of unemployment were to deny its existence.

When, finally, this year, after attempts at concealment and minimizing had failed, it was at last forced to recognize the fact of suffering among millions of unemployed, appropriations of federal funds for assistance to states were finally made.

I think it is fair to point out that a complete program of unemployment relief was on my recommendation actually under way in the state of New York over a year ago; and that in Washington relief funds in any large volume were not provided until this summer, and at that they were pushed through at the demand of Congress rather than through the leadership of the President of the United States.

At the same time, I have constantly reiterated my conviction that the expenditures of cities, states, and the federal government must be reduced in the interest of the nation as a whole. I believe that there are many ways in which such reduction of expenditures can take place, but I am utterly unwilling that economy should be practised at the expense of starving people.

We must economize in other ways, but it shall never be said that the American people have refused to provide the necessities of life for those who, through no fault of their own, are unable to feed, clothe, and house themselves. The first obligation of government is the protection of the welfare and well-being, indeed the very existence, of its citizens.

* * *

The next question asks my attitude toward appropriations for public works as an aid to unemployment. I am perfectly clear as to the principles involved in this case also.

From the long-range point of view it would be advisable for governments of all kinds to set up in times of prosperity what might be called a nest egg to be used for public works in times of depression. That is a policy which we should initiate when we get back to good times.

But there is the immediate possibility of helping the emergency through appropriations for public works. One question, however, must be answered first because of the simple fact that these public works cost money.

We all know that government treasuries, whether local or state or federal, are hard put to it to keep their budgets balanced; and, in the case of the federal Treasury, thoroughly unsound financial policies have made its situation not exactly desperate but at least threatening to future stability if the policies of the present administration are continued.

All public works, including federal, must be considered from the point of view of the ability of the government Treasury to pay for them. There are two ways of paying for public works. One is by the sale of bonds. In principle, such bonds should be issued only to pay for self-sustaining projects or for structures which will without question have a useful life over a long period of years. The other method of payment is from current revenues, which in these days means in most cases added taxes. We all know that there is a very definite limit to the increase of taxes above the present level.

From this point, therefore, I can go on and say that, if funds can be properly provided by the federal government for increased appropriations for public works, we must examine the character of these public works. I have already spoken of that type which is self-sustaining. These should be greatly encouraged. The other type is that of public works which are honestly essential to the community. Each case must rest on its own merits.

It is impossible, for example, to say that all parks or all playgrounds are essential. One may be and another may not be. If a school, for instance, has no playground, it is obvious that the furnishing of a playground is a necessity to the community. But if the school already has a playground and some people seek merely to enlarge it, there may be a very definite question as to how necessary that enlargement is.

Let me cite another example. I am much interested in providing better housing accommodations for the poor in our great cities. If a slum area can be torn down and new modern buildings put up, I should call that almost a human necessity; but, on the other hand, the mere erection of new buildings in some other part of the city while allowing the slums to remain raises at once a question of necessity. I am confident that the federal government working in cooperation with states and cities can do much to carry on increased public works and along lines which are sound from the economic and financial point of view.

Now I come to another question. I am asked whether I favor a system of unemployment insurance reserves made compulsory by the states, supplemented by a system of federally coordinated state employment offices to facilitate the reemployment of jobless workers.

The first part of the question is directly answered by the Democratic platform which advocates unemployment insurance under state laws.

This is no new policy for me. I have advocated unemployment insurance in my own state for some time, and, indeed, last year six Eastern governors were my guests at a conference which resulted in the drawing up of what might be called an idea plan of unemployment insurance.

This type of insurance is not a cure-all but it provides at least a cushion to mitigate unemployment in times of depression. It is sound if, after starting it, we stick to the principle of sound insurance financing. It is only where governments, as in some European countries, have failed to live up to these sound principles that unemployment insurance has been an economic failure.

As to the coordinated employment offices, I can only tell you that I was for the bills sponsored by Senator Wagner of my own state and passed by the Congress. They created a nationally coordinated system of employment offices operated by the individual states with the advisory cooperation of joint boards of employers and employees.

To my very great regret this measure was vetoed by the President of the United States. I am certain that the federal government can, by furnishing leadership, stimulate the various states to set up and coordinate practical, useful systems.

DISCUSSION QUESTIONS

1. Franklin Roosevelt's call for a New Deal and the importance of government investment in "public works" as a way of helping the economy get out of the Great Depression and get people back to work sounds very similar to President Obama's call for more investment in the nation's infrastructure. What is the proper role of the government in helping people get jobs? Should this be left to the private sector, or should the national government invest more in building highways, bridges, and airports to get more people back to work?

2. FDR's famous line from this speech is, "The first obligation of every government is the protection of the welfare and well-being, indeed the very existence, of its citizens." Do you agree? If so, how do you define the limits of that obligation?

67

"Against the Proposed New Deal"

Herbert Hoover

This campaign is more than a contest between two men. It is more than a contest between two parties. It is a contest between two philosophies of government.

We are told by the opposition that we must have a change, that we must have a new deal. It is not the change that comes from normal development of national life to which I object but the proposal to alter the whole foundations of our national life which have been builded through generations of testing and struggle, and of the principles upon which we have builded the nation. The expressions our opponents use must refer to important changes in our economic and social system and our system of government, otherwise they are nothing but vacuous words. And I realize that in this time of distress many of our people are asking whether our social and economic system is incapable of that great primary function of providing security and comfort of life to all of the firesides of our 25 million homes in America, whether our social system provides for the fundamental development and progress of our people, whether our form of government is capable of originating and sustaining that security and progress.

This question is the basis upon which our opponents are appealing to the people in their fears and distress. They are proposing changes and so-called new deals which would destroy the very foundations of our American system.

Our people should consider the primary facts before they come to the judgment—not merely through political agitation, the glitter of promise, and the discouragement of temporary hardships—whether they will support changes which radically affect the whole system which has been builded up by 150 years of the toil of our fathers. They should not approach the question in the despair with which our opponents would clothe it.

Our economic system has received abnormal shocks during the past three years, which temporarily dislocated its normal functioning. These shocks have in a large sense come from without our borders, but I say to you that our system of government has enabled us to take such strong action as to prevent the disaster which would otherwise have come to our nation. It has enabled us further to develop measures and programs which are now demonstrating their ability to bring about restoration and progress.

We must go deeper than platitudes and emotional appeals of the public platform in the campaign if we will penetrate to the full significance of the changes which our opponents are attempting to float upon the wave of distress and discontent from the difficulties we are passing through. We can find what our opponents would do after searching the record of their appeals to discontent, group and sectional interest. We must search for them in the legislative acts which they sponsored and passed in the Democratic-controlled House of Representatives in the last session of Congress. We must look into measures for which they voted and which were defeated. We must inquire whether or not the presidential and vice-presidential candidates have disavowed these acts. If they have not, we must conclude that they form a portion and are a substantial indication of the profound changes proposed.

And we must look still further than this as to what revolutionary changes have been proposed by the candidates themselves.

We must look into the type of leaders who are campaigning for the Democratic ticket, whose philosophies have been well known all their lives, whose demands for a change in the American system are frank and forceful. I can respect the sincerity of these men in their desire to change our form of government and our social and economic system, though I shall do my best tonight to prove they are wrong. I refer particularly to Senator Norris, Senator La Follette, Senator Cutting, Senator Huey Long, Senator Wheeler, William R. Hearst and other exponents of a social philosophy different from the traditional American one. Unless these men feel assurance of support to their ideas, they certainly would not be supporting these candidates and the Democratic Party. The seal of these men indicates that they have sure confidence that they will have voice in the administration of our government.

I may say at once that the changes proposed from all these Democratic principals and allies are of the most profound and penetrating character. If they are brought about, this will not be the America which we have known in the past.

Let us pause for a moment and examine the American system of government, of social and economic life, which it is now proposed that we should alter. Our system is the product of our race and of our experience in building a nation to heights unparalleled in the whole history of the world. It is a system peculiar to the American people. It differs essentially from all others in the world. It is an American system.

It is founded on the conception that only through ordered liberty, through freedom to the individual, and equal opportunity to the individual will his initiative and enterprise be summoned to spur the march of progress.

It is by the maintenance of equality of opportunity and therefore of a society absolutely fluid in freedom of the movement of its human particles that our individualism departs from the individualism of Europe. We resent class distinction because there can be no rise for the individual through the frozen strata of classes, and no stratification of classes can take place in a mass livened by the free rise of its particles. Thus in our ideals the able and ambitious are able to rise constantly from the bottom to leadership in the community.

This freedom of the individual creates of itself the necessity and the cheerful willingness of men to act cooperatively in a thousand ways and for every purpose as occasion arises; and it permits such voluntary cooperations to be dissolved as soon as they have served their purpose, to be replaced by new voluntary associations for new purposes.

There has thus grown within us, to gigantic importance, a new conception. That is, this voluntary cooperation within the community. Cooperation to perfect the social organization; cooperation for the care of those in distress; cooperation for the advancement of knowledge, of scientific research, of education; for cooperative action in the advancement of many phases of economic life. This is self-government by the people outside of government; it is the most powerful development of individual freedom and equal opportunity that has taken place in the century and a half since our fundamental institutions were founded.

It is in the further development of this cooperation and a sense of its responsibility that we should find solution for many of our complex problems, and not by the extension of government into our economic and social life. The greatest function of government is to build up that cooperation, and its most resolute action should be to deny the extension of bureaucracy. We have developed great agencies of cooperation by the assistance of the government which promote and protect the interests of individuals and the smaller units of business. The Federal Reserve System, in its strengthening and support of the smaller banks; the Farm Board, in its strengthening and support of the farm cooperatives; the Home Loan Banks, in the mobilizing of building and loan associations and savings banks; the Federal Land Banks, in giving independence and strength to land mortgage associations; the great mobilization of relief to distress, the mobilization of business and industry in measures of recovery, and a score of other activities are not socialism—they are the essence of protection to the development of free men.

The primary conception of this whole American system is not the regimentation of men but the cooperation of free men. It is founded upon the conception of responsibility of the individual to the community, of the responsibility of local government to the state, of the state to the national government.

It is founded on a peculiar conception of self-government designed to maintain this equal opportunity to the individual, and through decentralization it brings about and maintains these responsibilities. The centralization of government will undermine responsibilities and will destroy the system.

Our government differs from all previous conceptions, not only in this decentralization but also in the separation of functions between the legislative, executive, and judicial arms of government, in which the independence of the judicial arm is the keystone of the whole structure.

It is founded on a conception that in times of emergency, when forces are running beyond control of individuals or other cooperative action, beyond the control of local communities and of states, then the great reserve powers of the federal government shall be brought into action to protect the community. But when these forces have ceased, there must be a return of state, local, and individual responsibility.

The implacable march of scientific discovery with its train of new inventions presents every year new problems to government and new problems to the social order. Questions often arise whether, in the face of the growth of these new and gigantic tools, democracy can remain master in its own house, can preserve the fundamentals of our American system. I contend that it can; and I contend that this American system of ours has demonstrated its validity and superiority over any other system yet invented by human mind.

It has demonstrated it in the face of the greatest test of our history— that is the emergency which we have faced in the past three years.

When the political and economic weakness of many nations of Europe, the result of the World War and its aftermath, finally culminated in collapse of their institutions, the delicate adjustment of our economic and social life received a shock unparalleled in our history. No one knows that better than you of New York. No one knows its causes better than you. That the crisis was so great that many of the leading banks sought directly or indirectly to convert their assets into gold or its equivalent with the result that they practically ceased to function as credit institutions; that many of our citizens sought flight for their capital to other countries; that many of them attempted to hoard gold in large amounts. These were but indications of the flight of confidence and of the belief that our government could not overcome these forces.

Yet these forces were overcome—perhaps by narrow margins—and this action demonstrates what the courage of a nation can accomplish under the resolute leadership in the Republican Party. And I say the Republican Party, because our opponents before and during the crisis, proposed no constructive program; though some of their members patriotically supported ours. Later on the Democratic House of Representatives did develop the real thought and ideas of the Democratic Party, but it was so destructive that it had to be defeated, for it would have destroyed, not healed.

In spite of all these obstructions, we did succeed. Our form of government did prove itself equal to the task. We saved this nation from a quarter of a century of chaos and degeneration, and we preserved the savings, the insurance policies, gave a fighting chance to men to hold their homes. We saved the integrity of our government and the honesty of the American dollar. And we installed measures which today are bringing back recovery. Employment, agriculture, business—all of these show the steady, if slow, healing of our enormous wound.

I therefore contend that the problem of today is to continue these measures and policies to restore this American system to its normal functioning, to repair the wounds it has received, to correct the weaknesses and evils which would defeat that system. To enter upon a series of deep changes, to embark upon this inchoate new deal which has been propounded in this campaign, would be to undermine and destroy our American system.

Discussion Questions

1. State governments have always played a role in regulating the economy, from consumer protection to using tax breaks as a way to attract business investment within a state's borders. What kind of economic activities are best regulated at the state level? When should the federal government play a role?

2. Which of the activities that the government performs do you consider essential? Why?

3. Hoover's arguments against government bureaucracy and in favor of individual and community responsibility resonate today with the Tea Party supporters. What similarities do you see between Hoover's arguments and the current opponents of big government?

68

"The Rise and Fall of the GDP"

Jon Gertner

"Gross Domestic Product," or GDP, is a familiar economic term: It is a standard measure of overall economic activity, the amount of money that is spent during a particular period of time. Politicians are quick to take credit when the GDP grows, for growth is a sign of economic expansion. And when communities are concerned about the environmental or quality-of-life impact of a new development or industrial site, community and business leaders reassure them by pointing to the economic growth that will result.

But is all growth good growth? Jon Gertner argues that GDP is an inaccurate measure of overall economic well-being. Higher GDP does not necessarily mean we are better off, because it includes all types of spending—even spending that results from waste (gasoline burned by cars sitting in traffic jams), unhealthy activities (consumption of cholesterol-laden foods and the cardiologists' bills that often result), or high-spending consumerism (buying a new car every few years or the newest electricity-hog appliances). By comparing "high GDP man" and "low GDP man," Gertner makes it clear that the person spending more and contributing more to the economy may not be acting in the nation's best interests. He also uses the analogy of a car dashboard that tells the driver only how fast she is going and conveys no other information about how the car is functioning. Political leaders would be better served by a "human development index" that would reveal the nation's performance according to measures of health, education, the environment, employment, material well-being, interpersonal connectedness, and political engagement, rather than simply growth.

Whatever you may think progress looks like—a rebounding stock market, a new house, a good raise—the governments of the world have long held the view that only one statistic, the measure of gross domestic product, can really show whether things seem to be getting better or getting worse. GDP is an index of a country's entire economic output—a tally of, among many other things, manufacturers' shipments, farmers' harvests, retail sales and construction spending. It's a figure that compresses the immensity of a national economy into a single data point of surpassing density. The conventional feeling about GDP is that the more it grows, the better a country and its citizens are doing. In the U.S., economic activity plummeted at the start of 2009 and only started moving up during the second half of the year. Apparently things are moving in that direction still. In the first quarter of this year, the economy again expanded, this time by an annual rate of about 3.2 percent.

All the same, it has been a difficult few years for GDP. For decades, academics and gadflies have been critical of the measure, suggesting that it is an inaccurate and misleading gauge of prosperity. What has changed more recently is that GDP has been actively challenged by a variety of world leaders, especially in Europe, as well as by a number of international groups, like the Organization for Economic Cooperation and Development. The GDP, according to arguments I heard from economists as far afield as Italy, France, and Canada, has not only failed to capture the well-being of a 21st-century society but has also skewed global political objectives toward the single-minded pursuit of economic growth. "The economists messed everything up," Alex Michalos, a former chancellor at the University of Northern British Columbia, told me recently when I was in Toronto to hear his presentation on the Canadian Index of Well-Being. The index is making its debut this year as a counterweight to the monolithic gross domestic product numbers. "The main barrier to getting progress has been that statistical agencies around the world are run by economists and statisticians," Michalos said. "And they are not people who are comfortable with human beings." The fundamental national measure they employ, he added, tells us a good deal about the economy but almost nothing about the specific things in our lives that really matter.

In the U.S., one challenge to the GDP is coming not from a single new index, or even a dozen new measures, but from several hundred new measures—accessible free online for anyone to see, all updated regularly. Such a system of national measurements, known as State of the USA, will go live online this summer [see www.stateoftheusa.org]. Its arrival comes at an opportune moment, but it has been a long time in the works. In 2003, a government official named Chris Hoenig was working at the U.S. Government Accountability Office, the investigative arm of Congress, and running a group that was researching ways to evaluate national progress. Since 2007, when the project became independent and took the name State of the USA, Hoenig has been guided by the advice of the National Academy of Sciences, an all-star board from the academic and business worlds and a number of former leaders of federal statistical agencies. Some of the country's elite philanthropies—including the Hewlett, MacArthur and Rockefeller foundations—have provided grants to help get the project started.

* * *

Those involved with the self-defined indicators movement—people like Hoenig, as well as supporters around the world who would like to dethrone GDP—argue that achieving a sustainable economy, and a sustainable society, may prove impossible without new ways to evaluate national progress. Left unanswered, however, is the question of which indicators are the most suitable replacements for, or most suitable enhancements to, GDP. Should they measure educational attainment or employment? Should they account for carbon emissions or happiness? As Hoenig himself is inclined to say, and not without some enthusiasm, a new panel of national measures won't necessarily settle such arguments. On the contrary, it will have a tendency to start them.

High-GDP Man vs. Low-GDP Man

For now at least, GDP holds almost unassailable sway, not only as the key national indicator for the economic health of the United States but also for that of the rest of the world's developed countries, which employ a standardized methodology—there's actually a handbook—to calculate their economic outputs. And, as it happens, there are some good reasons that everyone has depended on it for so long. "If you want to know why GDP matters, you can just put yourself back in the 1930 period, where we had no idea what was happening to our economy," William Nordhaus, a Yale economist who has spent a distinguished career thinking about economic measurement, told me recently. "There were people then who said things were fine and others who said things weren't fine. But we had no comprehensive measures, so we looked at things like boxcar loadings." If you compare the crisis of 1930 with the crisis of 2008, Nordhaus added, it has made an enormous difference to track what's happening in the economy through indexes like GDP. Such knowledge can enable a quick and informed policy response, which in the past year took shape as a big stimulus package, for example. To Nordhaus, in fact, the GDP—the antecedents of which were developed in the early 1930s by an economist named Simon Kuznets at the federal government's request—is one of the greatest inventions of the 20th century. "It's not a machine or a computer," he says, "and it's not the way you usually think of an invention. But it's an awesome thing."

*   *   *

* * * For years, economists critical of the measure have enjoyed spinning narratives to illustrate its logical flaws and limitations. Consider, for example, the lives of two people—let's call them High-GDP Man and Low-GDP Man. High-GDP Man has a long commute to work and drives an automobile that gets poor gas mileage, forcing him to spend a lot on fuel. The morning traffic and its stresses aren't too good for his car (which he replaces every few years) or his cardiovascular health (which he treats with expensive pharmaceuticals and medical procedures). High-GDP Man works hard, spends hard. He loves going to bars and restaurants, likes his flat-screen televisions and adores his big house, which he keeps at 71 degrees year round and protects with a state-of-the-art security system. High-GDP Man and his wife pay for a sitter (for their kids) and a nursing home (for their aging parents). They don't have time for housework, so they employ a full-time housekeeper. They don't have time to cook much, so they usually order in. They're too busy to take long vacations.

As it happens, all those things—cooking, cleaning, home care, three-week vacations and so forth—are the kind of activity that keep Low-GDP Man and his wife busy. High-GDP Man likes his washer and dryer; Low-GDP Man doesn't mind hanging his laundry on the clothesline. High-GDP Man buys bags of prewashed salad at the grocery store; Low-GDP Man grows vegetables in his garden. When High-GDP Man wants a book, he buys it; Low-GDP Man checks it out of the library. When High-GDP Man wants to get in shape, he joins a gym; Low-GDP Man digs out an old pair of Nikes and runs through the neighborhood. On his morning commute, High-GDP Man drives past Low-GDP Man, who is walking to work in wrinkled khakis.

By economic measures, there's no doubt High-GDP Man is superior to Low-GDP Man. His salary is higher, his expenditures are greater, his economic activity is more robust. You can even say that by modern standards High-GDP Man is a bigger boon to his country. What we can't really say for sure is whether his life is any better. In fact, there seem to be subtle indications that various "goods" that High-GDP Man consumes should, as some economists put it, be characterized as "bads." His alarm system at home probably isn't such a good indicator of his personal security; given all the medical tests, his health care expenditures seem to be excessive. Moreover, the pollution from the traffic jams near his home, which signals that business is good at the local gas stations and auto shops, is very likely contributing to social and environmental ills. And we don't know if High-GDP Man is living beyond his means, so we can't predict his future quality of life. For all we know, he could be living on borrowed time, just like a wildly overleveraged bank.

GDP vs. Human Development Index

* * *

Most criticisms of GDP have tended to fall into two distinct camps. The first group maintains that GDP itself needs to be fixed. High-GDP Man and Low-GDP Man have to become one, in effect. This might entail, for starters, placing an economic value on work done in the home, like housekeeping and child care. Activities that are currently unaccounted for, like cooking dinner at your own stove, could also be treated the same as activities that are now factored into GDP, like food prepared in a restaurant. Another fix might be to cease giving only positive values to events that actually detract from a country's well-being, like hurricanes and floods; both boost GDP through construction costs.

The second group of critics, meanwhile, has sought to recast the criticism of GDP from an accounting debate to a philosophical one. Here things get far more complicated. The argument goes like this: Even if GDP was revised as a more modern, logical GDP 2.0, our reliance on such a measure suggests that we may still be equating economic growth with progress on a planet that is possibly overburdened already by human consumption and pollution. The only way to repair such an imbalance would be to institutionalize other national indicators (environmental, say, or health-related) to reflect the true complexity of human progress. Just how many indicators are required to assess societal health—3? 30? 300, à la State of the USA?—is something economists have been struggling with for years as well.

So far only one measure has succeeded in challenging the hegemony of growth-centric thinking. This is known as the Human Development Index, which turns 20 this year. The HDI is a ranking that incorporates a nation's GDP and two other modifying factors: its citizens' education, based on adult literacy and school-enrollment data, and its citizens' health, based on life-expectancy statistics. The HDI, which happens to be used by the United Nations, has plenty of critics. For example, its three-part weightings are frequently criticized for being arbitrary; another problem is that minor variations in the literacy rates of developed nations, for example, can yield significant differences in how countries rank.

One economist who helped create the Human Development Index was Amartya Sen, a Nobel laureate in economics who teaches at Harvard.

* * *

* * * Sen joined the Nobel laureate Joseph Stiglitz and the French economist Jean-Paul Fitoussi on a commission established by President Nicolas Sarkozy of France to consider alternatives to GDP.

* * *

* * * [T]he commission endorsed both main criticisms of the GDP: the economic measure itself should be fixed to better represent individuals' circumstances today, and every country should also apply other indicators to capture what is happening economically, socially and environmentally. The commission sought a metaphor to explain what it meant. Eventually it settled on an automobile.

Suppose you're driving, Stiglitz told me. You would like to know how the vehicle is functioning, but when you check the dashboard there is only one gauge. (It's a peculiar car.) That single dial conveys one piece of important information: how fast you're moving. It's not a bad comparison to the current GDP, but it doesn't tell you many other things: How much fuel do you have left? How far can you go? How many miles have you gone already? So what you want is a car, or a country, with a big dashboard—but not so big that you can't take in all of its information.

The question is: How many measures beyond GDP—how many dials on a new dashboard—will you need? Stiglitz and his fellow academics ultimately concluded that assessing a population's quality of life will require metrics from at least seven categories: health, education, environment, employment, material well-being, interpersonal connectedness and political engagement. They also decided that any nation that was serious about progress should start measuring its "equity"—that is, the distribution of material wealth and other social goods—as well as its economic and environmental sustainability. "Too often, particularly I think in an American context, everybody says, 'We want policies that reflect our values,' but nobody says what those values are," Stiglitz told me. The opportunity to choose a new set of indicators, he added, is tantamount to saying that we should not only have a conversation about recasting GDP. We should also, in the aftermath of an extraordinary economic collapse, talk about what the goals of a society really are.

Taking the Environment Into Account

The report from the Stiglitz-Sen-Fitoussi commission isn't a blueprint, exactly—it's more like open-source software, posted online for anyone to download, discuss and modify. It doesn't tell countries how they should measure progress. It tells them how they should think about measuring progress. One challenge here—something that the commission's members well understood—is that recommending new indicators and actually implementing them are very different endeavors. Almost everyone I spoke with in the indicators movement, including Chris Hoenig at State of the USA, seems to agree that at the moment our reach exceeds our grasp. When I met with Rebecca Blank, the undersecretary of commerce for economic affairs, whose job it is to oversee the data agencies that put together GDP, she noted that new national measures depend on more than a government's willingness; they also necessitate additional financing, interagency cooperation and great leaps in the science of statistical analysis. Blank wasn't averse to some of the commission's recommendations—indeed, she recently endorsed the idea, proposed by Steve Landefeld at the Bureau of Economic Analysis, that our national accounts add a "household perspective" that represents individuals' economic circumstances better than GDP. "But some of the constraint is we don't have the money to do it," she told me, referring to various new measures. "Some of the constraint is we know how to do it, but we need to collect additional data that we don't currently have. And some of the constraint is that we don't really know how to do it quite yet."

Environmental and sustainability indicators offer a few good examples of how big the challenge is. A relatively easy first step, several members of the Stiglitz commission told me, would be to build in a "depletion charge" to GDP for the natural resources—oil, gas, timber and even fisheries—

that a country transforms into dollars. At the moment, we don't do this; it's as if these commodities have no value until they are extracted and sold. A charge for resource depletion might not affect GDP in the United States all that much; the country is too big and too thoroughly based on knowledge and technology industries for the depletion costs of things like coal mining and oil drilling to make much of an impact. On the other hand, in countries like Saudi Arabia and China, GDP might look different (that is to say, lower) if such a charge were subtracted from their economic outputs. Geoffrey Heal, a professor at Columbia who worked on the environmental aspects of the commission's report, told me that including resource depletion in the national accounts—something the U.S. considered in the early 1990s and then abandoned for political reasons—could be implemented within a year if the world's developed nations agreed to do it. After that, he suggests, a next step might be to subtract from GDP the cost of the health problems—asthma and early deaths, for instance—caused by air pollutants like sulfur dioxide.

But environmental accounting gets more difficult. "We can put monetary values on mineral stocks, fisheries and even forests, perhaps," Heal says. "But it's hard to put a monetary value on alteration of the climate system, loss of species and the consequences that might come from those." On the other hand, Heal points out, you have to decide to measure something difficult before you can come up with a technique for measuring it. That was the case when the U.S. decided to create national accounts on economic production during the Great Depression. What the Stiglitz commission ultimately concluded was that it's necessary to make a few sustainability dials on the dashboard simply raw data—registering things like a country's carbon footprint or species extinctions—until we figure out how to give the effects approximate monetary values. Maybe in 10 years, Heal guesses, economists would be able to do that.

To Heal, making a real and rapid effort at calculating these costs and then posting the information is imperative. According to Heal, we have no sense of how much "natural capital"—our stocks of clean air and water and our various ecosystems—we need to conserve to maintain our economy and our quality of life. "If you push the world's natural capital below a certain level," Heal asks, "do you so radically alter the system that it has a long-term impact on human welfare?" He doesn't know the answer. Yet, he adds, if we were to pass that point—and at present we have no dials to indicate whether we have—then we couldn't compensate for our error through technological innovation or energy breakthroughs. Because by then it would be too late.

Putting a Number on Happiness

As difficult as it might be to compile sustainability indicators, it's equally challenging to create measures that describe our social and emotional lives. In this area, there's a fair amount of skepticism from the academic establishment about putting happiness onto a national dashboard of well-being. William Nordhaus of Yale told me that some of the measurements are "absurd." Amartya Sen, too, told me that he has reservations about the worth of statistics that purport to describe human happiness.

Stiglitz and his colleagues nevertheless concluded that such research was becoming sufficiently rigorous to warrant its possible inclusion. At first the connection to GDP can be puzzling. One explanation, however, is that while our current economic measures can't capture the larger effects of unemployment or chronic depression, providing policy makers with that information may influence their actions. "You might say, If we have unemployment, don't worry, we'll just compensate the person," Stiglitz told me. "But that doesn't fully compensate them." Stiglitz pointed to the work of the Harvard professor Robert Putnam, who served on the Stiglitz-Sen-Fitoussi commission, which suggests that losing a job can have repercussions that affect a person's social connections (one main driver of human happiness, regardless of country) for many years afterward.

When I caught up with Putnam, he said that the "damage to this country's social fabric from this economic crisis must have been huge, huge, huge." And yet, he noted, "We have plenty of numbers about the economic consequences but none of the numbers about the social consequences." Over the past decade, Putnam has been working on measures—having to do with church attendance, community involvement and the like—to quantify our various social links; just recently, the U.S. Census Bureau agreed to include questions of his in some of its monthly surveys. Still, his efforts are a work in progress. When I asked Putnam whether government should be in the business of fostering social connections, he replied, "I don't think we should have a government Department of Friendship that introduces people to one another." But he argued that just as registering the social toll of joblessness would add a dimension of urgency to the unemployment issue, it seemed possible that measuring social connections, and putting those measures on a national dashboard, could be in society's best interests. As it happens, the Canadian Index of Well-Being will contain precisely such a measure; and it's very likely that a related measure of "social capital," as it's often called, will become a State of the USA indicator too. "People will get sick and die, because they don't know their neighbors," Putnam told me. "And the health effects of social isolation are of the same magnitude as people smoking. If we can care about people smoking, because that reduces their life expectancy, then why not think about social isolation too?"

It seems conceivable, in fact, that including various measures of emotional well-being on a national dashboard could lead to policies quite different from what we have now. "There's an enormous inequality of suffering in society," Daniel Kahneman told me recently. By his estimate, "if you look at the 10 percent of people who spend the most time suffering, they account for almost half of the total amount of suffering." Kahneman suggested that tremendous social and economic gains could therefore be made by dealing with the mental-health problems—depression, say—of a relatively small fraction of the population. At the same time, he added, new measures of emotional well-being that he has been working on might soon give us a more enlightened perspective on the complex relationship between money and happiness.

Currently, research suggests that increased wealth leads us to report increased feelings of satisfaction with our lives—a validation, in effect, that higher GDP increases the well-being in a country. But Kahneman told me that his most recent studies, conducted with the Princeton economist Angus Deaton, suggest that money doesn't necessarily make much of a difference in our moment-to-moment happiness, which is distinct from our feelings of satisfaction. According to their work, income over about $70,000 does nothing to improve how much we enjoy our activities on a typical day. And that raises some intriguing questions. Do we want government to help us increase our sense of satisfaction? Or do we want it to help us get through our days without feeling misery? The two questions lead toward two very different policy options. Is national progress a matter of making an increasing number of people very rich? Or is it about getting as many people as possible into the middle class?

The Political Resistance

* * *

As for the effects of such changes, Stiglitz told me, "What we measure affects what we do, and better measurement will lead to better decisions, or at least different decisions." But until the developed nations of the world actually move beyond GDP—a big if—this remains a reasoned hypothesis only. A lingering question is whether some government officials, perceiving dangers in a new measurement system, might conclude that such an overhaul would wreak political havoc and therefore ought to be avoided. A heightened focus on environmental indicators, for starters, could give environmental legislation a far greater urgency. And a revision of economic measures presents other potential policy complications.

It has long been the case, for example, that the GDP of the United States outpaces that of European countries with higher taxes and greater government spending; it has thus seemed reasonable to view our economic growth as a vindication of a national emphasis on free markets and entrepreneurship. But things look different if you see the measure itself as flawed or inadequate. We take shorter vacations than Europeans, for instance, which is one reason their GDP is lower than ours—but that could change if our indicators start putting a value on leisure time. Some of the disparity, meanwhile, between the U.S. and various European countries, Stiglitz argued, is a statistical bias resulting from the way GDP formulas account for public-sector benefits. In other words, the services received from the government in a country like Sweden—in public education, health care and child care, among other things—are likely undervalued. Rejiggering the measures of prosperity would almost certainly challenge our self-perceptions, Stiglitz said, perhaps so much so that in the U.S. we might begin to ask, Is our system working as well for most people as we think it has been?

*   *   *

Discussion Questions

1. If all growth (increases in spending) is not necessarily good growth, how can we distinguish between "good" growth and "bad" growth? Of the criteria mentioned for the "human development index," which would be the most difficult to measure? Do you think other things should be included in the measure?

2. In public policy debates, analysts often distinguish "economic" indicators—inflation, unemployment, consumer spending—from "social" indicators, such as crime, divorce, school dropout rates, and teen pregnancies. In light of Gertner's argument, is this separation appropriate? Why or why not?

3. Do you think the Stiglitz-Sen-Fitoussi Commission will make any headway with political leaders (in terms of getting their index implemented)? What political obstacles would they face?

Debating the Issues: Is Income Inequality a Problem?

By any measure, income and wealth are distributed unequally in the United States. That may not come as a surprise, but the degree to which wealth and income are concentrated might be. According to recent Census figures, household income at the ninetieth percentile (meaning that 10 percent of households earned more income, and 89 percent less) was nearly twelve times household income at the tenth percentile. According to the Congressional Research Service, the top 1 percent of households held 34.5 percent of the nation's wealth. The bottom 50 percent held 1.1 percent in 2010. This means that the top 1 percent held over thirty-one times the wealth of the entire bottom half of the country. In 1989, the ratio was only 10:1.

The fact of income inequality is indisputable. Whether that inequality has negative effects (and what to do about it) is a more complicated question. To many, high levels of income inequality signify gross failure of basic norms of fairness, and has harmful consequences for cohesion, civic life, and ultimately, even political stability. In this view, income inequality is both a cause and a consequence of political inequality, as the rich are better equipped to rig the system in their favor through favorable tax laws and regulations that further protect and concentrate wealth. Those who aren't wealthy wind up with the scraps: underfunded public schools, dangerous neighborhoods, crumbling infrastructure, inadequate services, and on and on. Others maintain that inequality is not a serious problem, and that even if it were, the alternative—draconian policies that forcefully redistribute wealth—is even worse. Moreover, since nobody can say what distribution of income would be fair, any attempt to achieve balance is arbitrary.

The two readings in this debate clash directly on this point. Timothy Noah, author of *The Great Divergence*, which claims that inequality is at crisis proportions, summarized his argument in a series of columns in the online journal *Slate*. Here, he focuses on the consequences of excessive inequality. Apart from the fundamental unfairness—working class people unable to amass resources, take a day off, or achieve any sense of economic security, while the wealthy enjoy gated communities and lives of privilege—inequality has a number of corrosive effects that go well beyond this: lower economic growth, bad health outcomes for those at the bottom, and driving the middle class into the ranks of the poor. Noah specifically attacks the main arguments made by those who dismiss the idea that income inequality is either not worth worrying about, or is actually a good thing.

Did Noah provide a caricature of the argument that inequality may be a positive? Richard Epstein, a professor at New York University Law School, makes the argument that Noah dismisses: that inequality is actually a good thing, not because it gives people an incentive to work their way up the income ladder, but because the policies needed to remedy it make everybody worse off (through lower economic growth and coercive rules). The only way to reduce inequality is through tax policies that transfer wealth from those who have wealth to those who do not. Those policies not only do not work, Epstein argues, but they have the effect of eliminating aggregate wealth. Part of the problem is that when governments redistribute wealth, groups compete for the right to transfer those resources to themselves (Epstein notes the success of labor unions, big business, and agricultural interests in doing this, and suggests that income redistribution is no different). And part of the problem is that forced exchange via government coercion is, by definition, less efficient than voluntary exchange. The result may be less inequality, but also less wealth.

69

"Why We Can't Ignore Growing Income Inequality"

Timothy Noah

Clarence the Angel: We don't use money in heaven.
George Bailey: Comes in pretty handy down here, bub.
—Frank Capra's *It's A Wonderful Life* (1946)

The Declaration of Independence says that all men are created equal, but we know that isn't true. George Clooney was created better-looking than me. Stephen Hawking was born smarter, Evander Holyfield stronger, Jon Stewart funnier, and Warren Buffett better able to understand financial markets. All these people have parlayed their exceptional gifts into very high incomes—much higher than mine. Is that so odd? Odder would be if Buffett or Clooney were forced to live on my income, adequate though it might be to a petit-bourgeois journalist. Lest you conclude my equanimity is in any way unique (we Slate writers are known for our contrarianism), Barbara Ehrenreich, in her 2001 book *Nickel and Dimed*, quotes a woman named Colleen, a single mother of two, saying much the same thing about the wealthy families whose floors she scrubs on hands and knees. "I don't mind, really," she says, "because I guess I'm a simple person, and I don't want what they have. I mean, it's nothing to me."

It is easy to make too much of this, and a few conservatives have done so in seeking to dismiss the importance (or even existence) of the Great Divergence. Let's look at their arguments.

Inequality is good. Every year the American Economic Association invites a distinguished economist to deliver at its annual conference the Richard T. Ely Lecture. Ely, a founder of the AEA and a leader in the Progressive movement, would have been horrified by the 1999 lecture that Finis Welch, a professor of economics (now emeritus) at Texas A&M, delivered in his name. Its title was "In Defense of Inequality."

Welch began by stating that "all of economics results from inequality. Without inequality of priorities and capabilities, there would be no trade, no specialization, and no surpluses produced by cooperation." He invited his audience to consider a world in which skill, effort, and sheer chance played no role whatsoever in what you got paid. The only decision that would affect your wage level would be when to leave school. "After that, the clock ticks, and wages follow the experience path. Nothing else matters. Can you imagine a more horrible, a more deadening existence?"

But something close to the dystopia Welch envisioned already exists for those toiling in the economy's lower tiers. Welch should have a chat with his office receptionist. Or he could read *Nickel and Dimed*, or the 2010 book *Catching Out* by Dick J. Reavis, a contributing editor at *Texas Monthly* who went undercover as a day laborer.

Waitresses, construction workers, dental assistants, call-center operators—people in these jobs are essentially replaceable, and usually have bosses who don't distinguish between individual initiative and insubordination. Even experience is of limited value, because it's often accompanied by diminishing physical vigor.

Welch said that he believed inequality was destructive only when "the low-wage citizenry views society as unfair, when it views effort as not worthwhile, when upward mobility is impossible or so unlikely that its pursuit is not worthwhile." Colleen's comment would appear to suggest that the first of these conditions has not been met. But that's only because I omitted what she went on to say: "But what I would like is to be able to take a day off now and then . . . if I had to . . . and still be able to buy groceries the next day." Colleen may not begrudge the rich the material goods they've acquired through skill, effort, and sheer chance, but that doesn't mean she thinks her own labors secure her an adequate level of economic security. Clearly, they don't.

Welch judged the growing financial rewards accruing to those with higher levels of education a good thing insofar as they provided an incentive to go to college or graduate school. But for most of the 20th century, smaller financial incentives attracted enough workers to meet the economy's growing demand for higher-skilled labor. That demand isn't being met today, as Harvard economists Claudia Goldin and Lawrence Katz have shown. Welch also said that both women and blacks made income gains during the Great Divergence (duly noted in our installment on race and gender, though the gains by blacks were so tiny that it's more accurate to say blacks didn't lose ground). But that's hardly evidence that growing income inequality unrelated to gender or race doesn't matter. Finally, Welch argued that the welfare state has made it too easy not to work at all. But the Great Divergence had a more significant impact on the working middle class than on the destitute.

Income doesn't matter. In most contexts, libertarians can fairly be said to place income in very high regard. Tax it to even the slightest degree and they cry foul. If government assistance must be extended, they prefer a cash transaction to the provision of government services. The market is king, and what is the market if not a mighty river of money?

Bring up the topic of growing income inequality, though, and you're likely to hear a different tune. Case in point: "Thinking Clearly About Economic Inequality," a 2009 Cato Institute paper by Will Wilkinson. Income isn't what matters, Wilkinson argues; consumption is, and "the weight of the evidence shows that the run-up in consumption inequality has been considerably less dramatic than the rise in income inequality." Wilkinson concedes that the available data on consumption are shakier than the available data on income; he might also have mentioned that consumption in excess of income usually means debt—as in, say, subprime mortgages. The thought that the have-nots are compensating for their lower incomes by putting themselves (and the country) in economically ruinous hock is not reassuring.

Wilkinson further argues that consumption isn't what matters; what matters is utility gained from consumption. Joe and Sam both own refrigerators. Joe's is a $350 model from Ikea. Sam's is an $11,000 state-of-the-art Sub-Zero. Sam gets to consume a lot more than Joe, but whatever added utility he achieves is marginal; Joe's Ikea fridge "will keep your beer just as cold." But if getting rich is only a matter of spending more money on the same stuff you'd buy if you were poor, why bother to climb the greasy pole at all?

Next Wilkinson decides that utility isn't what matters; what matters is buying power. Food is cheaper than ever before. Since lower-income people spend their money disproportionately on food, declining food prices, Wilkinson argues, constitute a sort of raise. Never mind that Ehrenreich routinely found, in her travels among the lower middle class, workers who routinely skipped lunch to save money or brought an individual-size pack of junk food and called that lunch. Reavis reports that a day laborer's typical lunch budget is $3. That won't buy much. The problem isn't the cost of food per se but the cost of shelter, which has shot up so high that low-income families don't have much left over to spend on other essentials.

Declining food prices constitute a sort of raise for higher-income people too. But Wilkinson writes that the affluent spend a smaller share of their budget on food and a much larger share on psychotherapy and yoga and cleaning services. And since services like these are unaffected by foreign competition or new efficiencies in manufacturing, Wilkinson argues, providers can charge whatever they like.

Tell it to Colleen! I recently worked out with my new cleaning lady what I would pay her. Here's how the negotiation went. I told her what I would pay her. She said, "OK." According to the Bureau of Labor Statistics, the median income for a housekeeper is $19,250, which is $2,800 below the poverty line for a family of four.

A more thoughtful version of the income-doesn't-matter argument surfaces in my former *Slate* colleague Mickey Kaus' 1992 book *The End of Equality*. Kaus chided "Money Liberals" for trying to redistribute income when instead they might be working to diminish social inequality by creating or shoring up spheres in which rich and poor are treated the same. Everybody can picnic in the park. Everybody should be able to receive decent health care. Under a compulsory national service program, everybody would be required to perform some civilian or military duty.

As a theoretical proposition, Kaus' vision is appealing. Bill Gates will always have lots more money than me, no matter how progressive the tax system becomes. But if he gets called to jury duty he has to show up, just like me. When his driver's license expires, he'll be just as likely to have to take a driving test. Why not expand this egalitarian zone to, say, education, by making public schools so good that Gates' grandchildren will be as likely to attend them as mine or yours?

But at a practical level, Kaus' exclusive reliance on social equality is simply inadequate. For one thing, the existing zones of social equality are pretty circumscribed. Neither Gates nor I spend a lot of time hanging around the Department of Motor Vehicles. Rebuilding or creating the more meaningful spheres—say, public education or a truly national health care system—won't occur overnight. Nurturing the social-equality sphere isn't likely to pay off for a very long time.

Kaus would like to separate social equality from income equality, but the two go hand in hand. In theory they don't have to, but in practice they just do. Among industrialized nations, those that have achieved the greatest social equality are the same ones that have achieved the greatest income equality. France, for example, has a level of income inequality much lower than that of most other countries in the Organization for Economic Cooperation and Development. It's one of the very few places where income inequality has been going down. (Most everywhere else it's gone up, though nowhere to the degree it has in the United States.) France also enjoys what the World Health Organization calls the world's finest health care system (by which the WHO means, in large part, the most egalitarian one; this is the famous survey from 2000 in which the U.S. ranked 37th).

Do France's high marks on both social equality and income equality really strike you as a coincidence? As incomes become more unequal, a likelier impulse among the rich isn't to urge or even allow the government to create or expand public institutions where they can mix it up with the proles. It's to create or expand private institutions that will help them maintain separation from the proles, with whom they have less and less in common. According to Jonathan Rowe, who has written extensively about social equality, that's exactly what's happening in the United States. In an essay titled "The Vanishing Commons" that appeared in *Inequality Matters*, a 2005 anthology, Rowe notes that Congress has been busy extending copyright terms and patent monopolies and turning over public lands to mining and timber companies for below-market fees. "In an 'ownership' society especially," Rowe writes, "we should think about what we own in common, not just what we keep apart."

Inequality doesn't create unhappiness. Arthur C. Brooks, president of the American Enterprise Institute, argued this point in *National Review* online in June. What drives entrepreneurs, he wrote, is not the desire for money but the desire for earned success. When people feel they deserve their success, they are happy; when they do not, they aren't. "The money is just the metric of the value that the person is creating."

Brooks marshaled very little evidence to support his argument, and what evidence he did muster was less impressive than he thought. He made much of a 1996 survey that asked people how successful they felt, and how happy. Among the 45 percent who counted themselves "completely successful" or "very successful," 39 percent said they were very happy. Among the 55 percent who counted themselves at most "somewhat successful," only 20 percent said they were happy. Brooks claimed victory with the finding that successful people were more likely to be happy (or at least to say they were), by 19 percentage points, than less-successful people. More striking, though, was that 61 percent of the successful people—a significant majority—did not say they were "very happy." Nowhere in the survey were the successful people asked whether they deserved their happiness.

Let's grant Brooks his generalization that people who believe they deserve their success are likelier to be happy than people who believe they don't. It makes intuitive sense. But Brooks's claim that money is only a "metric" does not. Looking at the same survey data, Berkeley sociologist Michael Hout found that from 1973 to 2000 the difference between the affluent and the poor who counted themselves either "very happy" or "not too happy" ranged from 19 percentage points to 27. Among the poor, the percentage who felt "very happy" fell by nearly one-third from 1973 to 1994, then crept up a couple of points during the tight labor market of the late 1990s. Hout also observed that overall happiness dropped a modest 5 percent from 1973 to 2000.

Quality of life is improving. This argument has been made by too many conservatives to count. Yes, it's true that an unemployed steel worker living in the 21st century is in many important ways better off than the royals and aristocrats of yesteryear. Living conditions improve over time. But people do not experience life as an interesting moment in the evolution of human societies. They experience it in the present and weigh their own experience against that of the living. Brooks cites (even though it contradicts his argument) a famous 1998 study by economists Sara Solnick (then at the University of Miami, now at the University of Vermont) and David Hemenway of the Harvard School of Public Health. Subjects were asked which they'd prefer: to earn $50,000 while knowing everyone else earned $25,000, or to earn $100,000 while knowing everyone else earned $200,000. Objectively speaking, $100,000 is twice as much as $50,000. Even so, 56 percent chose $50,000 if it meant that would put them on top rather than at the bottom. We are social creatures and establish our expectations relative to others.

Inequality isn't increasing. This is the boldest line of conservative attack, challenging a consensus about income trends in the United States that most conservatives accept. (Brooks: "It is factually incorrect to argue that income inequality has not risen in America—it has.") Alan Reynolds, a senior fellow at Cato, made the case in a January 2007 paper. It was a technical argument hinging largely on a critique of the tax data used by Emmanuel Saez and Thomas Piketty in the groundbreaking paper we looked at in our installment about the superrich. But as Gary Burtless of Brookings noted in a January 2007 reply, Social Security records "tell a simple and similar story." A Congressional Budget Office analysis, Burtless wrote, addressed "almost all" of Reynolds's objections to Saez and Piketty's findings, and confirmed "a sizable rise in both pre-tax and after-tax inequality." Reynolds's paper didn't deny notable increases in top incomes, but he argued that these were because of technical changes in tax law and/or to isolated and unusual financial events. That, Burtless answered, was akin to arguing that, "adjusting for the weather and the season, no homeowner in New Orleans ended up with a wet basement" after Hurricane Katrina.

That income inequality very much matters is the thesis of the 2009 book *The Spirit Level*, by Richard Wilkinson and Kate Pickett, two medical researchers based in Yorkshire. The book has been criticized for overreaching. Wilkinson and Pickett relate income inequality trends not only to mental and physical health, violence, and teenage pregnancy, but also to global warming. But their larger point—that income inequality is bad not only for people on the losing end but also for society at large—seems hard to dispute. "Modern societies," they write,

> will depend increasingly on being creative, adaptable, inventive, well-informed and flexible communities, able to respond generously to each other and to needs wherever they arise. These are characteristics not of societies in hock to the rich, in which people are driven by status insecurities, but of populations used to working together and respecting each other as equals.

The United States' economy is currently struggling to emerge from a severe recession brought on by the financial crisis of 2008. Was that crisis brought about by income inequality? Some economists are starting to think it may have been. David Moss of Harvard Business School has produced an intriguing chart that shows bank failures tend to coincide with periods of growing income inequality. "I could hardly believe how tight the fit was," he told the *New York Times*. Princeton's Paul Krugman has similarly been considering whether the Great Divergence helped cause the recession by pushing middle-income Americans into debt. The growth of household debt has followed a pattern strikingly similar to the growth in income inequality (see the final graph). Raghuram G. Rajan, a business school professor at the University of Chicago, recently argued on the New Republic's Web site that "let them eat credit" was "the mantra of the political establishment in the go-go years before the crisis." Christopher Brown, an economist at Arkansas State University, wrote a paper in 2004 affirming that "inequality can exert a significant drag on effective demand." Reducing inequality, he argued, would also reduce consumer debt. Today, Brown's paper looks prescient.

Heightened partisanship in Washington and declining trust in government have many causes (and the latter slide predates the Great Divergence). But surely the growing income chasm between the poor and middle class and the rich, between the Sort of Rich and the Rich, and even between the Rich and the Stinking Rich, make it especially difficult to reestablish any spirit of *e pluribus unum*. Republicans and Democrats compete to show which party more fervently opposes the elite, with each side battling to define what "elite" means. In a more equal society, the elite would still be resented. But I doubt that opposing it would be an organizing principle of politics to the same extent that it is today.

I find myself returning to the gut-level feeling expressed at the start of this series: I do not wish to live in a banana republic. There is a reason why, in years past, Americans scorned societies starkly divided into the privileged and the destitute. They were repellent. Is it my imagination, or do we hear less criticism of such societies today in the United States? Might it be harder for Americans to sustain in such discussions the necessary sense of moral superiority?

What is the ideal distribution of income in society? I couldn't tell you, and historically much mischief has been accomplished by addressing this question too precisely. But I can tell you this: We've been headed in the wrong direction for far too long.

70

"Three Cheers for Income Inequality"

Richard A. Epstein

Taxing the top one percent even more means less wealth and fewer jobs for the rest of us.

The 2008 election was supposed to bring to the United States a higher level of civil discourse. Fast-forward three years and exactly the opposite has happened. A stalled economy brings forth harsh recriminations. As recent polling data reveals, the American public is driven by two irreconcilable emotions. The first is a deep distrust of government, which has driven the approval rate for Congress below ten percent. The second is a strong egalitarian impulse that directs its fury to the top one percent of income earners. Thus the same people who want government to get out of their lives also want government to increase taxes on the rich and corporations. They cannot have it both ways.

I voiced some of my objections to these two points in an interview on PBS, which sparked much controversy. The topic merits much more attention.

What are the origins of inequality? Start with a simple world in which all individuals own their labor. Acting in their self-interest (which includes that of family and friends), they seek to improve their lot in life. They cannot use force to advance their own position. Thus, they are left with two alternatives: individual labor and cooperative voluntary ventures.

Voluntary ventures will normally emerge only when all parties to them entertain expectations of gain from entering into these transactions. In some cases, to be sure, these expectations will be dashed. All risky ventures do not pan out. But on average and over time, the few failures cannot derail the many successes. People will make themselves better off.

The rub is that they need not do so at even rates. The legitimate origin of the inequality of wealth lies in the simple observation that successful actors outperform unsuccessful ones, without violating their rights. As was said long ago by Justice Pitney in *Coppage v. Kansas*, "it is from the nature of things impossible to uphold freedom of contract and the right of private property without at the same time recognizing as legitimate those inequalities of fortune that are the necessary result of the exercise of those rights."

So why uphold this combination of property and contract rights? Not because of atavistic fascination for venerable legal institutions. Rather, it is because voluntary exchanges improve overall social welfare. This works in three stages.

First, these transactions, on average, will make all parties to them better off. The only way the rich succeed is by helping their trading partners along the way.

Second, the successes of the rich afford increased opportunities for gain to other people in the form of new technologies and businesses for others to exploit.

Third, the initial success of the rich businessman paves the way for competitors to enter the marketplace. This, in turn, spurs the original businessman to make further improvements to his own goods and services.

In this system, the inequalities in wealth pay for themselves by the vast increases in wealth.

Any defense of wealth inequalities through voluntary means is, however, subject to a powerful caveat: The wealth must be acquired by legitimate means, which do not include aid in the form of state subsidies, state protection, or any other special gimmick. The rich who prosper from these policies do not deserve their wealth. Neither does anyone else who resorts to the same tactics.

As an empirical matter, large businesses, labor unions, and agricultural interests that have profited from government protections have drained huge amounts of wealth from the system. Undoing these protections may or may not change the various indices of inequality. But it will increase the overall size of the pie by improving the overall level of system efficiency.

The hard question that remains is this: To what extent will the United States, or any other nation, profit by a concerted effort to redress inequalities of wealth?

Again the answer depends on the choice of means. Voluntary forms of redistribution through major charitable foundations pose no threat to the accumulation of wealth. Indeed, they spur its creation by affording additional reasons to acquire levels of wealth that no rational agent could possibly consume.

Forced transfers of wealth through taxation will have the opposite effect. They will destroy the pools of wealth that are needed to generate new ventures, and they will dull the system-wide incentives to create wealth in the first place. There are many reasons for this system-wide failure.

First, the use of state coercion to remedy inequalities of wealth is not easily done. The most obvious method for doing so is by creating subsidies for people at the bottom, which are offset by high rates of taxation for people at the top. The hope is that high taxes will do little to blunt economic activity at the high end, while the payments will do little to dull initiative at the low end.

But this program is much more difficult to implement than is commonly supposed. The process of income redistribution opens up opportunities for powerful groups to secure transfers of wealth to themselves. This does nothing to redress inequalities of wealth. Even if these political players are constrained, there is still no costless way to transfer wealth up and down the income scale.

The administrative costs of running a progressive income tax system are legion. Unfortunately, that point was missed in a recent op-ed. Writing in the *New York Times*, Cornell economist Robert H. Frank plumped hard for steeper progressive income tax rates as a way to amend income inequality.

Yet matters are not nearly as simple as he supposes. In his view, the source of complexity in the current income tax code lies in the plethora of special interest provisions that make it difficult to calculate income by recognized standard economic measures. Thus, he thinks that it is "flatly wrong" to think that the flat tax will result in tax simplification. After all, it is just as easy to read a tax schedule that has progressive rates as one that has a uniform flat rate.

But more than reading tax schedules is at stake. First, one reason why the internal revenue code contains such complexity is its desire to combat the private strategies that people, especially those in the top one percent, use to avoid high levels of taxation. Anyone who has spent time in dealing with family trusts and partnerships, with income averaging, with the use of real estate shelters, and with foreign investments, knows just how hard it is to protect the progressive rate schedule against manipulation.

Second, the creation of these large tax loopholes is not some act of nature. Frank, like so many defenders of progressive taxation, fails to realize that progressive rates generate huge pressures to create new tax shelters. Lower the overall tax rates and the pressure to create tax gimmicks with real economic costs diminishes. Overall social output is higher with a flat tax than it is with a progressive one.

Third, the dangers posed by the use of progressive taxation are not confined to these serious administrative issues. There are also larger questions of political economy at stake. The initial question is just how steep the progressive tax ought to be. Keep it too shallow, and it does little to generate additional public revenues to justify the added cost of administration. Make it too steep, and it will reduce the incentives to create wealth that are always unambiguously stronger under a flat tax system. But since no one knows the optimal level of progressivity, vast quantities of wealth are dissipated in fighting over these levels. The flat tax removes that dimension of political intrigue.

Fourth, sooner or later—and probably sooner—high tax rates will kill growth. Progressives like Frank operate on the assumption that high taxation rates have little effect on investment by asking whether anyone would quit a cushy job just to save a few tax dollars. But the situation is in reality far more complex. One key to success in the United States lies in its ability to attract foreign labor and foreign capital to our shores. In this we are in competition with other nations whose tax policies are far more favorable to new investment than ours. The loss of foreign people and foreign capital is not easy to observe because we cannot identify with certainty most of the individuals who decide to go elsewhere. But we should at the very least note that there is the risk of a brain drain as the best and brightest foreign workers who came to the United States in search of economic opportunity ultimately may return home. They will likely not want to brave the hostile business climate that they see in the United States.

Fifth, sophisticated forms of tax avoidance are not limited to foreign laborers. Rich people have a choice of tax-free and taxable investments. They can increase transfers to family members in order to reduce the incidence of high progressive taxation. They can retire a year sooner, or go part-time to reduce their tax burdens. And of course, they can fight the incidence of higher taxation by using their not inconsiderable influence in the tax arenas.

Sixth, the inefficiencies created by a wide range of tax and business initiatives reduces the wealth earned by people in that top one percent, and thus the tax base on which the entire redistributive state depends. Defenders of progressive taxation, like Frank, cite the recent report of the Congressional Budget Office, which shows huge increases of wealth in the top one percent from 1979 to 2007. The top one percent increased its wealth by 275 percent in those years. The rest of the income distribution lagged far behind.

Unfortunately, the CBO report was out of date the day it was published. We now have tax data available that runs through 2009, which shows the folly of seeking to rely on heavier rates of taxation on the top one percent. The Tax Foundation's October 24, 2011 report contains this solemn reminder of the risks of soaking the rich in bad times:

> In 2009, the top 1 percent of tax returns paid 36.7 percent of all federal individual income taxes and earned 16.9 percent of adjusted gross income (AGI), compared to 2008 when those figures were 38.0 percent and 20.0 percent, respectively. Both of those figures—share of income and share of taxes paid—were their lowest since 2003 when the top 1 percent earned 16.7 percent of adjusted gross income and paid 34.3 percent of federal individual income taxes.

It is worth adding that the income of the top one percent also dropped 20 percent between 2007 and 2008, with a concomitant loss in tax revenues.

There are several disturbing implications that flow from this report. The first is that these figures explain the vulnerability in bad times of our strong dependence on high-income people to fund the transfer system. The current contraction in wealth at the top took place with only few new taxes. The decline in taxable income at the top will only shrink further if tax rates are raised. A mistake, therefore, in setting tax rate increases could easily wreck the entire system. Indeed, the worst possible outcome would be for high taxation to lower top incomes drastically. Right now, for better or worse, the entire transfer system of the United States is dependent on the continued success of high-income earners whom the egalitarians would like to punish.

Put otherwise, if a person at the middle of the income distribution loses a dollar in income, the federal government loses nothing in income tax revenues. Let a rich person suffer that decline and the revenue loss at the federal level is close to 40 percent, with more losses at the state level. The slow growth policies of the last three years have cost far more in revenue from the top one percent than any increase in progressive taxation could possibly hope to achieve. The more we move toward an equal income policy, the more we shall need tax increases on the middle class to offset the huge revenue losses at the top. Our current political economy makes the bottom 99 percent hostage to the continued success of the rich.

The dangers of the current obsession with income inequality should be clear. The rhetorical excesses of people like Robert Frank make it ever easier to champion a combination of high taxation schemes coupled with ever more stringent regulations of labor and capital markets. Together, these schemes spell the end of the huge paydays of the top one percent. Those earners depend heavily on a growth in asset value, which is just not happening today.

But what about the flat tax? Frank and others are right to note that a return to the flat tax will result in an enormous redistribution of income to the top one percent from everyone else. But why assume that the current level of progressivity sets the legitimate baseline, especially in light of the current anemic levels of economic growth? What theory justifies progressive taxation in the first place? The current system presupposes that this nation can continue to fund the aspirations of 99 percent out of the wealth of the one percent. That will prove to be unsustainable. A return to a flatter tax (ideally a flat tax) will have just the short-term consequences that Frank fears. It will undo today's massively redistributivist policies. But it will also go a long way toward unleashing growth in our heavily regulated and taxed economy.

The United States is now in the midst of killing the goose that lays the golden eggs. That current strategy is failing in the face of economic stagnation, even with no increase in tax rates. It will quickly crumble if tax increases are used to feed the current coalition of unions and farmers who will receive much of the revenue, while the employment prospects of ordinary people languish for want of the major capital investments that often depend on the wealth of the privileged one percent of the population.

The clarion call for more income equality puts short-term transfers ahead of long-term growth. Notwithstanding the temper of the times, that siren call should be stoutly resisted. Enterprise and growth, not envy and stagnation, are the keys to economic revival.

Discussion Questions:

1. How much inequality is too much? Can you define a standard for judging whether a given distribution of income is sufficiently unfair to justify government redress? In practical terms, if the top 1 percent of households control 34 percent of wealth, is that too much? What would a reasonable concentration be?

2. Ultimately, arguments against using government power to create a more equal (or, if you prefer, a less unequal) income distribution reduce to the position that even if inequality is bad, it is the price we must pay for a free society. Is that right? Does this mean that *all* redistributive policies are improper?

3. Are there ways of reducing income inequality that do not require the types of coercion that Epstein criticizes? What might they be?

CHAPTER 14

Government and Society

71

"Providing Social Security Benefits in the Future: A Review of the Social Security System and Plans to Reform It"

David C. John

There is wide agreement that Social Security requires major reforms if it is to continue to provide economic security to retirees. The baby boom generation will be retiring soon and the amount of money paid in benefits will exceed payroll taxes that are used to fund the system by 2016. The program has been running a surplus for the past two decades, but the government has been spending this money and giving the Social Security trust fund special Treasury bonds that will be repaid with general revenue between 2016 and 2038, when the bonds will be gone. By 2030 there will be only 2.2 workers for every retiree, which means that this "pay as you go" program will be facing a series of increasingly difficult choices about how to meet its obligations.

At the heart of the debate are two contrasting perspective of what the Social Security system should accomplish, both deeply rooted in American political culture: Should we view Social Security as a national guarantee of basic income for all individuals in their retirement, no matter what? Or should Social Security be an individualistic program that permits people to succeed—or fail—based on the choices that they make? To put it another way, is Social Security a social welfare program or an investment program? David C. John weighs into this controversy by outlining some principles for Social Security reform, providing an overview of five plans for reform, and then discussing the central characteristics of the Social Security program that are necessary for understanding the debate over reform. John is a strong supporter of personal retirement accounts (PRA), which would allow workers to invest a portion of their Social Security taxes. However, as John notes, none of these plans addresses the "transition problem." That is, because Social Security is a "pay as you go" program—today's workers pay for the Social Security benefits of today's retirees—if today's workers are allowed to take a portion of their Social Security taxes and put them in a PRA, this means that there will be even less money to pay for the current obligations to retirees than under the current system, at least for the next several decades. John writes, "Neither the current system nor any of the proposed reform plans comes close to closing the gap."

Social Security is the best-loved American government program, but how it works and is financed is almost completely unknown. Most Americans have a vague idea that they pay taxes for their benefits and that their benefits are linked somehow to their earnings. Many also know that the program is in trouble and needs to be "fixed" sometime soon to deal with the retirement of the baby boomers. Beyond this, their knowledge of the facts is severely limited and often colored by rumors and stories.

Most politicians exploit this lack of knowledge and limit their statements on Social Security to platitudes and vague promises. To make matters worse, reformers tend either to be content with similar platitudes or to speak in such detail that few outside the policy world can understand what they are saying. The simple fact is that today's Social Security is extremely complex, and any reform plan that is more than fine words will be similarly complex.

This paper attempts to simplify the reform debate by comparing various plans (including the current system) side by side. Each of the six sections of this paper compares how the current system and the reform plans handle a specific subject. Only reform plans that have been scored by Social Security's Office of the Chief Actuary are included in this comparison, using numbers contained in the 2003 Report of the Social Security Trustees. * * *

While looking at just one or two sections of special interest may be tempting, this approach would probably be misleading. For the best effect, each section should be considered together with the other sections in order to form a complete picture of the plan. Using simply one section by itself to judge an entire plan will not yield an accurate result.

Seven Important Rules for Real Social Security Reform

Information in this side-by-side comparison is based on Social Security's scoring memos for each plan and conclusions that can be drawn from information contained in those memos. While there are many good points in the reform plans examined in this analysis, this is not an endorsement of any proposal by the author or The Heritage Foundation. Instead, this comparison provides details of specific plans. However, it would be wise for reformers to follow a set of general principles to ensure that any

Social Security reform both resolves Social Security's problems and provides workers with greater retirement security. Those principles are listed below.

This comparison of plans makes no effort to examine whether the Social Security reform plans included in it meet or violate any or all of the principles.

Principles for Social Security Reform

- **The benefits of current retirees and those close to retirement must not be reduced.** The government has a moral contract with those who currently receive Social Security retirement benefits, as well as with those who are so close to retirement, that they have no other options for building a retirement nest egg. If the benefits of younger workers cannot be maintained given the need to curb the burgeoning cost of the program, then they should have the opportunity to make up the difference by investing a portion of their Social Security taxes in a personal retirement account.
- **The rate of return on a worker's Social Security taxes must be improved.** Today's workers receive very poor returns on their Social Security payroll taxes. As a general rule, the younger a worker is or the lower his or her income, the lower his or her rate of return will be. Reform must provide a better retirement income to future retirees without increasing Social Security taxes. The best way to do this is to allow workers to divert a portion of their existing Social Security taxes into a personal retirement account that can earn significantly more than Social Security can pay.
- **Americans must be able to use Social Security to build a nest egg for the future.** A well-designed retirement system includes three elements: regular monthly retirement income, dependent's insurance, and the ability to save for retirement. Today's Social Security system provides a stable level of retirement income and does provide benefits for dependents. But it does not allow workers to accumulate cash savings to fulfill their own retirement goals or to pass on to their heirs. Workers should be able to use Social Security to build a cash nest egg that can be used to increase their retirement income or to build a better economic future for their families. The best way to do this is to establish, within the framework of Social Security, a system of personal retirement accounts.
- **Personal retirement accounts must guarantee an adequate minimum income.** Seniors must be able to count on a reasonable and predictable minimum level of monthly income, regardless of what happens in the investment markets.
- **Workers should be allowed to fund their Social Security personal retirement accounts by allocating some of their existing payroll tax**

dollars to them. Workers should not be required to pay twice for their benefits—once through existing payroll taxes and again through additional income taxes or contributions used to fund a personal retirement account. Moreover, many working Americans can save little after paying existing payroll taxes and so cannot be expected to make additional contributions to a personal account. Thus Congress should allow Americans to divert a portion of the taxes that they currently pay for Social Security retirement benefits into personal retirement accounts.

- **For currently employed workers, participation in the new accounts must be voluntary.** No one should be forced into a system of personal retirement accounts. Instead, currently employed workers must be allowed to choose between today's Social Security and one that offers personal retirement accounts.
- **Any Social Security reform plan must be realistic, cost-effective and reduce the unfunded liabilities of the current system.** True Social Security reform will provide an improved total retirement benefit. But it should also reduce Social Security's huge unfunded liabilities by a greater level than the "transition" cost needed to finance benefits for retirees during the reform. Like paying points to obtain a better mortgage, Social Security reform should lead to a net reduction in liabilities.

The Social Security System and Plans for Reform

The Current System

Social Security currently pays an inflation-indexed monthly retirement and survivors' benefit, based on a worker's highest 35 years of earnings. Past earnings are indexed for average wage growth in the economy before calculating the benefit. The benefit formula is progressive, meaning that lower-income workers receive a benefit equal to a higher proportion of their average income than upper-income workers receive. The program is expected to continue to collect more in payroll taxes than it pays out in benefits until about 2018.

Unused payroll taxes are borrowed by the federal government and replaced by special-issue Treasury bonds. After the system begins to pay out more than it receives, the federal government will cover the resulting cash flow deficits by repaying the special-issue Treasury bonds out of general revenues. When the bonds run out in about 2042, Social Security benefits will automatically be reduced to a level equal to incoming revenue. This is projected to require a 27 percent reduction in 2042, with greater reductions after that.

The DeMint Plan

Representative Jim DeMint (R-SC) has introduced a voluntary personal retirement account (PRA) plan that would establish progressively funded voluntary individual accounts for workers under age 55 on January 1, 2005. The amount that goes into each worker's account would vary according to income, with lower-income workers able to save a higher percentage. For average-income workers, the account would equal about 5.1 percent of income.

The government would pay the difference between the monthly benefit that can be financed from an annuity paid for by using all or some of the PRA and the amount that the current system promises. The sum of the annuity and the government-paid portion of Social Security would be guaranteed at least to equal benefits promised under the current system, and 35 percent of PRA assets would be invested in government bonds to help pay for any Social Security cash flow deficits. This proportion would be reduced gradually in the future. General revenue money would be used to pay for additional cash flow deficits.

The Graham Plan

Senator Lindsay Graham (R-SC) has proposed a plan that would give workers under age 55 (in 2004) three options. (Workers above the age of 55 would be required to remain in the current system and would receive full benefits.)

Under *Option 1*, workers would establish PRAs funded with part of their existing payroll taxes, equal to 4 percent of pay up to a maximum of $1,300 per year. Workers' benefits would be reduced by changing the benefit indexing formula from the current wage growth index to one based on consumer prices. Over time, this change would reduce benefits for workers at all income levels, but the effect on lower-income workers would be eased by a mandated minimum benefit of at least 120 percent of the poverty level for workers with a 35-year work history. The government-paid monthly benefit would be further reduced to reflect the value of the PRA. This reduction would be calculated using the average earnings of government bonds so that, if the PRA earned more than government bonds, the total monthly benefit would be higher. Option 1 also raises survivor benefits to 75 percent of the couple's benefit for many survivors.

Option 2 is essentially the same as Option 1, but without PRAs. The government would pay all benefits for workers who choose this option. Option 2 includes both the basic benefit reduction and the minimum benefit requirement.

Option 3 pays the same level of benefits promised under current law, but workers who select this option would pay higher payroll taxes in return. Initially, the payroll tax rate for retirement and survivors benefits would increase from 12.4 percent of income to 14.4 percent of income (counting both the worker's and the employer's shares of the tax). In subsequent years, the tax rate would continue to climb in 0.25 percent increments.

The Smith Plan

Representative Nick Smith (R–MI) has proposed a voluntary PRA plan that would create personal retirement savings accounts funded with an amount equal to 2.5 percent of income, paid out of existing payroll taxes. This would increase to 2.75 percent of income in 2025 and could become larger after 2038 if Social Security has surplus cash flows. Retirement and survivors' benefits would be reduced by an amount equal to the value of lifetime account contributions plus a specified interest rate.

The Smith plan would also make many changes in Social Security's benefit formula, mainly affecting middle-income and upper-income workers. These changes would eventually result in most workers receiving a flat monthly benefit of about $550 in 2004 dollars. It would also gradually increase the retirement age for full benefits and require that all newly hired local and state workers be covered by Social Security. The Smith plan transfers $866 billion from general revenues to Social Security between 2007 and 2013 to help cover cash flow deficits and allows additional general revenue transfers when needed after that.

The Ferrara Plan

Peter Ferrara, Director of the International Center for Law and Economics, has proposed a plan that would create voluntary PRAs that would be funded according to a progressive formula that allows lower-income workers to save a higher proportion of their payroll taxes than upper-income workers. Average-income workers could save about 6.4 percent of their income. Workers would be guaranteed that the total of their PRA-generated benefits and government-paid monthly benefits would at least equal the benefits promised under the current system.

Any Social Security cash flow deficits that remain would be financed through general revenue transfers equal to a 1 percent reduction in the growth rate of all government spending for eight years, the corporate income taxes deemed to result from the investment of personal account contributions, and issuing about $1.4 trillion in "off-budget" bonds. Under the Ferrara plan, these bonds would be considered a replacement for the existing system's unfunded liability and thus would not increase the federal debt.

The Orszag-Diamond Plan

Peter Orszag, Senior Fellow at the Brookings Institution,* and Peter Diamond, Institute Professor of Economics at the Massachusetts Institute of Technology, have developed a plan that does not include any form of PRA

*Peter Orszag was President Obama's Budget Director at the Office of Management and Budget until July 2010. He now is at the Council on Foreign Relations [Editors].

or government investment of Social Security trust fund money in private markets. Instead, it gradually changes the benefit formula to reduce benefits for moderate-income and upper-income workers and requires that all state and local government workers come under Social Security. It would also gradually reduce benefits by raising the age at which workers could receive full benefits. Workers could still retire earlier, but at lower benefits. Benefits would increase for lower-income workers, widows, and the disabled.

In addition, the plan would gradually increase the payroll tax for all workers from the current 12.4 percent of income to 15.36 percent of income in 2078. It would also raise the earnings threshold on Social Security taxes—thus requiring higher-income workers to pay additional payroll taxes—and impose a new 3 percent tax on income above the earnings threshold. Workers would not receive any credit toward benefits for income covered by this new tax.

*   *   *

1. Personal Retirement Accounts

What Is This, and Why Is It Important?

Allowing workers to invest a portion of their Social Security taxes is the only alternative to raising Social Security taxes or reducing Social Security benefits. However, personal retirement accounts are not all equal. The money that goes into the PRAs could come from diverting a portion of existing Social Security taxes or from some other source.

Similarly, the size of the accounts (usually expressed as a percentage of the worker's pay) is important. While larger accounts would temporarily increase the amount of additional funds required to pay benefits to retirees, they would also accumulate a pool of money faster than smaller accounts and finance a greater portion of benefits in future years. This can reduce the amount of additional tax dollars needed in future decades.

Finally, how the PRAs are invested is important. Even though they show steady growth over time stocks and commercial bonds are generally more volatile than government bonds. Investing a portion of the PRAs in government bonds makes the accounts slightly less volatile while providing some of the additional dollars needed to pay benefits to current retirees.

2. Retirement and Survivors Benefits

What Is This, and Why Is It Important?

Other than creating personal retirement accounts that allow workers to self-fund all or a portion of their Social Security retirement benefits, most reform plans deal with the program's coming deficits by either changing the level of retirement benefits promised or finding ways to increase program revenues. This section examines how various reform plans treat promised retirement benefits.

Social Security uses a complex formula to calculate an individual worker's retirement benefits. Subtle changes in this formula can cause a large change in benefits over time. For instance, changing how past income is indexed to a constant purchasing power will have only a minor impact for the first several years. However, the effect is cumulative and after several decades will result in major changes in benefits.

Similarly, seemingly minor changes in "bend points" or other aspects of the benefit formula can, over the long term, cause major changes in benefits for upper-income and/or moderate-income workers. It is even possible to use the benefit formula to approximate an increase in the full retirement age without actually raising it. Thus, a plan could still allow workers to quality for "full retirement benefits" at 65, 66, or 67 but award them full retirement benefits (as defined under the current system) only if they wait to retire until a later age.

The first question that any plan must answer is whether it would pay the full level of benefits promised under the current system. If so, it must deal with how to pay the cost, since the current system cannot afford to pay for all of the promised benefits. Other important questions include whether the plan proposes benefit changes (usually reductions) if workers do not choose to have a personal retirement account, protects lower-income workers (who more often have an interrupted work history) by instituting some sort of minimum benefit level, and/or addresses the low benefits for certain lower-income, widowed, and disabled workers under the current system.

3. Payroll Taxes

What Is This, and Why Is It Important?

Increasing Social Security payroll taxes would be one way to pay projected cash flow deficits. This method is closer to the self-funding that has characterized the system so far, but raising payroll taxes has significant drawbacks. Alternatives to payroll tax increases include instituting some form of personal retirement account to increase the return on taxes, reducing benefits, and using significant amounts of general revenue money to cover Social Security's cash flow deficits.

Currently, all workers pay 5.3 percent of their income to pay for Social Security retirement and survivors benefits. In 2004, this tax will be paid on the first $87,700 of an employee's income.* Employers match this tax for a total of 10.6 percent of each worker's income. In addition, both employer and employee pay an additional 0.9 percent of the worker's income (1.8

---

*This threshold is indexed and changes every year. It was $110,800 in 2010 [Editors].

percent total) for Social Security disability benefits. Thus, the employer and employee pay a total Social Security payroll tax of 12.4 percent.

Additional payroll taxes could be collected in three ways:

- The overall tax rate could be increased. However, this imposes higher taxes on all income groups and could reduce employment in the economy by making it more expensive to hire additional workers.
- The tax could be imposed on income levels above the threshold, currently at $87,700. In the short run, this would increase revenues, but since retirement benefits are paid on all income taxed for Social Security, it would also eventually increase the amount of benefits the system would have to pay each year and offset the amount raised through the higher taxes.
- Payroll taxes could be disconnected from the benefit formula. This could take the form of a new tax paid on income above the current $87,700 earnings threshold, collecting taxes on income up to the $87,700 level but counting only income up to $60,000 or some other level toward benefits, or some combination of the two. In either case, this type of tax would break the link between taxes and income that has existed since Social Security began in 1935. To date, neither the right nor the left has been willing to break this link for fear that it would be the first step toward turning Social Security into a welfare system. Both sides have worried that such a move—or even the perception of such a move—would undermine the program's widespread support among the American people.

4. Social Security's Unfunded Liability

What Is This, and Why Is It Important?

Both the current Social Security system and every plan to reform it will require significant amounts of general revenue money in addition to the amount collected through payroll taxes. This additional money is necessary to reduce the difference between what Social Security currently owes and what it will be able to pay.

In the reform plans, the transition cost represents a major reduction from the unfunded liability of the current program. Even though the reform plans are expensive, all of them would require less additional money than the current system. However, both the amount and the timing of this additional money would vary depending on the plan.

The amount of additional money that is needed can be measured according to two different systems. Both measurements give valuable information.

Present value reflects the idea that a dollar today has more value to a person than that same dollar has sometime in the future. It gives an idea of when the additional money is needed by giving greater weight to money needed in the near future than to an equal amount needed further in the future. In addition to showing the amount of money needed, a higher present value number indicates that money is needed sooner rather than later. [The present value of the unfunded liability ranges from $929 billion in the Orszag-Diamond plan to $7.6 trillion in the Ferrara plan.]

The *sum of the deficits* indicates the total amount of additional money that will be needed. This measure gives $100 needed today the same weight as $100 needed in 15 years. This measure adds up only the future cash flow deficits; it does not include cash flow surpluses because the government does not have any way to save or invest that money for future use. Using both of these measurements gives a better picture of the situation than using just one. [The sum of the deficits of the unfunded liability ranges from $7.1 trillion in the Graham plan to $16.4 trillion in the Ferrara plan.]

Paying for the current system or any of the reform plans will require Congress to balance Social Security's needs against those of the rest of the economy. In general, as more additional dollars are needed for the current system or a reform plan, less money will be available for other government programs and the private sector.

As this burden on the general federal budget increases and persists, Congress would find it increasingly more difficult to come up with that money, and it would become increasingly less likely that such a plan would really be paid for on schedule. This is especially true for the current system, which will incur the massive deficits to pay all of the promised benefits.

*   *   *

5. Paying for Social Security's Unfunded Liability

What Is This, and Why Is It Important?

Both the current Social Security program and all of the proposed reform plans will require large amounts of general revenue money to cover the annual cash flow deficits. Exactly when that money is first needed, how many years it will be needed, and the total amount that will be needed varies from plan to plan. Avoiding use of general revenue money would require either reducing Social Security benefits enough to eliminate the annual deficits or imposing new taxes to generate sufficient revenue. Neither the current system nor any of the proposed reform plans comes close to closing the gap.

Some plans do specify sources for the needed general revenues, but these are handicapped by the fact that no Congress can bind the hands of a future Congress. Thus, even if Congress did pass a plan that specified the source of the needed general revenues, a future Congress could change the plan by a majority vote. The only way to avoid this uncertainty would be for Congress to pass and the states to ratify the plan as a constitutional amendment—which would be prohibitively difficult.

In short, both the current system and all known reform plans would have to find the necessary general revenues from some combination of four sources: borrowing additional money collecting more taxes than needed to fund the rest of the government, reducing other government spending, or reducing Social Security benefits more than is called for under either current law or any of the reform plans.

The most important thing to remember is that the existing Social Security system and the reform plans all face this problem. This is not a weakness that is limited to PRA plans or any other reform plan. The only question is when the cash flow deficits begin and how large they will be.

Current Law

Current law makes no provision for funding Social Security's unfunded liability. The program has no credit line with the U.S. Treasury, and when its trust fund promises are exhausted, current law will require it to reduce benefits.

The DeMint Plan

While some press releases connected with Representative DeMint's plan suggest that some of its general revenue needs could be generated by reducing the growth of federal spending, no language specifying where the general revenues would come from is included in his legislation.

The Graham Plan

Senator Graham's plan includes a commission that would recommend reductions in corporate welfare and redirect the savings to reduce his plan's unfunded liability. At best, a reduction in corporate welfare would generate only part of the needed general revenue. The commission would produce a legislative proposal that would then be considered by Congress.

Because the commission would be created by the same legislation that implements Graham's Social Security reforms, its recommendations could not even be considered until after the plan is enacted. As a result, passage of the Graham plan does not guarantee that these revenues would be available. Regardless of what the commission recommended, a future Congress could reject the proposed cuts in corporate welfare. In that case, Congress would have to come up with another method to raise the needed revenue.

The Smith Plan

Other than the proposed benefit changes that would partially reduce Social Security's unfunded liability, the Smith plan does not specify how it would pay cash flow deficits.

The Ferrara Plan

The Ferrara plan includes three mechanisms designed to create the needed general revenues.

First, it would mandate a 1 percent reduction in the growth of all federal spending (including entitlements such as Social Security) for at least eight years and redirect that revenue to Social Security. Since Congress cannot legally force a subsequent Congress to follow a set course of action, the only enforcement mechanism available is a constitutional amendment. As a result, the Ferrara plan simply appropriates to Social Security the amount of revenue that would result if Congress were to reduce spending growth. In practice, a future Congress could choose not to reduce spending growth and, instead, just let the deficit grow larger or generate the necessary revenue in some other way.

Second, the Ferrara plan would transfer to Social Security the amount of corporate income taxes that could potentially result from the investment of personal accounts in corporate stocks and bonds. This is not a new or higher tax. This transfer is intended to reflect the taxes that would be paid at the current 35 percent corporate tax rate. Since SSA does not conduct dynamic scoring, this transfer is based on the static assumption that two-thirds of the stocks and bonds held through personal accounts reflect domestic corporate investment.

Third, the Ferrara plan would borrow about $1.4 trillion in special off-budget bonds. However, there is no practical way to create off-budget bonds that would not count against the federal debt. Even if there were, such a move would reduce the amount of transparency in the federal budget.

The Orszag-Diamond Plan

While the Orszag-Diamond plan includes both some benefit reductions and benefit increases for widows, the disabled, and low-income workers, the two elements of the plan are roughly equal. It reduces Social Security's unfunded liability using tax increases contained in the plan, including an increase in the payroll tax rate, a gradual increase in the amount of income subject to Social Security taxes, and a new 3 percent tax on any salary income not subject to Social Security taxes.

6. Making Social Security a Better Deal for Workers

What Is This, and Why Is It Important?

In the long run, a reform plan should do more than just preserve the current Social Security system with its many flaws. While a key requirement of any reform plan is to provide a stable, guaranteed, and adequate level of benefits at an affordable cost, it should do more.

The current system fails to allow workers to build any form of nest egg for the future. Instead, it is the highest single tax for about 80 percent of workers. In return, each worker receives a life annuity that ends with the death(s) of the worker, the surviving spouse (if there is one), or young children (if any). In today's world, where two-earner families are increasingly the norm, the current system even limits survivor benefits to the higher of either the deceased spouses benefits or the surviving spouse's benefits. Whichever account is lower, no matter how long that spouse worked, is marked paid in full and extinguished.

At a minimum, a reform plan should allow workers to pass on some of what they earned and paid in Social Security taxes to improve their spouse's retirement benefits. It should also allow workers the flexibility to use their entire account for retirement benefits or take a smaller retirement benefit and use the balance to pay for a grandchild's college education, start a small business, or pass on money to a later generation.

In judging whether each proposed reform would be better for America's workers, readers may differ sharply. However, while most summaries and studies examine Social Security reform from the viewpoint of federal budget impact, tax rates, and the survivability of the system, few consider the overall impact of reform on the workers it was designed to benefit in the first place. Social Security should not be reformed or "saved" for its own sake, but only if it more effectively provides the benefits workers need at a price they can afford.

DISCUSSION QUESTIONS

1. The only plan that does not include partial privatization is the Orszag-Diamond plan. This could be called the "tough medicine" plan because the solvency of Social Security is accomplished through benefit reductions and tax increases. It is the only one of the plans that is funded through cuts and tax increases. Is the tough medicine worth it? Or do you agree with John that PRAs must be part of the overall reform?

2. One alternative to partial privatization that is not mentioned here is to have the federal government invest the Social Security surplus in the stock market or corporate bonds (as every state retirement system in the country does). This would, in theory, provide a high investment return, but critics claim it would also give the government too

much leverage (as a large shareholder) over the activities of private corporations. Would this be a legitimate role for the government to play in the economy? Can you think of other ways in which the existing system could be reformed, other than turning portions of the fund over to individuals?

3. Are the broad objectives initially established for Social Security—income security for old age, income redistribution, and risk-sharing across the population and across generations—still appropriate today? Are individuals more able to plan for and manage their retirement income today than in the 1930s or even the 1980s? Why or why not? What do you see as the major advantages and disadvantages of the current Social Security system and the plan for partial privatization?

72

"American Business, Public Policy, Case Studies, and Political Theory"

Theodore J. Lowi

Before Lowi's article appeared in 1964, many social scientists analyzed public policy through case studies that focused on one particular policy and its implementation. Lowi argued that what the social sciences lacked was a means to cumulate, compare, and contrast the diverse findings of these studies. We needed, in other words, a typology of policy making. In the article below, Lowi argues that different types of public policies produce different patterns of participation. Public policies can be classified as distributive, regulatory, or redistributive, each with its own distinctive "arena of power." For example, public policies that provide benefits to a single congressional district, group, or company can be classified as distributive. In the distributive arena of power, policy beneficiaries are active in seeking to expand or extend their benefits, but there is no real opposition. Rather, legislators build coalitions premised upon "mutual non-interference" interests, and their representatives seek particular benefits, such as a research and development contract, a new highway, or a farm subsidy, but they do not oppose the similar requests of others. The regulatory and redistributive policy arenas also display distinctive dynamics and roles that participants in the process play. Lowi's work was important not only for providing a classification scheme by which social scientists could think more systematically about different public policies, but for proposing that we study "politics" as a consequence of different types of public policy. Traditionally, social scientists have studied politics to see what kinds of policies are produced.

What is needed is a basis for cumulating, comparing, and contrasting diverse findings. Such a framework or interpretative scheme would bring the diverse cases and findings into a more consistent relation to each other and would begin to suggest generalizations sufficiently close to the data to be relevant and sufficiently abstract to be subject to more broadly theoretical treatment.

* * *

The scheme is based upon the following argument: (1) The types of relationships to be found among people are determined by their expectations—by what they hope to achieve or get from relating to others. (2) In politics, expectations are determined by governmental outputs or policies. (3) Therefore, a political relationship is determined by the type of policy at stake, so that for every type of policy there is likely to be a distinctive type of political relationship. If power is defined as a share in the making of policy, or authoritative allocations, then the political relationship in question is a power relationship or, over time, a power structure.

*   *   *

There are three major categories of public policies in the scheme: distribution, regulation, and redistribution. These types are historically as well as functionally distinct, distribution being almost the exclusive type of national domestic policy from 1789 until virtually 1890. Agitation for regulatory and redistributive policies began at about the same time, but regulation had become an established fact before any headway at all was made in redistribution.

These categories are not mere contrivances for purposes of simplification. They are meant to correspond to real phenomena—so much so that the major hypotheses of the scheme follow directly from the categories and their definitions. Thus, *these areas of policy or government activity constitute real arenas of power.* Each arena tends to develop its own characteristic political structure, political process, elites, and group relations. What remains is to identify these arenas, to formulate hypotheses about the attributes of each, and to test the scheme by how many empirical relationships it can anticipate and explain.

Areas of Policy Defined

(1) In the long run, all governmental policies may be considered redistributive, because in the long run some people pay in taxes more than they receive in services. Or, all may be thought regulatory because, in the long run, a governmental decision on the use of resources can only displace a private decision about the same resource or at least reduce private alternatives about the resource. But politics works in the short run, and in the short run certain kinds of government decisions can be made without regard to limited resources. Policies of this kind are called "distributive," a term first coined for nineteenth-century land policies, but easily extended to include most contemporary public land and resource policies; rivers and harbors ("pork barrel") programs; defense procurement and R & D [research and development]; labor, business, and agricultural "clientele" services; and the traditional tariff. Distributive policies are characterized by the ease with which they can be disaggregated and dispensed unit by small unit, each unit more or less in isolation from other units and from any general rule. "Patronage" in the fullest meaning of the word can be taken as a synonym for "distributive." These are policies that are virtually not policies at all but are highly individualized decisions that only by accumulation can be called a policy. They are policies in which

the indulged and the deprived, the loser and the recipient, need never come into direct confrontation. Indeed, in many instances of distributive policy, the deprived cannot as a class be identified, because the most influential among them can be accommodated by further disaggregation of the stakes.

(2) Regulatory policies are also specific and individual in their impact, but they are not capable of the almost infinite amount of disaggregation typical of distributive policies. Although the laws are stated in general terms ("Arrange the transportation system artistically." "Thou shalt not show favoritism in pricing."), the impact of regulatory decisions is clearly one of directly raising costs and/or reducing or expanding the alternatives of private individuals ("Get off the grass!" "Produce kosher if you advertise kosher!"). Regulatory policies are distinguishable from distributive in that in the short run the regulatory decision involves a direct choice as to who will be indulged and who deprived. Not all applicants for a single television channel or an overseas air route can be propitiated. Enforcement of an unfair labor practice on the part of management weakens management in its dealings with labor. So, while implementation is firm-by-firm and case-by-case, policies cannot be disaggregated to the level of the individual or the single firm (as in distribution), because individual decisions must be made by application of a general rule and therefore become interrelated within the broader standards of law. Decisions cumulate among all individuals affected by the law in roughly the same way. Since the most stable lines of perceived common impact are the basic sectors of the economy, regulatory decisions are cumulative largely along sectoral lines; regulatory policies are usually disaggregable only down to the sector level.

(3) Redistributive policies are like regulatory policies in the sense that relations among broad categories of private individuals are involved and, hence, individual decisions must be interrelated. But on all other counts there are great differences in the nature of impact. The categories of impact are much broader, approaching social classes. They are, crudely speaking, haves and have-nots, bigness and smallness, bourgeoisie and proletariat. The aim involved is not use of property but property itself, not equal treatment but equal possession, not behavior but being. The fact that our income tax is in reality only mildly redistributive does not alter the fact of the aims and the stakes involved in income tax policies. The same goes for our various "welfare state" programs, which are redistributive only for those who entered retirement or unemployment rolls without having contributed at all. The nature of a redistributive issue is not determined by the outcome of a battle over how redistributive a policy is going to be. Expectations about what it *can* be, what it threatens to be, are determinative.

Arenas of Power

Once one posits the general tendency of these areas of policy or governmental activity to develop characteristic political structures, a number of hypotheses become compelling. And when the various hypotheses are accumulated, the general contours of each of the three arenas begin quickly to resemble, respectively, the three "general" theories of political process identified earlier. The arena that develops around distributive policies is best characterized in the terms of [E. E.] Schattschneider's findings. The regulatory arena corresponds to the pluralist school, and the school's general notions are found to be limited pretty much to this one arena. The redistributive arena most closely approximates, with some adaptation, an elitist view of the political process.

(1) The distributive arena can be identified in considerable detail from Schattschneider's case study alone. What he and his pluralist successors did not see was that the traditional structure of tariff politics is also in largest part the structure of politics of all those diverse policies identified earlier as distributive. The arena is "pluralistic" only in the sense that a large number of small, intensely organized interests are operating. In fact, there is even greater multiplicity of participants here than the pressure-group model can account for, because essentially it is a politics of every man for himself. The single person and the single firm are the major activists.

* * *

When a billion-dollar issue can be disaggregated into many millions of nickel-dime items and each item can be dealt with without regard to the others, multiplication of interests and of access is inevitable, and so is reduction of conflict. All of this has the greatest of bearing on the relations among participants and, therefore, the "power structure." Indeed, coalitions must be built to pass legislation and "make policy," but what of the nature and basis of the coalitions? In the distributive arena, political relationships approximate what Schattschneider called "mutual non-interference"—"a mutuality under which it is proper for each to seek duties [indulgences] for himself but improper and unfair to oppose duties [indulgences] sought by others." In the area of rivers and harbors, references are made to "pork barrel" and "log-rolling," but these colloquialisms have not been taken sufficiently seriously. A log-rolling coalition is not one forged of conflict, compromise, and tangential interest but, on the contrary, one composed of members who have absolutely nothing in common; and this is possible because the "pork barrel" is a container for unrelated items. This is the typical form of relationship in the distributive arena.

The structure of these log-rolling relationships leads typically, though not always, to Congress; and the structure is relatively stable because all who have access of any sort usually support whoever are the leaders. And there tend to be "elites" of a peculiar sort in the Congressional committees whose jurisdictions include the subject matter in question. Until recently, for instance, on tariff matters the House Ways and Means Committee was virtually the government. Much the same can be said for Public Works on rivers and harbors. It is a broker leadership, but "policy" is best understood as cooptation rather than conflict and compromise.

*   *   *

(2) The regulatory arena could hardly be better identified than in the thousands of pages written for the whole polity by the pluralists. But, unfortunately, some translation is necessary to accommodate pluralism to its more limited universe. The regulatory arena appears to be composed of a multiplicity of groups organized around tangential relations. . . . Within this narrower context of regulatory decisions, one can even go so far as to accept the most extreme pluralist statement that policy tends to be a residue of the interplay of group conflict. This statement can be severely criticized only by use of examples drawn from non-regulatory decisions.

As I argued before, there is no way for regulatory policies to be disaggregated into very large numbers of unrelated items. Because individual regulatory decisions involve direct confrontations of indulged and deprived, the typical political coalition is born of conflict and compromise among tangential interests that usually involve a total sector of the economy. Thus, while the typical basis for coalition in distributive politics is uncommon interests (log-rolling), an entirely different basis is typical in regulatory politics. The pluralist went wrong only in assuming the regulatory type of coalition is *the* coalition.

*   *   *

What this suggests is that the typical power structure in regulatory politics is far less stable than that in the distributive arena. Since coalitions form around shared interests, the coalitions will shift as the interests change or as conflicts of interest emerge. With such group-based and shifting patterns of conflict built into every regulatory issue, it is in most cases impossible for a Congressional committee, an administrative agency, a peak association governing board, or a social elite to contain all the participants long enough to establish a stable power elite. Policy outcomes seem inevitably to be the residue remaining after all the reductions of demands by all participants have been made in order to extend support to majority size. But a majority-sized coalition of shared interests on one issue could not possibly be entirely appropriate for some other issue. In regulatory decision-making, relationships among group leadership elements and between them on any one or more points of governmental access are too unstable to form a single policy-making elite. As a consequence, decision-making tends to pass from administrative agencies and Congressional committees to Congress, the place where uncertainties in the policy process have always been settled. Congress as an institution is the last resort for breakdowns in bargaining over policy, just as in the case of parties the primary is a last resort for breakdowns in bargaining over nominations. No one leadership group can contain the conflict by an almost infinite subdivision and distribution of the stakes. In the regulatory political process, Congress and the "balance of power" seem to play the classic role attributed to them by the pluralists.

* * *

(3) Issues that involve redistribution cut closer than any others along class lines and activate interests in what are roughly class terms. If there is ever any cohesion within the peak associations, it occurs on redistributive issues, and their rhetoric suggests that they occupy themselves most of the time with these. In a ten-year period just before and after, but not including, the war years [World War II], the Manufacturers' Association of Connecticut, for example, expressed itself overwhelmingly more often on redistributive than on any other types of issues.

* * *

Where the peak associations, led by elements of Mr. Mills's power elite,* have reality, their resources and access are bound to affect power relations. Owing to their stability and the impasse (or equilibrium) in relations among broad classes of the entire society, the political structure of the redistributive arena seems to be highly stabilized, virtually institutionalized. Its stability, unlike that of the distributive arena, derives from shared interests. But in contrast to the regulatory arena, these shared interests are sufficiently stable and clear and consistent to provide the foundation for ideologies.

* * *

. . . Finally, just as the nature of redistributive policies influences politics towards the centralization and stabilization of conflict, so does it further influence the removal of decision-making from Congress. A decentralized and bargaining Congress can cumulate but it cannot balance, and redistributive policies require complex balancing on a very large scale. What [William] Riker has said of budget-making applies here: ". . . legislative governments cannot endure a budget. Its finances must be totted up by party leaders in the legislature itself. In a complex fiscal system, however, haphazard legislative judgments cannot bring revenue into even rough alignment with supply. So budgeting is introduced—which transfers financial control to the budget maker. . . ." Congress can provide exceptions to principles and it can implement those principles with elaborate standards of implementation as a condition for the concessions that money-providers will make. But the makers of principles of redistribution seem to be the holders of the "command posts."

---

*According to C. Wright Mills, a small network of individuals, which he called the "power elite," controls the economy, the political system, and the military [*Editors*].

None of this suggests a power elite such as Mills would have had us believe existed, but it does suggest a type of stable and continual conflict that can only be understood in class terms. The foundation upon which the social-stratification and power-elite school rested, especially when dealing with national power, was so conceptually weak and empirically unsupported that its critics were led to err in the opposite direction by denying the direct relevance of social and institutional positions and the probability of stable decision-making elites. But the relevance of that approach becomes stronger as the scope of its application is reduced and as the standards for identifying the scope are clarified. But this is equally true of the pluralist school and of those approaches based on a "politics of this-or-that policy."

*   *   *

DISCUSSION QUESTIONS

1. Provide examples of each type of policy that Lowi discusses (distributive, regulatory, and redistributive).

2. If you were a member of Congress, which type of policy would you try to emphasize if your main interest was in getting re-elected?

3. Are there any types of policies that do not seem to fit Lowi's framework? Do some policies fit more than one category?

Debating the Issues: Health Care Reform

Figuring out how to provide health care services is one of the hardest issues that confronts democracies. Most industrialized countries have created "single payer" systems, in which health care is provided (either entirely or largely) by government agencies, with universal coverage and paid for through taxes. The systems in Canada and Great Britain are examples. These systems provide universal access, though critics argue that they inevitably ration care, have long wait times, and limit access to advanced treatments. Relying largely on private coverage is an attractive option for people who can afford insurance, but can result in millions of people without access to services.

One thing is certain, though: health care is expensive, and increasing costs pose significant problems for individuals and governments. In the United States, we spend about one-sixth of GDP on health care services, close to $3 trillion in 2011. Per capita, we spend about twice what other industrialized countries spend. Yet about 50 million Americans lacked health insurance, and we do worse on key measures of public health, such as life expectancy and infant mortality, than many other countries.

The passage of the Affordable Care Act (ACA, or "Obamacare" to its critics) did not end the controversy over what to do about health care in the United States, and the reaction since its 2010 passage has been a continuation of longstanding disputes over affordability, access, and the reach of government. The key feature of the new law is a mandate that everyone purchase health insurance; those who do not will have to pay a fine. Other elements include an expansion of Medicaid and new rules that prohibit insurance companies from denying coverage or charging higher premiums based on pre-existing conditions.

Supporters of the law say it achieves the goal of providing universal access to health care, will help slow the growth of health care costs, and will ease the problem of paying for the costs of providing services to the uninsured. Some are unhappy that the law did not create a "single payer" system; in this view, leaving insurance companies intact—even giving them millions of new customers through the mandate—perpetuates the problem of profit-driven business providing services.

Critics see it very differently: they insist that "insurance" is not the same as "access," and believe that the law will result in higher costs, longer wait times, and less innovation. Many object strongly to the mandate, arguing that it expands government power by forcing people to purchase a product (health insurance) that they may not want or need. In 2012, the Supreme Court ruled in *National Federation of Independent Business v. Sebelius* that the mandate was a constitutional exercise of Congress's taxation power, ending the main effort to overturn the law. In Congress, Republicans introduced bills to repeal the law altogether (none passed).

The readings here provide different perspectives on the ACA. Serafini offers the views of health care experts, most of whom think that the law will provide nearly universal coverage, though they are less confident about the law's effect on costs and quality. Levin sees the law as a complete disaster that will increase costs, reduce access, and distort the entire health care system. He argues that we need to restore a degree of market discipline—where individuals have a direct incentive to make efficient decisions about their own care—and insists that there is no way to improve the ACA. The only option is outright repeal.

Condon addresses the concern that a major piece of social legislation was adopted on a pure party line vote. Unlike earlier laws—Social Security, Medicare, Civil Rights, Voting Rights—the ACA was passed without a single Republican voting for the bill on final passage (one House Republican voted for an earlier version of the bill). There are risks, he concludes, to this kind of process, although he believes that the burden is on Republicans to offer an option instead of repeal.

73

"Grading Health Reform: Experts Assess Whether the Bill Delivers on Its Promises"

Marilyn Werber Serafini

The primary objectives of health care reform were clear long before Congress took up the issue last year: slow the growth of health care spending, insure more people, improve the quality of care—and do it all without busting the federal budget. *National Journal* this week asked twenty health care experts across the political spectrum how the bill that President Obama signed into law on Tuesday measures up against those yardsticks.

The experts generally agreed that the new law comes close to achieving the objective of providing insurance to all Americans and does a fairly good job of making coverage affordable and available to consumers. But the experts also said that the law falls short of promises to lower skyrocketing health care spending, and they concluded that it doesn't do enough to improve the quality of health care.

* * *

Our judges gave each candidate's plan a series of numerical grades, from 1 to 10, depending on how close they thought it would come to achieving a given goal, such as covering the uninsured. A score of 10 indicated that the plan would come extremely close to reaching the goal, while a score of 1 meant that it would not come at all close.

National Journal tried to craft the survey questions to elicit objective assessments rather than partisan or ideological views. Regarding the uninsured, for example, we asked the judges how close each proposal would come to providing health insurance for all Americans. *NJ* did not want answers that reflected the judges' political leanings or personal views about whether a given plan was the best—or even a good—approach.

*   *   *

A Big Step Toward Universal Coverage

The Congressional Budget Office estimates that the health care reform law will provide coverage to 31 million of the 47 million Americans currently uninsured. Many of the people who won't be covered are illegal immigrants who are ineligible for federal assistance in obtaining insurance.

None of the twenty experts gave the law a perfect score of 10 for providing coverage, although all but two gave it high marks. Indeed, in this category, President Obama received the same grade that he did as a candidate.

During the campaign Obama recommended a narrower mandate requiring only that parents purchase insurance for their children; in contrast, the new law requires many adults to also get coverage. Most people without health insurance will have to pay one of two penalties, whichever is greater: either a fixed fine, starting at $95 in 2014, rising to $325 in 2015, and to $695 in 2016; or a percentage of taxable income, starting at 1.0 percent in 2014 and rising to 2.5 percent in 2016.

People with annual incomes below 100 percent of the federal poverty line ($10,830 for an individual and $22,050 for a family of four) are exempt from the penalties.

The law will significantly expand Medicaid, the federal-state health care program for the poor, to as many as 13 million additional beneficiaries. Beginning in 2014, Medicaid eligibility will extend to people with annual earnings lower than 133 percent of the federal poverty line ($14,440 for an individual).

Some judges took 1 or 2 points off their scores in this category because they advocated tougher penalties for failure to purchase insurance. Paul Ginsburg, president of the Center for Studying Health System Change, said, "I expect that the mandate will be refined in response to experience."

Ed Howard, executive vice president of the Alliance for Health Reform, called the law "a good start," and Jeffrey Levi, executive director of the Trust for America's Health, agreed. "Clearly, a significant group of people will be left out of this reform," he said. "But the addition of over 30 million Americans to the insurance roll is a monumental step of major proportions. But those who are left out will continue to need a safety net—hence the importance of the provisions expanding funding for community health centers and public health."

Gail Wilensky, a senior fellow at Project Hope who was Medicare administrator during the presidency of George H. W. Bush, noted that according to CBO estimates, "the percentage of people without insurance would drop from the current 15 percent to 5 percent, which is two-thirds of the way to universal coverage."

Elizabeth McGlynn, associate director of the health program at Rand, said that based on her think tank's microsimulation modeling, the percentage of uninsured would be reduced by 53 to 57 percent. She called that "a substantial improvement," although she added that it "would not achieve universal coverage." McGlynn concluded, "A large portion of the uninsured would be eligible for, but not enrolled in, Medicaid."

The Lewin Group actuary, John Sheils, said that his firm's model indicates that the law covers 60 percent of the uninsured population but only 43 percent of care that is currently uncompensated. "Very-low-income people exempt from the mandate account for much of this," he said.

According to Joe Antos, an American Enterprise Institute scholar, the goal shouldn't be reducing the number of uninsured but increasing the number of people who have access to appropriate care. "There is nothing in the bill that assures this," he said. Over time, Heritage Foundation Vice President Stuart Butler cautioned, although almost all citizens and legal residents will get coverage, "it may not be of the type, cost, and quality that they would like."

Some conservative opponents argue that an insurance mandate is unconstitutional and sets a worrisome precedent for government power. More than a dozen states have already filed lawsuits challenging the constitutionality of the requirement.

Many health reform advocates are also concerned, but for different reasons. They worry that some people will ignore the mandate—especially those who are young and healthy and see little need for health insurance. America's Health Insurance Plans, which represents insurers, shares this apprehension. Insurers agreed early on to stop denying policies to people with pre-existing conditions and in poor health in exchange for universal coverage.

Minor Impact on Quality of Care

Many of National Journal's health care experts are disappointed that the new law won't do more to improve the quality of health care. "The main focus of the legislation is on coverage expansion, not on improving quality or consumer decision-making," said Elizabeth McGlynn, associate director of the health program at Rand. "The bill contains provisions that would increase the information available to consumers; however, there are no direct incentives for consumers to use that information or to change the decisions they would have otherwise made."

The key, said Paul Ginsburg, president of the Center for Studying Health System Change, is implementing research into medical effectiveness. The new law funds research on so-called comparative effectiveness to evaluate the success of various medical treatments.

But American Enterprise Institute scholar Joe Antos worries that even the most-sophisticated [sic] consumers will have trouble interpreting and applying comparative-effectiveness results. "Sensible consumers will continue to rely on the advice of their doctors, which depends on the community standard of practice, the patient's specific circumstances, how services are paid for, and other factors. Patients are increasingly also seeking information on the Internet, which can lead some to demand inappropriate treatments."

Jeffrey Levi, executive director of Trust for America's Health, shares Antos's concern. "It's one thing to do the comparative-effectiveness research and quality assessment; it's another for consumers to take that information to heart and apply it to their own situations."

Quality may also differ for those getting insurance through an exchange and those in employer-sponsored plans, said Heritage Foundation Vice President Stuart Butler. Those in exchanges will have "a lot more choice and information," he said, predicting that employers will react to extra fees by restricting coverage and shifting costs.

Few experts were optimistic that doctors, hospitals, and other medical providers will gain the tools to improve care using best practices. "The bill promotes comparative-effectiveness research but does nothing to increase adherence to guidelines," said Lewin Group actuary John Sheils. "Adherence is the problem. There is overwhelming evidence in the literature showing that doctors do not follow guidelines."

Former Senate Majority Leader Tom Daschle noted that changes resulting from the research will not come "for some time." And even when the results of comparative-effectiveness research are more readily available, "probably past the 10-year mark," according to Antos, "their appropriate application depends critically on the specific patient's circumstances. Judgment will remain the driving factor, unless future Congresses attempt to impose uniform standards on medical practice."

Grace-Marie Turner, president of the Galen Institute, worries that comparative-effectiveness studies "are historically out of date long before the studies are finalized." What may have a greater effect on quality of care is the funding that President Obama included in last year's economic stimulus law to encourage doctors to adopt electronic medical records. "Considerable work must be done to help physicians who are in solo and small group practice use emerging tools," she said.

Although former Medicare Administrator Gail Wilensky called the law's direction positive, she stressed that much depends on what happens with pilot and demonstration projects that the law establishes for Medicare. The law authorizes pilot projects to test so-called accountable care organizations and the bundling of payments to medical providers. The idea is to get medical providers to better coordinate patient care. The government and private insurers, in turn, could then more effectively base payments on performance.

The experts were somewhat skeptical that the reforms will encourage medical providers to compete for patients based on quality and price. Conservatives were especially critical, but liberals didn't give high scores either.

Competition will change, Butler said, but not to meet that goal. "In Medicaid, Medicare, and in the more regulated private system, the incentive will increase to compete by cutting costs and avoiding certain patients to achieve a reasonable return amid tighter fee schedules," he said.

Bill Gets Low Score For Cost Control

Bringing health care spending in line with the economy's growth rate has been a priority since Washington began talking about health reform decades ago. During the 2008 presidential campaign, judges gave Barack Obama's proposal a score of only 3 for controlling costs.

In rating the newly passed reforms, the scores were nearly as low. Former Medicare Administrator Gail Wilensky noted that the law will institute some "promising" pilot projects for coordinating medical care in Medicare and for testing ways to pay doctors and hospitals. Still, Heritage Foundation Vice President Stuart Butler said that the law will increase, not decrease, the growth rate of total health spending.

"While the bill contains provisions that may ultimately lead to reductions," Elizabeth McGlynn, Rand health program associate director said, her think tank's projections indicate that, "with the exception of payment reform options, most would have a relatively small effect on the growth rate in health spending."

The actuary for the Centers for Medicare and Medicaid Services "reports that health spending will continue to grow faster than the economy, even assuming that future Congresses cut Medicare spending as prescribed in the bill," American Enterprise Institute scholar Joe Antos contended, adding, "This objective is probably impossible to meet even over the long term given the aging populace."

Brookings Institution senior fellow Henry Aaron is more optimistic about the long-term forecast; and Ed Howard, executive vice president of the Alliance for Health Reform, said that "most of what is possible is at least put in place, but will take time to have impact."

Many health care economists had high hopes for a so-called Cadillac tax to discourage employers from offering overly generous benefits. With less coverage, the theory goes, people will have to pay more out of their own pockets and thus become thriftier about purchasing medical services. But the final law watered down the tax and delayed its implementation. The tax on high-end insurance plans will apply to health plan premiums greater than $10,200 for individual coverage and $27,500 for families; it won't kick in until 2018.

Scores were somewhat higher, although mixed, when *National Journal* asked whether the federal government will get its money's worth from the law. "In terms of government spending per net newly insured individual, the expected value of the services obtained should exceed the cost to the federal government," McGlynn responded.

Butler, however, argued that the law is based on a "very high taxpayer cost for coverage expansions that could have been achieved at much lower cost." In scoring the law on its cost, Butler wanted to know whether zero was an option. "It has been 'funded' with new taxes and 'savings' that will not materialize. It is thus actually being funded with debt obligations on future generations."

Grace-Marie Turner, president of the Galen Institute, particularly worries about Medicare savings, which mostly come from decreasing payments to the Medicare Advantage program.

One-quarter of Medicare recipients get their insurance coverage from health maintenance organizations, preferred provider groups, and even some private fee-for-service plans as part of Medicare Advantage. But the program has been controversial because the government pays participating insurers about 14 percent more per beneficiary than it pays for the care of seniors in Medicare's traditional fee-for-service program.

"Richard Foster, Medicare's chief actuary, warned Congress that making the deep cuts to Medicare contained in the Senate bill 'represent an exceedingly difficult challenge' and, if sustained, would cause one out of five hospitals and nursing homes to become unprofitable," Turner said. "Congress is highly unlikely to allow this to happen, requiring even more tax dollars and deficit spending. This legislation is not paid for, even with half a trillion dollars in cuts to Medicare and half a trillion in new taxes. Political pressures will intensify to provide ever larger subsidies to more and more people and to impose strict price controls on providers. Coverage restrictions inevitably will follow. So, no, reform is not funded with existing health care dollars."

Paul Ginsburg, president of the Center for Studying Health System Change, countered that the government would have cut Medicare Advantage costs even if reform legislation had not passed, "although perhaps less sharply."

74

"Repeal: Why and How Obamacare Must Be Undone"

Yuval Levin

In the days since the enactment of their health care plan, Democrats in Washington have been desperately seeking to lodge the new program in the pantheon of American public-policy achievements. House Democratic whip James Clyburn compared the bill to the Civil Rights Act of 1964. Vice President Biden argued it vindicates a century of health reform efforts by Democrats and Republicans alike. House speaker Nancy Pelosi said "health insurance reform will stand alongside Social Security and Medicare in the annals of American history."

Even putting aside the fact that Social Security and Medicare are going broke and taking the rest of the government with them, these frantic forced analogies are preposterous. The new law is a ghastly mess, which began as a badly misguided technocratic pipe dream and was then degraded into ruinous incoherence by the madcap process of its enactment.

The appeals to history are understandable, however, because the Democrats know that the law is also exceedingly vulnerable to a wholesale repeal effort: Its major provisions do not take effect for four years, yet in the interim it is likely to begin wreaking havoc with the health care sector—raising insurance premiums, health care costs, and public anxieties. If those major provisions do take effect, moreover, the true costs of the program will soon become clear, and its unsustainable structure will grow painfully obvious. So, to protect it from an angry public and from Republicans armed with alternatives, the new law must be made to seem thoroughly established and utterly irrevocable—a fact on the ground that must be lived with; tweaked, if necessary, at the edges, but at its core politically untouchable.

But it is no such thing. Obamacare starts life strikingly unpopular and looks likely to grow more so as we get to know it in the coming months and years. The entire House of Representatives, two-thirds of the Senate, and the president will be up for election before the law's most significant provisions become fully active. The American public is concerned about spending, deficits, debt, taxes, and overactive government to an extent seldom seen in American history. The excesses of the plan seem likely to make the case for alternative gradual and incremental reforms only stronger.

And the repeal of Obamacare is essential to any meaningful effort to bring down health care costs, provide greater stability and security of coverage to more Americans, and address our entitlement crisis. Both the program's original design and its contorted final form make repairs at the edges unworkable. The only solution is to repeal it and pursue genuine health care reform in its stead.

From Bad to Worse

To see why nothing short of repeal could suffice, we should begin at the core of our health care dilemma.

Conservative and liberal experts generally agree on the nature of the problem with American health care financing: There is a shortage of incentives for efficiency in our methods of paying for coverage and care, and therefore costs are rising much too quickly, leaving too many people unable to afford insurance. We have neither a fully public nor quite a private system of insurance, and three key federal policies—the fee-for-service structure of Medicare, the disjointed financing of Medicaid, and the open-ended tax exclusion for employer-provided insurance—drive spending and costs ever upward.

The disagreement about just how to fix that problem has tended to break down along a familiar dispute between left and right: whether economic efficiency is best achieved by the rational control of expert management or by the lawful chaos of open competition.

Liberals argue that the efficiency we lack would be achieved by putting as much as possible of the health care sector into one big "system" in which the various irregularities could be evened and managed out of existence by the orderly arrangement of rules and incentives. The problem now, they say, is that health care is too chaotic and answers only to the needs of the insurance companies. If it were made more orderly, and answered to the needs of the public as a whole, costs could be controlled more effectively.

Conservatives argue that the efficiency we lack would be achieved by allowing price signals to shape the behavior of both providers and consumers, creating more savings than we could hope to produce on purpose, and allowing competition and informed consumer choices to exercise a downward pressure on prices. The problem now, they say, is that third-party insurance (in which employers buy coverage or the government provides it, and consumers almost never pay doctors directly) makes health care too opaque, hiding the cost of everything from everyone and so making real pricing and therefore real economic efficiency impossible. If it were made more transparent and answered to the wishes of consumers, prices could be controlled more effectively.

That means that liberals and conservatives want to pursue health care reform in roughly opposite directions. Conservatives propose ways of introducing genuine market forces into the insurance system—to remove obstacles to choice and competition, pool risk more effectively, and reduce the inefficiency in government health care entitlements while helping those for whom entry to the market is too expensive (like Americans with pre-existing conditions) gain access to the same high quality care. Such targeted efforts would build on what is best about the system we have in order to address what needs fixing.

Liberals, meanwhile, propose ways of moving Americans to a more fully public system, by arranging conditions in the health care sector (through a mix of mandates, regulations, taxes, and subsidies) to nudge people toward public coverage, which could be more effectively managed. This is the approach the Democrats originally proposed last year. The idea was to end risk-based insurance by making it essentially illegal for insurers to charge people different prices based on their health, age, or other factors; to force everyone to participate in the system so that the healthy do not wait until they're sick to buy insurance; to align various insurance reforms in a way that would raise premium costs in the private market; and then to introduce a government-run insurer that, whether through Medicare's negotiating leverage or through various exemptions from market pressures, could undersell private insurers and so offer an attractive "public option" to people being pushed out of employer plans into an increasingly expensive individual market.

Conservatives opposed this scheme because they believed a public insurer could not introduce efficiencies that would lower prices without brutal rationing of services. Liberals supported it because they thought a public insurer would be fairer and more effective.

But in order to gain sixty votes in the Senate last winter, the Democrats were forced to give up on that public insurer, while leaving the other components of their scheme in place. The result is not even a liberal approach to escalating costs but a ticking time bomb: a scheme that will build up pressure in our private insurance system while offering no escape. Rather than reform a system that everyone agrees is unsustainable, it will subsidize that system and compel participation in it—requiring all Americans to pay ever-growing premiums to insurance companies while doing essentially nothing about the underlying causes of those rising costs.

Liberal health care mavens understand this. When the public option was removed from the health care bill in the Senate, Howard Dean argued in the *Washington Post* that the bill had become merely a subsidy for insurance companies, and failed completely to control costs. Liberal health care blogger Jon Walker said, "The Senate bill will fail to stop the rapidly approaching meltdown of our health care system, and anyone is a fool for thinking otherwise." Markos Moulitsas of the Daily Kos called the bill "unconscionable" and said it lacked "any mechanisms to control costs."

Indeed, many conservatives, for all their justified opposition to a government takeover of health care, have not yet quite seen the full extent to which this bill will exacerbate the cost problem. It is designed to push people into a system that will not exist—a health care bridge to nowhere—and so will cause premiums to rise and encourage significant dislocation and then will initiate a program of subsidies whose only real answer to the mounting costs of coverage will be to pay them with public dollars and so increase them further. It aims to spend a trillion dollars on subsidies to large insurance companies and the expansion of Medicaid, to micromanage the insurance industry in ways likely only to raise premiums further, to cut Medicare benefits without using the money to shore up the program or reduce the deficit, and to raise taxes on employment, investment, and medical research.

The case for averting all of that could hardly be stronger. And the nature of the new law means that it must be undone—not trimmed at the edges. Once implemented fully, it would fairly quickly force a crisis that would require another significant reform. Liberals would seek to use that crisis, or the prospect of it, to move the system toward the approach they wanted in the first place: arguing that the only solution to the rising costs they have created is a public insurer they imagine could outlaw the economics of health care. A look at the fiscal collapse of the Medicare system should rid us of the notion that any such approach would work, but it remains the left's preferred solution, and it is their only plausible next move—indeed, some Democrats led by Iowa senator Tom Harkin have already begun talking about adding a public insurance option to the plan next year.

Because Obamacare embodies a rejection of incrementalism, it cannot be improved in small steps. Fixing our health care system in the wake of the program's enactment will require a big step—repeal of the law before most of it takes hold—followed by incremental reforms addressing the public's real concerns.

The Case for Repeal

That big step will not be easy to take. The Democratic party has invested its identity and its future in the fate of this new program, and Democrats control the White House and both houses of Congress. That is why the conservative health care agenda must now also be an electoral agenda—an effort to refine, inform, and build on public opposition to the new program and to the broader trend toward larger and more intrusive, expensive, and fiscally reckless government in the age of Obama. Obamacare is the most prominent emblem of that larger trend, and its repeal must be at the center of the conservative case to voters in the coming two election cycles.

The design of the new law offers some assistance. In an effort to manipulate the program's Congressional Budget Office score so as to meet President Obama's goal of spending less than $1 trillion in its first decade, the Democrats' plan will roll out along a very peculiar trajectory. No significant entitlement benefits will be made available for four years, but some significant taxes and Medicare cuts—as well as regulatory reforms that may begin to push premium prices up, especially in the individual market—will begin before then. And the jockeying and jostling in the insurance sector in preparation for the more dramatic changes that begin in 2014 will begin to be felt very soon.

To blunt the effects of all this, the Democrats have worked mightily to give the impression that some attractive benefits, especially regarding the rules governing insurance companies, will begin immediately. This year, they say, insurance companies will be prevented from using the pre-existing medical condition of a child to exclude that child's parents from insurance coverage, and a risk-pool program will be established to help a small number of adults who are excluded too. Additionally, insurance policies cannot be cancelled retroactively when someone becomes sick, some annual and lifetime limits on coverage are prohibited, and "children" may stay on their parents' insurance until they turn 26. Obamacare's champions hope these reforms might build a constituency for the program.

But these benefits are far too small to have that effect. The pre-existing condition exclusion prohibits only the refusal to cover treatment for a specific disease, not the exclusion of a family from coverage altogether, and applies only in the individual market, and so affects almost no one. More than half the states already have laws allowing parents to keep adult children on their policies—through ages varying from 24 to 31. And the other new benefits, too, may touch a small number of people (again, mostly in the individual market, where premiums will be rising all the while), but will do nothing to affect the overall picture of American health care financing. CBO scored these immediate reforms as having no effect on the number of uninsured or on national health expenditures.

The bill will also have the government send a $250 check to seniors who reach the "donut hole" gap in Medicare prescription drug coverage this year—and the checks will go out in September, just in time for the fall elections. But the checks will hardly make up for the significant cuts in Medicare Advantage plans that allow seniors to choose among private insurers for their coverage. Those cuts begin in 2011, but the millions of seniors who use the program will start learning about them this year—again, before the election—as insurance companies start notifying their beneficiaries of higher premiums or cancelled coverage.

We are also likely to see some major players in health insurance, including both large employers and large insurers, begin to take steps to prepare for the new system in ways that employees and beneficiaries will find disconcerting. Verizon, for instance, has already informed its employees that insurance premiums will need to rise in the coming years and retiree benefits may be cut. Caterpillar has said new taxes and rules will cost the company $100 million in just the next year, and tractor maker John Deere has said much the same. Such announcements are likely to be common this year, and many insurers active in the individual market are expected to begin curtailing their offerings as that market looks to grow increasingly unprofitable under new rules.

These early indications will help opponents of the new law make their case. But the case will certainly need to focus most heavily on what is to come in the years after this congressional election: spending, taxes, rising health care costs, cuts in Medicare that don't help save the program or reduce the deficit, and a growing government role in the management of the insurance sector.

The numbers are gargantuan and grim—even as laid out by the Congressional Budget Office, which has to accept as fact all of the legislation's dubious premises and promises. If the law remains in place, a new entitlement will begin in 2014 that will cost more than $2.4 trillion in its first ten years, and will grow faster than either Medicare or private-sector health care spending has in the past decade.

Rather than reducing costs, Obamacare will increase national health expenditures by more than $200 billion, according to the Obama administration's own HHS actuary. Premiums in the individual market will increase by more than 10 percent very quickly, and middle-class families in the new exchanges (where large numbers of Americans who now receive coverage through their employers will find themselves dumped) will be forced to choose from a very limited menu of government-approved plans, the cheapest of which, CBO estimates, will cost more than $12,000. Some Americans—those earning up to four times the federal poverty level—will get subsidies to help with some of that cost, but these subsidies will grow more slowly than the premiums, and those above the threshold will not receive them at all. Many middle-class families will quickly find themselves spending a quarter of their net income on health insurance, according to a calculation by Scott Gottlieb of the American Enterprise Institute.

Through the rules governing the exchanges and other mechanisms (including individual and employer insurance mandates, strict regulation of plan benefit packages, rating rules, and the like), the federal government will begin micromanaging the insurance sector in an effort to extend coverage and control costs. But even CBO's assessment does not foresee a reduction in costs and therefore an easing of the fundamental source of our health care woes.

To help pay for the subsidies, and for a massive expansion of Medicaid, taxes will rise by about half a trillion dollars in the program's first ten years—hitting employers and investors especially hard, but quickly being passed down to consumers and workers. And the law also cuts Medicare, especially by reducing physician and hospital payment rates, by another half a trillion dollars—cuts that will drastically undermine the program's operation as, according to the Medicare actuary, about 20 percent of doctors and other providers who participate in the program "could find it difficult to remain profitable and, absent legislative intervention, might end their participation." And all of this, CBO says, to increase the portion of Americans who have health insurance from just under 85 percent today to about 95 percent in ten years.

Of course, this scenario—for all the dark prospects it lays out—assumes things will go more or less as planned. CBO is required to assume as much. But in a program so complex and enormous, which seeks to take control of a sixth of our economy but is profoundly incoherent even in its own terms, things will surely not always go as planned. The Medicare cuts so essential to funding the new entitlement, for instance, are unlikely to occur. Congress has shown itself thoroughly unwilling to impose such cuts in the past, and if it fails to follow through on them in this case, Obamacare will add hundreds of billions of additional dollars to the deficit. By the 2012 election, we will have certainly begun to see whether the program's proposed funding mechanism is a total sham, or is so unpopular as to make Obamacare toxic with seniors. Neither option bodes well for the program's future.

Some of the taxes envisioned in the plan, especially the so-called Cadillac tax on high-cost insurance, are also unlikely to materialize quite as proposed, adding further to the long-term costs of the program. And meanwhile, the bizarre incentive structures created by the law (resulting in part from the elimination of the public insurance plan which was to have been its focus) are likely to cause massive distortions in the insurance market that will further increase costs. The individual market will quickly collapse, since new regulations will put it at an immense disadvantage against the new exchanges. We are likely to see significant consolidation in the insurance sector, as smaller insurers go out of business and the larger ones become the equivalent of subsidized and highly regulated public utilities. And the fact that the exchanges will offer subsidies not available to workers with employer-based coverage will mean either that employers will be strongly inclined to stop offering insurance, or that Congress will be pressured to make subsidies available to employer-based coverage. In either case, the program's costs will quickly balloon.

Perhaps worst of all, the law not only shirks the obligation to be fiscally responsible, it will also make it much more difficult for future policymakers to do something about our entitlement and deficit crisis. Obamacare constructs a new entitlement that will grow more and more expensive even more quickly than Medicare itself. Even if the program were actually deficit neutral, which it surely won't be, that would just mean that it would keep us on the same budget trajectory we are on now—with something approaching trillion-dollar deficits in each of the next ten years and a national debt of more than $20 trillion by 2020—but leave us with much less money and far fewer options for doing anything about it.

In other words, Obamacare is an unmitigated disaster—for our health care system, for our fiscal future, and for any notion of limited government. But it is a disaster that will not truly get under way for four years, and therefore a disaster we can avert.

This is the core of the case the program's opponents must make to voters this year and beyond. If opponents succeed in gaining a firmer foothold in Congress in the fall, they should work to begin dismantling and delaying the program where they can: denying funding to key provisions and pushing back implementation at every opportunity. But a true repeal will almost certainly require yet another election cycle, and another president.

The American public is clearly open to the kind of case Obamacare's opponents will need to make. But keeping voters focused on the problems with the program, and with the reckless growth of government beyond it, will require a concerted, informed, impassioned, and empirical case. This is the kind of case opponents of Obamacare have made over the past year, of course, and it persuaded much of the public—but the Democrats acted before the public could have its say at the polls. The case must therefore be sustained until that happens. The health care debate is far from over.

Toward Real Reform

Making and sustaining that case will also require a clear sense of what the alternatives to Obamacare might be—and how repeal could be followed by sensible incremental steps toward controlling health care costs and thereby increasing access and improving care.

Without a doubt, the Democrats' program is worse than doing nothing. But the choice should not be that program or nothing. The problems with our health care system are real, and conservatives must show the public how repealing Obamacare will open the way to a variety of options for more sensible reforms—reforms that will lower costs and help those with pre-existing conditions or without affordable coverage options, but in ways that do not bankrupt the country, or undermine the quality of care or the freedom of patients and doctors to make choices for themselves.

Republicans this past year offered a variety of such approaches, which varied in their ambitions, costs, and forms. A group led by representatives Paul Ryan and Devin Nunes and senators Tom Coburn and Richard Burr proposed a broad measures that included reforms of Medicare, Medicaid, the employer-based coverage tax exclusion, and malpractice liability and would cover nearly all of the uninsured. The House Republican caucus backed a more modest first step to make high-risk pools available to those with pre-existing conditions, enable insurance purchases across state lines, pursue tort reform, and encourage states to experiment with innovative insurance regulation. Former Bush administration official Jeffrey Anderson has offered an approach somewhere between the two, which pursues incremental reforms through a "small bill." Other conservatives have offered numerous other proposals, including ways of allowing small businesses to pool together for coverage, the expansion of Health Savings Accounts and consumer-driven health care (which Obamacare would thoroughly gut), and various reforms of our entitlement system.

All share a basic commitment to the proposition that our health care dilemmas should be addressed through a series of discrete, modest, incremental solutions to specific problems that concern the American public, and all agree that the underlying cause of these problems is the cost of health coverage and care, which would be best dealt with by using market forces to improve efficiency and bring down prices.

The approach to health care just adopted by President Obama and the Democratic Congress thoroughly fails to deal with efficiency and cost, and stands in the way of any meaningful effort to do so. It is built on a fundamental conceptual error, suffers from a profound incoherence of design, and would make a bad situation far worse. It cannot be improved by tinkering. It must be removed before our health care crisis can be addressed.

If we are going to meet the nation's foremost challenges—ballooning debt, exploding entitlements, out-of-control health care costs, and the task of keeping America strong and competitive—we must begin by making Obamacare history. We must repeal it, and then pursue real reform.

75

"Even After Big Victory, Health Care Future Uncertain"

George E. Condon, Jr.

President Obama's stunning victory on Thursday in the Supreme Court is a surprising validation of his dogged refusal to give ground on his 2008 campaign promise to provide health insurance for the millions of Americans who live in daily dread of disease or sickness. Just about everybody not on the White House staff expected a conservative high court to invalidate key parts of the law Obama pushed through Congress in 2010. But the president prevailed, dealing a severe blow to Republican hopes to ride "Obamacare" to big victories in November.

But before the White House gets too carried away in celebration, the reality is that the Court's decision, as historic as it is, does not guarantee the survival of the law that is the signature accomplishment of Obama's first term in office. This big legal victory gives the president a second chance to do what he flubbed the first time—persuade the country that this is not a partisan exercise. For even after this decision, the health care law still is far from the permanent reform he envisioned when he hailed its passage as answering "the call of history." More than two years later, it remains deeply unpopular despite surviving this legal challenge. Its implementation faces threats of sabotage and its repeal is only as far away as the next election that empowers Republicans to keep their promises. And it is far from a sure political winner in the upcoming election.

This was not how the White House expected it to be. They believed that the country would come to like the new law once they saw that it provided them benefits and understood that it did not threaten their own health insurance plans. But what was an article of faith in 2010 and 2011 has run aground in 2012. Polling shows that individual components are popular. But, as indicated in an ABC News/ *Washington Post* poll released on Wednesday, that doesn't mean people like the overall bill any better. In fact, the survey, conducted June 20–24, shows that 52 percent dislike what has been dubbed "Obamacare" while only 36 percent view it favorably.

That the president now understands these numbers was evident from his statement in the East Room. In victory, he was restrained and serious—no dancing in the end zone when the game is only in the third quarter. And there were certainly no claims that the law has been a political winner, only open acknowledgment that the long debate has been "divisive" and the wry observation that "it should be pretty clear by now that I didn't do this because it was good politics." He well knows the political challenges ahead.

Even on a day when the president's lawyers celebrate doing their job well, it is clear that most of these political and practical problems could have been averted or at least moderated if Obama had taken a different approach when he was crafting the legislation. He might have heard that "call from history." But he didn't heed the lessons of history. He was willing to be the first president since the Civil War to attempt to ram through a major social change—a program that would touch just about every American—on a party-line vote with no support in Congress from the opposing party. Full of hubris and with complete control of both Congress and the White House, the president's advisers did not feel the need for bipartisanship in 2009. They viewed it as a luxury, not a necessity.

Other presidents pushing big programs grasped the futility of trying to shut out the minority party. Even those who had large enough majorities to force their wishes on Congress understood that they needed their accomplishments to appear legitimate to the people and so survive the inevitable change in political cycles that would shift power in Washington. Certainly, Presidents Franklin Roosevelt and Lyndon Johnson understood that. Roosevelt settled for far less than he wanted in Social Security in 1935, complaining privately that it "had been chiseled down to a conservative pattern." But he won over sixteen of the twenty-one Republicans in the Senate and eighty-one of the ninety-six Republicans in the House. In the next election, in 1936, those who campaigned to repeal Social Security seemed out of the mainstream. GOP presidential nominee Alf Landon was in a minority when he argued that the law was "unjust, unworkable, stupidly drafted, and wastefully financed." He lost all but two states.

Three decades later, Johnson, who won his first congressional race in that 1936 election and had studied FDR, showed he had learned the lesson. Again, he had big majorities. But Johnson made sure that he did not pass the Civil Rights Bill of 1964, Medicare in 1965, or the Voting Rights Act of 1965 without significant Republican votes. On both civil rights bills, the GOP margins were even bigger than the Democratic margins. Medicare was closer, but drew thirteen Republican votes in the Senate and seventy in the House. "We had overwhelming Democratic majorities in the House and the Senate," recalled former Democratic Rep. Lee Hamilton, who was a freshman from Indiana in 1965. "He could have passed any bill he wanted to. He had the votes. But he chose to negotiate with the Republicans because he did not want to pass such an important bill on a party-line vote . . . As a result, Medicare was able to be implemented effectively. It had legitimacy."

That, added Hamilton, who now heads the Center on Congress at Indiana University, "has to be the model." When you pass a major piece of legislation on a party-line vote, he said, "It makes it extremely difficult to implement the legislation effectively, because there are so many ways the opposition can interfere, disrupt, delay, or block the implementation of the legislation." Certainly, that has been the case with health care. And it remains a threat even after Thursday's Supreme Court ruling. Finding a way to win over some Republicans will be a major imperative after November's election.

The White House, of course, howls in protest at any suggestion the president did not make a good-faith effort to enlist Republicans. Aides point to the much-ballyhooed seven-hour bipartisan health care "summit" at Blair House in February 2010 and to repeated invitations to Republicans to come on board. But the process was flawed from the beginning when the White House left the writing of the bill to Democrats, gave little support to the "Gang of Fourteen" or the "Gang of Six", and made it clear that there would be no give on medical–malpractice reform even though that could have wooed Republicans. And there was very little personal reaching out by the president to individual GOP members or senators.

But this Court decision, said former Democratic Rep. Tony Coelho, gives the president something he needed going into the election. "It makes him look strong and look like a leader," he said. "It helps diminish the notion that it is a partisan political deal." Coelho, who was in the House for eleven years representing a California district, was a House staffer when Medicare passed. He places the blame for the lack of Republican votes on the 2010 health care law on the early decision by GOP leaders to oppose anything the president offered.

"Today's leadership has a hard time cutting deals with Democrats," he said.

Now, because of the Supreme Court, the pressure shifts back to Republicans to explain why they want to repeal a measure that the Court has judged to be constitutional and that offers some attractive things to voters. And the opportunity is there for Democrats to show skeptical voters—especially those crucial independents who now may be willing to take a second look—that there is something in this law for them.

DISCUSSION QUESTIONS

1. One way of thinking about the tradeoffs inherent in health care is to imagine that there are three main goals of any system: access to services, affordability, and advanced treatments. But you can only choose two. How should we manage these tradeoffs? Are there any ways to select an optimal balance?

2. The conservative case for reform argues that the only way to achieve it is to put individuals back in control of their own decisions, and making them accountable for the costs. The liberal case for reform argues that this is impossible, because there is no way that people can ever make these decisions. (If you were offered the choice of an advanced MRI for $ 1,000, or a less sensitive CT scan for $200, how would you choose?) Is there any way to resolve this?

3. If you could design a health care system from scratch, what would it look like—private, public, or a combination? What role would values and attitudes about government play?

CHAPTER 15

Foreign Policy and World Politics

76

"The Age of Open Society"

George Soros

"Globalization" refers, generally speaking, to the diffusion of interests and ideologies across national borders. Proponents of globalization point to the hope that it will encourage global economic development, and foster universal human rights that are not dependent on where someone happens to live. Critics fall into two camps. One consists of those who fear that globalization will undermine national sovereignty and lead to a "one world" government that leaves everyone at the mercy of distant bureaucrats and officials. The other camp consists of those who see globalization as a smokescreen for corporate hegemony, where multinational corporations exploit workers in countries with low wages, few job protections, and lax environmental regulation, all in the name of higher profits.

George Soros, an investor who made billions of dollars in currency speculation and is now a philanthropist who promotes democracy, believes that economic globalization and political globalization are out of sync: although capital and markets move freely across national boundaries, political institutions do not. A global "open society" would, in his view, insure that the political and social needs of all countries are met (not simply the needs of industrialized nations, whose interests tend to dominate international markets), and would foster the development of stable political and financial institutions. This would require a broad international organization, either as part of the United Nations or as an independent institution. It would have to be based on the idea that certain interests transcend questions of national sovereignty.

Global politics and global economics are dangerously out of sync. Although we live in a global economy characterized by free trade and the free movement of capital, our politics are still based on the sovereignty of the state. International institutions exist, but their powers are limited by how much authority states are willing to confer on them. At the same time, the powers of the state are limited by the freedom of capital to escape taxation and regulation by moving elsewhere. This is particularly true of the countries at the periphery of the global capitalist system, whose economic destiny depends on what happens at the center.

This state of affairs would be sustainable if the market mechanism could be trusted to satisfy social needs. But that is not the case.

We need to find international political arrangements that can meet the requirements of an increasingly interdependent world. These arrangements ought to be built on the principles of open society. A perfect society is beyond our reach. We must content ourselves with the next best thing: a society that holds itself open to improvement. We need institutions that allow people of different views, interests, and backgrounds to live together in peace. These institutions should assure the greatest degree of freedom compatible with the common interest. Many mature democracies come close to qualifying as open societies. But they refuse to accept openness as a universal principle.

How could this principle of openness be translated into practice? By the open societies of the world forming an alliance for this purpose. The alliance would have two distinct but interrelated goals: to foster the development of open society within individual countries; and to establish international laws, rules of conduct, and institutions to implement these norms.

It is contrary to the principles of open society to dictate from the outside how a society should govern itself. Yet the matter cannot be left entirely to the state, either. The state can be an instrument of oppression. To the extent possible, outside help should take the form of incentives; the evolution of open society requires aid for economic and institutional development. Punitive measures, though sometimes unavoidable, tend to be counterproductive.

Unfortunately, positive intervention is out of favor because of an excessive faith in the magic of the marketplace. There is an alliance of democratic countries, NATO, capable of military intervention, but there is no similar alliance to engage in constructive intervention. This open-society alliance ought to have a much broader membership than NATO, and it must include nongovernmental members as well as heads of state. As former U.S. Secretary of State Henry Kissinger points out, states have interests but no principles; we cannot rely on them to implement the principle of openness.

Democratic governments are, however, responsive to the wishes of their electorates. Therefore, the impulse for the alliance has to come from the people, not from their leaders. Citizens living in open societies must recognize a global open society as something worth sacrifice. This responsibility rests in particular with the United States, the sole surviving superpower and the dominant force in the global capitalist system. There can be no global open society without its leadership. But the United States has become carried away by its success and fails to see why it should subordinate its self-interest to some nebulous common principle. The United States jealously guards its sovereignty and behaves as if it ought to be the sole arbiter of right and wrong. Washington will have to undergo a significant change of heart before it is ready to lead an open-society alliance.

The alliance, if it comes to pass, must not lose sight of its own fallibity. Foreign aid, though very valuable, is notoriously inefficient. Rule-based incentives are more promising. The international financial architecture needs to be redesigned to help give underdeveloped countries a leg up. Incentives would be conditional on each country's success in establishing open political and financial institutions.

The alliance could act within the United Nations, or it could go it alone. But a commitment to such an alliance would offer an opportunity to reform the United Nations. The noble intentions enunciated in the preamble of the U.N. Charter can never be attained as long as the United Nations remains a rigid association of sovereign states. But there is ample room for improvement, and an open-society alliance would be a start. Perhaps one day, then, historians will look back at these years to come as the Age of Open Society.

Discussion Questions

1. Is Soros's suggestion about an open society practical? Do you think there are circumstances under which nations would agree to such a proposal?

2. How, if at all, will globalization change notions about national identity? Do you think that, twenty-five or fifty years from now, being a U.S. citizen—or a citizen of any other country—will have the same meaning as it does now?

"Reality Check"

PETER D. SUTHERLAND

Peter Sutherland confronts the arguments against globalization. Over the past few years, protesters have disrupted meetings of international economic organizations (especially the World Trade Organization, an institution created to foster global free trade). Susan George, a critic of the World Trade Organization, gave the flavor of the arguments against globalization in a recent article in the journal The Nation: *" 'Free trade' as managed by the World Trade Organization and reinvigorated at the recent negotiations in Doha is largely the freedom of the fox in the henhouse. Despite the advance on generic drugs for pandemics such as AIDS, tuberculosis and malaria, the South's needs are shelved and the transnationals continue to run the show according to their own preferred rules." Sutherland has little patience with such protests, and believes that protesters are motivated by a simplistic and inaccurate view of what globalization is about: "The notion that globalization is an international conspiracy on the part of industrial-country governments and large firms to marginalize the poorest nations, to exploit low wages and social costs wherever they may be found . . . and even to undermine human rights and cut away democratic processes that stand in the way of ever more open markets is, of course, utter nonsense." He disagrees that international trade organizations ignore the needs of poor countries, and argues that increased global trade is (and has been) the most effective mechanism of economic development. At the same time, he offers some suggestions on how to ensure that existing institutions are strengthened.*

The Seattle Ministerial Conference of the World Trade Organization (WTO) demonstrated with disturbing force the huge confusions that haunt the public mind and much of global politics about the nature of trade and the process now known as globalization. The notion that globalization is an international conspiracy on the part of industrial-country governments and large firms to marginalize the poorest nations, to exploit low wages and social costs wherever they may be found, to diminish cultures in the interests of an Anglo-Saxon model of lifestyle and language, and even to undermine human rights and cut away democratic processes that stand in the way of ever more open markets is, of course, utter nonsense. Yet the Seattle demonstrations vividly exhibited the worrying tendency to equate these concerns and others to the existence and potential development of the World Trade Organization, the institutional and legal face of the world trade system.

This outpouring of misconceived, ill-understood propaganda against a system that has brought vast gains to most nations over the past few decades is extraordinarily dangerous. It is a threat to the prospects of a better life for many millions, perhaps billions, of people at the start of the new millennium. If left unquestioned and unchallenged in the interests of political correctness or political advantage, this sentiment could set the cause of economic and social development back 20 years. This threat is made all the more serious by the difficult new challenges facing governments today. Still, Seattle showed more clearly some of the institutional difficulties of managing effective decision-making processes, with over 100 countries truly interested and involved in managing the geopolitical realities of the 21st century.

The Biggest Straw Man

In order to understand the dangers implied by attacks on the WTO, one must first distinguish between "globalization" and the World Trade Organization. Neither as a body of international law nor as a governmental institution can the WTO be regarded as synonymous with globalization. The WTO, like its predecessor the General Agreement on Tariffs and Trade (GATT), is a collection of rules and undertakings voluntarily entered into and implemented by governments on the basis of consensus among those governments to provide a predictable, stable, and secure environment in which all types of firms can trade and invest. A small transfer of national sovereignty (insofar as any purely intergovernmental structure can affect sovereignty) in the interest of internationally enforceable disciplines brings economic gains for all and prevents economic muscle from being the sole arbiter of commercial advantage. It is easy to argue that in a period when business is as likely to be conducted at the global level as at the national, the WTO recovers a degree of sovereignty for governments that otherwise find themselves no longer able to influence significant aspects of their economic future.

Of course, open and secure markets have encouraged global trade and investment. They have provided jobs, consumer choice, and rising personal wealth in large parts of the world, including many developing countries. Governments everywhere want to see their firms able to trade, and they actively seek inward investment by foreign firms. But that is not the whole story of globalization. The WTO has had only a marginal effect on other significant elements, most of which relate to the mobility of people, information, culture, technology and capital. Air transport, telecommunications, the media, and now the internet are four of the most crucial drivers of globalization. While they are not without their dangers or inadequacies, few would seriously argue that they have not brought widespread benefits. These innovations represent the positive face of the global economy.

Are the more troublesome aspects of globalization really a reflection of the trading system, or do they represent quite different policy failures, including poor education and training, misplaced and inefficient government intervention in industry, corruption in both the public and private sectors, poor governance, crime, lack of transparency in regulatory systems, inadequate or inappropriate social security and pensions systems, and so on? Admittedly, the trading system has not always provided the right results; for instance, it ought to be able to deliver more for the least-developed countries, even if it cannot solve all their problems. However, equating the WTO with the difficulties of the global economy risks damaging a system which has given much and still has more to offer. Such thinking also neglects the importance of the WTO's fundamental role in simply facilitating trade and investment. The tendency to turn to the trade rules to resolve every challenge facing mankind—the environment, human rights, and labor standards—is almost as dangerous as the desire to dismantle the system in order to halt a process of globalization that is beyond the realm of any institution.

Fruits of the Uruguay Round

The first thing governments need to do in the current atmosphere of sometimes dubiously motivated protest and fear is to stop apologizing for the WTO and start defending it. The GATT helped create three decades of remarkably healthy economic growth. It succeeded in a low-profile manner because, in the 1950s and 1960s, high customs duties could be brought down steadily without attracting much political controversy. By the time the Uruguay Round was launched in 1986, the world was left with the hard cases of international trade. Negotiators finally had to face up to protectionism in the most sensitive industries of the developed countries, particularly in textiles, clothing, footwear, agriculture, steel, and automobiles. They also came to realize that the next stages of reducing protection and opening markets, and thus reestablishing the kind of trade growth spurred by the GATT, would mean moving some of the focus of negotiation from conditions at the border (such as tariffs and quota restrictions) to the heart of domestic regulation and sectoral support.

Immense political effort was required at the highest levels of government, but the Uruguay Round succeeded and established the WTO in the process. The advances made on all fronts cannot be underestimated. Policies in agriculture underwent a revolution: all market-access restrictions were translated into transparent tariffs, and the process of winding back the most distorting features of domestic support and export subsidies was initiated. A higher level of practical liberalization for farm goods might have been preferred, but the fundamental policy changes are irreversible and provide the basis to go further next time. Similarly, in textiles and clothing all the countries maintaining heavy quantitative controls on imports are committed to phasing them out. It will take nearly ten years, but the agreement at Uruguay marked a fundamental change of heart and direction.

Many other trade rules were amended, clarified, or added to the system. The practice of "negotiating" so-called "voluntary export restraints" affecting automobiles, steel, cutlery, and many other products for which consumers were forced to pay far more than was reasonable was outlawed. Some of the most damaging features of anti-dumping practices were cut back. Modern rules on technical barriers to trade and health and safety regulation were also put in place.

An agreement requiring intellectual property rights to be available and enforceable in all WTO countries was concluded for the first time, despite doubts and difficulties in some industrial and developing countries. There were two final jewels in the crown. First, an agreement on trade in services brought GATT-like disciplines and concessions in sectors as diverse as banking, telecommunications, professional services, travel, tourism, and the audio-visual industry. Financial services and telecommunications were the subject of additional valuable packages of concessions in the past three years, and the new negotiations, beginning this year, will take the process of progressive liberalization in the services sector much further. Second, the entire body of WTO disciplines and concessions was made enforceable through a tough dispute-settlement procedure that has now been used in nearly 200 cases.

It has become almost an article of faith that while all of these developments were good for the industrialized countries and some of the more advanced developing countries, many poorer countries lost out. Some critics suggest that these countries did not benefit from the results of the round, and that they were, in fact, further marginalized and impoverished. According to these critics, such marginalization is not surprising because developing countries had little or no voice in the negotiations that culminated in agreement at the end of 1993.

Such a position is an insult to the abilities of the many developing country trade negotiators who participated fully in the Uruguay Round. Although I took responsibility at a comparatively late stage, I can attest to the effectiveness and strength of purpose of these officials and ministers from poorer nations. They had considerable influence on the original development of the Uruguay Round agenda; worked assiduously through the eight-year process of examination and elucidation of issues, and negotiation of texts; and were in the foreground during the tough final months of bargaining. Certainly the United States, the European Union, and Japan were more influential, and many of the Uruguay Round texts pay particular attention to their interests. But the developing countries succeeded for the first time in any trade round in melding an influence on the final outcome quite disproportionate to their share of world trade. The WTO is very much their institution and the rules of world trade are as much their rules as those of the industrial countries.

Myths and Realities

So, if it is untrue that developing countries were ignored in the establishment of the WTO, is it at least true that they saw few practical benefits in terms of trade and investment? Again, the answer is no. A few measures demonstrating the long-term trends rather than the short-term aberrations bolster the point. Are developing countries benefiting from more open industrial-country markets? The answer is yes; despite the fall in trade during 1997 because of the drop in commodity prices and the Asian financial crisis, the share of developing countries and the transition economies in the imports of developed countries increased to 25 percent in 1998 from 22.8 percent in 1994. Has the developing countries' share in world trade grown? Again, yes. Despite the setbacks of 1997–1998, the latest WTO figures show that the share of developing countries in world exports of manufactures in 1998 was one percent higher than in 1994, and 6.4 percent higher than in 1990. The same overall growth trend can be observed for merchandise exports generally as well as agricultural products.

What about investment? Have developing countries seen an inward flow of productive investment, as they should if they offer more open markets with stable trade regimes based upon WTO disciplines? As with trade, the picture is mixed, with considerable variations in performance. However, figures from the UN Conference on Trade and Development show that overall inward foreign direct investment (FDI) flows to the developing world rose steadily and consistently from an average of US$35 billion a year in the period 1987–92 to US$166 billion in 1998. Taken as a percentage of gross fixed capital formation, FDI inflows to developing countries rose from an average of 3.9 percent in the period 1987–92 to 10.3 percent in 1998.

There is nothing fundamentally wrong with the system that calls for a wholesale rethinking on behalf of the developing countries. It is accepted that some developing countries have had difficulty in implementing some Uruguay Round commitments. Political and conceptual difficulties have hampered the implementation of certain intellectual property commitments in countries like India. In some of the poorest economies, the absence of solid institutional and technological infrastructure has made the implementation of agreements such as those on customs valuation and health and safety standards difficult. But patience and the right kind of technical assistance can resolve such problems over time. They are not evidence of a systemic failure in the WTO.

Indeed, many developing countries are successfully integrating themselves into the global economy through their commitment to WTO obligations. The failure of the Seattle meeting effectively blocked the continuation of that process or, at the very least, reduced opportunities for further progress. Essentially all that remains is the potential for negotiations on trade in services and agriculture that were mandated in the Uruguay Round agreements. This is not a small agenda, and any successful conclusion in the near future remains in question.

What has been lost or suspended is a larger and, in some respects more urgent, agenda. Developing countries have clearly been denied much that they rightly expected in the implementation of Uruguay Round commitments. They had reasonable demands that industrial countries implement in better faith the agreement to phase out textiles and clothing quotas. The agricultural agreement should have brought them more commercial advantage than has been the case. Antidumping legislation has continued to operate too stringently to the disadvantage of poorer countries. On the other hand, these countries have sometimes had difficulties in meeting their own obligations. That is hardly surprising since they have been required to go much further, much faster than was ever expected of industrial countries. In most cases, additional time needed for implementation of commitments should willingly be provided along with generous technical assistance efforts and the necessary funding for institutional capacity-building.

The least developed countries have been denied the duty-free treatment in market access that has long been promised and discussed in the context of a new round. The entire world has lost the commercial opportunities that would have sprung from global tariff and non-tariff-barrier negotiations covering industrial products. It is estimated that a 50 percent reduction in industrial tariffs would raise some US$270 billion in global income per year, and that developing countries could benefit from as much as 95 percent of the gains from liberalizing trade in manufactures.

Before the Next Round

Perhaps those opportunities will re-emerge, but the immediate priority is not to rush to launch a new round. Governments need to learn the lessons of the Seattle meeting and prepare the ground for the multilateral trading system to move forward on the basis of willing consensus among governments. I would propose four major areas as needing profound reconsideration.

First, coherence in trade policymaking is needed. Until now, this has tended to mean cooperation between the secretariats of the WTO and other major international institutions like the World Bank and the International Monetary Fund. Coherence should now take on a different meaning. It should ensure that the stances of WTO member governments in trade negotiations reflect a domestic consensus. Government departments must coordinate effectively among themselves so that, for instance, environmental, public health, or development concerns are factored into trade-policy decision-making early on. Governments must listen to and work with many different constituencies in an open and transparent manner. Only then can the WTO be clear of the foolish charge that it is some form of government-business conspiracy.

Second, negotiations and decision-making within the WTO itself need to become more coherent and effective. This may require a high level management structure in Geneva, perhaps based upon a restricted constituency-based management or advisory board. Senior policy-makers should come to Geneva regularly to set the body's business in the fullest context, including financial development, environmental concerns, and other considerations. Moreover, both the preparatory process and the Seattle ministerial meeting demonstrated that while full transparency is vital—and the institution will have to steel itself to become yet more open—efficient and effective decision-making is necessary if continued paralysis is to be avoided. Of course, negotiating positions may often be so far apart that compromise is simply not possible. Recent history suggests, however, that the techniques of negotiating in a multilateral environment are either inoperable or have been forgotten.

Third, careful consideration must now be given to the speed and intensity with which a new round or any other effort to extend the trading system is pursued. There can be little doubt that the Seattle meeting was both premature and over-burdened with proposals that were poorly thought-out, unnecessary, or premature. Is there really an urgent need to launch a broad-based new trade round in the immediate future? If one believes that neither agriculture nor services negotiations can progress outside such a round, then perhaps the answer is a qualified "yes." But, if the reality is such that an early start would be unlikely to move forward with any conviction, then perhaps governments should take a deep breath and await a more propitious time. Nothing would damage the WTO's image further than another failed attempt to initiate a round.

Fourth, regardless of a new round, governments must now live up to their responsibilities and start energetically defending the principles on which the WTO is based. A "human face" for the trading system is appropriate if it does not serve to undermine the foundations of the system and the huge gains it has provided humanity over the past fifty years. It is perfectly possible to understand and respond to the concerns of those who doubt the value of the system without holding it hostage to local politics. The critics must understand that however justified their causes, the world would not be a better place without the WTO and without continued efforts to make it still more effective for all its members.

This is a turning point for the global trading system. How governments respond to the challenges raised by the Seattle Ministerial Conference could have an overwhelming influence on the contribution that the institution can have on the creation of a better society in the future. Globalization remains a fact and an opportunity. The WTO is one of the most effective instruments at our disposal for translating the opportunity into the reality of improved welfare for billions of citizens. There is no question that it could be a better instrument. But it is the best that we have at our disposal and are likely to have in the future. Governments must learn to use it wisely, change it carefully, and support it convincingly.

DISCUSSION QUESTIONS

1. Many critics of globalization argue that allowing goods and capital to move freely across borders only moves jobs to countries with the cheapest (and most exploitable) labor forces. Supporters argue that these jobs, even though they might not pay much by Western standards, still provide much better opportunities for people in developing nations than would otherwise be available. Who do you think has the better case?

2. Does your campus have organizations active in "anti-sweatshop" organizations? (These groups, among other things, have encouraged universities to ensure that clothing and other gear with university symbols are not made by child labor or in dangerous factories). What impact have these organizations had on student opinion?

3. What is the alternative to globalization? What costs are associated with, for example, protecting domestic jobs from being exported? What are the benefits of such protection?

DEBATING THE ISSUES: IS THE WORLD STILL A DANGEROUS PLACE?

September 11, 2001 was a defining moment in American history. People will forever remember where they were on that date, much as people in an earlier generation recall where they were when they learned President Kennedy had been shot. The attacks were an emphatic demonstration that the world was a dangerous place.

A common belief in the intelligence community before 9/11 was that terror groups might actually possess a nuclear weapon, but none would dare to use it. After 9/11, this changed to a belief that terror groups did not possess a nuclear weapon, but would not hesitate to use one if they did. In response, the United States launched wars in Afghanistan and Iraq (the first of which became the longest war ever fought in American history, and the latter of which was extremely controversial), created a new security apparatus, reorganized entire swaths of society and the economy (as anyone who has flown in the last twelve years knows), and spent trillions of dollars in the fight against terrorism. Critics of these efforts argued that we were overreacting, as the threat was far less grave than perceived. Supporters countered that the new vigilance stopped many subsequent efforts to attack targets in the United States, from efforts to bring down airliners to plots to set off bombs in Times Square and destroy the New York Federal Reserve building.

After twelve years, can we say anything about how safe we are? The readings here consist of a debate that took place in the pages of the journal *Foreign Affairs*. Zenko and Cohen maintain that the United States is far safer than most realize, and that political leaders are exaggerating the threat for their own purposes, mostly electoral gain. It is not just the United States that is safer: they argue that the world is in fact a safer place to be than at any time in the past sixty years. There are fewer armed conflicts, fewer terrorist attacks, zero prospects for a superpower confrontation, unquestioned U.S. military supremacy, and more free nations. Even the nightmare scenario of a nuclear attack—whether from Iran, North Korea, or a terrorist group—is more a function of previous anxiety over a nuclear war with the Soviet Union than a realistic assessment of current threats. What the United States needs now, they conclude, is a balanced security policy that deals with actual problems that exist instead of the remote chance (the "1 percent doctrine") of a serious threat.

Miller disagrees. Even though the United States does not face any meaningful challenge to its military superiority, that does not mean that dangers are entirely absent. Given the instability of existing and potential nuclear powers, there is a threat that a crisis could lead to a nuclear confrontation (as well as the possibility that a rogue state may soon have both a nuclear weapon and the missile technology to threaten the United States directly). China and Russia as well could easily pose a threat to Asia or Europe. Add to this the unstable mix of failed states and non-state actors, and the world remains a dangerous place.

78

"Clear and Present Safety: The United States Is More Secure Than Washington Thinks"

MICAH ZENKO AND MICHAEL A. COHEN

Last August, the Republican presidential contender Mitt Romney performed what has become a quadrennial rite of passage in American presidential politics: he delivered a speech to the annual convention of the Veterans of Foreign Wars. His message was rooted in another grand American tradition: hyping foreign threats to the United States. It is "wishful thinking," Romney declared, "that the world is becoming a safer place. The opposite is true. Consider simply the jihadists, a near-nuclear Iran, a turbulent Middle East, an unstable Pakistan, a delusional North Korea, an assertive Russia, and an emerging global power called China. No, the world is not becoming safer."

Not long after, U.S. Secretary of Defense Leon Panetta echoed Romney's statement. In a lecture last October, Panetta warned of threats arising "from terrorism to nuclear proliferation; from rogue states to cyber attacks; from revolutions in the Middle East to economic crisis in Europe, to the rise of new powers such as China and India. All of these changes represent security, geopolitical, economic, and demographic shifts in the international order that make the world more unpredictable, more volatile and, yes, more dangerous." General Martin Dempsey, chairman of the Joint Chiefs of Staff, concurred in a recent speech, arguing that "the number and kinds of threats we face have increased significantly." And U.S. Secretary of State Hillary Clinton reinforced the point by claiming that America resides today in a "very complex, dangerous world."

Within the foreign policy elite, there exists a pervasive belief that the post–Cold War world is a treacherous place, full of great uncertainty and grave risks. A 2009 survey conducted by the Pew Research Center for the People and the Press found that 69 percent of members of the Council on Foreign Relations believed that for the United States at that moment, the world was either as dangerous as or more dangerous than it was during the Cold War. Similarly, in 2008, the Center for American Progress surveyed more than 100 foreign policy experts and found that 70 percent of them believed that the world was becoming more dangerous. Perhaps more than any other idea, this belief shapes debates on U.S. foreign policy and frames the public's understanding of international affairs.

There is just one problem: It is simply wrong. The world that the United States inhabits today is a remarkably safe and secure place. It is a world with fewer violent conflicts and greater political freedom than at virtually any other point in human history. All over the world, people enjoy longer life expectancy and greater economic opportunity than ever before. The United States faces no plausible existential threats, no great-power rival, and no near-term competition for the role of global hegemon. The U.S. military is the world's most powerful, and even in the middle of a sustained downturn, the U.S. economy remains among one of the world's most vibrant and adaptive. Although the United States faces a host of international challenges, they pose little risk to the overwhelming majority of American citizens and can be managed with existing diplomatic, economic, and, to a much lesser extent, military tools.

This reality is barely reflected in U.S. national security strategy or in American foreign policy debates. President Barack Obama's most recent National Security Strategy aspires to "a world in which America is stronger, more secure, and is able to overcome our challenges while appealing to the aspirations of people around the world." Yet that is basically the world that exists today. The United States is the world's most powerful nation, unchallenged and secure. But the country's political and policy elite seem unwilling to recognize this fact, much less integrate it into foreign policy and national security decision-making.

The disparity between foreign threats and domestic threatmongering results from a confluence of factors. The most obvious and important is electoral politics. Hyping dangers serves the interests of both political parties. For Republicans, who have long benefited from attacking Democrats for their alleged weakness in the face of foreign threats, there is little incentive to tone down the rhetoric; the notion of a dangerous world plays to perhaps their greatest political advantage. For Democrats, who are fearful of being cast as feckless, acting and sounding tough is a shield against GOP attacks and an insurance policy in case a challenge to the United States materializes into a genuine threat. Warnings about a dangerous world also benefit powerful bureaucratic interests. The specter of looming dangers sustains and justifies the massive budgets of the military and the intelligence agencies, along with the national security infrastructure that exists outside government—defense contractors, lobbying groups, think tanks, and academic departments.

There is also a pernicious feedback loop at work. Because of the chronic exaggeration of the threats facing the United States, Washington overemphasizes military approaches to problems (including many that could best be solved by nonmilitary means). The militarization of foreign policy leads, in turn, to further dark warnings about the potentially harmful effects of any effort to rebalance U.S. national security spending or trim the massive military budget—warnings that are inevitably bolstered by more threat exaggeration. Last fall, General Norton Schwartz, the U.S. Air Force chief of staff, said that defense cuts that would return military spending to its 2007 level would undermine the military's "ability to protect the nation" and could create "dire consequences." Along the same lines, Panetta warned that the same reductions would "invite aggression" from enemies. These are puzzling statements given that the U.S. defense budget is larger than the next 14 countries' defense budgets combined, and that the United States still maintains weapons systems designed to fight an enemy that disappeared 20 years ago.

Of course, threat inflation is not new. During the Cold War, although the United States faced genuine existential threats, American political leaders nevertheless hyped smaller threats or conflated them with larger ones. Today, there are no dangers to the United States remotely resembling those of the Cold War era, yet policy-makers routinely talk in the alarmist terms once used to describe superpower conflict. Indeed, the mindset of the United States in the post–9/11 world was best (albeit crudely) captured by former Vice President Dick Cheney. While in office, Cheney promoted the idea that the United States must prepare for even the most remote threat as though it were certain to occur. The journalist Ron Suskind termed this belief "the one percent doctrine," a reference to what Cheney called the "one percent chance that Pakistani scientists are helping al Qaeda build or develop a nuclear weapon." According to Suskind, Cheney insisted that the United States must treat such a remote potential threat "as a certainty in terms of our response."

Such hair-trigger responsiveness is rarely replicated outside the realm of national security, even when the government confronts problems that cause Americans far more harm than any foreign threat. According to an analysis by the budget expert Linda Bilmes and the economist Joseph Stiglitz, in the ten years since 9/11, the combined direct and indirect costs of the U.S. response to the murder of almost 3,000 of its citizens have totaled more than $3 trillion. A study by the Urban Institute, a nonpartisan think tank, estimated that during an overlapping period, from 2000 to 2006, 137,000 Americans died prematurely because they lacked health insurance. Although the federal government maintains robust health insurance programs for older and poor Americans, its response to a national crisis in health care during that time paled in comparison to its response to the far less deadly terrorist attacks.

Rather than Cheney's one percent doctrine, what the United States actually needs is a 99-percent doctrine: a national security strategy based on the fact that the United States is a safe and well-protected country and grounded in the reality that the opportunities for furthering U.S. interests far exceed the threats to them. Fully comprehending the world as it is today is the best way to keep the United States secure and resistant to the overreactions that have defined its foreign policy for far too long.

Better Than Ever

The United States, along with the rest of the world, currently faces a period of economic and political uncertainty. But consider four long-term global trends that underscore just how misguided the constant fear-mongering in U.S. politics is: the falling prevalence of violent conflict, the declining incidence of terrorism, the spread of political freedom and prosperity, and the global improvement in public health. In 1992, there were 53 armed conflicts raging in 39 countries around the world; in 2010, there were 30 armed conflicts in 25 countries. Of the latter, only four have resulted in at least 1,000 battle-related deaths and can therefore be classified as wars, according to the Uppsala Conflict Data Program: the conflicts in Afghanistan, Iraq, Pakistan, and Somalia, two of which were started by the United States.

Today, wars tend to be low-intensity conflicts that, on average, kill about 90 percent fewer people than did violent struggles in the 1950s. Indeed, the first decade of this century witnessed fewer deaths from war than any decade in the last century. Meanwhile, the world's great powers have not fought a direct conflict in more than 60 years—"the longest period of major power peace in centuries," as the Human Security Report Project puts it. Nor is there much reason for the United States to fear such a war in the near future: no state currently has the capabilities or the inclination to confront the United States militarily.

Much of the fear that suffuses U.S. foreign policy stems from the trauma of 9/11. Yet although the tactic of terrorism remains a scourge in localized conflicts, between 2006 and 2010, the total number of terrorist attacks declined by almost 20 percent, and the number of deaths caused by terrorism fell by 35 percent, according to the U.S. State Department. In 2010, more than three-quarters of all victims of terrorism—meaning deliberate, politically motivated violence by nonstate groups against noncombatant targets—were injured or killed in the war zones of Afghanistan, Iraq, Pakistan, and Somalia. Of the 13,186 people killed by terrorist attacks in 2010, only 15, or 0.1 percent, were U.S. citizens. In most places today—and especially in the United States—the chances of dying from a terrorist attack or in a military conflict have fallen almost to zero.

As violence and war have abated, freedom and democratic governance have made great gains. According to Freedom House, there were sixtynine electoral democracies at the end of the Cold War; today, there are 117. And during that time, the number of autocracies declined from 62 to 48. To be sure, in the process of democratizing, states with weak political institutions can be more prone to near-term instability, civil wars, and interstate conflict. Nevertheless, over time, democracies tend to have healthier and better-educated citizens, almost never go to war with other democracies, and are less likely to fight nondemocracies.

Economic bonds among states are also accelerating, even in the face of a sustained global economic downturn. Today, 153 countries belong to the World Trade Organization and are bound by its dispute-resolution mechanisms. Thanks to lowered trade barriers, exports now make up more than 30 percent of gross world product, a proportion that has tripled in the past 40 years. The United States has seen its exports to the world's fastest-growing economies increase by approximately 500 percent over the past decade. Currency flows have exploded as well, with $4 trillion moving around the world in foreign exchange markets every day. Remittances, an essential instrument for reducing poverty in developing countries, have more than tripled in the past decade, to more than $440 billion each year. Partly as a result of these trends, poverty is on the decline: in 1981, half the people living in the developing world survived on less than $1.25 a day; today, that figure is about one-sixth. Like democratization, economic development occasionally brings with it significant costs. In particular, economic liberalization can strain the social safety net that supports a society's most vulnerable populations and can exacerbate inequalities. Still, from the perspective of the United States, increasing economic interdependence is a net positive because trade and foreign direct investment between countries generally correlate with long-term economic growth and a reduced likelihood of war.

A final trend contributing to the relative security of the United States is the improvement in global health and well-being. People in virtually all countries, and certainly in the United States, are living longer and healthier lives. In 2010, the number of people who died from AIDS-related causes declined for the third year in a row. Tuberculosis rates continue to fall, as do the rates of polio and malaria. Child mortality has plummeted worldwide, thanks in part to expanded access to health care, sanitation, and vaccines. In 1970, the global child mortality rate (deaths of children under five per 1,000) was 141; in 2010, it was 57. In 1970, global average life expectancy was 59, and U.S. life expectancy was 70. Today, the global figure is just under 70, and the U.S. figure is 79. These vast improvements in health and well-being contribute to the global trend toward security and safety because countries with poor human development are more war-prone.

Phantom Menace

None of this is meant to suggest that the United States faces no major challenges today. Rather, the point is that the problems confronting the country are manageable and pose minimal risks to the lives of the overwhelming majority of Americans. None of them—separately or in combination—justifies the alarmist rhetoric of policy-makers and politicians or should lead to the conclusion that Americans live in a dangerous world.

Take terrorism. Since 9/11, no security threat has been hyped more. Considering the horrors of that day, that is not surprising. But the result has been a level of fear that is completely out of proportion to both the capabilities of terrorist organizations and the United States' vulnerability. On 9/11, al Qaeda got tragically lucky. Since then, the United States has been preparing for the one percent chance (and likely even less) that it might get lucky again. But al Qaeda lost its safe haven after the U.S.-led invasion of Afghanistan in 2001, and further military, diplomatic, intelligence, and law enforcement efforts have decimated the organization, which has essentially lost whatever ability it once had to seriously threaten the United States.

According to U.S. officials, al Qaeda's leadership has been reduced to two top lieutenants: Ayman al-Zawahiri and his second-in-command, Abu Yahya al-Libi. Panetta has even said that the defeat of al Qaeda is "within reach." The near collapse of the original al Qaeda organization is one reason why, in the decade since 9/11, the U.S. homeland has not suffered any large-scale terrorist assaults. All subsequent attempts have failed or been thwarted, owing in part to the incompetence of their perpetrators. Although there are undoubtedly still some terrorists who wish to kill Americans, their dreams will likely continue to be frustrated by their own limitations and by the intelligence and law enforcement agencies of the United States and its allies."

As the threat from transnational terrorist groups dwindles, the United States also faces few risks from other states. China is the most obvious potential rival to the United States, and there is little doubt that China's rise will pose a challenge to U.S. economic interests. Moreover, there is an unresolved debate among Chinese political and military leaders about China's proper global role, and the lack of transparency from China's senior leadership about its long-term foreign policy objectives is a cause for concern. However, the present security threat to the U.S. mainland is practically nonexistent and will remain so. Even as China tries to modernize its military, its defense spending is still approximately one-ninth that of the United States. In 2012, the Pentagon will spend roughly as much on military research and development alone as China will spend on its entire military.

While China clumsily flexes its muscles in the Far East by threatening to deny access to disputed maritime resources, a recent Pentagon report noted that China's military ambitions remain dominated by "regional contingencies" and that the People's Liberation Army has made little progress in developing capabilities that "extend global reach or power projection." In the coming years, China will enlarge its regional role, but this growth will only threaten U.S. interests if Washington attempts to dominate East

Asia and fails to consider China's legitimate regional interests. It is true that China's neighbors sometimes fear that China will not resolve its disputes peacefully, but this has compelled Asian countries to cooperate with the United States, maintaining bilateral alliances that together form a strong security architecture and limit China's room to maneuver.

The strongest arguments made by those warning of Chinese influence revolve around economic policy. The list of complaints includes a host of Chinese policies, from intellectual property theft and currency manipulation to economic espionage and domestic subsidies. Yet none of those is likely to lead to direct conflict with the United States beyond the competition inherent in international trade, which does not produce zero-sum outcomes and is constrained by dispute-resolution mechanisms, such as those of the World Trade Organization. If anything, China's export-driven economic strategy, along with its large reserves of U.S. Treasury bonds, suggests that Beijing will continue to prefer a strong United States to a weak one.

Nuclear Fear

It is a matter of faith among many American politicians that Iran is the greatest danger now facing the country. But if that is true, then the United States can breathe easy: Iran is a weak military power. According to the International Institute for Strategic Studies, Iran's "military forces have almost no modern armor, artillery, aircraft or major combat ships, and UN sanctions will likely obstruct the purchase of high-technology weapons for the foreseeable future."

Tehran's stated intention to project its interests regionally through military or paramilitary forces has made Iran its own worst enemy. Iran's neighbors are choosing to balance against the Islamic Republic rather than fall in line behind its leadership. In 2006, Iran's favorability rating in Arab countries stood at nearly 80 percent; today, it is under 30 percent. Like China's neighbors in East Asia, the Gulf states have responded to Iran's belligerence by participating in an emerging regional security arrangement with the United States, which includes advanced conventional weapons sales, missile defenses, intelligence sharing, and joint military exercises, all of which have further isolated Iran.

Of course, the gravest concerns about Iran focus on its nuclear activities. Those fears have led to some of the most egregiously alarmist rhetoric: at a Republican national security debate in November, Romney claimed that an Iranian nuclear weapon is "the greatest threat the world faces." But it remains unclear whether Tehran has even decided to pursue a bomb or has merely decided to develop a turnkey capability. Either way, Iran's leaders have been sufficiently warned that the United States would respond with overwhelming force to the use or transfer of nuclear weapons. Although a nuclear Iran would be troubling to the region, the United States and its allies would be able to contain Tehran and deter its aggression—and the threat to the U.S. homeland would continue to be minimal.

Overblown fears of a nuclear Iran are part of a more generalized American anxiety about the continued potential of nuclear attacks. Obama's National Security Strategy claims that "the American people face no greater or more urgent danger than a terrorist attack with a nuclear weapon." According to the document, "international peace and security is threatened by proliferation that could lead to a nuclear exchange. Indeed, since the end of the Cold War, the risk of a nuclear attack has increased."

If the context is a state-against-state nuclear conflict, the latter assertion is patently false. The demise of the Soviet Union ended the greatest potential for international nuclear conflict. China, with only 72 intercontinental nuclear missiles, is eminently deterrable and not a credible nuclear threat; it has no answer for the United States' second-strike capability and the more than 2,000 nuclear weapons with which the United States could strike China.

In the past decade, Cheney and other one-percenters have frequently warned of the danger posed by loose nukes or uncontrolled fissile material. In fact, the threat of a nuclear device ending up in the hands of a terrorist group has diminished markedly since the early 1990s, when the Soviet Union's nuclear arsenal was dispersed across all of Russia's 11 time zones, all 15 former Soviet republics, and much of eastern Europe. Since then, cooperative U.S.–Russian efforts have resulted in the substantial consolidation of those weapons at far fewer sites and in comprehensive security upgrades at almost all the facilities that still possess nuclear material or warheads, making the possibility of theft or diversion unlikely. Moreover, the lessons learned from securing Russia's nuclear arsenal are now being applied in other countries, under the framework of Obama's April 2010 Nuclear Security Summit, which produced a global plan to secure all nuclear materials within four years. Since then, participants in the plan, including Chile, Mexico, Ukraine, and Vietnam, have fulfilled more than 70 percent of the commitments they made at the summit.

Pakistan represents another potential source of loose nukes. The United States' military strategy in Afghanistan, with its reliance on drone strikes and cross-border raids, has actually contributed to instability in Pakistan, worsened U.S. relations with Islamabad, and potentially increased the possibility of a weapon falling into the wrong hands. Indeed, Pakistani fears of a U.S. raid on its nuclear arsenal have reportedly led Islamabad to disperse its weapons to multiple sites, transporting them in unsecured civilian vehicles. But even in Pakistan, the chances of a terrorist organization procuring a nuclear weapon are infinitesimally small. The U.S. Department of Energy has provided assistance to improve the security of Pakistan's nuclear arsenal, and successive senior U.S. government officials have repeated what former Secretary of Defense Robert Gates said in

January 2010: that the United States is "very comfortable with the security of Pakistan's nuclear weapons."

A more recent bogeyman in national security debates is the threat of so-called cyberwar. Policy-makers and pundits have been warning for more than a decade about an imminent "cyber-Pearl Harbor" or "cyber-9/11." In June 2011, then Deputy Defense Secretary William Lynn said that "bits and bytes can be as threatening as bullets and bombs." And in September 2011, Admiral Mike Mullen, then chairman of the Joint Chiefs of Staff, described cyber attacks as an "existential" threat that "actually can bring us to our knees."

Although the potential vulnerability of private businesses and government agencies to cyber attacks has increased, the alleged threat of cyberwarfare crumbles under scrutiny. No cyber attack has resulted in the loss of a single U.S. citizen's life. Reports of "kinetic-like" cyber attacks, such as one on an Illinois water plant and a North Korean attack on U.S. government servers, have proved baseless. Pentagon networks are attacked thousands of times a day by individuals and foreign intelligence agencies; so, too, are servers in the private sector. But the vast majority of these attacks fail wherever adequate safeguards have been put in place. Certainly, none is even vaguely comparable to Pearl Harbor or 9/11, and most can be offset by common sense prevention and mitigation efforts.

A New Approach

Defenders of the status quo might contend that chronic threat inflation and an overmilitarized foreign policy have not prevented the United States from preserving a high degree of safety and security and therefore are not pressing problems. Others might argue that although the world might not be dangerous now, it could quickly become so if the United States grows too sanguine about global risks and reduces its military strength. Both positions underestimate the costs and risks of the status quo and overestimate the need for the United States to rely on an aggressive military posture driven by outsized fears.

Since the end of the Cold War, most improvements in U.S. security have not depended primarily on the country's massive military, nor have they resulted from the constantly expanding definition of U.S. national security interests. The United States deserves praise for promoting greater international economic interdependence and open markets and, along with a host of international and regional organizations and private actors, more limited credit for improving global public health and assisting in the development of democratic governance. But although U.S. military strength has occasionally contributed to creating a conducive environment for positive change, those improvements were achieved mostly through the work of civilian agencies and nongovernmental actors in the private and non-profit sectors. The record of an overgrown post–Cold War U.S. military is far more mixed. Although some U.S.-led military efforts, such as the NATO intervention in the Balkans, have contributed to safer regional environments, the U.S.-led wars in Afghanistan and Iraq have weakened regional and global security, leading to hundreds of thousands of casualties and refugee crises (according to the Office of the UN High Commissioner for Refugees, 45 percent of all refugees today are fleeing the violence provoked by those two wars). Indeed, overreactions to perceived security threats, mainly from terrorism, have done significant damage to U.S. interests and threaten to weaken the global norms and institutions that helped create and sustain the current era of peace and security. None of this is to suggest that the United States should stop playing a global role; rather, it should play a different role, one that emphasizes soft power over hard power and inexpensive diplomacy and development assistance over expensive military buildups.

Indeed, the most lamentable cost of unceasing threat exaggeration and a focus on military force is that the main global challenges facing the United States today are poorly resourced and given far less attention than "sexier" problems, such as war and terrorism. These include climate change, pandemic diseases, global economic instability, and transnational criminal networks—all of which could serve as catalysts to severe and direct challenges to U.S. security interests. But these concerns are less visceral than alleged threats from terrorism and rogue nuclear states.They require long-term planning and occasionally painful solutions, and they are not constantly hyped by well-financed interest groups. As a result, they are given short shrift in national security discourse and policy making.

To avoid further distorting U.S. foreign policy and to take advantage of today's relative security and stability, policy-makers need to not only respond to a 99 percent world but also solidify it. They should start by strengthening the global architecture of international institutions and norms that can promote U.S. interests and ensure that other countries share the burden of maintaining global peace and security. International institutions such as the UN (and its affiliated agencies, such as the International Atomic Energy Agency), regional organizations (the African Union, the Organization of American States, the European Union, and the Association of Southeast Asian Nations), and international financial institutions can formalize and reinforce norms and rules that regulate state behavior and strengthen global cooperation, provide legitimacy for U.S. diplomatic efforts, and offer access to areas of the world that the United States cannot obtain unilaterally.

American leadership must be commensurate with U.S. interests and the nature of the challenges facing the country. The United States should not take the lead on every issue or assume that every problem in the world demands a U.S. response. In the majority of cases, the United States should "lead from behind"—or from the side, or slightly in the front—but rarely, if ever, by itself. That approach would win broad public support.

According to the Chicago Council on Global Affairs' most recent survey of U.S. public opinion on international affairs, less than 10 percent of Americans want the country to "continue to be the preeminent world leader in solving international problems." The American people have long embraced the idea that their country should not be the world's policeman; for just as long, politicians from both parties have expressed that sentiment as a platitude. The time has come to act on that idea.

If the main challenges in a 99 percent world are transnational in nature and require more development, improved public health, and enhanced law enforcement, then it is crucial that the United States maintain a sharp set of nonmilitary national security tools. American foreign policy needs fewer people who can jump out of airplanes and more who can convene roundtable discussions and lead negotiations. But owing to cuts that began in the 1970s and accelerated significantly during its reorganization in the 1990s, the U.S. Agency for International Development (USAID) has been reduced to a hollow shell of its former self. In 1990, the agency had 3,500 permanent employees. Today, it has just over 2,000 staffers, and the vast majority of its budget is distributed via contractors and nongovernmental organizations. Meanwhile, with 30,000 employees and a $50 billion budget, the State Department's resources pale in comparison to those of the Pentagon, which has more than 1.6 million employees and a budget of more than $600 billion. More resources and attention must be devoted to all elements of nonmilitary state power—not only USAID and the State Department but also the Millennium Challenge Corporation, the National Endowment for Democracy, and a host of multilateral institutions that deal with the underlying causes of localized instability and ameliorate their effects at a relatively low cost. As U.S. General John Allen recently noted, "In many respects, USAID's efforts can do as much—over the long term—to prevent conflict as the deterrent effect of a carrier strike group or a marine expeditionary force." Allen ought to know: He commands the 100,000 U.S. troops fighting in Afghanistan.

Upgrading the United States' national security toolbox will require reducing the size of its armed forces. In an era of relative peace and security, the U.S. military should not be the primary prism through which the country sees the world. As a fungible tool that can back up coercive threats, the U.S. military is certainly an important element of national power. However, it contributes very little to lasting solutions for 99 percent problems. And the Pentagon's enormous budget not only wastes precious resources; it also warps national security thinking and policy making. Since the military controls the overwhelming share of the resources within the national security system, policy-makers tend to perceive all challenges through the distorting lens of the armed forces and respond accordingly. This tendency is one reason the U.S. military is so big. But it is also a case of the tail wagging the dog: the vast size of the military is a major reason every challenge is seen as a threat.

More than 60 years of U.S. diplomatic and military efforts have helped create a world that is freer and more secure. In the process, the United States has fostered a global environment that bolsters U.S. interests and generally accepts U.S. power and influence. The result is a world far less dangerous than ever before. The United States, in other words, has won. Now, it needs a national security strategy and an approach to foreign policy that reflect that reality.

79

"National Insecurity: Just How Safe Is the United States?"

PAUL D. MILLER

Micah Zenko and Michael Cohen ("Clear and Present Safety," March/April 2012) argue that "the world that the United States inhabits today is a remarkably safe and secure place." The country faces no "existential" threats, great-power war is unlikely, democracy and prosperity have spread, public health has improved, and few international challenges place American lives at risk." In light of these developments, they argue, the United States is safer today than it was during the Cold War.

The biggest problem with this argument is the authors' narrow definition of what constitutes a threat to the United States: a situation that poses existential danger or causes immediate bodily harm or death to U.S. citizens. This threshold is shortsighted and unrealistically high. If the same framework were applied to the twentieth century, then the outbreak of World War I and the German invasion of Poland in 1939 would not have been considered threats to the United States. But U.S. strategists then understood that because their country was a primary beneficiary and architect of the world order, any threat to that order was a threat to the United States itself.

So, too, today, there are major challenges to the global order that endanger U.S. national security, whether or not they pose existential or immediate threats. They include nuclear-armed autocracies, the spread of failed states and the rogue actors who operate from within them, and a global Islamist insurgency. Because the United States has lacked a single superpower rival and has focused chiefly on defeating terrorism and al Qaeda, it has underestimated the danger from all three.

Atomic Autocracies

The single greatest danger to global peace and to the United States is the presence of powerful autocratic states armed with nuclear weapons. Democracies, including those with atomic weapons, generally share a similar view of the world as the United States and thus rarely pose threats. Unlike during the Cold War, when the United States faced only two nuclear-armed autocratic adversaries, China and the Soviet Union, now it may soon face five: Russia, China, North Korea, Pakistan (if civilian rule there proves illusory and relations with the United States continue to deteriorate), and Iran (should its nuclear program succeed). All these countries are at least uncooperative with, if not outright hostile to, the United States. Zenko and Cohen are sanguine about the prospects of great-power war, but a militarized crisis involving nuclear weapons states is more likely today than at any time in decades.

Russia no longer purports to lead a global revolution aimed at overthrowing all capitalist states, but its contemporary ideology—authoritarian, nationalist, and quasi-imperialist—threatens Europe's future freedom and territorial integrity. The Kremlin was likely involved in the 2007 cyberattack on Estonia, a NATO ally, which targeted the country's parliament, government offices, banks, and media organizations. And in 2008, Russia invaded Georgia, which had been promised future NATO membership. As his popularity at home erodes, Russian president Vladimir Putin may once again allow a foreign crisis to escalate to win nationalist plaudits. For more than seventy years, U.S. policy-makers have equated Europe's security with that of the United States; it is that notion that gives credence to the U.S. presidential candidate Mitt Romney's contention that Russia is the United States' "number one geopolitical foe."

Meanwhile, China clearly poses a greater danger today than it did during the Cold War. The United States and China fought to a bloody stalemate in the Korean War and remained enemies for the next two decades. But crippled by economic weakness, in 1972, Beijing embraced diplomatic relations with Washington. China's power quickly grew as the country liberalized its economy and modernized its military. It is now a formidable power, armed with nuclear weapons and a ballistic missile capability, and it has invested heavily in building up its navy. Its increasing strength has emboldened it to aim more overtly at reducing U.S. influence in East Asia. The same Pentagon report that Zenko and Cohen cite to calm fears about China also notes that "Beijing is developing capabilities intended to deter, delay, or deny possible U.S. support for [Taiwan] in the event of conflict. The balance of cross-Strait military forces and capabilities continues to shift in the mainland's favor." And because U.S. relations with China are prone to regular crises, as during the Tiananmen Square massacre in 1989 and after the accidental U.S. bombing of the Chinese embassy in

Belgrade in 1999, a militarized confrontation with China is more likely today than at any point since the Korean War.

In addition to Russia and China, there may soon be up to three more nuclear autocracies hostile to the United States. North Korea and Iran are avowed enemies of the United States, and distrust between the United States and Pakistan has never been higher. Pakistan and North Korea tested nuclear weapons in 1998 and 2006, respectively, and Iran will almost certainly develop a nuclear weapons capability. (To be sure, a U.S. or Israeli strike could temporarily delay Iran's nuclear program. But such an attack might well provoke a wider war, illustrating once again the dangers rife in the international system.) All three states have invested in medium and long-range ballistic missiles that could hit U.S. allies, and despite the failure of North Korea's recent missile test, the United States must take seriously the possibility that any of these three states could soon be able to produce missiles that could hit the U.S. homeland. North Korea's nuclear arsenal is very small, and it would take years for Iran to accumulate a nuclear stockpile. But these states need only a few dozen warheads to pose a major challenge to the United States. What is more, because of their technological and conventional military weakness, North Korea, Pakistan, and Iran have sought to level the playing field by investing in unconventional capabilities or terrorist organizations, the latter of which could be used to carry out a nuclear attack.

Pirates and Terrorists and Hackers, Oh My!

In addition to traditional threats from nuclear-armed states, the United States faces dangers that it rarely or never encountered during the Cold War: failed states and the rogue actors that operate from within them, including pirates, organized criminals, drug cartels, terrorists, and hackers.

Zenko and Cohen correctly observe that these kinds of dangers have often been overblown. There is nothing new about pirates and terrorists, for example, and they have rarely been more than a nuisance. What is new are their increased capabilities to threaten the United States, capabilities magnified by technology, globalization, and state failure. Travel and communication have become easier, weapons technology is more lethal, and the growing number of lawless countries offers fertile ground for rogue actors to operate with impunity. At the same time, U.S. border, port, and infrastructure security has not kept up. Osama bin Laden harmed the United States in a way that would have been inconceivable for a non-state actor during the Cold War. And even if the United States can prevent another 9/11 or a crippling cyberattack, the aggregate effects of an increasing number of malicious nonstate actors include rising costs of sustaining the global liberal order, a slowing of the gears of normal diplomatic and economic exchange, and heightened public suspicion and uncertainty.

The most dangerous threat of this type is what the counterterrorism scholar David Kilcullen has called the global Islamist insurgency, consisting of campaigns by Islamist militants to erase Western influence in Muslim countries, replace secular governments in the Muslim world with hard-line regimes, and eventually establish the supremacy of their brand of Islam across the world. Some Islamist organizations have directly targeted the United States and its allies in dozens of attacks and attempted attacks over the last decade. Of these groups, Zenko and Cohen mention only al Qaeda, and they repeat the Obama administration's claim that the organization is near defeat. The claim is wrong, but even if it were true, it would be irrelevant: al Qaeda is only the most famous member of a global network of Islamist movements that oppose the United States. If such a movement were to take over any country, that country would offer a safe haven to al Qaeda and its affiliates, allies, and copycats. But if one were to seize control of Pakistan, with its nuclear weapons, or Saudi Arabia, with its oil wealth, the resulting regime would pose a major threat to global order.

During the Cold War, the only phenomenon comparable to today's proliferation of militant Islamist groups was the Soviet Union's sponsorship of communist insurgencies around the world. But the Islamist movements will likely prove more resilient and more dangerous, because they are decentralized, their ideology does not rest on the fate of one particular regime, and globalization has made it easier for them to operate across borders. There is also a greater risk that Islamists will acquire and use weapons of mass destruction, since they are not accountable to one particular sponsoring power that can be deterred.

Zenko and Cohen are right that the United States needs to reinvest in its tools of soft power, including diplomacy and development. But those tools are not enough to cope with hostile states armed with nuclear weapons, rogue actors empowered by technology and globalization, and a worldwide network of insurgent and terrorist groups that claim they have a religious duty to oppose the United States. In attempting to manage or defeat these threats, the United States cannot afford to reduce its military capabilities, as Zenko and Cohen advise. Waiting to respond to dangers only once they threaten the very existence of the United States, instead of trying to prevent them from materializing, is an irresponsible basis for foreign policy.

Zenko and Cohen Reply

In "Clear and Present Safety," we argued that the world the United States inhabits is a remarkably safe place and that politicians, government officials, military leaders, and national security experts regularly overstate threats to the country. In this regard, Paul Miller's response is not an indictment of our thesis but a strong corroboration.

Indeed, it is hard to imagine a better example than Miller's response of how potential challenges are regularly inflated in order to justify an ever-expanding national security infrastructure. Miller relies on alarmist, worst-case scenarios and dubious historical analogies. Even worse, he displays a surprising lack of confidence in the United States' ability to respond to emerging challenges.

In Miller's dystopian worldview, every potential provocation, no matter how far-fetched, both is likely to occur and requires a militarized response.

Take his approving citation of Mitt Romney's claim that Russia is the United States' "number one geopolitical foe." Despite his halfhearted caveat that Moscow "no longer purports to lead a global revolution aimed at overthrowing all capitalist states," he still seems to believe that a demographically, economically, and diplomatically weakened Russia is bent on imperiling European security. Reading Miller, one would never know that a massive, 28-state military alliance, comprising 3.5 million active-duty troops and close to 2,500 nuclear weapons, exists in large measure to block Russian revanchist aspirations.

Miller claims that "Iran will almost certainly develop a nuclear weapons capability." That Tehran has decided to pursue nuclear weapons, however, would be news to the Office of the Director of National Intelligence and the International Atomic Energy Agency, neither of which shares Miller's view. Even if Iran did go nuclear, there is little reason to believe that the United States could not contain it, just as it has contained numerous other nuclear powers since World War II.

Miller speaks of a global Islamist insurgency and warns grimly that Pakistan or Saudi Arabia could be taken over by radical Islamists. These are doomsday scenarios that have been batted around for the last decade but are unlikely to materialize. This is largely because jihadist groups have shown little actual ability to seize power in these countries, where they enjoy paltry public support.

Miller also argues that any authoritarian state with a few dozen nuclear weapons would "pose a major challenge to the United States." But he omits the motive for these countries to seek nuclear weapons—defense—and discounts the United States' own formidable nuclear deterrent. In the past ten years, North Korea has developed a small nuclear capability, but that acquisition has had little effect on the strategic balance on the Korean Peninsula because of U.S. conventional and nuclear weapons deployed in the theater. What is striking, although Miller mentions the failure of Pyongyang's most recent missile test, it seems to have had no impact on his dire prediction of a North Korean missile threat to the U.S. homeland.

Finally, Miller argues that "a militarized confrontation with China is more likely today than at any point since the Korean War." His basis for this assertion is that U.S.–Chinese relations "are prone to regular crises," such as those during the Tiananmen Square massacre in 1989 and following the accidental U.S. bombing of the Chinese embassy in Belgrade in 1999. But neither of these disputes, nor the many others that have occasionally roiled relations in the last two decades, came even close to provoking a militarized conflict.

The reason is both obvious and important: neither Washington nor Beijing has any interest in going to war, and both have employed formal and informal mechanisms to prevent conflict, including the exchange of special envoys, the Military Maritime Consultative Agreement, and mutual membership in the World Trade Organization. Indeed, the U.S.–Chinese relationship has been defined by intermittent cooperation and mutual interest on such issues as curbing nuclear proliferation, enhancing global economic stability, and even putting in place sanctions against Iran. And as the recent incident involving the Chinese dissident Chen Guangcheng demonstrated, neither side wants to openly confront the other. So it remains a mystery why Miller contends that "China clearly poses a greater danger today than it did during the Cold War."

Just as Miller overestimates the threats the United States faces, he also underestimates Washington's ability to respond to those challenges. The United States has unmatched intelligence and analytic capabilities and some of the world's best diplomats. Its defense budget is larger than those of the next fourteen countries combined and supports over 2,000 operationally deployed nuclear weapons; an air force of some 4,000 aircraft; a navy with 285 ships, including 11 carrier strike groups; and 770,000 active-duty soldiers and marines. Even if this budget is reduced by eight percent over the coming decade, as Congress agreed it would be as part of the 2011 debt-limit agreement, the men and women who protect the country and its interests will still be able to meet the challenges that may come their way.

Miller is right to conclude that "waiting to respond to dangers only once they threaten the very existence of the United States, instead of trying to prevent them from materializing, is an irresponsible basis for foreign policy." He is wrong, however, about the appropriate strategy and tools to stop these dangers from emerging.

Our essay argued that the United States must rebalance its national security strategy to de-emphasize the currently dominant role of the military. Miller apparently disagrees, but he never explains why a highly militarized foreign policy can best manage the challenges facing the United States in the twenty-first century. Even if one accepts Miller's darkly pessimistic worldview, it does not necessarily follow that the armed forces should take the lead in carrying out U.S. foreign policy. If the past decade demonstrated anything, it is that military action is not always the best way to keep the country safe and healthy, especially if one wants to avoid the accompanying cost in blood and treasure and a host of unintended consequences.

Since September 11, 2001, U.S. defense spending has grown by 70 percent, intelligence spending by 100 percent, and homeland security spending by 300 percent. Miller implicitly argues that these efforts have not made the United States any safer. But he refuses to provide any alternatives, sticking to the same pattern of overreaction that our essay addressed. It makes little sense to continue to base U.S. national security strategy on such a flawed premise and yet expect a different outcome.

DISCUSSION QUESTIONS:

1. Is it useful to think in terms of probabilities—a 1 percent chance of an attack, or even a 0.01 percent chance—when the consequences of a nuclear detonation in New York, or Tokyo, or London would be unthinkable? Shouldn't governments do everything possible to prevent this? Or is it necessary to think in terms of costs and benefits?

2. What do you see as the major security threats to the United States over the next ten years? Twenty-five years? Fifty years? Is there any realistic way of assessing such threats, and planning how to deal with them?

Appendix

Marbury v. Madison (1803)

The power of judicial review—the authority of the federal courts to determine the constitutionality of state and federal legislative acts—was established early in the nation's history in the case of Marbury v. Madison *(1803). While the doctrine of judicial review is now firmly entrenched in the American judicial process, the outcome of* Marbury *was by no means a sure thing. The doctrine had been outlined in* The Federalist, *No. 78, and had been relied on implicitly in earlier, lower federal court cases, but there were certainly sentiments among some of the Founders to suggest that only Congress ought to be able to judge the constitutionality of its acts.*

The facts leading up to the decision in Marbury v. Madison *tell an intensely political story. Efforts to reform the federal judiciary had been ongoing with the Federalist administration of President Adams. Following the defeat of the Federalist party in 1800 and the election of Thomas Jefferson as president, the Federalist Congress passed an act reforming the judiciary. The act gave the outgoing president Adams authority to appoint several Federalist justices of the peace before Jefferson's term as president began. This would have enabled the Federalist party to retain a large measure of power.*

Marbury was appointed to be a justice of the peace by President Adams, but his commission, signed by the president and sealed by the secretary of state, without which he could not assume office, was not delivered to him before President Jefferson took office March 4, 1803. Jefferson refused to order James Madison, his secretary of state, to deliver the commission. Marbury, in turn, filed an action in the U.S. Supreme Court seeking an order—called a writ of mandamus—directing the secretary of state to compel the delivery of the commission.

The Constitution grants the Supreme Court original jurisdiction in only a limited number of cases—those involving ambassadors, public ministers, and those in which a state is a party; in the remaining cases, the Court has authority only as an appellate court. When it acts according to its original jurisdiction, the Court exercises initial authority over a controversy, just like a trial court, as distinguished from the more limited authority it exercises when a case is presented as an appeal from a lower court's decision.

In 1789, Congress passed legislation setting up the federal courts, called the Judiciary Act of 1789. That legislation gave the Supreme Court the original authority to "issue writs of mandamus in cases warranted by the principles and usage of law. . . ." Thus, the ultimate question in Marbury v. Madison *was whether Congress could, by statute, enlarge the original jurisdiction of the Court.*

The Court first considered whether Marbury's appointment was complete— and therefore irrevocable—before Jefferson took office. Under the law, the appointment was deemed complete when the president signed the commission and the secretary of state sealed it; the appointment was a completed fact at that time, and was not dependent upon delivery. Therefore, the Court found that Marbury was entitled to his commission. The Court then decided that by withholding the commission, Secretary of State Madison was violating Marbury's legal rights. The remaining question was whether the Supreme Court could issue an order compelling the delivery of the commission.

Chief Justice Marshall delivered the opinion of the Court.

. . . It is, then, the opinion of the Court,

1st. That by signing the commission of Mr. Marbury, the President of the United States appointed him a justice of peace for the county of Washington, in the District of Columbia; and that the seal of the United States, affixed thereto by the Secretary of State, is conclusive testimony of the verity of the signature, and of the completion of the appointment, and that the appointment conferred on him a legal right to the office for the space of five years.

2d. That, having this legal title to the office, he has a consequent right to the commission; a refusal to deliver which is a plain violation of that right, for which the laws of his country afford him a remedy.

It remains to be inquired whether,

3d. He is entitled to the remedy for which he applies. This depends on,

1st. The nature of the writ applied for; and,

2d. The power of this court.

* * *

This . . . is a plain case for a mandamus, either to deliver the commission, or a copy of it from the record; and it only remains to be inquired,

Whether it can issue from this court.

The act to establish the judicial courts of the United States authorizes the Supreme Court "to issue writs of mandamus in cases warranted by the principles and usages of law, to any courts appointed, or persons holding office, under the authority of the United States."

The Secretary of State, being a person holding an office under the authority of the United States, is precisely within the letter of the description, and if this court is not authorized to issue a writ of mandamus to such an officer, it must be because the law is unconstitutional, and therefore absolutely incapable of conferring the authority, and assigning the duties which its words purport to confer and assign.

The constitution vests the whole judicial power of the United States in one Supreme Court, and such inferior courts as congress shall, from time to time, ordain and establish. This power is expressly extended to all cases arising under the laws of the United States; and, consequently, in some form, may be exercised over the present case; because the right claimed is given by a law of the United States.

In the distribution of this power it is declared that "the Supreme Court shall have original jurisdiction in all cases affecting ambassadors, other public ministers and consuls, and those in which a state shall be a party. In all other cases, the Supreme Court shall have appellate jurisdiction."

* * *

To enable this court, then, to issue a mandamus, it must be shown to be an exercise of appellate jurisdiction, or to be necessary to enable them to exercise appellate jurisdiction.

* * *

It is the essential criterion of appellate jurisdiction, that it revises and corrects the proceedings in a cause already instituted, and does not create that cause. . . . [Y]et to issue such a writ to an officer for the delivery of a paper, is in effect the same as to sustain an original action for that paper, and, therefore, seems not to belong to appellate, but to original jurisdiction.

The authority, therefore, given to the Supreme Court, by the act establishing the judicial courts of the United States, to issue writs of mandamus to public officers, appears not to be warranted by the constitution; and it becomes necessary to inquire whether a jurisdiction so conferred can be exercised.

The question, whether an act, repugnant to the constitution, can become the law of the land, is a question deeply interesting to the United States; but, happily, not of an intricacy proportioned to its interest. It seems only necessary to recognize certain principles, supposed to have been long and well established, to decide it.

That the people have an original right to establish, for their future government, such principles, as, in their opinion, shall most conduce to their own happiness is the basis on which the whole American fabric has been erected. The exercise of this original right is a very great exertion; nor can it, nor ought it, to be frequently repeated. The principles, therefore, so established, are deemed fundamental. And as the authority from which they proceed is supreme, and can seldom act, they are designed to be permanent.

This original and supreme will organizes the government, and assigns to different departments their respective powers. It may either stop here, or establish certain limits not to be transcended by those departments.

The government of the United States is of the latter description. The powers of the legislature are defined and limited; and that those limits may not be mistaken, or forgotten, the constitution is written. To what purpose are powers limited, and to what purpose is that limitation committed to writing, if these limits may, at any time, be passed by those intended to be restrained? The distinction between a government with limited and unlimited powers is abolished, if those limits do not confine the persons on whom they are imposed, and if acts prohibited and acts allowed, are of equal obligation. It is a proposition too plain to be contested, that the constitution controls any legislative act repugnant to it; or, that the legislature may alter the constitution by an ordinary act.

Between these alternatives there is no middle ground. The constitution is either a superior paramount law, unchangeable by ordinary means, or it is on a level with ordinary legislative acts, and, like other acts, is alterable when the legislature shall please to alter it.

If the former part of the alternative be true, then a legislative act contrary to the constitution is not law: if the latter part be true, then written constitutions are absurd attempts, on the part of the people, to limit a power in its own nature illimitable.

Certainly all those who have framed written constitutions contemplate them as forming the fundamental and paramount law of the nation, and, consequently, the theory of every such government must be, that an act of the legislature, repugnant to the constitution, is void.

This theory is essentially attached to a written constitution, and, is consequently, to be considered, by this court, as one of the fundamental principles of our society. It is not therefore to be lost sight of in the further consideration of this subject.

If an act of the legislature, repugnant to the constitution, is void, does it, notwithstanding its invalidity, bind the courts, and oblige them to give it effect? Or, in other words, though it be not law, does it constitute a rule as operative as if it was a law? This would be to overthrow in fact what was established in theory; and would seem, at first view, an absurdity too gross to be insisted on.

* * *

It is emphatically the province and duty of the judicial department to say what the law is. Those who apply the rule to particular cases, must of necessity expound and interpret that rule. If two laws conflict with each other, the courts must decide on the operation of each.

So if a law be in opposition to the constitution; if both the law and the constitution apply to a particular case, so that the court must either decide that case conformably to the law, disregarding the constitution; or conformably to the constitution, disregarding the law; the court must determine which of these conflicting rules governs the case. This is of the very essence of judicial duty.

If, then, the courts are to regard the constitution, and the constitution is superior to any ordinary act of the legislature, the constitution, and not such ordinary act, must govern the case to which they both apply.

Those, then, who controvert the principle that the constitution is to be considered, in court, as a paramount law, are reduced to the necessity of maintaining that courts must close their eyes on the constitution, and see only the law.

This doctrine would subvert the very foundation of all written constitutions. It would declare that an act which, according to the principles and theory of our government, is entirely void, is yet, in practice, completely obligatory. It would declare that if the legislature shall do what is expressly forbidden, such act, notwithstanding the express prohibition, is in reality effectual. It would be giving to the legislature a practical and real omnipotence, with the same breath which professes to restrict their powers within narrow limits. It is prescribing limits, and declaring that those limits may be passed at pleasure.

That it thus reduces to nothing what we have deemed the greatest improvement on political institutions, a written constitution, would of itself be sufficient, in America, where written constitutions have been viewed with so much reverence, for rejecting the construction. But the peculiar expressions of the constitution of the United States furnish additional arguments in favour of its rejection.

The judicial power of the United States is extended to all cases arising under the constitution.

Could it be the intention of those who gave this power, to say that in using it the constitution should not be looked into? That a case arising under the constitution should be decided without examining the instrument under which it arises?

This is too extravagant to be maintained.

In some cases, then, the constitution must be looked into by the judges.

. . . [I]t is apparent, that the framers of the constitution contemplated that instrument as a rule for the government of courts, as well as of the legislature.

Why otherwise does it direct the judges to take an oath to support it? This oath certainly applies in an especial manner, to their conduct in their official character. How immoral to impose it on them, if they were to be used as the instruments, and the knowing instruments, for violating what they swear to support!

The oath of office, too, imposed by the legislature, is completely demonstrative of the legislative opinion on this subject.

*   *   *

Why does a judge swear to discharge his duties agreeably to the constitution of the United States, if that constitution forms no rule for his government? If it is closed upon him, and cannot be inspected by him?

If such be the real state of things, this is worse than solemn mockery. To prescribe, or to take this oath, becomes equally a crime.

It is also not entirely unworthy of observation, that in declaring what shall be the supreme law of the land, the constitution itself is first mentioned; and not the laws of the United States generally, but those only which shall be made in pursuance of the constitution, have that rank.

Thus, the particular phraseology of the constitution of the United States confirms and strengthens the principle, supposed to be essential to all written constitutions, that a law repugnant to the constitution is void; and that courts, as well as other departments, are bound by that instrument.

McCulloch v. Maryland (1819)

Early in the nation's history, the U.S. Supreme Court interpreted the powers of the national government expansively. The first Supreme Court case to directly address the scope of federal authority under the Constitution was McCulloch v. Maryland *(1819). The facts were straightforward: Congress created the Bank of the United States—to the dismay of many states that viewed the creation of a national bank as a threat to the operation of banks within their own state borders. As a result, when a branch of the Bank of the United States was opened in Maryland, that state attempted to limit the bank's ability to do business under a law that imposed taxes on all banks not chartered by the state.*

In an opinion authored by Chief Justice Marshall, the Court considered two questions: whether Congress had the authority to create a national bank; and whether Maryland could in turn tax it. Marshall's answer to these two questions defends an expansive theory of implied powers for the national government and propounds the principle of national supremacy with an eloquence rarely found in judicial decisions.

CHIEF JUSTICE JOHN MARSHALL delivered the opinion of the Court.

The first question made in the cause is, has Congress power to incorporate a bank? The power now contested was exercised by the first Congress elected under the present constitution. The bill for incorporating the Bank of the United States did not steal upon an unsuspecting legislature, and pass unobserved. Its principle was completely understood, and was opposed with equal zeal and ability. . . . In discussing this question, the counsel for the state of Maryland have deemed it of some importance, in the construction of the constitution, to consider that instrument not as emanating from the people, but as the act of sovereign and independent states. The powers of the general government, it has been said, are delegated by the states, who alone are truly sovereign; and must be exercised in subordination to the states, who alone possess supreme dominion. . . . No political dreamer was ever wild enough to think of breaking down the lines which separate the states, and of compounding the American people into one common mass. Of consequence, when they act, they act in their states. But the measures they adopt do not, on that account, cease to be the measures of the people themselves, or become the measures of the state governments.

From these conventions the constitution derives its whole authority. The government proceeds directly from the people; is "ordained and established" in the name of the people; and is declared to be ordained, "in order to form a more perfect union, establish justice, insure domestic tranquility, and secure the blessings of liberty to themselves and to their posterity." The assent of the states, in their sovereign capacity, is implied in calling a convention, and thus submitting that instrument to the people. But the people were at perfect liberty to accept or reject it; and their act was final. It required not the affirmance, and could not be negatived, by the state governments. The constitution, when thus adopted, was of complete obligation, and bound the state sovereignties.

The government of the Union, then (whatever may be the influence of this fact on the case), is, emphatically, and truly, a government of the people. In form and in substance it emanates from them. Its powers are granted by them, and are to be exercised directly on them, and for their benefit.

This government is acknowledged by all to be one of enumerated powers. The principle, that it can exercise only the powers granted to it, is now universally admitted. But the question respecting the extent of the powers actually granted, is perpetually arising, and will probably continue to arise, as long as our system shall exist. The government of the United States though limited in its powers, is supreme; and its laws, when made in pursuance of the constitution, form the supreme law of the land, "anything in the constitution or laws of any state to the contrary notwithstanding."

* * *

A constitution, to contain an accurate detail of all the subdivisions of which its great powers will admit, and of all the means by which they may be carried into execution, would partake of the prolixity of a legal code, and could scarcely be embraced by the human mind. It would probably never be understood by the public. Its nature, therefore, requires, that only its great outlines should be marked, its important objects designated, and the minor ingredients which compose those objects be deduced from the nature of the objects themselves. . . . in considering this question, then, we must never forget, that it is a constitution we are expounding.

Although, among the enumerated powers of government, we do not find the word "bank" or "incorporation," we find the great powers to lay and collect taxes; to borrow money; to regulate commerce; to declare and conduct a war; and to raise and support armies and navies. The sword and the purse, all the external relations, and no inconsiderable portion of the industry of the nation, are entrusted to its government. . . . [I]t may with great reason be contended, that a government, entrusted with such ample powers, on the due execution of which the happiness and prosperity of the nation so vitally depends, must also be entrusted with ample means for their execution. The power being given, it is the interest of the nation to facilitate its execution. It can never be their interest, and cannot be presumed to have been their intention, to clog and embarrass its execution by withholding the most appropriate means. . . . It is, then, the subject of fair inquiry, how far such means may be employed.

The government which has a right to do an act, and has imposed on it the duty of performing that act, must, according to the dictates of reason, be allowed to select the means.

* * *

But the constitution of the United States has not left the right of Congress to employ the necessary means, for the execution of the powers conferred on the government, to general reasoning. To its enumeration of powers is added that of making "all laws which shall be necessary and proper, for carrying into execution the foregoing powers, and all other powers vested by this constitution, in the government of the United States, or in any department [or officer] thereof."

The counsel for the state of Maryland have urged various arguments, to prove that this clause . . . is really restrictive of the general right, which might otherwise be implied, of selecting means for executing the enumerated powers.

. . . [Maryland argues that] Congress is not empowered by it to make all laws, which may have relation to the powers conferred on the government, but such only as may be "necessary and proper" for carrying them into execution. The word "necessary" is considered as controlling the whole sentence, and as limiting the right to pass laws for the execution of the granted powers, to such as are indispensable, and without which the power would be nugatory. That it excludes the choice of means, and leaves to Congress, in each case, that only which is most direct and simple.

Is it true, that this is the sense in which the word "necessary" is always used? . . . We think it does not. If reference be had to its use, in the common affairs of the world, or in approved authors, we find that it frequently imports no more than that one thing is convenient, or useful, or essential to another. To employ the means necessary to an end, is generally understood as employing any means calculated to produce the end, and not as being confined to those single means, without which the end would be entirely unattainable.

Let this be done in the case under consideration. The subject is the execution of those great powers on which the welfare of a nation essentially depends. It must have been the intention of those who gave these powers, to insure, as far as human prudence could insure, their beneficial execution. This could not be done by confiding the choice of means to such narrow limits as not to leave it in the power of Congress to adopt any which might be appropriate, and which were conducive to the end. This provision is made in a constitution intended to endure for ages to come, and consequently, to be adapted to the various crises of human affairs. To have prescribed the means by which government should, in all future time, execute its powers, would have been to change, entirely, the character of the instrument, and give it the properties of a legal code. It would have been an unwise attempt to provide, by immutable rules, for exigencies which, if foreseen at all, must have been seen dimly, and which can be best provided for as they occur. To have declared that the best means shall not be used, but those alone without which the power given would be nugatory, would have been to deprive the legislature of the capacity to avail itself of experience, to exercise its reason, and to accommodate its legislation to circumstances. If we apply this principle of construction to any of the powers of the government, we shall find it so pernicious in its operation that we shall be compelled to discard it.

*   *   *

We admit, as all must admit, that the powers of the government are limited, and that its limits are not to be transcended. But we think the sound construction of the constitution must allow to the national legislature that discretion, with respect to the means by which the powers it confers are to be carried into execution, which will enable that body to perform the high duties assigned to it, in the manner most beneficial to the people. Let the end be legitimate, let it be within the scope of the constitution, and all means which are appropriate, which are plainly adapted to that end, which are not prohibited, but consist with the letter and spirit of the constitution, are constitutional.

*   *   *

It being the opinion of the court that the act incorporating the bank is constitutional, and that the power of establishing a branch in the state of Maryland might be properly exercised by the bank itself, we proceed to inquire: Whether the state of Maryland may, without violating the constitution, tax that branch?

That the power of taxation is one of vital importance; that it is retained by the states; that it is not abridged by the grant of a similar power to the government of the Union; that it is to be concurrently exercised by the two governments; are truths which have never been denied. But, such is the paramount character of the constitution that its capacity to withdraw any subject from the action of even this power, is admitted. . . . [T]he paramount character [of the Constitution] would seem to restrain, as it certainly may restrain, a state from such other exercise of this power as is in its nature incompatible with, and repugnant to, the constitutional laws of the Union. A law, absolutely repugnant to another, as entirely repeals that other as if express terms of repeal were used.

* * *

This great principle is, that the constitution and the laws made in pursuance thereof are supreme; that they control the constitution and laws of the respective states, and cannot be controlled by them. From this, which may be almost termed an axiom, other propositions are adduced as corollaries, on the truth or error of which, and on their application to this case, the cause has been supposed to depend. These are, 1st. That a power to create implies a power to preserve. 2d. That a power to destroy, if wielded by a different hand, is hostile to, and incompatible with, these powers to create and to preserve. 3d. That where this repugnance exists, that authority which is supreme must control, not yield to that over which it is supreme.

. . . [T]axation is said to be an absolute power, which acknowledges no other limits than those expressly prescribed in the constitution, and like sovereign powers of every other description, is trusted to the discretion of those who use it. But the very terms of this argument admit that the sovereignty of the state, in the article of taxation itself, is subordinate to, and may be controlled by the constitution of the United States. How far it has been controlled by that instrument must be a question of construction. In making this construction, no principle not declared can be admissible, which would defeat the legitimate operations of a supreme government.

* * *

All subjects over which the sovereign power of a state extends, are objects of taxation; but those over which it does not extend, are, upon the soundest principles, exempt from taxation. . . . The sovereignty of a state extends to everything which exists by its own authority, or is introduced by its permission; but does it extend to those means which are employed by Congress to carry into execution—powers conferred on that body by the people of the United States? We think it demonstrable that it does not. Those powers are not given by the people of a single state. They are given by the people of the United States, to a government whose laws, made in pursuance of the constitution, are declared to be supreme. Consequently, the people of a single state cannot confer a sovereignty which will extend over them.

If we apply the principle for which the state of Maryland contends, to the constitution generally, we shall find it capable of changing totally the character of that instrument. We shall find it capable of arresting all the measures of the government, and of prostrating it at the foot of the states. The American people have declared their constitution, and the laws made in pursuance thereof, to be supreme; but this principle would transfer the supremacy, in fact, to the states. If the controlling power of the states be established; if their supremacy as to taxation be acknowledged; what is to restrain their exercising this control in any shape they may please to give it? Their sovereignty is not confined to taxation. That is not the only mode in which it might be displayed. The question is, in truth, a question of supremacy; and if the right of the states to tax the means employed by the general government be conceded, the declaration that the constitution, and the laws made in pursuance thereof, shall be the supreme law of the land, is empty and unmeaning declamation.

*   *   *

We are unanimously of opinion, that the law passed by the legislature of Maryland, imposing a tax on the Bank of the United States, is unconstitutional and void. This opinion does not deprive the states of any resources which they originally possessed. It does not extend to a tax paid by the real property of the bank, in common with other real property within the state, nor to a tax imposed on the interest which the citizens of Maryland may hold in this institution, in common with other property of the same description throughout the state. But this is a tax on the operations of the bank, and is, consequently, a tax on the operation of an instrument employed by the government of the Union to carry its powers into execution. Such a tax must be unconstitutional.

Reversed.

Barron v. Baltimore (1833)

The declaration made in Barron v. Baltimore *(1833) that citizenship had a dual aspect—state and national—set the terms of the Supreme Court's interpretation of the Bill of Rights for nearly a century. The reasoning of the case proved persuasive even after the adoption of the Fourteenth Amendment, as the federal courts refused to extend the protections of the federal Constitution to citizens aggrieved by the actions of state or local governments.*

Barron brought suit in a federal court claiming that the city of Baltimore had appropriated his property for a public purpose without paying him just compensation. He asserted that the Fifth Amendment to the Constitution operated as a constraint upon both state and federal governments.

CHIEF JUSTICE JOHN MARSHALL delivered the opinion of the Court.

. . . The question presented is, we think, of great importance, but not of much difficulty. The constitution was ordained and established by the people of the United States for themselves, for their own government, and not for the government of the individual states. Each state established a constitution for itself, and in that constitution, provided such limitations and restrictions on the powers of its particular government, as its judgment dictated. The people of the United States framed such a government for the United States as they supposed best adapted to their situation and best calculated to promote their interests. The powers they conferred on this government were to be exercised by itself; and the limitations on power, if expressed in general terms, are naturally, and, we think, necessarily, applicable to the government created by the instrument. They are limitations of power granted in the instrument itself; not of distinct governments, framed by different persons and for different purposes.

If these propositions be correct, the fifth amendment must be understood as restraining the power of the general government, not as applicable to the states. In their several constitutions, they have imposed such restrictions on their respective governments, as their own wisdom suggested; such as they deemed most proper for themselves. It is a subject on which they judge exclusively, and with which others interfere no further than they are supposed to have a common interest.

*   *   *

Had the people of the several states, or any of them, required changes in their constitutions; had they required additional safe-guards to liberty from the apprehended encroachments of their particular governments; the remedy was in their own hands, and could have been applied by themselves. A convention could have been assembled by the discontented state, and the required improvements could have been made by itself.

. . . Had Congress engaged in the extraordinary occupation of improving the constitutions of the several states, by affording the people additional protection from the exercise of power by their own governments, in matters which concerned themselves alone, they would have declared this purpose in plain and intelligible language.

But it is universally understood, it is a part of the history of the day, that the great revolution which established the constitution of the United States, was not effected without immense opposition. Serious fears were extensively entertained, that those powers which the patriot statesmen, who then watched over the interests of our country, deemed essential to union, and to the attainment of those unvaluable objects for which union was sought, might be exercised in a manner dangerous to liberty. In almost every convention by which the constitution was adopted, amendments to guard against the abuse of power were recommended. These amendments demanded security against the apprehended encroachments of the general government—not against those of the local governments. In compliance with a sentiment thus generally expressed, to quiet fears thus extensively entertained, amendments were proposed by the required majority in congress, and adopted by the states. These amendments contain no expression indicating an intention to apply them to the state governments. This court cannot so apply them.

We are of opinion, that the provision in the fifth amendment to the constitution, declaring that private property shall not be taken for public use, without just compensation, is intended solely as a limitation on the exercise of power by the government of the United States, and is not applicable to the legislation of the states. We are, therefore, of opinion, that there is no repugnancy between the several acts of the general assembly of Maryland, given in evidence by the defendants at the trial of this cause, in the court of that state, and the constitution of the United States. This court, therefore, has no jurisdiction of the cause, and it is dismissed.

This cause came on to be heard, on the transcript of the record from the court of appeals for the western shore of the state of Maryland, and was argued by counsel: On consideration whereof, it is the opinion of this court, that there is no repugnancy between the several acts of the general assembly of Maryland, given in evidence by the defendants at the trial of this cause in the court of that state, and the constitution of the United States; whereupon, it is ordered and adjudged by this court, that this writ of error be and the same is hereby dismissed, for the want of jurisdiction.

Roe v. Wade (1973)

One of the most significant changes in constitutional interpretation in the last three decades has been the Court's willingness to look beyond the explicit language of the Bill of Rights to find unenumerated rights, such as the right to privacy. In discovering such rights, the Court has engaged in what is known as substantive due process analysis—defining and articulating fundamental rights—distinct from its efforts to define the scope of procedural due process, when it decides what procedures the state and federal governments must follow to be fair in their treatment of citizens. The Court's move into the substantive due process area has generated much of the political discussion over the proper role of the Court in constitutional interpretation.

The case that has been the focal point for this debate is Roe v. Wade, *the 1973 case that held that a woman's right to privacy protected her decision to have an abortion. The right to privacy in matters relating to contraception and childbearing had been recognized in the 1965 decision of* Griswold v. Connecticut, *and was extended in subsequent decisions culminating in* Roe. *The theoretical issue of concern here relates back to the incorporation issue: Should the Supreme Court be able to prohibit the states not only from violating the express guarantees contained in the Bill of Rights, but its implied guarantees as well?*

Texas law prohibited abortions except for "the purpose of saving the life of the mother." The plaintiff challenged the constitutionality of the statute, claiming that it infringed upon her substantive due process right to privacy.

JUSTICE BLACKMUN delivered the opinion of the Court.

. . . [We] forthwith acknowledge our awareness of the sensitive and emotional nature of the abortion controversy, of the vigorous opposing views, and the deep and seemingly absolute convictions that the subject inspires. One's philosophy, one's experiences, one's exposure to the raw edges of human existence, one's religious training, one's attitudes toward life and family and their values, and the moral standards one establishes and seeks to observe, are all likely to affect one's thinking [about] abortion. In addition, population growth, pollution, poverty, and racial overtones tend to complicate and not to simplify the problem. Our task, of course, is to resolve the issue by constitutional measurement, free of emotion and of predilection. We seek earnestly to do this, and, because we do, we have inquired into, and in this opinion place some emphasis upon, medical and medical-legal history and what that history reveals about man's attitudes toward the abortion procedure over the centuries.

* * *

[The Court here reviewed ancient and contemporary attitudes toward abortion, observing that restrictive laws date primarily from the late nineteenth century. The Court also reviewed the possible state interests in restricting abortions, including discouraging illicit sexual conduct, limiting access to a hazardous medical procedure, and the states' general interests in protecting fetal life. The Court addressed only the third interest as a current legitimate interest of the state.]

. . . The Constitution does not explicitly mention any right of privacy. In a line of decisions, however, . . . the Court has recognized that a right of personal privacy, or a guarantee of certain areas or zones of privacy, does exist under the Constitution. . . . This right of privacy, whether it be founded in the Fourteenth Amendment's concept of personal liberty and restrictions upon state action, as we feel it is, or, as the District Court determined, in the Ninth Amendment's reservation of rights to the people, is broad enough to encompass a woman's decision whether or not to terminate her pregnancy. The detriment that the State would impose upon the pregnant woman by denying this choice altogether is apparent. Specific and direct harm medically diagnosable even in early pregnancy may be involved. Maternity, or additional offspring, may force upon the woman a distressful life and future. Psychological harm may be imminent. Mental and physical health may be taxed by child care. There is also the distress, for all concerned, associated with the unwanted child, and there is the problem of bringing a child into a family already unable, psychologically and otherwise, to care for it. In other cases, as in this one, the additional difficulties and continuing stigma of unwed motherhood may be involved. All these are factors the woman and her responsible physician necessarily will consider in consultation.

On the basis of elements such as these, appellants and some amici [friends of the Court] argue that the woman's right is absolute and that she is entitled to terminate her pregnancy at whatever time, in whatever way, and for whatever reason she alone chooses. With this we do not agree. Appellants' arguments that Texas either has no valid interest at all in regulating the abortion decision, or no interest strong enough to support any limitation upon the woman's sole determination, is unpersuasive. The Court's decisions recognizing a right of privacy also acknowledge that some state regulation in areas protected by that right is appropriate. As noted above, a State may properly assert important interests in safeguarding health, in maintaining medical standards, and in protecting potential life. At some point in pregnancy, these respective interests become sufficiently compelling to sustain regulation of the factors that govern the abortion decision. The privacy right involved, therefore, cannot be said to be absolute. In fact, it is not clear to us that the claim asserted by some amici that one has an unlimited right to do with one's body as one pleases bears a close relationship to the right of privacy previously articulated in the Court's decisions.

* * *

We therefore conclude that the right of personal privacy includes the abortion decision, but that this right is not unqualified and must be considered against state interests in regulation.

Where certain "fundamental rights" are involved, the Court has held that regulation limiting these rights may be justified only by a "compelling state interest," and that legislative enactments must be narrowly drawn to express only the legitimate state interests at stake.

. . . The District Court held that the appellee failed to meet his burden of demonstrating that the Texas statute's infringement upon Roe's rights was necessary to support a compelling state interest. . . . Appellee argues that the State's determination to recognize and protect prenatal life from and after conception constitutes a compelling state interest. As noted above, we do not agree fully with either formulation.

The appellee and certain amici argue that the fetus is a "person" within the language and meaning of the Fourteenth Amendment. In support of this they outline at length and in detail the well-known facts of fetal development. If this suggestion of personhood is established, the appellant's case, of course, collapses, for the fetus' right to life is then guaranteed specifically by the Amendment. The appellant conceded as much on reargument. On the other hand, the appellee conceded on reargument that no case could be cited that holds that a fetus is a person within the meaning of the Fourteenth Amendment.

The Constitution does not define "person" in so many words. Section 1 of the Fourteenth Amendment contains three references to "person." The first, in defining "citizens," speaks of "persons born or naturalized in the United States." The word also appears both in the Due Process Clause and in the Equal Protection Clause. "Person" is used in other places in the Constitution. . . . But in nearly all these instances, the use of the word is such that it has application only postnatally. None indicates, with any assurance, that it has any possible pre-natal application.

All this, together with our observation, that throughout the major portion of the 19th century prevailing legal abortion practices were far freer than they are today, persuades us that the word "person," as used in the Fourteenth Amendment, does not include the unborn.

. . . The pregnant woman cannot be isolated in her privacy. She carries an embryo and, later, a fetus, if one accepts the medical definitions of the developing young in the human uterus. . . . The situation therefore is inherently different from marital intimacy, or bedroom possession of obscene material, or marriage, or procreation, or education, with which [earlier cases defining the right to privacy] were concerned. As we have intimated above, it is reasonable and appropriate for a State to decide that at some point in time another interest, that of health of the mother or that of potential human life, becomes significantly involved. The woman's privacy is no longer sole and any right of privacy she possesses must be measured accordingly.

Texas urges that, apart from the Fourteenth Amendment, life begins at conception and is present throughout pregnancy, and that, therefore, the State has a compelling interest in protecting that life from and after conception. We need not resolve the difficult question of when life begins. When those trained in the respective disciplines of medicine, philosophy, and theology are unable to arrive at any consensus, the judiciary, at this point in the development of man's knowledge, is not in a position to speculate as to the answer.

. . . In view of all this, we do not agree that, by adopting one theory of life, Texas may override the rights of the pregnant woman that are at stake. We repeat, however, that the State does have an important and legitimate interest in preserving and protecting the health of the pregnant woman, whether she be a resident of the State or a nonresident who seeks medical consultation and treatment there, and that it has still *another* important and legitimate interest in protecting the potentiality of human life. These interests are separate and distinct. Each grows in substantiality as the woman approaches term and, at a point during pregnancy, each becomes "compelling."

With respect to the State's important and legitimate interest in the health of the mother, the "compelling" point, in the light of present medical knowledge, is at approximately the end of the first trimester. This is so because of the now established medical fact . . . that until the end of the first trimester mortality in abortion is less than mortality in normal child-birth. It follows that, from and after this point, a State may regulate the abortion procedure to the extent that the regulation reasonably relates to the preservation and protection of maternal health. Examples of permissible state regulation in this area are requirements as to the qualifications of the person who is to perform the abortion; as to the licensure of that person; as to the facility in which the procedure is to be performed, that is, whether it must be a hospital or may be a clinic or some other place of less-than-hospital status; as to the licensing of the facility; and the like.

This means, on the other hand, that, for the period of pregnancy prior to this "compelling" point, the attending physician, in consultation with his patient, is free to determine, without regulation by the State, that in his medical judgment the patient's pregnancy should be terminated. If that decision is reached, the judgment may be effectuated by an abortion free of interference by the State.

With respect to the State's important and legitimate interest in potential life, the "compelling" point is at viability. This is so because the fetus then presumably has the capability of meaningful life outside the mother's womb. State regulation protective of fetal life after viability thus has both logical and biological justifications. If the State is interested in protecting fetal life after viability, it may go so far as to proscribe abortion during that period except when it is necessary to preserve the life or health of the mother.

Measured against these standards, the Texas Penal Code, in restricting legal abortions to those "procured or attempted by medical advice for the purpose of saving the life of the mother," sweeps too broadly. The statute makes no distinction between abortions performed early in pregnancy and those performed later, and it limits to a single reason, "saving" the mother's life, the legal justification for the procedure. The statute, therefore, cannot survive the constitutional attack made upon it here.

*   *   *

Reversed.

Brown v. Board of Education of Topeka, Kansas (1954)

Brown v. Board of Education *(1954) was a momentous opinion, invalidating the system of segregation that had been established under* Plessy v. Ferguson *(1896). However, the constitutional pronouncement only marked the beginning of the struggle for racial equality, as federal courts got more and more deeply involved in trying to prod recalcitrant state and local governments into taking steps to end racial inequalities.*

The Brown case involved appeals from several states. In each case, the plaintiffs had been denied access to public schools designated only for white children under a variety of state laws. They challenged the Plessy v. Ferguson *(1896) "separate but equal" doctrine, contending that segregated schools were by their nature unequal.*

Chief Justice Warren first discussed the history of the Fourteenth Amendment's equal protection clause, finding it too inconclusive to be of assistance in determining how the Fourteenth Amendment should be applied to the question of public education.

CHIEF JUSTICE WARREN writing for the majority.

. . . The doctrine of "separate but equal" did not make its appearance in this Court until 1896, in the case of *Plessy v. Ferguson,* involving not education but transportation. American courts have since labored with the doctrine for over a half a century. In this Court, there have been six cases involving the "separate but equal" doctrine in the field of public education.

* * *

In the instant cases, [the question of the application of the separate but equal doctrine to public education] is directly presented. Here, . . . there are findings below that the Negro and white schools involved have been equalized, or are being equalized, with respect to buildings, curricula, qualifications and salaries of teachers, and other "tangible" factors. Our decision, therefore, cannot turn on merely a comparison of these tangible factors in the Negro and white schools involved in each of the cases. We must look instead to the effect of segregation itself on public education.

In approaching this problem, we cannot turn the clock back to 1868 when the [Fourteenth] Amendment was adopted, or even to 1896 when *Plessy v. Ferguson* was written. We must consider public education in the light of its full development and its present place in American life throughout the Nation. Only in this way can it be determined if segregation in public schools deprives these plaintiffs of the equal protection of the laws.

Today, education is perhaps the most important function of state and local governments. Compulsory school attendance laws and the great expenditures for education both demonstrate our recognition of the importance of education to our democratic society. It is required in the performance of our most basic responsibilities, even service in the armed forces. It is the very foundation of good citizenship. Today it is a principal instrument in awakening the child to cultural values, in preparing him for later professional training, and in helping him to adjust normally to his environment. In these days, it is doubtful that any child may reasonably be expected to succeed in life if he is denied the opportunity of an education. Such an opportunity, where the state has undertaken to provide it, is a right which must be made available to all on equal terms.

We come then to the question presented: Does segregation of children in public schools solely on the basis of race, even though the physical facilities and other "tangible" factors may be equal, deprive the children of the minority group of equal educational opportunities? We believe that it does.

In *Sweatt v. Painter*, in finding that a segregated law school for Negroes could not provide them equal educational opportunities, this Court relied in large part on "those qualities which are incapable of objective measurement but which make for greatness in a law school." In *McLaurin v. Oklahoma State Regents*, the Court, in requiring that a Negro admitted to a white graduate school be treated like all other students, again resorted to intangible considerations: ". . . his ability to study, to engage in discussions and exchange views with other students, and, in general, to learn his profession." Such considerations apply with added force to children in grade and high schools. To separate them from others of similar age and qualifications solely because of their race generates a feeling of inferiority as to their status in the community that may affect their hearts and minds in a way unlikely ever to be undone. The effect of this separation on their educational opportunities was well stated by a finding in the Kansas case by a court which nevertheless felt compelled to rule against the Negro plaintiffs:

"Segregation of white and colored children in public schools has a detrimental effect upon the colored children. The impact is greater when it has the sanction of the law; for the policy of separating the races is usually interpreted as denoting the inferiority of the Negro group. A sense of inferiority affects the motivation of a child to learn. Segregation with the sanction of law, therefore, has a tendency to [retard] the educational and mental development of Negro children and to deprive them of some of the benefits they would receive in a racial[ly] integrated school system." Whatever may have been the extent of psychological knowledge at the time of *Plessy v. Ferguson*, this finding is amply supported by modern authority. Any language in *Plessy v. Ferguson* contrary to this finding is rejected.

We conclude that in the field of public education the doctrine of "separate but equal" has no place. Separate educational facilities are inherently unequal. Therefore, we hold that the plaintiffs and others similarly situated for whom the actions have been brought are, by reason of the segregation complained of, deprived of the equal protection of the laws guaranteed by the Fourteenth Amendment. This disposition makes unnecessary any discussion whether such segregation also violates the Due Process Clause of the Fourteenth Amendment.

Because these are class actions, because of the wide applicability of this decision, and because of the great variety of local conditions, the formulation of decrees in these cases presents problems of considerable complexity. On reargument, the consideration of appropriate relief was necessarily subordinated to the primary question—the constitutionality of segregation in public education. We have now announced that such segregation is a denial of the equal protection of the laws.

United States v. Nixon (1974)

The Supreme Court has had few occasions to rule on the constitutional limits of executive authority. The Court is understandably reluctant to articulate the boundaries of presidential and legislative power, given the Court's own somewhat ambiguous institutional authority. In the case that follows, however, the Court looked at one of the ways in which the Constitution circumscribes the exercise of presidential prerogative.

United States v. Nixon *(1974) involves claims to executive authority. President Richard Nixon was implicated in a conspiracy to cover up a burglary of the Democratic Party Headquarters at the Watergate Hotel in Washington, D.C., during the 1972 re-election campaign. The Special Prosecutor assigned to investigate the break-in and file appropriate criminal charges asked the trial court to order the President to disclose a number of documents and tapes related to the cover-up in order to determine the scope of the President's involvement. The President produced edited versions of some of the materials, but refused to comply with most of the trial court's order, asserting that he was entitled to withhold the information under a claim of "executive privilege."*

CHIEF JUSTICE BURGER delivered the opinion of the Court.

In the District Court, the President's counsel argued that the court lacked jurisdiction to issue the subpoena because the matter was an intra-branch dispute between a subordinate and superior officer of the Executive Branch and hence not subject to judicial resolution. That argument has been renewed in this Court with emphasis on the contention that the dispute does not present a "case" or "controversy" which can be adjudicated in the federal courts. The President's counsel argues that the federal courts should not intrude into areas committed to the other branches of Government. He views the present dispute as essentially a "jurisdictional" dispute within the Executive Branch which he analogizes to a dispute between two congressional committees. Since the Executive Branch has exclusive authority and absolute discretion to decide whether to prosecute a case, it is contended that a President's decision is final in determining what evidence is to be used in a given criminal case.

. . . Although his counsel concedes the President has delegated certain specific powers to the Special Prosecutor, he has not "waived nor delegated to the Special Prosecutor the President's duty to claim privilege as to all materials which fall within the President's inherent authority to refuse to disclose to any executive officer." The Special Prosecutor's demand for the items therefore presents, in the view of the President's counsel, a political question since it involves a "textually demonstrable" grant of power under Art. II. . . .

The demands of and the resistance to the subpoena present an obvious controversy in the ordinary sense, but that alone is not sufficient to meet constitutional standards. In the constitutional sense, controversy means more than disagreement and conflict; rather it means the kind of controversy courts traditionally resolve. Here at issue is the production or nonproduction of specified evidence deemed by the Special Prosecutor to be relevant and admissible in a pending criminal case. It is sought by one official of the Government within the scope of his express authority; it is resisted by the Chief Executive on the ground of his duty to preserve the confidentiality of the communications of the President. Whatever the correct answer on the merits, these issues are "of a type which are traditionally justiciable."

* * *

. . . We turn to the claim that the subpoena should be quashed because it demands "confidential conversations between a President and his close advisors that it would be inconsistent with the public interest to produce." The first contention is a broad claim that the separation of powers doctrine precludes judicial review of a President's claim of privilege. The second contention is that if he does not prevail on the claim of absolute privilege, the court should hold as a matter of constitutional law that the privilege prevails over the subpoena. . . .

* * *

[*The Court discussed its authority to interpret the Constitution, concluding that it had full power to adjudicate a claim of executive privilege.*]

In support of his claim of absolute privilege, the President's counsel urges two grounds one of which is common to all governments and one of which is peculiar to our system of separation of powers. The first ground is the valid need for protection of communications between high government officials and those who advise and assist them in the performance of their manifold duties; the importance of this confidentiality is too plain to require further discussion. Human experience teaches that those who expect public dissemination of their remarks may well temper candor with a concern for appearances and for their own interests to the detriment of the decisionmaking process. Whatever the nature of the privilege of confidentiality of presidential communications in the exercise of Art. II powers the privilege can be said to derive from the supremacy of each branch within its own assigned area of constitutional duties. Certain powers and privileges flow from the nature of enumerated powers; the protection of the confidentiality of presidential communications has similar constitutional underpinnings.

The second ground asserted by the President's counsel in support of the claim of absolute privilege rests on the doctrine of separation of powers. Here it is argued that the independence of the Executive Branch within its own sphere, insulates a president from a judicial subpoena in an ongoing criminal prosecution, and thereby protects confidential presidential communications.

However, neither the doctrine of separation of powers, nor the need for confidentiality of high level communications, without more, can sustain an absolute, unqualified presidential privilege of immunity from judicial process under all circumstances. The President's need for complete candor and objectivity from advisers calls for great deference from the courts. However, when the privilege depends solely on the broad, undifferentiated claim of public interest in the confidentiality of such conversations, a confrontation with other values arises. Absent a claim of need to protect military, diplomatic or sensitive national security secrets, we find it difficult to accept the argument that even the very important interest in confidentiality of presidential communications is significantly diminished by production of such material for *in camera* inspection with all the protection that a district court will be obliged to provide.

The impediment that an absolute, unqualified privilege would place in the way of the primary constitutional duty of the judicial branch to do justice in criminal prosecutions would plainly conflict with the function of the courts under Art. III. In designing the structure of our Government and dividing and allocating the sovereign power among three coequal branches, the Framers of the Constitution sought to provide a comprehensive system, but the separate powers were not intended to operate with absolute independence. To read the Art. II powers of the President as providing an absolute privilege as against a subpoena essential to enforcement of criminal statutes on no more than a generalized claim of the public interest in confidentiality of nonmilitary and nondiplomatic discussions would upset the constitutional balance of "a workable government" and gravely impair the role of the court under Art. III.

Since we conclude that the legitimate needs of the judicial process may outweigh presidential privilege, it is necessary to resolve those competing interests in a manner that preserves the essential functions of each branch. The rights and indeed the duty to resolve that question does not free the judiciary from according high respect to the representations made on behalf of the President. The expectation of a President to the confidentiality of his conversations and correspondence, like the claim of confidentiality of judicial deliberations, for example, has all the values to which we accord deference for the privacy of all citizens and added to those values the necessity for protection of the public interest in his responsibilities against the inroads of such a privilege on the fair administration of criminal justice. The interest in preserving confidentiality is weighty indeed and entitled to great respect. However we cannot conclude that advisers will be moved to temper the candor of their remarks by the infrequent occasions of disclosure because of the possibility that such conversations will be called for in the context of a criminal prosecution.

On the other hand, the allowance of the privilege to withhold evidence that is demonstrably relevant in a criminal trial would cut deeply into the guarantee of due process of law and gravely impair the basic function of the courts. A President's acknowleged need for confidentiality in the communications of his office is general in nature, whereas the constitutional need for production of relevant evidence in a criminal proceeding is specific and central to the fair adjudication of a particular criminal case in the administration of justice. Without access to specific facts a criminal prosecution may be totally frustrated. The President's broad interest in confidentiality of communications will not be vitiated by disclosure of a limited number of conversations preliminarily shown to have some bearing on the pending criminal cases.

We conclude that when the ground for asserting privilege as to subpoenaed materials sought for use in a criminal trial is based only on the generalized interest in confidentiality, it cannot prevail over the fundamental demand of due process of law in the fair administration of criminal justice. The generalized assertion of privilege must yield to the demonstrated, specific need for evidence in a pending criminal trial.

*   *   *

In this case the President challenges a subpoena served on him as a third party requiring the production of materials for use in a criminal prosecution on the claim that he has a privilege against disclosure of confidential communications. He does not place his claim of privilege on the ground they are military or diplomatic secrets. As to these areas of Art. II duties the courts have traditionally shown the utmost deference to presidential responsibilities. No case of the Court, however, has extended this high degree of deference to a President's generalized interest in confidentiality. Nowhere in the Constitution, as we have noted earlier, is there any explicit reference to a privilege of confidentiality; yet to the extent this interest relates to the effective discharge of a President's powers, it is constitutionally based.

*   *   *

[*The Court distinguished this case from cases involving claims against the president while acting in an official capacity.*]

Mr. Chief Justice Marshall sitting as a trial judge in the *Burr* case was extraordinarily careful to point out that: "[I]n no case of this kind would a Court be required to proceed against the President as against an ordinary individual." Marshall's statement cannot be read to mean in any sense that a President is above the law, but relates to the singularly unique role under Art. II of a President's communications and activities, related to the performance of duties under that Article. Moreover, a President's communications and activities encompass a vastly wider range of sensitive material than would be true of any "ordinary individual." It is therefore necessary in the public interest to afford presidential confidentiality the greatest protection consistent with the fair administration of justice. The need for confidentiality even as to idle conversations with associates in which casual reference might be made concerning political leaders within the country or foreign statesmen is too obvious to call for further treatment. We have no doubt that the District Judge will at all times accord the presidential records that high degree of deference suggested in *United States v. Burr,* and will discharge his responsibility to see to it that until released to the Special Prosecutor no *in camera* [private] material is revealed to anyone. This burden applies with even greater force to excised material; once the decision is made to excise, the material is restored to its privileged status and should be returned under seal to its lawful custodian.

Affirmed.

United States v. Lopez (1995)

How far does Congress's authority extend with respect to the states? Since the 1930s, when a liberalization of Supreme Court doctrine cleared the way for an expansion of federal authority, Congress has relied on a loose interpretation of the Commerce Clause to justify extensive involvement in state and local affairs. (Congress can also shape what states do, for example, by placing conditions upon the receipt of federal funds). In 1990, Congress enacted the Gun-Free School Zones Act, making possession of a firearm in designated school zones a federal crime. When Alfonso Lopez, Jr., was convicted of violating the act, his lawyer challenged the constitutionality of the law, arguing that it was "invalid as beyond the power of Congress under the Commerce Clause." In a striking reversal of interpretation, the Supreme Court agreed and declared the law invalid, holding that banning guns in schools was too far removed from any effect on interstate commerce to warrant federal intervention. Critics of the decision argued that the Court's reasoning might invalidate a large body of federal crime and drug legislation that relies on the connection between regulated activity and interstate commerce. Sup-

*porters maintained that the decision marked a new era of judicial respect for fed-
eralism and state autonomy.*

CHIEF JUSTICE REHNQUIST delivered the opinion of the Court.

In the Gun-Free School Zones Act of 1990, Congress made it a federal
offense "for any individual knowingly to possess a firearm at a place that
the individual knows, or has reasonable cause to believe, is a school zone."
The Act neither regulates a commercial activity nor contains a requirement that the possession be connected in any way to interstate commerce.
We hold that the Act exceeds the authority of "Congress to regulate Commerce . . . among the several States. . . ." (U.S. Constitution Art. I, 8, cl. 3).

On March 10, 1992, respondent, who was then a 12th-grade student,
arrived at Edison High School in San Antonio, Texas, carrying a concealed
.38 caliber handgun and five bullets. Acting upon an anonymous tip,
school authorities confronted respondent, who admitted that he was carrying the weapon. He was arrested and charged under Texas law with firearm possession on school premises. The next day, the state charges were
dismissed after federal agents charged respondent by complaint with
violating the Gun-Free School Zones Act of 1990.

A federal grand jury indicted respondent on one count of knowing
possession of a firearm at a school zone, in violation of 922(q) [the relevant
section of the Act of 1990]. Respondent moved to dismiss his federal
indictment on the ground that 922(q) "is unconstitutional as it is beyond
the power of Congress to legislate control over our public schools." The
District Court denied the motion, concluding that 922(q) "is a constitutional exercise of Congress' well-defined power to regulate activities in
and affecting commerce, and the 'business' of elementary, middle and
high schools . . . affects interstate commerce." Respondent waived his right
to a jury trial. The District Court conducted a bench trial, found him guilty
of violating 922(q), and sentenced him to six months' imprisonment and
two years' supervised release.

On appeal, respondent challenged his conviction based on his claim
that 922(q) exceeded Congress' power to legislate under the Commerce
Clause. The Court of Appeals for the Fifth Circuit agreed and reversed
respondent's conviction. It held that, in light of what it characterized as
insufficient congressional findings and legislative history, "in the full
reach of its terms, is invalid as beyond the power of Congress under the
Commerce Clause." Because of the importance of the issue, we granted
certiorari and we now affirm.

We start with first principles. The Constitution creates a Federal Government of enumerated powers. As James Madison wrote, "[t]he powers
delegated by the proposed Constitution to the federal government are
few and defined. Those which are to remain in the State governments are

numerous and indefinite." (*The Federalist*, No. 45). This constitutionally mandated division of authority was adopted by the Framers to ensure protection of our fundamental liberties. Just as the separation and independence of the coordinate branches of the Federal Government serves to prevent the accumulation of excessive power in any one branch, a healthy balance of power between the States and the Federal Government will reduce the risk of tyranny and abuse from either front.

[*For the next several pages Rehnquist reviews the evolution of interpretations of the Commerce Clause, starting with* Gibbons v. Ogden *(1824). This case established the relatively narrow interpretation of the Commerce Clause in which the Court prevented* states *from interfering with interstate commerce. Very rarely did cases concern Congress's power. The 1887 Interstate Commerce Act and the 1890 Sherman Antitrust Act expanded Congress's power to regulate intrastate commerce "where the interstate and intrastate aspects of commerce were so mingled together that full regulation of interstate commerce required incidental regulation of intrastate commerce," arguing that the Commerce Clause authorized such regulation. Several New Deal era cases,* NLRB v. Jones & Laughlin Steel Corp. *(1937),* United States v. Darby *(1941), and* Wickard v. Filburn *(1942) broadened the interpretation of the Commerce Clause.*]

Jones & Laughlin Steel, Darby, and *Wickard* ushered in an era of Commerce Clause jurisprudence that greatly expanded the previously defined authority of Congress under that Clause. In part, this was a recognition of the great changes that had occurred in the way business was carried on in this country. Enterprises that had once been local or at most regional in nature had become national in scope. But the doctrinal change also reflected a view that earlier Commerce Clause cases artificially had constrained the authority of Congress to regulate interstate commerce.

But even these modern-era precedents which have expanded congressional power under the Commerce Clause confirm that this power is subject to outer limits. In *Jones & Laughlin Steel*, the Court warned that the scope of the interstate commerce power "must be considered in the light of our dual system of government and may not be extended so as to embrace effects upon interstate commerce so indirect and remote that to embrace them, in view of our complex society, would effectually obliterate the distinction between what is national and what is local and create a completely centralized government." Since that time, the Court has heeded that warning and undertaken to decide whether a rational basis existed for concluding that a regulated activity sufficiently affected interstate commerce.

* * *

Consistent with this structure, we have identified three broad categories of activity that Congress may regulate under its commerce power. First, Congress may regulate the use of the channels of interstate com-

merce. Second, Congress is empowered to regulate and protect the instrumentalities of interstate commerce, or persons or things in interstate
commerce, even though the threat may come only from intrastate activities. Finally, Congress' commerce authority includes the power to regulate those activities having a substantial relation to interstate commerce,
those activities that substantially affect interstate commerce.

Within this final category, admittedly, our case law has not been clear
whether an activity must *affect* or *substantially affect* interstate commerce
in order to be within Congress' power to regulate it under the Commerce
Clause. We conclude, consistent with the great weight of our case law, that
the proper test requires an analysis of whether the regulated activity *substantially affects* interstate commerce.

We now turn to consider the power of Congress, in the light of this
framework, to enact 922(q) [The Gun-Free School Zones Act]. The first two
categories of authority may be quickly disposed of: 922(q) is not a regulation of the use of the channels of interstate commerce, nor is it an attempt
to prohibit the interstate transportation of a commodity through the
channels of commerce; nor can 922(q) be justified as a regulation by which
Congress has sought to protect an instrumentality of interstate commerce
or a thing in interstate commerce. Thus, if 922(q) is to be sustained, it must
be under the third category as a regulation of an activity that substantially affects interstate commerce.

First, we have upheld a wide variety of congressional Acts regulating
intrastate economic activity where we have concluded that the activity
substantially affected interstate commerce. Examples include the regulation of intrastate coal mining; intrastate extortionate credit transactions,
restaurants utilizing substantial interstate supplies, inns and hotels catering to interstate guests, and production and consumption of home-grown
wheat. These examples are by no means exhaustive, but the pattern is
clear. Where economic activity substantially affects interstate commerce,
legislation regulating that activity will be sustained.

Even *Wickard*, which is perhaps the most far reaching example of Commerce Clause authority over intrastate activity, involved economic activity in a way that the possession of a gun in a school zone does not. Roscoe
Filburn operated a small farm in Ohio, on which, in the year involved, he
raised 23 acres of wheat. It was his practice to sow winter wheat in the fall,
and after harvesting it in July to sell a portion of the crop, to feed part of it
to poultry and livestock on the farm, to use some in making flour for
home consumption, and to keep the remainder for seeding future crops.
The Secretary of Agriculture assessed a penalty against him under the
Agricultural Adjustment Act of 1938 because he harvested about 12 acres
more wheat than his allotment under the Act permitted. The Act was
designed to regulate the volume of wheat moving in interstate and foreign commerce in order to avoid surpluses and shortages, and concomitant fluctuation in wheat prices, which had previously obtained. The

Court said, in an opinion sustaining the application of the Act to Filburn's activity, "One of the primary purposes of the Act in question was to increase the market price of wheat and to that end to limit the volume thereof that could affect the market. It can hardly be denied that a factor of such volume and variability as home-consumed wheat would have a substantial influence on price and market conditions. This may arise because being in marketable condition such wheat overhangs the market and, if induced by rising prices, tends to flow into the market and check price increases. But if we assume that it is never marketed, it supplies a need of the man who grew it which would otherwise be reflected by purchases in the open market. Home-grown wheat in this sense competes with wheat in commerce" (317 U.S., at 128).

Section 922(q) is a criminal statute that by its terms has nothing to do with *commerce* or any sort of economic enterprise, however broadly one might define those terms. Section 922(q) is not an essential part of a larger regulation of economic activity, in which the regulatory scheme could be undercut unless the intra-state activity were regulated. It cannot, therefore, be sustained under our cases upholding regulations of activities that arise out of or are connected with a commercial transaction, which viewed in the aggregate, substantially affects interstate commerce.

Second, 922(q) contains no jurisdictional element which would ensure, through case-by-case inquiry, that the firearm possession in question affects interstate commerce. . . . 922(q) has no express jurisdictional element which might limit its reach to a discrete set of firearm possessions that additionally have an explicit connection with or effect on interstate commerce.

*   *   *

The Government's essential contention, in fine, is that we may determine here that 922(q) is valid because possession of a firearm in a local school zone does indeed substantially affect interstate commerce. The Government argues that possession of a firearm in a school zone may result in violent crime and that violent crime can be expected to affect the functioning of the national economy in two ways. First, the costs of violent crime are substantial, and, through the mechanism of insurance, those costs are spread throughout the population. Second, violent crime reduces the willingness of individuals to travel to areas within the country that are perceived to be unsafe. The Government also argues that the presence of guns in schools poses a substantial threat to the educational process by threatening the learning environment. A handicapped educational process, in turn, will result in a less productive citizenry. That, in turn, would have an adverse effect on the Nation's economic well-being. As a result, the Government argues that Congress could rationally have concluded that 922(q) substantially affects interstate commerce.

We pause to consider the implications of the Government's arguments. The Government admits, under its "costs of crime" reasoning, that Congress could regulate not only all violent crime, but all activities that might lead to violent crime, regardless of how tenuously they relate to interstate commerce. Similarly, under the Government's "national productivity" reasoning, Congress could regulate any activity that it found was related to the economic productivity of individual citizens: family law (including marriage, divorce, and child custody), for example. Under the theories that the Government presents in support of 922(q), it is difficult to perceive any limitation on federal power, even in areas such as criminal law enforcement or education where States historically have been sovereign. Thus, if we were to accept the Government's arguments, we are hardpressed to posit any activity by an individual that Congress is without power to regulate.

Although Justice Breyer argues that acceptance of the Government's rationales would not authorize a general federal police power, he is unable to identify any activity that the States may regulate but Congress may not. Justice Breyer posits that there might be some limitations on Congress' commerce power such as family law or certain aspects of education. These suggested limitations, when viewed in light of the dissent's expansive analysis, are devoid of substance.

Justice Breyer focuses, for the most part, on the threat that firearm possession in and near schools poses to the educational process and the potential economic consequences flowing from that threat. Specifically, the dissent reasons that (1) gun-related violence is a serious problem; (2) that problem, in turn, has an adverse effect on classroom learning; and (3) that adverse effect on classroom learning, in turn, represents a substantial threat to trade and commerce. This analysis would be equally applicable, if not more so, to subjects such as family law and direct regulation of education.

For instance, if Congress can, pursuant to its Commerce Clause power, regulate activities that adversely affect the learning environment, then, a fortiori, it also can regulate the educational process directly. Congress could determine that a school's curriculum has a "significant" effect on the extent of classroom learning. As a result, Congress could mandate a federal curriculum for local elementary and secondary schools because what is taught in local schools has a significant "effect on classroom learning," and that, in turn, has a substantial effect on interstate commerce.

Justice Breyer rejects our reading of precedent and argues that "Congress . . . could rationally conclude that schools fall on the commercial side of the line." Again, Justice Breyer's rationale lacks any real limits because, depending on the level of generality, any activity can be looked upon as commercial. Under the dissent's rationale, Congress could just as easily look at child rearing as "fall[ing] on the commercial side of the line" because it provides a "valuable service" namely, to equip [children] with the skills they need to survive in life and, more specifically, in the workplace. We do not doubt that Congress has authority under the Commerce

Clause to regulate numerous commercial activities that substantially affect interstate commerce and also affect the educational process. That authority, though broad, does not include the authority to regulate each and every aspect of local schools.

Admittedly, a determination whether an intrastate activity is commercial or noncommercial may in some cases result in legal uncertainty. But, so long as Congress' authority is limited to those powers enumerated in the Constitution, and so long as those enumerated powers are interpreted as having judicially enforceable outer limits, congressional legislation under the Commerce Clause always will engender "legal uncertainty." As Chief Justice Marshall stated in *McCulloch v. Maryland*, (1819), "The [federal] government is acknowledged by all to be one of enumerated powers. The principle, that it can exercise only the powers granted to it . . . is now universally admitted. But the question respecting the extent of the powers actually granted, is perpetually arising, and will probably continue to arise, as long as our system shall exist." The Constitution mandates this uncertainty by withholding from Congress a plenary police power that would authorize enactment of every type of legislation. Congress has operated within this framework of legal uncertainty ever since this Court determined that it was the judiciary's duty "to say what the law is." Any possible benefit from eliminating this "legal uncertainty" would be at the expense of the Constitution's system of enumerated powers.

*   *   *

These are not precise formulations, and in the nature of things they cannot be. But we think they point the way to a correct decision of this case. The possession of a gun in a local school zone is in no sense an economic activity that might, through repetition elsewhere, substantially affect any sort of interstate commerce. Respondent was a local student at a local school; there is no indication that he had recently moved in interstate commerce, and there is no requirement that his possession of the firearm have any concrete tie to interstate commerce.

To uphold the Government's contentions here, we would have to pile inference upon inference in a manner that would bid fair to convert congressional authority under the Commerce Clause to a general police power of the sort retained by the States. Admittedly, some of our prior cases have taken long steps down that road, giving great deference to congressional action. The broad language in these opinions has suggested the possibility of additional expansion, but we decline here to proceed any further. To do so would require us to conclude that the Constitution's enumeration of powers does not presuppose something not enumerated, and that there never will be a distinction between what is truly national and what is truly local. This we are unwilling to do.

For the foregoing reasons the judgment of the Court of Appeals is Affirmed.

The Declaration of Independence

In Congress, July 4, 1776

When in the course of human events, it becomes necessary for one people to dissolve the political bands which have connected them with another, and to assume among the Powers of the earth, the separate and equal station to which the Laws of Nature and of Nature's God entitle them, a decent respect to the opinions of mankind requires that they should declare the causes which impel them to the separation.

We hold these truths to be self-evident, that all men are created equal, that they are endowed by their Creator with certain unalienable rights, that among these are Life, Liberty and the pursuit of Happiness. That to secure these rights, Governments are instituted among Men, deriving their just powers from the consent of the governed. That whenever any Form of Government becomes destructive of these ends, it is the Right of the People to alter or to abolish it, and to institute new Government, laying its foundation on such principles and organizing its powers in such form, as to them shall seem most likely to effect their Safety and Happiness. Prudence, indeed, will dictate that Governments long established should not be changed for light and transient causes; and accordingly all experience hath shown, that mankind are more disposed to suffer, while evils are sufferable, than to right themselves by abolishing the forms to which they are accustomed. But when a long train of abuses and usurpations, pursuing invariably the same Object evinces a design to reduce them under absolute Despotism, it is their right, it is their duty, to throw off such Government, and to provide new Guards for their future security.—Such has been the patient sufferance of these Colonies; and such is now the necessity which constrains them to alter their former Systems of Government. The history of the present King of Great Britain is a history of repeated injuries and usurpations, all having in direct object the establishment of an absolute Tyranny over these States. To prove this, let Facts be submitted to a candid world.

He has refused his Assent to Laws, the most wholesome and necessary for the public good.

He has forbidden his Governors to pass Laws of immediate and pressing importance, unless suspended in their operation till his Assent should be obtained; and when so suspended, he has utterly neglected to attend to them.

He has refused to pass other Laws for the accommodation of large districts of people, unless those people would relinquish the right of Representation in the Legislature, a right inestimable to them and formidable to tyrants only.

He has called together legislative bodies at places unusual, uncomfortable, and distant from the depository of their public Records, for the sole purpose of fatiguing them into compliance with his measures.

He has dissolved Representative Houses repeatedly, for opposing with manly firmness his invasions on the rights of the people.

He has refused for a long time, after such dissolutions, to cause others to be elected; whereby the Legislative powers, incapable of Annihilation, have returned to the People at large for their exercise; the State remaining in the mean time exposed to all the dangers of invasion from without, and convulsions within.

He has endeavoured to prevent the population of these States; for that purpose obstructing the Laws for Naturalization of Foreigners; refusing to pass others to encourage their migrations hither, and raising the conditions of new Appropriations of Lands.

He has obstructed the Administration of Justice, by refusing his Assent to Laws for establishing Judiciary Powers.

He has made Judges dependent on his Will alone, for the tenure of their offices, and the amount and payment of their salaries.

He has erected a multitude of New Offices, and sent hither swarms of Officers to harrass our People, and eat out their substance.

He has kept among us, in times of peace, Standing Armies without the Consent of our legislature.

He has affected to render the Military independent of and superior to the Civil Power.

He has combined with others to subject us to a jurisdiction foreign to our constitution, and unacknowledged by our laws; giving his Assent to their Acts of pretended Legislation:

For quartering large bodies of armed troops among us:

For protecting them, by a mock Trial, from Punishment for any Murders which they should commit on the Inhabitants of these States:

For cutting off our Trade with all parts of the world:

For imposing Taxes on us without our Consent:

For depriving us in many cases, of the benefits of Trial by jury:

For transporting us beyond Seas to be tried for pretended offences:

For abolishing the free System of English Laws in a neighbouring Province, establishing therein an Arbitrary government, and enlarging its Boundaries so as to render it at once an example and fit instrument for introducing the same absolute rule into these Colonies:

For taking away our Charters, abolishing our most valuable Laws, and altering fundamentally the Forms of our Governments:

For suspending our own Legislatures, and declaring themselves invested with Power to legislate for us in all cases whatsoever.

He has abdicated Government here, by declaring us out of his Protection and waging War against us.

He has plundered our seas, ravaged our Coasts, burnt our towns, and destroyed the lives of our people.

He is at this time transporting large armies of foreign mercenaries to compleat the works of death, desolation and tyranny, already begun with circumstances of Cruelty & perfidy scarcely paralleled in the most barbarous ages, and totally unworthy the Head of a civilized nation.

He has constrained our fellow Citizens taken Captive on the high Seas to bear Arms against their Country, to become the executioners of their friends and Brethren, or to fall themselves by their Hands.

He has excited domestic insurrections amongst us, and has endeavored to bring on the inhabitants of our frontiers, the merciless Indian Savages, whose known rule of warfare, is an undistinguished destruction of all ages, sexes, and conditions.

In every stage of these Oppressions we have Petitioned for Redress in the most humble terms: Our repeated Petitions have been answered only by repeated injury. A Prince, whose character is thus marked by every act which may define a Tyrant, is unfit to be the ruler of a free people.

Nor have we been wanting in attention to our British brethren. We have warned them from time to time of attempts by their legislature to extend an unwarrantable jurisdiction over us. We have reminded them of the circumstances of our emigration and settlement here. We have appealed to their native justice and magnanimity, and we have conjured them by the ties of our common kindred to disavow these usurpations, which, would inevitably interrupt our connections and correspondence. They too must have been deaf to the voice of justice and of consanguinity. We must, therefore, acquiesce in the necessity, which denounces our Separation, and hold them, as we hold the rest of mankind, Enemies in War, in Peace Friends.

WE, THEREFORE, the Representatives of the UNITED STATES OF AMERICA, in General Congress, Assembled, appealing to the Supreme Judge of the world for the rectitude of our intentions, do, in the Name, and by Authority of the good People of these Colonies, solemnly publish and declare, That these United Colonies are, and of Right ought to be FREE AND INDEPENDENT STATES; that they are Absolved from all Allegiance to the British Crown, and that all political connection between them and the State of Great Britain, is and ought to be totally dissolved; and that as Free and Independent States, they have full Power to levy War, conclude Peace, contract Alliances, establish Commerce, and to do all other Acts and

Things which Independent States may of right do. And for the support of this Declaration, with a firm reliance on the protection of Divine Providence, we mutually pledge to each other our Lives, our Fortunes and our sacred Honor.

The foregoing Declaration was, by order of Congress, engrossed, and signed by the following members:

John Hancock

NEW HAMPSHIRE
Josiah Bartlett
William Whipple
Matthew Thornton

MASSACHUSETTS BAY
Samuel Adams
John Adams
Robert Treat Paine
Elbridge Gerry

RHODE ISLAND
Stephen Hopkins
William Ellery

CONNECTICUT
Roger Sherman
Samuel Huntington
William Williams
Oliver Wolcott

NEW YORK
William Floyd
Philip Livingston
Francis Lewis
Lewis Morris

NEW JERSEY
Richard Stockton
John Witherspoon
Francis Hopkinson
John Hart
Abraham Clark

PENNSYLVANIA
Robert Morris
Benjamin Rush
Benjamin Franklin
John Morton
George Clymer
James Smith
George Taylor
James Wilson
George Ross

DELAWARE
Caesar Rodney
George Read
Thomas M'Kean

MARYLAND
Samuel Chase
William Paca

Thomas Stone
Charles Carroll,
    of Carrollton

VIRGINIA
George Wythe
Richard Henry Lee
Thomas Jefferson
Benjamin Harrison
Thomas Nelson, Jr.
Francis Lightfoot Lee
Carter Braxton

NORTH CAROLINA
William Hooper
Joseph Hewes
John Penn

SOUTH CAROLINA
Edward Rutledge
Thomas Heyward, Jr.
Thomas Lynch, Jr.
Arthur Middleton

GEORGIA
Button Gwinnett
Lyman Hall
George Walton

Resolved, That copies of the Declaration be sent to the several assemblies, conventions, and committees, or councils of safety, and to the several commanding officers of the continental troops; that it be proclaimed in each of the United States, at the head of the army.

The Federalist, No. 10

James Madison

To the People of the State of New York:

Among the numerous advantages promised by a well-constructed Union, none deserves to be more accurately developed than its tendency to break and control the violence of faction. The friend of popular governments never finds himself so much alarmed for their character and fate, as when he contemplates their propensity to this dangerous vice. He will not fail, therefore, to set a due value on any plan which, without violating the principles to which he is attached, provides a proper cure for it. The instability, injustice, and confusion introduced into the public councils, have, in truth, been the mortal diseases under which popular governments have everywhere perished; as they continue to be the favorite and fruitful topics from which the adversaries to liberty derive their most specious declamations. The valuable improvements made by the American constitutions on the popular models, both ancient and modern, cannot certainly be too much admired; but it would be an unwarrantable partiality, to contend that they have as effectually obviated the danger on this side, as was wished and expected. Complaints are everywhere heard from our most considerate and virtuous citizens, equally the friends of public and private faith, and of public and personal liberty, that our governments are too unstable; that the public good is disregarded in the conflicts of rival parties; and that measures are too often decided, not according to the rules of justice and the rights of the minor party, but by the superior force of an interested and overbearing majority. However anxiously we may wish that these complaints had no foundation, the evidence of known facts will not permit us to deny that they are in some degree true. It will be found, indeed, on a candid review of our situation, that some of the distresses under which we labor have been erroneously charged on the operation of our governments; but it will be found, at the same time, that other causes will not alone account for many of our heaviest misfortunes; and, particularly, for that prevailing and increasing distrust of public engagements, and alarm for private rights, which are echoed from one end of the continent to the other. These must be chiefly, if not wholly, effects of the unsteadiness and injustice with which a factious spirit has tainted our public administrations.

By a faction, I understand a number of citizens, whether amounting to a majority or minority of the whole, who are united and actuated by some common impulse of passion, or of interest, adverse to the rights of other citizens, or to the permanent and aggregate interests of the community.

There are two methods of curing the mischiefs of faction: the one, by removing its causes; the other, by controlling its effects.

There are again two methods of removing the causes of faction: the one, by destroying the liberty which is essential to its existence; the other, by giving to every citizen the same opinions, the same passions, and the same interests.

It could never be more truly said than of the first remedy, that it is worse than the disease. Liberty is to faction what air is to fire, an aliment without which it instantly expires. But it could not be less folly to abolish liberty, which is essential to political life, because it nourishes faction, than it would be to wish the annihilation of air, which is essential to animal life, because it imparts to fire its destructive agency.

The second expedient is as impracticable as the first would be unwise. As long as the reason of man continues fallible, and he is at liberty to exercise it, different opinions will be formed. As long as the connection subsits between his reason and his self-love, his opinions and his passions will have a reciprocal influence on each other; and the former will be objects to which the latter will attach themselves. The diversity in the faculties of men, from which the rights of property originate, is not less an insuperable obstacle to a uniformity of interests. The protection of these faculties is the first object of government. From the protection of different and unequal faculties of acquiring property, the possession of different degrees and kinds of property immediately results; and from the influence of these on the sentiments and views of the respective proprietors, ensues a division of the society into different interests and parties.

The latent causes of faction are thus sown in the nature of man; and we see them everywhere brought into different degrees of activity, according to the different circumstances of civil society. A zeal for different opinions concerning religion, concerning government, and many other points, as well of speculation as of practice; an attachment to different leaders ambitiously contending for pre-eminence and power; or to persons of other descriptions whose fortunes have been interesting to the human passions, have, in turn, divided mankind into parties, inflamed them with mutual animosity, and rendered them much more disposed to vex and oppress each other than to co-operate for their common good. So strong is this propensity of mankind to fall into mutual animosities, that where no substantial occasion presents itself, the most frivolous and fanciful distinctions have been sufficient to kindle their unfriendly passions and excite their most violent conflicts. But the most common and durable source of factions has been the various and unequal distribution of property. Those who hold and those who are without property have ever formed distinct interests in society. Those who are creditors, and those who are debtors, fall under a like discrimination. A landed interest, a manufacturing interest, a mercantile interest, a moneyed interest, with many lesser interests, grow up of necessity in civilized nations, and divide them into different classes, actuated by different sentiments and views. The regulation of these various and interfering interests forms the principal task of modern legislation, and involves the spirit of party and faction in the necessary and ordinary operations of the government.

No man is allowed to be a judge in his own cause, because his interest would certainly bias his judgment, and, not improbably, corrupt his integrity. With equal, nay with greater reason, a body of men are unfit to be both judges and parties at the same time; yet what are many of the most important acts of legislation, but so many judicial determinations, not indeed concerning the rights of single persons, but concerning the rights of large bodies of citizens? and what are the different classes of legislators but advocates and parties to the causes which they determine? Is a law proposed concerning private debts? It is a question to which the creditors are parties on one side and the debtors on the other. Justice ought to hold the balance between them. Yet the parties are, and must be, themselves the judges; and the most numerous party, or, in other words, the most powerful faction must be expected to prevail. Shall domestic manufactures be encouraged, and in what degree, by restrictions on foreign manufactures? are questions which would be differently decided by the landed and the manufacturing classes, and probably by neither with a sole regard to justice and the public good. The apportionment of taxes on the various descriptions of property is an act which seems to require the most exact impartiality; yet there is, perhaps, no legislative act in which greater opportunity and temptation are given to a predominant party to trample on the rules of justice. Every shilling with which they overburden the inferior number is a shilling saved to their own pockets.

It is in vain to say that enlightened statesmen will be able to adjust these clashing interests and render them all subservient to the public good. Enlightened statesmen will not always be at the helm. Nor, in many cases, can such an adjustment be made at all without taking into view indirect and remote considerations, which will rarely prevail over the immediate interest which one party may find in disregarding the rights of another or the good of the whole.

The inference to which we are brought is, that the *causes* of faction cannot be removed, and that relief is only to be sought in the means of controlling its *effects*.

If a faction consists of less than a majority, relief is supplied by the republican principle, which enables the majority to defeat its sinister views by regular vote. It may clog the administration, it may convulse the society;

but it will be unable to execute and mask its violence under the forms of the Constitution. When a majority is included in a faction, the form of popular government, on the other hand, enables it to sacrifice to its ruling passion or interest both the public good and the rights of other citizens. To secure the public good and private rights against the danger of such a faction, and at the same time to preserve the spirit and the form of popular government, is then the great object to which our inquiries are directed. Let me add that it is the great desideratum [desire] by which this form of government can be rescued from the opprobrium under which it has so long labored, and be recommended to the esteem and adoption of mankind.

By what means is this object attainable? Evidently by one of two only. Either the existence of the same passion or interest in a majority at the same time must be prevented, or the majority, having such coexistent passion or interest, must be rendered by their number and local situation unable to concert and carry into effect schemes of oppression. If the impulse and the opportunity be suffered to coincide, we well know that neither moral nor religious motives can be relied on as an adequate control. They are not found to be such on the injustice and violence of individuals, and lose their efficacy in proportion to the number combined together, that is, in proportion as their efficacy becomes needful.

From this view of the subject it may be concluded that a pure democracy, by which I mean a society consisting of a small number of citizens, who assemble and administer the government in person, can admit of no cure for the mischiefs of faction. A common passion or interest will, in almost every case, be felt by a majority of the whole; a communication and concert result from the form of government itself; and there is nothing to check the inducements to sacrifice the weaker party or an obnoxious individual. Hence it is that such democracies have ever been spectacles of turbulence and contention; have ever been found incompatible with personal security or the rights of property; and have in general been as short in their lives as they have been violent in their deaths. Theoretic politicians, who have patronized this species of government, have erroneously supposed that by reducing mankind to a perfect equality in their political rights, they would, at the same time, be perfectly equalized and assimilated in their possessions, their opinions, and their passions.

A republic, by which I mean a government in which the scheme of representation takes place, opens a different prospect, and promises the cure for which we are seeking. Let us examine the points in which it varies from pure democracy, and we shall comprehend both the nature of the cure and the efficacy which it must derive from the Union.

The two great points of difference between a democracy and a republic are: first, the delegation of the government in the latter to a small number of citizens elected by the rest; secondly, the greater number of citizens and greater sphere of country over which the latter may be extended.

The effect of the first difference is, on the one hand, to refine and enlarge the public views, by passing them through the medium of a chosen body of citizens, whose wisdom may best discern the true interest of their country, and whose patriotism and love of justice will be least likely to sacrifice it to temporary or partial considerations. Under such a regulation, it may well happen that the public voice, pronounced by the representatives of the people, will be more consonant to the public good than if pronounced by the people themselves, convened for the purpose. On the other hand, the effect may be inverted. Men of factious tempers, of local prejudices, or of sinister designs, may by intrigue, by corruption, or by other means, first obtain the suffrages, and then betray the interests of the people. The question resulting is, whether small or extensive republics are more favorable to the election of proper guardians of the public weal; and it is clearly decided in favor of the latter by two obvious considerations.

In the first place, it is to be remarked that, however small the republic may be, the representatives must be raised to a certain number in order to guard against the cabals of a few; and that, however large it may be, they must be limited to a certain number in order to guard against the confusion of a multitude. Hence, the number of representatives in the two cases not being in proportion to that of the two constituents, and being proportionally greater in the small republic, it follows that, if the proportion of fit characters be not less in the large than in the small republic, the former will present a greater option and consequently a greater probability of a fit choice.

In the next place, as each representative will be chosen by a greater number of citizens in the large than in the small republic, it will be more difficult for unworthy candidates to practise with success the vicious arts by which elections are too often carried; and the suffrages of the people being more free, will be more likely to centre in men who possess the most attractive merit and the most diffusive and established characters.

It must be confessed that in this, as in most other cases, there is a mean, on both sides of which inconveniences will be found to lie. By enlarging too much the number of electors, you render the representative too little acquainted with all their local circumstances and lesser interests: as by reducing it too much, you render him unduly attached to these, and too little fit to comprehend and pursue great and national objects. The federal Constitution forms a happy combination in this respect; the great and aggregate interests being referred to the national, the local and particular to the State legislatures.

The other point of difference is, the greater number of citizens and extent of territory which may be brought within the compass of republican than of democratic government; and it is this circumstance principally which renders factious combinations less to be dreaded in the former than in the latter. The smaller the society, the fewer probably will be the distinct parties and interests composing it; the fewer the distinct parties and interests, the more frequently will a majority be found of the same party; and the smaller the number of individuals composing a majority, and the smaller the compass within which they are placed, the more easily will they concert and execute their plans of oppression. Extend the sphere, and you take in a greater variety of parties and interests; you make it less probable that a majority of the whole will have a common motive to invade the rights of other citizens; or if such a common motive exists, it will be more difficult for all who feel it to discover their own strength and to act in unison with each other. Besides other impediments, it may be remarked that, where there is a consciousness of unjust or dishonorable purposes, communication is always checked by distrust in proportion to the number whose concurrence is necessary.

Hence, it clearly appears that the same advantage which a republic has over a democracy in controlling the effects of faction is enjoyed by a large over a small republic,—is enjoyed by the Union over the States composing it. Does the advantage consist in the substitution of representatives whose enlightened views and virtuous sentiments render them superior to local prejudices and to schemes of injustice? It will not be denied that the representation of the Union will be most likely to possess these requisite endowments. Does it consist in the greater security afforded by a greater variety of parties, against the event of any one party being able to outnumber and oppress the rest? In an equal degree does the increased variety of parties comprised within the Union, increase this security. Does it, in fine, consist in the greater obstacles opposed to the concert and accomplishment of the secret wishes of an unjust and interested majority? Here, again, the extent of the Union gives it the most palpable advantage.

The influence of factious leaders may kindle a flame within their particular States, but will be unable to spread a general conflagration through the other States. A religious sect may degenerate into a political faction in a part of the Confederacy; but the variety of sects dispersed over the entire face of it must secure the national councils against any danger from that source. A rage for paper money, for an abolition of debts, for an equal division of property, or for any other improper or wicked project, will be less apt to pervade the whole body of the Union than a particular member of it; in the same proportion as such a malady is more likely to taint a particular county or district, than an entire State.

In the extent and proper structure of the Union, therefore, we behold a republican remedy for the diseases most incident to republican government. And according to the degree of pleasure and pride we feel in being republicans, ought to be our zeal in cherishing the spirit and supporting the character of Federalists.

PUBLIUS

The Constitution of the United States of America

Annotated with references to the Federalist Papers;
bracketed material is by the editors of this volume.

Federalist Paper Number and Author

[PREAMBLE]

84 (Hamilton)

We the People of the United States, in Order to form a more perfect Union, establish Justice, insure domestic Tranquility, provide for the common defence, promote the general Welfare, and secure the Blessings of Liberty to ourselves and our Posterity, do ordain and establish this Constitution for the United States of America.

ARTICLE I

Section 1

[LEGISLATURE POWERS]

10, 45 (Madison)

All legislative Powers herein granted shall be vested in a Congress of the United States, which shall consist of a Senate and House of Representatives.

Section 2

[HOUSE OF REPRESENTATIVES, HOW CONSTITUTED, POWER OF IMPEACHMENT]

39 (Madison)
45 (Madison)
52–53, 57 (Madison)

The House of Representatives shall be composed of Members chosen every second Year by the People of the several States, and the Electors in each State shall have the Qualifications requisite for Electors of the most numerous Branch of the State Legislature.

52 (Madison), 60 (Hamilton)

No Person shall be a Representative who shall not have attained to the Age of twenty five Years, and been seven Years a Citizen of the United States, and who shall not, when elected, be an Inhabitant of that State in which he shall be chosen.

54 (Madison)

Representatives and *direct Taxes** shall be apportioned among the several States which may be included within this Union,

* [Modified by Sixteenth Amendment.]

according to their respective Numbers, *which shall be determined by adding to the whole Number of free Persons, including those bound to Service for a Term of Years,* and excluding Indians not taxed, *three-fifths of all other Persons.** The actual Enumeration shall be made within three Years after the first Meeting of the Congress of the United States, and within every subsequent Term of ten Years, in such Manner as they shall by Law direct. The Number of Representatives shall not exceed one for every thirty Thousand, but each State shall have at Least one Representative; *and until such enumeration shall be made, the State of New Hampshire shall be entitled to chuse three, Massachusetts eight, Rhode Island and Providence Plantations one, Connecticut five, New-York six, New Jersey four, Pennsylvania eight, Delaware one, Maryland six, Virginia ten, North Carolina five, South Carolina five and Georgia three.†*

54
(Madison)

58
(Madison)

55–56
(Madison)

When vacancies happen in the Representation from any State, the Executive Authority thereof shall issue Writs of Election to fill such Vacancies.

79
(Hamilton)

The House of Representatives shall chuse their Speaker and other Officers; and shall have the sole Power of Impeachment.

Section 3

[THE SENATE, HOW CONSTITUTED, IMPEACHMENT TRIALS]

39, 45
(Madison),
60
(Hamilton),

The Senate of the United States shall be composed of two Senators from each State, *chosen by the Legislature thereof,‡* for six Years; and each Senator shall have one Vote.

62–63
(Madison)
59
(Hamilton)

Immediately after they shall be assembled in Consequence of the first Election, they shall be divided as equally as may be into three Classes. The Seats of the Senators of the first Class shall be vacated at the Expiration of the second Year, of the second Class at the Expiration of the fourth Year, and of the third Class at the Expiration of the sixth Year, so that one third may be chosen every second Year: *and if Vacancies happen by Resignation, or otherwise, during the Recess of the Legislature of any State, the Executive thereof may make temporary Appointments until the next Meeting of the Legislature, which shall then fill such Vacancies.§*

68
(Hamilton)

62
(Madison),
64 (Jay)

No person shall be a Senator who shall not have attained to the Age of thirty Years, and been nine Years a Citizen of the United States, and who shall not, when elected, be an Inhabitant of that State for which he shall be chosen.

---

* [Modified by Fourteenth Amendment.]
† [Temporary provision.]
‡ [Modified by Seventeenth Amendment.]
§ [Modified by Seventeenth Amendment.]

The Vice-President of the United States shall be President of the Senate, but shall have no Vote, unless they be equally divided.

39
(Madison),
65–67, 79
(Hamilton)
65
(Hamilton)
84
(Hamilton)

The Senate shall chuse their other Officers, and also a President pro tempore, in the Absence of the Vice-President, or when he shall exercise the Office of President of the United States.

The Senate shall have the sole Power to try all Impeachments. When sitting for that Purpose, they shall be on Oath or Affirmation. When the President of the United States is tried, the Chief Justice shall preside: And no Person shall be convicted without the Concurrence of two thirds of the Members present.

Judgment in Cases of Impeachment shall not extend further than to removal from Office, and disqualification to hold and enjoy any Office of honor, Trust or Profit under the United States: but the Party convicted shall nevertheless be liable and subject to Indictment, Trial, Judgment and Punishment, according to Law.

Section 4

[ELECTION OF SENATORS AND REPRESENTATIVES]

59–61
(Hamilton)

The Times, Places and Manner of holding Elections for Senators and Representatives, shall be prescribed in each State by the Legislature thereof; but the Congress may at any time by Law make or alter such Regulations, except as to the Place of Chusing Senators.

*The Congress shall assemble at least once in every Year, and such Meeting shall be on the first Monday in December, unless they shall by Law appoint a different Day.**

Section 5

[QUORUM, JOURNALS, MEETINGS, ADJOURNMENTS]

Each House shall be the Judge of the Elections, Returns and Qualifications of its own Members, and a Majority of each shall constitute a Quorum to do Business; but a smaller Number may adjourn from day to day, and may be authorized to compel the Attendance of absent Members, in such Manner, and under such Penalties as each House may provide.

Each House may determine the Rules of its Proceedings, punish its Members for disorderly Behavior, and, with the Concurrence of two-thirds, expel a Member.

Each House shall keep a Journal of its Proceedings, and from time to time publish the same, excepting such Parts as may in their Judgment require Secrecy; and the Yeas and Nays of the

---

*[Modified by Twentieth Amendment.]

Members of either House on any question shall, at the Desire of one-fifth of those Present, be entered on the Journal.

Neither House, during the Session of Congress, shall, without the Consent of the other, adjourn for more than three days, nor to any other Place than that in which the two Houses shall be sitting.

Section 6

[COMPENSATION, PRIVILEGES, DISABILITIES]

The Senators and Representatives shall receive a Compensation for their Services, to be ascertained by Law, and paid out of the Treasury of the United States. They shall in all Cases, except Treason, Felony and Breach of the Peace, be privileged from Arrest during their Attendance at the Session of their respective Houses, and in going to and returning from the same; and for any Speech or Debate in either House, they shall not be questioned in any other Place.

55 (Madison), 76 (Hamilton)
No Senator or Representative shall, during the Time for which he was elected, be appointed to any civil Office under the authority of the United States, which shall have been created, or the Emoluments whereof shall have been increased during such time; and no Person holding any Office under the United States, shall be a Member of either House during his Continuance in Office.

Section 7

[PROCEDURE IN PASSING BILLS AND RESOLUTIONS]

66 (Hamilton)
All bills for raising Revenue shall originate in the House of Representatives; but the Senate may propose or concur with Amendments as on other Bills.

69, 73 (Hamilton)
Every Bill which shall have passed the House of Representatives and the Senate, shall, before it become a Law, be presented to the President of the United States; If he approve he shall sign it, but if not he shall return it, with his Objections to that House in which it shall have originated, who shall enter the Objections at large on their Journal, and proceed to reconsider it. If after such Reconsideration two-thirds of that House shall agree to pass the Bill, it shall be sent, together with the Objections, to the other House, by which it shall likewise be reconsidered, and if approved by two thirds of that House it shall become a Law. But in all such Cases the Votes of both Houses shall be determined by Yeas and Nays, and the Names of the Persons voting for and against the Bill shall be entered on the Journal of each House respectively. If

any Bill shall not be returned by the President within ten Days (Sundays excepted) after it shall have been presented to him, the Same shall be a Law, in like Manner as if he had signed it, unless the Congress by their Adjournment prevent its Return, in which Case it shall not be a Law.

69, 73
(Hamilton)

Every Order, Resolution, or Vote to which the Concurrence of the Senate and House of Representatives may be necessary (except on a question of Adjournment) shall be presented to the President of the United States; and before the Same shall take Effect, shall be approved by him, or being disapproved by him, shall be repassed by two-thirds of the Senate and House of Representatives, according to the Rules and Limitations prescribed in the Case of a Bill.

Section 8

[POWERS OF CONGRESS]

The Congress shall have Power

30–36
(Hamilton),

41
(Madison)

To lay and collect Taxes, Duties, Imposts and Excises, to pay the Debts and provide for the common Defence and general Welfare of the United States; but all Duties, Imposts and Excises shall be uniform throughout the United States;

56
(Madison)

42, 45, 56
(Madison)

To borrow money on the Credit of the United States;

To regulate Commerce with foreign Nations, and among the several States, and with the Indian Tribes;

32
(Hamilton),

To establish an uniform Rule of Naturalization, and uniform Laws on the subject of Bankruptcies throughout the United States;

42
(Madison)

To coin Money, regulate the Value thereof, and of foreign Coin, and fix the Standard of Weights and Measures;

42
(Madison)

To provide for the Punishment of counterfeiting the Securities and current Coin of the United States;

42
(Madison)

To establish Post Offices and Post Roads;

42
(Madison)

43
(Madison)

To promote the Progress of Science and useful Arts, by securing for limited Times to Authors and Inventors the exclusive Right to their respective Writings and Discoveries;

81
(Hamilton)

To constitute Tribunals inferior to the supreme Court;

42
(Madison)

To define and Punish Piracies and Felonies committed on the high Seas, and Offenses against the Law of Nations;

41
(Madison)

To declare War, grant Letters of Marque and Reprisal, and make Rules concerning Captures on Land and Water;

23, 24, 26
(Hamilton),

To raise and support Armies, but no Appropriation of Money to that Use shall be for a longer Term than two Years;

41
(Madison)

To provide and maintain a Navy;

To make Rules for the Government and Regulation of the land and naval forces;

29
(Hamilton)
To provide for calling forth the Militia to execute the Laws of the Union, suppress Insurrections and repel Invasions;

29
(Hamilton),
56
(Madison)
To provide for organizing, arming, and disciplining the Militia, and for governing such Part of them as may be employed in the Service of the United States, reserving to the States respectively, the Appointment of the Officers, and the Authority of training the Militia according to the discipline prescribed by Congress;

32
(Hamilton),
43
(Madison)

43
(Madison)
To exercise exclusive Legislation in all Cases whatsoever, over such District (not exceeding ten Miles square) as may, by Cession of particular States, and the Acceptance of Congress, become the Seat of the Government of the United States, and to exercise like Authority over all Places purchased by the Consent of the Legislature of the State in which the Same shall be, for the Erection of Forts, Magazines, Arsenals, dock-Yards, and other needful Buildings;—And

29, 33
(Hamilton)

44
(Madison)
To make all Laws which shall be necessary and proper for carrying into Execution the foregoing Powers, and all other Powers vested by this Constitution in the Government of the United States, or in any Department or Officer thereof.

Section 9

[SOME RESTRICTIONS ON FEDERAL POWER]

42
(Madison)
The Migration or Importation of such Persons as any of the States now existing shall think proper to admit, shall not be prohibited by the Congress prior to the Year one thousand eight hundred and eight, but a tax or duty may be imposed on such Importation, not exceeding ten dollars for each Person.*

83, 84
(Hamilton)
The privilege of the Writ of *Habeas Corpus* shall not be suspended, unless when in Cases of Rebellion or Invasion the public Safety may require it.

84
(Hamilton)
No Bill of Attainder or ex post facto Law shall be passed.

No Capitation, or other direct, Tax shall be laid, unless in Proportion to the Census or Enumeration herein before directed to be taken.†

No Tax or Duty shall be laid on Articles exported from any State.

32
(Hamilton)
No Preference shall be given by any Regulation of Commerce or Revenue to the Ports of one State over those of another: nor shall Vessels bound to, or from, one State, be obliged to enter, clear, or pay Duties in another.

No Money shall be drawn from the Treasury, but in Consequence of Appropriations made by Law; and a regular Statement

* [Temporary provision.]
† [Modified by Sixteenth Amendment.]

and Account of the Receipts and Expenditures of all public Money shall be published from time to time.

39
(Madison),
84
(Hamilton)

No Title of Nobility shall be granted by the United States: And no Person holding any Office of Profit or Trust under them, shall, without the Consent of the Congress, accept of any present, Emolument, Office, or Title, of any kind whatever, from any King, Prince or foreign State.

Section 10

[RESTRICTIONS UPON POWERS OF STATES]

33
(Hamilton),
44
(Madison)

No State shall enter into any Treaty, Alliance, or Confederation; grant Letters of Marque and Reprisal; coin Money; emit Bills of Credit; make any Thing but gold and silver Coin a Tender in Payment of Debts; pass any Bill of Attainder, ex post facto Law, or Law impairing the Obligation of Contracts, or grant any Title of Nobility.

32
(Hamilton),
44
(Madison)

No State shall, without the Consent of the Congress, lay any Imposts or Duties on Imports or Exports, except what may be absolutely necessary for executing its inspection Laws: and the net Produce of all Duties and Imposts, laid by any State on Imports or Exports, shall be for the Use of the Treasury of the United States; and all such Laws shall be subject to the Revision and Controul of the Congress.

No State shall, without the Consent of Congress, lay any duty of Tonnage, keep Troops, or Ships of War in time of Peace, enter into any Agreement or Compact with another State, or with a foreign Power, or engage in War, unless actually invaded, or in such imminent Danger as will not admit of Delay.

ARTICLE II

Section 1

[EXECUTIVE POWER, ELECTION, QUALIFICATIONS OF THE PRESIDENT]

39
(Madison),
70, 71, 84
(Hamilton)

The executive Power shall be vested in a President of the United States of America. *He shall hold his Office during the Term of four years, and, together with the Vice-President, chosen for the same Term, be elected, as follows:**

69, 71
(Hamilton)

39, 45
(Madison),

Each State shall appoint, in such Manner as the Legislature thereof may direct, a Number of Electors, equal to the whole Number of Senators and Representatives to which the State may be entitled in the Congress: but no Senator or Representative, or

---

* [Number of terms limited to two by Twenty-second Amendment.]

Person holding an Office of Trust or Profit under the United

68, 77
(Hamilton)

States, shall be appointed an Elector.

The electors shall meet in their respective States, and vote by ballot for two Persons, of whom one at least shall not be an Inhabitant of the same State with themselves. And they shall make a List of all the Persons voted for, and of the Number of Votes for each; which List they shall sign and certify, and transmit sealed to the Seat of the Government of the

66
(Hamilton)

*United States, directed to the President of the Senate. The President of the Senate shall, in the Presence of the Senate and House of Representatives, open all the Certificates, and the Votes shall then be counted. The Person having the greatest Number of Votes shall be the President, if such Number be a Majority of the whole Number of Electors appointed; and if there be more than one who have such Majority, and have an equal Number of Votes, then the House of Representatives shall immediately chuse by Ballot one of them for President; and if no Person have a Majority, then from the five highest on the List the said House shall in like Manner chuse the President. But in chusing the President, the Votes shall be taken by States, the Representation from each State having one Vote; a quorum for this Purpose shall consist of a Member or Members from two-thirds of the States, and a Majority of all the States shall be necessary to a Choice. In every Case, after the Choice of the President, the Person having the greatest Number of Votes of the Electors shall be the Vice-President. But if there should remain two or more who have equal Votes, the Senate shall chuse from them by Ballot the Vice-President.**

The Congress may determine the Time of chusing the Electors, and the Day on which they shall give their Votes; which Day shall be the same throughout the United States.

No Person except a natural born Citizen, or a Citizen of the United States, at the time of the Adoption of this Constitution, shall be eligible to the Office of President; neither shall any Person be eligible to that Office who shall not have attained to the Age of

64 (Jay)

thirty-five Years, and been fourteen Years a Resident within the United States.

In Case of the Removal of the President from Office, or his Death, Resignation, or Inability to discharge the Powers and Duties of the said Office, the same shall devolve on the Vice-President, and the Congress may by Law provide for the Case of Removal, Death, Resignation or Inability, both of the President and Vice-President, declaring what Officer shall then act as President, and such Officer shall act accordingly, until the Disability be removed, or a President shall be elected.

The President shall, at stated Times, receive for his Services, a

73, 79
(Hamilton)

Compensation, which shall neither be encreased nor diminished

* [Modified by Twelfth and Twentieth Amendment.]

during the Period for which he shall have been elected, and he shall not receive within that Period any other Emolument from the United States, or any of them.

Before he enter on the Execution of his Office, he shall take the following Oath or Affirmation:—"I do solemnly swear (or affirm) that I will faithfully execute the Office of President of the United States, and will to the best of my Ability, preserve, protect and defend the Constitution of the United States."

Section 2

[POWERS OF THE PRESIDENT]

69, 74
(Hamilton)
The President shall be Commander in Chief of the Army and Navy of the United States, and of the Militia of the several States, when called into the actual Service of the United States; he may require the Opinion, in writing, of the principal Officer in each of the executive Departments, upon any Subject relating to the Duties of their respective Offices, and he shall have Power to Grant Reprieves and Pardons for Offenses against the United States, except in Cases of Impeachment.

74
(Hamilton)
69
(Hamilton)
74
(Hamilton)
42
(Madison)
64 (Jay),
66
(Hamilton)
He shall have Power, by and with the Advice and Consent of the Senate, to make Treaties, provided two thirds of the Senators present concur; and he shall nominate, and by and with the Advice and Consent of the Senate, shall appoint Ambassadors, other public Ministers and Consuls, Judges of the Supreme Court, and all other Officers of the United States, whose Appointments are not herein otherwise provided for, and which shall be established by Law: but the Congress may by Law vest the Appointment of such inferior Officers, as they think proper, in the President alone, in the Courts of Law, or in the Heads of Departments.

42
(Madison),

66, 69,
76, 77
(Hamilton)

67, 76
(Hamilton)
The President shall have Power to fill up all Vacancies that may happen during the Recess of the Senate, by granting Commissions which shall expire at the End of their next Session.

Section 3

77
(Hamilton)
69, 77
(Hamilton)
[POWERS AND DUTIES OF THE PRESIDENT]
He shall from time to time give to the Congress Information of the State of the Union, and recommend to their Consideration such Measures as he shall judge necessary and expedient; he may, on extraordinary Occasions, convene both Houses, or either of them, and in Case of Disagreement between them, with Respect to the Time of Adjournment, he may adjourn them to such Time as he shall think proper; he shall receive Ambassadors and other public Ministers; he shall take Care that the Laws be faithfully

77
(Hamilton)
69, 77
(Hamilton)
42
(Madison),
69, 77
(Hamilton)

78
(Hamilton)
executed, and shall Commission all the Officers of the United States.

Section 4

[IMPEACHMENT]

39
(Madison),
69
(Hamilton)
The President, Vice-President and all civil Officers of the United States, shall be removed from Office on Impeachment for, and Conviction of, Treason, Bribery, or other high Crimes and Misdemeanors.

ARTICLE III

Section 1

[JUDICIAL POWER, TENURE OR OFFICE]

81, 82
(Hamilton)
65
(Hamilton)
78, 79
(Hamilton)
The judicial Power of the United States, shall be vested in one Supreme Court, and in such inferior Courts as the Congress may from time to time ordain and establish. The Judges, both of the supreme and inferior Courts, shall hold their Offices during good Behavior, and shall, at stated Times, receive for their Services a Compensation, which shall not be diminished during their Continuance in Office.

Section 2

[JURISDICTION]

80
(Hamilton)
The judicial Power shall extend to all Cases, in Law and Equity, arising under this Constitution, the Laws of the United States, and Treaties made, or which shall be made, under their Authority;—to all Cases affecting Ambassadors, other public Ministers and Consuls;—to all Cases of admiralty and maritime Jurisdiction;—to Controversies to which the United States shall be a party;— to Controversies between two or more States;—*between a State and Citizens of another State;*—between Citizens of different States,— between Citizens of the same State claiming Lands under Grants of different States, *and between a State,* or the Citizens thereof, *and foreign States, Citizens or Subjects.**

81
(Hamilton)
In all Cases affecting Ambassadors, other public Ministers and Consuls, and those in which a State shall be Party, the supreme Court shall have original Jurisdiction. In all the other Cases before mentioned, the Supreme Court shall have appellate Jurisdiction, both as to Law and Fact, with such Exceptions, and under such Regulations as the Congress shall make.

---

* [Modified by the Eleventh Amendment.]

83, 84
(Hamilton)

The Trial of all Crimes, except in Cases of Impeachment, shall be by Jury; and such Trial shall be held in the State where the said Crimes shall have been committed; but when not committed within any State, the Trial shall be at such Place or Places as the Congress may by Law have directed.

Section 3

[TREASON, PROOF, AND PUNISHMENT]

43
(Madison),

98
(Hamilton)

Treason against the United States, shall consist only in levying War against them, or in adhering to their Enemies, giving them Aid and Comfort. No Person shall be convicted of Treason unless on the Testimony of two Witnesses to the same overt Act, or on Confession in open Court.

43
(Madison),
84
(Hamilton)

The Congress shall have Power to declare the Punishment of Treason, but no Attainder of Treason shall work Corruption of Blood, or Forfeiture except during the Life of the Person attained.

ARTICLE IV

Section 1

[FAITH AND CREDIT AMONG STATES]

42
(Madison)

Full Faith and Credit shall be given in each State to the public Acts, Records, and judicial Proceedings of every other State. And the Congress may by general Laws prescribe the Manner in which such Acts, Records and Proceedings shall be proved, and the Effect thereof.

Section 2

[PRIVILEGES AND IMMUNITIES, FUGITIVES]

80
(Hamilton)

The Citizens of each State shall be entitled to all Privileges and Immunities of Citizens in the several States.

A Person charged in any State with Treason, Felony, or other Crime, who shall flee from Justice, and be found in another State, shall on demand of the executive Authority of the State from which he fled, be delivered up, to be removed to the State having Jurisdiction of the Crime.

*No Person held to Service or Labour in one State, under the Laws thereof, escaping into another, shall, in Consequence of any Law or Regulation therein, be discharged from such Service or Labour, but shall be delivered up on Claim of the Party to whom such Service or Labour may be due.**

---

* [Repealed by the Thirteenth Amendment.]

Section 3

[ADMISSION OF NEW STATES]

43
(Madison)

New States may be admitted by the Congress into this Union; but no new States shall be formed or erected within the Jurisdiction of any other State; nor any State be formed by the Junction of two or more States, or Parts of States, without the Consent of the Legislatures of the States concerned as well as of the Congress.

43
(Madison)

The Congress shall have Power to dispose of and make all needful Rules and Regulations respecting the Territory or other Property belonging to the United States; and nothing in this Constitution shall be so construed as to Prejudice any Claims of the United States, or of any particular State.

Section 4

[GUARANTEE OF REPUBLICAN GOVERNMENT]

39, 43
(Madison)

The United States shall guarantee to every State in this Union a Republican Form of Government, and shall protect each of them against Invasion; and on Application of the Legislature, or of the Executive (when the Legislature cannot be convened) against domestic Violence.

ARTICLE V

[AMENDMENT OF THE CONSTITUTION]

39, 43
(Madison)
85
(Hamilton)

The Congress, whenever two-thirds of both Houses shall deem it necessary, shall propose Amendments to this Constitution, or, on the Application of the Legislatures of two-thirds of the several States, shall call a Convention for proposing Amendments, which, in either Case, shall be valid to all Intents and Purposes, as Part of this Constitution, when ratified by the Legislatures of three-fourths of the several States, or by Conventions in three-fourths thereof, as the one or the other Mode of Ratification may be proposed by the Congress; *Provided that no Amendment which may be made prior to the Year One thousand eight hundred and eight shall in any Manner affect the first and fourth Clauses in the Ninth Section of the first Article;* and that no State,

43
(Madison)

without its Consent, shall be deprived of its equal Suffrage in the Senate.

---

* [Temporary provision.]

ARTICLE VI

[DEBTS, SUPREMACY, OATH]

43
(Madison)
All Debts contracted and Engagements entered into, before the Adoption of this Constitution, shall be as valid against the United States under this Constitution, as under the Confederation.

27, 33
(Hamilton),
39, 44
(Madison)
This Constitution, and the Laws of the United States which shall be made in Pursuance thereof; and all Treaties made, or which shall be made, under the Authority of the United States, shall be the supreme Law of the Land; and the Judges in every State shall be bound thereby, any Thing in the Constitution or Laws of any State to the Contrary notwithstanding.

27
(Hamilton),
44
(Madison)
The Senators and Representatives before mentioned, and the Members of the several State Legislatures, and all executive and judicial Officers, both of the United States and of the several States, shall be bound by Oath or Affirmation, to support this Constitution; but no religious Test shall ever be required as a Qualification to any Office or public Trust under the United States.

ARTICLE VII

[RATIFICATION AND ESTABLISHMENT]

39, 40, 43
(Madison)
The Ratification of the Conventions of nine States, shall be sufficient for the Establishment of this Constitution between the States so ratifying the Same.*

Done in Convention by the Unanimous Consent of the States present the Seventeenth Day of September in the Year of our Lord one thousand seven hundred and Eighty seven and of the Independence of the United States of America the Twelfth. *In Witness* whereof We have hereunto subscribed our Names,

G:⁰ WASHINGTON—
Presidt, and Deputy
from Virginia

---

* [The Constitution was submitted on September 17, 1787, by the Constitutional Convention, was ratified by the conventions of several states at various dates up to May 29, 1790, and became effective on March 4, 1789.]

New Hampshire	JOHN LANGDON	Delaware	GEO READ
	NICHOLAS GILMAN		GUNNING BEDFOR JUN
Massachusetts	NATHANIEL GORHAM		JOHN DICKINSON
	RUFUS KING		RICHARD BASSETT
			JACO: BROOM
Connecticut	WM SAML JOHNSON	Maryland	JAMES MCHENRY
	ROGER SHERMAN		DAN OF ST THOS. JENIFER
New York	ALEXANDER HAMILTON		DANL CARROLL
New Jersey	WIL: LIVINGSTON	Virginia	JOHN BLAIR—
	DAVID BREARLEY		JAMES MADISON JR.
	WM PATERSON	North Carolina	WM BLOUNT
	JONA: DAYTON		RICHD DOBBS SPAIGHT
Pennsylvania	B FRANKLIN		HU WILLIAMSON
	THOMAS MIFFLIN	South Carolina	J. RUTLEDGE
	ROBT MORRIS		CHARLES COTESWORTH PINCKNEY
	GEO. CLYMER		CHARLES PINCKNEY
	THOS. FITZSIMONS		PIERCE BUTLER
	JARED INGERSOLL		
	JAMES WILSON	Georgia	WILLIAM FEW
	GOUV MORRIS		ABR BALDWIN

Amendments to the Constitution

Proposed by Congress and Ratified
by the Legislatures of the Several States,
Pursuant to Article V of the Original Constitution.

Amendments I–X, known as the Bill of Rights, were proposed by Congress on September 25, 1789, and ratified on December 15, 1791. Federalist Papers comments, mainly in opposition to a Bill of Rights, can be found in #84 (Hamilton).

AMENDMENT I

[FREEDOM OF RELIGION, OF SPEECH, AND OF THE PRESS]

Congress shall make no law respecting an establishment of religion, or prohibiting the free exercise thereof; or abridging the freedom of speech, or of the press; or the right of the people peaceably to assemble, and to petition the Government for a redress of grievances.

AMENDMENT II

[RIGHT TO KEEP AND BEAR ARMS]

A well regulated Militia, being necessary to the security of a free State, the right of the people to keep and bear Arms, shall not be infringed.

AMENDMENT III

[QUARTERING OF SOLDIERS]

No Soldier shall, in time of peace be quartered in any house, without the consent of the Owner, nor in time of war, but in a manner to be prescribed by law.

Amendment IV

[SECURITY FROM UNWARRANTABLE SEARCH AND SEIZURE]

The right of the people to be secure in their persons, houses, papers, and effects, against unreasonable searches and seizures, shall not be violated, and no Warrants shall issue, but upon probable cause, supported by Oath or affirmation, and particularly describing the place to be searched, and the persons or things to be seized.

Amendment V

[RIGHTS OF ACCUSED PERSONS IN CRIMINAL PROCEEDINGS]

No person shall be held to answer for a capital, or otherwise infamous crime, unless on a presentment or indictment of a Grand Jury, except in cases arising in the land or naval forces, or in the Militia, when in actual service in time of War or public danger; nor shall any person be subject for the same offence to be twice put in jeopardy of life or limb; nor shall be compelled in any Criminal Case to be a witness against himself, nor be deprived of life, liberty, or property, without due process of law; nor shall private property be taken for public use, without just compensation.

Amendment VI

[RIGHT TO SPEEDY TRIAL, WITNESSES, ETC.]

In all criminal prosecutions, the accused shall enjoy the right to a speedy and public trial, by an impartial jury of the State and district wherein the crime shall have been committed, which district shall have been previously ascertained by law, and to be informed of the nature and cause of the accusation; to be confronted with the witnesses against him; to have compulsory process for obtaining Witnesses in his favor, and to have the Assistance of Counsel for his defence.

Amendment VII

[TRIAL BY JURY IN CIVIL CASES]

In suits at common law, where the value in controversy shall exceed twenty dollars, the right of trial by jury shall be preserved, and no fact tried by a jury shall be otherwise re-examined in any Court of the United States, than according to the rules of the common law.

AMENDMENT VIII

[BAILS, FINES, PUNISHMENTS]
Excessive bail shall not be required, nor excessive fines imposed, nor cruel and unusual punishments inflicted.

AMENDMENT IX

[RESERVATION OF RIGHTS OF PEOPLE]
The enumeration in the Constitution, of certain rights, shall not be construed to deny or disparage others retained by the people.

AMENDMENT X

[POWERS RESERVED TO STATES OR PEOPLE]
The powers not delegated to the United States by the Constitution, nor prohibited by it to the States, are reserved to the States respectively, or to the people.

AMENDMENT XI

[Proposed by Congress on March 4, 1794; declared ratified on January 8, 1798.]

[RESTRICTION OF JUDICIAL POWER]
The Judicial power of the United States shall not be construed to extend to any suit in law or equity, commenced or prosecuted against one of the United States by Citizens of another State, or by Citizens or Subjects of any foreign State.

AMENDMENT XII

[Proposed by Congress on December 9, 1803; declared ratified on September 25, 1804.]

[ELECTION OF PRESIDENT AND VICE-PRESIDENT]
The Electors shall meet in their respective states, and vote by ballot for President and Vice-President, one of whom, at least, shall not be an inhabitant of the same state with themselves; they shall name in their ballots

the person voted for as President, and in distinct ballots the person voted for as Vice-President, and they shall make distinct lists of all persons voted for as President, and of all persons voted for as Vice-President, and of the number of votes for each, which lists they shall sign and certify, and transmit sealed to the seat of the government of the United States, directed to the President of the Senate;—The President of the Senate shall, in presence of the Senate and House of Representatives, open all the certificates and the votes shall then be counted;—The person having the greatest number of votes for President, shall be the President, if such number be a majority of the whole number of Electors appointed; and if no person have such majority, then from the persons having the highest numbers not exceeding three on the list of those voted for as President, the House of Representatives shall choose immediately, by ballot, the President. But in choosing the President, the votes shall be taken by states, the representation from each state having one vote; a quorum for this purpose shall consist of a member or members from two-thirds of the states, and a majority of all the states shall be necessary to a choice. And if the House of Representatives shall not choose a President whenever the right of choice shall devolve upon them, before the fourth day of March next following, then the Vice-President shall act as President, as in the case of the death or other constitutional disability of the President. The person having the greatest number of votes as Vice-President, shall be the Vice-President, if such number be a majority of the whole number of Electors appointed, and if no person have a majority, then from the two highest numbers on the list, the Senate shall choose the Vice-President; a quorum for the purpose shall consist of two-thirds of the whole number of Senators, and a majority of the whole number shall be necessary to a choice. But no person constitutionally ineligible to the office of President shall be eligible to that of Vice-President of the United States.

AMENDMENT XIII

[Proposed by Congress on January 31, 1865; declared ratified on December 18, 1865.]

Section 1

[ABOLITION OF SLAVERY]

Neither slavery nor involuntary servitude, except as a punishment for crime whereof the party shall have been duly convicted, shall exist within the United States, or any place subject to their jurisdiction.

Section 2

[POWER TO ENFORCE THIS ARTICLE]
Congress shall have power to enforce this article by appropriate legislation.

AMENDMENT XIV

[Proposed by Congress on June 13, 1866, declared ratified on July 28, 1868.]

Section 1

[CITIZENSHIP RIGHTS NOT TO BE ABRIDGED BY STATES]
All persons born or naturalized in the United States, and subject to the jurisdiction thereof, are citizens of the United States and of the State wherein they reside. No state shall make or enforce any law which shall abridge the privileges or immunities of citizens of the United States; nor shall any State deprive any person of life, liberty, or property, without due process of law; nor deny to any person within its jurisdiction the equal protection of the laws.

Section 2

[APPORTIONMENT OF REPRESENTATIVES IN CONGRESS]
Representatives shall be apportioned among the several States according to their respective numbers, counting the whole number of persons in each State, excluding Indians not taxed. But when the right to vote at any election for the choice of electors for President and Vice-President of the United States, Representatives in Congress, the Executive and Judicial officers of a State, or the members of the Legislature thereof, is denied to any of the male inhabitants of such State, being twenty-one years of age, and citizens of the United States, or in any way abridged, except for participation in rebellion, or other crime, the basis of representation therein shall be reduced in the proportion which the number of such male citizens shall bear to the whole number of male citizens twenty-one years of age in such State.

Section 3

[PERSONS DISQUALIFIED FROM HOLDING OFFICE]
No person shall be a Senator or Representative in Congress, or elector of President and Vice-President, or hold any office, civil or military, under the United States, or under any State, who, having previously taken an

oath, as a member of Congress, or as an officer of the United States, or as a member of any State legislature, or as an executive or judicial officer of any State, to support the Constitution of the United States, shall have engaged in insurrection or rebellion against the same, or given aid or comfort to the enemies thereof. But Congress may by a vote of two-thirds of each House, remove such disability.

Section 4

[WHAT PUBLIC DEBTS ARE VALID]

The validity of the public debt of the United States, authorized by law, including debts incurred for payment of pensions and bounties for services in suppressing insurrection or rebellion, shall not be questioned. But neither the United States nor any State shall assume or pay any debt or obligation incurred in aid of insurrection or rebellion against the United States, or any claim for the loss or emancipation of any slave; but all such debts, obligations and claims shall be held illegal and void.

Section 5

[POWER TO ENFORCE THIS ARTICLE]

The Congress shall have power to enforce, by appropriate legislation, the provisions of this article.

AMENDMENT XV

[Proposed by Congress on February 26, 1869; declared ratified on March 30, 1870.]

Section 1

[BLACK SUFFRAGE]

The right of citizens of the United States to vote shall not be denied or abridged by the United States or by any State on account of race, color, or previous condition of servitude.

Section 2

[POWER TO ENFORCE THIS ARTICLE]

The Congress shall have power to enforce this article by appropriate legislation.

AMENDMENT XVI

[Proposed by Congress on July 12, 1909; declared ratified on February 25, 1913.]

[AUTHORIZING INCOME TAXES]

The Congress shall have power to lay and collect taxes on incomes, from whatever source derived, without apportionment among the several States, and without regard to any census or enumeration.

AMENDMENT XVII

[Proposed by Congress on May 13, 1912; declared ratified on May 31, 1913.]

[POPULAR ELECTION OF SENATORS]

The Senate of the United States shall be composed of two Senators from each State, elected by the people thereof, for six years; and each Senator shall have one vote. The electors in each State shall have the qualifications requisite for electors of the most numerous branch of the State Legislature.

When vacancies happen in the representation of any State in the Senate, the executive authority of such State shall issue writs of election to fill such vacancies: Provided, That the Legislature of any State may empower the executive thereof to make temporary appointments until the people fill the vacancies by election as the Legislature may direct.

This amendment shall not be so construed as to affect the election or term of any Senator chosen before it becomes valid as part of the Constitution.

AMENDMENT XVIII

[Proposed by Congress December 18, 1917; declared ratified on January 29, 1919.]

Section 1

[NATIONAL LIQUOR PROHIBITION]

After one year from the ratification of this article, the manufacture, sale, or transportation of intoxicating liquors within, the importation thereof into, or the exportation thereof from the United States and all territory subject to the jurisdiction thereof for beverage purposes is hereby prohibited.

Section 2

[POWER TO ENFORCE THIS ARTICLE]
Congress and the several states shall have concurrent power to enforce this article by appropriate legislation.

Section 3

[RATIFICATION WITHIN SEVEN YEARS]
This article shall be inoperative unless it shall have been ratified as an amendment to the Constitution by the legislatures of the several states, as provided in the Constitution, within seven years from the date of the submission hereof to the states by Congress.*

Amendment XIX

[Proposed by Congress on June 4, 1919; declared ratified on August 26, 1920.]

[FEMALE SUFFRAGE]
The right of the citizens of the United States to vote shall not be denied or abridged by the United States or by any state on account of sex.

Congress shall have power, by appropriate legislation, to enforce this article by appropriate legislation.

Amendment XX

[Proposed by Congress on March 2, 1932; declared ratified on February 6, 1933.]

Section 1

[TERMS OF OFFICE]
The terms of the President and Vice-President shall end at noon on the 20th day of January, and the terms of Senators and Representatives at noon on the 3rd day of January, of the years in which such terms would have ended if this article had not been ratified; and the terms of their successors shall then begin.

---

* [Repealed by the Twenty-first Amendment.]

Section 2

[TIME OF CONVENING CONGRESS]

The Congress shall assemble at least once in every year, and such meeting shall begin at noon on the 3rd day of January, unless they shall by law appoint a different day.

Section 3

[DEATH OF PRESIDENT-ELECT]

If, at the time fixed for the beginning of the term of the President, the President-elect shall have died, the Vice-President-elect shall become President. If a President shall not have been chosen before the time fixed for the beginning of his term, or if the President-elect shall have failed to qualify, then the Vice-President-elect shall act as President until a President shall have qualified; and the Congress may by law provide for the case wherein neither a President-elect nor a Vice-President-elect shall have qualified, declaring who shall then act as President, or the manner in which one who is to act shall be selected, and such person shall act accordingly until a President or Vice-President shall have qualified.

Section 4

[ELECTION OF THE PRESIDENT]

The Congress may by law provide for the case of the death of any of the persons from whom the House of Representatives may choose a President whenever the right of choice shall have devolved upon them, and for the case of the death of any of the persons from whom the Senate may choose a Vice-President whenever the right of choice shall have devolved upon them.

Section 5

[AMENDMENT TAKES EFFECT]

Sections 1 and 2 shall take effect on the 15th day of October following ratification of this article.

Section 6

[RATIFICATION WITHIN SEVEN YEARS]

This article shall be inoperative unless it shall have been ratified as an amendment to the Constitution by the legislatures of three-fourths of the several States within seven years from the date of its submission.

Amendment XXI

[Proposed by Congress on February 20, 1933; declared ratified on December 5, 1933.]

Section 1

[NATIONAL LIQUOR PROHIBITION REPEALED]

The eighteenth article of amendment to the Constitution of the United States is hereby repealed.

Section 2

[TRANSPORTATION OF LIQUOR INTO "DRY" STATES]

The transportation or importation into any State, Territory, or Possession of the United States for delivery or use therein of intoxicating liquors, in violation of the laws thereof, is hereby prohibited.

Section 3

[RATIFICATION WITHIN SEVEN YEARS]

The article shall be inoperative unless it shall have been ratified as an amendment to the Constitution by conventions in the several States, as provided in the Constitution, within seven years from the date of the submission hereof to the States by the Congress.

Amendment XXII

[Proposed by Congress on March 21, 1947; declared ratified on February 26, 1951.]

Section 1

[TENURE OF PRESIDENT LIMITED]

No person shall be elected to the office of the President more than twice, and no person who has held the office of President or acted as President for more than two years of a term to which some other person was elected President shall be elected to the Office of the President more than once. But this Article shall not apply to any person holding the office of President when this Article was proposed by the Congress, and shall not prevent any person who may be holding the office of President, or acting as President, during the term within which this Article becomes operative from holding the office of President or acting as President during the remainder of such term.

Section 2
[RATIFICATION WITHIN SEVEN YEARS]

This Article shall be inoperative unless it shall have been ratified as an amendment to the Constitution by the legislatures of three-fourths of the several states within seven years from the date of its submission to the States by the Congress.

Amendment XXIII

[Proposed by Congress on June 21, 1960; declared ratified on March 29, 1961.]

Section 1
[ELECTORAL COLLEGE VOTES FOR THE DISTRICT OF COLUMBIA]

The District constituting the seat of Government of the United States shall appoint in such manner as the Congress may direct:

A number of electors of President and Vice-President equal to the whole number of Senators and Representatives in Congress to which the District would be entitled if it were a State, but in no event more than the least populous State; they shall be in addition to those appointed by the States, but they shall be considered, for the purposes of the election of President and Vice-President, to be electors appointed by a State; and they shall meet in the District and perform such duties as provided by the twelfth article of amendment.

Section 2
[POWER TO ENFORCE THIS ARTICLE]

The Congress shall have power to enforce this article by appropriate legislation.

Amendment XXIV

[Proposed by Congress on August 27, 1963; declared ratified on January 23, 1964.]

Section 1

[ANTI-POLL TAX]

The right of citizens of the United States to vote in any primary or other election for President or Vice-President, for electors for President or Vice-President, or for Senator or Representative in Congress, shall not be denied or abridged by the United States or any State by reason of failure to pay any poll tax or other tax.

Section 2

[POWER TO ENFORCE THIS ARTICLE]

The Congress shall have power to enforce this article by appropriate legislation.

AMENDMENT XXV

[Proposed by Congress on July 7, 1965; declared ratified on February 10, 1967.]

Section 1

[VICE-PRESIDENT TO BECOME PRESIDENT]

In case of the removal of the President from office or his death or resignation, the Vice-President shall become President.

Section 2

[CHOICE OF A NEW VICE-PRESIDENT]

Whenever there is a vacancy in the office of the Vice-President, the President shall nominate a Vice-President who shall take office upon confirmation by a majority vote of both houses of Congress.

Section 3

[PRESIDENT MAY DECLARE OWN DISABILITY]

Whenever the President transmits to the President pro tempore of the Senate and the Speaker of the House of Representatives his written declaration that he is unable to discharge the powers and duties of his office, and until he transmits to them a written declaration to the contrary, such powers and duties shall be discharged by the Vice-President as Acting President.

Section 4

[ALTERNATE PROCEDURES TO DECLARE AND TO END
PRESIDENTIAL DISABILITY]

Whenever the Vice-President and a majority of either the principal officers of the executive departments or of such other body as Congress may
by law provide, transmit to the President pro tempore of the Senate
and the Speaker of the House of Representatives their written declaration
that the President is unable to discharge the powers and duties of his
office, the Vice-President shall immediately assume the powers and duties
of the office as Acting President.

Thereafter, when the President transmits to the President pro tempore
of the Senate and the Speaker of the House of Representatives his written
declaration that no inability exists, he shall resume the powers and duties
of his office unless the Vice-President and a majority of either the principal officers of the executive department or of such other body as Congress
may by law provide, transmit within four days to the President pro tempore of the Senate and the Speaker of the House of Representatives their
written declaration that the President is unable to discharge the powers
and duties of his office. Thereupon Congress shall decide the issue, assem-
bling within 48 hours for that purpose if not in session. If the Congress,
within 21 days after receipt of the latter written declaration, or, if Congress is not in session, within 21 days after Congress is required to assemble, determines by two-thirds vote of both houses that the President is
unable to discharge the powers and duties of his office, the Vice-President
shall continue to discharge the same as Acting President; otherwise, the
President shall resume the powers and duties of his office.

Amendment XXVI

[Proposed by Congress on March 23, 1971; declared ratified on June 30, 1971.]

Section 1

[EIGHTEEN-YEAR-OLD SUFFRAGE]

The right of citizens of the United States, who are eighteen years of age
or older, to vote shall not be denied or abridged by the United States or by
any State on account of age.

Section 2

[POWER TO ENFORCE THIS ARTICLE]

The Congress shall have power to enforce this article by appropriate legislation.

Amendment XXVII

[LIMITING CONGRESSIONAL PAY CHANGES]
[Proposed by Congress on September 25, 1789; ratified on May 7, 1992.]

No law varying the compensation for the services of the Senators and Representatives shall take effect until an election of Representatives shall have intervened.

Acknowledgments

Akihil Reed Amar: "Second Chances," (c) 2013 The Atlantic Media Co., as first published in *The Atlantic Magazine*. All rights reserved. Distributed by Tribune Media Services.

George Annas: From *The New England Journal of Medicine*, George J. Annas, "Jumping Frogs, Endangered Toads, and California's Medical-Marijuana Law," vol. 353, issue 21. Copyright (c) 2005 Massachusetts Medical Society. Reprinted with permission from Massachusetts Medical Society.

Matt Bai: "How Much Has Citizens United Changed the Political Game?" From *The New York Times*, July 17, 2012 © 2012 *The New York Times*. All rights reserved. Used by permission and protected by the Copyright Laws of the United States. The printing, copying, redistribution, or retransmission of this Content without express written permission is prohibited.

Charles Beard: Reprinted with the permission of Scribner, a Division of Simon & Schuster, Inc., from *An Economic Interpretation of the Constitution of the United States* by Charles A. Beard. Copyright © 1913 and 1935 by The Free Press. Copyright renewed © 1941 by Charles A. Beard. Copyright renewed © 1963 by William Beard and Miriam B. Vagts. All rights reserved.

The Cato Institute: "Privatization," *Cato Handbook for Policy Makers, 7th ed.* © 2009, The Cato Institute, Cato Handbook for Policymakers. Used by permission.

Tim Cavanaugh: "Beware Obama's Big Ideas." *Reason*, February 2013, *Reason* magazine and Reason.com.

Adam Clymer: "Triumphant Obama Faces New Foe in 'Second-Term Curse'." From *The New York Times*, November 7, 2012 © 2012 *The New York Times*. All rights reserved. Used by permission and protected by the Copyright Laws of the United States. The printing, copying, redistribution, or retransmission of this Content without express written permission is prohibited.

George E. Condon, Jr. "Even After Big Victory, Health Care Future Uncertain." Reprinted with permission from *National Journal*, June 28, 2012. Copyright 2012 by National Journal Group, Inc. All rights reserved.

Chandler Davidson: "The Historical Context of Voter Photo-ID Laws." *PS, political science & politics* by American Political Science Association Reproduced with permission of CAMBRIDGE UNIVERSITY PRESS in the format reprint in a book/ebook/anthology via Copyright Clearance Center.

Alexis de Tocqueville: "Political Association in the United States" (pp. 189-195) from *Democracy in America* by Alexis de Tocqueville. Edited by J.P. Mayer and Max Lerner. Translated by George Lawrence. English translation copyright © 1965 by Harper & Row, Publishers, Inc. Reprinted by permission of HarperCollins Publishers.

Ross Douthat: "The Marriage Ideal." From *The New York Times*, August 8, 2010 © 2010 *The New York Times*. All rights reserved. Used by permission and protected by the Copyright Laws of the United States. The printing, copying, redistribution, or retransmission of this Content without express written permission is prohibited.

Ronald Dworkin: "The Decision That Threatens Democracy." From *The New York Review of Books*. Copyright © 2010 by Ronald Dworkin.

Chris Edwards and Jeff Patch: "Corporate Welfare and Earmarks," *Cato Handbook for Policymakers*, 7th Edition, pp. 277-279, 283-287. Reproduced with permission of The Cato Institute.

Daniel Elazar: "The Political Subcultures of the United States" from *American Mosaic: The Impact of Space, Time, and Culture on American Politics*, pp. 229-36, 239-46. We have made diligent efforts to contact the copyright holder to obtain permission to reprint this selection. If you have information that would help us, please write to Permissions Department, W. W. Norton & Company, Inc., 500 Fifth Avenue, New York, NY 10110.

Richard Epstein: "Three Cheers for Income Inequality." Reprinted from Defining Ideas, November 8, 2011, with the permission of the publisher, the Hoover Institution. Copyright © 2011 by the Board of Trustees of the Leland Stanford Junior University.

James Fallows: "How to Save the News." (c) 2010 The Atlantic Media Co., as first published in *The Atlantic Magazine*. All rights reserved. Distributed by Tribune Media Services.

Richard Fenno: "U.S. House Members in Their Constituencies: An Exploration," *The American Political Science Review*, Vol. 71, No. 3 (Sep., 1977), pp. 883-917. Copyright © 1977 American Political Science Association. Reprinted with the permission of Cambridge University Press.

Morris P. Fiorina: "The Decline of Collective Responsibility in American Politics" from *Daedalus*, Vol. 109, No. 3, Summer 1980. © 1980 by The American Academy of Arts and Sciences. Reprinted by permission of MIT Press Journals.

"Letter to the Editor," in *Commentary* (May 2006). Reprinted by permission of the author.

"What Culture Wars?" in *The Wall Street Journal* (July 14, 2004). Reprinted by permission of the author.

Edward B. Foley: "Is There a Middle Ground in the Voter ID Debate?," Election Law @ Moritz, Ohio State University, Sept. 6, 2005. Reprinted by permission of the author.

Brian Friel: "Inhofe: Earmarks Are Good For Us." Reprinted with permission from *National Journal*, March 5, 2010. Copyright 2010 by National Journal Group, Inc. All rights reserved.

George Gallup: "Polling the Public" from *A Guide to Public Opinion Polls*. © 1944 Princeton University Press, 1948 revised 2nd. Edition, 1975 renewed. Reprinted by permission of Princeton University Press.

William Galston: "Telling Americans to Vote, Or Else." From *The New York Times*, November 5, 2011 © 2011 *The New York Times*. All rights reserved. Used by permis-

Sanford Levinson: Chapter 1, "The Ratification Referendum," *Our Undemocratic Constitution: Where the Constitution Goes Wrong (And How We the People Can Correct It)* by Sanford Levinson, pp. 11-24. Copyright © 2006 by Oxford University Press, Inc. Reprinted with permission of Oxford University Press.

Eric Liu: "Sworn Again Americans." This essay originally appeared in *Democracy: A Journal of Ideas*, issue #24.

Theodore J. Lowi: "American Business, Public Policy, Case Studies, and Political Theory." Copyright © 1964 Trustees of Princeton University. Reprinted with permission of Cambridge University Press.

David Mayhew: "Congress: The Electoral Connection" from *Congress: The Electoral Connection* (1974). Copyright © 1974 by Yale University Press. Reprinted with the permission of Yale University Press.

Louis Menand: "The Unpolitical Animal: How Political Science Understands Voters." Copyright © Louis Menand. Granted with the permission of the author.

Paul Miller: "National Insecurity: Just How Safe is the United States?" Reprinted by permission of *Foreign Affairs*, (no. 3, July/August 2012). Copyright 2012 by the Council on Foreign Relations, Inc. www.ForeignAffairs.com.

Richard Morin: "Choice Words: If You Can't Understand Our Poll Questions, Then How Can We Understand Your Answers?" From *The Washington Post*, © 1999 *The Washington Post*. All rights reserved. Used by permission and protected by the Copyright Laws of the United States. The printing, copying, redistribution, or retransmission of the Material without express written permission is prohibited.

Richard Neustadt: "The Power to Persuade." *Presidential Power: The Politics of Leadership from FDR to Carter*, 1st Edition, © 1980, pp. 26-43. Reprinted by permission of Pearson Education, Inc., Upper Saddle River, NJ.

Timothy Noah: "The United States of Inequality, Part 10: Why We Can't Ignore Growing Income Inequality." From *Slate*, © 2010 The Slate Group All rights reserved. Used by permission and protected by the Copyright Laws of the United States. The printing, copying, redistribution, or retransmission of the Material without express written permission is prohibited.

David O'Brien: "The Court in American Life." From *Storm Center: The Supreme Court in American Politics, Third Edition* by David M. O'Brien. Copyright © 1993, 1990, 1986 by David M. O'Brien. Used by permission of W. W. Norton & Company, Inc.

Mancur Olson: "The Logic of Collective Action," from *Rise and Decline of Nations* (1982). Copyright © 1982 by Yale University Press. Reprinted with the permission of Yale University Press.

Richard Peltz-Steele: "Dismantling Federalism Is A Shortcut With A Very Steep Price," Forbes, 7/08/2012. Reprinted by permission of Richard J. Peltz-Steele, U Mass Law School.

Paul Peterson: "The Price of Early Federalism." From *The Price of Federalism*. Copyright © 1995. Reprinted with the permission of The Brookings Institution, Washington, DC.

Markus Prior: "News vs. Entertainment: How Increasing Media Choice Widens Gaps in Political Knowledge and Turnout", *American Journal of Political Science*, Vol

49, Issue 3, pp. 577-589. Copyright © 2005, John Wiley & Sons. Reprinted with permission.

Nicol Rae: "Be Careful What You Wish For: The Rise of Responsible Parties in American National Politics." Reprinted, with permission, from the Annual Review of Political Science. Volume 10 © 2007 by Annual Reviews www.annual reviews.org.

Justin Raimondo: "The Libertarian Case Against Gay Marriage," *The American Conservative*, April 1, 2011. Reprinted with permission, Copyright *The American Conservative*.

Jonathan Rauch: "Earmarks Are a Model, Not a Menace." Reprinted with permission from *National Journal*, March 14, 2009. Copyright 2010 by National Journal Group, Inc. All rights reserved.

"In Defense of Prejudice." Copyright © 1995 by Harper's Magazine. All rights reserved. Reproduced from the May issue by special permission.

"Objections to These Unions." Copyright 2004 Jonathan Rauch.

Gerald Rosenberg: *The Hollow Hope Can Courts Bring About Social Change?* (University of Chicago Press, 1993). © 1991 by The University of Chicago

Jay Sekulow: "State sovereignty is the issue." SCOTUSblog (Jun. 25, 2012), http://www.scotusblog.com/2012/06/online-symposium-scotus-on-az-immigration-state-sovereignty-is-the-issue.

Marilyn Serafini: "Grading Reform." Excerpted with permission from *National Journal*, March 27, 2010. Copyright 2010 by National Journal Group, Inc. All rights reserved.

Bradley Smith: "Citizens United We Stand," *The American Spectator*, Vol. 43, No. 4, May 2010, pp. 14-17. Reprinted by permission of *The American Spectator* and Spectator.org.

Rogers M. Smith: "Beyond Tocqueville, Myrdal and Hartz: The Multiple Traditions in America" pp. 549-550, 558-563. *The American Political Science Review*, Volume 87, Issue 03 (September 1993). Copyright © 1993 American Political Science Association. Reprinted with the permission of Cambridge University Press.

George Soros: "The Age of Open Society." From *The New Era*. Reprinted with the permission of the author.

Paul Starr: "Goodbye to the Age of Newspapers (Hello to a New Era of Corruption)," *The New Republic*, March 4, 2009. Reprinted by permission of *The New Republic*, © 2009 TNR II, LLC.

Peter Sutherland: "Reality Check." *Harvard International Review* (Winter 2000). Reprinted with permission of the publisher.

Hans von Spakowsky: "Requiring Identification by Voters," Testimony before the Texas Senate, Delivered March 10, 2009. © 2010, The Heritage Foundation. Reprinted by permission of The Heritage Foundation.

David B. Truman: "The Alleged Mischiefs of Faction" from *The Governmental Process* (Knopf, 1971). Reprinted with permission of Edwin M. Truman.

Steven M. Warshawsky: "What Does It Mean To Be An American?," *American Thinker*, July 2, 2007. Reprinted by permission of the author.

Jenine R. Wedel: "Federalist No. 70: Where does the Public Begin and End?", *Public Administration Review*, December, 2011, pages S118-S127. Reprinted by permission of Copyright Clearance Center on behalf of John Wiley & Sons, Inc.

James Q. Wilson: "How Divided Are We?" Reprinted from *Commentary*, February 2006, by permission; copyright © 2006 by Commentary, Inc.

"What Government Agencies Do and Why They Do It." Copyright © 1991 James Wilson. Reprinted by permission of Basic Books, a member of the Perseus Books Group.

Gordon S. Wood: From *The Creation of the American Republic, 1776-1787* by Gordon S. Wood. Published for the Omohundro Institute of Early American History and Culture. Copyright © 1970 by the University of North Carolina Press; new preface copyright © 1998 by the University of North Carolina Press. Used by permission of the publisher. www.uncpress.unc.edu.

Micah Zenko and Michael A. Cohen: "Clear and Present Safety: The United States is More Secure Than Washington Thinks." Reprinted by permission of *Foreign Affairs* (no. 2, March/April 2012). Copyright 2012 by the Council on Foreign Relations, Inc. www.ForeignAffairs.com.